Third Edition

Contemporary Direct and Interactive Marketing

Lisa D. Spiller
Christopher Newport University
Newport News, Virginia

Martin Baier
Bernardsville, New Jersey

RĀCOM
COMMUNICATIONS

Third Edition
Contemporary Direct and Interactive Marketing
Lisa D. Spiller
Christopher Newport University, Newport News, Virginia
Martin Baier
Bernardsville, New Jersey

CIP Data available from the Library of Congress

ISBN 978-1-933199-37-5

Editor & Publisher: Richard Hagle
Associate Editor: Cheryl Wilson
Design: Sans Serif Design
Credits and acknowledgments borrowed from other sources and reproduced, with permission, in this text-book appear on appropriate page within text.

Copyright © 2012 by
Racom Communications
150 N. Michigan Ave.
Suite 2800
Chicago, IL 60601

Brief Table of Contents

Contents

Preface

Welcome to the third edition of *Contemporary Direct and Interactive Marketing*!

We wrote this book to help you understand and use the theories behind modern direct and interactive marketing and learn how to apply these theories in your classes and in your career. You will be reading about direct/interactive marketing concepts, methods, and applications. In other courses, you may have studied psychology and human behavior, the basics of advertising, communications theory and practice, and even accounting. In this book, you will see how many disciplines converge in the field of direct marketing to form a discipline that changes with time but is creative, useful, successful, and even fun! When reading the following chapters, we hope you will be able to apply many concepts you have already studied and learn how they are essential to successful marketing. We also hope that as you consider your career, whether in marketing or a related field, you will have found it helpful to understand how so many activities we all undertake daily are affected by direct and interactive marketing. In some sense, we are all marketers and consumers, and we all become involved in the techniques of direct and interactive marketing.

Decades ago, direct marketers gathered customer names and addresses, created mailing lists, established relationships with customers, and sold goods and services on a one-on-one basis to customers via mail and telephone. Today, much has changed and much has remained the same. Direct marketers are still concerned with creating relationships with each customer and maximizing customer value by serving individual customer needs on a personal basis; however, computer technology, customer databases, and digital and social media have dramatically changed the speed and effectiveness of these activities. More and more companies and organizations are using the direct and interactive model as their primary method for business transactions. This third edition recognizes the growth of various digital marketing formats as the newest format for conducting direct and interactive marketing today. Although mobile and digital marketing is similar to direct mail in that it targets messages on a personal one-on-one basis with great precision and effectiveness, it does so with much greater speed of transmission and enables an immediate customer response and excellent measurability and analysis. Today's consumers desire both the speed and the control that the new digital and social media formats provide. Marketers must include these important mediums in their direct marketing campaigns.

Direct marketing has always been accountable and measurable, and now with the various digital media formats and computer technology, it is more interactive and precise than ever before. This third edition builds on the traditional foundations of direct marketing that are still applicable today, and it extends into the future where continuous digital innovations are transforming the marketing landscape. The new media of yesterday have become mainstream media today. We cannot begin to envision what changes are ahead. But one thing is certain: traditional direct and interactive marketing principles will still apply. This edition builds on these traditional foundations, captures the new media and methods, and explores the future innovations of direct and interactive marketing.

Using this book

This edition contains the following four major section: (1) Build, Develop and Measure Direct and Interactive Marketing Strategies; (2) Create and Place Direct and Interactive Marketing Campaigns; (3) Serve and Adapt to Customers and Markets; and (4) Applications, Examples, and Careers in Direct and Interactive Marketing. Individual chapters within these major sections deal with such subjects as database marketing and customer relationship management, developing lists and profiling customers, testing, measuring and analyzing campaigns, planning value propositions, creating compelling message and media strategies, fulfilling the offer, serving the customer, understanding environmental, ethical, and legal issues, exploring international strategies, and applying direct and interactive marketing. Each chapter includes the key terms in bold type, end-of-chapter summaries, review questions, exercises, and cases. The material does not progress from easy to difficult, but it does progress logically from an introduction to application.

To be successful in any course, you must read each chapter carefully and outline key concepts along the way. The opening vignette for each chapter will give you a "real world example" that provides a sense of what that chapter will address. Read each opening vignette *prior* to each chapter. Each chapter contains state-of-the-art direct and interactive marketing content, many pictures and images, and numerous applications and examples to drive home important concepts. We provide discussion questions at the end of each chapter to assist you in reviewing the important concepts along with mini-exercises to enable you to critically think about and apply the content of each chapter. Keep your eyes and ears open to the marketing world around you and you will be able to easily understand and apply the concepts, strategies, tools and techniques of direct and interactive marketing that have become mainstream marketing in today's world.

Acknowledgments

We are the authors and personally responsible for this comprehensive book, but we hasten to acknowledge lots of input and assistance from many individuals. Much has been derived from our direct marketing career experiences: from the firms that provided us with the opportunities and field laboratories, from our work colleagues at these firms, as well as from literally hundreds of other direct marketers who have shared their own successes and failures with us. In college classrooms, many seeds were planted by those who taught us. Our own presentations of concepts and theory have been considerably enriched by challenging and perceptive interaction with students.

We are especially grateful to the following people who have contributed information to select chapters of our textbook: Dr. Elizabeth Young for coauthoring the Testing, Measuring and Analyzing Customers and Campaigns chapter, along with the Instructor's Manual and Test Item File, and for her excellent reviewing and editing assistance; Dave Marold of Eastern Michigan University for his networking assistance, his constant motivation and support, and his many excellent reviews and contributions, and especially for coauthoring several of the new end-of-chapter cases with us; Dr. Matt Sauber of Eastern Michigan University for his valuable reviews and contributions on the new end-of-chapter cases and select chapter material; Charles George for his excellent contributions to the Mobile, Text and Telephone and Digital and Social Media chapters, and for allowing us to feature him in an end-of-chapter case. Our special thanks to Matt Sauber, David Marold and Alicia Anderson of Eastern Michigan University for allowing us to reprint their "Domino's Pizza: Growing Sales with Technology" comprehensive case and to Vicki Rowland and Kaitlin Rogers for coauthoring the Peninsula SPCA comprehensive case.

We are grateful to the talented and dedicated people at The Martin Agency for allowing us to feature their agency in Appendix A, for their contributions to and assistance with Appendix B and several opening vignettes and cases featuring their clients. Our special praise goes to Barbara Joynes and Terry Thompson (who make *everything* happen at The Martin Agency!) for their generosity of time and talent and for their firm belief in direct marketing education. We are also grateful to the following people at The Martin Agency for their assistance with select opening vignettes and cases: Steve Bassett, Liz Toms, Kathryn Leake, Neill McIvor, Tedd Aurelius, Courtney Faudree, Leslie Griles and Colton Payne.

We extend great appreciation to the kind people at Busch Gardens/Water Country USA for providing many excellent contributions, examples and images throughout the third edition. We offer special thanks and praise to Dan Dipiazzo, Vice-President of Marketing, and his talented team including Nancy Henry and Bruce Wilson.

We owe special gratitude to Chuck Applebach of the Virginia Beach Convention & Visitors Bureau for his assistance and important contributions to the third edition in many areas. We are also thankful for the kind and timely assistance of Greg Ward and Justine Thompson of BCF Boom Your Brand, the creative agency for the Virginia Beach Convention & Visitors Bureau.

We are truly grateful for the administrative and secretarial support of Crystal Kernan, Tricia Lorandi, and Clare Maliniak. We recognize and appreciate the research assistance of two CNU students: Jeff Ball and Adam Baker. We owe much thanks Suzanne Spiller for her valuable contributions to several chapters.

We are indebted to the many business professionals who kindly assisted in providing case information and textbook examples. In addition to those mentioned above, these include:

- Amy Hart, Hauser's Jewelers
- Kurt Ruf, RUF Strategic Solutions
- Joe Pych, NextMark
- Ruthie Keefe and Francy Hughes, BlueSky Creative, Inc.
- Florence Camenzind and Mark Honeyball, Chevrolet Europe
- Mary Eckenrode, and Denise Meine-Graham, Cheryl's
- Michael Sparling, 1-800-FLOWERS.com
- Mike Simmons and Ken Gammage, Directed Electronics
- Vicki Rowland, Peninsula SPCA
- Janel Mootrey and Lisa Mihalcik, Zappos.com, Inc.
- Amber Nettles, The Daily Press
- Elizabeth Baran, Dick's Sporting Goods, Inc.
- Jenelle Allemon, Domino's Pizza
- Ted Ward, GEICO
- Siobhan Werhan, Hi-Ho Silver
- Jody Wagner and Anne Walsh, Jody's Popcorn
- Deanna Williams, Macy's Inc.
- Karen Rice Gardiner, National Geographic Society
- Carrie Schweikart, QuadDirect
- David Noonan, Mountain Gear
- Jessica Wharton, Newport News/Williamsburg International Airport (PHF)
- Sylvia Weinstein, Oyster Pointer and Newport News Kidsville News
- Peter Samuel, PING
- Sandra Jarvis, Peace Frogs, Inc.
- Brenda Snow, Kristen Kennedy and Blake Burnette, Snow Companies
- Chris Mainz, Southwest Airlines
- Roger Phelps and Cama Poffenberger, STIHL, Inc.
- William Leber, Swisslog Logistics, Inc.
- Matt White, White & Partners
- Courtney Darden, Williamsburg Winery
- Wendy Weber, Crandall Associates

Many reviewers at various institutions provided valuable comments and suggestions for this and the previous editions. We are grateful to the following colleagues for their thoughtful inputs and recommendations:

Third Edition Reviewers

- Janel Bell, Alabama State University
- Shawn Grain Carter, Fashion Institute of Technology
- John Cronin, Western Connecticut State University

- Susan Jones, Ferris State University
- Eric Larson, Villanova University
- Harvey Markovitz, Pace University
- Dave Marold, Eastern Michigan University
- Henry Greene, Central Connecticut University
- Jack Mandel, Nassau Community College

Second Edition Reviewers

- Robert M. Cosenza, University of Mississippi
- Dale Lewison, University of Akron
- Mark A. Neckes, Johnson and Wales University
- Carol Scovotti, University of Wisconsin, Whitewater

First Edition Reviewers

- Dennis B. Arnett, Texas Tech University
- Bruce C. Bailey, Otterbein College
- Dave Blackmore, University of Pittsburgh at Bradford
- Deborah Y. Cohn, Yeshiva University
- John J. Cronin, Western Connecticut State University
- Wenyu Dou, University of Nevada, Las Vegas
- F. Robert Dwyer, University of Cincinnati
- James S. Gould, Pace University
- Richard A. Hamilton, University of Missouri, Kansas City
- Susan K. Harmon, Meddle Tennessee State University
- Sreedhar Kavil, St. John's University
- Barry Langford, Florida Gulf Coast University
- Marilyn Lavin, University of Wisconsin, Whitewater
- Paula M. Saunders, Wright State University
- Donald Self, Auburn University, Montgomery
- Carmen Sunda, University of New Orleans
- William Trombetta, St. Joseph's University
- Ugur Yucelt, Pennsylvania State University, Harrisburg

Finally, we owe many thanks to our families for their constant support and encouragement—James "Dooley," Suzanne, Chad, and Jack Spiller, and Dorothy Baier and Donna Baier Stein. To them, we dedicate this book.

Lisa Spiller
Martin Baier

About the Authors

As a team, Lisa Spiller and Martin Baier provide a blend of experience uniquely suited to writing a direct marketing text. Dr. Spiller is an award-winning professor with more than 25 years of experience teaching direct marketing to undergraduate business students. Martin Baier, a legendary member of the Direct Marketing Association's Hall of Fame and author of the very first direct marketing textbook, was a highly successful direct marketing professional who dedicated more than 35 years to academia in an attempt to bridge the gap between what is learned in the classroom and what is practiced in the business world. In 1984, the two met at the University of Missouri, Kansas City, where Baier taught the graduate direct marketing classes and Spiller taught the undergraduate direct marketing classes. The rest is history . . . and their years of teaching experience and knowledge of direct marketing are captured in this text.

Lisa D. Spiller

Lisa Spiller is a professor of marketing in the Joseph W. Luter III School of Business at Christopher Newport University in Newport News, Virginia. She has been teaching direct marketing courses to undergraduate business students for more than 25 years and has helped her university pioneer a major in direct and interactive marketing. Dr. Spiller's marketing students have won the coveted Collegiate Gold ECHO Award from the Direct Marketing Association in 2003, 2005, 2007 and 2011, the Collegiate Silver ECHO Award in 2002. Her students have also received the Gold Collegiate Marketing Award for Excellence and Innovation (MAXI) from the Direct Marketing Association of Washington Educational Foundation (DMAW-EF) in 2004, 2005, 2006, 2007, 2009, and 2011; the Collegiate Silver MAXI Award in 2002, 2003 and 2010; and the Guy Yolton Creative Direct Mail Award in 2002, 2004, 2005, 2007 and 2009.

Dr. Spiller was named the Direct Marketing Educational Foundation (DMEF) Robert B. Clark Outstanding Direct Marketing Educator in 2005. She was the inaugural recipient of the DMAW-EF O'Hara Leadership Award for Direct and Interactive Marketing Education in 2008. Professor Spiller has received awards for her teaching, including the inaugural CNU Alumni Society Faculty Award for Excellence in Teaching and Mentoring in 2007; Faculty Advisor Leader Awards from the DMEF in 2002, 2003, 2005, 2007 and 2011; a Distinguished Teaching Award in 1997 from the DMEF; and the Elmer P. Pierson Outstanding Teacher Award in 1987 from the University of Missouri, Kansas City. Her research studies, the majority of which have been related to some aspect of direct and database marketing, have been published in numerous journals. Dr. Spiller served on the Abstract Editorial Board of the *Journal of Interactive Marketing* for ten years, was an Academic Representative on the DMEF Board of Trustees for two years, and has been a member of the Academic Advisory Board of the DMAW-EF for more than a decade.

Dr. Spiller received her B.S.B.A. and M.B.A. degrees from Gannon University and her Ph.D. from the University of Missouri, Kansas City. Prior to joining academia, Spiller held positions as a marketing director with an international company and as an account executive with an advertising agency. Through the years, she has served as a marketing consultant to many organizations. Dr. Spiller possesses a true passion for teaching and has been a strong advocate of direct and interactive marketing education throughout her entire academic career.

Martin Baier

Martin Baier has been a direct marketing consultant and educator since retiring in 1987 as executive vice president of the marketing group at Old American Insurance Company. He is founder of the Center for Direct Marketing Education and Research in the Henry Bloch School of Business and Public Administration of the University of Missouri, Kansas City (UMKC), where he served for 25 years as adjunct professor. He has consulted with a variety of organizations now involved in or adopting the discipline of direct marketing. His education includes an M.A. in economics (1970), a B.A. in business administration (1943), and a B.S. in economics (1943)—all from UMKC. His *Elements of Direct Marketing,* the first college textbook on the subject, was published by McGraw-Hill in 1983. A Japanese edition was published by Nikkei in Tokyo in 1985; an international student edition was published in Singapore in 1986. His *How to Find and Cultivate Customers through Direct Marketing* was published by NTC Business Books in 1996. *Contemporary Database Marketing: Concepts and Applications,* coauthored with Kurtis Ruf and Goutam Chakraborty, is an interactive college textbook/CD, published by Racom Books in 2001.

Martin Baier has been affiliated with many professional organizations and listed in *Who's Who in Finance and Industry* and in *Who's Who in Advertising.* He has taught direct marketing at many universities and has conducted numerous seminars throughout the United States and in Europe, Australia, New Zealand, and Asia. His presentation of "ZIP Code—New Tool for Marketers" in the January–February 1967 *Harvard Business Review* created substantial interest and caused the *Kansas City Star* to name him the "Father of ZIP Code Marketing."

He was inducted into the Direct Marketing Association Hall of Fame in 1989. The DMEF presented him its Ed Mayer Award, and the Direct Marketing Insurance Council named him Direct Marketing Insurance Executive of the Year, both in 1983. The Mail Advertising Service Association honored him with its Miles Kimball Award in 1990. The Ed Sisk Award for Direct Marketing Vision was presented to him by the Direct Marketing Association of Washington Educational Foundation in 1994. The Andi Emerson 1995 Award, for contribution of outstanding service to the direct marketing creative community, was awarded to him by the Direct Marketing Creative Guild and the John Caples Awards Board. In 1995, he was elected International Fellow of the Institute of Direct Marketing (U.K.) in recognition of exceptional services to the profession. The New England Direct Marketing Association honored him with a Lifetime Achievement Award in 1996.

## PART 1

Build, Develop and Measure Direct and Interactive Marketing Strategies

## CHAPTER 1

Examining the Processes and Applications of Direct and Interactive Marketing

OPENING VIGNETTE: PEACE FROGS

Like most college students, Catesby Jones needed some extra cash, so in 1985 he decided to create beach volleyball shorts to sell around campus at the University of Virginia. He wanted an unusual design that would appeal to his target market, so he arranged an eye-catching assortment of national flags all over the boxer shorts. To put flair into his design, Catesby added a frog holding two digits in the air, forming a peace sign. After receiving numerous orders, he began manufacturing and selling the unique boxer shorts from his dorm room. Soon he began selling other items featuring the creative peace-signing frog, such as the T-shirt featured in Figure 1-1.

Catesby saw the potential in his creation, so he and a few buddies decided to place a $15,000 direct marketing advertisement in *Rolling Stone* magazine. The advertisement generated a total of 1,000 orders. By the time Catesby finished his degree in international relations, he was already four years into what would become his passion and a very successful business.

Peace Frogs began to dispense products through multichannel distribution using a mail-order catalog, retail stores—company-owned and licensed (from wholesale to department stores and specialty retailers)—and on the Internet at www.peacefrogs.com. (See Figure 1-2.) These channels allowed the company to distribute its products to a vast number of consumers and save resources through cross-marketing. They also helped create brand recognition and loyalty because the consumer could see the merchandise at many different outlets.

FIGURE 1-1. Peace Frogs Hope T-shirt. Used with permission of Peace Frogs, Inc.

Now a million-dollar company, Peace Frogs operates a 37,000 square feet distribution center at its home office in Gloucester, Virginia. This multipurpose facility houses Peace Frogs' merchandise, ordering systems, and a retail store. The 25 employees who work in the distribution center try to ensure that customers are completely satisfied.

The company not only has unique clothing, it has also found a distinctive way to distribute merchandise—by psychedelically painted VW vans driving the roads and highways of the United States. Peace Frogs chose this vehicle, shown in Figure 1-3, both as a means of transportation and as a marketing statement, a representation of "reliability and freedom." As it did with its products, the company has taken something ordinary and transformed it into a unique message that leaves a distinct impression and has a positive impact on its customers. The peace frog and its related "positively peaceful thinking" message have become a significant symbol to which many can relate.

FIGURE 1-2. Peace Frogs Web page. Used with permission of Peace Frogs, Inc.

FIGURE 1-3. Peace Frogs van. Used with permission of Peace Frogs, Inc.

The company's line now includes T-shirts, sweatshirts, hats, boxer shorts, lounge pants, jewelry, accessories, and school supplies. In the process of building a business through direct marketing, Catesby Jones showed that with dedication, hard work, and daring to be a little different, people can make an impact.

The Scope of Direct and Interactive Marketing

Find us on Facebook!

Follow us on Twitter!

Connect with us on LinkedIn!

Watch us on YouTube!

FIGURE 1-4. Social media icons.

Visit our Web site! Click here! Text this number now! Call this toll-free number! Complete the bottom portion of this mailer and return it in the enclosed postage paid envelope! Clip this coupon and visit our store! The use of direct and interactive marketing in today's business world is booming! Direct and interactive marketing is now at the center of the communications revolution and is being used by businesses, organizations, associations, and individuals across the world with great fervor. More than a decade ago, Roland Rust and Richard Oliver foretold the rise of direct marketing at the expense of traditional advertising. They claimed:

> Mass media advertising as we know it today is on its deathbed. . . . Advertising agencies are restructuring to accommodate a harsher advertising reality, . . . direct marketing is stealing business away from traditional advertising, and the growth of sales promotion and integrated marketing communications both come at the expense of traditional advertising.[1]

Practitioners and scholars suggest a paradigm shift in marketing, fueled by the growth in the use of direct marketing techniques, is under way. New digital and social media marketing developments are dramatically changing how marketers create and communicate customer value. Today's marketers must know how to leverage new information, communication, and distribution technologies to connect more effectively with customers in this digital age.[2] For many companies, direct marketing—especially in its most recent transformation, digital marketing, including mobile and social networking—constitutes a complete business model. This new direct model is quickly changing the way companies think about building relationships with customers.[3] Given the many technological advances, marketers are increasingly using direct marketing applications to reach and interact with consumers on a personal basis.

Today, direct marketing is a fundamental marketing tool in a growing variety of businesses. Direct marketing grew faster than almost every other marketing activity for the latter part of the twentieth century.[4] Total direct marketing advertising expenditures are projected to grow 4.9 percent annually through 2014. In addition, while spending on digital data is only a small portion of the overall data spending mix, it is projected to triple in size by 2012.[5] These statistics strongly suggest that direct marketing is becoming an integral element in the marketing manager's arsenal worldwide. The economic impact of direct and interactive marketing is simply mind-boggling! With this much emphasis being placed on direct and interactive marketing, it is important to understand what it is and how it is used.

Characteristics and Growth of Direct and Interactive Marketing

Despite its growth, there is no agreement about exactly what direct marketing is. Both practitioners and academicians grapple with a contemporary conceptual definition. Unquestionably, the concept known as direct marketing continues to evolve. However, its definition provides a framework from which we can improve our understanding and determine the critical elements of its process. The definition you are about to read is the result of years of scholarly research involving a content analysis of direct marketing definitions published in direct marketing, principles of marketing, integrated marketing communication, and advertising textbooks.[6]

Definition and Description

DIRECT MARKETING *is a database-driven interactive process of directly communicating with targeted customers or prospects using any medium to obtain a measurable response or transaction via one or multiple channels.* This definition identifies database, interactivity, direct communications, target customers, measurable response, and one or multiple channels as key dimensions in direct marketing activities. It encompasses not only what direct marketing is but the characteristics that make it unique.

Direct marketing is characterized by:

- Customer/prospect databases that make one-to-one targeting possible.
- A view of customers as assets with lifetime value.
- Ongoing relationships and affinity with customers.
- Data-based market segmentation.
- Research and precise experimentation (testing).
- Benefit-oriented direct response advertising.
- Measurement of results and accountability for costs.
- Interactivity with customers on a personalized, individualized basis.
- Multimedia direct response communication.
- Multichannel fulfillment and distribution.

Direct marketing is *database-driven* marketing. It is a process, a discipline, a strategy, a philosophy, an attitude, a collection of tools and techniques. In summary, its goal is to *create* and *cultivate* customers, regardless of whether these customers are themselves consumers, buyers for industrial organizations, or potential donors or voters. It is a way to market a for-profit business or a not-for-profit organization. Its principles apply to marketing activities targeting both business consumers (B2B) and final consumers (B2C). Today, direct marketing is being used by many traditional brand advertisers, and many experts believe that all marketing is converging.

The Convergence of Direct Marketing and Brand

Historically, direct marketing and traditional brand advertising were two separate disciplines. **Brand marketing** was mass marketing, and direct marketing was niche marketing. Brand marketers primarily used newspapers and broadcast media (television and radio) to get products or services recognized and preferred by masses of consumers, whereas direct marketers predominantly used direct mail and catalogs with customized offers designed for individual customers to motivate a specific response that could be tracked and measured to determine its effectiveness and resulting sales. Figure 1-5 overviews the inherent differences between these two disciplines.

FIGURE 1-5. Comparison between direct marketing and traditional brand marketing.

Direct Marketing	Traditional Marketing
Direct selling to individuals with customers identifiable by name, address, and purchase behavior	Mass selling with buyers identified as broad groups sharing common demographic and psychographic characteristics
Products have the added value of distribution direct to the customer, an important benefit	Product benefits do not typically include distribution to the customer's door
The medium is the marketplace	The retail outlet is the marketplace
Marketing controls the product all the way through delivery	The marketer typically loses control as the product enters the distribution channel
Advertising is used to generate an immediate transaction, an inquiry, or an order	Advertising is used for cumulative effect over time for building image, awareness, loyalty, and benefit recall; purchase action is deferred
Repetition of offers, promotional messages, toll-free numbers, and Web addresses are used within the advertisement	Repetition of offers and promotional messages are used over a period of time
Customer feels a high perceived risk—product bought unseen and recourse is distant	Customer feels less risk—has direct contact with the product and direct recourse

According to the Direct Marketing Association, the clear distinction between direct marketing and brand marketing has blurred with the digital revolution. Most companies now have a virtual storefront in the form of a Web site. Companies have the ability to store, track, and target information about consumers like never before. Direct marketing strategies, such as displaying URLs, toll-free numbers, e-mail addresses, and calls to action, have found their way into TV and radio spots, print ads, mobile ads, and text messages, Web sites, e-mails, blogs, social networks, online videogames, and almost every other type of media. Direct marketing's versatility, measurability, and undeniable return on investment have gradually garnered the respect of even the most traditional brand advertisers and agencies.[7] Direct marketers are also recognizing the importance of creating and reinforcing brand strategies at the individual level. Therefore, direct marketing and brand strategies are now viewed as complementary, and when applied correctly, they can create a synergistic marketing effect. Although these two disciplines have come from vastly different origins, they are indeed converging, with many companies recognizing the value of their combined marketing strategies.

Today, companies and organizations of all different sizes and types are integrating branding with their self-promotional direct marketing strategies. An excellent example is a creative boutique in Leesburg, Virginia, called MindZoo. This direct marketing agency, specializing in the development of highly customized direct marketing programs for newspapers, retailers, and consumer product and service providers, began in the basement of President Randy Jones's home in 2001. Jones's background included 10 years with Gannett, selling everything from classified advertising to database marketing services. The name MindZoo, intended as a whimsical description of Jones's nonconformist creative process, allows him and his staff an almost unlimited number of ways to integrate the zoo-branded theme into his direct response materials. MindZoo's brand begins with a distinctive logo with embedded animal eyes. As shown in Figure 1-6, MindZoo's creative materials have run the gamut from a customized Zoo Map on the homepage of the company's Web site to the inclusion of stuffed animals placed in zebra-lined gift bags in its direct mail packages and media kits.

Jones and the Zoo Crew strategically incorporate branding into all of the agency's direct marketing activities. Prospective clients get a taste of MindZoo's creative talent long before they begin to use its services.

FIGURE 1-6.
MindZoo's
promo materials.

Today, direct marketing is used by virtually every organization in every sector, including political, governmental, and sports. Its history is rich, and its future is seemingly unlimited!

Factors Affecting the Growth of Direct and Interactive Marketing

The first mail-order catalogs are said to have appeared in Europe in the mid-fifteenth century, soon after Gutenberg's invention of movable type.[8] There is record of a gardening catalog, the predecessor of today's colorful seed and nursery catalogs, issued by William Lucas, an English gardener, as early as 1667. From these beginnings there followed a proliferation of catalogs during the post–Civil War period when agrarian unrest, through the National Grange, fueled the popular slogan "eliminate the middleman." Then, as now, mail-order catalogs reflected social and economic change.

While mail-order merchandise catalogs were becoming more accepted, new cultural, social, and economic phenomena were breeding another form of mail order. The versatility of laser printing, personalization possibilities of inkjet printing, advances in press technology, and computerized typesetting are important examples of how the printing process is becoming more conducive to the "demassification" of the printed word. Further enhancing the growth of direct marketing, during the 1960s and to this day, has been the increasing availability of advertising media (other than direct mail) suitable for direct response advertising, especially those geared to highly defined market segments. The same evolution has been occurring in the broadcast media, television and radio, through special cable programming geared to market segments, along with the convenience of toll-free telephone calling. The phone itself has become another major medium for direct marketers, enhanced by cellular and wireless technologies.

The Internet has surely changed the way most consumers make purchases and the way most companies conduct business today. Virtually all companies and organizations not only have a Web site but are actively employing interactive digital marketing strategies including blogging, search engine marketing (SEM), online social networking, and mobile and text marketing.

The social and economic changes that have given impetus to the burgeoning rise of direct marketing since the mid-twentieth century have been coupled with equally impressive advances in the technology used in various elements of direct marketing. A few of these technological and social advances are worth mentioning.

PRINTING TECHNOLOGY. The versatility of laser printing, personalization of inkjet printing, advances in press technology, and computerized typesetting are important examples of how the printing process is becoming more conducive to the demassification of the printed word. Desktop publishing enables businesses to create newsletters, brochures, and other print materials that can have a highly professional look at a fraction of former costs. Graphic capabilities have also taken major strides. Compare, for example, the carnival cover design of the 1976 Oriental Trading Company catalog with its present carnival catalog cover design shown in Figure 1-7. Indeed, much has changed!

FIGURE 1-7. Oriental Trading catalog covers.

CREDIT CARDS. Since the advent of credit cards during the 1950s, there has been enormous growth of mail order as a selling method. Credit cards greatly enhanced and expedited transactions, which up to that time had been mainly cash or check with order. The ready availability of worldwide credit systems, together with rapid electronic funds transfer, has contributed to the feasibility and viability of direct marketing by simultaneously offering convenience and security.

PERSONAL COMPUTERS. Personal computers have made possible the record keeping, work operation, and model building that are so much a part of the art and science of direct marketing. The complex maintenance of lists and the retrieval of data associated with them are just two examples of the computer's contribution. Of course, the use of highly sophisticated analysis can mean the difference between direct marketing success and failure.

CHANGING CONSUMER LIFESTYLES. As travel becomes more expensive and communication becomes less expensive, there is further impetus to the use of mail, telephone, and Internet. Mailed catalogs, Web sites, and toll-free telephone numbers provide the convenience of shopping from home. Furthermore, as more women have entered the workforce, families are placing a greater emphasis on time utilization. Once a leisurely pastime, shopping has become more of a chore, especially for the majority of households in which both spouses work. The advent of mail order and the Web have made anytime day-or-night shopping even more convenient for these working spouses.

NEGATIVE ASPECTS OF RETAILING. Many consumers enjoy shopping in traditional retail stores. However, there is a strong belief that traditional retail shopping has a number of negative aspects associated with it. Some of these include inadequate parking facilities; concerns about safety; long walking distances; uninformed sales clerks; difficulties in locating retail sales personnel; long waiting lines at check-out; in-store congestion; difficulty in locating certain sizes, styles, or colors of products; and the hassle of juggling packages out of the retail stores. For these consumers, direct marketing, with all of its modern methods and conveniences, has been a welcome alternative.

The foregoing social and technological factors have served to not only popularize the use of direct and interactive marketing over the years but also affect the way direct and interactive marketing activities are carried out today. If the logic of direct and interactive marketing has become the logic of all marketing, its process must be explored and mastered. Let's investigate the process involved in conducting direct and interactive marketing.

The Processes of Direct and Interactive Marketing

Direct marketing guru Edward Nash once said: "Direct marketing is somewhat like laser surgery: a powerful, precise, and very effective tool in the hands of professionals, but a potential disaster in the hands of amateurs. We must approach it as if we are surgeons, not butchers, as if we are cabinetmakers, not carpenters."[9] The process of direct and interactive marketing is presented in the model featured in Figure 1-8. This model is parallel with the definition of direct marketing provided earlier in this chapter. The model recognizes the importance of responses that are measurable and the value of customer data in driving direct marketing strategies. It also encompasses the strategic use of multiple channels—a topic that is of emerging importance to direct marketers.

First and foremost, direct marketing activities are based on their historical foundations. Inherent to the effectiveness of the direct and interactive marketing process is the constant focus on customers. *Customers* are the life-blood of an organization.[10] Enterprise thrives on customers. They are the reason for its existence. The creation and cultivation of customers is what direct marketing is all about. Much has been written in recent times about **customer relation-**

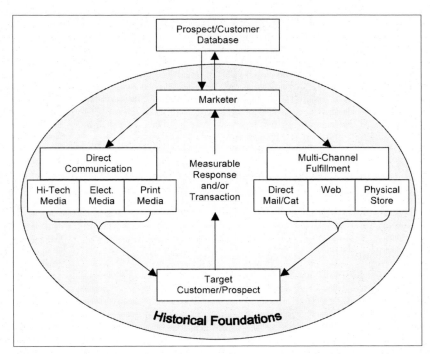

FIGURE 1-8. Direct & interactive marketing model.

ship management (CRM). We examine *interactive customer relationships,* as well as the related subjects of customer affinity and loyalty, pointing to the need for determining the lifetime value of a customer in greater detail in Chapters 2, 4 and 11.

Although new media like the Internet change the mechanism by which direct marketing activities are performed, its cornerstone—database-driven direct response communications—remains in effect today. In addition, the quality of the targeted list or database segment is critical to direct marketing success. That success is determined by measuring response rates. The formula for success remains constant—reaching the *right* people with the *right* offer using the *right* creative approach. Now let's detail the process of direct and interactive marketing.

Here is a brief overview of the direct and interactive marketing process. The marketer sends out a customized direct response communication via any type of medium to customers or prospective customers on the basis of the information the marketer has about that customer or prospect. In the case of prospecting efforts, because customer data do not yet exist in the company's database, the company often rents a list of prospective customers based on specific selection criteria. The targeted customer or prospect receives that communication and responds directly to the company or organization via multiple channel options. The customer response, which could take many different forms (inquiry, transaction, donation, visit, vote, etc.), is entered into the company database and is processed. Once processed, the customer's response is fulfilled and delivery of the requested product, service, or information is provided directly to that customer. Then, the entire process begins again with the direct marketer using the data contained in its database to distribute more customized messages to select recipients and the process continues. Let's examine each component of the process in greater detail.

Direct Communication 1:1

The goal of direct marketers is to interact with customers on a one-to-one basis, with reference to the information obtained and stored about each customer in the customer database. Direct

FIGURE 1-9.
BlueSky
personalized
advertisement.

marketers then provide the customer with information and product/service offers that are relevant to each customer's needs and wants. This, too, is different from the activities of traditional
marketers, who normally attempt to communicate with customers on a mass or segmented basis
but not normally on a personal individual basis. Direct marketers actively seek out and identify
those target customers to whom they will connect and send a catalog or some follow-up correspondence. An example of the personalization in direct and interactive marketing can be seen in
the advertisement featured in Figure 1-9.

Multiple Media

While direct mail and direct response advertising are items within the historical foundations,
direct marketing is not dependent on any one medium. In fact, it demonstrates that many media
may be used to directly communicate with prospects and customers. Thus, media are basically
placed into three categories: high-tech, electronic, and print media. High-tech media include:
Internet, e-mail, search engines, blogs, online social networking, mobile marketing, text messaging, and whatever new digital formats emerge in the future. This dimension stresses the importance of interactivity and acknowledges that direct marketing will continue to evolve with
technological advances. In addition to the Internet, practitioners also consider electronic media
like telemarketing and direct response television to be powerful vehicles for directly communicating with customers. Print media, such as newspapers, magazines, brochures, flyers, catalogs
and mail order are media options for direct marketing practitioners. Of course there are a
plethora of innovative ways to encourage consumers to visit Web sites, and these will be discussed later in the book.

Measurable Response

The single most notable differentiating feature of direct marketing is that it always seeks to generate a *measurable response.* This response can take the form of an order, an inquiry about the
product or service, or traffic driven to a Web site or brought into a store. The activities of direct
marketing are *measurable,* and the direct marketer must be *accountable,* always relating results to
costs. Unlike most of the activities of traditional brand advertising—creating awareness for a
product, service, or organization or enhancing the image of a product, brand, or a company—
direct marketing activities can always be measured by the response of targeted customers and/or
prospects. Most direct response ads today include a strong call-to-action along with a URL
encouraging consumers to visit a Web site, as the advertisement for the City of Virginia Beach in
Figure 1-10 illustrates.

Database

The key technological tool that enables the building and maintenance of long-term relationships
is the database. One of the most important tasks of direct marketing is capturing these customer

FIGURE 1-10. Virginia Beach "Be Yourself" advertisement. Used with permission by the City of Virginia Beach Convention & Visitors Bureau.

responses and storing them in a database. The creation of a database enables direct marketers to target their best prospects and best customers, build customer relationships, and maintain long-term customer loyalty—the hallmarks of CRM. Thus, the goal of direct marketers is not just to make a sale but to *create a customer!* Although traditional marketers have a long history of building relationships with customers, their activities and interactions with them are not normally measurable, accountable, or captured and recorded in a database.

Customer Relationships

Successful direct marketing relies on building strong customer relationships. While relationship building is referred to in many different ways (e.g., relationship marketing, one-to-one marketing, permission marketing, and CRM), the end result is the same—mutually beneficial long-term bonds between buyer and seller. The success of that relationship is measured in terms of lifetime customer value. Successful relationships also require respect for and protection of personal information shared by customers. Customer bonds with the seller strengthen when he or she trusts that the information shared is protected. Direct marketers have long known the long-term value of customers and have exercised CRM strategies to retain them.

Multichannel Fulfillment

Direct response communication is intended to generate a measurable action (such as order, inquiry, charitable donation, or vote for a candidate) via multiple channels. Of course, each customer response generates information that is stored in the organization's database and is used by the direct marketer in future marketing activities. The customer selects the desired channel, such as a visit to a Web site or store or a phone call. Direct marketers must process or fulfill each customer's response, regardless of whether it is an inquiry or an order. These are the customer service and fulfillment activities, which are often called "back-end" marketing. They include delivery of information or order shipment directly to the target customer. Multichannel fulfillment is also called **multichannel distribution** because it refers to a marketer using several (two or more) competing channels of distribution to reach the same target consumer. By practicing multichannel distribution, direct marketers may incur greater expense but normally yield greater customer satisfaction by enabling customers to select their preferred shopping channels. Some customers prefer product delivery to their doorstep, and others won't purchase the product without careful personal examination of it, including trying it on for size and style decisions.

For example, Victoria's Secret, the well-known marketer of women's fashions and lingerie, uses three competing channels of distribution. First, its catalogs are mailed to its database of customers and prospective customers and contain both its toll-free number and Web address for consumers to place direct orders; second, its Web site permits consumers to shop online at www.VictoriasSecret.com; and third, its retail stores are located in most major shopping malls, enabling consumers to come into the store to browse and purchase the merchandise in person. These three channels of distribution may compete with one another for the same target customer's order, and yet if the company didn't offer all of these options, it might lose potential customers to other marketers. Multichannel fulfillment or distribution offers multiple options for today's increasingly demanding consumer. The bottom line: Consumers want choices! Multichannel fulfillment gives them exactly that.

Now that we have examined the process of direct and interactive marketing, you might be wondering: how does the marketer carry out these processes for each individual customer on a one-to-one basis? The answer lies in precise measurement and analysis and proper targeting. The marketer follows each direct and interactive marketing campaign with a response analysis that examines the results for effectiveness. He or she can then initiate future communication designed specifically for each target customer by using the customer information stored in the database. The process begins again: each direct response communication builds on the relationship the direct marketer has with each individual customer and reinforces that customer's loyalty to the company or organization. We'll expand on each of these characteristics of direct marketing and interactive marketing in subsequent chapters in this textbook.

Applications of Direct and Interactive Marketing

You can immediately recognize a direct response advertisement, regardless of the medium used, by noting whether the reader, listener, or viewer is requested to take an immediate action: visit a Web site, text a given number, reply to an e-mail, mail an order form, call a phone number, come to a store or event, fill in a coupon, ask for a salesperson to call, send a contribution, vote for a particular candidate, or attend a meeting. If there is such a request, it is an example of direct marketing.

Users of Direct and Interactive Marketing

At some time or another, virtually every business and every organization—charitable, political, educational, cultural, and civic—and every individual uses direct response advertising and, indeed, has a database for doing so. As individuals, we use e-mail or direct mail whenever we send greeting cards, wedding invitations, and birth or graduation announcements. Job hunters find that Web sites and social media networks are an excellent way to get their résumés to prospective employers. Businesses, especially small businesses, use a variety of media for direct response advertising and employ many of the other elements of direct marketing. This is true of giant corporations as well as small retailers and industrial service organizations.

Today, most companies are realizing the great value direct and interactive marketing brings. Nearly all companies have increased their online marketing activities, particularly the use of e-mail and social media platforms, to take advantage of the customization, personalization, selectivity and cost-savings each presents. See Figure 1-11 for an example of a geographically-targeted e-mail from Busch Gardens.

FIGURE 1-11.
Busch Gardens
e-mail.

Let's look at a sampling of the many applications of the tools and techniques of database-driven direct marketing in use.

Business-to-Business

B2B direct marketing is the process of providing goods and services to industrial market intermediaries, as opposed to ultimate final consumers. Although the distinction is not always easy to make, we differentiate industrial goods from consumer goods based on their ultimate use. **Industrial goods** are generally used as raw materials or in the fabrication of other goods. Whereas iron ore is almost always an industrial good, a personal computer can be either an industrial or a consumer good, depending on its ultimate use. For example, the DuPont Personal Protection group uses direct and interactive marketing to promote its protective apparel to two primary customer segments: emergency responders and industrial workers (Figure 1-12)

Although the number of industrial organizations is but a fraction of the number of consumers, the volume of purchasing is as great in the industrial market as it is in the consumer market. The buying power of industrial organizations is highly concentrated, however, within certain industries (e.g., manufacturing), and there are also heavy concentrations regionally and geographically. This buying power is often measured by various forms of activity, such as manufacturing, wholesaling, retailing, mining, agriculture, and construction.

In comparing B2B transactions with business-to-consumer (B2C) transactions, we should note that consumer purchases are often consummated at the seller's location (e.g., clothing bought at a retail store). In industrial buying, the seller normally comes to the buyer's location (e.g., a computer installation sold to a chain of retail stores). A major factor contributing to the increasing use of direct marketing by businesses and industries is the rising cost of these per-

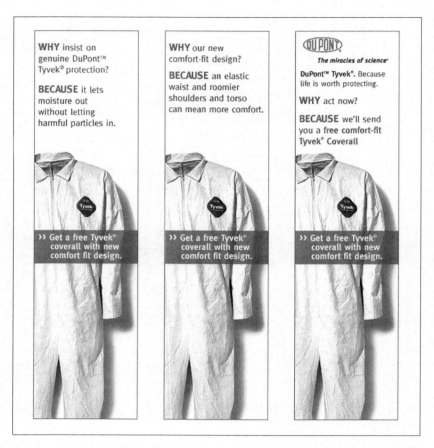

FIGURE 1-12.
Tyvek online
banner ad. Used
with permission
of DuPont.

sonal sales calls made to a buyer's location. Please note that this cost is per *call*, not per *sale*; it takes multiple calls to make one sale.

In contrasting business buyers with consumer buyers, apparent differences between these are sometimes exaggerated. Individual buyers within business organizations are obviously also consumers in their own rights. Conversely, many consumers also wear different hats when they are at work as industrial buyers. Some B2B businesses, recognizing this comparison, have gone so far as to look at the demographics of buyers within organizations at the same time as they look at the demographics of organizations themselves. A comparison of database demographics, contrasting consumer and industrial markets, is shown in Figure 1-13. These characteristics are not all-inclusive, of course, but they do indicate some interesting differences and, at the same time, similarities.

All buyers—consumers as well as industrial organizations—have a name and address. Beyond that identification, a consumer's age can be important in product differentiation as can the years a company has been in business. The gender of an industrial buyer may very well have the same influence as it does on that buyer making a purchase as a consumer. A consumer's income can be looked at in the same light as an organization's revenue, just as a consumer's wealth can be looked at in the same light as an organization's net worth. Though many marketers see lists of business buyers being different from lists of consumers, we argue that there is as much sameness as there is difference!

The tools and techniques of direct marketing used by businesses are basically the same as those for consumer direct marketing, as presented throughout this textbook. These tools and techniques are used in industrial markets to:

CONSUMER	*INDUSTRIAL*
Name/Address	Name/Address
Source code	Source code
Age	Year started
Gender	Gender of decision maker
Income	Revenue
Wealth	Net worth
Family size	Number of employees
Children	Parent firm or subsidiary
Occupation	Line of business
Credit evaluation	Credit evaluation
Education	Education of decision makers
Urban/rural resident	Headquarters/branch
Own or rent home	Private or public ownership
Ethnic group	Minority ownership
Interests	Interests of decision makers
Life-style of ZIP area	Socio-economics of location
Mail respondent	Mail respondent
Transactions & R/F/M	Transactions & R/F/M

FIGURE 1-13. Comparison of demographic items in consumer and industrial direct marketing.

- generate qualified "leads" for salesperson follow-up.
- achieve direct sales remotely (i.e., via catalogs and Web sites).
- reinforce all sales efforts.
- introduce new products.
- develop new markets and applications.
- build industrial customer goodwill.
- conduct industrial market research.

B2B marketers, like B2C marketers, combine relational databases to obtain information about their customers *as well as their customers' customers*. They perform statistical analyses to identify their own best customers and then seek prospects that look like these.

Nonprofit Organizations

Direct marketing is ideal for nonprofit organizations because it is measurable, accountable, targeted, cost-effective, and requires a direct response—qualities that are all of particular importance to organizations that exist to support and advance a cause. Nonprofit organizations serve as a forum for the creation and distribution of new ideas. These organizations, like hospitals and universities, may deliver services. The American Cancer Society and the March of Dimes actively support advancing medical research in an attempt to find a cure for diseases. Mothers Against Drunk Driving (MADD) focuses on safety issues. What they all have in common is that they want people to know about their cause and respond to their pleas for support. This response could be in the form of a donation to a charitable organization or help to achieve any number of an organization's communication objectives. Any nonprofit organization can effectively use direct marketing to achieve its communication objectives. An example of nonprofit direct marketing can be seen in the Peninsula Society for the Prevention of Cruelty to Animals (PSPCA) e-mail presented in Figure 1-14.

FIGURE 1-14. Peninsula SPCA e-mail. Used with permission of Peninsula Society for the Prevention of Cruelty to Animals.

What nonprofit organizations employ direct marketing strategies to achieve their goals and objectives? The answer is probably *every* organization. Most health-concerned organizations, such as the American Cancer Society, the American Heart Association, the American Diabetes Association, and the American Lung Association, avidly practice direct marketing to obtain donations to support research for their worthy causes. Organizations concerned with protecting the environment, such as the World Wildlife Fund, the Nature Conservancy, and the Rails-to-Trails Conservancy, use direct marketing.

Educational institutions have long relied on direct marketing to obtain student enrollments, offer continuing education courses, raise funds, garner political support, and communicate with alumni and the larger community. Other nonprofit organizations include those concerned with helping our youth, such as Big Brothers Big Sisters, Boys & Girls Club of America, and the Rappahannock River Rats Youth Hockey Association. Nonprofit organizations also exist to protect women, such as the Miles Foundation and Battered Women's Organization, whereas others exist to provide support to minorities, such as An Achievable Dream. In summary, nonprofit organizations are using a variety of media and direct marketing tactics to generate awareness of their causes and to obtain volunteers, donors, and friends. The next section explores how political organizations are using direct marketing to promote both their cause and their candidates.

Political Organizations

Do you want to be elected president, governor, or mayor? Do you want to be elected to a school board? Do you want to build support or raise funds for the National Women's Political Caucus or Planned Parenthood? Do you want to overcome objections of legislatures to conversion of railroad rights-of-way to Rails-to-Trails? Do you want to garner political and financial support for environmental causes like the Nature Conservancy, World Wildlife Fund, American Rivers, and starving elk? If you answered "yes" to any of the above questions, you will rely on direct marketing activities to obtain votes and financial support!

The Internet is a valuable tool used by political parties and candidates to raise funds , secure campaign volunteers and win votes. However, political direct marketing activities are not always aimed at raising money. The Internet also permits the parties to send customized messages to specific groups and individuals and to use online discussions and instant messaging in support of their candidates. In today's sophisticated world, political organizations use unique analytical tools, such as micro-targeting, to create specific offers designed to woo voters.

Political micro-targeting, also referred to as *narrowcasting,* is aggregating groups of voters based on data about them available in databases and on the Internet—to target them with tailor-made messages.[11] Political parties gather personal information about voters to deliver narrowly targeted messages calculated to influence their votes. Micro-targeting goes beyond traditional segmentation bases to gather data at the individual level. This information can include magazine subscriptions, real estate records, consumer transaction data, demographics, lifestyle data, geography, psychographics, voter history, and survey response data. Micro-targeting can add great value to political marketing activities.

Political micro-targeting is used by political parties to determine which voters care about specific campaign issues. For example, research has shown that all people who regularly attend church are not alike. Political micro-targeting can be used to identify those churchgoers who would be more interested in hearing a Democratic message of social justice.[12] Given that direct and interactive marketing messages can be personalized and delivered to individuals on a one-to-one basis, micro-targeting is seen as a powerful tool for directing appropriate messages to voters. For example, in 2008, the Obama Presidential campaign employed micro-targeting techniques to its e-mail strategy and created hyper-segmented e-mails that provided readers with customized messaging.[13] In conclusion, political micro-targeting helps campaigns deliver more effective messages to specific individuals and households by tracking and analyzing information on a person-by-person basis.

Political organizations are not the only public administrative bodies to narrowly target select groups of individuals. A wide variety of governmental organizations regularly apply direct and interactive marketing strategies as well. This is the topic of our next section.

Governmental Organizations

The government has relied on direct marketing for many of its public interactions. The U.S. Postal Service (USPS) distributes direct mail to both end users and organizational consumers to promote its many products and services. Direct mailers encourage final consumers to purchase uniquely designed stamps, online postage services, as well as schedule convenient and time-saving pick-up and delivery services.

All branches of the military use direct and interactive marketing for targeted recruiting to high school juniors and seniors. Figure 1-15 presents some of the direct mail pieces being used by the U.S. Department of the Navy in its recruiting activities. Note the variety of motivational headlines it uses: "No sense hiding from the hero you were born to be." "How many people can put world traveler on their resume?" "Jump-start your life." The copy of each direct mail piece is compelling, promoting the benefits—world travel, exposure to cutting-edge technology, opportunity for college education, respect, and the ability to make a difference—associated with joining the military.

Beyond the U.S. military, many other governmental entities use direct and interactive marketing on a regular basis. Just think about the travel and tourism industry where most destination marketing organizations and convention and visitor bureaus fund their promotional efforts through local and state tax dollars. Most state and local tourism organizations use direct and interactive marketing because it produces campaign results that are measurable and attributable

FIGURE 1-15. U.S. Navy direct mailers. Use of the Department of the Navy's Accelerate Your Life® marks is granted with permission of the Department of the Navy and does not constitute an endorsement of any author, publisher or product thereof, by the Department of the Navy or the Department of Defense.

FIGURE 1-15.
continued.

to specific media, like media sourcing, response rates, conversion rates, and sales revenue generated from visiting tourists. The City of Virginia Beach concentrates its direct marketing efforts on prospective tourists in the northeast region of the United States. This geographic region is important because the city's convenient location makes it only a day's drive for two-thirds of the nation's population. The Convention and Visitors Bureau of the City of Virginia Beach distributes its Vacation Planner featured in Figure 1-16 to anyone who requests travel information about the City of Virginia Beach.

Often hand-in-hand with travel and tourism marketing is sports marketing, because the direct response that both of these marketers are often seeking is in the form of visitation. Let's now explore how sports organizations utilize direct and interactive marketing activities.

Sports Organizations

A variety of direct marketing strategies and tactics are frequently used by sports organizations to help them achieve their objectives. Virtually all sports team marketers share the common objective of filling the seats of their stadium, arena, park, or rink with loyal fans cheering them on to victories. Of course, sports marketers would prefer if these fans purchased season tickets and supported the home team for the entire season and not just one game. Sports marketers may

FIGURE 1-16. City of Virginia Beach vacation planner. Used with permission of the City of Virginia Beach Convention & Visitors Bureau.

also be interested in obtaining corporate sponsors or hosting fundraising events. These are additional areas where direct marketing can be applied in an especially effective manner. However, before you begin to think about the glamour and fun associated with sports marketing, you should be aware of its unique challenges.

One uncontrollable variable that often presents a challenge to direct marketing to gain attendance for an upcoming game is the record and reputation of the visiting team. When the home team plays against a big contender or rival, or a team with an excellent winning record, securing attendance is much easier. When the contender doesn't have a good reputation or record, it is much more difficult to fill the seats. Similarly, the record of the home team is an important component of sports marketing. A winning team is easily marketed. Everyone wants to support a winning team! But when the team is not performing well, the task of selling season tickets becomes quite a challenge.

Promoting special events to regular season ticket holders is another common communication objective. Often sports organizations will partner with nonprofit organizations to hold special events to raise funds for a specific cause. For example, the Norfolk Admirals Hockey Team supported a breast cancer cause by creatively painting the ice pink! The Admirals donated a portion of ticket sales to the cause, auctioned off pink hockey sticks and autographed jerseys, held a pregame Women's Hockey 101 Clinic, and provided educational materials.

FIGURE 1-17.
Cover of the
Norfolk Tides
sponsorship
brochure. Used
with permission
of Norfolk Tides
Baseball Club.

Of course, sports marketers also use direct marketing activities to prospect for new fans by offering group discounts. It is also common for sports marketers to promote attendance at select games that might not naturally garner a high attendance.

So far we've discussed how sports marketers use direct marketing activities targeting final consumers (B2C). However, equally important is their efforts to market to business consumers (B2B). Most sports marketers actively promote to business consumers to obtain sponsorship support for their team. Many of these activities entail direct marketing strategies and tactics. As Figure 1-17 shows, the Norfolk Tides Baseball Club offers a variety of sponsorship packages to prospective sponsors. Prospective sponsors are asked to respond by placing a phone call to the number provided at the bottom of the brochure or by visiting the Norfolk Tides Web site. These brochures are distributed via postal mail to both current and prospective sponsors.

Summary

Direct marketing is a database-driven interactive process of directly communicating with targeted customers or prospects using any medium to obtain a measurable response or transaction via one or multiple channels. Almost all types of businesses can and do conduct direct and interactive marketing activities, including organizations and individuals whose goal is to establish long-term relationships with their customers. Direct and interactive marketing uses many different types of media and formats, including direct mail, catalogs, newspaper, magazine, radio, television, phone, Internet, hand-held devices, and mobile. The industry has a long history and has experienced rapid growth primarily due to credit cards, computers, advances in the printing industry, changing lifestyles of consumers, and the negative aspects of in-store retailing.

Customers are at the heart of the direct and interactive marketing process. The main goal of the direct and interactive marketing process is to develop and strengthen long-term relationships with customers.

Key Terms

direct marketing
brand marketing
customer relationship management (CRM)
multichannel distribution/
   multichannel fulfillment

business-to-business (B2B)
   direct marketing
industrial goods
political micro-targeting

Review Questions

1. Name and elaborate on the characteristics that distinguish *direct* from *traditional* brand marketing.

2. What is meant by measurability of and accountability for marketing decisions?

3. What is the difference between a list and a database?

4. Write an overview of the components of the direct and interactive marketing process and model.

5. "Direct marketing is an aspect of marketing characterized by *measurability* and *accountability* with reliance on *databases*." Explain this statement.

6. Discuss the historical roots and the emergence of direct marketing; how has it been influenced by technological, economic, and social change?

7. Compare and elaborate on the changes in graphic design between the 1947 and 2008 catalog covers of Oriental Trading Company shown in Figure 1-7.

8. How does the Internet fit into the total marketing scheme of things and the distinguishing characteristics of direct marketing?

9. What is direct response advertising and how does it relate to direct mail as well as print, broadcast, and Web sites?

10. Describe the use of direct marketing by a business. Describe its use by a nonbusiness organization. Describe how it fits into the political scheme of things.

Exercise

Think of your favorite cuisine. Pretend you have just opened a restaurant featuring all of your favorite foods.

a. How will your marketing plan use direct marketing techniques to build your business?

b. Pretend a year has gone by and you have been successfully operating your restaurant. How will your direct marketing activities change over the next few years?

Critical Thinking Exercise

You have just decided to run for mayor of your town. Think about the political campaign you want to conduct and identify the various direct and interactive marketing strategies you will utilize in your campaign. From a direct and interactive marketing perspective, what can and should you do to uniquely position yourself to be perceived as the better candidate and win votes? What steps will you take in creating your campaign? How will you connect with voters in your town? What mediums will you select to communicate your message?

CASE: Cheryl's

This case is an example of how a company effectively uses multichannel marketing in growing a business. It demonstrates how a new entrepreneurial venture was successfully launched on a very small budget by concentrating on direct-response communication channels, CRM, and measurement. The case specifically details how a company manages multiple channels in serving its customers. It is proof that direct and interactive marketing can work for any company, organization, or entrepreneur—regardless of size.

As a learning experience, the student should focus on the basic elements of direct marketing, including marketing research, database development, CRM, measurability and accountability, and multichannel distribution. Then, examine how direct and interactive marketing strategies and techniques play an integral role in the development and execution of a successful twenty-first-century business. Let's see what you can learn from this inspiring tale of a successful entrepreneur.

In 1981, together with her college roommate, Caryl Walker, and equipped with an old-fashioned cookie recipe from her grandmother Elsie, Cheryl Krueger launched her entrepreneurial business venture. What began as a single cookie store has now evolved into a multimillion-dollar business. Today, the company headquartered in Westerville, Ohio, now named Cheryl's, is a multichannel marketer with retail stores, catalog, a growing Internet business, and a business gift division. What was the secret ingredient in building this successful business?

Cheryl started with $40,000, a degree in home economics/business, and seven years of retail experience. She began by opening one retail store. For the first five years, Cheryl worked two jobs to support the business. In 1985, she came on board full-time, and the company began to broaden its offering to include gifts and desserts along with an expanded dessert line, which now includes brownies, cheesecake, pies, and cakes.

FIGURE 1-18. Cheryl's logo.

Today, Cheryl's team of associates strives to be the best. Its goal is to be the #1 Food Gifting E-commerce destination. That includes having a customer-centered focus throughout the entire business. The company prides itself in putting the customer first. An overall philanthropic ethos exists throughout the company culture, from free shipping to military (APO/FPO), involvement with cancer research, and a collaboration with the Make-A-Wish Foundation. Customer relationships are the key to any successful business. That is especially true for food and gift companies because of the large number and wide variety of competitors that exist in the industry. Therefore, building and maintaining customer relationships has been a focus of the company right from the beginning.

In 2005, Cheryl sold the company to 1-800-FLOWERS.COM. 1-800-FLOWERS.COM is the world's leading florist and gift shop. Additionally, 1-800-FLOWERS.COM is composed of individually branded companies that include The Popcorn Factory®, 1-800-Baskets.com®, Fannie

May®, Wine Tasting Network® and many others. This family of brands offers opportunities for Cheryl's to build relationships with many new customers across the entire 1-800-FLOWERS.COM enterprise.

Building and Maintaining Customer Relationships

Customer relationship management is made possible through the development and use of a customer database. Cheryl's preferred customers receive certain offers and benefits that are not available to other customers. These special benefits are presented as a "surprise and delight" to the preferred customers. The special offers are most often delivered to individual customers via direct mail or e-mail communication.

The company maintains an internal customer database; however, it also works closely with an outside vendor to ensure data hygiene is maintained. Additionally, this is an enterprise-wide customer database/data warehouse that enables them to better understand and market to all enterprise customers. Therefore, any customer who has interacted with any of the 1-800-FLOWERS.COM brands will be listed in the enterprise-wide customer database. For example, someone who asks to receive a catalog from The Popcorn Factory, makes a purchase from 1-800-FLOWERS.COM, or receives a gift from Cheryl's, will be housed in the central database. There are many benefits to this system for both the individually branded companies and for all enterprise-wide customers. For example, wouldn't it be great for Cheryl's to know how many Popcorn Factory customers purchase birthday products each month so Cheryl's could send these customers a timely e-mail reminder the following year? This is just one example of the potential benefit of understanding a customer's place in life, so to speak. This type of customer lifestyle data will lead to the delivery of more appropriate and timely need-satisfying offerings from all enterprise-wide businesses.

Some important considerations when maintaining a customer database include—as mentioned earlier—data hygiene—ensuring that the information contained in the database is current, accurate, and not duplicated. Customer data hygiene involves basics such as employing National Change of Address (NCOA) and Address Standardization on the database, as well as on direct mail campaigns, to save considerable marketing dollars lost when mailing to invalid addresses. Also, customer identification and matching are important parts of data hygiene to avoid duplicate records, which would potentially result in a customer receiving multiple or irrelevant marketing communication. For example, when Cheryl's is able to identify that Customer Record X and Customer Record Y are actually the same person, the company can combine that customer's order history, contact preferences, and so on to optimize the profile of that customer, which will lead to cost savings and more efficient and effective marketing contact(s).

Database analysis is also important to Cheryl's. The company tracks several customer metrics such as buyer file size, retention rate of existing and new customers, number of new customers, purchase frequency, average order value, net promoter score, and so on to be able to market to and interact with its customers effectively. Cheryl's has developed a customer persona. "Katherine"—the name Cheryl's customer has been given—comes to "life" through this process—she not only has a name but also a face, a personality. Decisions the company will make will be viewed through the eyes of this fictitious customer.

Seeking New Customers

Prospecting efforts include cross-promotions with its enterprise-wide "family of brands." The company actively seeks out new customers via catalog prospecting both within the family of brands and through list rental and exchange agreements with competitors as well as other retailers who have a similar customer profile. The best prospecting methods for the company are

FIGURE 1-19. Cheryl's online catalog. Used with permission of Cheryl&Co®.

when prospective customers have an opportunity to view or sample its products. Cheryl's products are awesome, and the company consistently achieves high marks from its current customers via surveys. The company's buttercream frosted cookie is certainly what many consumers consider its "best foot forward" both from a visual presentation and a taste standpoint. Consumers also attest to the beautiful presentation of Cheryl's products, which is why catalog mailings are important prospecting methods. However, with environmental concerns, the increasing cost of postage, and the ever-growing online shopping audience it is has become increasingly important for Cheryl's to focus on its online marketing activities.

Cheryl's online activities including paid search, affiliate marketing, social media and natural search (search engine optimization). Cheryl's has a Facebook page, a Twitter account and a Blog. While the company is still in the beginning stages of understanding what its fans, friends and customers are most interested in, it has quickly learned that having contests and giving away Cheryl's cookies and gifts are a popular way to engage its audience! Figure 1-19 shows Cheryl's online catalog.

Multichannel Marketing Methods

Cheryl's retail stores account for about 8 percent of sales, with telephonic, Internet and Business Gift Services—a department dedicated to business-to-business sales accounting for 78 percent. 14 percent comes from QVC, cross-brand efforts and wholesale. Today, the most rapidly growing channel is its Internet business. Certainly a portion of these orders are driven by consumers receiving the Cheryl's catalog.

Cheryl's strives to align the customer experience regardless of what channel they choose to use. For instance, when a catalog is mailed out, often the company will feature the items that are on the catalog cover or on pages two or three in the catalog on the home page of its Web site. This same product line will also be "center stage" in Cheryl's retail stores. This provides a consistently branded image and message to those customers who shop via multiple channels.

Conclusion

Today, Cheryl's is a tremendous business success. Why? It is due to a combination of several things. First, it is because of the excellent quality products and strong focus on serving its customers. Second, its success is because of the application of savvy direct and interactive marketing strategies to maintain customers and reach out to new ones. Third, business success is due in part to offering customers multiple channels from which they can purchase products. Fourth, Cheryl's is a member of the well-known 1-800-FLOWERS.COM family of brands, which provides excellent cross-branding and cross-selling opportunities. And finally, as the saying goes, the proof is in the pudding (or in this case, in the cookies). Bon appetit!

Case Discussion Questions

1. What are the most important direct marketing concepts Cheryl's has employed to grow its business?
2. What additional offers might Cheryl's offer to its customers to connect with them and serve their needs and desires?

Notes

1. Roland T. Rust and Richard W. Oliver (1994), "The Death of Advertising," *Journal of Advertising,* 23(4), 71–77.
2. Philip Kotler and Gary Armstrong (2008), *Principles of Marketing,* 12th ed. (Englewood Cliffs, NJ: Prentice Hall).
3. Gary Armstrong and Philip Kotler (2007), *Marketing: An Introduction,* 8th ed. (Englewood Cliffs, NJ: Prentice Hall).
4. Herbert Katzenstein and William S. Sachs (1992), *Direct Marketing,* 2nd ed. (New York: Macmillan).
5. The DMA Statistical Fact Book, 2011 ed. (New York: The Direct Marketing Association, 2011) p. 1.
6. Carol Scovotti and Lisa D. Spiller (2006), "Revisiting the Conceptual Definition of Direct Marketing: Perspectives from Practitioners and Scholars," *Marketing Management Journal,* 16(2), 188–202.
7. *The Integration of DM & Brand, 2007* ed. (New York: Direct Marketing Association, 2007), p. xxiii.
8. Many of the early historical references contained in this section are based on documentation prepared by Nat Ross for the Direct Marketing Association.
9. Edward L. Nash (1993), *Database Marketing: The Ultimate Marketing Tool* (New York: McGraw-Hill).
10. Martin Baier (1996), *How to Find and Cultivate Customers through Direct Marketing* (Lincolnwood, IL: NTC Business Books), p. 3ff.
11. "Political Microtargeting," SourceWatch, 2008, retrieved on May 19, 2008, http://www.sourcewatch.or/index.php?title=Political_microtargeting.
12. "The 2008 Tools Campaign: Microtargeting," New Politics Institute, retrieved on April 29, 008, http://www.newpolitics.net/content_areas/new_tools_campaign/microtargeting.
13. Rahaf Harfoush, (2009), *Yes We Did: An Inside Look at How Social Media Build the Obama Brand,* Berkeley, CA: New Riders, p. 48.

## CHAPTER 2

Building Databases, Rewarding Customers, and Managing Relationships

OPENING VIGNETTE: DICK'S SPORTING GOODS SCORECARD® REWARDS PROGRAM

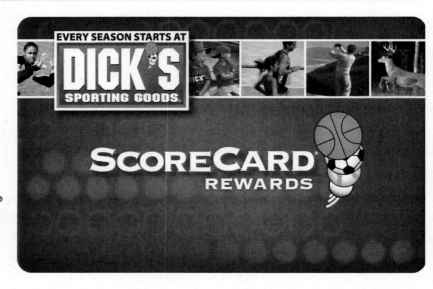

FIGURE 2-1.
Dick's Sporting
Goods ScoreCard®
rewards program
card. Used with
permission of
Dick's Sporting
Goods, Inc.

He shops. He scores! Dick's Sporting Goods ScoreCard® Rewards Program enables its customers to earn rewards while making purchases at any of its stores or online. Customers may register for the ScoreCard® Rewards Program for free. Once registered, members earn points each time they shop at Dick's Sporting Goods and are awarded a $10 reward certificate for every 300 points they earn. Program members may also receive exclusive deals, new product alerts, and insider access via its direct marketing programs.

So, you don't like basketball? Are you a runner or a golfer? Might you enjoy water sports? If so, what kind of water sports do you prefer—motorized or paddle sports? Members of the Dick's Sporting Goods ScoreCard® Rewards Program also receive specialized direct marketing catalogs and programs based upon their sports preferences and past purchase history. Therefore, if you are a ScoreCard® Rewards Program member and you are a runner who has purchased running shoes at Dick's Sporting Goods, you will likely know that the month of May is National Runner's Month. How will you know? Because you would have received the Dick's Sporting Goods *Runner's Gear Guide* containing exclusive offers for ScoreCard® Rewards Program members.

The Runner's Gear Guide presents a wide variety of merchandise associated with running, such as running shoes, clothes, watches, water bottles and other accessories. This year's Runner's Gear Guide also contained 14 inspirational stories of why people run, coupons to score bonus points with the purchase of a pair of athletic shoes or athletic apparel, and a special offer to go to NationalRunnersMonth.com to register to win a Dick's Sporting Goods shopping spree! The Runner's Gear Guide also encourages you to go to Dick's Sporting Goods' Facebook page to share your own running story with the company.

Let's say you are a ScoreCard® Rewards Program member who enjoys water sports and has recently purchased a canoe from Dick's Sporting Goods. You will likely receive Dick's Sporting Goods Paddle Sports Gear Guide. Similar to the Runner's Gear Guide, it features special offers on a wide variety of kayaks, canoes, paddles, storage racks, accessories and water apparel. In addition, it presents short stories about topics related to paddle sports, such as how to choose the right kayak and water safety rules. The Paddle Sports Gear Guide also contains coupons for discounts on purchases related to paddle sports, along with special bonus point offers.

In conclusion, Dick's Sporting Goods makes shopping fun and easy while it creates value for its customers. With its ScoreCard® Rewards Program, the company is able to connect with its customers on a personalized basis uniquely tailored to each customer's lifestyle and activities. Dick's Sporting Goods illustrates the value of using its customer rewards program to build and enhance its customer database and initiate and maintain customer relationships, the topic of this chapter.

All direct marketers seek to maximize the profits of their business. Two ways to achieve this are attracting new customers and encouraging your current customers to buy more from you. However, it is very well established that a new customer acquisition program may *not* be as profitable as a customer retention program. Did you know that it costs (on average) about eight to ten times more money to acquire a new customer than it does to keep a current one?[1] Thus, direct marketers may be better served by directing their marketing efforts toward retaining the customers they already have. This is the concept behind database-driven direct marketing, which is the focus of this chapter. We also discuss what a customer database is, its importance in developing customer loyalty, and how to build, maintain, secure, and use a customer database. In addition, this chapter discusses database enhancement and database analytics. Finally, we discuss the importance of CRM and PRM.

Customer Database

A **customer database** is a list of customer names to which the marketer has added additional information in a systematic fashion. Just as a house list contains active as well as inactive customers, inquirers, and referrals, so does an organization's customer database. Thus we can think of a customer database as a computerized house list that contains more than merely a listing of customer names.

A customer database is the key to developing strong customer relationships and retaining current customers. It is the vehicle through which a company documents comprehensive information about each customer. This information could include the consumer's past purchases (buying patterns), demographics (age, birthday, income, marital status, etc.), psychographics (activities, interests, and opinions), and much more. Marketers use this information to direct all future marketing activities with each customer on an individual basis. For example, the customer database is used for such purposes as lead generation, lead qualification, sale of a product or service, and promotional activities. Armed with this information, marketers are able to develop a closer relationship with each customer on a personalized basis. The stronger the relationship with each customer, the more likely that customer will continue purchasing from the company. That is why current customers, with whom the direct marketer already has an established relationship, are more likely to be retained as future customers.

How does a company retain its customers? By keeping the customer satisfied and happy. Highly satisfied customers tend to be loyal customers, and loyal customers generate greater profits for an organization over their lifetime of patronage. This is due to the following reasons:

1. Loyal customers tend to increase their spending over time. These customers are better to have and more profitable than other customers.[2]

2. Loyal customers cost less to serve than new customers. Repeat customers have greater familiarity with an organization's processes and procedures and therefore are more quickly and easily served.

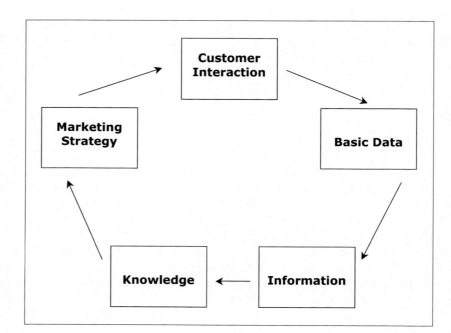

FIGURE 2-2.
Database
development
process

3. Loyal customers are normally happy customers who tell others about the organization, commonly referred to as word-of-mouth advertising, which in turn generates additional business.

4. Loyal customers are less price sensitive than are new customers. They see value in their relationship with the organization and may spend more freely because of their high level of satisfaction with the company.

In addition, according to Frederick Reichheld, author of *The Loyalty Effect,* a five-percentage-point increase in customer retention in a typical company will increase profits by more than 25 percent—and growth by more than 100 percent.[3] The task of creating and maintaining loyal customers is what CRM is all about. In an attempt to retain current customers, marketers invest in programs and activities to create and enhance customer loyalty. The development of a customer database is the first step in this process.

Database Development

Developing a customer database for marketing purposes is an ordered process. It begins with obtaining basic data about customers. This is followed by the task of converting that data into relevant information for the company. Then the company uses that information to produce knowledge about its customers and their preferences. Armed with that knowledge, a company can develop strategy to better communicate with and serve its customers. Finally, customer interaction will likely yield additional valuable customer data for the company. Figure 2-2 provides a flowchart of the process.

However, in building a customer database, the management must first determine the company's primary goals. For example, an organization might want to get to know its customers better to develop more effective future promotional activities. Other objectives may include selling them different products/services, thanking them for their patronage, encouraging referral business, introducing a new product or service, distributing information about an upcoming event or sale, or introducing a new staff member or employee . . . the list goes on! Customer loyalty programs are commonly used in the process of creating a customer database.

Customer Loyalty Programs

Customer loyalty programs are programs sponsored by an organization or company to encourage customer repeat purchases through program enrollment processes and the distribution of awards and/or benefits. Airlines, hotels, cruise lines, retail stores, and many other organizations have rewarded customer loyalty through structured programs for years.

Organizations primarily offer customer loyalty programs to strengthen customer relationships. Loyalty programs are also used to develop or provide additional information to a company's customer database. The beauty of customer loyalty programs is that you can obtain information about customers on a direct basis and use this information to more effectively target customers' future needs and wants.

Examples of Loyalty Programs

Southwest Airlines encourages long-term customer relationships and fosters a customer-driven approach to generating loyalty through its *Rapid Rewards* frequent flyer program. (See Figure 2-3.) The program, which began in 1987, was recently redesigned and its features were refined with insights gathered from its customers.

Members of the Rapid Rewards program earn points for every dollar they spend with Southwest and a number of designated partner companies. Customers may redeem these points for award travel with unlimited availability and freedom from blackout dates. Points do not expire as long as a member's account stays active within a 24-month period. As can be seen in Figure 2-4, Southwest Airlines embraces nearly every opportunity, including signage throughout airport terminals and promotional messages printed on its napkins and bags of peanuts, to advertise its Rapid Rewards program and drive customers to its Web site to enroll.

Customers may even sign up for a Rapid Rewards credit card for which points are earned after every purchase. (See Figure 2-5.) Southwest's most frequent customers who fly 25 or more one-way flights or earn 35,000 points in a calendar year also earn "A-List" status. This preferred status carries many perks such as priority boarding, priority check-in, and bonus Rapid Rewards points.

Southwest's Rapid Rewards program is an excellent example of how companies strengthen relationships with customers and reward valuable customers for their loyalty. Establishing a customer loyalty program is not only a great way to reward customers, but it is also an excellent mechanism for collecting data from customers.

FIGURE 2-3. SWA Rapid Rewards logo. Used with permission of Southwest Airlines.

FIGURE 2-4.
Airport sign &
napkin and
peanuts.
Photographs by
Adam Baker. Used
with permission
of Adam Baker.

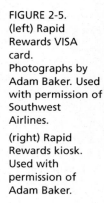

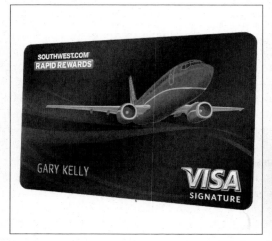

FIGURE 2-5.
(left) Rapid
Rewards VISA
card.
Photographs by
Adam Baker. Used
with permission of
Southwest
Airlines.

(right) Rapid
Rewards kiosk.
Used with
permission of
Adam Baker.

Source Data

The information contained in a customer database is called **source data.** Each direct marketer must determine the particular source data needed for the organization's customer database—which often varies based on the specific products or services or the competitive situation of the direct marketer. Collecting data that will not be used simply drives up the organization's marketing costs. Within their house records, direct marketers usually capture certain key data, such as product preferences or credit experience, if relevant. Many companies today collect much of their customer data through online registration forms and even automatic online data collection methods. An important piece of data that many companies record is the source code of each customer. The **source code** indicates the media, media vehicle, or means by which the person has responded to become a customer. These codes should be very specific and may include sources such as participation at a specific event, referral from another customer, referral from an employee.

Companies like Amazon.com automatically collect from viewers of their Web sites information such as computer Internet Protocol (IP) addresses, item searches and browsing activity, and purchase history. Through the use of cookies, in which Amazon.com stores specific identifying information on customer computers, the company can offer personalized features, including "Recommended for You" items, relevant advertisements on other Web sites, and item storage in

ASSUMPTIONS:

Recency of Transaction:	20 Points If within Past 3 Months
	10 Points If within Past 6 Months
	5 Points If within Past 9 Months
	3 Points If within Past 12 Months
	1 Point If within Past 24 Months
Frequency of Transaction:	Number of Purchases within 24 Months Times 4 Points Each (Maximum: 20 Points)
Monetary Value of Transaction:	Gross Dollar Volume of Purchases within 24 Months Times 10% (Maximum: 20 Points)
Weighting Assumption:	Recency = 5
	Frequency = 3
	Monetary = 2

EXAMPLE:

Cust.	Purchase #	Recency	Assigned Points	(x5) Wght. Points	Frequency	Assigned Points	(x3) Wght. Points	Monetary	Assigned Points	(x2) Wght. Points	Total Wght. Points	Cum. Points
A	#1	3 Mths.	20	100	1	4	12	$ 30	3	6	118	118
A	#2	9 Mths.	5	25	1	4	12	$100	10	20	57	175
A	#3	24 Mths.	1	5	1	4	12	$ 50	5	10	27	202
B	#1	12 Mths.	3	15	2	8	24	$500	20	40	79	79
C	#1	3 Mths.	20	100	1	4	12	$100	10	20	132	132
C	#2	6 Mths.	10	50	1	4	12	$ 60	6	12	74	206
C	#3	12 Mths.	3	15	2	8	24	$ 70	7	14	53	259
C	#4	24 Mths.	1	5	1	4	12	$ 20	2	4	21	280

FIGURE 2-6. R/F/M Values.

the company's online shopping cart. Amazon.com discloses this automatic data collection through its privacy policy accessible online.[4]

Some of the basic data marketers should collect for a customer database are the customer's name and address including ZIP code, telephone number, and e-mail address. Many direct marketers document how the customer first learned about the product or service. Additional data called **transactional data** include what products each customer has purchased, how recently (recency) and how often (frequency), and how much the customer spends (monetary). This information provides an avenue to analyze each customer through some variation of the **recency/ frequency/monetary (R/F/M)** assessment. By carrying the date and volume of purchases in the master list record over a period of time, marketers can determine the transaction record of each customer in a given period, which helps determine the future potential of that customer.

Assessment

The exact R/F/M formulation for each direct marketer naturally varies according to the importance given to each of the variables in relation to each other. For some promotions, marketers might need to manipulate their calculations by weighting one of the factors, so that, for example, the results will show those customers who had purchased most recently. More sophisticated direct marketers use multivariate statistical techniques to mathematically determine the R/F/M weights and use them with greater reliability.

Figure 2-6 shows how to evaluate customers on a mailing list according to the combined R/F/M values of their transactions over time. For purposes of this example, the following weights are assigned to the variables: recency ($\times$ 5), frequency ($\times$ 3), and monetary ($\times$ 2). In the example, three customers (identified as A, B, and C) have a purchase history calculated over a 24-month period. We assigned numerical points to each transaction, according to the derived R/F/M formula and further weighted these points. The resulting cumulative point calculations—202 for A, 79 for B, and 280 for C—indicate a potential preference for customer C. C's R/F/M history, and perhaps A's as well, justify spending more promotion dollars. Customer B might be an unlikely promotion dollar risk. To apply R/F/M assessments, marketers must keep the customer database—especially the transaction data—current by means of continuous database maintenance.

Database Maintenance

A database is a perishable commodity that needs constant oversight and maintenance. Direct marketers must establish maintenance schedules and adhere to them rigorously. An initial requirement for proper list maintenance is that the list be compiled and developed in a uniform manner. Only when such uniformity exists within a computerized list is it possible to use match codes with any assurance of control.

Database maintenance activities include identifying and eliminating any duplicate records, identifying consumer names that appear on a number of different direct marketing response lists, and keeping the customer records current. Let's look more closely at each of these activities.

Match Codes and Merge-Purge

A serious and often cumbersome problem in compiling and maintaining lists is the potential for duplicating the same individual or organization, not only within house lists but also within and between response and compiled lists and even between these lists and house lists. Given that most lists are computerized, marketers can extract from a name/address record abbreviated information about this record. This abbreviation is called a **match code,** and it is constructed so that each individual record can be matched with each other record. Because such matching requires a tremendous amount of computer memory, the match code is abbreviated to minimize the need for such storage. The match code abbreviation should be designed so that it addresses each area where errors are likely to occur within key parts of a record, such as transposition within a street address number as shown in the example here.

Ann Stafford	Ann Stafford
9330 West Arlington Road	3930 West Arlington Road
Alexandria, VA 22301	Alexandria, VA 22301

An example of a simple 18-digit match code derived from the name/address is shown in Figure 2-7. Quite often, direct marketers add other data to the match code, such as a unique identification number or an expiration date for a magazine subscription. Mailing labels for catalogs or periodicals often demonstrate match codes of this type. An example is the ten-digit customer number used by the Newport News catalog of Spiegel Brands. This unique customer number reveals information about the particular market segment to which each customer belongs, their credit card status, whether they are a member of the Newport News Discount Club, and more.

An alternative to match codes is a unique identification number, such as a Social Security number, which identifies only one individual, but the customer or prospect has to provide this number for the marketer to be able to use it. Today, many consumers are not willing to provide their Social Security numbers due to privacy protection considerations.

Using the abbreviated match codes, the computerized **merge-purge process** identifies and deletes duplicate names/addresses *within* house lists. It can also eliminate names on house lists from outside response or compiled lists the marketer is using for new customer solicitation. Thus, the organization's own house list will not be duplicated within that promotion effort to prospects. The merge-purge process can eliminate duplication between these outside response and compiled lists as well.

Merge-purge is a highly sophisticated and complex process, but essentially it generates a match code for each name/address on each list, and these match codes, potentially many million of them at a time, are matched with every other name on the list in sequence. Duplications are identified for special handling (which we discuss later).

Position	Item	Description
1	State	A unique alpha-numeric code assigned to each state
2-5	ZIP code	Last 4 numbers of 5-digit ZIP code
6-8	Surname	1st, 3rd, and 4th alpha characters of surname or business name
9-12	Address	House or business number
13-15	Address	1st, 3rd, and 4th alpha characters of street name
16	Surname	Alpha-numeric count of characters in surname
17	Given name	Alpha initial of first name
18	Given name	Alpha-numeric count of characters in first name

EXAMPLE ADDRESS

Ann Stafford
9330 West Arlington Rd
Alexandria, VA 22301

DERIVED MATCH CODE

8 2 3 0 1 S A F 9 3 3 0 A L I 8 A 3
1 2 3 4 5 6 7 8 9 10 11 12 13 14 15 16 17 18

FIGURE 2-7. Match codes.

% DUPLICATION (OR MULTI-BUYERS)	TOTAL NUMBER OF NAMES/ADDRESSES MERGED					
	100,000	500,000	1,000,000	2,500,000	5,000,000	10,000,000
5%	$1,000	$ 5,000	$10,000	$ 25,000	$ 50,000	$100,000
10%	$2,000	$10,000	$20,000	$ 50,000	$100,000	$200,000
15%	$3,000	$15,000	$30,000	$ 75,000	$150,000	$300,000
20%	$4,000	$20,000	$40,000	$100,000	$200,000	$400,000
25%	$5,000	$25,000	$50,000	$125,000	$250,000	$500,000
30%	$6,000	$30,000	$60,000	$150,000	$300,000	$600,000

Assumption: Mailing cost is $200 per thousand names mailed (or not mailed).

FIGURE 2-8. Economic value of merge-purge.

It is doubtful that a "perfect" match code could be developed, one that would compensate for *all* the idiosyncrasies and potential errors inherent in a name/address record. However, the one shown in Figure 2-8 has a pretty good track record.

As demonstrated in the direct mail example shown in Figure 2-9, even a 5 percent "hit" rate, eliminating the need to mail 5 percent duplications, can result in substantial savings. This is especially true when several million name/address records are merged and purged. Thus, identifying a duplication of 15 percent of the names, when one million names on various lists are merged and purged, would eliminate 150,000 pieces of unnecessary mail. At an assumed cost of $200 per thousand names mailed, this would result in a savings of $30,000. Against this savings, of course, would be the cost of the merge-purge itself, possibly as much as $10 per thousand names examined or $10,000 for a one million name/address input.

The merge-purge process can also effectively remove names of individuals who have expressed a desire not to receive solicitation as well as those who are poor credit risks or otherwise undesirable customers. Figure 2-8, adapted from an actual merge-purge procedure, displays the manner of showing duplicate names/addresses on two or more lists. Both name and address variations are shown.

Name	Address	City	State	Zip
Samantha Fox	12353 N. Oak Drive	Arlington	VA	22301
Samantha Fox	12353 N. Oak Drive	Arlington	VA	22301
Christina Smith	250 Elders Drive	Arlington	VA	22301
C Smith	250 Elders Drive	Arlington	VA	22301
Jerry Matthis	9372 Nasaw St	Arlington	VA	22301
Jerry Matthis	9372 Nasaw St	Arlington	VA	22301
Dale Armstrong	700 Mosac Ln	Arlington	VA	22301
Nancy Armstrong	700 Mosac Ln	Arlington	VA	22301
Steven Samson	3662 S 11th St	Arlington	VA	22301
Steve Samson	3662 S 11th St	Arlington	VA	22301
Regina Jones	251 12th Ave	Arlington	VA	22301
Regina Jones	252 12th Ave	Arlington	VA	22301
Elaine Lowell	261 N Second St	Arlington	VA	22301
Claire Lowell	261 N 2nd St	Arlington	VA	22301
Carson Snyder	690 42nd St	Arlington	VA	22301
Carson Snyder	690 42nd St	Arlington	VA	22301
Catherine Marlin	Apt 963 561 N 5th St	Arlington	VA	22301
Catherine Marlin	561 N 5th St	Arlington	VA	22301
Elizabeth Parks	68 Waverly Lane	Arlington	VA	22301
Elizabeth Parks	68 Waverly Ln	Arlington	VA	22301
Elizabeth Parks	68 Waverly Ln N	Arlington	VA	22301
Elizabeth Parks	68 Waverly Ln N	Arlington	VA	22301

FIGURE 2-9. Duplicate records.

Multibuyers

Eliminating duplicate names/addresses, saving costs, and minimizing irritation to those receiving duplicate mailings all are obvious advantages of the merge-purge process. But there is another, possibly even greater advantage. If the same name/address is found on two or more response lists simultaneously, that individual may be a better prospect for a direct marketing offer because he or she is a **multibuyer.** Experimentation has shown, in fact, that those whose names appear on three lists have a higher response rate than those appearing on two lists. Likewise, names appearing on four lists are even more responsive.

In addition to identifying multibuyers, direct marketers perform database maintenance activities to keep their customer records current and accurate. These activities are discussed in the next section.

Keeping Records Current

If incorrect addresses or phone numbers result in misdirected advertising promotions, the cost is twofold: (1) the wasted contact, and (2) the sacrifice of potential response. That is what is at stake if the direct marketer does not keep his or her records current. In an effort to keep customer records current and accurate, direct marketers regularly perform change of address investigations, nixie removal, and record status updates. Let's examine each of these activities in greater detail.

Whenever possible, direct marketers request address corrections through the postal service. The U.S. Postal Service assures that mail prepaid with first-class postage is automatically returned if undeliverable or else forwarded without charge if the new address is known. In the latter instance, for a fee, the change of address notification can be sent back to the direct marketer. In the case of advertising mail, the use of the "address correction requested" legend on the mailing envelope guarantees prepayment of any return postage and service fees. There are many variations of this particular list correction service relative to either individual mail or catalog mail, concerning forwarding or return postage guarantees.

Additionally, direct marketers encourage the recipient of mail to inform them of any change of address or phone number. If available, customers are encouraged to reference a unique account code when requesting changes. If the account number is unavailable, customers are asked to provide both the old and new address—the former for entering into the system and removing the old record, and the latter for future addressing.

Using the "address correction requested" service on each and every customer mailing is not necessary; once or twice a year should suffice to clean the database. Using the legend more frequently, because of lags in handling times, could result in duplication of returned mail and unnecessary duplication of costs. The term **nixie** refers to mail that has been returned by the U.S. Postal Service because it is undeliverable as addressed, often due to a simple error in the street address or the ZIP code. Possibly, the person to whom the piece is addressed is deceased or has moved and left no forwarding address. The marketer will remove such names from the mailing list; unless the list owner can obtain updated information, they cannot be reinstated. According to the U.S. Census Bureau, about 14 percent or 40 million Americans move each year.[5] Perhaps this is why e-mail addresses are quickly becoming the preferred address—because they do not necessarily change each time the person moves to a new geographical location. However, some Internet service providers are local, and if you move to a new location, you have to change your e-mail address. Also, keep in mind that many consumers switch Internet providers due to personal preferences, and many more prefer to change their screen names.

The U.S. Postal Service, for a nominal handling fee, will provide direct marketers with correct address information, if available. Often, however, mail addressed to a deceased person will go to the surviving spouse. Business mail to an individual who has changed positions or even left an organization will go to the replacement in that position. Although the U.S. Postal Service will not send notifications in such instances, some direct marketers correct their lists in other ways. Special notices might periodically be sent with mailings requesting list correction. Additionally, sales representatives may request consumer information changes each time he or she calls on a customer. In some cases, the mail recipient sends such notice directly. Other ways list owners can update their lists include news items, periodic updates from telephone and other directories, and public records such as birth and death notices and marriage and divorce proceedings.

Changes in telephone numbers should be made periodically to house lists that are used to access customers by telephone. Customers who have changed to unlisted numbers should be contacted by mail or an effort should be made to obtain these numbers.

It is important to perform database maintenance not only from the perspective of nixie and otherwise undeliverable mail but also to keep the record status of customers up to date. List owners should enter new orders from customers into the database promptly because they have a major impact on the R/F/M formulation described earlier. Such prompt record keeping also avoids unnecessary mailings, telephone calls, or e-mails to customers who already have what the direct marketer is offering.

Database Security

Customer databases are assets, much the same as buildings, equipment, and inventories. Because their value is intangible, however, databases are not easily insurable (except for replacement or duplication costs) even if we can determine their future value. Unlike other assets, they're portable, especially when an entire database can be placed on a single computer disk.

For these reasons, marketers must take special precautions to prevent theft, loss, or unauthorized use of the database and to guarantee the information privacy rights of all consumers.

Information Privacy

As we address in greater detail later in Chapter 12, organizations that maintain a customer database also have a responsibility to safeguard the personal information contained in it. The dramatic growth of online marketing has also led to new challenges for protecting the privacy of customer information. Online consumer databases contain a wide variety of personal identification information, and if security is breached, this information may be accessible by those with intentions of identity theft and scamming. A 2011 customer database breach involving major multi-channel marketing provider Epsilon resulted in the compromising of names and/or e-mail addresses of some individuals. Access to these types of information could lead to e-mail "phishing," in which individuals receive realistic but unauthorized e-mails that seek to obtain more personal information such as social security numbers and passwords. Though the unauthorized access in Epsilon's case likely only affected around two percent of the marketing provider's clients, the subsequent obligation of companies such as Marriott and Hilton to send informational alerts regarding the incident to their member database placed Epsilon at risk of tarnishing its positive reputation.[6]

Direct marketers must use the information only in a highly ethical manner and honor any consumer requests to have their personal information kept confidential—which means not sharing it with other direct marketers. Therefore, regular database maintenance should include activities to protect the information privacy rights of consumers, as well as to ensure that the information in each database record is accurate and kept up to date.

Proper Database Storage

A logical first step in database security is the provision of adequate storage. Usually, such storage protects against natural hazards of fire and water damage, as well as theft or unauthorized use. To discourage theft, marketers should limit and control access to database files at all times. This often involves certain passwords used to protect the database and permit only select individuals access to the information stored in the database. Should records become lost, adequate backup should be available in the form of duplicate records at a remote location.

List Seeding

Direct marketers have developed a variety of marking techniques to ensure that their customer lists are not misappropriated or misused, especially when rented to outside parties. One commonly used technique is called salting or seeding a list. **Seeding (salting)** a list is when the direct marketer places decoys, which are either incorrect spellings or fictitious names that appear nowhere else, on the customer list so as to track and identify any misuse. Although a seeded list may reveal such misuse, it may not lead to the guilty person. Marketers should construct identification programs like seeding so that the decoy names will not be removed through match coding. Of course the decoy names should be confidential and access to them limited.

Direct marketers discourage list theft by placing seeds on lists. Direct marketers must communicate their use of list seeds to all parties involved in the list industry. By fully disclosing the actions to protect their lists, direct marketers may discourage list theft.

Database Uses and Applications

Once we have captured and stored data, we can convert it into real information to better serve customers and maximize profitability. The uses of a customer database are virtually endless; we discuss some of the more common ones in this chapter. Keep in mind that the real beauty of a customer database is that it enables direct marketers to communicate with small market segments or individual customers without other customers knowing. This kind of communication secrecy, also called **stealth marketing,** enables direct marketers to extend different types of offers to individual customers on the basis of their customer information.

For example, Harris Teeter, a regional grocery store, sends elaborate gifts on a regular basis to its *very best* customers. These customers also receive a $10 Harris Teeter gift card at Thanksgiving along with a personally signed thank-you letter from the store manager. Gifts of lesser value and thank-you letters not containing the gift card may be sent to those regular customers who are *not as valuable* to Harris Teeter, based on the amount spent. Furthermore, Harris Teeter may send other direct mail letters containing coupons encouraging other customers (those even *less valuable*) to shop more often at Harris Teeter. This kind of one-on-one communication is made possible by analyzing the source data contained in a customer database. This is critical to successful direct marketing because building customer relationships is most effectively carried out on a one-to-one basis. The ability to know one's customers and communicate with them individually is the basic premise of a customer database for direct marketers.

Using a Customer Database

Though there are a million ways to use a database, let's explore eight of the more common uses.

1. *Profile customers.* By developing a geographic, demographic, social, psychological, and behavioral profile of their customers, direct marketers can better understand the various consumer market segments they serve. For example, Carnival Cruise Line has 10 cruise line brands, with more than nine million customers, 65 percent being repeat customers.[7] Imagine all of the information its database has on its customers' prior travel habits and interests and how the company may use this data to profile its customers. Carnival collects information regarding passenger anniversaries and birthdays, what cruises passengers took, what they paid, their sailing dates, how many people traveled in their party, and whether they traveled with children. This information enables the company to better understand the needs of their typical customers.

2. *Retain the best customers.* According to the well-known 80/20 principle, approximately 80 percent of an organization's business is generated by 20 percent of its customers. Thus, it is critical that direct marketers analyze their customer database to determine who their best customers are and to spend more effort (and promotional dollars) in keeping these customers satisfied and coming back for more! Just think of the Harris Teeter example. Harris Teeter can afford to spend more money in terms of promotional dollars to keep those customers who spend more money in groceries satisfied and coming back on a regular basis. Harris Teeter cannot justify sending its occasional shoppers gifts and personally signed thank-you notes from the store manager.

3. *Thank customers for their patronage.* All customers deserve to be recognized and thanked for their decision to purchase from a given organization. This is especially true when the direct marketer has a number of competitors from whom the customer could have purchased. Customers expect to be satisfied with their purchase decisions; however, follow-up activities can often provide an avenue for future dialogue with each customer to ensure that satisfaction. Thanking customers is also an effective way to both reinforce

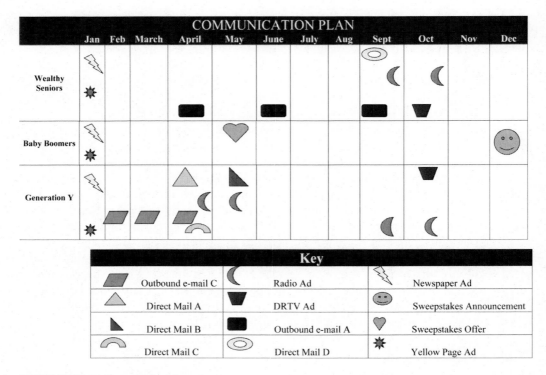

FIGURE 2-10. Communication plan.

purchase decisions and promote future purchases. An example is the thank-you letter containing a bumper sticker that is mailed to an individual who makes a donation to a state or local police association. Donors take pride in displaying those bumper stickers, which state, "I Am a Proud Supporter of the Virginia State Police."

4. *Capitalize on cross-selling and continuity selling opportunities.* **Cross-selling** refers to selling your current customers products and services that are related (and even unrelated) to the products/services they currently purchase from your organization. By analyzing the products and services your customers have purchased from you, you can identify and capitalize on numerous cross-selling opportunities. **Continuity selling** has also been referred to as "club offers"; here consumers purchase on a regular basis—either weekly, monthly, quarterly, or annually. *Time* magazine, for example, cross-sells its other publications—*People, Sports Illustrated, Fortune*—to certain current subscribers.

5. *Develop a customer communication program.* As mentioned earlier, the real beauty and power of a customer database is that it enables the direct marketer to communicate on a one-to-one basis with each customer. Thus, the company can segment its promotional strategies based on the customer group and individual with whom it is communicating. For example, newer customers could receive "welcome" letters, while established customers might receive "thank you for your loyalty" letters. Of course, each customer does not know what is being communicated to other customers. Unlike general advertising, a customer database also enables customized marketing communications to occur between the company and its customers without the competition knowing. This is another powerful use of the customer database. As Figure 2-10 reveals, customer communication plans or programs are targeted, tailored, and timed communications with

select members or segments of the customer population. These are planned communications and most models depict a 12-month communication program.

Many companies, such as Smithfield Foods featured in Figure 2-11, send e-newsletters to their customers. In the e-newsletter, Smithfield encourages its customers to "Tailgate with Smithfield" and offers its customers a sampling of great new recipes to try out for grilling at the game or at home.

Finally, a customer communication program implies two-way communication. Direct marketers use customer feedback to revise and improve their marketing activities to better serve the customer and maximize profitability. Examples of customer communication programs are numerous. Hotels, airlines, grocery stores, nonprofit organizations, magazines, and just about every direct marketer creates and uses one to guide its customer and prospect communications. If you purchase a new car, chances are likely that you will receive a variety of follow-up communications from the automobile manufacturer. Say you purchased a Honda Civic. The first message you receive should be a "thank you" for your purchase. Next might be a mini-survey to assess the quality of your Honda shopping experience. After that, you might receive a number of updates about what is new at Honda and regular reminder notices about when you should bring your Civic back to the dealer for servicing. Of course, at some point in time, Honda will suggest that it is time to trade your Civic in for a new one!

6. **Perform marketing research.** The database is a natural arena for direct marketers to conduct marketing research to better understand the current and future needs and wants of their customers. Marketing research gathers, classifies, and analyzes information about customers. This information is normally "problem-specific" or "purpose-specific." For example, if the direct marketer is thinking of bringing a new product or service to the market, investigating the potential response from current customers is a natural application of marketing research. Marketing research activities can include customer satisfaction surveys, new product research, customer needs assessments, brand preference studies, media preference research, and much more.

For example, many hotels send send surveys via e-mail following customer stays. Hilton and Marriott and their associated brands are consistent with this approach, asking how expectations have been met, and even sending reminders to complete surveys that have not yet been completed and returned.

7. **Generate new customers.** We've seen that analyzing the customer database enables the direct marketer to develop profiles of its average customers and its best customers. Armed with this information, direct marketers can seek out new customers who may have needs and wants similar to those of their current customers. This also enables direct marketers to rent response or compiled lists of prospects who match the profile of their best customers and target them with promotional offers to attract new customers. This is a much more effective and efficient way to generate new customers than merely blanketing the mass audience with advertisements in the hope that someone with a need or desire for the product/service will respond.

Another very effective way to generate new customers is via referrals. Current customers can be sent offers to encourage their relatives and friends to become customers as well. Many companies provide a "forward to friend" option in their e-mail communications with customers. Here's an example of how a company has both thanked its customers and generated referrals at the same time. One benefit that a Busch Gardens pass member has is the ability to purchase discounted tickets for friends and family. Based on the level of the pass, the discount is either $12 or $15 off a single-day ticket. Shown in Figure 2-12, as a way of offering a bigger discount and to drive spring visitation prior to

FIGURE 2-11.
Smithfield Foods
e-Newsletter.
Used with
permission of
Smithfield Foods.

the launch of a new ride, Busch Gardens mailed postcards to all annual pass members offering a 50 percent discount on single-day tickets good for up to six tickets. The park received a 2.2 percent response rate and gained new customers.

8. ***Send customized offers.*** We've seen that analyzing the customer database enables a direct marketer to develop a profile of consumer needs and wants. It also enables direct marketers to create customized offers to individuals or market segments within the customer database. Customized offers often are sent via direct mail or outbound e-mail. E-mail is generally more cost effective, and it enables companies to easily target customers who are members of a company's loyalty program. Of course, all companies provide the opportunity for customers to opt out of receiving such e-mail communication. An excellent example of a company that sends valuable customized offers to its loyalty program members is Barnes & Noble. Its members receive weekly communication about new book titles and special offers for extra discounts on these featured book titles. Various offers encourage the sale of DVDs or used books, and sometimes these offers are limited to online shopping. As Figure 2-13 shows, occasionally members receive free gift offers, like a free book light, when they spend a specified amount or special limited time offers to obtain an extra discount on their in-store or online purchases.

FIGURE 2-12.
Busch Gardens
Best Spring
Ever postcard.

FIGURE 2-13.
Barnes & Noble
offers. Used with
permission of
Barnes & Noble
Inc.

These are examples of how a company communicates regularly with its customers by sending customized offers. Keep in mind that the more data a direct marketer has about its customers, the more specific and customized the offers can be. For that reason, most direct marketers regularly update customer records and, whenever possible, incorporate new information to their customer records. This process is called *database enhancement,* and it is discussed later in this chapter. However, every direct marketer will regularly analyze the data contained in its customer database to learn more about its customers to more effectively serve them. This process is called *database analytics,* and it is the key to effectively using a customer database for all purposes. Let's discuss database analytics in greater detail.

FIGURE 2-13.
continued.

Performing Database Analytics

Database analytics is where the direct marketer analyzes customer information housed within the customer database to draw inferences about an individual customer's needs. This relies on customer profiling, modeling, and data mining. **Data mining** uses statistical and mathematical techniques to extract knowledge from data contained within a database. It is the process of using software tools to find relevant information from large amounts of data, typically an enterprise data warehouse, and using the results for strategic business decision making.

A variety of database tools permit assessment of single-variable information. However, the multivariable patterns can allow assessment of causes and effects in the business process. The true value of the integrated data warehouse can be found by leveraging decision support tools, such as online analytical processing (OLAP) to mine the data for hidden patterns. OLAP has long been the domain of business analysts and statisticians. Today, sophisticated new tools enable business analysis capabilities via the data warehouse throughout the entire organization. Previous tools provided only static reports, offering little flexibility in terms of what a user could glean or screen from the warehouse. With OLAP, users can slice and dice the data from a summary level down into the detail of the data record. Marketers can obtain information on customers by region or by revenue and do it all from their desktop. An example might be a direct mail transaction database in which responders are evaluated by different demographic characteristics. The analysis could allow the marketing team to select specific prospects from large compiled files that fit common customer profiles.

Let's take a look at another example. Teradata, a division of NCR, analyzed the sales data of a well-known retailer and found some interesting correlations. Based on the analysis, Teradata found a direct relationship between the purchases of beer and diapers in the evening hours.[8] On investigation, the retailer found that this was occurring because husbands were being sent out on Saturday night to buy diapers and subsequently purchased beer as an impulse item. Thus, retailers and merchandisers wanting to predict and model future consumer behavior use information like the beer and diapers relationship in their attempts to maximize the effectiveness of their marketing efforts. This example points to the fact that data analytics are only valuable if the new knowledge gained enables the users of the information to make *actionable decisions*. Yes, beer and diapers were found to be positively correlated, but most retailers would not rearrange their stores to stock these items side by side.

The secret to database analytics is for marketers to be able to identify their most and least valuable customers and clarify demographic and behavioral statistics that apply to each population. Then they must be able to clearly identify the differences between the two groups. Marketers use data analytics to make strategic business decisions to retain current customers and attract new ones. Think of it this way: if you can clearly identify specific differences between your "best" or most valuable customer and your least valuable customer, then you will know how to "mine" the most likely best customers from prospect lists and databases. Although this seems like common sense, many businesses do not take the time to analyze, evaluate, and act on this critical knowledge.

The drivers to using analytical data revolve around cost, value, and accuracy: cost of the analysis, long-term value (or lifetime value) of a current or prospective customer, and accuracy of the data to be used in strategic decision making. There is a plethora of data available to marketers, at a wide range of costs and detail. The key is in obtaining the most current, relevant, and accurate data to add to your existing customer database. The process of adding data to a customer database is the topic of the next section.

Database Enhancement

Database enhancement is adding and overlaying information to customer records to better describe and understand the customer. Direct marketers also call it "appending" the database. It is a means to an end, not an end in and of itself. There are at least three specific reasons to enhance a customer database:

1. To learn more about the customer.

2. To increase the effectiveness of future promotional activities targeted to current customers.

3. To better prospect for new customers who are similar to current customers.

The kinds of information that enhance a database in this way include geographic, demographic, social, and psychological data. We can obtain the data either *internally* or *externally*.

Internal Data Enhancement

Direct marketers can obtain information *internally* when they conduct marketing research activities with their existing customers. Of course, each customer must be willing to furnish the given data. Examples of information that direct marketers, such as Carnival Cruise Lines, Dell Computers, or Hallmark Cards, can collect internally from their customers include:

- Age
- Gender
- Income
- Marital status
- Family composition
- Street address
- E-mail address
- Length of time at current residence
- Size of household
- Type of housing
- Telephone number
- Preferred contact method
- Do not mail (preference)
- Lifestyle data

Direct marketers cannot gather all enhancement data internally; therefore, they must rely on some external sources as well. For example, when applying for a JC Penney credit card, the company must obtain some historical information about your credit rating prior to approving your application and establishing the limit of your line of credit.

External Data Enhancement

Direct marketers purchase external data from many different sources. They purchase data compiled by companies like Experian, Equifax, R. L. Polk, and Claritas and electronically overlay this information onto their customer databases. The data are usually demographic, although some companies compile consumer lifestyle and leisure activity data. Claritas offers several products designed to assist direct marketers with customer database enhancement. Claritas Market Place File Enhancement helps direct marketers gain a better understanding of their customers and prospects. The behavioral profiles associated with this enhancement service include a variety of consumer buying behaviors, either from syndicated data or Claritas's own audits. Customer addresses can be standardized, geocoded, and appended with segmentation information in a matter of minutes. Claritas Consumer Point, customer targeting and strategic market planning software, connects a direct marketer's customer file with market data to expose hidden gaps in existing and untapped markets. Consumer Point's Internet-based data access provides insights into the most up-to-date segment distribution, behavioral profiles, and demographic/consumer demand data for targeting profitable customers and strategic market planning.

Examples of the data that direct marketers may obtain to enhance their customer database externally include:

- Geographic address
- Telephone number

- Gender of head of household
- Length of time of residence
- Number of adults at residence
- Number of children at residence
- Income
- Occupation
- Marital status
- Make of automobiles owned

Companies like Equifax, Experian, Ruf Strategic Solutions, and Claritas purchase census data from the government, sometimes for small geographic areas known as census tracts; direct marketers can purchase the data from these intermediary firms for a fee. Census data can help identify:

- Specific age segments (e.g., adults aged 18 to 24)
- One-person households
- Households with children
- Households with specified income levels
- Households with homes greater than specified values
- Adults with some college education
- Adults in college
- Adults with specified occupations

Finally, firms can purchase external data about businesses, rather than final consumers. Companies such as Dun & Bradstreet and Experian collect data on businesses and make it available to direct marketers for a fee. Such data can include:

- Company name/address/telephone number
- Industrial classification code
- Number of employees
- Gross sales
- Primary products produced
- Branch locations
- Name/title of key employees

In summary, direct marketers enhance their customer database in an effort to better serve the future needs and wants of their customers. This should result in a stronger relationship with each customer. While each customer is valuable to the direct marketer, all customers are not of equal value. Let's examine how direct marketers manage relationships with their customers.

Customer Relationship Management

Market share has shifted to customer share, competition to collaboration, and mass marketing to integrated interactive relationship marketing. Technology has shifted also. Interactivity, spurred by the commercial development of the Internet, now allows marketers to address customers as individuals, gather and remember their responses, and reduce the amount of time necessary to make strategic decisions about how customers make purchase decisions. The marketer's tool kit has also been enhanced by the convergence of technologies such as high-speed computing, expanding communication bandwidth, massive national databases, enhanced statistical decision support tools and campaign management. This convergence has allowed for the development of **customer relationship management**, an integrated system that delivers a single source transactional database of up-to-date customer information throughout an entire organization and maximizes the total value of the customer relationship and organize the outbound communication driven by database marketing.

Within all of this innovation, however, many companies have lost sight of the foundations of experimentation that have been the cornerstone of database marketing in the past. CRM provides a variety of sales, marketing, and service functions that allow interaction with prospects or customers across the organization and multiple media channels. The main benefit is that all information, from prospect communication to sales close to service history, are tracked and used for management of treatment for that customer and future prospects based on patterns that emerge with analytics.

Customer relationship management tools should be employed to track all of the outbound media touch points from a company, including e-mail, direct mail, SMS text messaging, banner ad marketing, direct response TV, and traditional channels such as radio, newspaper and magazine ads. A new form of CRM that has analytic tools embedded into the media planning and measurement modules allows scoring of response touch point data in real-time so a marketer can modify and customize its campaigns to target lists or media channels that are delivering higher value return on investment. Ruf Strategic Solutions was one of the first vendors to offer Intelligent CRM or I-CRM in its product called NAVIGATOR . This product allows the marketer to immediately access the marketing results through an online dashboard linked to the marketing database. Campaign management, forecasting trends, media analysis, and data mining capabilities are connected to enable timely, results-oriented decisions for successful customer relationships. An I-CRM tool typically contains:

1. Multichannel Marketing: Communicate with your customers across all touch points through a fully integrated data warehouse and sharpen your targeting skills to maximize response rates and reduce waste.

2. Marketing Automation: Simplify complex processes, obtain instant access to key performance indicators, and compare results from different periods or campaigns in order to gauge business trends.

3. Campaign Management: Manage and measure every campaign from list selection, based upon any combination of variables from your database, through results tracking and campaign ROI.

4. E-mail Marketing: Effortlessly deliver high volumes of e-mails, create customized and personalized messages, and obtain detailed response reports.

5. Analytical Tools: Gain actionable intelligence with powerful tools such as OLAP, which can quickly identify the reasons behind customer actions, and Web Analytics, which can enhance your Web visitors' experiences.

6. Data Services: Enhance, consolidate, and standardize of all your data into one comprehensive database.

In summary, I-CRM tools give marketers the real-time intelligence needed to be successful in modifying marketing spending and tracking market changes in a timely fashion. The goal of CRM is to allow the entire organization to be cohesive in how it communicates with each customer and manage that customer experience as if it has distinct knowledge of needs and prior support issues. This is a "closed-loop" process, as shown in Figure 2-14.

Full-circle marketing, which is based on the fact that not all customers are created equal, is

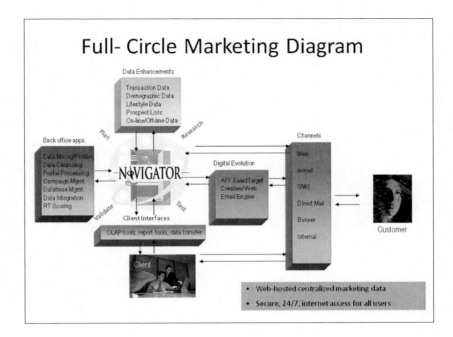

FIGURE 2-14. Ruf's Full-Circle marketing process. Used with permission of RUF™ Strategies Solutions.

an innovative marketing strategy that brings database marketing to a new level. Because customers change over time, marketers' communication with them must follow these changes if they are to maintain optimum lifetime value. The framework for this full-circle approach includes four dimensions that are at the heart of the experimental technique. This foundation includes planning, research, testing, and validation and then repeats in a never-ending feedback loop.

CRM has been evolving over the years and, with proper assessment of the organization process and readiness to adapt to a data and customer-centric strategy, can lead to significant business competitive advantage. It's amazing when you consider that most residential and business consumers take the underpinnings of a highly sophisticated CRM system or platform for granted. Such systems include everything from point of contact to "is it available?" and "when will I receive it?" to a problem or complaint. By focusing on CRM at the initial point of contact, the company has a far better chance of nurturing a long-term relationship that generates satisfaction for the customer and revenue or value for the company. Understanding customer value is a necessary element in the development of effective marketing strategies.

Customer Value

All customers are not of equal value to a company or organization. We can categorize customers according to the strength of their relationship to our company or organization. As Figure 2-15 reveals, customers can be placed in a hierarchy with the least valuable at the bottom and the most valuable at the top. *Suspects* are those prospective consumers that you think may have a need or want for your company's product or service. *Prospects* are qualified "hand-raisers" who have identified themselves as having an interest in your company or organization. Prospects may have visited your Web site or dialed your toll-free number. Your *customers* have placed an order with your company. They could be called "single buyers" as you do not know if they will return for a repeat purchase. *Clients* are multibuyers. These are repeat customers with whom you have an established relationship. At the top of the customer hierarchy are your *advocates*. These customers are your most valuable customers. They generate the most revenue for your company.

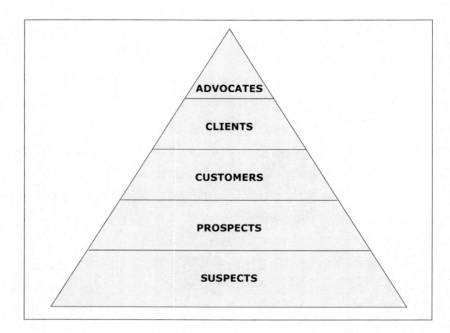

FIGURE 2-15.
Customer
hierarchy.

In direct marketing, the emphasis is on discerning between one-time buyers versus multi-buyers. A customer who has purchased twice is a proven repeat buyer and is far more likely to purchase again than a one-timer. Thus, marketing strategies are tailored to convert one-time buyers into multibuyers and expend fewer resources on them as they age, relative to multibuyers. Additionally, for companies that are multichannel (direct mail, Web, retail), those customers who purchase from more than one channel tend to be more valuable in the long run than those who purchase from a single channel. This has to be carefully evaluated to factor out the fact that a multichannel buyer is, ipso facto, a multibuyer. Thus, companies must determine what, if any, additional value for being a multichannel buyer comes above the multibuyer status.

Marketers must keep in mind that customers who buy once and never buy again have a one-time value. Prospective customers who never make a purchase usually cost the company in unrequited advertising and possibly service dollars. However, customers who buy frequently have a maximized or enhanced value to the company. Why? It's simple. As we mentioned earlier in this chapter, a company's best customers are loyal to the company, require less customer service and assistance, spend more per transaction, and generate valuable referrals. This combination adds up to greater value for the company. That is precisely why most companies have a customer-centric focus.

Therefore, a company's CRM strategies that focus on customers' wants and needs at the earliest possible touch point and make their experience long-lasting and sustainable, prove their worth in value. As with all direct and interactive marketing, what is measurable is what translates into knowing what defines value. Although all facets of measurability are important to the direct model, a company that knows the economic worth or value of its customers is the most defining. The value of customers over their lifetime allows a company to claim these customers as assets on its balance sheet. Hence, the importance of LTV.

Lifetime Value of a Customer

The **lifetime value of a customer (LTV)** can be calculated as the discounted stream of net revenues that a customer will generate over the period of his or her lifetime of patronage with a company.[9] The information for calculating LTV is derived from transactions recorded in an organization's database.

Whenever we gain or retain a customer as a result of good customer relations, we earn not only the revenue generated in one month or one year but also the *present value* of the *future profits* generated for as long as the customer remains active as a customer.[10] Just think . . . if a business were to be totally consumed in a fire, its tangible assets such as buildings, equipment, and inventory could be rebuilt in time, and each of these tangible assets is likely to be covered by insurance. The business would continue. However, if an organization lost its database of customers, an intangible but very valuable asset, the business likely could not continue. Without customers, there is no business! You might argue, well, the business would simply have to go out and get new customers. That may be true, but it would require much greater effort and cost than most companies could sustain.

Direct marketers spend a major portion of their time, effort, and money developing lists of customers and qualified prospects. In fact, many in direct marketing believe that such lists, along with descriptive databases, are in fact the key ingredients that differentiate *direct* marketing from general marketing. Therefore, direct marketers especially should view their customers as assets, as investments. They are the lifeblood of a direct marketing organization from which future sales accrue at a cost that is generally significantly lower than that attributed to the first sale.

It follows that if a marketing expenditure can result in the acquisition of *new* customers who will generate value over future time, that action is desirable even though the initial cost to obtain those customers might be greater than the short-term return on that investment. Some might call this long-term return on investment, LTV, the cost of goodwill. Savvy direct marketers call it "the value of a customer."

Naturally, when a new customer is acquired, the direct marketer does not know whether that customer will make only a single purchase or become an ongoing customer. The direct marketer cannot determine if that customer will purchase only low-margin products that have limited profitability or purchase without paying attention to price at all. However, direct marketers know that in most cases the cost of acquiring customers will yield a positive return on the investment. In Chapter 4 we explain how to calculate customer LTV and explore the implications of this important metric.

One-on-One Personalized Marketing

Segmentation analysis allows the company or organization to treat the customer with one-to-one personalization and customization. Just as the corner grocer of the past could anticipate his customers' exact needs, current modeled propensities can project likely results from variable treatment of millions of respondents. Everything from the offer, price, and graphic design can be changed, customized, and personalized for a single customer in a nanosecond with information on who is entering your Web site or responding at your fulfillment center. Many travel destinations use response scores to modify the fulfillment kit that will be delivered to the inquirer. For example, a senior with an affinity for art will be sent the museum tour piece, and the middle-aged household with highly active lifestyles will get the adventure kit. This type of customization and personalization is the result of detailed market segmentation made possible by customer and prospect database analysis.

The concept of micro-targeting has become a hot topic in marketing today as we mentioned earlier in Chapter 1. **Micro-targeting** is one-on-one personalized marketing, based on advanced, precise psychographic and lifestyle data. One of the benefits of one-on-one marketing is that you are able to deliver your message to a select customer or prospect (or group of them) without others knowing about it. Earlier in this chapter we presented that concept of stealth marketing.

SOCIAL NETWORKS THAT OBAMA JOINED In 2008 Presidential Election	
AsianAve	Flickr
BlackPlanet	GLEE
Digg	LinkedIn
DNC PartyBuilder	MiGente
Econs	MyBatanga
Eventful	MySpace
Facebook	Twitter
FaithBase	YouTube

FIGURE 2-16. Obama social networks.

This type of communication flies below the radar and can be thought of as the opposite of mass marketing. Micro-targeting abandons the concept of the big idea for an advertising campaign because those ideas included standardized offers and mass media communications. As more companies shift promotional budget allocations to more targeted media, such as e-mail, direct mail, special events, and trade shows, micro-targeting will continue to grow in both usage and applications.

Here's an example of how micro-targeting was cunningly used by candidate Obama in his 2008 presidential election campaign. Obama was the first candidate to build profiles on social networks that targeted online communities that already existed—such as the minority communities, including MiGente, BlackPlanet, FaithBase, and AsianAve.[11] Of course the profile or message content varied and was tailored so that it resonated with each specific online market segment. For example, in Obama's FaithBase profile, he focussed on his own faith values, while on GLEE, an online community for Gays, Lesbians, and Everyone Else, Obama discussed his efforts to encourage and support equality.[12] The Obama campaign team created a number of official Facebook profiles that targeted specific demographics, including Veterans for Obama, Women for Obama, and African Americans for Obama.[13] As Figure 2-16 reveals, the Obama campaign identified and joined 16 different social networks in which to interact and share unique campaign messages designed for each online community type.[14]

In summary, as consumers' lives become more fragmented, and their interests become more specialized, micro-targeting and customized communications will continue to be a growing area for marketers.

Partner Relationship Management (PRM)

Earlier in this chapter we discussed the important concept of CRM. Now we'll discuss **partner relationship management** (**PRM**). PRM is where companies work closely with partners in other companies or departments to generate greater value to customers. In today's busy world, companies are networking with other companies and relying on partnerships to more effectively and efficiently serve the needs of their customers. Marketers cultivate relationships with prospective partners just as they cultivate relationships with their customers. According to Randy Jones of MindZoo, "Partner marketing represents one of the most effective ways to increase the visibility and open rate of your direct mail programs while decreasing your promotion costs and improving your return on investment."[15]

Often, companies and organizations engage in relationships with multiple partners to support a cause. In this instance, the partners share a common goal or objective in that they want to promote and support a worthy cause. That is why these types of partnership strategies are often

FIGURE 2-17.
The *Washington Post*
and XM Radio. Used
with permission of
The Washington Post
and MindZoo, LLC.
Photo by Kim Kirby,
www.jimkirbyphoto.com

called **cause-related marketing**. Selecting the right partner is one of the most important decisions in PRM. Critical to a successful PRM program is the identification of a partner or partners who can benefit from reaching your desired target audience.[16] Those PRM programs that are mutually beneficial to all partners will yield great success.

Let's explore an example of a mutually beneficial direct marketing partnership. The *Washington Post* and XM Radio teamed up to acquire new subscribers. As Figure 2-17 presents, these partners executed a direct mail campaign targeting urban young professionals with a contest that enabled responding new *Post* subscribers to automatically be entered to win an XM2go portable receiver and three months of XM Radio service. The *Washington Post* was responsible for this promotion and the majority of associated costs. XM Radio provided, at no charge to the *Washington Post*, products and services for contest winners, plus paid for 25 percent of total program costs. Basically, XM Radio was able to reach the target market for less than the cost of Standard A postage. This shows that partner relationships can provide cost-effective marketing venues.

Summary

A customer is the company's most important asset. Customer retention is more beneficial to most companies than is new customer acquisition. A customer database is a tool used to retain customers. It enables a company to establish and strengthen relationships with customers by allowing them to interact with each customer on a personalized basis. The information captured and stored in a database provides the company with knowledge about the particular needs, wants, and interests of each customer. Armed with this knowledge, marketers are better able to develop products and services that will satisfy each customer's needs and wants. In addition, the information housed in the customer database may assist the marketer in more effectively communicating with each customer. The end result is this: a highly satisfied customer, a loyal customer!

Database marketing employs a number of activities designed to acquire, store, and use customer information. Database marketing activities commonly include customer loyalty programs, such as the many airline, hotel, and grocery programs. In addition, direct marketers regularly assess the value of their customers. This may include applying the recency/frequency/monetary assessment and calculating the LTV over a period of time. Of course, direct marketers must keep their customer database current and accurate for it to be of value. Direct marketers perform common database maintenance activities, such as applying match codes and a merge-purge process to identify and delete duplicate customer records, identifying multibuyers, and performing status updates to keep each record current. Direct marketers also carry out a variety of activities designed to safeguard their database against improper use or theft. Some of these activities include salting or seeding their customer lists, applying access passwords, and ensuring information privacy protection for their customers. Each of these database marketing activities is critical in maintaining strong customer relationships, which, in turn, lead to the retention of customers. Database analytics, including data mining, are enabling marketers to better understand their current customers and target key prospects. CRM programs are highly valuable and are growing in popularity. PRM enables companies to pool their databases and achieve synergies to attract new customers.

Key Terms

customer database
customer loyalty programs
source data
source code
transactional data
recency/frequency/monetary (R/F/M)
match code
merge-purge process
multibuyer
nixie
seeding
salting

stealth marketing
cross-selling
continuity selling
database analytics
data mining
database enhancement
customer relationship management (CRM)
lifetime value of a customer (LTV)
micro-targeting
partner relationship management (PRM)
 cause-related marketing

Review Questions

1. What is a *customer loyalty program?* Identify three customer loyalty programs with which you are familiar. What are the benefits to each of the organizations sponsoring these loyalty programs?

2. When building a customer database, what must an organization first determine? What must they first identify?

3. What is a *match code?* Explain its importance for database development and maintenance.

4. Describe the activities required to maintain a customer database? How often do you think database maintenance should be performed?

5. What is the purpose of the merge-purge process? How does it work?

6. If incorrect addresses or phone numbers result in misdirected advertising promotions, what is the cost to the organization? How can this be avoided?

7. Explain the value of applying the recency/frequency/monetary assessment to an organization's customer database. Is it possible to determine when an organization should place more weight on one of the three variables over the other? If so, explain why. If not, explain why not.

8. Describe the value of database analytics. Provide examples of what can be learned via data mining.

9. Explain what is meant by the term *lifetime value of a customer*. Why is it important?

10. Imagine that you have recently started a new business venture and that you already have a database of 10,000 customers. You are going to a financial institution to obtain a loan to expand your business. The financial officer asks you, "What is the biggest asset of your business?" How will you respond? Provide support for your answer using the information presented in this chapter.

Exercise

Congratulations! You have just been hired as the marketing director for a local grocery store chain. They have just launched a customer loyalty program, and one of your main responsibilities will be to oversee this program. What strategies and tactics will you employ in promoting the program to entice customers to become members? Also, how do you plan on generating real value for program members? Finally, what source data will you gather, and how do you intend to use the source data contained in the database?

Critical Thinking Exercise

Research a few customer loyalty/rewards programs which utilize either a mobile device, e-mail address, or consumer Web site account. Do you think these programs are successful? What could or should be altered about each program to make it more customer-focused? Which program do you think is most successful? Why?

CASE: Nevada Tourism

Building, maintaining, analyzing and using customer databases for marketing purposes is what this chapter is all about. That is precisely what this case focuses on. The customers are tourists and the vacation destination is Nevada.

Nevada

When many people think about tourism in the state of Nevada, images come to mind of flashing lights adorning tall buildings and crowds of people bustling around from restaurants to shows and from casino to casino. The words that might be associated with Las Vegas, Nevada are "thrilling" and "exciting" and "alive." But, this is only part of what the great state has to offer tourists as there is so much more to be discovered beyond Las Vegas.

Nevada's vast public lands, coupled with its plentiful sunshine (more than 300 days of sunshine a year) provide a plethora of outdoor recreational opportunities, such as hiking, biking, golfing, fishing and hunting. Nevada offers many historic landmarks, cultural experiences, as well as some of the finest resort spas, for its tourists to enjoy. Nevada offers its guests year-round activities including a winter wonderland of skiing, snowboarding and snowmobiling fun.

Promoting Nevada's many tourist attractions is the primary purpose of the Nevada Commission on Tourism.

Tourism Marketing Objectives

The Nevada Commission on Tourism (NCOT) needed a cost-effective solution to generate high-quality, electronic leads, dubbed "Eleads," for travel to their state. NCOT was interested in a more focused approach to actually engaging customer interactions and lead creation versus traditional awareness-building campaigns that do not optimize marketing ROI. The objective was to drive new prospective travelers to the NCOT Web site to share travel information and capture their contact information for future marketing campaigns.

With the strategic knowledge and technological ingenuity of Ruf Strategic Solutions (a.database marketing and business intelligence company located in Olathe, Kansas), an ELead Generation and Customer Relationship Management (CRM) program was developed and implemented for NCOT. Ruf's Performance-Based Marketing solution was able to electronically deliver qualified leads to NCOT's CRM system (Navigator), while validating, verifying and enhancing lead data. The Performance-Based Marketing solution also recalibrated lead generation settings to ensure increased returns for NCOT. Let's explore how this lead generation program worked, and how *well* it worked to deliver high-quality leads (prospective Nevada tourists) to NCOT.

The E-lead Generation and CRM Program

Creative, yet simple advertisements as shown in Figure 2-18, promoting vacationing in the state of Nevada were placed throughout hundreds of publisher sites enticing interested tourists to respond to obtain their free Nevada Visitors Guide. Once the prospective tourist responded, Ruf's database system would go to work verifying and validating each response or "lead" to the national compiled household database in its data center. Ruf's system also enhanced each lead record by appending rich demographic and psychographic information. These qualified and enhanced leads were then automatically added to Nevada's CRM database and sent the requested Nevada Visitors Guide. Based on any expressed individual preferences, as well as enhancement data analytics, select prospective tourists would also receive content-specific e-mails tailored to their lifestyle and other follow-up marketing communication to strengthen the relationship.

How did NCOT determine which prospects should receive follow-up communications beyond responding to the prospect's initial request for tourist information? How did NCOT determine which leads should not be proactively followed beyond the initial reply? Also, how did NCOT's CRM system know what type of follow-up information to send prospects along with the format of such communication? The answer: Data analytics. Each lead was not only verified, validated and enhanced, it was analyzed for its *quality* and weighed for *follow-up*.

Program Analytics

While there are many different criteria that may be used to assess the quality of a lead, Ruf and NCOT decided there were three main factors that should be used to determine the quality of a lead for Nevada. These factors are:

1. Are they engaged? Did they click on links in Nevada e-mails sent after the lead was acquired? If so, this action provided valuable datum that was entered into NCOT's CRM database.

FIGURE 2-18.
Nevada tourist ads.
Used with permission
of RUF™ Strategies
Solutions.

2. Can they be reached? What was the percent of e-mail addresses retained over time and what was the e-mail delivery rate?

3. Do they resemble rural Nevada visitors? How many leads were similar to the top quintile of the Nevada (excluding Las Vegas) tourist profile and do they live in a state that has a high propensity to visit Nevada?

NCOT's CRM strategy was determined based on an analysis of the above three factors. The first two factors required analysis of the metrics provided regarding each prospect's interaction with Nevada's marketing communication outreach. The third factor required both analytics and predictive modeling. The leads were analyzed and compared with the current NCOT customer database to determine whether each lead had the propensity of becoming a valuable Nevada tourist in the future. Thus, database analysis was used to track, measure, and shape NCOT's marketing activities.

Program Results and Analysis

This Elead program was not only tailored, targeted, and well timed to respond to the varied interests of prospective Nevada tourists, but it was also a cost-effective marketing program for NCOT. According to David Peterson of NCOT, "Ruf Strategic Solutions has made this lead generation program so easy for us! It has become one of the most cost effective ways for us to generate leads who are interested in traveling to Nevada. We pay for exactly what we get with not waste and the qualified leads automatically appear in Navigator, our online CRM system, with dashboard gauges to show optimum lead sources and thus, streamlines our fulfillment process."

Analysis of the metrics proved that the ELead Generation and CRM program highly efficient and effective for NCOT as presented in Figure 2-19. During the first year in which the program was conducted, the Elead program used only 15 percent of NCOT's marketing budget and produced nearly 67 percent of all NCOT leads, with 62 percent of collateral requests being attributed to Eleads as well. Similarly, the program was responsible for acquiring more new e-mail addresses than any other Nevada program. Moreover, database analysis showed that prospects acquired via Eleads opted in for and were receptive to ongoing NCOT messaging at a higher rate than other NCOT marketing programs.

Further analysis revealed that people who respond to Elead campaigns greatly resembled visitors of rural Nevada with 45 percent of the leads falling into the top quintile (20 percent) of the most valuable Nevada tourist profile. The cost per lead was significantly less for Elead cam-

FY10 Scoring Report	Lead Count	% of Leads	Ever Clicked	Emails Retained	Email Delivery	Like NV Visitors	Campaigns Providing Largest # of Leads
Pay-for-Performance Internet Initiatives (Ruf Campaigns)	68,167	66.74%	7.0%	59.5%	31.4%	47.6%	Ruf E-Network, eMiles *33% of the leads were just acquired in April. Not yet clicked
Misc. Broadcast/Print/Internet	16,290	15.95%	22.9%	44.5%	96.9%	15.3%	Google Organic Search
General Print Campaign	12,640	12.37%	26.1%	55.0%	93.9%	22.9%	Endless Vacation, Sunset, Nat'l Geographic Traveler
NCOT Collateral Materials	1,841	1.80%	24.8%	52.8%	95.7%	15.8%	Adventure Guide, Visitors Guide, Nevada State Parks
Outbound e-Newsletter Communications	1,112	1.09%	90.8%	81.5%	93.8%	22.6%	eNewsletter
Co-Ops (TV, Print, Internet)	792	0.78%	19.5%	65.1%	96.4%	17.9%	Ski Lake Tahoe
Syndication, Local Cable, Time Warner, Local Broadcast	658	0.64%	17.4%	68.2%	97.0%	57.2%	KCBS Website, FOX KVVU Vegas
Paid Search Campaigns	227	0.22%	20.1%	54.3%	96.3%	36.5%	Google Paid Search
Direct Response Nat'l Cable TV	221	0.22%	10.6%	71.4%	95.8%	28.3%	Discovery Channel, CNN, Travel Channel, Weather Channel
Local Broadcast TV	128	0.13%	33.3%	15.0%	97.5%	52.1%	NBC Affiliates
Golf Direct and eMarketing	36	0.04%	88.6%	80.0%	91.4%	35.3%	eNewsletter
Ski Direct and eMarketing	31	0.03%	85.2%	70.4%	96.3%	34.6%	Ski Email eNewsletter
Totals/Averages	**102,143**	**100%**	**26.6%**	**61.4%**	**95.2%**	**29.3%**	

FIGURE 2-19. Scoring report table. Used with permission of RUF™ Strategies Solutions.

not including outbound emails

BEST   Average   Worst   Internal eNewsletter Excluded

paigns than for other prospecting sources (average $7 for Elead campaigns compared to $79 for other sources.) Finally, 100 percent of Eleads had an e-mail address compared with 69 percent for other prospecting campaign sources.

Conclusion

This case is an excellent example of a highly effective lead generation and CRM program. It also demonstrates the use and effectiveness of e-mail as a lead generating and relationship building medium with prospects. The leads generated by the Elead program described in this case were 100 percent accountable and measurable. Many Elead programs can be targeted to a specific geographic area and can target niche markets, such as ski and golf prospects as well. Such targeting can lead to more effective relationship marketing.

Building and strengthening relationships with prospects and customer is what database marketing and CRM is all about. In this case, Ruf 's Performance-Based Marketing program has enabled NCOT to effectively and inexpensively engage with highly qualified prospective travelers to the state of Nevada.

Case Discusssion Questions

1. Explain why generating high-quality electronic leads, "Eleads," is superior to traditional awareness-building campaigns in maximizing marketing ROI.

2. Discuss the data collection methods—e.g., e-mail, telephone, online chat—that the Nevada Commission on Tourism (NCOT) uses to obtain high-quality, electronic leads, "Eleads," in response to NCOT advertisements. What is the mechanism to capture and extract these data and add them to Ruf's database system?

3. Visit Ruf Strategic Solutions Web site, www.ruf.com, and click on TRAVELYTICS—marketing solutions built for the truism industry. Explain how Ruf's marketing analytics help travel and tourism organizations to discover, reach, acquire tourists and grow return on marketing investment.

Notes

1. "Love Those Loyalty Programs: But Who Reaps the Real Rewards?" *Knowledge @ Wharton,* April 4, 2007; "Marketing," retrieved January 28, 2008, knowledge.wharton.upenn.edu/article.cfm?articleid=1700. Ron Shevlin, "The Cost of Acquisition versus the Cost of Retention," August 1, 2007, retrieved January 28, 2008, marketingroi.wordpress.com/2007/08/01/debunking-marketing-myths-the-cost-of-acquisition-versus-the-cost-of-retention.

2. Arthur Midleton Hughes, "How to Retain Customers" (n.d.) retrieved February 8, 2008, www.crm2day.com/editorial/EEEZpkplyyYXurvQw1.php.

3. Frederick F. Reichheld (1996), *The Loyalty Effect: The Hidden Force behind Growth, Profits and Lasting Value* (Cambridge, MA: Harvard Business School Press).

4. http://www.amazon.com/gp/help/customer/display.html?ie=UTF8&nodeId=468496http://www.amazon.com/gp/help/customer/display.html?ie=UTF8&nodeId=468496#cookies, retrieved May 6, 2011.

5. http://www.homeinsight.com/details.asp?url_id=7&WT.cg_n=Publications&WT.cg_s=0&GCID=bhph1, U.S. Census Bureau Research, retrieved May 7, 2011.

6. http://www.epsilon.com/News%20&%20Events/Press_Releases_2011/Alliance_Data_Provides_Statement_Surrounding_Unauthorized_Entry_Incident_at_Epsilon_Subsidiary/p1061-l3

7. http://phx.corporate-ir.net/phoenix.zhtml?c=140690&p=irol-reportsother4 (2010 Annual Report), retrieved May 6, 2011.

8. "Taking Data Mining beyond Beer and Diapers," (August, 2002) *iStart: New Zealand's e-Business Portal;* retrieved from www.istart.co.nz/index/HM20/PCO/PV21906/EX224/CS22580.

9. Martin Baier, Kurtis M. Ruf, and Goutam Chakraborty (2002), *Contemporary Database Marketing: Concepts and Applications* (Evanston, IL: Racom), p. 151.

10. Adapted from Jon Anton and Natalie L. Petouhoff (2002), *Customer Relationship Management: The Bottom Line to Optimizing Your ROI* (Upper Saddle River, NJ: Prentice Hall), p. 138.

11. Rahaf Harfoush, *Yes We Did: An Inside Look at How Social Media Built the Obama Brand,* (Berkeley, CA: New Riders 2009), p. 138

12. Ibid.

13. Ibid. p. 139.

14. Ibid., p. 140

15. Randy Jones, *Partner Marketing,* whitepaper (Leesburg, VA: MindZoo).

16. Ibid.

Determining Lists and Segmenting Markets

OPENING VIGNETTE: NEXTMARK

Finding new customers is an important activity for all businesses and organizations. Therefore, effective customer prospecting is considered a highly valuable task in enabling a company or organization to grow. But how do direct marketers identify and locate the "right" prospects? The answer: they rent lists. A list is a specifically defined group of organizations or individuals who possess common characteristics. There are lists available for almost anything and everything. Just name it, and there's a list for it! Unfortunately, many marketing professionals don't realize how many highly targeted prospect lists are available to them because they do not have the right tools.

The challenge for most direct marketers is to locate appropriate lists that will enable them to communicate with prospects that are likely to have a need or desire for their products or services. Fortunately, this task has become much easier due to the advances in technology, the availability of lists, and companies like NextMark. NextMark, headquartered in Hanover, New Hampshire, is a leading provider of list commerce technology. (See Figure 3-1.)

Joe Pych founded NextMark in 1999 with the vision of streamlining the direct marketing process, particularly the mailing list procurement process. The company has quickly risen to the top of its industry, serving marketing professionals, list brokers, and list managers. NextMark's innovations include being the first to apply modern search technologies to the problem of finding mailing lists; the first to syndicate access to mailing list information through Web sites such as Direct Magazine, Multichannel Merchant, and the Direct Marketing Association; and the first to build the biggest and most up-to-date index of mailing lists in the world. More than 5,000 users from 1,500 companies can attest to the value of NextMark's services.

In 2005, NextMark unveiled a free list finder service to provide access to insider information on virtually every list on the market—which totals more than 60,000 lists! As revealed in Figure 3-2, a simple click on the Find Lists tab on NextMark's Web site will take you to the list finder. Simply type in the keyword for the kind of list that you wish to locate and voilà! An entire page of lists pertaining to your keyword is likely to appear! What happened? The NextMark's list

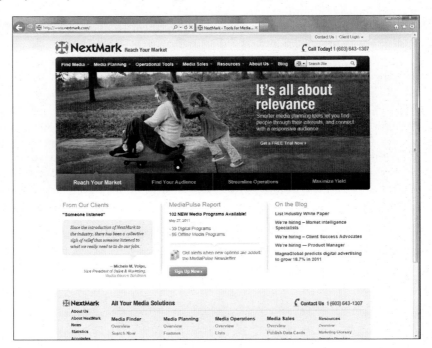

FIGURE 3-1. NextMark home page. Used with permission of NextMark, Inc.

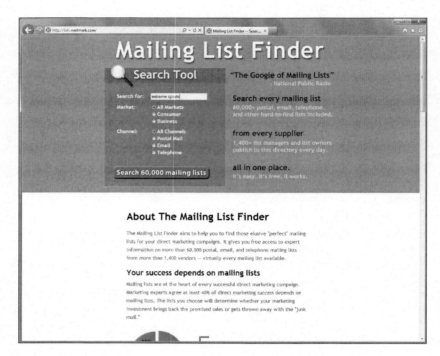

FIGURE 3-2.
NextMark Online
list finder service.
Used with
permission of
NextMark, Inc.

finder search engine identified the most relevant and popular lists based on your keyword. Each of these lists will have an associated rank—which indicates the "relevance" or fit of the data card to the specific set of search criteria used, and, in addition, the type of channel for which the list is available, such as postal mail, e-mail, telephone, insert, or stuffer. Next, click on the list that you want to further explore and in seconds, a data card appears for that particular list. Each data card includes detailed information about the list along with buttons to request additional information and to place orders.

NextMark does not own or manage any of the lists found on its Web site. Instead, it works with more than 1,400 suppliers—the list managers—to promote their lists through the list finder. According to Joe Pych, "The main purpose of NextMark's new list finder service is to raise awareness of the excellent specialized lists that are available and to make them more accessible." Many companies are partnering with NextMark to make this service even more valuable. In some ways, NextMark is building the technology to help eliminate the administrative headaches associated with developing lists and discovering markets. So if you want to effectively prospect for new customers, visit NextMark at www.nextmark.com and explore its list finder—you will be pleasantly surprised at how easy prospecting can be with highly targeted lists.

Developing lists and discovering markets is the topic of this chapter. We explore the different types of lists, identify the key players in the list industry, and explain how to evaluate lists. Then we'll discuss how to use lists and market segmentation to effectively develop new markets and prospect for new customers.

Lists as Market Segments

Lists and data are at the very core of direct marketing. Lists identify prospects as well as customers who have something in common. Perhaps these individuals made a response or transaction with the direct marketer. Perhaps the prospects on a list are all females who enjoy surfing as a hobby. Or a different list could identify all of the customers who purchased a surfboard from a certain sporting goods store within a given year. Yet another list could possess the names and addresses of males between the ages of 20 and 25 who are independently wealthy and own a horse! Therefore, lists cannot be thought of as mere mailing lists, because customers and potential customers on marketing lists are often reachable through media other than direct mail, such as e-mail, mobile, text, telephone, the Internet, magazines, newspaper, television, and radio. Lists are the marketplace, the "place" of the four P's of marketing (product, place, price, and promotion). A list denotes a market segment. Therefore, it follows that the direct marketer needs to accumulate data about the customers and prospects on its list(s). Marketers must identify relevant geographic, demographic, social, psychological, and behavioral information using information they discover about their customers to identify prospects with similar characteristics. In the case of customer lists, the direct marketer needs to record activity in terms of responses or transactions. What direct response medium triggered the activity? Did the person buy, inquire, or take some other action? What product was involved? Did the customer pay by credit card? Direct marketers also want to know how frequently the activity occurs, how recently it last occurred, and the dollar amount of the transaction.

A Perishable Commodity

A list is a perishable commodity. Not only does the degree of activity (or inactivity) fluctuate, which means a list could be less valuable tomorrow than it is today, but the people and organizations on lists are far from static. They move. They marry. They divorce. They die. Their attitudes change. In 12 months, for example, as many as 25 percent of the addresses on an average customer list could change.

The direct marketer must not only be aware of the condition of lists acquired from others but also be assured that the maintenance of the house list is current and adequate. Otherwise, part of the communication with an out-of-date list will be undeliverable and result in cost without potential benefit. List maintenance involves not only name and address correction but also continual updating of the data within the customer's record.

Data about a list are also perishable. No direct marketer wants to distribute messages indiscriminately. He wants to make sure not only that the message is delivered, it is also delivered to the right prospect. Direct marketers are particularly sensitive to the downside of indiscriminate mass communication, not only in terms of the waste of resources but also in terms of the possible antagonism sparked among non-prospects.

Technology has dramatically improved the manner by which direct marketers create, store, rent or acquire, and use lists. Today, the lists of almost all direct marketers are computerized and sophisticated. However, most direct marketing lists originated long before the computer age—and were housed on simple index cards. With computerization came the ability to research, rent, and test various lists and conduct precise market segmentation of house lists. Your objective in reading this chapter is to better understand how lists are developed, tested, segmented, used and analyzed.

Types of Lists

There are three basic types of lists. In descending order of importance to the direct marketer, these are:

1. House lists
2. Response lists
3. Compiled lists

HOUSE LISTS. These four segments of a house list may be among an organization's most valuable assets, inasmuch as they generate future business at a cost much less than that of acquiring responses from outside lists. It is not uncommon for a house list to be four times or even ten times as productive as an outside list with which there is no existing customer relationship.

The kind and degree of customer activity is also relevant in terms of products purchased as well as the recency, frequency, and dollar value of such purchases. The source of the customer as well as the promotional strategy the marketer used to acquire that customer is information that can also help determine future response. The original list source and whether this source was direct mail, space advertising, broadcast media, the Internet, or even a salesperson have a bearing on future productivity. With inquiries, there is only an expression of interest rather than an actual purchase. Although this information is important, inquiries do not have equal value compared with customer purchase information. With referrals, the recommendation by a customer of the organization could offer an advantage, especially when the name of the present customer can be used in the promotional effort sent to the referred prospect.

RESPONSE LISTS. **Response lists** are the house lists of other organizations. In terms of future productivity, these lists rate right behind house lists. Obviously, the lists of those direct marketers offering similar products and services will yield the greater potential for response to a similar or even directly competitive offer. A customer who has subscribed to a news magazine by mail, *USA Today,* for example, could be an ideal prospect for a competitive news magazine, such as *Newsweek.* Similarly, a consumer who has purchased fitness equipment by mail could be an ideal prospect for a sporting goods store such as the Sports Authority. The first important qualification is that the name on a list from an outside source has a history of response to direct marketed offers. The second and possibly equally important characteristic would be an indication of response to a similar direct marketed offer. Beyond this could be a history of purchase of related items. Those who have purchased gourmet meat products, for example, might be good prospects for gourmet fruit products. They might even be good prospects for classical records or a book on interior decorating.

Lists of directly competitive firms, if available, are obvious choices. On the other hand, one of the real challenges to direct marketers is to determine *why* the purchaser of a home study course by mail, for example, might be a particularly good prospect for a book club.

Like an organization's house lists, other response lists should be looked at in terms of geographics, demographics, and social and psychological factors. They should also be segmented by type of response and/or ultimate transaction or purchase. Direct marketers should consider response lists in terms of source as well as the promotional strategy that caused them to be responsive in the first place.

COMPILED LISTS. Usually falling behind both house lists and response lists in expectations are compiled lists. **Compiled lists** are lists generated by a third party or market research firm. Individuals on compiled lists do *not* have a response history. Examples of such lists include phone directory listings; automobile and driver's license registrations; the newly married and the newly born; high school and college student rosters; public records such as property tax rolls and voter lists; rating services, such as Dun & Bradstreet; and a multitude of rosters such as those for

FIGURE 3-3.
The Wall Street Journal
program. Used with
permission of *The Wall
Street Journal* and
MindZoo, LLC. Photo
by Kim Kirby,
www.jimkirbyphoto.com

service and civic organizations. Other potential sources of compiled lists include manufacturer warranty cards and coupon redemptions.

Although compiled lists typically do not have a response qualification built into them, market segmentation techniques coupled with sophisticated computer systems for duplication identification make possible selection of the best prospects (those most likely to effect a response or transaction) from very large compiled lists. Modern technology can also cross-identify characteristics of compiled lists, such as phone or automobile registration lists, with known response and thus further improve response potential. Combining a response list with an automobile registration list and further identifying those on the response lists who own a minivan, for example, is a way of identifying responsive households with children. Direct marketers use compiled lists in market segmentation and in further qualifying response and house lists. Let's take a look at an example of how direct marketers can effectively use compiled lists. The *Wall Street Journal* wanted to promote to one of its most challenging segments—college students. With their limited financial resources, college students have historically been a very difficult sale. The *Wall Street Journal* used a customized student segmentation strategy based on a profile of its current college student subscribers to determine high-probability prospect student responders for its nationwide direct mail campaign, shown in Figure 3-3. This profile data—major, class year, and most responsive geographical school locations—served as select criteria for obtaining student prospect data from a variety of compiled lists and data sources. The campaign was highly effective, with overall response rates three times greater than that of previous direct mail campaigns that targeted the college student market segment.

Development of House Lists

The discussion of house lists earlier anticipates that direct marketers must compile and develop the list along with relevant data through some appropriate mechanical means. Computerized systems hold a great deal of flexibility as well as long-range economy.

The marketer must first determine just what useful data, other than accurate names and addresses, it needs to qualify individual members of the list, how to collect and record it, and in

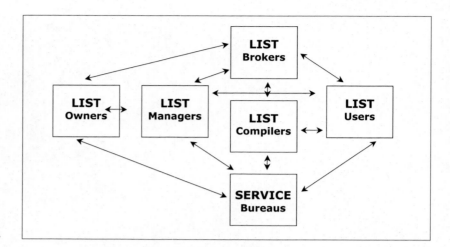

FIGURE 3-4.
The List Industry.

what form. Consider, too, just what purpose the data will serve in the future. Keep in mind that collection of information costs money and must therefore produce benefits commensurate with its cost. How will the data be used, and can they be analyzed and evaluated properly?

The List Industry

List owners and list users often come together through the efforts of list brokers, list managers, list compilers, and even service bureaus. Typically, marketers rent response lists under an arrangement allowing them to make a specific use of the data. Sometimes they buy compiled lists outright; there is no limit on the number of times mailings may be sent to these names. List owners usually maintain rented response lists, so these lists often have better deliverability than compiled lists that have not been updated regularly. Figure 3-4 shows the relationship between the various members in the list industry. Service bureaus interact with all members of the list industry, providing expertise in the areas of data processing and analysis. Check out www.fastlist.com and www.alistnow.com for more information on list building.

List Users

Virtually every direct marketer uses lists. For example, Victoria's Secret, L. L. Bean, Lands' End, Eddie Bauer, Cabela's, and Macy's all use lists. There are literally thousands of response and compiled lists available from which to choose, and the starting point is usually the direct marketer's own list.

A direct marketer using lists must obviously know its own customer profile to match it against available lists. Sometimes the marketer will use only segments of these lists, selecting them according to geographic, demographic, social, psychological, or behavioral characteristics. Matching one's house list against potential response and compiled lists is in itself a stimulating exercise. It often provides the direct marketer with basic knowledge of the marketplace the marketer can use to develop new products and determine successful promotional strategies.

List Owners

List owners are those who describe and acquire prospects who show potential of becoming customers of the list user. A key attribute of direct marketing, aside from its measurability and accountability, is the acquisition of lists and data about the individuals or organizations on these lists. Every direct marketer is a list owner. The lists that the marketer compiles during new business acquisition activities are described as house lists.

Although the primary reason for acquiring house lists is to build and perpetuate an organization through contact with its customers, many direct marketers view their house lists as profit centers in their own right. Firms rent their house lists to other direct marketers, under specified conditions, and this activity becomes an important source of added revenue. Nearly all credit card companies participate in list rental activities. Also, if you subscribe to any major magazines, your name appears on the magazine's house list.

All respondents to a renter's offer become additions to the renter's own house list. Under the usual rental arrangement, the rented list may be mailed only one time, and the list owner must approve the offer in advance. Directly competitive offers may not be approved except in an exchange that occurs when two competitive list owners provide each other with comparable numbers of their respective house lists or lists of active or inactive buyers.

An obvious advantage of renting a list rather than purchasing it outright (as is sometimes done with compiled lists) is that the list owner maintains the list, keeping it current and accurate. Another obvious advantage is that the names on such lists have a history of responding to direct marketing activity; thus they are termed "response" lists. A history of prior response, whether by mail, phone, or the Internet, is another important advantage to direct marketers.

Owners of response lists or compiled lists provide descriptions of them in a standard format, such as the example shown in Figure 3-5. The information on a list card normally includes list quantities, market segments available, pricing, general description of the list, demographic profile, including available list selections (such as age, gender, ZIP code, state, marital status, products purchased), as well as mechanical considerations, such as the type of addressing and ordering instructions. Lists are priced on a cost-per-thousand (CPM) basis. The costs of lists can range from less than $10 per thousand names for large quantities of broad-based compiled lists to more than $100 per thousand for highly selective, up-scale response lists. The average list rental charge of approximately $40 to $50 per thousand for one-time use usually includes provision of these names on either labels or disks for computer processing. List selections (also called "selects") normally carry a fee of $5 to $25 per thousand depending on the list, with the majority priced at $10 per thousand. These list selections enable direct marketers to narrow the list and properly choose specific narrowed segments of prospects contained within each list population. The process of choosing list selects from a given list is a form of precise market segmentation, which we discuss in detail later in this chapter. Each list is a segment and by applying list selections to a list, direct marketers can pinpoint certain prospects with a high degree of selectivity and accuracy.

Not all direct marketers make their house lists available for use by others. Perhaps the list contains proprietary information, or the list owner wishes to safeguard a very valuable asset from improper use. For example, some nonprofit organizations never rent their donor lists to ensure privacy. Most colleges and universities do not allow their student lists to be used by other businesses. Can you think of some businesses that would like to rent the list of students enrolled at your school? Some list owners also feel that there is a tendency for a list to wear itself out. Even offers that do not directly compete can vie with each other for discretionary spending, these list owners contend.

The counterargument is that it is virtually impossible for individuals and organizations to be left off response or compiled lists. Thus, although a list owner has a proprietary interest in a house list, individuals and organizations on the list will inevitably appear on lists owned by others. Another counterargument contends that the more opportunities individuals and organizations are provided, the more likely they are to respond.

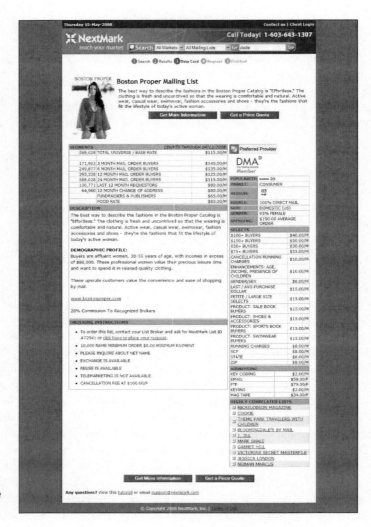

FIGURE 3-5.
NextMark list
card. Used with
permission of Joe
Pych, NextMark.

List Brokers

Like real estate brokers or stockbrokers, **list brokers** serve as intermediaries who bring list users and list owners together. They do not actually own lists but serve as middlemen in the industry. In so doing, they perform the following functions:

- Find new lists.
- Verify information.
- Report on performance.
- Check instructions.
- Clear offers.
- Check mechanics.
- Clear mailing date.
- Work out timing.
- Ensure delivery date.

List brokers are specialists in the process of bringing list owners and list users together. They should have a very clear picture of the products of the list owner as well as the needs of the list user. List brokers usually work on a commission basis, which is paid by the list owner.

List Managers

Although list rental can be an attractive profit center, direct marketers usually run it as a by-product of their basic business. Thus they often try to maximize returns from this activity through list managers. **List managers** represent the interests of list owners and assume the responsibility, on behalf of list owners, of keeping in contact with list brokers and lists users. They perform the advertising and sales functions and often maintain the lists they manage in their own facility. Like list brokers, list managers receive a commission from the list owner.

List Compilers

Organizations that develop lists and data about them, often serving as their own list managers and list brokers, are called **list compilers.** The form of list compilation they do is different from what direct marketers do in developing their own house lists through generation of responses and/or transactions.

List compilers usually develop their lists from public records (such as drivers' licenses or motor vehicle registrations), newspaper clippings, directories, warranty cards, and trade show registrations. In fact, the compiler owns such lists and then resells them, rather than renting them for one-time use. Instead of regularly maintaining such lists, compilers usually recompile periodically. Names and addresses in phone directories, for example, are compiled regularly, at least annually, on issuance of newly published volumes.

Service Bureaus

Service bureaus provide data processing, data mining, outsourcing, online analytical processing (OLAP), and other services to support the interchange of lists and database information within the direct marketing industry. Some of the larger direct marketing companies have their own service departments that perform this function on a regular basis.

List Research and Analysis

Renting lists and using them to prospect for new customers, clients, donors, members, voters, or whatever the marketer needs can be a critical element in the execution of a successful direct marketing campaign. But before you can rent a list you must first determine the type of list you need for your campaign—business or consumer lists, postal, e-mail, or telephone lists—and the lists that are available to be rented. That requires list research. Then, once you have rented the list (or lists) and have used it to implement your marketing campaign, you will want to evaluate how well that list worked in producing new customers. That requires list measurement and analysis. Let's explore these two important activities. We will begin by walking through the online list research process available at NextMark.com. NextMark is a great "go-to" source for information about available data and marketing lists.

List Research

The list research process begins with having precise knowledge about your customers in order to pinpoint most likely prospective customers. We will discuss in greater detail the specific data that can be used to segment consumers later this chapter. As was explained in Chapter 2, your cus-

FIGURE 3-6.
NextMark Find
Media screen
page. Used with
permission of
NextMark, Inc.

tomer database can and should be used as a starting point to better understand your customers. First, using your customer database, you should analyze and develop a profile of your current customers. You will also want to determine your most valuable customers. Know that your most likely prospective customers will normally resemble your current customers. Thus, you will want to find and rent those lists of prospects that resemble your current customers—especially the profile of your *best* (most valuable) customers.

Here's an example. Let's say your customers are 25-34 years old with sports interests, both conventional and extreme. Not only do they enjoy football and basketball but they also are into hanggliding, surfing, skateboarding, winter sports, robot wars, etc. Your *best* customers are interested in extreme sports that have speed, height, danger and a high level of physical exertion associated with them. You go to www.NextMark.com and you key in "Extreme Sports" into its media list finder as shown in Figure 3-6 and hit enter to begin the list search. The NextMark search engine will run your query against all data cards in the set you selected and display the results.

Within a few seconds you will be able to view the "extreme sports results." As presented in Figure 3-7, this is a listing of all lists associated with extreme sports that are available for list rental along with each list's rank, title and size. All search results are sorted by rank. Rank is based on the "responsiveness" of a list and to the specific set of search criteria. Each data card will receive a different rank each time a new search in conducted via the NextMark list media finder.

Now you may begin to browse through all of the lists to find those that best match your desired prospect. In order to do so, you will need to determine which of these lists have buyer profiles similar to your *best* customer profile. With a simple click on any of the lists you can access each list's data card, which will provide the details you need to review to determine which list (or lists) might best suit your needs. As shown in Figure 3-8, each data card is arranged in two columns. The wider left column includes the list title, summary, description information and list segments. The right column contains availability and ordering information as well as list details such as universe, provider or source, and *selects*. List selects detail the various geographic, demographic and lifestyle variables that are available for that particular list.

FIGURE 3-7. NextMark "Extreme Sports" results screen page. Used with permission of NextMark, Inc.

FIGURE 3-8. NextMark "Extreme Sports" list card. Used with permission of NextMark, Inc.

The decision of "which list or lists might work best" for a given marketing campaign should be based on an evaluation of the descriptions, market segments and *selections* available for each list. Each data card reveals the source of the list, minimum quantity that can be rented, types of lists available (postal mail e-mail, telephone), along with other information. In addition, each list card will display its popularity score, which is based on how often the list has been rented. Once you have concluded your evaluation, you may select your lists and place your order to rent the list(s). However, if the "extreme sports results" did not provide you with the lists you are seeking, then you may refine your search by entering different key terms into the list media finder and begin a new search. For example, perhaps you want to narrow your extreme sports search to find only those lists associated with "snow sports." You may do so and the search engine will continue to narrow its search and display results for each search conducted.

List Measurement and Analysis

Record keeping is essential to properly evaluate the profitability of response lists as well as compiled lists. Record keeping includes accurate measurement of results and evaluation of response differences. Evaluating the productivity of a list you have rented and used for a marketing campaign begins with selecting and using a **key code,** a unique identifier placed on the response device or order form *prior* to sending a promotional piece to prospective customers. Key codes can be simple preprinted numbers identifying the source of the list, or they can be so complex as to incorporate not just the source but the category of list, type of product offered by the list owner, or even the degree of prior direct marketing activity. Unique tracking codes can also be created for e-mail lists, mobile and text messaging campaigns.

Direct marketers structure key codes so that they can accumulate information across several individual lists by different categories. Thus, the direct marketer can tabulate response not only by individual lists but also by sources of list, product lines, geographic location (ZIP code), and a variety of other broad qualifiers. The marketer then groups individual lists into such categories and makes assumptions about the overall efficiency of certain list sources, particular ZIP codes, or specific product lines.

Marketers should keep ongoing records of lists and monitor them even if they frequently contact the names on the list. The character and nature of lists change over time, just as the character and nature of the list owner's business may change. Many direct marketers have achieved the highest response rate when they have used so-called hotline names. **Hotline names** (also called "hotline buyers") are those most recently acquired, but there is no consensus in the industry about what chronological period "recent" describes. Many lists specify "three-month hotline" or "six-month hotline" to detail the name categories by recency.

Response differences can occur as a result of timing alone. Certain exogenous factors over which the direct marketer can exert no control (beyond the quality of the list itself), such as economic conditions or climate variations, can have a profound effect on results when lists are developed over a period of time. Other uncontrollable factors include major events or even catastrophes that divert public attention from the everyday.

Certain offers, such as a catalog of Christmas gifts, are timely and target seasonal differences in consumer buying habits. Some offers can be affected by the income tax season or by the vacation season. Some direct marketers try to time their promotional efforts so as to avoid arrival during any type of holiday event, especially those that take people outdoors. For example, if Lands' End were to send consumers a catalog offering winter sweaters in the early portion of summer, when most consumers are enjoying wearing light summer clothing, the response to their offer may be affected by the season. In addition, offers with expiration dates may need to be lengthened during the summer months due to the fact that many consumers take summer vacations and are not at home to receive their mail.

Even for nonseasonal offers, however, an apparent month-to-month cycle affects direct response advertising. All other factors being equal, many direct marketers have noted these ebbs and flows. For example, Bally's and other fitness centers probably receive a greater response to their direct marketing efforts during the months of January and February, although they are open for business 12 months a year. Each direct marketer should develop an index of monthly responses and determine which month generates the highest relative response. Noting monthly variances is useful to the direct marketer who is testing lists on an ongoing basis. It makes it possible to consider the variable of timing in comparing one list with another when these are released during different months of the year. In summary, marketers rely on list analysis to predict future response from lists or segments of lists and to determine future list strategies.

Many companies experience peaks and valleys in response rates based on the products and services they offer. In addition, an organization's customer database is also likely to be segmented, because not all customers have the same needs, wants, or interests. Thus, direct marketers must apply the principles of market segmentation prior to interacting with customers on a personalized basis. Customers can be served best by organizations that know their characteristics. The concept and theory of market segmentation and its special relevance in both consumer and business direct marketing are the subjects of the next section.

The Nature of Market Segmentation

Because all buyers are not alike, marketers have developed ways to place them into groups or market segments, according to geographic, demographic, social, psychological, or behavioral factors. These market segments are the focal points of product differentiation and positioning. Direct marketers have been using market segmentation strategies in their efforts to effectively promote and distribute products and services to consumers for many years. Think of a sports magazine. Its readers are probably interested in many different sports. It could easily identify its golf enthusiast consumers and offer them golf products and services. Likewise, it could offer its tennis-playing readers tennis equipment and clothing.

Market segmentation is a strategy devised to attract and meet the needs of a specific submarket. These subgroups are referred to as **market segments.** A company may direct marketing strategies at several market segments. Each segment should be homogeneous (that is, its members should be similar to one another), heterogeneous (meaning its members should all be different from the members of other segments), and substantial in size (so as to be profitable).

Product Differentiation

Marketers target products and services to select market segments, rather than the total market, unless the product or service is unique and appeals equally to everyone. Many times it is necessary to *differentiate* products for particular market segments and *position* these products so that they will have special appeal to the intended market. **Product differentiation** is a strategy that uses innovative design, packaging, and positioning to make a clear distinction between products and services serving the same market segment. Product differentiation, like market segmentation, is an alternative to price competition. The difference might be real or simply an advertised difference. For example, a brand of toothpaste that contains fluoride is intrinsically different from one that does not. An airline may call its Boeing 777 aircraft a Star-Stream Jet without making it any different from the planes of its competitors. Product differentiation can distinguish a product from that of its competitors.

Product Positioning

Product positioning is the way the product is defined by consumers on important attributes. It enables consumers to rank products or services according to perceived differences between competing products or brands within a single product category.

Marketers can position products based on quality, size, color, distribution method, time of day the product is used, time of year, and price. Examples include Nike: "Just do it"; M&M's:

"Melts in your mouth, not in your hands"; Taco Bell: "Think outside the bun"; Avis: "We Try Harder." Most big-ticket marketers, such as the manufacturers of Rolex watches and Mercedes-Benz automobiles, thrive by positioning their products as exclusive, high-quality items. So do the well-known direct marketers of specialty products like Harry and David, Brookstone, and Victoria's Secret.

Segmenting Business Markets

Like consumer markets, business markets break down into smaller, more homogeneous segments of the heterogeneous total industrial market.

STANDARD INDUSTRIAL CLASSIFICATION (SIC). The **Standard Industrial Classification (SIC)** coding system developed by the federal government serves as a basis for classifying statistical data and has been widely used by government, trade associations, and business enterprises. SIC codes classify business customers by the main economic activity in which they engage. All major activities are assigned a two-digit code number. Some of the major industry divisions include (but are not limited to) agriculture, mining, construction, manufacturing, transportation, wholesale trade, retail trade, financial services, and public administration.

As a company's business activity becomes more specialized, up to six digits can be added to the SIC code to identify subgroups. SIC codes can also designate the primary and secondary lines of a business as well as additional segmentation information based on the following statistical data: sales volume, credit rating, age of business, number of employees, net financial worth, and subsidiary and geographic location. Most direct marketers have used SIC codes in conjunction with proprietary information as the primary tool for segmenting business and industrial consumers. However, SIC codes posses certain limitations and are no longer in such wide use.

NORTH AMERICAN INDUSTRY CLASSIFICATION SYSTEM (NAICS). The **North American Industry Classification System (NAICS,** pronounced "nakes") has replaced the SIC coding system. Many business people felt that the SIC system failed to recognize the growth of information technology, the service industry, high technology, and international trade. The NAICS system offers several improvements over the SIC system. Figure 3-9 overviews the main differences between them.

The first improvement is relevance. NAICS identifies over 350 new industries, including high-tech areas, and 9 new service industry sectors that now contribute to the economy. The second improvement is comparability. NAICS was developed by the United States, Canada, and Mexico to produce comparable data for all three nations. Industries are identified by a six-digit code to accommodate a larger number of sectors and allow greater flexibility in designating subsectors. The first five digits denote the NAICS levels common to all three NAFTA (North American Free Trade Agreement) countries, whereas the sixth digit accommodates user needs in individual countries. NAICS is a two- through six-digit hierarchical classification code system. A complete and valid NAICS code contains six digits. Figure 3-10 shows the hierarchical structure of NAICS.

The third improvement is consistency. NAICS uses a consistent principle: businesses that use similar production processes are grouped together. This is entirely different from the SIC system, which focused on the industries served. The fourth improvement is adaptability. NAICS will be reviewed every five years, so classifications and information keep up with the changing economy. Finally, quality has been improved with key measures of U.S. economic activity such as retail services, manufacturers' shipments, and service industry receipts.[1]

SIC Codes	NAICS Codes
SIC codes classify establishments by the type of activity in which the business is primarily engaged.	NAICS is based on a production-oriented, or a supply-based, conceptual framework.
SIC is a 4-digit code.	NAICS is a 6-digit code.
SIC system lacked current information.	NAICS will be reviewed every five years so classifications will change with the economy.
SIC have 10 classifying sectors: • Agriculture, Forestry, and Fishing • Mining • Construction • Manufacturing • Transportation, Communications, and Public Utilities • Wholesale Trade • Retail Trade • Finance, Insurance, and Real Estate • Services • Public Administration	NAICS have 20 classifying divisions: • Agriculture, Forestry, Fishing, and Hunting • Mining • Construction • Manufacturing • Utilities • Transportation and Warehousing • Wholesale Trade • Retail Trade • Accommodation and Food Services • Finance and Insurance • Real Estate and Rental and Leasing • Information • Professional, Scientific, and Technical Services • Administrative Support; Waste Management and Remediation Services • Educational Services • Health Care and Social Assistance • Arts, Entertainment, and Recreation • Other Services (except Public Administration) • Public Administration • Management of Companies and Enterprises

FIGURE 3-9. Comparison of SIC codes and NAICS codes. Source: NAICS Association Web Site, accessed online at http://www.naics.com/info.htm, February 2003

xx	Industry Sector
xxx	Industry Subsector
xxxx	Industry Group
xxxxx	Industry
xxxxxx	U.S., Canadian, or Mexican national Specific

FIGURE 3-10. NAICS hierarchical.

The Bases for Market Segmentation

The needs, wants, or interests of the consumers belonging to various market segments differ. However, it would be almost impossible to conduct marketing research for every product and service that could determine which market segment each consumer would best fit into; therefore marketers use other, more general indicators for segmenting markets. These indicators include geographic, demographic, social, psychological, and behavioral factors. A brief overview is provided here.

Geographic Segmentation

Potential geographic subdivisions range in size from the country as a whole down through census divisions and federal reserve districts to states, counties, trading areas, cities, towns, census tracts, neighborhoods, and even individual city blocks. In addition, there are numerical codes such as ZIP codes, geocodes, telephone area codes, computer "match" codes, and territory and route numbers. Once upon a time, census tract numbers were the best means of geographical segmentation. Do you know which census tract you live in? Most people probably do not. However, our ZIP code number *is* meaningful, and everyone knows that number.

FIGURE 3-11.
Busch Gardens
New York and
Carolina ads.
Used with
permission of
Busch Gardens.

An important form of geographic market segmentation is that which recognizes inherent differences among those buyers who reside in central cities, suburban, urban fringe, and rural areas. Geographic location can also affect the future purchase activity of consumers. For example, the level of consumer interest in purchasing nursery plants or snow blowers is often related to the climate of the geographic area in which the consumer lives.

Let's examine an example of geographic segmentation. Busch Gardens targets most of its communication to consumers geographically, accounting for different vacation interests, ticket offers and other communication points that vary by market. Some of these efforts are overt in appealing to residents of a particular region, such as the park's recent campaigns touting Busch Gardens as the place "Where _____ Goes to Get Away," with different city names inserted in the appropriate regions shown in Figure 3-11. More often the communication is more subtle, with elements tailored slightly to highlight particular offers or events of greater interest to a specific geographical market.

Population changes within geographic areas, such as the decreasing population of a specific geographic area or the high mobility of the population in another, have significance to the marketer. Census data is invaluable for research regarding the changing geographic and demographic profile of the American population. The recent Census CD Neighborhood Change Database (NCDB) is a powerful product that presents decades of census tract series data. Additional information about this produce is available at www.geolytics.com.

Another geographic segmentation tool, the **Global Positioning System (GPS),** associates latitude and longitude coordinates with street addresses. Direct marketers use this system to identify geographic locations, establish business sites, locate competition, measure distance, and generate data about the demographics of a business location. Given this information, combined with the technological mapping capabilities of most businesses, a direct marketer can better determine the business penetration and market potential in certain geographical areas.

Today, computer systems are capable of analyzing **Geographic Information Systems (GIS)** to help better understand data related to geographic areas. A GIS is a computer system capable of capturing, storing, analyzing, and displaying geographically referenced information identified according to location.[2] A GIS can help you answer questions and solve problems by looking at your data in a way that is quickly understood and easily shared.[3] The GIS software leader is ERSI, which provides a full spectrum of ready-to-use geospatial data products delivered either as a Web service or as packaged media.[4]

Demographic Segmentation

Demographics are identifiable and measurable statistics that describe the consumer population. The primary unit of observation in demography is the individual; the family unit and household are secondary concerns. Common demographic variables include age, gender, education level, income level, occupation, and type of housing.

There are three main sources for such data: (1) population enumeration, as in a census; (2) registration on the occurrence of some event, such as birth, marriage, or death; and (3) sample surveys or tabulation of special groups. The data obtained in these ways are generally available for marketing and other uses from governmental sources, especially the Census Bureau.

It is often wise to tabulate the effect of the interaction of many demographic variables at the same time. For example, it is highly valuable for a direct marketer to know the marital status of a certain 25-year-old male consumer. Just think of two male consumers, both aged 25; one might be married with two children and the other single with no children. These two consumers probably belong in totally different market segments based on their market needs. In this case, the more demographic data you can collect, the better. Often, a single demographic statistic can be misleading.

Marketers know that currency is the key to accuracy and validity of demographic data. *Changes* in demography, such as when someone marries or has a baby, have significant marketing implications.

Social Factor Segmentation

Social factors include a person's culture, subculture, social class rank, peer group references, and reference individual(s). Social factors demonstrate the impact that other people in our society have on our decision-making process and consumption activities.

Society may well have an impact on our behavior beyond our control. For example, **reference groups** (also called "peer groups") are the people a consumer turns to for reinforcement. This reinforcement normally comes *after* the consumer makes a purchase decision. Reference groups may have a direct and powerful influence on the consumption behavior of adolescents and teenagers. A **reference individual** is a person a consumer turns to for advice. This person or persons will influence the consumer *before* he or she makes a purchase decision. Therefore, reference individuals normally have a stronger impact on consumer decision making than do reference groups.

Psychographic Segmentation

Psychographics is the study of lifestyles, habits, attitudes, beliefs, and value systems of individuals. Even though buyers may have common geographic, demographic, and social characteristics, they often have different buying characteristics. Psychographic segmentation divides consumers into different groups based on lifestyle and personality variables. Individual buyer behavior is influenced not only by geographic, demographic, and social factors but also by variables that are more difficult to define, such as environment, self-perception, and lifestyles. When marketers can identify and measure these influences, they can use them effectively in segmenting mailing lists.

Direct marketers have the ability to identify psychographic market segments and thus predict potential consumer response by recognizing and evaluating the simultaneous appearance of a prospect's name on a variety of lists. For example, a registered owner of a particular type of automobile might also appear on the subscriber lists of the *Wall Street Journal* and *Better Homes and Gardens* as well as the customer lists of upscale catalogs such as Neiman Marcus and Gump's. This same prospect might even be a contributor to Planned Parenthood and a member of the National Geographic Society. When merged, such multiple list identifiers can describe the psychographics of consumers (activities, interests, and opinions) more specifically than consumer surveys. Another means of psychographic identification of specific prospects is a comprehensive data file developed by Equifax under the trade name "Lifestyle Selector." The Lifestyle Selector is the direct marketing industry's largest and most comprehensive database of self-reported consumer information. More than 500 response segments cover all aspects of how consumers live, what they spend their money on, and what interests they possess. This file is primarily derived from two sources: responses to consumer surveys and product registration cards filled out voluntarily by consumers after they have completed a product purchase. Included for each of the 47 million consumer names and addresses are a variety of demographic characteristics and activities or hobbies. It is possible for a consumer direct marketer to develop a psychographic and demographic profile of his or her company's house lists by matching the lists with the Lifestyle Selector and extend his or her prospect base by adding other names from the data file.

Thus, measurement of environmental influences within geographic units combined with demographic and psychographic indicators derived from list cross-referencing and other expressions of activities, interests, and opinions all interact to enable the direct marketer to reach individual consumers within market segments. Such list selection is obviously more efficient and can be more effective than directing pinpointed messages to the total marketplace.

Behavioral Market Segmentation

The actions taken by consumers are certainly a viable base for market segmentation. The specific types of products and services consumers have purchased, the time the transactions took place, the method or location of their purchases, and the method of payment they choose can all reveal similarities among consumers. Each behavioral factor can indicate a consumer preference that may be shared by other consumers, consequently identifying a market segment.

"Cookies" provide marketers with the ability to segment consumers according to their online activity. A **cookie** is an electronic tag or identifier that is placed on a personal computer. Cookies are a tool for recognizing Web users again after they have interacted with a marketer's Web site in some capacity. The process is quite simple: whenever a Web site visitor makes a request to a Web server, that server has the opportunity to set a cookie on the personal computer that made the request. The Web site host can then use the cookie for tracking beyond the initial click to determine how often that visitor returns to the Web site, the length of time of each visit, and the particular Web pages visited, which can often detail the specific products or services in which the visitor is interested. Cookies provide valuable insight into consumer behavior.

Using Multiple Segmentation Bases

Relying on a single base for segmenting markets and selecting customers is rarely effective. Most direct marketers use multiple segmentation bases—such as combining geographic data with behavioral data. Thus, within a single ZIP code area, several smaller segments may exist on the basis of behavioral differences, like products purchased. A good example of multivariable segmentation is "geodemographic" segmentation. Several companies, including Claritas, Experian, Acxiom, and MapInfo, combine U.S. census data with consumer lifestyle patterns to profile customers by geographic areas. These services enable marketers to choose segments wisely based on multivariable segmentation data.

Claritas, featured in Figure 3-12, began geodemographic segmentation in 1976 by analyzing data, isolating key factors, and developing a clustering system. This clustering system began with two key drivers: age and income. But as Claritas quickly discovered, there was more than just age and income that needed to be evaluated. The statisticians who created PRIZM realized the importance of creating segments based on the demographics that correlate directly with consumer *behavior*.

A new version of the PRIZM system was created in 2003 using the 2000 census to replace the earlier system, which used the 1990 census. Beyond having nearly a third more new seg-

FIGURE 3-12.
Claritas PRIZM
Advertisement.
Used with
permission of
Claritas, a Nielsen
Company.

ments, and 66 in total, the key enhancement to the system was to allow marketers to shift from a five-digit ZIP code to Census Tract to Block Group to ZIP+4, all the way down to household level—all within a set of 14 social groups. Each social group contains creatively named segments that tend to cluster together. For example, the "Urban Uptown" group contains the nation's wealthiest urban consumers and has the following five segments: "Young Digerati," "Money and Brains," "Bohemian Mix," "The Cosmopolitans," and "American Dreams." Although this group is diverse in terms of housing styles and family sizes, residents share an upscale perspective that is reflected in their marketplace selections. Figure 3-13 shows some examples of the unique segments from a variety of social groups that Claritas created based on geodemographic analysis.

Claritas also provides an online service, MyBestSegments.com, which can help guide marketing campaigns and media strategies for specific market segments. Customer segmentation profiling information included in MyBestSegments encompasses PRIZM and a variety of categories about consumer markets, including travel, eating out, shopping, auto purchases, and

Examples of Unique Claritas PRIZM Segments:

• **Close-In Couples:** Predominantly African-American couples, 55-year-old plus, that live in older homes in urban neighborhoods, high school educated, empty nesting, enjoying secure and comfortable retirements

• **Winners Circle:** A collection of mostly 35- to 54-year old couples with large families in new-money subdivisions. Surrounding their homes are the signs of upscale living: recreational parks, golf courses, and upscale malls surround their homes. With a median income of over$100,000, these residents are big spenders who like to travel, ski, go out to eat, and shop at clothing boutiques.

• **Home Sweet Home:** Mostly under 55, these residents tend to be upper-middle-class married couples living in mid-size homes with few children, they have attended college and hold professional and white-collar jobs, they have fashioned comfortable lifestyles, filling their homes with toys, TV's and pets

• **Up-and-Comers:** Mostly in their twenties, single, many are recent college graduates who are into athletic activities, the latest technology and nightlife entertainment

• **Shotguns & Pickups:** These Americans tend to be young, working-class couples with large families, most have two or more kids, they live in small homes and manufactured housing, nearly a third of the residents live in mobile homes and many own hunting rifles and pickup trucks

Source: PRIZM Segment Narratives. Reprinted with permission from Claritas, A Nielsen Company, April, 2008.

FIGURE 3-13. Examples of Claritas PRIZM segments. Used with permission of Claritas, a Nielsen Company.

more. Demographic data are also available. Plus, these data are continually updated to be in sync with Claritas's Market Place suite of products for additional consumer behavior data. Visit MyBestSegments (www.claritas.com/MyBestSegments/Default.jsp) to explore the "ZIP Code Look-Up" feature of this system, which allows you to plug in your ZIP code to obtain a profile of your neighborhood's top five segments, along with some descriptive detail about each segment's lifestyle traits. While visiting the MyBestSegment site, you may also want to investigate the "Segment Look-Up" feature, which provides detailed descriptions of each of its 66 unique market segments. As Figure 3-14 shows, direct marketers that subscribe to Claritas can quickly and easily obtain details about the best segments to target for a specific offer and additional customer profiling information.

ZIP Code Areas as Market Segments

ZIP code areas, although originally conceived and developed by the U.S. Postal Service for the purpose of sorting and distributing mail, have become a convenient and logical method of geo-

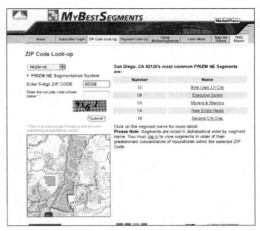

FIGURE 3-14. MyBestSegments.com web pages. Used with permission of Caritas, a Nielsen Company.

graphic segmentation, especially in direct marketing. ZIP code areas have become a key basis for market segmentation in direct marketing, combining the characteristics of geographic, demographic, social, psychological, and behavioral factors. The value of ZIP codes for marketers is based on the simple fact that the codes tend to enclose homogeneous neighborhoods and geographical boundaries.

The old saying "birds of a feather flock together," explains why ZIP code areas constitute market segments. Because people with like interests tend to cluster and because their purchase decisions are frequently influenced by their desire to emulate their friends, neighbors, and community innovators, ZIP code areas provide the means to *identify* clusters of households that have a high degree of *homogeneity*. This homogeneity is inherent in the manner in which ZIP code areas have been constructed and relies on accepted principles of reference group theory as well as the concept of environmental influences on buyer behavior.

Marketers can use ZIP code areas in many specific ways; we outline some of them in Figure 3-15.

Geographic Structure

The socioeconomic usefulness of these units, especially from a direct marketing perspective, results from the three criteria the U.S. Postal Service used in establishing each ZIP code:

1. A hub city is at the center of each cluster of ZIP code areas (termed a sectional center) that is the natural center of local transportation.

2. An average of 40 to 75 individual post offices lie within each sectional center, resulting in units with fairly consistent population density.

3. Each natural transportation hub is about 2 to 3 hours' driving time away from the farthest post office in the sectional center.

An obvious convenience of these geographic units which sets them apart from commonly used divisions such as counties is that each household and business within the unit is readily identifiable by a five-digit number assigned to it as a part of its street address. In dissecting the ZIP code, you will find that the first digit of the five-digit codes identifies one of ten (0 through 9) geographic areas of the nation, with the digit ascending from east to west. These regions are identified in Figure 3-16.

- Establish and define market segments, including sales potentials based on environmental data about the unit.
- Evaluate direct marketing results performance, based on a measurement of actual penetration against the projected potential, and realign market segments as such analysis warrants.
- Process inquiries and orders more efficiently and effectively without need for reference to a map, since the address immediately identifies the sales territory.
- Forecast more accurately based on objective analysis of the marketplace rather than on a collection of individual opinions about it.
- Pinpoint market segments in relation to profits.
- Increase regional and national advertising effectiveness when direct mail, magazines, or newspapers are used.
- Determine optimum distribution centers.
- Set up a territorial rating system for credit evaluation and perform continuing analysis of accounts receivable.
- Conduct market research, especially if demographic cross sections or probability sampling is called for.
- Develop differentiated products that have special interest to specific market segments that can be defined by ZIP code areas, certain educational levels, or target occupation groups, for example.
- Analyze penetration of present customers according to specific ZIP code area characteristics to more effectively direct and control marketing efforts.
- Identify growth areas, with updated demographics.
- Direct new product sampling more effectively.
- Control inventories according to historical territorial patterns.
- Coordinate data processing and information systems through use of the ZIP code as part of the computerized "match code."
- Distribute seasonal and climate-oriented products and information on a chronological schedule by ZIP code area.

FIGURE 3-15. Uses of ZIP Code Area Data.

The next two digits of the five-digit number identify a major city or major distribution point (sectional center) within a state. The last two digits of the five-digit ZIP code fall into two geographic categories: (1) key post offices in each area, which normally have stations and branches in the city's neighborhoods; and (2) a series of associated small town or rural post offices served by the sectional center transportation hub or a specific neighborhood or delivery unity within a city.

ZIP+4

Figure 3-17 summarizes what the five-digit ZIP code designations represent. The U.S. Postal Service has added a four-digit extension to the original five-digit code. The sixth and seventh digits denote a *sector* and the last two denote a *segment* within a sector. These additional four digits permit mail to be sorted to carrier delivery routes. An example of the meaning of the additional four-digits is as follows:

- Digits 6 and 7—could denote the location of a specific organization, like a university.
- Digits 8 and 9—could represent a specific segment or department within the university, perhaps the office of admissions.

Clustering Areas to Segments

A key advantage of ZIP code areas is that they can be combined like building blocks to suit the individual need of the direct marketer relative to product differentiation or promotional strategy.

FIGURE 3-16. ZIP Code National Area Designations.

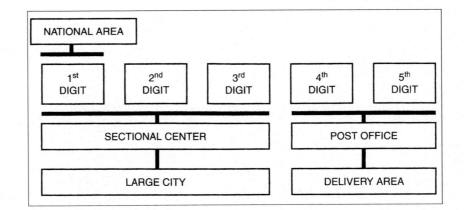

FIGURE 3-17.
ZIP Code digit
designations

A ZIP code–based marketing information system enables direct marketers to know more about their markets and organize them according to local transportation patterns. Many major coupon distributors segment their markets on the basis of ZIP code areas. These companies also know which ZIP code areas possess a heavy concentration of residential households and coupon users.

Availability of Statistical Data

During the past few decades, increasing amounts of data for ZIP code areas have become available. Some of these include organizations' own records along with consumer survey data compiled by the Census Bureau, Market Research Institute (MRI), and Simmons Market Research Bureau.

ZIP Code Business Patterns is a service published by the U.S. Census Bureau. It presents data on the total number of establishments, employment, and payroll for more than 40,000 5-digit ZIP Code areas nationwide.[5] ZIP Code Business Patterns provides segmentation information that is invaluable for direct marketers.

Summary

Most direct marketers conduct market segmentation to serve consumer needs and wants in an optimal way. Lists are important market segmentation tools. There are three basic types of lists: house, response, and compiled. Each list is of value for direct marketers, although house lists are considered the most valuable. The list industry is comprised of list owners, list users, list brokers, list managers, list compilers, and service bureaus. Each member plays an important role in the list rental activities of direct marketers. Direct marketers strive to keep lists current and accurate. House lists normally hold a customer's name, address, and pertinent contact information. In addition, most direct marketers rent lists in an attempt to prospect for new customers. List rental strategies are made simple today due to computerized databases services with search techniques, such as NextMark's list services. List selections afford direct marketers the opportunity to further segment a list using a variety of segmentation variables. Direct marketers segment final consumers according to geographic, demographic, social, psychological, and behavioral characteristics. Often times, multiple variables are used to segment markets, such as geodemographic segmentation. Direct marketers also segment businesses or industrial consumers according to SIC codes or the NAICS. Direct marketers consider ZIP code areas to be geographic market segments that provide important customer information.

Key Terms

house lists
response lists
compiled lists
list owners
list brokers
list managers
list compilers
service bureaus
key code
hotline names
market segmentation
market segments

product differentiation
product positioning
North American Industry Classification
    System (NAICS)
Global Positioning System (GPS)
Geographic Information Systems (GIS)
demographics
reference groups
reference individual
psychographics
cookie

Review Questions

1. What is *market segmentation* and how do direct marketers use it?

2. How is segmenting industrial markets different from segmenting final consumer markets?

3. Overview the differences between SIC codes and NAICS. Name some companies who might use industrial classifications in segmenting their industrial or business consumer market.

4. What are *psychographics?* In what way are they useful to direct marketers?

5. In the four-digit extension of an original five-digit ZIP code, what does each of the numbers stand for?

6. How can ZIP codes help achieve product differentiation or promotional strategy?

7. What type of list is most important to an organization? Why?

8. Identify a few products or services that probably incur response differences attributable to timing.

9. Explain the difference between a *list user* and a *list owner.*

10. What are list brokers, list managers, and list compilers each responsible for?

Exercise

As a Nike employee, it is your responsibility to create a house list for the company. Create a list and include all the important characteristics about customers that would be beneficial to making the company most profitable. Keep in mind, Nike sells many different types of products, so you would want the organization of your house list to be segmented accordingly. If you were to rent lists to augment your house list, where would you go to find appropriate lists? What other types of companies would have lists that would interest you?

Critical Thinking Exercise

Identify a list of which you are a member. How did you become a member of this list? What is the profile of the other members of this list? How are you similar? Describe a few companies and organizations that might be interested in renting this list. What is your level of receptiveness to the offers these companies might present to you?

CASE: Virginia Beach Tourism

Do you like to travel? Do you enjoy taking a vacation? If so, you are among the millions or billions or perhaps zillions of people who do! Tourism is a powerful industry that affects many different businesses, including hotels, restaurants, retail outlets, attractions, transportation providers and meeting facilities. In 2009, approximately 5.6 million overnight adult guests visited Virginia Beach and spent roughly $1.06 billion. This visitor spending was also responsible for generating 11,596 jobs and $91.6 million in taxes and fees paid to the City of Virginia Beach and the Commonwealth of Virginia from those industries that have direct contact with visitors. The total economic impact of visitor spending was $1.4 billion. Indeed, Virginia Beach travel and tourism is big business. Tourism is also an industry comprised of many different types of consumers with vastly different needs, wants and desires to which tourism marketers must strategically appeal.

This case is designed to help you to better understand how a vacation destination is able to segment its market to attract a wide variety of prospective tourists. The vacation destination is Virginia Beach, Virginia, a place that literally has something for everyone. However, to be effective in marketing to a diverse leisure traveler population, its marketing strategies must be customized and targeted to cater to each consumer group's interests and desires. Before we discuss Virginia Beach's marketing strategies, let's take a stroll down its beautiful boardwalk and take a glance at Virginia Beach as a vacation destination.

FIGURE 3-18. Virginia Beach Coastline. Used with permission by the City of Virginia Beach Convention & Visitors Bureau.

Why Visit Virginia Beach?

A tourist favorite, the Virginia Beach resort area features a three-mile long nationally acclaimed boardwalk along the Atlantic Ocean with separate bike path—a combination perfect for strolling, running, biking, roller blading, renting a surrey or just taking in the sights and sounds of the beach scene. Hotels, restaurants, unique shops, a fishing pier and even playgrounds for the kids are all wrapped up in a park-like atmosphere that goes on for miles. Live musical and family-friendly entertainment is offered nightly during the summer months along Atlantic Avenue and at four oceanfront stages. Parasailing, jet ski rental, ocean kayaking, boat tours and charter fishing trips are all available to tourists. Virginia Beach offers numerous venues to engage tourists. For example, the 800,000-gallon Virginia Aquarium & Marine Science Center is one of the best aquariums and live animal habitats in the country featuring river otters, harbor seals, Loggerhead sea turtles, stingrays and sharks as well as hundreds of hands-on exhibits, an outdoor aviary and nature trail and a 3D IMAX® theater.

Who's the Target Market?

The primary target market for overnight visitation to Virginia Beach can be divided into two categories—final consumers and organizational consumers—each with its own subset of defined market segments. These include:

- Leisure Travelers (Such as: families, singles without children, sports enthusiasts, and the mature market.)
- Meeting Planners / Event Planners / Sports Planners (Including: social, military, educational, religious and fraternal organizations, and more.)

The secondary market includes group tour operators, motor coach operators and group tour planners. This case focuses on how Virginia Beach targets various prospective leisure travelers.

Geographically, Virginia Beach concentrates its direct marketing efforts on prospective tourists in the Northeast region of the United States. This geographic region is important because the city's convenient location makes it only a day's drive for two-thirds of the nation's population. Therefore, the top geographic target markets include the following:

- Washington, D.C.
- Richmond/Petersburg, VA
- Roanoke/Lynchburg, VA
- Philadelphia, PA
- New York, NY
- Pittsburgh, PA

- Cleveland, OH
- Baltimore, MD
- Hampton Roads, VA
- Harrisburg, PA
- Raleigh, NC

Now that you know what geographical markets are targeted by Virginia Beach, let's explore how it customizes its marketing and media strategies to attract specific demographic and behavioral segments of tourists.

Virginia Beach's Marketing and Media Strategy

Virginia Beach employs a multi-media marketing strategy including magazines, interactive/ online, broadcast television and radio, as well as select newspapers. Its marketing strategy is designed to achieve two objectives: (1) to generate awareness of Virginia Beach as a quality, year-round destination; and (2) to drive traffic to its tourism Web sites, *VisitVirginiaBeach.com* and *LiveTheLife.com*. Virginia Beach marketers have used list rental strategies to identify e-mail lists that might prove to be useful in connecting with prospective tourists. They have recently run a dedicated Virginia Beach e-mail campaign with lists from WeatherBug, eTarget Media, iExplore, Orbitz, Sherman's Travel, Daily Candy, New York Times, Washington Post, Raleigh News & Observer, eBrains, and The Baltimore Sun.

Virginia Beach's Segmentation Strategy

The secret to successful tourism marketing for Virginia Beach lies in its highly segmented marketing initiatives designed to drive prospective tourists to its easy-to-navigate Web site, and once there, enable each prospect to quickly locate the information of interest. This marketing strategy is uniquely customized and tailored to each demographic and behavioral consumer segment.

Here's how it works: First, Virginia Beach researches each consumer market segment's desires and develops a series of creative messages tailored to each segment's professed desires regarding *what each group lives for* in a beach vacation. Next, Virginia Beach places advertisements with unique Web site URLs created explicitly for each segment in specific media vehicles that strategically reach each traveler segment. Then, when each prospective traveler visits the Virginia Beach Web site, he or she immediately views select Web pages containing vacation information about Virginia Beach that is of specific interest. For example, prospective sports enthusiast travelers will view the Web pages featuring photos and descriptions regarding the

FIGURE 3-19. Virginia Beach Web pages. Used with permission by the City of Virginia Beach Convention & Visitors Bureau.

FIGURE 3-20.
(left) Virginia Beach
LIVEFORTHECRUISE.com
ad. Used with
permission by the
City of Virginia Beach
Convention & Visitors
Bureau

FIGURE 3-21.
(right) Virginia Beach
LIVEFORTHESPINCYCLE.
com ad. Used with
permission by the
City of Virginia Beach
Convention & Visitors
Bureau

wide variety of sports events and activities offered at Virginia Beach as presented in Figure 3-19. Of course, each prospect is free to explore the entire Web site as it is easy to navigate and chock full of information and enticing photos and videos.

Let's take a look at precisely how Virginia Beach targets each leisure traveler segment.

SINGLES WITHOUT CHILDREN. So you are single, without children, and searching for a vacation destination for you and your friends. You might locate an advertisement and information about Virginia Beach on a travel Web site or via search engine optimization with Google, Yahoo/Bing or Facebook. As Figure 3-20 shows, the Virginia Beach advertisements that you will find will contain messages tailored to your specific interests such as taking a bike ride along the boardwalk. The ad encourages you to visit "LIVEFORTHECRUISE.COM" to learn more about what a vacation in Virginia Beach has to offer you.

FAMILIES. Pretend for a moment that you are a mom or a dad with a family of three young children and you're planning a beach vacation. As a parent, you might see an advertisement for Virginia Beach in a magazine such as *Good Housekeeping* or *Working Mother*. An example of the advertisement you will see is shown in Figure 3-21. The ad is targeting families with a specific a call-to-action to come play on the beach and visit "LIVEFORTHESPINCYCLE.COM."

SPORTS ENTHUSIASTS If you are a sports enthusiast, you are likely interested in surfing, kayaking, running, or fishing when you visit Virginia Beach. Perhaps you want to learn more about its Annual Sand Soccer Tournament or its Rock n' Roll 1/2 Marathon. You may see ads such as those featured in Figure 3-22 that provide unique URLs, "LIVEFORTHEBIGONE.COM" and "LIVEFORCLOSEENCOUNTERS.COM" encouraging you to visit the specific Virginia Beach microsite to obtain more information.

MATURE CONSUMERS. Fast-forward your life by about 30 or 40 years and think about what you might want from a vacation at Virginia Beach when you are a bit older. You will still enjoy vacationing, but your desires will be different than they are now. You might see Virginia Beach advertisements in *Coastal Living* magazine or on *WashingtonPost.com*. Those ads will be tailored to your interests, which may include taking a walk along the boardwalk or enjoying a couple of afternoons spent on the fairways. (See Figure 3-23.)

FIGURE 3-22.
Virginia Beach
LIVEFORTHEBIGONE.com
and LIVEFORTHE CLOSE
ENCOUNTER.com ads.
Used with permission by
the City of Virginia Beach
Convention & Visitors
Bureau.

FIGURE 3-23.
Virginia Beach
LIVEFORTHEFAIRWAY.com
ad. Used with permission
by the City of Virginia
Beach Convention &
Visitors Bureau.

Conclusion

When you are a vacation destination that offers something for everyone, you must carefully segment your market and identify the geographic, demographic and behavioral sub-groups that exist. As you have seen in this case, the Virginia Beach resort area offers an ideal example of how to employ effective market segmentation strategies by targeting specific segments or niches of consumers with customized and creative messages that appeal to each segment's precise needs, wants and interests. So, what vacation interests do you have? Go to VisitVirginiaBeach.com or LiveTheLife.com and you will surely find whatever you desire in a weekend getaway or a vacation destination.

Case Discussion Questions

1. Identify the segmentation variables discussed in the case to classify potential tourists who vacation at Virginia Beach. Can you think of other variables that can group destination vacationers, with common interests and attraction to Virginia Beach? Describe how such group(s) can be targeted.

2. The case describes the target Virginia Beach vacationers as leisure travelers, meetings and convention planners and group tour organizers / operators. Describe the marketing and media strategies Virginia Beach Convention and Visitors Bureau uses to target these groups.

3. Virginia Beach is described as a quality, year-around vacation destination. Yet the sports, entertainment, and leisure activities depicted on its Web site are all summer bound. Imagine a family is planning to vacation in Virginia Beach during the month of November. What recreational, sight-seeing, and cultural activities can you recommend to such a family?

Notes

1. From the North American Industry Classification System (NAICS) Web site, http://www.census.gov/naics, February 2008.

2. http://erg.usgs.gov/isb/pubs/gis_poster, March 17, 2008.

3. http://www.gis.com/whatisgis/index.html, March 17, 2008.

4. http://www.ersi.com/index.html, March 17, 2008.

5. http://censtats.census.gov/cbpnaic/cbpnaic.shtml, retrieved May 28, 2011.

## CHAPTER 4

Testing, Measuring and Analyzing Customers and Campaigns

OPENING VIGNETTE:
THE NATIONAL GEOGRAPHIC SOCIETY OFFER TEST

The National Geographic Society (NGS) is one of the world's largest nonprofit scientific and educational organizations. Founded in 1888 to "increase and diffuse geographic knowledge," the Society works to inspire people to care about the planet. Like all direct and interactive marketing organizations, NGS is always striving to maximize the rate of response it obtains on its membership offers. Its membership offer includes its "product," which is a subscription for 12 issues of National Geographic Magazine.

In January, April, and October of each year The NGS sends membership promotion mailings to approximately 18,000,000 households in the United States and Canada. The NGS tests its

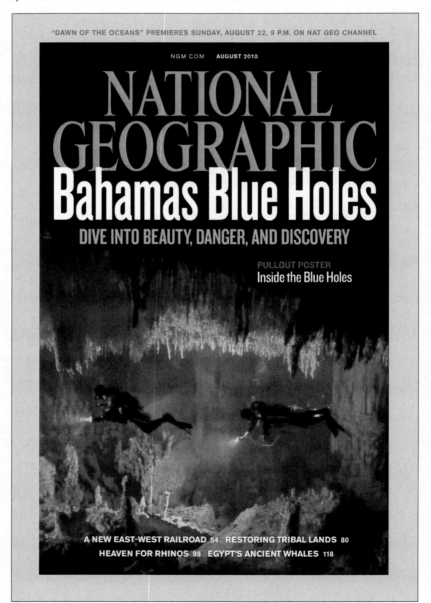

FIGURE 4-1. *National Geographic Magazine.* Used with permission of National Geographic Society.

offers, premiums, prices, mailing lists, payment options, and creative approaches to attract new members for its organization. The most common type of test is normally an **offer test**. When conducting a test, The NGS takes 10 percent of the total mailing quantity and uses that for tests. A test offer for The NGS will have no less than 25,000 recipients.

The NGS conducted pricing and payment term offer tests to determine the impact that these offers had on response rates. As shown in Figure 4-2, The NGS tested two Bill-Me-Later price offers ($18 and $15) against its *control* Bill-Me-Later offer ($12, plus $3.95 for shipping which totals $15.95) and a credit card payment offer. The control is the offer that has historically generated the highest rate of response for the organization.

An analysis of the results of the offer test is used to determine the most effective offer to be sent to a larger sample of prospective members. How does The NGS decide "what works best?" The NGS uses the following criteria:

> The highest net per net subscription, which means how much money did the organization obtain after it found the lowest cost per order, then adjusted for those who did not submit payment (as this was a Bill-Me-Later offer); and

> The offer that beat the control offer by at least 7 percent.

If two tests earned the same response rate, cost the same, and seemed like they would gener-

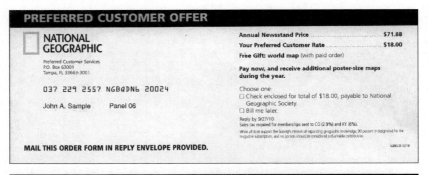

FIGURE 4-2. National Geographic Society offer reply cards. Used with permission of National Geographic Society.

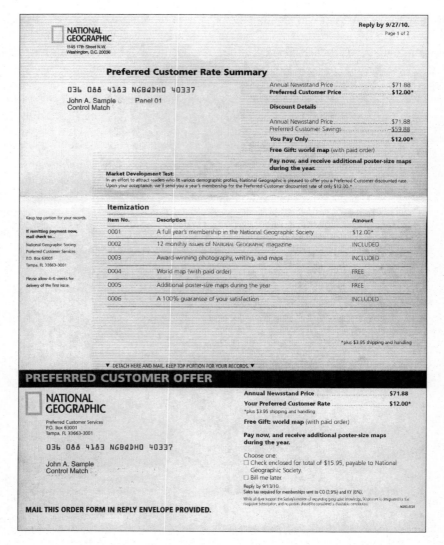

FIGURE 4-2.
continued.

ate the same amount of renewal (repeat business), the NGS would consider the additional factors of:

1. Which one has a smaller environmental footprint—less paper, less trucking, less ink, etc.

2. Which one more effectively extends its mission? For example, for several years, The NGS used a direct mail package that included a free world map in it. This package gave people a map with which to follow the news, trace their cultural heritage, locate earthquakes, etc. So The NGS educated 10 million people at a time. Even though 97 percent of the people who received the offer did not order the NGS magazine, they all got a useful tool to understand geography. And that is what The NGS is all about.

3. Which one takes the least amount of time to manufacture and get into the mail.

As can be concluded, response rates are the key metric used to make strategic campaign decisions, but there are other important factors to be analyzed as well. Analysis of the metrics generated from a test is critical to decision making. Direct marketers must conduct tests, measure response rates and analyze results in order to make good business decisions to maximize profitability and meet organizational objectives. That's precisely what this chapter will discuss.

Testing

Testing, also known as **experimentation**, manipulates one or more controllable factors, called **independent variables,** to determine their influence on various events or outcomes, called **dependent variables.** Testing is especially prevalent in direct marketing. In a test, the direct marketer creates an environment in which controls serve to pinpoint the causes of behavior differences among respondents. This method of gathering data requires close adherence to statistical techniques to ensure validity. Because direct marketers rely heavily on experimentation, we look closely at certain relevant tools and techniques of statistics in this chapter. Some examples of direct marketing questions that call for experimentation are the following:

- How does frequency of mailing to a particular record on a database affect total response?
- How can direct marketers benefit from the Web?
- Is it possible to increase profits by servicing small industrial accounts totally by mail, telephone, or online, rather than using personal salespeople?
- How productive are various segments of a total market?
- Is a newspaper advertisement more effective in color than in black and white?
- What is the best season to offer spring-blooming bulbs to be planted in the fall?
- What is the most profitable pricing strategy?

Independent variables could be the product or service offered, its price structure, or some attribute of the promotional strategy used in the offer. They can also describe the demography or geography of a market. Independent variables should reflect the situation in the real world, for example, the age, gender, marital status, or ZIP code of residence of a respondent. Marketers should generally evaluate only one independent variable at a time. Certain advanced statistical techniques, however, such as multivariate correlation and regression analysis, offer the opportunity to measure the interaction of many independent variables simultaneously. Although direct marketers may investigate many different independent variables, they commonly use the following four types of tests.

List Tests

Investigating whether certain lists will generate a higher response rate than other lists is an ongoing task for most direct marketers. Direct marketers constantly test the lists they use—for both prospective customers and current customers. Most will test a small sample of a prospect list prior to renting the entire list for new customer acquisition purposes. Most list brokers permit small samples of prospect lists to be rented for list testing.

Offer Tests

Offer tests, whether incentives, such as free shipping or discounted shipping, percentage discount or dollar discount, have an impact on the rate of response to the offer. In other words, do the incremental sales generated by the promotional offer offset the forgone shipping revenue or discounts given?

Creative Tests

Creative tests address issues such as design, layout, copy, images, photographs, and much more. Most direct marketers have a printed catalog. One common creative test has to do with the design of the catalog cover. Thus, a test would be conducted to determine whether a test cover creative beat a control cover. This would require testing either a unique design or an alternative style of the control cover design. It could also include variations in images, such as a certain photographed model, or copy compared to the control design or norm. Let's take a closer look at an example.

The American Heart Association decided to test six copy approaches in the form of teasers displayed on the outside of the mailing envelope. These six envelope teasers would be tested against each other and also against the control, the envelope that the fundraiser had been using successfully in the past, but which had no teaser at all.

These seven envelope panels (six tests and one control), included a letter, contribution form, and reply envelope enclosed in each mailing envelope. These forms were essentially the same for all seven packages except for the beginning of the letter, which emphasized the teaser copy approach that was featured on the outside mailing envelope. The American Heart Association sent these mailings to their current donors as well as "cold" prospects, those who had not given a contribution before. The response from each group and for each copy approach was tabulated separately through key coding appearing on the contribution form.

These tested copy approaches are shown in Figure 4-3.

Effort	Copy Approach
1	Use the enclosed FREE GIFT.
2	Emergency Heart Attack Card Enclosed.
3	4 years ago Billy Thompson's dad would have died . . .
4	If you have ever worried about having a heart attack . . .
5	You hold lives in your hands . . . TODAY . . . AND THAT'S IMPORTANT!
6	We'd like to show you how you can help save a life. YOURS.
7	(Control) No teaser copy.

The response results were these:		
The best package:	6	We'd like to show you how you can help save a life. YOURS.
Good packages:	4	If you have ever worried about having a heart attack . . .
	3	4 years ago Billy Thompson's dad would have died . . .
Poor packages:	1	Use the enclosed FREE GIFT.
	5	You hold lives in your hands . . . TODAY . . . AND THAT'S IMPORTANT!
	7	No teaser copy.
	2	Emergency Heart Attack Card Enclosed.

FIGURE 4.3. Tested copy approaches. Used with permission of National Geographic Society.

Source: This case was originally developed by Freeman F. Gosden, Jr., President of Smith-Hemmings-Gosden, Direct Response Advertising, El Monte, California, who conducted the test from which it was derived.

The results of this test proved that teaser copy on the outer envelope was an effective creative approach to use in a fundraising campaign and enabled the American Heart Association to then utilize the most effective teaser copy in its subsequent mailings.

Contact Strategy Tests

This common type of test is related to a direct marketer's customer database. Contact strategy tests investigate whether altering the number of catalogs sent to a group of customers over a specific period can have an impact on sales or profit. Direct marketers often include additional variables, such as using e-mail or other types of direct mail contacts, in the contact strategy tests. In essence, what combination of contacts will maximize the sales or profits associated with each particular customer or select market segment?

In direct marketing, the number of responses or transactions is often the dependent variable. In other research situations the dependent variable could be favorable or unfavorable reactions to a product or overall rating of a brand preference. At least three levels of observation are normally needed for measurement. Direct marketing tests usually take place in a field setting, but marketers do sometimes conduct them under laboratory conditions. In a laboratory, marketers must be sure that the setting is realistic and that the subjects are representative. It would not be appropriate, for example, to use college students in a laboratory setting to test a product geared to the senior citizen market.

Designing the Test

Valid experiments are characterized by (1) the presence of a **control group** on which the experiment is not conducted but that is otherwise identical to the test group and (2) **random assignment** of subjects to both test and control groups so that differences between groups occur by chance alone. Let's examine another example of a creative test. Busch Gardens wanted to determine if a mailer that contained a flap promoting a free Christmas Town ticket with the purchase of a two-year pass sold more passes than the same mailer not including the flap. Both mailers, shown in Figure 4-4, contained exactly the same offer—the only difference was that one creative

FIGURE 4-4. Busch Gardens Free Christmas Town Ticket mailers. Used with permission of Busch Gardens.

piece specifically highlighted the free ticket. A total of 36,000 direct mail pieces were sent to a random sample of Busch Gardens Pass Members. A test group of 25 percent received the mailer without the extra flap promoting a free Christmas Town ticket with the purchase, while 75 percent served as the control group and received the mailer that contained the extra flap. Results showed that the mailer with the flap containing the free ticket communication performed 30 percent higher than the test group. Busch Gardens concluded that the additional costs incurred in printing the mailer with the extra flap were justifed based on the measured results of the creative test.

It is naive to compare responses from two groups that are not randomly selected and may not be similar in their composition. Consider, for example, the often repeated statement that those who receive a college education earn more in their lifetimes than those who do not. The two groups are not comparable, and thus it would be foolish to draw a conclusion that college education in and of itself causes higher lifetime income. It is conceivable that the drive that caused the student to enter college in the first place also affects lifetime income.

Common forms of experimental design measure the effect of an experiment as the difference between what is observed about the dependent variable of the test group and what is observed about the dependent variable of the control group. But even with control and randomization, there is still no guarantee that the two groups are identical. Differences between them that arise by chance alone may be substantial.

Adequate scheduling of experiments, their timely release, and key coding are vital. Marketers should devise a comprehensive schedule to describe the purpose of the experiment and also its various components, costs, and expected results for the test segment as well as the control.

Tracking Responses and Measuring Test Results

Obviously, response differences to a product offering—between tests and control—cannot be measured unless there is a complete record of results for all segments of the experiment. There must be a means to identify the sources of these results. This is accomplished through **key codes** placed on each response device, such as an order form, to make it easy to record results. In direct mail, the key code can be a unique number or other identifier placed on the order form. When the phone is used for response, the key code can be a unique telephone number, a departmental number, or an individual's name. Many direct marketers using the phone or a Web site ask respondents for the key code printed in the advertisement or on the label of a catalog to which they are responding. This is an excellent tracking device where the code will vary based on the element being tested.

Let's examine a test that utilized a highly specific tracking device. Busch Gardens wanted to determine how much it needed to give away in the form of a price discount on its single pass tickets. Busch Gardens runs various types of promotions and offers throughout its operating season and wanted to test offer thresholds to determine if they were giving away more than necessary. One way in which this offer variation was tested was for summer discounts, specifically for pass members to use for visiting friends and relatives. The primary objective was to determine how much a free ticket would influence visitation versus a 50 percent discounted ticket. Due to the significant level of the discount, offers were uniquely bar-coded and included in summer newsletters mailed to each pass member household. The shaded grey area that appears at the bottom right corner of each coupon as shown in Figure 4-5 contained the unique bar code. The two offers were equally split and randomly sent to a total of 100,000 households; each offer representing 50,000. The test results showed that 75 percent of visits were made by the free ticket and Busch Gardens was able to conclude that the free offer was a significantly higher motivator to generate a visit.

FIGURE 4-5. Busch Gardens discount ticket coupon test. Used with permission of Busch Gardens.

Today most direct marketers are multichannel merchants, and their customers' orders are often placed via the company's Web site or at a retail location without a key code. Tracking these responses and correctly linking the results of tests back to a customer database is crucial. The objective is to find ways to match the orders placed on the Web site or in the retail stores that were driven or caused by the specific catalog, offer, or direct mailing that is being tested. Typically, direct marketers use "matchback" rules to track most accurately the results of these tests when key codes are not used. **Matchback** simply refers to the process by which an order response is tracked back to the original source (catalog or offer) from which it was generated. For example, suppose a customer places an online order for a pair of shoes. The direct marketer's task is to determine what specific offer or catalog was responsible for motivating that customer to place the order.

Measuring results involves comparing the response rate generated by the control format versus that of the test format. In direct marketing, the control is normally that direct mail format, package, offer, creative, and so on that has proven time and time again to generate the highest rate of response. When the results of a test shows that a test format or package "beats" or surpasses that of a control format or package, the direct marketer faces a strategic decision. At this point many direct marketers decide to perform additional testing to validate that the new test format is repeatedly more successful in generating a higher response rate than that of the control format prior to determining which format to use for its rollout. Therefore, the validity in measuring test results is crucial to direct marketers.

Let's look at how a direct marketer conducts a creative test. Calico Corners, a high-end retailer of custom draperies, furniture and home accessories, recently conducted a **split test** on a direct mailer. A split test is where two or more samples are taken from the same list, each considered to be representative of the entire list and used for package tests or to test the homogeneity of the list. An A/B split was performed on the prospect database with the A group receiving the control piece presented in Figure 4-5, and the B group receiving the same postcard and offer but an alternative creative design. Both the control and the alternative piece contained a key code to track which piece was responsible for the response and order. The control creative design won, with a response rate that was 11 percent higher than the alternate creative design. This sizable difference in response rate qualified the control creative piece for rollout.

In summary, direct marketers must track responses and measure results carefully to ensure the validity of a test. Assuming that the direct marketer has properly selected a sample of adequate size and designed and conducted the experiment itself in a valid manner, he or she must also know how to validate the difference between the results of the experiment group and its control group. Only by understanding this can direct marketers decide to change from one promotional strategy to another, from one market segment to another, or to adopt a new product in place of an old one.

Typically, in direct marketing experimentation, the mean response to a direct mail solicita-

FIGURE 4-6.
Calico Corners
"Control" piece.

tion is expressed as the average number of responses for each 1,000 pieces of mail sent out and attributable to the test (in which a single variable has been injected) in relationship to the control. That variable could be the mailing list used. Or it could be a pricing variance or a product difference. When we compare the test and the control, we must determine whether, in fact, the difference is real, in a statistical sense, or whether it might have occurred through chance alone. The difference in results must be further related to difference in cost, if there is any. In effect, one tests the hypothesis that there is no difference between the test and the control.

Hypothesis Testing

In testing a **hypothesis**—an assertion about the value of the parameter of a variable—the researcher decides, on the basis of observed facts such as the relative response to a test of variation in advertising copy, for example, whether an assumption seems to be valid. The way that the assumption is stated for purposes of testing it is called the **null hypothesis**, meaning that the researcher must state the hypothesis in such a way that it can be proved wrong. Assuming that the null hypothesis proves, in fact, to be *true* (meaning that the original hypothesis was not borne out by tests but when stated negatively—as a null hypothesis—it proves to be borne out by tests), we can determine the probability that should be assigned to an **alternative hypothesis.** Hypotheses are typically stated in negative terms; that is, a null hypothesis (H_0) versus an alternative hypothesis (H_a) in a form such as the following:

H_0: Direct mail response from the test promotion is at or below direct mail response from the control promotion.

H_a: Direct mail response from the test promotion is above direct mail response from the control promotion.

The null hypothesis then states that direct mail response *will not* be better than the control. Measurement sets out to *disprove* this null hypothesis. The probability of this happening might be very small, considering that the experiment involves new and untried copy intended to out-perform the control, which presumably is the best copy now available.

In the event the direct marketer decides to *reject the null hypothesis,* it is rejected in favor of the alternative hypothesis. In this instance, if the null hypothesis is rejected, it is done in favor of the alternative hypothesis because that test response *is* significantly better than the control response.

Some results, obviously, are more significant than others. A statistician puts a special inter-pretation on the word *significant,* associating it with a specific probability, often denoted by the Greek letter alpha (α), which is decided on prior to testing the hypothesis. The researcher might state that the null hypothesis will be rejected only if the result is significant at a level of, say, 0.05 (5 percent). That is, the test result must diverge enough from the control result so that such a result would occur with the probability of 0.05 or less if the hypothesis were true. The statement of a level of significance should be made *prior* to testing the hypothesis to avoid vacillation on the part of the researcher when the actual response is observed.

Two types of error can occur in tests of hypotheses. A **Type I error** results when the decision maker rejects the null hypothesis even though it is, in fact, true. In this instance the "wrong" decision allows an action when it should not. The probability of doing this is fixed and equal to α. Note that α determines a critical result so rare that it is preferred to reject the null hypothesis rather than believe that an event that rare actually occurred. Thus, ? measures the probability of committing a Type I error.

A **Type II error** occurs when the decision maker accepts the null hypothesis when it is in fact not true. In this instance, the wrong decision is to not do something when something should be done. The probability associated with a Type II error is called beta (β) and it is more difficult to measure than α, prior to conducting an experiment, because it requires a fixed value, other than the one assumed within the null hypothesis, around which confidence intervals associated with an alternative hypothesis can be based.

Statistical Evaluation of Differences

Frequently, when evaluating the results of an experiment and comparing the response from a test with the response from a control, we need to know whether a difference is (or is not) *sta-tistically significant.* The **chi-square (χ^2) test** is one way to determine such a difference.[1] The null hypothesis offered in making the determination is that there is, in fact, no difference between the response from the test and the response from the control. A statistic χ^2 is com-puted from the observed samples and compared with a chi-square distribution table that lists probabilities for a theoretical sampling distribution.

The shape of a χ^2 distribution varies according to the number of **degrees of freedom,** defined as the number of observations that are allowed to vary. The number of degrees of free-dom is determined by multiplying the number of observations in a row (minus 1) times the number of observations in a column (minus 1), thus, $(r-1)(c-1)$, where r is the number of rows and c is the number of columns. For example, the contingency table in Figure 4-7, expressed as "2 × 2" (and read "2 by 2") would involve just one degree of freedom, $(2-1) \times (2-1) = 1$. A table of this form can be used for evaluating the significance of the difference between a test and its control in an experiment.

The typical chi-square table, found in most statistical textbooks, will show critical values for 30 (or more) degrees of freedom for reference when as many as 30 observations are measured *against one another.* Because direct marketers are urged to test just one variable at a time (i.e., a single test against a single control, only the top row of the table)—that for one degree of

	Test	Control	Totals
Response	A	C	$A + C$
Nonresponse	B	D	$B + D$
Total mailed	$A + B$	$C + D$	$A + B + C + D = N$

The statistic χ^2 is computed as follows:

$$\chi^2 = \frac{N[/(A \times D) - (C \times B)/ - N/2]^2}{(A + B) \times (C + D) \times (A + C) \times (B + D)}$$

Here is a sample calculation:

	Test	Control	Totals
Response	200	100	300
Nonresponse	800	900	1700
Total mailed	1000	1000	2000

$$\chi^2 = \frac{2,000 \times [|180,000 - 80,000| - 1,000]^2}{1,000 \times 1,000 \times 300 \times 1,700}$$

$\chi^2 = 38.4$ . . . *which is significant at the 99 ++ % level since it exceeds the critical value in the χ^2 table for one degree of freedom for a significance level of 0.001, given as 10.83*

FIGURE 4-7.
Example of
Chi Square.

freedom—needs to be referenced. Here, then, are the critical values of a chi-square distribution for one degree of freedom along with associated probabilities:

> *Chi–square critical value of* 0.00016 = 0.99 *probability;* 0.00063 = 0.98; 0.0039 =0.95; 0.16 = 0.90; 0.064 = 0.80; 0.15 = 0.70; 0.46 = 0.50; 1.64 = 0.20; 2.71 = 0.10; 3.84 = 0.05; 5.41 = 0.02; 6.64 = 0.01; 10.83 = 0.001.

Put simply, the actual level of response of even a meticulously controlled experiment may not always be projected into the future. Conditions might be different. Thus, whereas the relationship between a test and its control may be the same, that is, one is still better than the other, the entire level of response for both might be either higher or lower than that originally experienced.

Structuring and Evaluating a Test

We conduct a test to make an adequate decision. To do this, the direct marketers must:

- sample a population.
- measure relevant variables, ideally one at a time.
- compute statistics using these measurements.
- infer something about the probability distributions that exist in the population.
- make a decision mindful of the chance of incurring a Type I error (when the decision maker rejects the null hypothesis even though it is true) or a Type II error (when the decision maker accepts the null hypothesis when it is *not* true).

Let's say that a direct marketer wants to test a new promotion strategy against his or her present strategy, to be offered to the control group in the experiment. Past experience indicates that he or she can expect a 2 percent response rate from the present promotion.

Here is a framework for implementation of the test:

1. State the hypothesis and convert it to a null hypothesis.

2. Develop, by a priori analysis, the assumptions required and compute the appropriate sample size.

3. Structure and perform the experiment.

4. Develop, by a posteriori analysis, statistics for judging hypothesis validity.

5. Make the decision.

This procedure sounds simple and appears to be reasonable. Let's follow it step by step:

Step 1. State the Hypothesis and convert it to a null hypothesis. The null hypothesis is

- H_0: Direct mail response from the test promotion is at or below direct mail response from the control promotion.

Although it is not necessary to state an alternative hypothesis at this stage, doing so could imply that he or she is hoping to reject the null hypothesis in favor of the alternative, that is, the test promotion would be better than the control, so that

- H_a: Direct mail response from the test promotion is above direct mail response from the control promotion.

Step 2. A Priori Analysis. The response level of 2 percent is the first of three assumptions. The second assumption is the significance level, which, when $\alpha = 0.05$, describes a confidence level of 95 percent. (The confidence level is equal to 1.0 minus α, thus 1.0—0.05 = 0.95, or 95 percent.) The final assumption relates to limit of error or variation around the mean or, more descriptively, the error limit we wish to maintain around the assumed level of response. In this example, we will assume 15 percent. Having established figures for our three assumptions, 2 percent response, 95 percent confidence level, and 15 percent limit of error, we can use the formula given earlier in this chapter to establish the sample size. The three assumptions and resultant sample size are summarized in Figure 4-8, which shows the effect of the 15-percent error limit. At a 95 percent confidence level, any response below 2.3 percent would not be better than a control response (as assumed) of 2.0 percent.

Step 3. Structure of the Test. Having determined (in the manner demonstrated earlier in this chapter) an objective sample size of 8,365 pieces to be mailed for the control and a comparable volume for the test promotion and having obtained the sample in a valid manner, he or she conducts the experiment through release of the test mailing versus the control mailing.

Expected (Assumed) Response Rate: 2%, 20/M pieces mailed.

Significance Level (α): .05

Confidence Level ($1.0 - \alpha$): 95%

Limits of Error:

<u>Percent Response/M Pieces Mailed</u>

+15% 20/M + 3/M = 23/M (2.3%)

−15% 20/M − 3/M = 17/M (1.7%)

Sample Size: 8,365 mailing pieces (determined separately)

FIGURE 4-8.
A Piori
assumptions and
sample size.

Step 4. A Posteriori Analysis. When all results are in, the direct marketing research examines the response from both the test and the control promotions. One evaluation procedure for determining whether an observed difference is (or is not) statistically significant is the chi-square (χ^2) test, as demonstrated earlier in this chapter.

Step 5. Make the Decision. The decision to accept or reject the promotion tested in the experiment should be clear-cut, based on the a posteriori analysis.

Conducting tests and measuring and analyzing test results to make good business decisions is only a part of the analytics involved in direct marketing. In the next sections, we'll explore more analytic concepts, including response rates, conversion rates, and how to calculate them; customer lifetime value; the concept of a lift; fixed and variable costs; margins; net order contribution; break-even and how to calculate it; and return on investment/return on advertising investment.

Direct marketing can be called successful, that is, creates *benefits*, when it gains new customers (or new orders from existing customers) for a company. We need to remember that direct marketing also has *costs*, e.g., conducting research, acquiring lists, creating advertising campaigns, and fulfilling orders. The goal is to create a marketing campaign that not only breaks even—that is, gains enough sales to pay for all costs—but results in a profit. To figure out how to be profitable and whether marketing activities are profitable, we need to understand a number of different concepts, terms, and formulas.

Using Math and Metrics to Determine the "Right" Target Market

As we have already established in earlier chapters, all consumers are not alike. They can be grouped into market segments on the basis of similar needs and wants. Most companies build profiles of their customers on the basis of the customer data they gather and store in their databases. We discussed the different types of data used for segmenting customers in Chapter 3. The actions taken by consumers are certainly a viable base for market segmentation. The most valuable customer information a company can collect is that which comes after the first sale or transaction. The specific types of products and services consumers have purchased, the time the transactions took place, the method or location of their purchases, and the method of payment they choose can all reveal similarities among consumers. Each behavioral factor can indicate a consumer preference that may be shared by other consumers, consequently identifying a market segment. The creation of a database enables direct marketers to analyze customer transaction data to determine the value of each customer. How does a database help you quantify customer value? How do you measure and calculate customer value? How do you use transaction data to determine customer value? Those are the questions we address in the next section.

Determining Customer Value

It is well established that some customers generate the majority of a company's transactions. We refer to that as the 80/20 principle—approximately 20 percent of a company's customers generate 80 percent of its profits. If that is true, then shouldn't marketers identify those top 20 percent and concentrate on keeping them happy and loyal to the company? Of course! But how do you identify which customers are in the top 20 percent? There are a number of different methods for calculating customer value, such as recency/frequency/monetary assessment, which was discussed in Chapter 2. Another method is to calculate customer value quantitatively via a value equation. Let's take a look at this method. To calculate average customer value, you should follow this four-step process:

1. Take a random sample of customers (active and inactive) who first bought from you about three years ago.

2. Add up the total dollar amount they have purchased in the three years since the date of their first purchase.

3. Divide by the number of customer records in your sample.

4. Multiply by the percentage that represents your average profit margin.

For example, let's pretend you now own a catalog operation selling household gifts. You are in your fourth year in business and want to calculate the average value of your customers. What do you do?

- You randomly select 1,000 customers who have been purchasing with your company for a minimum of three years and obtain a computer printout of their buying history. You see that these customers have placed 1,775 orders during this period with a total value of $89,300.

- You calculate your average profit margin on your household gift lines and determine it to be 20 percent.

- Now let's do the math! Dividing total sales by customers ($89,300 by 1,000) results in average sales of $89.30 per customer. Then, by multiplying that figure by the average profit margin percent (20 percent), you determine that average customer value is $17.86.

That figure represents what the average customer you acquired three years ago was worth to you in terms of future profits.

What if you were able to motivate your customers to spend twice as much? How much do the 1,000 customers now account for in terms of total sales? The answer is $178,600. Therefore, what is the average value of these customers now? Going through the rest of the calculations, the average customer is now worth $35.72. That figure tells you that you'll now be able to spend twice to acquire a new customer—$35.72 instead of $17.86!

The real benefit of calculating customer value is that it can be calculated on a segment or cluster basis, or on an individual basis. The process for calculating individual or segment customer values is basically the same; however, you would not select a "random" sample of customers but concentrate on the segment or cluster of interest. On the basis of these customer value calculations, you can determine which customers or customer segments are generating the most profitability for your company and concentrate on retaining those customers.

Why calculate the value of customers? Because . . .

- It determines how much each customer is worth to your organization.

- It tells you how much money you can afford to spend to acquire a new customer like your current customers.

- You need to identify your best customers in order to seek out new prospective customers who match the customer profiles of your best customers.

Determining customer value is important, but as described, it is based on past purchasing behavior. Customer lifetime value takes on more of an investment view where you regard your customers as investments in future profitability. Let's explore how to calculate customer lifetime value.

Calculating Customer Lifetime Value

As we discussed in Chapter 2 (as lifetime value), **customer lifetime value (CLTV)** is the present value of profits to be realized over the life of a customer's relationship with an organization. Customer relationships translate into customer retention, which usually means repeat customer

$$R \left[\frac{1 - \dfrac{1}{(1+i)^N}}{i} \right]$$

Where –
   R = Annual revenue from a loyal customer
   i = Annual relevant interest rate
   N = No. of periods in which a customer makes purchases

FIGURE 4-9.
Customer lifetime
value equation.

Source: Jon Anton and Natalie L. Petouhoff, *Customer Relationship Management: The Bottom Line to Optimizing Your ROI,*" (Upper Saddle River, NJ: Prentice Hall, 2002), 138.

purchases or transactions over time. When a customer is retained, it is not only the revenue generated in a one-month or one-year period that constitutes the value of that customer, it is the present value of the future stream of revenue that must be taken into consideration. This is the basic premise behind CLTV. Let's see how CLTV can be calculated. Refer to the equation shown in Figure 4-9.

Now let's look at an example to apply the formula and calculate CLTV. Let's assume that you own a fitness business. Based on customer database analysis, you can determine the following about a given customer:

- The stream of revenues from a specific customer is level across time at $25 per month or $300 per year.

- The interest rate (opportunity cost) is the bank rate paid on the money for which no other specific use is made and will be assumed to be 9 percent.

- The amount of time a typical customer stays with a company is three years.

Based on these assumptions, you can calculate CLTV using the formula, where

R = $300; I = 0.09; and N = 3. Therefore, the CLTV of this customer is $759.39.

You might increase a customer's LTV by enticing the customer to spend more on each transaction, thus increasing his or her annual stream of revenues. In addition, you might increase the length of time a customer stays loyal to a firm which in turn would lengthen the investment period. In summary, calculating CLTV is critical for those direct marketers who view their customers as investments.

Determining the "Right" Customer to Target

Quantifying customer value and CLTV can help marketers determine which current customers or prospective customers to target for future direct marketing campaigns. However, it is important to note that customer retention strategies normally generate greater profitability for companies than do new customer acquisition strategies. This is partially due to the value of the established relationship that current customers have with a given company. You must keep in

	Customer Acquisition Focus	Customer Retention Focus
FIGURE 4-10. Acquisition versus customer retention.	$150 to acquire customers = 6 $25 to retain customers = 5	$75 to acquire customers = 3 $100 to retain customers = 20

mind that strong customer relationships are directly correlated to strong customer loyalty, and loyal customers are less price-sensitive, spend more per transaction, cost less to serve, and generate positive word-of-mouth referrals! The bottom line: Loyal customers are more profitable!

Many marketers claim that it costs at least five times more to replace a customer than it does to retain a current customer. Mathematically, this can be easily calculated. For example, let's say it costs $5 to keep a customer happy and loyal to your firm (a customer retention strategy) and it costs $25 (five times $5) to replace a customer (a new customer acquisition strategy). Let's perform the math given a budget of $175. Figure 4-10 shows that if we allocate the majority of our budget on acquiring new customers, we net 11 customers. However, if we allocate the majority of our budget on retaining current customers, we acquire 23 customers. Given the same budget, the mathematical difference is significant.

The calculations show that it is more cost-effective to concentrate your direct and interactive marketing efforts on customer retention and customer relationship building than it is to concentrate on new customer acquisition. Of course, you will want to first focus on your most valuable customers and then search for customers who possess similar characteristics to these highly valued customers.

It sounds simple, right? But where do you look? How do you begin? How do you know which markets, market segments, or clusters of customers will be more likely to respond to your offer? One method is by conducting market penetration analysis. Let's examine that concept in greater detail.

Analyzing Market Penetration

Modeling techniques can correlate market penetration with demographics, lifestyle research, transaction data, and buyer behavior to reveal those markets that contain the largest proportion of a company's customers. **Market penetration** is the expressed percentage relationship of customers to some benchmark universe. Thus, it tells what percentage of the total universe of potential buyers are customers. Market penetration analysis may be performed on any universe, including ZIP code areas, product lines, customer market segments, or specific demographic categories, such as gender, age, or education. Market penetration is calculated by dividing the number of customers in a specific category (such as a ZIP code area) by the total number of people in that category (or ZIP code area). Let's take a look at the following example to better understand how market penetration is calculated and used.

Betty's Bakery is located in Erie, Pennsylvania, and is well known locally for offering delicious baked goods. Betty was able to create a customer list and collect information about her customers by offering weekly drawings for a free pie over the past year. She has determined that the 52 free pies were well worth the customer data she has now collected. Looking over the 5,000 customer cards, she noticed that her customers primarily reside in four ZIP code areas as shown in Figure 4-11.

Let's calculate the customer market penetration for each ZIP code area by dividing the number of Betty's customers in each area by the population for each respective ZIP code area. Figure 4-12 shows the market penetration for each ZIP code area.

Based on an analysis of these market penetrations, we can conclude that ZIP code area

Zip Code Area	Population	Betty's Customers
16501	17,050	1,384
16502	11,288	1,785
16503	10,035	876
16504	9,398	1,010

FIGURE 4-11. Betty's Bakery customer distribution.

Zip Code Area	Population	Betty's Customers	Market Penetration %
16501	17,050	1,384	8.1
16502	11,288	1,785	15.8
16503	10,035	876	8.7
16504	9,398	1,010	10.7

FIGURE 4-12. Betty's Bakery ZIP Code market penetration.

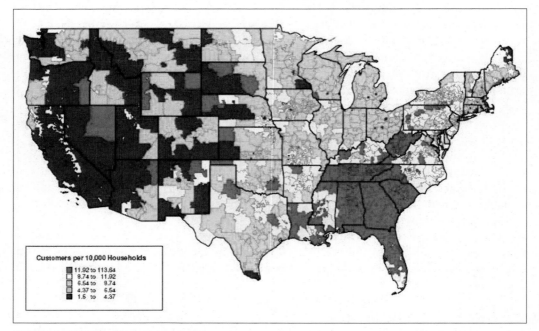

FIGURE 4-13. ZIP Code area penetration map.

16502 contains the largest proportion of Betty's customers, while area 16501 contains the smallest proportion. Thus market penetration analysis can assist Betty in determining which ZIP code area should be targeted for future direct mail promotions. Because it is well known that prospective customers are similar to current customers, Betty should target ZIP code area 16502 for new customer acquisition efforts. As shown in Figure 4-13, marketers often map their customers according to ZIP code area market penetration in order to visually reveal those geographic areas that should be targeted for future promotions.

Often, companies make the mistake of targeting the market in which they have the *least* penetration in an attempt to increase the presence in that specific market segment (for example, ZIP code area 16501). This is not normally a wise strategy because there is usually a reason that the consumers in that market are not responding to company offers in the first place. Perhaps these customers do not have a need or desire for the company's products or services. Therefore, a more effective strategy is to concentrate future marketing efforts on those market segments that contain larger customer penetrations.

Measurement Is the Key

The single most notable feature of direct and interactive marketing is that it always seeks a measurable response. Regardless of whether that response comes via a Web site, or from an in-store visit, or is a phone call to place an order or request additional information, all responses can be measured and evaluated. Thus, determining *what* to measure becomes the challenge. First and foremost, let's discuss how to calculate response rates to conduct response rate analysis.

Calculating Response Rates and Conducting Break-Even Analysis

Possibly the most frequently asked question in direct and interactive marketing is, "What response rate should I expect to my offer?" In reality, there is no universal or normal response rate. The rate can vary relative to such important considerations as the product itself as well as the demand for it, price competition, market preference, and the nature of the promotional offer. A preprinted insert in a Sunday newspaper will generate more response if there are no directly competitive offers in the same issue. A product in the early stages of its life cycle will create more attention and more interest than one that is generally available and displays little if any differentiation.

A more realistic question to be asked in evaluating the response to an offer is probably, "What response do I *need?*" What would it take to just **break even** on a particular offering? And, what response rate will give me a *profit?* We will discuss the concept of break-even in more detail in the next section, but let's look here at how knowing the number of sales it takes to break even allows us to calculate what we need to sell to earn a profit.

The formula for determining break-even point for a single promotion to a new customer is shown in Figure 4-14.

That is, if the marketer recovers promotion cost from the gross profit (beyond cost of goods sold and overhead) of the total number of units sold, he or she breaks even *on those sales.*

Figure 4-15 provides a worksheet for calculating the break-even point and profit at various levels of unit sales per thousand pieces of direct mail promotion. A variation of this worksheet can be used for any medium.

Lines 2 through 8 of the break-even calculation in Figure 4-15 represent production costs, totaling $17.69 (line 9) per copy of a book, *Practical Mathematics.* Order processing/collection costs (line 5) and costs of returns (line 6) are amortized and allocated to net sales, in the manner shown at the top of Figure 4-15.

Unit margin (also known as unit profit or unit contribution), calculated by subtracting $17.69 (line 9) from the selling price of $39.95 (line 1), is $22.26 (line 10). Unit margin divided into total promotion costs of $345.83 per thousand pieces mailed (line 11) provides break-even net sales (line 12). This is 15.54 units per thousand (M), or 1.55 percent. That is the answer to our earlier question: "What advertising response is needed to just break even?" Having calculated a break-even response rate of 1.55 percent, lines 13 to 20 of Figure 4-15 present alternative profit amounts at assumed alternative levels of net sales.

The calculation assumes the offering of only a single item and anticipates a desirable net profit at various levels of response beyond the break-even point. However, a more likely and realistic calculation for direct marketers uses *continuity,* and is applicable to long-term recovery

FIGURE 4-14.
Break-Even
Formula.

$$\text{Break-even number of sales} = \frac{\text{Promotion cost}}{\text{Unit margin (or profit) per sale}}$$

Product/Offer: *Practical Mathematics* @$39.95, net 30 days

Assumptions:		
# Promotions Mail'd	9,508	
Shipments Return'd	8%	
Sales Uncollectable	6%	

Order Processing/Collection Costs:		
Gross Orders	100@$1.80=$180.00	
Less: Returns	8@8% of 100	
Net Sales (A)	92@$0.50=$ 46.00	
Total	(B)	$226.00
Cost Per Net Sale (B/A) =		$2.46

Cost of Returns:		
Return Servicing		$1.30
Shipping/Delivery		$2.20
Total (C)		$3.50
Returns Project'd(D)	8%	
Cost Per Net Sale		$0.30
(C x D/1.00-D)		

Break-Even Calculation:

Line	Description		
1	Selling Price		$39.95
2	Cost-of-Goods Sold	$5.99	
3	G&A Allocation	$3.80	
4	Shipping/Delivery Costs	$2.20	
5	Processing/Collection Costs	$2.46	
6	Cost of Returns	$0.30	
7	Sales Uncollectable	$2.40	
8	Premium Gift Cost	$0.54	
9	Total Production Costs		$17.69
10	UNIT PROFIT (Line 1–Line 9)		$22.26
11	Total Promotion Costs per M Pieces Mailed		$345.83
	(includes database, print, mail, postage, overhead)		
12	BreakevenNtSales/M PiecesMailed(Line11/Line10)		15.54

Total Profit at Alternative Levels of Net Sales:

Line	Description							
13	Projected Net Sales per M Pieces Mailed	17	20	25	30	35	40	45
14	Less: Break-even Sales (Line 12)	15.54	15.54	15.54	15.54	15.54	15.54	15.54
15	Net Sales Earning Full Unit Pro (Line 13–Line 14)	1.46	4.46	9.46	14.46	19.46	24.46	29.46
16	Unit Profit (Line 10)	$22.26	$22.26	$22.26	$22.26	$22.26	$22.26	$22.26
17	Net Profit per M Pieces Mailed (Line 15 x Line 16)	32.61	99.39	210.69	322.00	433.30	544.61	655.91
18	M Pieces Mailed	9,508	9,508	9,508	9,508	9,508	9,508	9,508
19	Total Net Profit (Line17 x Line 18/1000)	$310.01	$944.98	$2,003.26	$3,061.55	$4,119.83	$5,178.11	$6,236.40
20	NtPr'fit %NtSales: Line19/Line1 x Line13 x Line18/1000	4.80%	12.44%	21.10%	26.87%	30.99%	34.08%	36.49%

FIGURE 4-15. Break-even worksheet.

of future time periods, such as that experienced by magazine publishers, insurance companies, fundraisers, and catalog merchandisers who expect repeat orders from new customers.

Response rates will also vary widely according to prequalification of the mailing list or the narrowness and appropriateness of market segments targeted. Typically, all other factors being equal, current customers will respond to an offer for a new product at a much higher level than will prospective customers. In addition, a company's more valuable customers, with whom a stronger customer relationship has been cultivated, will likely respond at much higher rates to company offers than will all other customers. This phenomenon is called a *lift*, and it can be mathematically measured and evaluated. Let's learn more about this valuable concept.

Calculating the Impact of a Lift

A **lift** is an increase in the average response rate due to making an offer to only those market segments or clusters that are predicted to be most responsive. A lift can be applied to any direct response communication where selectivity is involved. For example, if you are creating a direct mail campaign, a lift can decrease the mailing quantity needed (via selectivity) and increase the overall response rate. Thus, a lift will produce a double cost advantage for a company in its direct and interactive marketing efforts.

How is a lift calculated? Figure 4-16 shows that a lift is basically the *new* response rate divided by the *old* response rate (achieved prior to selectivity).

For example, let's say we distributed a direct mail package to all of the 10,000 clients in our database and it garnered a 2.0 percent response rate. Not bad, right? But could it be improved?

$$\text{Lift} = 100 \times \frac{\text{New response rate}}{\text{Old response rate}}$$

FIGURE 4-16. Lift Calculation equation.

$$\text{Lift} = 100 \times \frac{3.52}{2.00}$$

FIGURE 4-17. Example of lift calculation.

Maybe, via database analysis! Let's say we analyzed our database to identify those clients who purchased from our organization within the past month. Based on our analysis, we determine that 3,255 clients actively purchased from our company during that time period. For our next direct mail campaign, we decide to selectively mail to those 3,255 individuals instead of our entire client population. We have now decreased our costs (printing, production, postage) and achieve a response rate of 3.52 percent. What happened? That is what we call a lift. As Figure 4-17 shows, the lift for this example was 176 percent.

Most companies are striving to maximize response rates to their direct and interactive marketing campaigns. All else being equal, a lift can generally generate an increase in response rate due to greater selectivity and produce lower costs associated with the more precise, targeted niche promotional effort. However, beyond increasing response rates, most companies want to generate sales and maximize profitability.

Marketers evaluating the concept of a lift will normally seek to reduce any extraneous variables that may factor into the difference in response rates. Therefore, in an attempt to isolate and measure the impact of a lift, many marketers use a control group and an experimental group. These concepts were presented earlier in this chapter, but apply here as well. Once a direct marketing effort has been made to two different groups at the same time, the lift in response rates can be calculated. Marketers will also create and impose rules to more accurately measure lift on the marketing effort.

Beyond using a control and test group, some marketers have created a panel group that is reserved for calculating the potential lift in response rates. This method may be used to determine the impact that a catalog or mailing has had (if any) on customer response rates and transaction amounts. Thus, the concept of a lift can be applied to the measurement of almost any medium. For example, let's say we want to investigate the impact of catalog mailings on a company's Web site sales. We plan on mailing a million catalogs. So, we take a random sample of 100,000 customers and these customers will *not* receive the catalog in the mail. We then review the 21-day Web site sales at the household level and factor out sales for the group that did not receive the catalog mailer. The results show that those customers treated with receipt of a physical catalog generated sales of $1.10/online catalog, and those who did not actually receive the mailed catalog generated sales of $1/online catalog. Therefore, the implied Web lift due to catalog receipt is 10 percent. At the **source code** level, which identifies the medium by which the customer has responded to a given promotion, the measurement of a lift is complete. However, many marketers want to know additional details about responses at the customer or household level, which is a bit more sophisticated and entails more detailed database analysis.

Often consumer responses are in the form of an inquiry or request for additional information. These responses, called leads, afford the marketer the opportunity to convert those inquiries or leads into sales. This is called lead conversion and it is the topic of our next section.

Determining Conversion Rates

Conversion refers to the transfer of a prospective customer to an actual buying customer. Many consumers do not actually place an order or make a donation during their first interaction with a company or organization. In fact, the initial objective of a company's offer is often to entice the

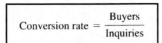

FIGURE 4-18.Conversion rate formula.

prospective customer to request additional information. This is the process of lead generation. These initial inquiries are then followed up with additional interaction between the company and the prospect, with the ultimate goal of new customer acquisition. The rate by which a company converts these leads into sales is called its **conversion rate.**

As Figure 4-18 reveals, a conversion rate is calculated by dividing the number of buyers by the number of inquiries, expressed as a percentage.

For example, let's say you have 1,000 inquiries and 300 of them have subsequently become buyers. You have a conversion rate of 30 percent. Achieving a high conversion rate is important because each direct marketing effort will likely cost the company additional dollars and will need to be allocated in a company's promotional budget. The concept of planning the direct marketing budget is the topic of our next section.

Planning the Direct Marketing Budget

To help us put together all the concepts we will be working with in this next section, let's create a mythical company: Permanent Wear (PW). This company produces all kinds of clothing from micro-fibers. Their director of marketing is Charlie Perry. This year, PW is introducing a new line of jeans for men and women. Their jeans will be more expensive than some other brands, but they can be washed and worn for a much longer time than regular cotton fabric jeans, and they look good! As part of their new line introduction, PW has to conduct research, evaluate its probable market, create a marketing campaign, prepare a budget, and decide how it will measure the success of its direct marketing campaign. Let's see how Charlie and PW do, using marketing math.

PW has conducted its research, segmented its market, rented and created lists, prioritized the media it wants to use for advertising, and generated some preliminary ideas for creative materials, so it's time for Charlie to develop his direct marketing budget. Many companies will use one of the following traditional approaches to establish how much money to allocate to marketing:

- Establish a percentage of probable sales revenue.
- Use last year's marketing budget, plus a small percentage increase.
- Make a good guess on how much is needed.

In direct marketing, the budget is a function of:

- Net order contribution of the item(s) sold.
- Media/sales costs.
- Response rates.
- Desired level of profitability.

Another difference between traditional marketing budgets and direct marketing budgets is that in direct marketing, campaign results are constantly monitored, and changes can be made in strategy even while the campaign is in progress—or before the next one is executed. Remember: Direct marketing is *always* measurable and accountable.

How to Begin: Estimating Costs

Each advertising campaign needs to be treated as an individual cost/profit exercise. So, in the case of PW, if Charlie is planning to use the Internet for one major introductory campaign of the new jeans, he will need to work up a budget for that campaign.

Where does he start? One way is to list all the elements he would like to use in the campaign as if he had an unlimited amount of money. For example, maybe he would like to run banner ads for one month on three major Web sites. Here are some of the elements he would have to include in his preliminary budget.

For the ad itself:

- Creative/production/cost of hiring a designer.
- Cost of the banner ad for 30 days on 3 Web sites.
- Cost of hiring someone to record and analyze the hits.

For the campaign:

- Fixed costs.
- Cost of goods sold.
- Variable costs (including fulfillment costs, credits and returns).

If Charlie wanted to create campaigns using other media, for example, direct mail, national television, magazine advertising, his advertising costs would involve different elements.

As Figure 4-19 shows, each medium has its own costs, but two constants are the costs of the *creative materials* (both the personnel to create them and the production and duplication) and the *media buy* (the cost of time or space to present the creative materials), except in direct mail and telephone marketing, where instead of media buy costs, Charlie would have mailing costs or personnel and telephone line rental costs.

The First Calculations: Margins, Fixed and Variable Costs

Let's say Charlie has added all his costs for his ideal Internet campaign, and they come to $3 million. Can PW afford this campaign? How many jeans can they sell and at what price to afford it and make money? Charlie has to look at some other factors. First, he needs to understand what the likely margins on sales of the new jeans are likely to be.

Let's start with total sales. If the new jeans retail for an average price of $88 a pair, and the company expects to sell 100,000 pairs in a year, then their **gross sales** or total sales would be: $88 × 100,000 = $8,800,000. But of course, it costs the company something to make and distribute the jeans. Therefore, we use the term **cost of goods sold** to include the **variable costs** that come into play when making and selling the jeans. PW knows that their cost of goods sold for this line of jeans will be $22 per pair. This includes the cost of manufacturing the fabric, sewing the jeans, shipping them out, processing orders, allowances for bad debt, and handling returns. Variable costs are those costs that vary with production. **Fixed costs** are those costs that do not vary with production. (See Figure 4-20 for examples.)

Another important concept here is the **unit margin** or trade margin (also called unit contribution or unit profit) that each sale provides. Remember, we talked about this in discussing response rates. This is like the concept of the gross margin except that the unit contribution is simply the amount that *each sale* provides to cover all other costs. In our example, the unit margin of each pair of jeans is $66.

$88	average selling price for one pair of jeans
−22	cost of goods sold/variable costs
$66	unit margin

This $66 is what is left over after a sale to cover all fixed costs, which, as we have seen, include the overhead necessary to run the entire business. Why do advertising costs count as fixed costs? Because the advertising dollars will be spent regardless of how many units are produced and

Medium	Creative Cost Elements	Related Costs
Broadcast	Script writer(s)	Cost of air time
	Talent (announcers, actors)	Cost of distributing
	Studio time/rental to film/tape	or disseminating
	Recording equipment	finished product to
	Crew (camera people, engineers, etc.)	broadcast outlets,
	Duplication equipment	e.g., by mail, satellite
	Discs, film, tape for duplication	Time buyer (if used)
	Rights to use copyrighted material	
	Pre-produced sound effects, pictures	
Electronic (Internet)	Artists/writers who create ads	Cost of placements
	Computer design software	Cost of site maintenance
Catalogs	Writers, artists, photographers	List creation/rental
	Rights to use copyrighted pictures, photos	List maintenance
	Materials: computer software, drawing	Production/duplication
	boards, artists' supplies	costs of catalog
Direct Mail	Writers, artists, photographers	Duplication costs
	Production equipment, e.g., computers,	List creation/rental
	design software, printers	List maintenance
	Paper stock/photo stock	Lettershop
		"Nixies" and returns
Out-of-Home:**		
Billboards	Writers, artists, photographers	Billboard rental
	Production equipment	Billboard maintenance
	Paper stock (if not provided by	
	billboard co. as part of rental)	
Buses	Writers, artists who create copy	Bus side rental
	Production equipment	Duplication costs
	Paper stock	
Point of sale	Same as for buses	Duplication costs
Print	Writers, artists, photographers	Space buy, e.g., in
	Production equipment and costs	newspaper, yellow
	Rights to copyrighted material	pages, magazine
Telemarketing	Writers to create scripts	Telephone lines
		Salaries for staff
		making/taking calls
		Computers and programs
		for call makers/takers

* For several of these media, e.g., broadcast, out-of-home, and print, there may be additional costs of working with personnel at an ad agency, if one is used.

** Other "out-of-home" media may include posters in subways, airports, other public places; aerial banners or other mobile media displays; table-top ads at large events. Generally, all of these will share the common creative costs of artists, writers, and photographers, plus any special space/place rental costs.

FIGURE 4-19. Costs of creative elements by media.

sold. It is going to cost Charlie the same amount to advertise on the Internet whether the company gets 3 orders or 3 million. The same is true of his advertising budgets for all other media: if he plans to spend $2 million this year on network television, that is a fixed cost, regardless of how many orders he gets as a result of this particular advertising campaign.

Another important concept comes into play here: the **allowable margin.** Many companies will establish an allowable margin for each promotional campaign. Basically, it represents the amount of money you have left over to cover advertising/promotion and profit after *all* other expenses have been deducted. It can be the same as the unit contribution or less, depending on whether fixed costs have been allocated to the product sales before the unit contribution has

Fixed Costs	Variable Costs
Rent/mortgage on facilities	Costs of goods sold, tied to production
Salaries of permanent staff	Commissions to sales people
Amortization of facilities	Order processing
Overhead of running company	Shipping, delivery, returns, restocking
Advertising	Costs of money (financing)
	Bad debt
	Fulfillment activities

FIGURE 4-20. Types of general fixed and variable costs

been figured. In our example with PW, we will assume that the allowable margin is the same as the unit contribution, that is, $66 per pair of jeans.

Net Profit and Breaking Even

The next concept we encounter is **net profit** or net profit margin. This is the amount of money the company will have (before taxes) after the fixed costs are subtracted from the gross revenues. Often, a company will set a goal for its net profit margin and measure its success for a product line in terms of whether this goal was obtained or not.

To know how many jeans have to be sold to make a profit, Charlie first needs to know how many jeans PW has to sell to break even before he adds in the cost of his advertising campaign. The simple formula for calculating break-even is:

$$\text{Break-even in units sold} = \frac{\text{Fixed Costs in Dollars}}{\text{Net Unit Margin in Dollars}}$$

We don't know what PW's fixed costs are on a per unit basis, but let's say the total fixed costs allocated to the jeans line are $6 million a year. Therefore, to break even on their new line of jeans:

$$\text{Break-even in units sold} = \frac{\$6,000,000}{\$66}$$

Break-even = 90,910 jeans

However, PW wants to do better than just break even: they want to make a profit. So let's say that they want a 20 percent profit before taxes over and above recovery of their fixed costs. (They could establish their profit target in other ways, e.g., as a percentage of the sale of each pair of jeans, or as fixed dollar number for the year based on increasing the profit percentage from a previous year.) Then we have to add 20 percent of the fixed costs *to* the fixed costs and recalculate the units to be sold:

$$
\begin{aligned}
\$6,000,000 &= \text{fixed costs} \\
\times\, .20 & \\
\hline
\$1,200,000 &= \text{profit} \\
+6,000,000 &= \text{fixed costs} \\
\hline
\$7,200,000 &= \text{new target to be achieved}
\end{aligned}
$$

$$\text{New target in units to be sold} = \frac{\$7,200,000}{\$66}$$

New target units: 109,091 jeans

Remember: Always add the desired profit margin (in dollars) to your other fixed costs to give yourself the new number to divide by the unit margin (in dollars).

This is the number of jeans PW would have to sell over one year to not only recover all fixed costs but to arrive at a 20 percent net profit before taxes. In our example of Charlie's Internet campaign, all he has to be concerned about is how many jeans *this particular campaign* will sell—and whether he can do better than break-even. He has initially calculated his costs for the Internet advertising as $3 million. His boss has told him that he expects to see a 10 percent profit on this specific campaign. That means adding $300,000 to the fixed costs of $3 million, giving Charlie $3,300,000 to work into our formula. We need to know how many total pairs of jeans it will require PW to sell to meet this target. Again we can use our break-even formula, realizing that we have already added a profit amount:

$$\text{Target units to be sold} = \frac{\$3,300,000}{\$66}$$

Target unitsto be sold: 50,000 jeans

At this point, Charlie needs to consult with others in the company. Is it reasonable to expect this one campaign to sell 50,000 jeans, which allows for covering fixed costs (before advertising), plus a profit, plus Charlie's Internet advertising campaign? If the company has no previous experience in the clothing field, it may be that they will want to test the market with a smaller campaign to start with. Or, Charlie's boss, the president, may feel that she has enough knowledge to predict that this is too ambitious a sales goal for the first campaign. We'll talk about how to compare a test with a roll-out later, but at this point, let's assume that Charlie's boss tells him to cut back on the costs of his Internet advertising campaign so that he can have a less ambitious sales target. He does this by cutting back to one Internet provider, AOL, which has quoted him $100,000 to run a banner ad on their home page for one month. He also has to pay a designer $15,000 to design the ad, and he has a contractor who will charge $5,000 for recording the hits. His new fixed-costs budget for the Internet campaign is $120,000. Because this is going to be a two-step campaign—in other words, PW will advertise on the Internet, then send samples to people who respond before actually getting any orders—Charlie is told that he can budget up to $1,200,000 for the second step of the campaign, the mail out of samples.

Since Charlie now has the advertising budget that he needs for this campaign, he recalculates the number of jeans he needs to sell to achieve his target of break-even:

$$\text{Units to be sold} = \frac{\$1,320,000 \text{ (fixed cost plus profit)}}{\$66 \text{ (unit margin in this campaign)}}$$

Units to be sold: 20,000 pairs of jeans

As we can see, if the variable costs in this campaign had risen even more, so would Charlie's target for sales. Or, if he could reduce his fixed costs (or his profit margin), then the total number of jeans to be sold would be reduced.

Cost per Inquiry/Cost per Order

In direct marketing, it is important to know how much it costs us to obtain a new customer and a new order. We can have basically four kinds of possible prospective customer behavior:

• People who are exposed to the campaign but do nothing (nonresponse).

- People who are exposed and inquire (inquiry response).
- People who are exposed, inquire, and buy (buyer response).
- People who are exposed and buy immediately (no inquiry).

Since there is a cost to doing any kind of marketing, we need to know how to calculate it for those who inquire and those who buy (those who do nothing don't figure into our calculation). We also need to understand that calculating costs and responses varies from medium to medium. Figure 4-21 shows the special calculations that need to be made in measuring the results in different media.

Let's look at an example in which PW uses Charlie's Web campaign to target 12 million customers. The campaign has two steps: The first step is intended to get people to request a sample of the jeans fabric. When PW mails back the fabric sample, they also send an order form. Their next step is to sell jeans based on this inquiry/mail-out campaign. They will have a **cost per inquiry (CPI)** which is sometimes called a **cost per lead (COL)**, and then a **cost per order (CPO)** or **cost per response (CPR)**. Figures 4-22 and 4-23 detail the elements included and the process involved in the calculations of CPI and CPO.

We don't know if Charlie was given targets for CPI or CPO in this campaign or a number of new customers to be obtained, but we do know that he achieved the following:

- His target for breaking even was 20,000 pairs of jeans sold, and they sold 24,000.
- In addition to making a profit on his campaign, the sales covered all the variable costs (at 25 percent of revenue) of the 24,000 pairs of jeans *before* the advertising costs were subtracted.

There is one more measure of success that we need to know about.

Medium	Special Calculations
Broadcast (radio/TV)	Cost of the schedule is the marketing cost Measurement of viewers reached based on rating points, e.g., number of responses divided by gross rating points*
Electronic (Internet)	Cost of Web site and maintenance are the marketing costs
Catalogs (treat each item as its own campaign)	Divide the number of pages by cost to determine cost per page Divide the number of items per page by cost per page to determine the marketing cost of each product
Clubs/Continuity Programs	Higher advertising allowables used here because customers are expected to buy beyond their first purchase
Direct Mail	Use total number mailed as basis to determine net profit
Print Advertising	Use circulation figures to determine net profit, e.g., number of responses divided by circulation

*Gross Rating Points are calculated by the "reach" of a commercial—how many people watch or listen to the program in which it is inserted (as measured by commercial ratings services such as Arbitron and Nielsen) times the frequency (number of times) the commercial is presented in a given program vehicle.

FIGURE 4-21. Special calculations for different media.

AOL subscribers:	12,000,000
Response rate:	5%
Total number of people responding:	600,000
Banner ad cost:	$120,000
Banner ad cost per thousand:	$10*
Cost per inquiry:	$.20**

*In marketing, costs are generally quoted in terms of how much it takes to reach 1,000 people via a given medium. In this example, PW knew that via AOL it could reach 12,000,000 people. If we divide 12,000,000 by 1,000, we get 12,000 "groups" of 1,000 people each. Therefore, we take the total banner ad cost of $120,000 and divide it by the 12,000 "groups" and say the "cost per thousand" is $10.
**To derive the "cost per inquiry," we take the total cost, $120,000, and divide it by the total number of people who inquired, 600,000, giving us a cost per inquiry of $.20. Note that this is a pure cost at this point—there is no profit associated with it.

FIGURE 4-22.
Cost per inquiry
of a banner ad
on AOL.

Mailings of fabric to AOL inquirers:	600,000
Response rate (% who ordered):	4%
Number of orders:	24,000
Average order price:	$ 88
Gross sales:	$2,112,000
Gross profit before advertising: @75% margin	1,584,000*
Cost of fabric mail-out campaign @$2.00 per mailing:	1,200,000
Advertising cost (inquiry campaign):	120,000
Promotional costs total:	1,320,000
Profit (or loss):	264,000
Cost per order:	55.00**
Profit (or loss) per new customer/order:	11.00***

*The company has a COGS of 25%, so they have a profit margin of 75% before advertising costs.
**The cost per order is derived by taking the total marketing costs ($1,200,000 + $120,000) and dividing their sum of $1,320,000 by the total orders of 24,000.
***Since there was a profit of $264,000 from the campaign, we divide that by the number of orders, 24,000, to get the "profit per order."

FIGURE 4-23.
Cost per order
based on the AOL
ad campaign.

Return on Investment/Return on Advertising Investment

It is important to note that the goal of an advertising campaign may *not* be to make a profit if, for example, the campaign focuses on a product introduction, achieving penetration in a new market, or even gaining market share. In these cases, the number of new customers acquired, new orders acquired, or total market share gained may be the measures of success. However, what *is* important is that these goals be clearly stated when the budget is being planned. At some point, of course, the company has to make money on the products it sells, so understanding the basics of how to calculate profit and loss are important.

One popular measurement tool in the business world is **return on investment,** or **ROI.** This is a simple calculation: net profit divided by the average amount invested in the company in a year. When we look specifically at calculating ROI for an advertising campaign, we need to know what the gross profit is for that campaign; remember: gross profit or margin is total sales less cost of goods sold (COGS). Then we subtract from the gross profit all the promotional (advertising) costs, which gives us a net profit (but without consideration for other fixed costs that the company incurs). We then divide this number by the total promotional costs. To express the answer in percentage terms, which is how we talk about ROI, for example, "his ROI in that campaign was 20 percent," we multiply the answer by 100. We can do this for Charlie's Web campaign for the jeans:

Gross Sales:	$2,112,000	
Less COGS:	- 528,000	(25% of gross sales)
Gross Margin:	$1,584,000	
Less Promo:	-1,320,000	
Net Profit:	$ 264,000	
ROI calculation:	$264,000	= .2
	$1,320,000	

ROI = .2 x 100 = **20%**

Is this a good ROI for Charlie? Well, we don't know if his boss gave him an ROI target. Since the jeans are a new product, it's possible that one of the company's goals was to gain a minimum number of orders while not losing money. Of course, a higher ROI is always better. If, for example, Charlie's campaign had sold two pairs of jeans for each order (without any additional promotional expenses), the gross margin would have doubled, and we would have the following numbers:

Gross Sales:	$4,224,000	
Less COGS:	- 1,056,000	(25% of gross sales)
Gross Margin:	$3168,000	
Less Promo:	-1,320,000	
Net Profit:	$1,848,000	
ROI calculation:	$\frac{\$1,848,000}{\$1,320,000} = 1.4$	

ROI = 1.4 x 100 = **140%**

Also, if Charlie had been able to cut his advertising costs, the ROI would have improved. Overall, though, it looks like Charlie did a reasonable job with his first campaign for the new jeans!

One more note: In doing the math to arrive at the proper ROI for an advertising campaign, there is another way to calculate the ROI. We can take the total number of units sold and *subtract* the units we know it takes to break even on the cost of the campaign; in other words, the number of units it will take to pay for the entire advertising campaign. We then multiply the remaining number of units sold, which will be earning full profit by the net unit contribution. Then, we can divide that net profit number by the cost of the campaign and arrive at the same ROI answer as we did above. Let's see how Charlie would calculate this.

Charlie's break-even units:	20,000
Total units sold:	24,000
Units earning full profit:	(24,000-20,000) = 4000 units (pairs of jeans)
Net Profit:	(4000 units x $66 net unit contribution)
	= $264,000
ROI for the advertising campaign:	$\frac{\$\ 264,000\ \text{profit}}{\$1,320,000\ \text{ad costs}} = .20$

ROI = .2 x 100 = **20% ROI**

Budgeting for Tests

Sometimes, a company will want to test a planned campaign on a small scale to see if the assumptions about costs and response levels are reasonable. In the case of PW and Charlie, he believes that direct mail might be a good way to market the new jeans, but he wants to run a test with a small sample. He has in mind a mailing that includes color pictures of people actively working and playing in the jeans, plus a small fabric sample—and of course an order form that can be returned, although he will provide the Web site address, a fax number, and a toll-free number for ordering also.

Charlie first has to determine his advertising allowable (sometimes called **allowable margin**), or the amount that can be spent to get an order while still allowing for media costs and the designated profit to be made. From previous experience and his budget projections, he believes that he can use an advertising allowable of $6.00 per unit (pair of jeans) ordered via direct mail. He has bought a mailing list from the magazine *Field and Stream,* and he plans to use just the portion of that list (people subscribing in four northeastern states) for his test campaign. This portion of the list has 2000 names. The cost per thousand is $900 for the test. We could also express this cost as $.90 per name:

> CPM = $900 for the test
> 2000 names on the mailing list
> 2000 divided by 1000 = 2 "groups" of 1000 names
> 2 (groups of 1000) x $900 (per group of 1000) = $1800 for the test
> $1800 divided by 2000 = $.90 per name

What Charlie is looking for is a response rate that either comes in at a cost of $6.00 per response or less than that.

Charlie sends out the mailing in April, with an offer that expires by the end of May. He gets a 5% response, or 100 orders:

> 2000 mail pieces x .05 response rate = 100 orders

It cost him $1800 to run the test. Did he achieve his $6.00 cost per order?

> $1800 divided by 100 orders = $18.00 per order

No! It cost him $18.00 per order, so, he decides to run a second test. This time, he eliminates the fabric sample from the mailing, which saves him the cost of the sample and also lowers his postage costs. He now has a CPM of $600. He picks 3000 names from the *Field and Stream* list, this time people from four southwestern states. This time, his budget looks like this:

> CPM = $600 for the test
> 3000 names on the mailing list
> 3000 divided by 1000 = 3 "groups" of 1000 names
> 3 (groups of 1000) × $600 (per group of 1000) = $1800 for the test

Charlie sends out the new test mailing in May and gets a 10% response, or 300 orders:

> 3000 mail pieces x .10 response rates = 300 orders

It cost him $1800 to run this test. Did he achieve his $6.00 cost per order?

> $1800 divided by 300 orders = $6.00

Yes! It cost him exactly $6.00 per order. You will note that he did several things that improved his CPO. He lowered his actual costs by not sending the sample. He used a different mailing list, perhaps with people more interested in the product. He ran the test later in the spring, perhaps a better buying time. He used more names.

Sometimes, of course, companies are willing to take a chance on rolling out a large campaign even if the test has not quite met their goals. Like Charlie, they may know of ways to cut costs, reach better prospects, or even pick a better time of year for the campaign. As we already know, varying the creative format, the message, and the price of products can make huge differences in how people react to advertising, but it's always a good idea to test first.

Analytic Application: Super Bowl Advertising

Suppose you are the marketing vice-president for a company that has just produced a truly revolutionary running shoe. You have a marketing budget of $5.4 million for the coming year, and since you are introducing the product next year, you decide to spend half of your budget, or $2.7

million, on one 30-second direct response television ad during the Super Bowl in January. The ad provides a Web site address that will allow your company to know when a hit has resulted from people seeing this particular ad. You get 1 million hits on that Web site after the Super Bowl telecast. Is this good? How many shoes did you eventually sell as a result? Did the ad pay for itself or not? Could you have done better by spending your money in some other form of advertising?

Let's say that of the one million visitors to your site, .035 percent ordered a pair of the shoes by visiting your Web site. You, of course, created a special Web address *just* for this commercial, so you could accurately evaluate how many responses and orders this one ad produced. Let's also say that a pair of the shoes at the price offered in this ad sold for $110, including shipping and handling. The variable costs come to $65. You had an advertising allowable of $8 per order. So, you can now make some calculations:

Selling Price:	$110.00
Variable Costs:	−65.00
Unit Margin:	$45.00

One million prospects (hits) × .035 response rate = 350,000 orders

Cost of your ad: $2,700,000

Break-even in units ordered: $\dfrac{\$2,700,000}{\$45}$

= 60,000 units to break even

Pairs of shoes sold:	350,000
Break even needed:	−60,000
Units at full profit:	290,000
Unit margin:	× $45

Net Profit: $13,050,000

ROI: Profit divided by ad costs: $\dfrac{\$13,050,000}{\$2,700,000}$ = 4.83 or 483% ROI

CPO: $2,700,000 divided by 350,000 = $7.71 versus an allowable of $8.

We now know you beat your advertising allowable and came in with a healthy profit, although we do not know if your boss gave you a higher ROI target. But 483 percent looks good! The point is not the numbers themselves, but that you now know how to make calculations that tell you how successful you have been—and very likely what you might want to consider doing (or not doing) in the future. In this case, it looks like the one-time Super Bowl ad worked well for your product introduction.

Summary

Direct marketing is research-oriented and is especially susceptible to the tools and techniques of testing and experimentation. In this chapter, we have looked at how valid tests can be constructed to manipulate the variables that a direct marketer would be likely to test, including lists, offers and creative materials. Experiments must be designed and sampling must be controlled so that results are measurable and accountable. Hypothesis testing enables such measurement. It is important to schedule experiments carefully and record results utilizing key codes to identify sources of response for accurate evaluation. Statistical differences in the results of tests may or may not be significant, and the direct marketer must know how to determine statistical significance.

Direct marketing mathematical calculations can also help you to determine which customers to target based on the calculation of customer value and CLTV. By calculating and analyzing response rates, lift, market penetration, and conversion rates, you may be able to create more effective future marketing strategies to grow the profitability of the organization. We saw, for example, how critical analyzing market penetration was to increased sales for Betty's Bakery. Indeed, quantitative analysis is important in direct and interactive marketing!

Finally, we looked at the steps Permanent Wear, and Charlie, its director of marketing, would take to plan the marketing budget. We discussed key concepts such as break-even analysis, net profit, cost per inquire/cost per order, return on investment (ROI) and budgeting for tests. The point of this extended example is that calculations can help you analyze how successful you have been with tests and campaigns and therefore what you might want to consider doing (or not doing) in future campaigns. The numbers themselves are necessary to success but alone are not sufficient. Marketers must measure and analyze them, i.e., knowing how to do marketing math, means everything to the direct marketer!

Key Terms

test	customer lifetime value (CLTV)
experiment	market penetration
independent variable	break even
dependent variable	source code
control group	conversion
random assignment	conversion rate
key codes	gross sales
matchback	cost of goods sold
split test	variable costs
hypothesis testing	fixed costs
null hypothesis	unit margin
alternative hypothesis	allowable margin
type I error	net profit
type II error	cost per inquiry (CPI)
chi-square test	cost per response (CPR)
degrees of freedom	return on investment (ROI)

Review Questions

1. Why do we bother to examine the costs of marketing? What should result from spending money on marketing?

2. Why calculate the value of customers?

3. What steps would you take to calculate average customer value?

4. How much more does it cost to replace a customer than to retain a current one?

5. How is a lift calculated? Why is it important to know about lifts?

6. Why is the concept of break-even important? Is this always a goal in a direct marketing campaign? What might be another goal of the campaign?

7. What are some examples of fixed costs and variable costs in a clothing manufacturing business like PW?

8. Why do advertising costs count as fixed costs?

9. In a specific direct marketing campaign, if we want to improve the ROI, what are some ways to do this?

10. Why would a marketing manager run a test of a direct marketing campaign before rolling it out? What would he or she be hoping to learn from the test?

Exercise

Let's see where Charlie at PW is with his direct marketing campaign for the new jeans. After two years, he has learned that using the Internet and direct mail are effective ways to attract new customers and retain current customers who make repeat buys. But he would like to gain market penetration. How could he plan to do this? How could he achieve a lift in response during the third year of the campaign? By now, his boss is looking at the increased costs of producing the jeans and tells Charlie to work toward a better ROI. What steps could Charlie take to do this?

Critical Thinking Exercise

Chad Stafford, director of a summer tennis camp, wanted to determine which offer he should use in promoting his tennis camp next summer. He wanted to determine which offer would work best to attract tennis players to register for the camp. He created the following two offers: (1) Free court time for a week at the country club; and (2) free tennis balls and a gift card to the country club tennis pro shop. Construct a test to help Chad determine what offer to use. What are the steps that must be taken in determining which offer to implement? Beyond the actual test results, what additional issues should be analyzed in order to make a good business decision?

CASE: Charles George, Artist, Entrepreneur, and Direct Response Mogul

Charles George was primarily an artist when he first discovered direct marketing. Since his first introduction to direct marketing, Charles has made a lifelong commitment to learning about and implementing new direct response marketing strategies. This passion and love for direct marketing, and also art has been a driving force behind his success as an artist and also in helping others realize their goals.

FIGURE 4-24. (left)"Staring in the Eyes" painting.Used with permission of Charles George.

FIGURE 4-25. (right) "Pride of the Plains" painting.Used with permission of Charles George.

Not Your Ordinary Artist

His knowledge of direct response marketing has opened up many doors for Charles. He has used direct marketing to sell art in galleries and murals to new moms and businesses. He has also owned retail stores that sell art and has worked with other corporations to promote and sell his art.

Moreover, he has used his knowledge of direct marketing to help other artists grow their businesses and increase their sales.

Making Direct Marketing Work for an Art Show

Recently Charles helped an artist, Matthew, who was just starting out and had a very small client list, to launch his career. Matthew had just been laid off from his job and was having a hard time supporting his wife and family. The two assets that Matthew did possess were his skill and passion for doing charcoal portraits and a list of 27 people who had purchased his charcoal portraits. What Matthew needed was a venue where he could host an art show. Charles advised that the best place to hold such an art show would be in Matthew's home. This would allow Matthew to invite clients to his home and give the entire show a very personal feel.

With the location decided, the first step in planning the show was to figure out a way to increase Matthew's list size and to get more people to the party. Since Matthew lives in Northern Virginia, one commonality is the community's love for the Washington Redskins. Two local Redskins jerseys were purchased at a thrift store and then autographs of the players on the jerseys were obtained by visiting a local meet and greet promotion with the Washington Redskins.

The second step in planning the art show was to create two gift baskets with other items that people would find valuable. The total amount spent on the items was $30 for each basket, including the Redskin jersey as the premier item in each basket. The third and fourth steps of the planning stage required picking a date for the art show and then mailing out the invitations for the show.

The invitations that were sent read: "On May 15 at 2:00 P.M., you are invited to attend Matthew's charcoal art show at his home where he will be showing his latest portraits. Bring a friend. The two people who bring the most friends will be rewarded with a personalized gift basket featuring a signed Washington Redskins football jersey. Please RSVP by May 8. I look forward to seeing you at the show!—Matthew."

Saturday afternoon at 2:00 P.M. was the time chosen to start the show, because Charles wanted this to be an event that the whole family could attend. This way if the mother of the family chose to have a family portrait created, but did not have a photo of the family with her, then the whole family would be there to be photographed, so Matthew could do the a multi-person portrait—which was more expensive, thus more profitable for Matthew, than a single portrait.

At the art show, Matthew's wife was initially responsible for mingling with guests and making sure that the light finger foods were always available. The two children were responsible for talking to people and offering them food. This allowed Matthew and Charles to mingle and to handle the sales of the show.

Upon the guests' arrival, Matthew welcomed clients and guests and walked them over to where the gift baskets were located. Each person who was originally invited filled out a contact card with name, address, phone, number and e-mail address and the number of guests they brought with them to the show. Getting these cards completed allowed Matthew to announce the winner of the gift baskets and to grow his database.

Thirty minutes after everyone arrived, Matthew talked about each charcoal portrait that he had hanging in his house. As each client and new guest became interested, Charles was there to help them with their own personal portrait.

At the end of the show, the results were:

- Number of people that filled out contact cards: 87.
- Number of new portraits commissioned: 4 (One portrait was commissioned by a grand-mother of her entire family, including children and grandchildren for $897.00).
- The price points on the other 3 portraits that were commissioned: $125, $215 and $215.
- Total sales of day from the initial show were $1,452.00.

Monday following the show, a personal thank you note was sent to everyone who attended. For the people who did not purchase a charcoal drawing, inside the thank-you note was enclosed a card made a special offer: "Purchase a charcoal portrait of at least two people by Saturday May 22nd and receive a 15% discount as a thank you for attending my art show on Saturday. Thank you again for attending.—Matthew."

Eighty-three of these cards with offers inside were sent and 7 more portraits were commissioned at the average price of $182.75 each. This resulted in an additional $1,279.25 in sales.

Finally, the following Monday, for the people who did not respond to the thank you offer, Matthew contacted them personally by phone to thank them again for coming. He also let them know that if they were to purchase a two-person portrait, while on the phone with him, he would include a third person for free. Matthew called 76 people, and eight people purchased, while on the phone, at $215 for each charcoal portrait. That brought the total sales of the phone initiative $1,720.

In addition, four people asked Matthew if they could host an in-home art show for him, where they could invite their friends to see his art. This allowed Matthew to grow his database of contacts even more and increase his sales. Most importantly, he learned a system that would allow him to launch his entire art career, provide for his family, and follow his passion of always wanting to make a living as an artist. The result of Charles' marketing consultation effort was 87 new people on Matthew's list and 19 charcoal portraits sold and $4,451.00 in revenue. Plus, four more opportunities to grow his list and increase sales. He was then able leverage this one event into an entire career for Matthew.

Leveraging Direct Marketing in Selling Art

Recently, Charles started the Art Marketing Institute (AMI) to help artists market and sell their art on a more formal level. The Art Marketing Institute is primarily Web based, but Charles incorporates both online and offline direct marketing strategies to help build AMI's list, acquire and retain new customers, and promote new products to help artists sell art. The commonalities of Charles' success are his knowledge and passion for direct marketing, art, technology, and helping other people.

FIGURE 4-26. Art Marketing Institute logo.

Growing the Art Marketing Institute's List

Let's look at a few ways that Charles grows the list of the Art Marketing Institute.

- Facebook Adwords: Charles uses Facebook ads to promote the Art Marketing Institute's fan page to get artists to become a fan and also to drive traffic to specific landing pages on the Web site to get artists to opt in to the e-mail list.
- Webinars, Teleseminars: webinars and teleseminars can send a massive amount of qualified traffic to a Web site and are among the fastest ways to grow a list.

- Banner Ads: Placing banners on targeted niche sites is a good way to drive qualified traffic to a Web site. Each banner can be measured against a control for response and conversion rates.

Each of the media that are used are sent to a specific landing page that is measurable, this way each direct marketing medium can be measured and tested against the control for that medium.

Monetizing the List by the Numbers

The Art Marketing Institute is direct marketing based through and through, whether the activity involves acquiring a new lead, maintaining a current customer, or making a special offer to a customer in the top 5 percent. As with all direct marketing, the primary focus is on the customer/client list and the relationship with those customers/clients on the list. Every strategy that is implemented is based on adding value to strengthen the relationship Charles has with each customer.

Now let's look at a few ways Charles maintains, builds value, and strengthens the relationships with other artists on his list, while monetizing the database:

1. Inbox Journal. This is similar to an e-mail newsletter that Charles sends out at least twice a week that informs artists about some marketing technique or strategy that will help them sell more of their art.

   Charles monetizes the Inbox Journal by three ways.

   a. Banner ads and special promotions within the e-mail that artists find valuable. These come in the form of promotions for his products and services to help artists and also other company's products and services that will benefit artists.

   b. Solo e-mails of other companies" products that are outside of the newsletter.

   c. List rental: the list rental business is a very lucrative business. In the future, this is a third option that Charles' intends to implement to further monetize Art Marketing Institute's list.

2. Promotion of New AMI Products: having a list that is responsive is the most powerful aspect of any direct marketing company. It allows the company to keep clients informed and promote new products by simply sending a series of e-mails, direct mail or via outbound telephone promotions.

3. Art Marketing Institute membership: This is one of the primary ways the Art Marketing Institute helps train artists to succeed in the marketplace. This is done through coaching calls, monthly tutorials on marketing art, and interviews with other successful artists. In exchange for access to the premium material, the artist pays the Art Marketing Institute a monthly fee.

For this example, we are just going to focus on the continuity aspect of this revenue model to illustrate how powerful continuity is when leveraged month after month.

The value of continuity:

1. It requires fewer customers to reach the targeted revenue goals.

2. It allows the marketer to spend more money to acquire a new customer than other competitors, while ultimately deriving higher revenues based on the initial investment.

3. It increases the value of each customer.

4. It builds loyal customers who are more inclined to purchase additional products at higher price points.

5. It dramatically increases the lifetime value of each customer.

For this example, we are going to focus on using Facebook ads to make self-liquidating offers (SLO) with an optional 30-day free trial (optional continuity). We will look at a few metrics, such as monthly revenue growth, response rates, and breakeven points. For this example, half of the people will accept the free trial offer and half of those people (25% of the initial people that purchase) will "stick" in the continuity for the second month (the billable month). We are also assuming a 5-month stick rate for each person in the continuity program. (See Figure 4-27 for the analytics associated with Art Marketing Institute.)

As you can see by this example, having continuity in place allows the business to spend more money to acquire a new customer because these customers are retained longer, and it also doesn't take as many customers to meet the financial goals of the organization as it does for companies that are just selling products that only allow one transaction per customer.

AMI Goal:	Get at Least 300 new customers per month and at least 75 new members in continuity each month	
	1% Conversion Rate	**2% Conversion Rate**
Total Monthly Ad Budget	6000	6000
Total Daily Budget	200	200
Price/Click	0.4	0.4
Total # of Clicks	500.00	500.00
Sale Conversion Rate of SLO	0.01	0.02
Total # of Sales	5	10
SLO Price	17.00	17.00
SLO Sales	85.00	170.00
Gross Profit	-115.00	-30.00
Break Even Point	12	12
Cost Per Order	40.00	20.00
Continuity Offer		
% Who Accept Each Day	0.5	0.5
# Who Accept Accept Each Day	2.5	5
Monthly Continuity		
30 Day Total Number in Continuity	75	150
Month 2 (1st Billable Month)		
30 Day Stick Rate	0.5	0.5
# Who Stick	37.5	75
AMI Monthly Membership Fee	47	47
Membership Revenue	$ 1,762.50	$ 3,525.00
Month 3		
Members From Month 2	75	150
30 Day Stick Rate	0.5	0.5
# Who Stick	37.5	75
AMI Monthly Membership Fee	47	47
Membership Revenue	$ 3,525.00	$ 7,050.00
Month 4		
Members From Month 3	75	150
30 Day Stick Rate	0.5	0.5
# Who Stick	37.5	75
AMI Monthly Membership Fee	47	47
Membership Revenue	$ 5,287.50	$ 10,575.00
Month 5		
Members From Month 4	75	150
30 Day Stick Rate	0.5	0.5
# Who Stick	37.5	75
AMI Monthly Membership Fee	47	47
Membership Revenue	$ 7,050.00	$ 14,100.00

FIGURE 4-27. Art Marketing Institute Analytics.

To learn more about Charles George you can visit his website at *www.CharlesGeorge.com* or *www.ArtMarketingInstitute.com.*

Case Discussion Questions

1. What additional techniques might be used to monetize the Art Marketing Institute's Inbox Journal? Which of these is likely to have the greatest impact? Why?

2. In the example shown on the spreadsheet, if the initial ad budget were doubled, and the click rate went to 6 percent, what would the final monthly revenue numbers look like? Would it be better to increase the budget to an even greater number of dollars?

3. If you assume a 12-month stick rate for each person in the continuity program, what would the 12th month revenue figures look like the spreadsheet example?

4. If the ad budget could be lowered to $5,000 but the click rates remained the same as in the spreadsheet example, when would the break-even point occur?

Notes

Other statistical techniques used for measuring significant differences include ANOVA (analysis of variance, the F-test), the t-test (for sample sizes through 30), and the Z-test (for sample sizes larger than 30).

## PART 2

Create and Place Direct and Interactive Marketing Campaigns

## CHAPTER 5

Planning and Creating a Value Proposition: The Offer

OPENING VIGNETTE: MOUNTAIN GEAR

Do you enjoy being outdoors? Do you like fresh air and beautiful scenery? How about hiking up a mountain on a crisp sunny afternoon? Or backpacking for days at a time? Are you interested in camping? How about partaking in a rock-climbing adventure? Or maybe you're fond of snow sports and enjoy the thrill of snowboarding or cross-country skiing? Perhaps you get pleasure out of cruising around a river or a lake in a kayak or canoe? How about fishing? Do any of these sound like fun? If so, go get your gear!

There are so many different ways to enjoy the outdoors, but to do so you'll need the right gear, clothing, accessories and equipment. Meet Mountain Gear, an outdoor cataloger with one retail store located in Spokane, Washington. Mountain Gear is considered a national and international expert in climbing, mountaineering and backpacking gear. It offers many different lines of products and a mirage of product items to serve just about any desire associated with outdoor adventures.

Mountain Gear offers the following five product categories: men's clothing, women's clothing, footwear, outdoor gear, and sale items. The company also offers the following seven product lines based on the outdoor activity type: climbing, camping and hiking, snow sports, trail running and fitness, canyoneering, paddle sports, and travel. Within each of these product lines, the company offers many different product groups. For example, in the camping and hiking activity line, Mountain Gear's customers may purchase tents, packs, sleeping bags and pads, headlamps, poles and tools, navigation and electronics, cookware and water filters, first aid and hygiene products, and chairs and furniture. Of course, the company offers a selection of different colors, models, and brands for each of these products groupings. Mountain Gear offers its customers a one-stop shopping haven when it comes to outdoor adventure products. However, Mountain Gear's customers are incredibly diverse in their needs and wants. For example, a customer who enjoys snowboarding may or may not be interested in camping, fishing, trail running or rock climbing. The challenge? How to target customers with relevant offers that match their outdoor adventure interests.

Mountain Gear wanted to expand its direct marketing efforts as a way to increase response and enhance its customer relationships. With the help of QuadDirect, an integrated communications provider, Mountain Gear implemented a highly segmented and personalized direct response campaign. The company segmented its customer base and created customized offers tailored to each segment's interests.

QuadDirect created a double-fold card that featured one of three different images to target different customer segments based on purchase histories. See Figure 5-1 for Mountain Gear's customized direct mailers. Each card also contained a personalized URL built around a product assortment targeted to the customer's interests. The card was mailed to 57,000 customers. The personalized URLs also promoted either e-mail sign-up with a sweepstakes promotion or a "refer-a-friend" offer if the customer had already signed up for e-mail notifications.

This campaign was a huge success for Mountain Gear. Customized offers tailored uniquely to customer's interests and behaviors proved to be highly effective. Response to the personalized mailer was 67 percent higher than response to postcards previously mailed to these same customer groups for similar marketing campaigns. Nearly 1,200 customers signed up for the Mountain Gear's e-mail list during the 14-day period of the promotion. Creating compelling and need-satisfying offers is how Mountain Gear is able to help thousands of people start amazing adventures and enjoy life-long hobbies.

In summary, planning and creating a value proposition or offer takes creative and strategic thinking. It must satisfy a need or want and entice consumers to take action. That is the topic of

FIGURE 5-1. Mountain Gear customized direct mailers. Used with permission of Mountain Gear.

this chapter. We define the offer, discuss the elements of an effective offer, the steps in planning the offer, the components of an offer, and how to create, target, and test the offer. In addition, this chapter examines a variety of different types of offers that have been successfully used by direct marketers through the years. Because creating the offer is both a science and an art, we can learn much from examining offers that have worked *as well as* those that have not worked.

What Is the Offer?

The **offer** is the value proposition to the prospect or customer stating what you will give the customer in return for taking the action your marketing communication asks him or her to take. In essence, it is the terms under which a direct marketer promotes a product or service. The offer encompasses both the manner of presentation by a direct marketer and the all-important request for a response.

Creating need-satisfying offers is a part of ongoing customer relationship management (CRM) that drives the direct marketing process. Without an attractive offer, consumers would not initially respond to an organization, and thus the customer relationship would never originate. Without continuous monitoring of customer needs and wants, direct marketers could not create appropriate offers to keep their customers satisfied and encourage them to return and purchase again and again. The offer is the all-important "front-end" activity in the CRM process.

The Offer as a Component of Direct Marketing Strategy

According to Edward Nash, author of *Direct Marketing: Strategy, Planning, Execution,* there are five essential elements of direct marketing strategy: product, offer, medium, distribution method, and creative.[1] The offer must be created with all of these five elements in mind. However, Nash claims that the offer is the element most quickly and easily revised for an improved result in the direct marketing effort. Nash claims, "even the slightest change in the price—whether it's in bold or buried in body copy or a coupon—can have dramatic effects on front-end performance."[2] Just think about all of the products that are priced at odd numbers, such as $19.99 or $199.97. These figures are pennies away from the even dollar amounts; however, consumers often perceive them to be far less. Research has proven that odd prices are very effective in generating consumer response; therefore, many direct marketers use odd prices in their offers.

Other direct marketers believe in the "40-40-20 rule," which states that the success of any direct marketing effort is 40 percent reliant on using the right lists, 40 percent reliant on having an effective offer, and 20 percent reliant on creating the right creative mix (copywriting, photographs, illustrations, etc.) in your direct marketing effort. However we may try to quantify its importance, the offer is clearly a major contributor to the success or failure of any direct marketing campaign.

Elements of an Effective Offer

To create an effective offer, the direct marketer must research and really know the target audience and the customers' likes, dislikes, "hot buttons," and, most of all, needs and wants. Without this information, it is difficult, at best, to create an effective offer. In addition, marketers must research how consumer needs and wants change. Direct marketers must constantly revise their offers, including the creative materials used to convey each offer. This normally requires printing a number of different catalogs or changing a company's Web site throughout the year to provide timely offers that appeal to consumers during a particular season or holiday. Figure 5-2 features a few of the various catalog covers used by well-known specialty food and gift direct marketer Harry and David when marketing to their customers. Note that the creative appeal used and the products offered are appropriate for each season or holiday.

According to Lois Geller, author of *Response: The Complete Guide to Profitable Direct Marketing,* effective offers have three characteristics: believability, involvement, and creativity.[3]

1. Believability. Using common sense when creating the offer can go a long way toward making it believable. An offer has to make sense to the consumer. It cannot give so much in the form of gifts or "freebies" that it makes the consumer wonder "what's wrong with

FIGURE 5-2.
Harry and David
seasonal offers.

the product or service?" For example, a sale offering 80 percent off at the end of a season makes sense to the consumer, because we all know that marketers need to make room for new inventory, but 80 percent off at any other time makes the consumer wonder "what's wrong with this product that it didn't sell?" Therefore, the offer should be believable.

2. Involvement. Geller believes that most shoppers suffer from what she calls the "glaze-over effect." She claims that some offers are so common that consumers' eyes simply glaze over when we see one.[4] For example, an offer of 10 or 15 percent discount is very common. It usually gets passed over. However, the offer that promises "buy one, get one at half price" is more exciting and appealing and may motivate the consumer to calculate his or her potential savings. The offer must attempt to get the consumer involved.

3. Creativity. The most creative offers usually get the highest response. Creativity can set your offer apart from all the other offers bombarding consumers. Geller believes that

"exclusive offers" are very appealing and should be featured prominently if the product or service is really exclusive to the market. "Exclusive" means that the product is in limited supply or not available in stores and is special to your company.[5] An example of an exclusive offer is:

"The recipe for these peanut butter balls has been in the Stafford family for 50 years. For decades, friends and neighbors have been savoring these tasty sweet treats. Buy one box of these peanut butter balls, and we'll throw in Grandma Stafford's special recipe for oatmeal cookies with a cinnamon swirl. You can't find this recipe in any cookbook or baker's magazine. We keep it so we can give it to our special customers. Enjoy!"

Planning the Offer

The right offer can sell almost anything, but it must be carefully planned. Let's walk through a four-step process that explains how heeding the details that can make or break an offer.

Step 1: Establish the Objectives of the Offer

What is the offer designed to do? Get orders? Generate sales leads? Sell subscriptions? Encourage repeat purchases or renewals? Introduce and sell new products? Increase the amount that the customer is presently purchasing? Raise funds? Without clearly established objectives, you won't be able to measure the success or failure of the offer—and remember that measurement is imperative in direct marketing.

The underlying objective of any offer is to maximize profitability for a company or organization. Two of the most common methods of achieving increased profitability are (1) encouraging repeat purchases from existing customers, and (2) encouraging a company's current customers to purchase additional related or unrelated products beyond what they normally buy. The three direct marketing strategies that achieve this profit-maximization objective are continuity selling, cross-selling, and up-selling. Let's take a look at each of these strategies.

Continuity selling describes offers that are continued on a regular basis, whether weekly, monthly, quarterly, or annual. These offers are also called "club offers" and are a hallmark of direct marketers, who want to acquire customers who will remain active for an extended period of time. In continuity selling, customers buy related products or services as a series of small purchases, rather than all at a single time. Books, magazine subscriptions, insurance policies, and many other products are sold by means of club offers, as are periodic shipments of fruit, cheese, or other food items. An example of continuity selling is provided in Figure 5-3. Harry and David's Fruit-of-the-Month Club offers consumers an opportunity to receive select fruit throughout the year. The customer can choose to give or receive the 3-Box Club, 5-Box Club, 8-Box Club, or the 12-Box Club.

The continuity selling offer includes a **positive option,** where the customer must specifically request shipment for each offer in a series, or a **negative option,** where the shipment is sent automatically unless the customer specifically requests that it not be. The negative option is a controversial marketing technique because some consumers don't realize that they must request the shipments be stopped or else they are responsible for paying for the products delivered. Most consumers normally expect to pay for what they order, but with negative option, they pay unless they request the shipment to be stopped. It is different from the norm. An example of a negative option club offer is a continuity mail-order marketer called Around-the-World-Shoppers Club. They ship a variety of unusual gift items monthly to subscribers, each month from a different foreign country. Of course, if the consumer receives an undesired shipment, it can be returned at any time for credit.

FIGURE 5-3.
Harry and David
club newsletter.

Another example of a negative option offer is a til-forbid. A **til-forbid (TF)** is an offer that prearranges continuing shipments on a specified basis and is renewed automatically until the customer instructs otherwise. TF offers are commonly used with insurance policies or magazine subscriptions. Other examples include some clubs, such as senior citizen groups or automobile clubs, which may include specific services with an annual membership fee.

Cross-selling offers new products to existing customers. The products may be related or unrelated to those the customers are already buying. For example, a purchaser of books and software might be offered other books and software or possibly an insurance policy, a home power tool, or a vacation package to a tropical resort. The most important element of successful cross-selling is the manner in which the customer views the direct marketer's reputation, reliability, and overall image.

Up-selling is the promotion of more expensive products or services over the product or service originally discussed or purchased. You might think of up-selling as suggestive selling, since the marketer is suggesting the more expensive product or service as opposed to the consumer requesting it.

In summary, continuity selling, cross-selling, and up-selling are important direct marketing strategies used to achieve different objectives when planning the offer. Each strategy has been used by direct marketers and has met with great success. It is important that the direct marketer decides which strategy he or she will employ when planning an offer.

Step 2: Decide on the Attractiveness of the Offer

Generally, the more attractive you can afford to make the offer, the better the response will be. How do you make an offer attractive? You dress it up with lots of freebies. However, direct marketers must be careful that the cost of the incentives like free gifts does not outweigh the added profit of the additional orders. This step entails close examination of both the objectives and the budget constraints within which the direct marketer must operate. An example of an attractive offer by Barnes & Noble appears in Figure 5-4. Note that this online offer is for two free gifts valued at $32.99.

Step 3: Reduce the Risk of the Offer

The direct marketing consumer bears risk, usually greater than in traditional retail buying, whenever he or she purchases a product without the added benefit of actually seeing, touching, feeling, and personally examining it. Therefore, the goal of the direct marketer is to reduce the perceived risk associated with purchasing the product unseen and unfelt.

Two basic components of the offer are designed to reduce the risk, a *free trial* or *examination period,* and a *money-back guarantee.* We talk about these in greater detail later in this chapter. For now, understand that their importance is magnified by their role in reducing the risk associated with any offer.

Step 4: Select a Creative Appeal

The appeal of an offer can be either rational or emotional. The rational appeal targets a consumer's logical buying motives. It presents facts in a logical, rational manner and targets basic needs such as those for food, shelter, clothing, and safety. An example of a rational appeal is the National Association of Letter Carriers' Food Drive. This organization distributes a direct mail postcard to residents asking them to help "stamp out hunger" by placing a food donation at their mailbox on a certain day before their letter carrier arrives. The carrier will pick up the food donation and deliver it to a local food bank or pantry. The offer is clear, logical, and does not attempt to invoke great emotion on the part of the local resident who is being asked for a food donation.

The emotional appeal focuses on a consumer's desires and feelings. It targets the consumer's wants, such as social status, prestige, power, recognition, and acceptance, as opposed to physical needs. An example of an emotional appeal is the offer extended by Emode, a leading self-assessment company. Their offer is for a free IQ test to see how smart you are. This assessment test can determine how your IQ score affects your ability to compete and provide a comparison to other people. Although the offer may pique the consumer's curiosity and may provide some nice-to-know information, it is appealing to a person's wants. Nobody *needs* to have this information. The type of appeal selected must be appropriate to the media used to distribute the offer. For example, if a direct marketer is making an online offer to regular or prospective customers, the offer must be direct and to the point because most people only spend a few seconds on Web

FIGURE 5-4.
Barnes & Noble
offer. Used with
permission of
Barnes & Noble
Inc.

sites. In addition, the offer must enable the consumer to respond via a quick click of the mouse or keyboard. The offer must include messages that encourage the consumer to "forward to a friend" or to "click here," as in the banner ad offer shown in Figure 5-5.

Regardless of the creative appeal used, each offer must have the same basic parts or components. Let's investigate the components that encompass the offer.

Components of the Offer

The components of the direct marketing offer fall into two categories: those that are required and must be present in all offers, and those that are optional and may be included depending on strategy and costs.[6] The *required* elements are product, price, payment terms, length of commit-

FIGURE 5-5. Busch Gardens Adventure banner ad.

ment, and risk-reduction mechanisms. The *optional* elements are incentives, multiple offers, and customer obligations.

Product or Service

The actual tangible product or intangible service is critical to the success of any offer, of course. It must satisfy the needs or wants of the target consumer to whom it is being presented. Physical features such as weight, dimensions, color, model, accessories, and any extended properties such as gift wrapping, alterations, delivery, and service are very important, as is the basic benefit the product will provide. Services have unique properties such as type of service, length of time or duration of the service, location, and frequency or schedule of the service. Appropriate timing of the offer can also affect the consumer's response, particularly if the product or service is seasonal, as we've discussed.

Marketers must understand these product or service features well to create an effective offer that garners a response from the target consumer. If the product/service itself does not satisfy the needs or wants of the consumer, then no matter how attractive you make the rest of the offer, it will be to no avail. Simply stated, consumers are not interested in purchasing products and services for which they have no need or desire.

Pricing and Payment Terms

Direct marketers must decide whether their price objective is to maximize profit or maximize sales. If the price is meant to generate the largest possible return on investment (ROI), that is, the objective is to maximize profit, then the direct marketer must use a **price skimming** strategy. This strategy establishes the price at the highest possible level to "skim the cream" off the top of the market and target only a select number of consumers who can *afford* to buy the product/service. Of course, a high price will result in fewer sales transactions but greater profitability per sale.

A **price penetration** strategy will help the direct marketer maximize sales volume. This strategy sets the price at a very low level so that almost any consumer who wants to buy the product can afford to do so.

The price elasticity of a product is another factor to take into account when establishing the price of the product. **Price elasticity** is the relative change in demand for a product given a change in its price. It measures the consumer's responsiveness or sensitivity to price changes. For example, let's pretend the Gap decreased the price of its jeans from $35 to $25. Would consumers buy two pairs of jeans instead of one? Let's also pretend Starbucks Coffee increased the price of their coffee by $2. Would consumers continue purchasing Starbucks, or would they switch to either a different brand of coffee or substitute product, such as hot cocoa or tea, instead of coffee? The direct marketer, in initially estimating the demand for products, first determines whether there is a price the market expects and then develops an estimate of the sales volume he or she expects at different price levels. If the consumer's demand for a product doesn't change substantially regardless of price increases, the product has an inelastic market demand. If, however, the consumer is very sensitive to price changes and market demand for the product decreases greatly as price increases, then the product has an elastic market demand. A product

Basic price statement	"One year supply for only $12.99"
Price stated as a fraction	"One-half off when ordered by May 1st"
Price stated by unit	"Now only $2.49 an issue"
Price savings stated by percentage	"Save 30% when ordered by May 1st"
Price savings stated by unit	"First two issues are free"
Price savings stated by dollar amount	"Save $25"
Price savings based on introduction	"Save $15 on your initial subscription"
Price savings based on multiple purchases	"Save $2.98 one two"
Price based on promotional offer	"Buy one, get one free"

FIGURE 5-6. Examples of price in an offer.

with an *elastic* market demand should usually be priced lower than an item with an *inelastic* market demand.

It is not just price level that is important. Equally important is the manner in which we state the price. Is it a buy-one-get-one-free offering? Is it a sale? Figure 5-6 shows various ways to present price in an offer.

Finally, payment method is a vital part of the offer. The payment methods direct marketers have offered in the past, cash with the order and collect on delivery, lacked convenience and often were a deterrent to ordering. On the other hand, an offer to absorb shipping costs if cash payment is sent with the order can be a distinct incentive.

A bill-me-later (BML) payment offer that includes credit card options, either the direct marketer's own, a bank card, or a travel and entertainment card, not only provides convenience but also spurs the customer not to procrastinate when placing an order. In certain cases, such as a free trial offer with full return privileges, the BML offer isn't just nice to have, it's a necessity.

Delayed payment is sometimes extended to provide installment terms. This option is usually confined to higher priced products and can be with or without an interest charge. Payment in installments is an attractive incentive to many consumers and such an offer can be a strong one. However, marketers must weigh the advantages of this incentive against the cost of financing the resulting accounts receivable, the potential for bad debts, and the ultimate return on the direct marketer's investment.

Trial or Examination Period

Typically, the buyer does not have the opportunity to see or feel the product before ordering. The free trial or free examination offer helps overcome this distinct disadvantage of ordering by mail or telephone.

The trial offer might be an introductory one requiring payment of a nominal amount, such as 25 cents for the first 30 days of coverage under an insurance policy or $1.97 for the first three months of subscription to a magazine. If the buyer's examination reveals that the insurance policy or magazine does not meet expectations, even the small introductory payment might be refunded.

Full return privileges are, of course, a vital part of any offer.

Guarantees

Direct marketers have been using guarantees for many years. In fact, the 1744 catalog of colonial America's first important printer, Benjamin Franklin, guaranteed customer satisfaction with the following statement on its front cover: "Those persons who live remote, by sending their orders and money to said B. Franklin, may depend on the same justice as if present."

A guarantee of "complete satisfaction or your money back" is an inherent necessity of direct marketing. This assurance, and the manner in which it is presented, is a vital part of the offer. L. L. Bean offered this "100 percent guarantee" in one of their recent catalogs:

> Our products are guaranteed to give 100% satisfaction in every way. Return anything purchased from us at any time if it proves otherwise. We will replace it, refund your purchase price or credit your credit card. We do not want you to have anything from L.L. Bean that is not completely satisfactory.

Certain direct marketers of collectible items even guarantee to buy back some products at a later time and certain direct marketers of insurance guarantee to accept all applicants for some types of policies. Guarantees have been developed for extended time periods. Some even offer "double your money back" if the buyer is less than completely satisfied.

Sweepstakes and Contests

Direct marketers have used sweepstakes and contests as an ordering stimulus. To avoid being considered a lottery, which requires a purchase as a condition for entry and is illegal in many states, a contest or sweepstakes must guarantee a winner, and making a purchase must not be a requirement, though it can be an option for entering. In addition, the law requires that the odds of winning the sweepstakes or contest be published on promotional materials. You should readily see that attractive prize offerings, such as trips to lavish resorts or big-ticket electronic devices such as flat-screen televisions, yield a large response in terms of contest or sweepstakes participation.

Random drawings to select winners are sometimes done in advance of the mailing, so that the contest will not be construed as a lottery. How can a direct marketer choose a winner before people enter the contest? That may seem odd; however, based on the mailing list that will be used to distribute the contest or sweepstakes offer, the direct marketer can actually select a name or multiple names and then if that person does not enter the contest, they will not be awarded the prize. Remember, lotteries require a prior purchase, whereas contests and sweepstakes only require an entry form to be submitted. A key to the success of sweepstakes and other forms of contests is getting the respondents involved in some way, such as by returning perforated tear-offs, die-cuts, tokens, and stamps, as well as by giving answers to questions, problems, or puzzles. Direct marketers should be creative when designing contest or sweepstakes entry forms.

Gifts and Premiums

An effective device for stimulating response to a direct marketing promotion is the offer of a free gift or premium either for purchasing or for simply examining or trying the product. Although such incentives increase response, as do sweepstakes and contests, they may also attract less qualified respondents in terms of credit-worthiness or final product acceptance.

Some gifts are termed "keepers," meaning that the customer can keep the premium whether or not they keep the product. To be most effective, the premium should be related to the product or the specific audience. Sometimes, direct marketers offer customers a choice between multiple gifts. In other situations, direct marketers keep the gift "a mystery" and consumers do not know what particular gift they will receive until it is delivered. It can have tangible and apparent value or the value can be intrinsic, such as a booklet containing advice. Sometimes the free gift offer can be as nominal as information or a price estimate.

Time Limits

A limited time offer typically specifies a deadline, an enrollment period, a charter membership, a limited edition, or a prepublication offer. An example of a limited time offer can be seen in Fig-

FIGURE 5-7.
Time limit offer
example. Used
with permission
of Busch Gardens.

ure 5-7. Most limited time offers provide an offer expiration date or they may use action phrases such as "act now!" or "pre-order now!" or "for a limited time only" or "hurry!" to encourage consumers to act quickly because the offer will expire after a certain date. The offer may also quote "while supplies last."

Do all offers possess all the components we've discussed? Probably not. However, these are the essential parts of most basic offers. Now you know the pieces of the puzzle, what do you do with them? You begin creating an offer for your consumers.

Creating an Offer

The offer is not independent of the entire direct marketing strategy. While creating it, marketers must keep the other strategic elements of direct marketing in mind, especially the needs and wants of the customer. Let's discuss the five steps direct marketers should follow when creating an offer.

Step 1: Perform Market Research

When direct marketers attempt to predict and determine consumer needs and wants, they often rely on certain indicators, such as geographic, demographic, social, psychological, and behavioral characteristics of the consumer. (These were overviewed in Chapter 3.) Direct marketers strive to understand consumer needs and wants, not merely predict them. Thus, they often conduct consumer research to determine what *motivates* the consumer to purchase a given product/service. After all, consumer motivations drive the purchase process. **Motivations** are needs that compel a person to take action or behave in a certain way, such as purchase a product/service. Consumers have both internal and external motivations for their behavior. Internal motivators can stem from basic physiological needs, such as hunger or thirst, or other needs, such as the need for acceptance. However, external motivators can take the form of advertisements, free samples, a sales pitch, or even a persuasive offer.

In any event, direct marketers must understand what needs the consumer is attempting to satisfy to effectively create offers that will meet these needs and wants. Direct marketers are concerned with creating, caring for, and keeping customers. They want to create a customer, not just make a sale! The difference between the two is that a sale means a one-time purchase, whereas a customer is someone who will come back and make repeat purchases from an organization throughout his or her lifetime. Thus, long-term CRM is a constant focus of direct marketers.

Therefore, the underlying theme in creating any offer is the consumer. The development of an offer cannot occur without an understanding of the consumer's needs and wants. Think of it in this way: creating an offer without careful analysis of consumer needs and wants is like driving off in a car without making sure there is gasoline in the tank! Not a good idea, right? It is only by carefully researching the consumer and the competitive situation that the direct marketer will have the needed information on which to create an offer. The market research data collected by the direct marketer also provides specific details pertaining to the terms of the offer.

Windstream Communications launched a direct marketing campaign called Windstream Movers Program, featuring customized offers based on consumer analysis. Intuitively, Windstream knew that movers into single-family dwelling units (SFDUs) were more likely to be new homeowners, and therefore more likely to need a landline, broadband, and television services. Movers into multi-family dwelling units (MFDUs) were more likely to be younger renters, and therefore, they might eschew traditional landlines in favor of cell phones. As a result, Windstream employed duplex laser printing to customize the offer and text to the moving consumer segments. As Figure 5-8 reveals, this was achieved by preprinting a single self-mailer format that allowed for individualized and customized messaging to premovers, new homeowners, and movers/renters. In addition, these unique offers were mailed on a weekly basis to be in-home as close to the move date as possible so that the timing of the offers would correspond to consumer needs.

Step 2: Determine the Terms of the Offer

Although brand names, packages, and labels along with advertising and other promotional strategies create product and supplier preferences, it is the quality of the product itself that must ultimately lead to repurchases. The quality (and this includes any warranty and service) must be consistent with customer expectations, and it is the terms of the offer that creates those expectations. Therefore, it is critical to meet (and even exceed) what is set forth by the terms of the offer.

Direct marketers must consider five specific product details when determining the terms of the offer. These product details include the following.

1. A Choice of Sizes. Whether the direct marketer will make the product available in a wide array of sizes, including extra-small, extra-large, and half-sizes, are specific details that

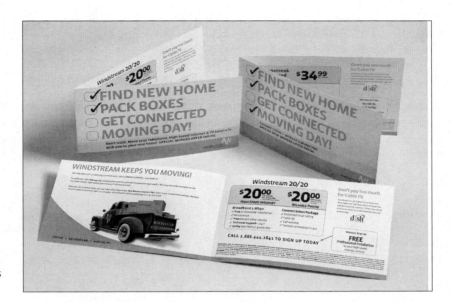

FIGURE 5-8. Windstream Communications offer.

must be determined. Another term of the offer pertaining to product sizes is whether the direct marketer will allow consumers to place a special order for an unusual size if desired. Direct marketers must spell out these specific product terms.

2. A Choice of Colors. Whether the direct marketer will make the product available in a wide variety of popular colors is an important product detail. In addition, can the consumer select certain colors to be mixed and matched with other colors when ordering products with more than one component or piece? For example, when placing an order with Victoria's Secret, can a consumer select a bathing suit top in one color or design and a bathing suit bottom in a different but coordinating color or design? Will the direct marketer allow consumers to place special orders for a unique color if desired? Direct marketers make these and similar determinations when creating the terms of an offer.

3. Product Specifications. Direct marketers must disclose the dimensions of the product including such elements as the weight, height, length, texture, and scent of the product in the offer. Direct marketers often use photographs or illustrations to depict the product; however, they must also be careful to spell out the exact specifications in words as well as photographs.

4. Product Accessories. Direct marketers must specifically state what product accessories are available. It is also important to specify which accessories are included with the purchase of the product and which can be purchased separately if so desired. Once again, the more specific the product details are identified in the offer, the smaller the chance of unmet consumer expectations.

5. Personalization. Personalization enhances the sale of a direct-marketed product, and thus should, if possible, be made available to the customer. The cornerstone of some very successful direct marketing companies has been offering personalized products.

Step 3: Target the Offer

In creating an offer and developing the copy or jargon that will position it, Donna Baier Stein and Floyd Kemske in their book, *Write on Target,* insist that every direct marketer or copywriter must ask themselves four essential questions:[7]

1. What am I selling?

2. Whom am I selling to?

3. Why am I selling this now?

4. What do I want my prospect to do?

They believe the key to effective direct marketing is unlocking the selling power that comes from knowing to whom you are targeting your offer. Knowing the target consumer requires market research on that target profile of consumers. It is only by knowing and understanding the target

FIGURE 5-9. Busch Gardens targeted offers. Used with permission of Busch Gardens.

consumer that the offer can be "right on target" to generate the maximum response rate. Of course, not all consumers are the same. There are differences (and similarities) between them. That is the basis of market segmentation and is also the starting point of effectively targeting an offer. Examples of targeted offers are shown in Figure 5-9. Busch Gardens markets to different niche groups such as corporations, emergency personnel, healthcare professionals and educators and must create targeted offers and customized promotional materials personalized for each respective segment.

The process of targeting the offer is directly related to the important concepts of market segmentation and product positioning we reviewed in Chapter 3. Market segmentation enables a marketer to view consumers as belonging to certain select groups based on shared characteristics and/or needs and wants. Thus, instead of trying to target a product or service to the total market, most marketers select certain groups of customers called market segments to which they will target their promotional efforts.

Positioning is a marketing strategy that enables marketers to understand how each consumer perceives a company's product or service. This perception is based in part on the strengths and weaknesses of the product or service compared to other competing products or services. By knowing what that perception is, we can more effectively create an offer and target it toward a particular consumer segment. Of course, offers may or may not generate a positive reaction or consumer response. This is why direct marketers normally test different offers to determine which one is most effective with a particular consumer market segment.

Step 4: Test the Offer

As presented in the previous chapter, testing is of great importance to the success of the offer. We might consider testing to be the ultimate consumer opinion poll. The research question we are asking each consumer is, of course, "does the offer make you want to buy the product or service?" If the offer is not attempting to sell something but trying to obtain a specific outcome, such as a vote for a politician or attendance at an upcoming meeting, does it make the target individual want to take the action for which the offer is requesting? The test determines the effectiveness of the offer and provides an answer to the critical question—does the offer *work?*

How do direct marketers conduct the tests? The answer is simple. They first determine what they want to test or investigate. For example, direct marketers may want to determine the free gift or premium they will offer consumers who make a purchase during some specified time period. Let's say a local restaurant wants to distribute direct mail offers to local residents in a particular ZIP code area to encourage consumers to patronize the restaurant. Prior to creating the offer, the restaurant wants to determine whether consumers will respond more readily to an offer for a free appetizer or a free dessert. Next, the direct marketer creates two direct mail cards, one containing the offer for the free appetizer and the other the offer for a free dessert, and mails these cards to a sample of consumers in the ZIP code area of interest. When consumers present these cards to the restaurant waiter or waitress, the cards are kept. At the end of the time period specified for the test, the direct marketer counts how many responses each free gift offer generated. The offer that generates the largest response wins the test. Direct marketers then use the test results to determine which free gift to include when creating the offer. Of course, direct marketers may perform multiple tests if they want to investigate other terms or components of the offer.

Lois Geller has offered a simple, four-step approach to testing the offer.[8]

1. Test only one feature at a time. When you are testing an offer, be sure to change only one variable at a time. If you change more than one variable, whether it is creative, product or service, or price, you will not know what variable change caused the change in consumer response.

2. Code your tests so you can measure results. Each version of a promotion must have its own specific/individual code so that you will know which offer has generated the best response. For example, if you are testing the same offer in two different magazines, the only difference between them should be the code printed on the response device so that when consumers respond to the offer, you will know which magazine was responsible for generating that consumer's order.

3. Keep accurate records. Record all coded tests so that you can measure and analyze the test results. Recording test results can be as simple as writing them in a ledger book, or as sophisticated as computing an ongoing summation in a computerized database.

4. Analyze test results and take action. Whenever a test for an offer is complete, you will want to know which offer polled best, in other words generated the largest consumer response rate, so that you repeat the most effective offer.

Marketers should test their offers on an ongoing basis. In fact, early testing of an offer on a small market segment, rather than waiting until the offer is complete and ready to be rolled out to the entire consumer market, saves time and money. Remember that given time and preparation, *all* components of an offer can be tested—one at a time. Keep in mind that the ultimate goal of testing is to determine what will work the best in generating a response from the consumer.

Step 5: Execute the Offer

Once the direct marketer performs marketing research, decides on the terms of the offer, appropriately targets the offer to the right consumer market segment, and employs tests on various components of the offer, it is time to execute the offer. The first part of offer implementation is where the direct marketer uses the results of each test to revise the offer and make it more attractive to consumers. Once the direct marketer makes the necessary revisions, he or she is now prepared to put the offer into action.

What does executing the offer mean? It means that the direct marketer must be ready to implement the decisions made thus far. The direct marketer must be poised and prepared to fulfill the terms of the offer at the time of implementation. This means that if a free gift is offered with a purchase, the direct marketer must have an adequate supply of the free gifts to distribute to those consumers making a purchase. If the direct marketer is offering a new innovative color of a given product, that new color of product is ready to be packaged and shipped as soon as an order is received from a consumer.

In summary, creating the offer is a step-by-step process that culminates when a consumer accepts the offer and carries out the action that the direct marketer has asked him or her to take. Direct marketers who follow the steps described in this section should find greater success in both the execution of the offer and consumer acceptance of that offer. Creating the offer is a bit of science and art. The science is the logical sequence of steps that direct marketers should follow when creating the offer, and the art is the many different kinds of offers that direct marketers can create. Let's take a look at some popular offers that are used in direct marketing.

Popular Offers

Although some offers may be unique and no offer is "right" for all situations, most are extensions of common offers that have stood the test of time. With that said, the following is an overview of nine popular offers.

1. Free gift offers. Providing a gift for inquiring, trying the product, purchasing the product, or for spending a certain dollar amount can be very effective, given the right situation.

2. Other free offers. Offering a free catalog, information booklet, estimate, demonstration, tour, delivery, and more is generally effective.

3. Discount offers. Everybody loves a bargain! Discounts can come in many different forms: cash discounts, quantity discounts, seasonal discounts, early bird discounts, and trade discounts to name a few. Discounts are most effective when the product or service has a well-established value. However, discounting the price can also generate a negative image. If a watch is priced at $15, consumers may perceive either that it is a bargain or it is simply "cheap." Therefore, direct marketers must use discount offers in conjunction with the promotional message that the offer is trying to convey.

4. Sale offers. Sale offers are similar to discount offers; there has to be a reason for the sale such as preseason sales, postseason sales, and holiday sales. Direct marketers often repeat seasonal sale offers on an annual basis if they are successful. Examples of sale offers include the Mother's Day sale or Presidents' Day sale. Sale offers, such as inventory reduction or clearance sales, provide an explanation for the sale and thus make it more believable to the prospect. Unlike discount offers, sale offers tend to be held at certain times of the year and usually provide explanatory terms for their existence.

5. Sample offers. Sample offers are designed to get the product into the hands of a prospective buyer. Usually, they are offered in conjunction with continuity selling. An example is a free sample issue of a magazine offered along with a trial year subscription.

6. Time-limit offers. Time-limit offers work because they force the consumer to make a decision by a certain time. It is normally more effective to use an exact date, as opposed to a time period (ten days), when implementing a time-limit offer. Examples of time-limit offers include magazine publishers who offer consumers a special price on a subscription if the consumers place their order by a specified date and amusement parks that offer consumers a free gift for purchasing a season pass by a specified date. In addition, book publishers commonly extend prepublication offers to consumers who place an order for a new book prior to the official publication date of the book. In this case, the publisher uses the prepublication orders to help in determining the printing quantity.

7. Guarantee offers. We've seen that guarantees are very common in direct marketing. Direct marketers commonly use money-back or extended guarantees. However, it is important to use common sense when offering time limits with the guarantee. For example, when selling fishing lures, be sure to allow enough time for the consumer to use the lures for a fishing season, prior to returning them if not satisfied.

8. Build-up-the-sale offer. The objective of a build-up-the-sale offer is to increase the dollar amount of the average order. An example is offering a volume of books for $19.95, and then offering the same volume of books, leather bound, for $24.95.

9. Sweepstakes offers. Contests or sweepstake offers add the element of excitement to an ordinary direct marketing appeal. There are, however, certain rules that must be followed in executing a sweepstakes offer. In addition, they may not be used in some states due to local restrictions.

These nine sample offers are only a few of the many creative types of offers that direct marketers have effectively used throughout the years. Jim Kobs, a leading authority in direct marketing, developed an extensive listing of tested, successful propositions. See Figure 5-10 for Kobs's 99 proven direct response offers.

99 PROVEN DIRECT RESPONSE OFFERS

Basic Offers
1. Right Price
2. Free Trial
3. Money-Back Guarantee
4. Cash with Order
5. Bill Me Later
6. Installment Terms
7. Charge Card Privileges
8. C.O.D.

Free Gift Offers
9. Free Gift for an Inquiry
10. Free Gift for a Trial Order
11. Free Gift for Buying
12. Multiple Free Gifts with a Single Order
13. Your Choice of Free Gifts
14. Free Gifts Based on Size of Order
15. Two-Step Gift Offer
16. Continuing Incentive Gifts
17. Mystery Gift Offer

Other Free Offers
18. Free Information
19. Free Catalog
20. Free Booklet
21. Free Fact Kit
22. Send Me a Salesman
23. Free Demonstration
24. Free "Survey of Your Needs"
25. Free Cost Estimate
26. Free Dinner
27. Free Film Offer
28. Free House Organ Subscription
29. Free Talent Test
30. Gift Shipment Service

Discount Offers
31. Cash Discount
32. Short-Term Introductory Offer
33. Refund Certificate
34. Introductory Order Discount
35. Trade Discount
36. Early Bird Discount
37. Quantity Discount
38. Sliding Scale Discount
39. Selected Discounts

Sale Offers
40. Seasonal Sales
41. Reason-Why Sales
42. Price Increase Notice
43. Auction-By-Mail

Sample Orders
44. Free Sample
45. Nominal Charge Samples
46. Sample Offer with Tentative Commitment
47. Quantity Sample Offer
48. Free Sample Lesson

Time Limit Offers
49. Limited Time Offers
50. Enrollment Periods

51. Pre-Publication Offer
52. Charter Membership (or Subscription) Offer
53. Limited Edition Offer

Guarantee Offers
54. Extended Guarantee
55. Double-Your-Money-Back Guarantee
56. Guaranteed Buy-Back Agreement
57. Guaranteed Acceptance Offer

Build-Up-The-Sale Offers
58. Multi-Product Offers
59. Piggyback Offers
60. The Deluxe Offer
61. Good-Better-Best Offer
62. Add-On Offer
63. Write-Your-Own-Ticket Offer
64. Bounce-Back Offer
65. Increase and Extension Offers

Sweepstakes Offers
66. Drawing Type Sweepstakes
67. Lucky Number Sweepstakes
68. "Everybody Wins" Sweepstakes
69. Involvement Sweepstakes
70. Talent Contests

Club & Continuity Offers
71. Positive Option
72. Negative Option
73. Automatic Shipments
74. Continuity Load-Up Offer
75. Front-End Load-Ups
76. Open-Ended Commitment
77. "No Strings Attached" Commitment
78. Lifetime Membership Fee
79. Annual Membership Fee

Specialized Offers
80. The Philanthropic Privilege
81. Blank Check Offer
82. Executive Preview Charge
83. Yes/No Offers
84. Self-Qualification Offer
85. Exclusive Rights for Your Trading Area
86. The Super Dramatic Offer
87. Trade-In Offer
88. Third party Referral Offer
89. Member-Get-A-Member Offer
90. Name-Getter Offers
91. Purchase-With-Purchase
92. Delayed Billing Offer
93. Reduced Down Payment
94. Stripped-Down Products
95. Secret Bonus Gift
96. Rush Shipping Service
97. The Competitive Offer
98. The Nominal Reimbursement Offer
99. Establish-the-Value Offer

FIGURE 5-10. Kobs's 99 proven offers.

Summary

In summary, planning the offer is a critical part of the success of any direct marketing campaign. It is reliant on a solid understanding of consumer needs and wants. All direct marketing offers are response-driven. Direct marketers must plan each offer. This planning includes establishing objectives, deciding on offer attractiveness, reducing offer risk, and selecting a creative appeal. Every offer consists of basic components and decisions that must be made by the direct marketer. These components include the product or service, pricing or payment terms, trial or examination period, guarantees, sweepstakes or contests, gifts or premiums, and time limits. Direct marketers must carefully create the offer to ensure success. The step-by-step process to follow when creating the offer involves performing marketing research, determining the terms of the offer, targeting the offer, testing the offer, and finally, revising and executing the offer. Direct marketers can create many different types of offers. Many direct marketers vary the offer based on the season. Some popular offers include free gift offers, discount offers, sale offers, sample offers, time-limit offers, guarantee offers, build-up-the-sale offers, and sweepstakes offers. These different types of offers have been presented in this chapter. In the next chapter you will learn how the creative strategy is used to position the offer to the target market.

Key Terms

offer	up-selling
continuity selling	price skimming
positive option	price penetration
negative option	price elasticity
til-forbid (TF)	motivations
cross-selling	positioning

Review Questions

1. Why is it important for direct marketers to understand consumer motivations when creating an offer? What can drive these motivations?

2. What is an *offer?* What are the elements of an effective offer?

3. What are the main differences between continuity selling, cross-selling, and up-selling?

4. What are the basic components to include in planning an offer?

5. Describe the four-step process to planning an offer. Is the order of this process important? Why or why not?

6. There are several popular offers. Name a few of the popular offers described in this chapter. How can you determine which offer will work best in a particular situation?

7. What are the four questions Donna Baier Stein and Floyd Kemske in their book *Write on Target* suggest every direct marketer or copywriter ask? What do they believe to be the key to effective direct marketing?

8. How do market segmentation and positioning strategies play a role in planning an offer?

9. Review Lois Geller's four-step approach to testing the offer. Apply these steps in the creation of a test to determine the best price for a new set of golf clubs.

10. Name the five specific product details direct marketers must consider when planning the offer. Select any direct marketing catalog and determine whether it provides each of these important product details.

Exercise

You are a part of the marketing team of a new brand of cola just introduced to the market. Your job is to plan the offer to promote the new product to the 21 to 35 age group via an online and direct mail campaign. As you already know, you have several variables to consider. To start with, examine the basic components to planning the offer. Next, follow the four steps to planning the offer. Of all the common popular offers presented in the chapter, which type of offer would you choose, or what combination would you use? Why do you think they would be effective?

Critical Thinking Exercise

Visit at least three Web sites of stores which are entirely virtual (have no bricks and mortar). Compare and contrast how each creates the offer using the steps given in the chapter. Name the one you think is most effective and provide justification for your choice.

CASE: Jody's Gourmet Popcorn

What you are about to read is a great example of how a company uses different offers to target different markets and achieve different objectives. It demonstrates how a direct marketer can use a variety of different offers to achieve numerous marketing objectives. It illustrates how planning an offer is critical when attempting to maximize customer value by creating, cultivating, and retaining customers.

Warning: If you like to snack, you are going to love this case! What you are about to discover is a company that makes delicious snacks that can be customized in more ways than you can imagine. In fact, if you can imagine a new product that the company doesn't already make, submit your idea and it might be selected as the company's newest product item. Let us introduce you to Jody's Gourmet Popcorn. (See Figure 5-11.)

Many people believe that popcorn is an American tradition. Can you imagine going to the movies and not smelling popcorn? For many Americans, a movie isn't any good unless you have a bucket of popcorn on your lap to go along with it. It is from that mindset that Jody Wagner

FIGURE 5-11. Jody's popcorn logo. Used with permission of Jody's Popcorn.

and her husband, Alan, started Jody's Gourmet Popcorn. When Jody and Alan lived in Chicago, a great date included a trip to a caramel corn store and a long walk munching on the delicacy. In fact, Alan incorporated caramel corn into his marriage proposal to Jody by presenting her with an engagement ring that was sealed inside a prize envelope placed inside a Cracker-Jack® box! Talk about a creative offer!

When Jody and Alan moved to Virginia Beach, they couldn't believe that the oceanfront resort lacked fresh caramel corn. Every summer, Jody knew that visitors to Virginia Beach were missing out. So, in 2005, Jody and Alan opened Jody's Gourmet Popcorn in Virginia Beach.

Today, you can purchase Jody's Gourmet Popcorn treats in Jody's Virginia Beach store, online or in select retail stores. Jody's products are also available at a number of festivals and special events. Let's explore how Jody and Alan built their company and the importance they placed on planning and creating a value proposition or offer.

Product Offers

When Jody and Alan first decided they wanted to start a gourmet popcorn business, they began to search for the best caramel corn recipe they could find. They tried recipe after recipe before they gave up and determined that they would have to create their own formula. Alan and Jody set up a laboratory in their garage and installed a commerical popper and caramelizer. Alan, a physcian and scientist, began working day and night to develop a sweet, crunchy, delicious carmel corn. "Amazing or Bust" was his motto. He finally found "amazing" perfection with his 53rd batch—which is now dubbed: *Secret Recipe 53 Caramel Corn*. Finding the right need-satisfying product is one of the first and most important steps in planning and creating an offer. (See Figure 5-12.)

Jody's Gourmet Popcorn opened in September 2005, offering four flavors of popcorn—Secret Recipe 53 Caramel Corn, Cinnamon Toast, White Cheddar, and Cheesy Jalapeño. Today, the store offers more than 23 flavors of popcorn and 15 flavors of fudge. Jody's products are made with only the finest, freshest, quality ingredients including lucious caramel, rich chocolate, savory cheeses, and Virginia peanuts. Jody's Gourmet Popcorn has earned the Kosher certification. The company offers customers the ability to customize both their popcorn and the containers or tins. Such customization makes Jody's Gourmet Popcorn a unique gift.

As shown in Figure 5-13, custom color popcorn can be manufactured for schools, organizations and special events. Custom Gourmet Popcorn Gift Tins that include tin desgins featuring different universities, professional sports teams, holidays and other specialized events are now

FIGURE 5-12.
Trio basics
popcorn bags.
Used with
permission of
Jody's Popcorn.

FIGURE 5-13.
VT Group
popcorn bags.
Used with
permission of
Jody's Popcorn.

offered to Jody's customers. Schools are encouraged to paticipate in a "Fun Raiser" and sell "Spirit Corn"—which is popcorn produced in their school colors. You can even purchase personalized popcorn for weddings and special events. If you can imagine it, Jody's can probably produce it!

Corporate gift giving is made easy with Jody's Gourmet Popcorn customized business gifts. These gifts may include personalized gift messages, custom labels for company logos and messages.

The final product offer that Jody's Gourmet Popcorn makes to its customers is this: If you have an idea for a new flavor or snack product that Jody doesn't currently offer, you may submit your idea to the company by e-mail at "goodnews@jodyspopcorn.com." If your idea is ultimately selected by the company, the product will be named after you and you will receive a lifetime supply of the item. Now there's a unique customized offer indeed!

Other Promotional Offers

Beyond product offers, Jody's Gourmet Popcorn offers a variety of promotional offers to its customers. For example, the company offers free shipping for domestic orders that amount to more than $50 with the promotion code of "FREESHIP." Also, a variety of offers are extended to customers via its Web site and Facebook page. The announcement of new, special popcorn varieties and promotions are provided on its Web site. One such example is Jody's offer of free bags of caramel popcorn with any order on National Caramel Corn Day.

The company communicates with its customers via its Web site, Facebook page, and Twitter account. Jody encourages customers to write a review of the company's products and provides a link to an external review Web site where they may do so. Jody's Gourmet Popcorn also offers a virtual tour of its 8,000 square-foot production facility through the company's YouTube channel. Free product samples are offered for distribution to product reviewers. Finally, Jody offers specialized branded merchandise including beach balls, mugs, shot glasses, and magnets.

Conclusion

In summary, regardless of who you are—student, parent, bride-to-be, company, charitable organization, etc—or what flavor of popcorn you desire, Jody's Gourmet Popcorn has a sweet offer for you. Rarely can you find a company that has more value propositions for its customers than Jody's Gourmet Popcorn. So, what are you waiting for? Visit www.jodyspopcorn.com and place your order so you can get a taste of a customized offer at its finest.

Case Discussion Questions

1. The company Web site portrays Jody's Gourmet Popcorn for gift giving. Identify occasions when consumers should be reminded to purchase and ship Jody's popcorn for gifts. Are there occasions that would be different for corporate gift giving? Why or why not?

2. The case mentions that Jody's Gourmet Popcorn can be customized and packaged for corporate gift giving. Discuss the different kinds of businesses Jody's Gourmet Popcorn could target for its products. What media mix or lists would you advise Jody's Gourmet Popcorn to utilize in reaching business prospects.

3. Visit Jody's Gourmet Popcorn site (www.jodyspopcorn.com) and identify the site's social networking applications. Suggest ways for Jody's Popcorn to enhance its social networking popularity and attract direct visitors/customers to its site by linking to affiliate sites.

4. Compare Jody's Gourmet Popcorn (www.jodyspopcorn.com) with other online popcorn businesses such as Colonel Gourmet Popcorn (www.colonelgorumetpopcorn.com), Kernel Encore Popcorn (www.kernelencorepopcorn.com), Snappy Popcorn (www.snappypopcorn.com), and the Popcorn Factory (www.thepopcornfactory.com). What are Jody's Popcorn's advantages vis-à-vis the competitors? What are its disadvantages?

Notes

1. Adapted from Edward L. Nash (2000), *Direct Marketing: Strategy, Planning, Execution,* 4th ed. (New York: McGraw-Hill).

2. Ibid., p. 25.

3. Adapted from Lois K. Geller (1996), *Response: The Complete Guide to Profitable Direct Marketing* (New York: Free Press).

4. Ibid., p. 26.

5. Ibid., p. 27.

6. Adapted from Mary Lou Roberts and Paul D. Berger (1999), *Direct Marketing Management,* 2nd ed. (Upper Saddle River, NJ: Prentice Hall).

7. Adapted from Ibid.

8. Adapted from Ibid.

## CHAPTER 6

Planning and Creating Compelling Message Strategies

OPENING VIGNETTE: AMERICAN CANCER SOCIETY

What happens when you create a social media campaign that combines an awesome nonprofit cause—the American Cancer Society—with an extremely popular celebrity, Justin Bieber? Instant success! This success is no small feat because in the social media world the nonprofit space is extremely crowded. A wide variety of nonprofit organizations are clamoring for attention urging viewers to join a movement, support a cause or event, or to donate . . . now! In order for any nonprofit organization to be successful in the digital space, it must break through the clutter and excite and engage the target audience. The message must be compelling and provide a strong call-to-action that emotionally connects with consumers. The message must not only seize the audience's attention, it must evoke the desired measurable response from its audience. Generate awareness and interest. Motivate the audience. Stimulate action. That's the creative formula that spells success!

FIGURE 6-1. American Cancer Society logo. Used with permission of American Cancer Society, Inc.

That is just what The Martin Agency in Richmond, Virginia, did for its client, the American Cancer Society (ACS), when it created the ACS—More Birthdays campaign. It was a brilliant campaign that broke through and grabbed the viewer's attention because it really connected with its target audience of women, 35 to 64 years old, especially those with a connection to cancer. (Figure 6-1.)

The campaign goals were to increase awareness for the American Cancer Society and its mission by driving the target audience to view YouTube postings and the ACS More Birthdays site. The campaign also had the goal of acquiring 10,000 Facebook fans. The campaign was a huge success in part because the creative strategy was simple, yet compelling. The ACS—More Birthdays campaign strategy was built on the fact that celebrity birthdays are a key trending topic on sites such as Google and Twitter. Therefore, a social media campaign that featured the birthdays of social media celebrity giants (Bieber, Usher, Mysto and Pizzi) made good sense. Here's how the campaign worked:

The ACS—More Birthdays campaign featured famous artists and musicians who, inspired by the American Cancer Society's work, created videos in which they performed the "Happy Birthday" song. These videos were turned into shareable e-cards and phone calls. The Martin Agency refreshed the content through new artist/musician video releases, and also periodic pushes focused on new content and social integrations. The Martin Agency created a mashup video to release on Justin Bieber's birthday (March 1st) and the video was released on YouTube and Facebook. The video was promoted via American Cancer Society's social media channels, as well as the celebrities' own social media channels.

Facebook fans had to "Like" the More Birthdays Facebook fan page in order to view the video there. (See Figure 6-2.) Two weeks after the video launch, the audio track was released as a free download on morebirthdays.com. A similar strategy of celebrity and media activation was used to drive thousands of follow-up visits to morebirthdays.com, which greatly expanded the American Cancer Society's online audience. In addition, Usher tweeted Justin wishing him a happy birthday and included references to the American Cancer Society, as well as a link to the video and urged their mutual fans to link and/or donate. As you might imagine, this set off a social frenzy of great proportions and to the great benefit of the American Cancer Society!

How well did the ACS—More Birthdays campaign work? The Facebook page and video was shared almost 100,000 times in the first week alone and viewed more than 500,000 times. There were 772,392 YouTube views, 19,373 Facebook Likes, 87,613 clicks to the Facebook landing tab from Usher's social posts, and 24,620 Tweets linking back to the landing tab during the campaign launch week alone All campaign goals were far exceeded in the first week and have continued to grow exponentially. With this campaign, the American Cancer Society's celebration of the victories against cancer was spread to more than 20 countries. Most importantly, this campaign

FIGURE 6-2.
FB page posts.

was a huge success in helping the American Cancer Society as it strives to create a world with less cancer and more birthdays.

Planning and creating compelling copy is what this chapter is about. In direct marketing terms, creativity encompasses the *content* of the direct mail package, direct response advertisement, Web site, or whatever media format is being used to convey the direct marketing offer. Creative strategies include decisions about the words, terms, symbols, designs, pictures, image, and media formats that will be used in direct marketing activities. The old cliché "it's not creative unless it sells" implies that the creative strategies must attain the objectives set forth by the direct marketer. These objectives may be to generate a response, transaction, political vote, or charitable donation. Regardless of the objectives, direct marketers make many decisions in planning and developing creative strategies. These decisions include types research to conduct, objectives to be set, brand and image, design and format, copywriting and graphics, and message creation and execution based on media selection. These are the key topics of this chapter.

Creating promotions in direct marketing requires a special kind of creativity with which this chapter is concerned. With emphasis on the "message" aspect of promotion, we discuss the need for conducting research and setting creative objectives. Then we explore copywriting and graphics techniques and strategies. Finally, we look at creating messages for specific media. The "media" themselves—print media (direct mail, magazines, newspapers), broadcast media (television, radio, telephone), and high-tech digital media (Internet, blogging, social networking, mobile)—will be dealt with in turn in later chapters, as will the adaptation of messages to all of them.

Creative Research

The creative process to develop compelling messages for any direct response promotion, in any format or in any medium, begins with research and leads to idea generation and finally copywriting. Direct marketers must really understand their target audiences. This includes customer preferences, buying patterns, offer and media preferences, contact preferences, and more. In the perspective of traditional economics, the demand from individual consumers is often viewed as a function of their monetary income or their accumulated wealth. In the real world, monetary income is not the *only* determinant of demand; in fact, it might not even be the major one. In addition to recognizing the real complexity of demand, the direct marketer also needs to study and understand buyer behavior.

What motivates buyers to take action? A buyer's ability to buy can be evaluated by well-understood demographic indicators such as income, wealth, age, gender, and marital status. However, buyer behavior is also influenced by environmental factors and psychographic indicators of lifestyle that are not readily identifiable or easily measurable. Marketers want to measure these environmental factors to determine the proneness to spend and the willingness to buy. To do this, they use such measurements as income in relation to what others are earning in some particular universe, such as a given ZIP Code area. Or, marketers may study consumers' purchase behavior, as well as their educational level and the social class standings. These can be important customer qualifications.

As social economist Thorstein Veblen observed,[1] the "conspicuous consumption" of a neighborhood can also be a qualifier of behavior. The basic concept of human ecology that behavior is a response to environmental influences tells us that a household with a $20,000 annual income located in a ZIP code area in which the median household income is $30,000 is likely to emulate that median level. The reverse is also true, with a $50,000 household tending to behave like its $30,000 ZIP code area neighbors. This tendency contributes to homogeneity of behavior within such areas, even though there is a variance of characteristics among and between individual households.

Discretionary household purchases under such circumstances are dependent not just on the *ability to buy* but also on the *proneness to spend*. Because this is such a potentially powerful economic force, direct marketers are well advised to understand it as they study the qualifications available within customer databases, the readership of magazines and newspapers, or the characteristics of television viewers and Internet browsers.

It is imperative for direct marketers to understand the economic and social differences among an infinite variety of consumers in the marketplace. They must also be aware of a vast number of factors motivating these individuals. The challenge to those responsible for creating compelling message strategies is to get inside the head of a buyer and to know what the benefits to the customer will be and what will motivate the customer to take action to gain them.

To plan effective messages, marketers must also understand how the consumer thinks and what he or she perceives. What are the key benefits each consumer is trying to obtain? In addition, direct marketers must research the competition to determine what other alternatives consumers have to fulfill their needs and desires. Armed with detailed knowledge about consumers, direct marketers can begin to plan and create effective messages that will not only get the attention and interest of consumers but hopefully stimulate action—if action is the objective.

Message Objectives

Planning and creating compelling messages also relies on the objective of the message. Is it intended to sell a product, generate a Web site visit, obtain a donation, evoke an inquiry, or secure a vote? Does the message have some other measurable intention? Is there more than one objective that must be taken into consideration? If so, there may be a need for more than one message strategy, based on differing consumer needs. In Chapter 3 we explored the need for segmenting consumers into homogeneous groups with similar needs, desires, and so on. Customer research can also determine which segments of consumers are more prone to respond based on the objectives of the message. Often, customized messaging is required to communicate effectively with different market segments of consumers. Therefore, long before you can create compelling messages, you must know all about your customers as well as the intention of your promotional message.

Direct marketers relate the costs of promotion to the results achieved from it. Managers need to see costs such as advertising and selling as adding value. Organizations work continually to improve efficiency of direct marketing by measuring its costs and its results accurately. It has been said that "if it weren't for advertising, you would pay more for most things you buy." The informational value of promotion makes this so through creation of demand resulting from product awareness by customers. Thus a key objective of creative copy is to generate a return on investment for the direct marketer. Of course, it is up to each individual direct marketer and creative campaign to determine exactly what the desired return should be.

Mindful that a major goal of marketing is to convey product benefits to present and potential customers, advertising professionals have vacillated in recent times between creative messages that create brand awareness, or are image building, and those more directed to immediate sales or response.

Many direct marketers do indeed feel that it's not creative unless it sells something! Though this is likely an exaggeration, we need to distinguish between advertising that promotes brand and builds long-term image and advertising that seeks an immediate response or transaction. The response could be in the form of a Web site visit, text message reply, telephone call, in-store visit, product or service purchase, donation, vote, participation, etc. Those creating direct marketing campaigns are more attuned to the latter objectives, but that is not to say they are oblivious to the former. Direct response copywriters must not only possess skill as a wordsmith but also create copy to achieve message objectives. In the words of "the Wizard of Ads," Roy Williams, "Average writers position the listener as an uninvolved bystander. Good writers position the listener as an interested observer. Great writers involve the listener as an active participant."[2] This entails many different copywriting and graphics techniques. Let's delve into that topic.

Copywriting Techniques

Every successful promotion has at its heart a concept and an offer . . . and blends product, price, and place in a way that provides benefits to a target market. As we presented in the previous chapter, customers will respond to offers if they provide benefits that appeal to them. Such benefits can be the physical attributes of a product, translated into terms that meet customer needs. Customers don't buy quarter-inch drill bits; they buy the ability to make quarter-inch holes! They don't buy power steering; they buy ease in parking a car parallel to a curb. Direct marketers therefore use promotion that is benefit oriented. They sell benefits in a manner that matches a customer's motivation.

Features versus Advantages versus Benefits

When asked why he was so adept at writing copy for Scott's grass seed, Charles B. Mills, a direct response copywriter at O. M. Scott's Lawn Products, replied, "Because I like to talk about your lawn, not about my seed." Airlines sell a vacation in some exotic place, not the trip to get there. Designers sell fashion and acceptance more than the practicality of clothing. Insurance companies sell security and peace of mind, not a paper contract. Elmer Wheeler, sales motivator, summed it up, saying, "Sell the sizzle, not the steak." Direct response advertisers rely on copy that emphasizes such benefits to motivate responders.

Vic Schwab, a successful advertising copywriter with such ability, described the copywriting art as "learning to think like a horse." As an illustration, he told the story of a farmer who had lost his horse. "How'd you find him so quickly?" asked a neighbor. To which the farmer replied: "Well, I just asked myself, if I were a horse, where would I go? I went there and there he was!" Schwab used this story to drive home his copywriter's maxim that you have to "show people an advantage." This meant, to Schwab, that *you had to know them!*

Today, a database can provide the knowledge that enables the trained copywriter to "think like a horse," to relate the benefits of offers to customers. Direct response copywriting is an art. Those who have the talent and have achieved a track record of success are much in demand. They have the ability to translate product features into advantages, these into benefits, and benefits into words, design, and graphics.

Phrases such as these typify compelling promotional copy:

- "An important message for persons over age 65."
- "Are you tired of the back-breaking work caring for your lawn?"
- "At last . . . a simple, effective way to rid your house of bugs."
- "Do you need more room in your house . . . or a new roof?"
- "Here's good news for taxpayers!"

Offers incorporating customer benefits are structured to incite action and overcome human inertia. An analytical technique for identifying benefits, FAB (features-advantages-benefits), appears in Figure 6-3.

As demonstrated in Figure 6-3, a washing machine might be of compact size, feature high spin speed, provide a variety of wash temperature choices, accommodate a range of colors, and might include a tumble dryer. These are *features* of the washing machine included in its manufacture—features often promoted in consumer advertising.

The direct response advertising copywriter seeks to translate these product features into advantages and, then, from these into benefits. Compact size, for example, provides the advantage of the machine fitting into a smaller space, the benefit being space saving. High spin, as another example, provides the advantage of clothes drying faster and the resulting benefit is the customer saving time. Figure 6-3 provides the direct response copywriter with a useful procedure for identifying benefits as a necessary prelude to actual copywriting.

Writing the Copy

Effective copywriting begins by determining the **big idea** and then creatively weaving that big idea into all aspects and elements of the creative campaign. Think of the big idea as a highlighted unique selling point or creative phrase that becomes the star or focal point of an entire promotional campaign. The big idea should become the company's tagline, logo, symbol, or slogan and should be consistently used throughout all creative strategies and materials. The big idea should be branded to create a synergy with real identity and meaning for the company or organization. In his book, *Guerrilla Creativity,* Jay Conrad Levinson refers to the big idea as a "meme." He defines a **meme** as a self-explanatory symbol, using words, action, sounds, or pictures that communicate an entire idea.[3] Levinson also contends that the following three things should be understood about a meme:[4]

> **Translating Features of a Washing Machine
> into Advantages and Then into Benefits**
>
> *Features* (what the product has):
> - compact size
> - high spin speed
> - wash temperature choice
> - range of colors
> - integrated tumble drier
>
> *Advantages* (what the features do):
> - fits into a smaller space
> - clothes dry faster
> - accommodates a full range of fabrics
> - offers choice to consumer
> - moves from wash to dry automatically
>
> *Benefits* (why customers buy):
> - space saving
> - time saving
> - does a good job
> - flexibility
> - convenience
> - economy
> - no more hand washing
> - choices
>
> *How to get from features to benefits*:
> ... imagination
> ... technology
> ... product design
> ... common sense

FIGURE 6-3.
Features/Benefits.

1. It's the lowest common denominator of an idea, a basic unit of communication.

2. It can alter human behavior, and in guerrilla marketing that means motivating people to buy whatever the guerilla offers.

3. It is simplicity itself, easily understandable in a matter of seconds.

How does a company create the big idea? Many different ways including: the Internet, competitors, customers, distributors, books, movies, and more. The big idea is often the result of individual or group brainstorming sessions. However, some of the best big ideas are created by simply honing a wild, off-the-wall idea. Creative experts say that many off-the-wall or potential big ideas usually come to mind when they least expect them. Some of these different moments may include when a copywriter is out jogging, socializing, or taking a shower! Levinson claims that the key to creating a persuasive idea comes from the well-known "shoes and eyes" theory. "Walk a mile in your customer's shoes and see things through his eyes."[5] Regardless of how the big idea is developed, it should be catchy, a real attention getter, and brief—not too many words, easy to recognize and remember. Of course, the big idea usually ties in with the company's overall copy appeal.

Let's examine some advertisements that demonstrate the use of effective persuasive copy. Take a look at the ads in Figure 6-4. You might notice how the Virginia Beach *Live the Life* brand or big idea is consistently used. Also, each ad has brief and catchy copy that dares the tourist to "be bold" or "be daring." Finally, in each ad both the "Virginia is for Lovers" tagline and the Virginia Beach Web site are strategically placed in the same location.

FIGURE 6-4.
Virginia Beach
"Be Bold" and
"Be Daring" ads.
Used with
permission by the
City of Virginia
Beach Convention
& Visitors Bureau.

Copy Appeals

The **copy appeal** is the basic underlying theme of the promotion or campaign. Most copy appeals are timeless because they stem from basic human needs—what people want to gain, save, avoid, or become. Some examples include the following:

> ***People want to gain*** self-confidence, improved appearance, time, professional advancement, increased enjoyment, personal prestige, popularity, praise from others, financial wealth.
>
> ***People want to save*** time, money, memories.
>
> ***People want to avoid*** criticism, physical pain, trouble, discomfort, embarrassment, work, worry, effort, emotional suffering.
>
> ***People want to become*** good citizens, creative, efficient, knowledgeable, good parents, physically fit, influential over others, popular, successful, recognized authorities, respected.

Copywriters must determine and use the appropriate copy appeal based on the desired response. There are three basic types of appeals: rational, emotional, and moral. *Rational* appeals emphasize logic and reasoning. They usually present facts and figures. *Emotional* appeals are irrational and may focus on love, pride, joy, and humor. *Moral* appeals emphasize ethics and target consumers' feelings of what is "right" or "proper" from an ethical perspective. In some cases, copywriters may use a combination of the three basic appeals.

Figure 6-5 provides several creative examples of effective copy appeals used in direct response advertisements. Each of these advertisements for Hauser's Jewelers, a family-owned upscale jewelry store located in Newport News, Virginia, presents a simple message laced with subtle humor.

Each of these advertisements has an attractive and effective layout featuring a creative headline, a picture of the featured jewelry, the Hauser's Jewelers name, and its address and Web site to encourage action. Moreover, each headline offers a message appeal that stems from the basic human desire of most men—to give a truly special and memorable gift. The copy in each advertisement stems from basic human desires, and it is presented in a humorous tone. This combination is what makes copy appeals highly effective.

Copywriting Formulas

Successful copywriting often follows a formula to keep copy flowing in a logical sequence. Several of these formulas, which have been used extensively for many years, are presented here.

FIGURE 6-5. Hauser's Jewelers ads. Used with permission of Hauser's Jewelers.

BOB STONE'S SEVEN-STEP FORMULA

1. Promise a benefit in your headline or first paragraph, your most important benefit.[6]
2. Immediately enlarge on your most important benefit.
3. Tell the reader exactly what he or she is going to get.
4. Back up your statements with proofs and endorsements.
5. Tell the reader what will be lost by not acting.
6. Rephrase your prominent benefits in the closing offer.
7. Incite action now.

A-I-D-A Of unknown origin, this formula has been used a great deal by direct response copywriters for many years:

1. Attract *Attention*
2. Arouse *Interest*
3. Stimulate *Desire*
4. Call for *Action*

P-P-P-P Created by Henry Hoke, Sr., and popularized by Edward N. Mayer Jr., two pioneer direct marketers, is this tried-and-true formula for direct response copywriting:

1. *Picture*—get attention early in copy to create desire.
2. *Promise*—tell what the product or service will do, describe its benefits to the reader.
3. *Prove*—show value, backed up with personal testimonials or endorsements.
4. *Push*—ask for the order.

STAR-CHAIN-HOOK L. E. "Cy" Frailey, who authored many books on letter writing, described "the star, the chain, and the hook" invented by another professional letter writer, Frank Dignan, as follows.[7]

1. Get the reader's favorable attention. Do it with an opening paragraph that is bright and brisk—*the star*.

2. Follow quickly with a flow of facts, reasons, and benefits, all selected and placed in the best order to transform attention to interest and finally to desire—*the chain*.

3. Suggest action and make it easy as possible—*the hook*.

KISS PRINCIPLE Of unknown origin, this creative copywriting formula stands for "keep it simple, stupid!" The KISS copywriting formula has been effectively used by creative geniuses for centuries. The basic premise is to keep the message simple and easy to understand and remember.

Figure 6-6 presents an excellent example of the KISS copywriting formula in creative design. The creative design on this oversized self-mailer postcard for Calico Corners, a high-end retailer of custom draperies, furniture, and home accessories, is divided into three portions. Each portion features a photograph and a simple message shown in a shadow box for prospective consumers. The message is bold and punchy. "Dream It." "Design It." "Done." It conveys the ease and simplicity involved in the thinking, buying, and implementing processes when new homeowners shop at Calico Corners.

FIGURE 6-6. CalicoCorners creative design. Used with permission of Calico Corners and MindZoo, LLC. Photo by Kim Kirby, www.jimkirbyphoto.com

Design and Graphics

Hand in hand with copy—the words, the expressions, the ideas, the meanings—go design and graphics—the art, the layout, the symbols, the effects. Here we include the impact of photographs, illustrations, type styles, paper, inks, size, and a variety of other attention-getting devices. Through design and graphics, the designer, like the copywriter, creates mood and feeling while getting and holding attention. In direct marketing the ultimate goal of the designer, like that of the copywriter, is to stimulate action, to generate measurable response. Thus, design (like copy) becomes a means and not an end—another element of the total promotion process.

The designer of direct marketing promotion has available a great many graphic techniques for use in a variety of media: direct mail, print, broadcast, digital video, and online, as well as posters and billboards. These include the following:

LAYOUTS. A **layout** positions copy and illustrations not only to gain attention but also to direct the reader through the message in the sequence intended by the copywriter. Compelling layouts make optimal use of type as well as white space, photographs along with illustrations, and other graphic techniques, including shapes, sizes, folds, die-cuts, and pop-ups. Figure 6-7 shows the effective use of a die-cut shape, as well as effective layout with multiple headlines, body copy, art, company logo, and response information.

ILLUSTRATIONS AND PHOTOGRAPHS. A compelling illustration can create attention. Photographs of products in use, especially showing people, can dramatize benefits. The designer, using graphic illustrations, can even extend to designed borders, highlighting copy elements for prominence, tint blocks, and emphasis of elements such as product features and response forms.

INVOLVEMENT DEVICES. Many direct response advertising devices spur action by **involvement devices** that engage the reader in some way. These include tokens, stamps, punch-outs, puzzles, premiums, and gadgets that the reader returns to the seller. Links and click buttons are natural involvement devices of Web sites.

TYPE. Designers use typefaces to suggest boldness or dignity, Old English or Asian, antiquity or space age, movement or emphasis, masculinity or femininity. They know that typefaces need to be relevant to the message, and they also need to be easily and instantly readable. Sizes of typefaces are a factor to consider, as are the thickness and complexity of the type's structure. When the designer uses more than one typeface or type size, these should blend, and the variety should not become complicated. Sometimes, to create emphasis, typefaces can be overprinted on one another and sometimes they are reversed, that is, white on color. Certain special designs become recognizable logotypes for organizations, such as the typefaces used in advertising for Victoria's Secrets, Nike and IBM.

PAPER. Here the designer is concerned with substance, texture, and finish as well as color, weight, size, and shape of paper. A linen or laid finish can denote elegance. A parchment stock can denote permanence. Paper can have a high-gloss finish for use in a catalog of upscale merchandise, or it can simulate the look of a newspaper to convey timeliness. Paper can convey the impression of the Yellow Pages of a phone book or the urgency of a telegram. Paper not only helps set the tone of a direct response advertisement but its texture, weight, and size can have substantial impact on cost.

INK. Like paper, ink can convey impressions through color, gloss, intensity, and placement. Ink selection must consider the paper and the printing process as well as design. Some inks are even available with fragrances, such as the smell of lavender or pine trees. Some can be embossed to simulate gold and silver coins. Some can be scraped off to reveal a printed message underneath. Some can be printed on unusual paper stock, such as cellophane, waxed paper, or foil.

FIGURE 6-7. ShipShapes direct mail, elephant. Used with permission of ShipShapes™.

COLOR. Much information has been developed about the physical and psychological effects of color since Sir Isaac Newton first associated basic colors with sunlight. We know that light, heat, and color have much in common. The darker the color, the more light and heat are absorbed. Certain colors, notably yellow, can be seen farther than others; black printed on yellow provides maximum readability. Some colors convey associations: purple implies royalty, red is associated with danger, green denotes safety, and blue is a "health" color (e.g., health insurance provided by Blue Cross). Psychologically, the "warm" colors (yellow, orange, red) stimulate, and the "cool" colors (blue, green, violet) sedate. Thus, the former might more likely encourage action if used in a direct response advertisement. Colors have different meanings to various cultures, to various ages, in various geographic locations; the direct response advertising designer needs to be aware of these.

The JCPenney Dorm Living direct mail piece featured in Figure 6-8 is an excellent example of effective layout. This direct mailer was designed to promote merchandise to incoming freshmen entering college for the first time and to motivate these students to shop from its online Dorm Shop at www.jcp.com. The creative design matched the branding established for the Dorm Shop so that online and direct mail branding strategies complemented each other.

The format presents products with compartmentalized product messages, such as "Must-Haves" and "Nice-To-Haves," where photographs and bullet points provide detailed lists for each category. A handy dorm shopping checklist is provided with product items listed under various

FIGURE 6-8. JCPenney dorm living promotion photo. Used with permission of JCPenney.

categories, such as eat, sleep, decorate, shower, clean, and travel. It uses a variety of type styles and colors along with enough white space to allow for easy reading. Notice how the photographs show the variety of different product colors available and how the front panel appears to be written on notebook paper. The offer of free shipping is circled to gain attention, and the Web site is clearly displayed repeatedly throughout the direct mail piece. Finally, the direct mail piece contains action words such as "Order Today" with multiple options for doing so, along with a promotional code to take advantage of the free shipping offer. Careful layout and design planning will boost the rate of response for any direct marketing creative format. Joining compelling messages with effective layout and design is indeed a formidable combination!

Creating Messages for Specific Media

The copywriting and graphics techniques discussed in the preceding sections apply to all the media used by direct response advertisers; however, special considerations must be made when creating promotional messages that include sight, sound, or movement. We'll examine the video and audio creative elements associated with the design of direct response television, radio, digital video, and online ads in the next section. We will discuss each medium in greater length in subsequent chapters.

Television

Television is especially suited to visualization of action as well as demonstration. Products appropriate for direct response TV include these, which are often bought on impulse: recordings, housewares, specialty items such as jewelry, and a variety of services.

A major limitation in creating direct response TV commercials is *time*. Commercial time is usually available in multiples of seconds: 10, 20, 30, 60, 90, and usually up to a maximum of 120 (two minutes). A maximum airtime of 2 minutes allows for approximately 200 spoken words. Because audio and visual images can be used simultaneously in TV, the old adage that "one picture is worth a thousand words" applies *if* the product is one that can be demonstrated, such as the "handy, dandy, utterly amazing kitchen slicer-dicer."

Marketers generally feel they need 20 seconds for attention getting, up to 75 seconds for demonstration, and the remaining 25 seconds of a typical 120-second spot announcement for specifying what action the customer can take by showing a mailing or Web site address, or telephone number. Because 120 seconds on prime-time television is usually too expensive for a direct response advertiser, most of these commercials appear during low-cost fringe time (early morning, late night, and weekend hours). Often, markets can be segmented through specific programs, such as movies or wrestling, usually aired at such other than prime times.

Many direct marketers have experienced profitable response rates using infomercials, which are program-style narrated commercials that may run as long as 30 minutes in other than prime time, usually on special-interest cable channels. Featured are products, such as exercisers or nutrition supplements, that can benefit from extensive demonstration and enjoy audience involvement.

CONCEPT. The logical starting point in creating direct response TV commercials is determining just what the advertising is about and what it is to do—its concept. It might be used as support, to call attention to a newspaper insert or a forthcoming direct mail package. Or to generate Web site traffic or get leads for sales follow-up. Or to produce orders or create in-store traffic. Unlike the case for direct mail or print media, there is no written record of the product's features and benefits for the audience to refer to at a later time. The TV viewer can't be expected to remember too much, so logic and clarity are important.

STORYBOARDS. The visual portion of a television commercial is shown through a series of illustrations, called **storyboards**, which outline the structure of the commercial, the graphics and photographs, and the video action. Most of these storyboards are now computerized, which makes commercial design much faster and easier. A storyboard essentially is a timeline that goes from top to bottom, with the top occurring first in the sequencing. The steps to creating a storyboard are:

1. Objectives: Think of your story as a video and decide what you want it to accomplish.
2. Setting: Establish the backdrop for your story.
3. Major ideas: Outline the main ideas or frames that may be used to portray your story.
4. Characters: Identify the characters that will appear in your story along with each character's specific role.
5. Plot: Determine the story's problem and solution, along with its climax.
6. Message: Decide on the story's primary meaning or purpose—the action you want the viewer to take based on your story.

Figures 6-9 and 6-10 show two storyboards created by White and Partners, a marketing and advertising agency located in Herndon, Virginia. The agency developed both storyboards for the production of direct response television commercials for one of its clients, Luray Caverns, a premier attraction in the Shenandoah Valley and Eastern America's largest and most popular caverns. These commercials were produced for the grand opening of its newest attraction, The Luray Valley Museum, a museum that tells the tale of the people of the Shenandoah Valley. The "Conestoga Wagon" commercial was 15 seconds long. The audio to accompany the video in the storyboard sequence shown in Figure 6-9 included music (Folk Appalachia, simple banjo and fiddle) and the following:

> **Voice Over:** "When you absolutely, positively, had to have it there . . . kind of on time . . . there was only one way to ship it."
>
> **Driver:** "HEAWWWWW!!!"
>
> **Voice Over:** "The Conestoga Wagon, on display at the Luray Valley Museum. Now open at Luray Caverns. What will you discover—"

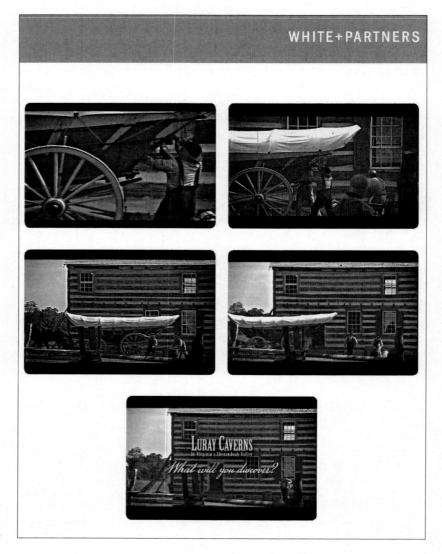

FIGURE 6-9.
Luray Caverns
"Wagon"
storyboards.
Used with
permission of
White & Partners.

The "Treasure" commercial was also 15 seconds long. The audio to accompany the video in the storyboard sequence shown in Figure 6-10 included fun, simple and playful music and the following:

> **Voice Over:** "While the little ones are busy . . . sifting for gems . . . you get to discover . . . the real treasure. Family fun is easy to find at the Luray Valley Museum. Now open at Luray Caverns. What will you discover?"

These television commercials were extremely effective in generating a response. Within a month of the commercials airing on television, tourist traffic to Luray Caverns had increased more than 10 percent when compared with the same period during the prior year.

SCRIPT. Although a script for a TV commercial containing no more than 200 words cannot verbally "explain" a product or service as thoroughly as a direct mail package or print advertisement, the combination of words with pictures and graphics, audio with video, can exert considerable impact. That is why one of the most effective uses of direct response TV is to support

FIGURE 6-10.
Luray Caverns
"Treasure"
storyboards.
Used with
permission of
White & Partners.

other direct response advertising media through copy, such as "Watch your mailbox for . . ." or "Watch for this offer in next Sunday's Chicago Tribune." A visualization of the insert to which attention is being drawn often accompanies this copy. An effective TV script needs to be tightly woven and fully coordinated with the visual and graphic elements involved. Like good letter copy or well-written print ads, the script needs to first get attention, through audio coupled with video and graphics, and then do its job in presenting product features and benefits as it gets the viewer involved and geared to action.

GRAPHICS. Direct response TV graphics begin with the words or script coordinated with the other elements that bring the message to life in both audio and video: images, actions, effects, and direction. Actors who deliver the words must be credible, professional, and appropriate to the product. Filming and editing are important so that words are synchronized with pictures. Written words are often superimposed on video to present localized response addresses or phone numbers. Television graphics are concerned with the interaction of audio and video so that the ultimate effect of the message on the viewer will be maximized.

PRODUCTION. The production team for a direct response TV commercial consists of a variety of highly specialized technicians, coordinated by a producer. Typical concerns at this juncture are whether to use motion picture film or videotape and live actors, animation, or still illustrations. Directors, actors, and graphic designers become involved, as do camera people and film editors. Decisions as to which to employ must relate costs to response.

Radio

The process of developing radio commercials is less complex than for television. Radio offers the additional advantage of flexibility in that live commercials, often read by a station announcer or known local personality, can be scheduled quickly. If need be, these can be revised right up to airtime. Radio commercials are far less expensive than TV, too, in airtime costs as well as production costs. Through use of particular radio station formats—easy listening, rock and roll, or news/talk programs—the direct response advertiser can develop a substantial degree of market segmentation. Positioning adjacent to particular programs, such as early morning farm programs or a popular disc jockey, can further segment markets. Positioning during morning and evening drive times, when office or factory workers are driving to and from their jobs, is another means of market segmentation.

Like other media, radio advertising must first get attention. Sometimes a radio personality reading a script, even in an ad-lib manner, can attract attention. If the product being sold involves music, a few bars or a few headline words can make an effective headline for a radio commercial.

The close and request for action are of special concern in using radio for direct response. Many times, radio listeners are performing another activity simultaneously, such as driving, reading a book, taking a shower, or doing household chores. Pencil and paper for writing down addresses and phone numbers are not readily available nor is it feasible for a listener to stop everything and get them. As a result, the most effective response instruction is one that is easy to remember such as "1-800-FLOWERS" or "1-800-PETMEDS." Repeating the address or number helps, too.

Digital Video

As we will present in Chapter 8, millions of people are viewing videos online and the trend is poised to continue and grow in the coming years. Thanks to YouTube, marketers now have a new digital format with which to spread their promotional messages, and the best part, it's free. More video content is uploaded to YouTube in 60 days than all three major U.S. television networks created in 60 years.[8] Given that videos will continue to be a highly popular and productive format, marketers must make sure their videos are created in such a manner that they appeal to their target customers or prospects.

Creating a video requires an ordered process. From iMovie to Final Cut to Windows Movie Maker, there are many different computer programs that allow users to create customized videos. The following information is a generalized description of the steps used to create a video that can be distributed through e-mail, YouTube, or even burned onto a CD or DVD. A step-by-step process to creating a video is as follows:

1. The first thing to do is prepare a **storyboard.** As previously discussed, a storyboard is an illustration of your outline of the video. This includes the story line, examples of images or videos that will be included, timing of the video (i.e., how long each frame will last, etc.) and the dialogue or words that will be used. The information in the storyboard will guide the creation of the video and will make it easier to weave ideas together

2. The next step is to **import** the images and videos that you will be featuring. Importing everything at once will make it easier to plan out the timing and sequence of your images and videos.

3. Next, put the videos and images in the **order** in which they should appear in the video. Some of your clips will need to be edited to decrease the time it will play or appear on the screen.

4. Now you may add in the transitions. **Transitions** are effects on the videos and images that allow the clip to move to the next scene or image. Most editing software will have different styles of transitions from which to choose.

5. Clipping the videos and images to perfect the timing is the next step in the process. **Clipping** is similar to cropping, but it relates to time instead of image size. By clipping the videos, the amount of time the video or image is shown can be extended or shortened. This process also includes selecting which parts of images or videos will be included. For example, if a video is 4 minutes long but you only want to include 2 minutes of the most exciting parts of it, you can use the clipping/cutting tool to select only those 2 minutes.

6. After clipping and transitions, a **sound overlay** can be added as part of the finishing touches. If the current videos or images have their own sounds and you would like to omit them, detach the audio files and then delete them. Depending upon the software used, each image or video segment with a sound file that may have to be detached will have to be deleted separately. After this is complete, import or add the audio file that will be played in the video. A voice recording may be used instead of music depending upon the needs for the video.

There are many other features that may be included in a video to make it more appealing and effective, such as titles, captions, special themes, and other video effects, however the above is a basic outline to get you through the process. The process of creating a video may be considered part art and part science. Despite what is involved in the process, creating an appealing video is important to do well so that your videos don't get lost in the endless stream of available videos to be viewed.

Internet

Creating effective direct response messages for the array of digital formats available on the Internet is vital in today's marketing world. Direct marketers must be mindful of a variety of special considerations when creating Internet ads. Let's explore some of the more important ones.

The first item to address in creating Internet promotions must be the dissemination of incentives for the prospect to visit a company's Web site in the first place. This is in contrast to the entrepreneur targeting the prospect, as is the case with direct mail or the telephone, as well as print and broadcast media. This is now typically being done through many formats, such as print, broadcast, mobile, SMS text messages, social media and Internet search engines, all of which can let a prospect know the location of the Web site, as well as benefits to accrue from browsing. We will discuss the Internet and digital and social media in greater detail in Chapter 10. For now, let's concentrate on the creation of compelling copy for Internet platforms.

The copywriter and the graphic designer must design a Web site, starting with its home page, so that the browser is motivated to becoming a customer. At this stage, everything we've said about creating promotions for all media—direct mail, print, and broadcast—apply as well to the Internet. Especially important, however, is the *sequencing* of each visit with clicks and links. *Information,* as needed, becomes a literal goldmine. The logic and convenience of ordering online is readily apparent. Of course, once a relationship has been established with a customer, then the Internet becomes an effective and efficient way of doing business.

Let's explore the message strategies used by Virginia Beach in its online promotion by reviewing its Web site.

FIGURE 6-11. Virginia Beach Convention & Visitor's home page. Used with permission by the City of Virginia Beach Convention & Visitors Bureau.

HOME PAGE. Virginia Beach's Web site in Figure 6-11 uses the four basic design principles: *alignment, proximity, repetition,* and *contrast.* There is horizontal alignment across the main navigation bar on the top of the page, as well as a vertical menu to enable visitors to quickly and easily locate desired information available on its Web site. The use of proximity and repetition in the vertical banner, such as the advertisements that run along the left side of the site, tie the various tourist features together, along with the bullet-point listing of recent news about what's happening in Virginia Beach. The eye is drawn to the page through the use of contrast with the different background colors, various font styles, and variety of colors in the primary image featured at the top of the page. This site also contains several key elements that consumers would expect to find on an interactive Web site. It enables prospective tourists to click on a file folder to request more information about accommodations, attractions, and packages directly from the site itself. The home page also offers visitors an opportunity to view a blog and select their preferred language.

OUTBOUND E-MAIL. Figure 6-12 provides an example of an outbound e-mail from the Peninsula SPCA. The e-mail shown in Figure 6-12 utilizes the principles of design with contrast between the black, blue and orange type and the use of an appealing image. The call to action "Vote Today!" is presented with great passion and is repeated twice: "Click Here to Vote" and in the "www.votetosavelives.org" link. The e-mail also encourages viewers to connect with the PSPCA via the additional calls to action: "Find us on Facebook" and "Follow us on Twitter" set off at the bottom of the e-mail surrounded by generous white space.

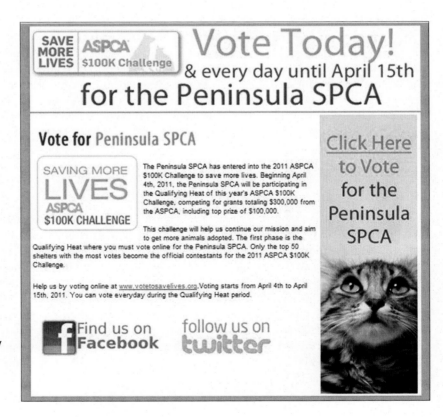

FIGURE 6-12. PSPCA "Vote Today" e-mail. Used with permission of Peninsula Society for the Prevention of Cruelty to Animals.

FIGURE 6-13. Busch Gardens Glory at the Gardens banners. Used with permission of Busch Gardens.

BANNER ADVERTISEMENTS. Banner ads, the digital equivalent of print ads, are created with the intent to engage the viewer and drive action. These ads have changed over time and now are truly interactive and integrated. These ads may be use sound, video, and flash animation. The ads may also include special forms such as floating ads, page takeovers and tearbacks designed to get the attention of the viewer. Let's examine an example of the creative design of banner ads. The banner ads for Busch Gardens' Glory at the Gardens concerts featured in Figure 6-13 employs motion to capture viewers' interest while maintaining branding for the event throughout the rotation of panels. The copy lines dissolve from frame to frame, highlighting the upcoming acts and dates, with a link on the final frame to the Busch Gardens Web site for full details on the series.

Summary

Direct response copywriting is both art and science, and those who have mastered it are very much in demand. FAB (features-advantages-benefits) analysis is often used by direct response copywriters to position products so that these provide benefits to users. There is a variety of copywriting formulas available to guide creative development and many of these are set forth in this chapter. Design and graphics are important adjuncts to copywriting, used to create attention and guide the reader through copy. These include the art, layout, symbols, and effects. Consideration should be given also to such factors as photographs, illustrations, type styles, paper, inks, size, and a variety of attention-getting techniques.

Development of direct response advertising must be concerned with the special characteristics of the medium to be used: direct mail, catalogs, print (magazines and newspapers), broadcast (television and radio), digital videos, telephone, and the Internet.

Key Terms

big idea
copy appeal
layout
involvement devices
storyboards

Review Questions

1. How do measurability and accountability, characteristics key to direct marketing, apply to advertising?
2. What, specifically, is *direct response advertising?* What makes it unique from all other types of advertising?
3. Why is an understanding of buyer motivations important in the creation of direct marketing promotions?
4. What do we mean by "features, advantages, benefits"? Give an example of each for a product of your choosing.
5. Why are design and graphics important in the creation of direct response advertising?
6. Name at least three elements of design that a direct marketer can use to create a message.
7. Name and explain one copywriting formula that has been successful throughout the years.
8. How do you create copy appeal? Give two examples.
9. Think about an advertising campaign you have seen recently. Who was the advertiser, and what was the "big idea" the advertiser was trying to convey? Was it successful?
10. What are some important considerations when creating message content for Internet and e-mail marketing?

Exercise

Busch Gardens, a well-known amusement park located in Virginia, is holding a contest for college students. The first-place prize is a season passport for two people to enjoy the park for a lifetime for each member of the winning team! The challenge is to identify as many features of the park as possible and their associated advantages. Then, you must convert each advantage into a benefit that the amusement park may use in marketing their park to consumers. You may select your target market customer, either (1) families or (2) young adults. Have fun and good luck!

Critical Thinking Exercise

Select one of your favorite advertisements and critically evaluate it according to the creative techniques and principles detailed in this chapter. Does it achieve its creative objectives? If so, how or in what way? If not, what about the ad is hindering its effectiveness?

CASE: Barely There

How does a creative idea for a direct and interactive marketing campaign originate? Is it a product of sheer genius? Or is it hatched when a bunch of brilliant minds get together and spit out off-the-wall ideas in a brainstorming session? Could it be the result of extensive research? Maybe it is based on a thorough understanding of the target customers' deepest desires? Or could it be just a stroke of good luck?

Whatever it takes, The Martin Agency in Richmond, Virginia, surely has it and has demonstrated sheer ingenuity when it created the Barely There campaign for its client, Hanesb rands. This case is a success story of creativity that really worked. It demonstrates the exceptional things that can happen when you combine commonsense thinking with clever ideas.

In direct and interactive marketing terms, creativity encompasses the content of whatever media format is being used to convey the offer. Creative strategies include decisions about the words, terms, symbols, designs, pictures, images, and media format. The old cliché "it's not creative unless it sells" implies that the creative strategies must attain the objectives set forth for the campaign. These objectives may be to generate a response, transaction, political vote, charitable donation, and so on. Regardless of the objectives, direct marketers must make many decisions about the creative elements included in a campaign. These decisions include brand and image building, copywriting and graphics, and message creation based on media selection. This case lets you explore how Hanesbrands and The Martin Agency made these decisions when they developed the direct and interactive marketing campaign for the Barely There Invisible Look collection of bras.

With a fraction of the advertising budget in comparison with category leaders, the company was intent on creating a more meaningful and intimate connection with women with the Barely There Invisible Look collection of bras. Hanesbrands challenged The Martin Agency to achieve this objective, and the company and agency worked together and did just that and more! After months of market research, positioning, and creative development, the end result was great success. Let's take a look at how this creative campaign was developed.

Research

The campaign was driven by innovative consumer research and then by the realization that the ultimate goal of bras for women was not to look sexy with their clothes off but to help them look and feel great with their clothes on. This realization was further developed when Hanesbrands began to gain consumer insights via research across the country.

The team flipped through a variety of fashion magazines, and all they saw were pretty women in pretty bras. In fact, the ads of the largest competitor in the lingerie industry, Victoria's Secret, featured beautiful models with perfect shapes and bras that fit perfectly. These models are often shown with slinky body parts, naked torsos, and stiletto heels. Where's the humanity? It seems that the intimate apparel category has been missing the mark for years, overlooking the underlying reason women wear bras in the first place—to help them look good in their clothes.

So the team got busy, and they uncovered that women try to avoid the dreaded "bad bra day" when bras don't fit right or don't look right. The team created a dictionary of "bad bra moments" and began to completely understand the consumer's perspective (the mono-boob, the quadra-boob, the puffed-up chicken chest). These bad bra moments were extremely annoying for most women. Research also found that millions of women are wearing ill-fitting bras. What many consumers really need is a friend to help them avoid bad bra moments. The solution? A new positioning strategy for Barely There intimates to be the bra brand to own to solve the most common universal bra problems and allow women never to have a bad bra day. The Invisible Look bra collection addresses the practical concerns women have about shape and fit.

Positioning

Positioning Barely There intimates as the brand that can help women look and feel better in their clothes was a new direction for the lingerie industry. The new campaign is viewed as part sales pitch and part public service announcement. It doesn't focus on the supermodels but illus-

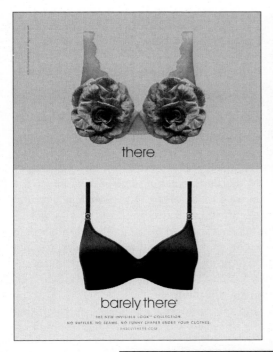

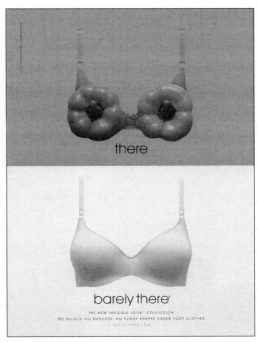

FIGURE 6-14.
Barely There print
advertisements.

trates the problems women often encounter with the wrong bra and provides practical solutions to correct the problem. The new positioning strategy fills a niche that is currently unfulfilled. Victoria's Secret may command the market segment of women desiring a sexier bra, but that still leaves a large portion of the consumer lingerie market to capture. The Martin Agency team, armed with its new dictionary of bad bra moments, seized the opportunity and history was made with a totally unique and entertaining creative campaign for the Barely There Invisible Look bra collection.

Creative Development

Due to the strategic direction and the desire to significantly drive brand awareness, the creative team found a simple way to convey the message using three words—two of which were the brand name. The result is a problem solution campaign, your bra is either "there" or "barely there." On the left is a bra that is bumpy or misshapen (labeled "There"). On the right is a smoothly shaped bra (labeled "Barely There"). The value proposition of the campaign was that other bras are painfully "there." Figure 6-14 shows a few of these creative executions.

The creative team at The Martin Agency had fun imagining all of the crazy shaped items that could be used to portray an ill-fitting bra. Of course, most women wouldn't intentionally stuff their shirts with cocktail umbrellas, red bell peppers, pine cones, or decorative bows, but many would be quick to admit that some bras do create the odd appearance of some of those items.

Color was also an important aspect to the creative development of the campaign. The creative team knew that the campaign needed to be both sophisticated and fashion-y as well as funny. The creative team decided to photograph the items attached to the garments rather than composite the images of the items and bras in postproduction. The art director strongly felt that it would be more "real," and this method would ensure the color and reflections would work with each other. Therefore, the campaign entailed a photo shoot with each bra presenting its own set of different challenges for the creative team and the photographers.

The result? A company and agency partnership that produced a brilliant campaign that clearly passes everyone's giggle test. The campaign is nationally acclaimed as it has won numerous creative awards. Finally, and most important, it effectively conveys a message along with a Web site, barelythere.com, where consumers can purchase a bra that will really make them feel and look good in their clothes.

Case Discussion Questions

1. What role did marketing research play in the development of the Barely There campaign? Could the campaign have been created without the background research? Why or why not?

2. Provide some examples of how this campaign converted the features of the Invisible Look bra collection into benefits.

3. Identify a few of the primary competitors for the Barely There Invisible Look collection of bras. What different copy appeals are being used by the various product line competitors? What makes the Barely There campaign different?

4. Would you categorize the copy appeal used in this campaign to be rational, emotional, or moral? Explain why. Do you think the use of a different appeal would have been more effective for marketing the Invisible Look bra collection?

Notes

1. Thorstein Veblen (1917), *The Theory of the Leisure Class* (London: Macmillan), p. 110.

2. Jay Conrad Levinson (2001), *Guerrilla Creativity,* (New York: Houghton Mifflin), p. 10.

3. Ibid., p. 2.

4. Ibid., p. 3.

5. Ibid., p. 13.

6. Bob Stone (2001), *Successful Direct Marketing Methods,* 7th ed. (New York: McGraw-Hill), pp. 294–395.

7. Ibid.

8. A Quick Guide To YouTube and Creating Your Own YouTube Channel, Marketing Profs, 2011, p. 1., www.marketingprofs.com/ . . . /a-quick-guide-to-youtube-creating-your-own-youtube-channel, retrieved May 23, 2011.

Designing and Employing Print

OPENING VIGNETTE: ZOO'S NEWS

With rising costs for postage and materials, coupled with declining response rates for the newspaper industry in general, it had become increasingly difficult for regional newspapers, with limited distribution potential, to achieve direct mail response rates that would result in acceptable profit margins. However, with limitations on telemarketing, newspapers have few cost-effective outlets remaining to target potential new subscribers. Plus, research shows direct mail subscribers tend to renew at higher rates. Given this situation, individual newspaper companies needed to find innovative ways to cost-effectively achieve new subscriber acquisition goals. The answer? Zoo's News!

FIGURE 7-1.
Zoo's News *Happy New(s) Year* Direct Mail Promotion. Used with permission of MindZoo, LLC Photo by Kim Kirby, www.jimkirbyphoto.com.

Zoo's News is an innovative direct mail product, developed by MindZoo, a direct marketing firm in Naples, Florida. It is a comprehensive subscription acquisition program that enables individual newspapers to pool their collective resources to gain significant economies of scale on creative development, printing, and production. As Figure 7-1 shows, this program was launched in January 2008 with seven regional newspapers featuring the seasonal theme of Happy New(s) Year. This award-winning creative concept enabled newspapers to link their content to popular New Year's resolutions.

The seven launch participants included the *Chicago Tribune, Atlanta Journal-Constitution, Newsday, Orlando Sentinel, South Florida Sun-Sentinel, Orange County Register,* and *Milwaukee Journal-Sentinel*. All seven newspapers selected their own prospect data from their in-house databases based on MindZoo's recommendation to mail to a mix of geodemographically selected nonsubscribers and former subscribers. The result was a series of seven different Happy New(s) Year direct mail solicitations hitting mailboxes from coast to coast with a total of 535,000 pieces in total distribution. By producing multiple versions of Zoo's News simultaneously, all participating newspapers enjoyed significant cost savings while taking advantage of the support of an award-winning agency supplier of direct mail services to the newspaper industry. Depending on the quantity chosen for mailing, participants saved 35 to 45 percent on the total cost of print and production for their Happy New(s) Year promotion, which greatly reduced the subsequent cost per order for all participants regardless of individual response rate. This seasonal approach has proven to be very effective for other solo mail programs developed on behalf of newspaper clients.

Zoo's News is an example of the advantages that can be obtained by partner marketing and innovative direct mail concepts. In this chapter we look at print media as direct marketers use them for direct response advertising.

Direct mail, in its various formats, is a print medium. Publications, magazines, and newspapers represent another form of printed communication. In contrast with direct mail ads, which are delivered individually, magazines and newspapers convey direct response advertising to groups of readers in a package along with other advertisements as well as editorial matter. In this chapter we examine direct mail (including self-mailers, classic packages, and catalogs), newspapers, magazines, and collateral printed materials—and their characteristics and advantages and disadvantages. We discuss the potential for market segmentation through readership of specific parts of a particular print medium at a particular time—sports or obituaries in today's newspaper, as examples. Let's begin with direct mail as it has long been the basic promotion format for direct marketers. It relies on mailing lists and data about the individuals or organizations on such lists to most effectively reach market segments.

Direct Mail

Direct marketers use virtually all forms of advertising media to generate measurable responses, including **direct mail.** According to the U.S. Postal Service, the average U.S. consumer receives about 22 pieces of mail per week, with 79 percent of households either reading or scanning the advertising mail they receive.[1] Not all direct mail is carried by the U.S. Postal Service, however; some goes by private carriers, such as FedEx, UPS, or other door-to-door distributors, such as newspaper carriers on their circulation rounds. Some is enclosed within newspapers and magazines. Sometimes marketers also combine several offers into a single package, such as coupons or other inserts into newspapers, or enclose offers with other mail or parcels, such as statement stuffers or package inserts. Among the various shapes of direct mailers, postcards are most likely to be read.[2]

Direct mail is one of the most selective media and offers great potential for personalization. It is very flexible (mainly because of the many different formats available) and is also extremely suitable for testing. Its inherent advantages, however, cause direct mail to be the most expensive medium per prospect reached. Even with a volume of 100,000 pieces, it may be difficult to distribute a traditional direct mail package (mailing envelope, computer-processed four-page letter, circular, order form, and business reply envelope) for less than $1 per piece. Direct mail costs normally include creative, art and preparation, printing production, mailing lists, computer processing, letter shop production, allocated fees, and postage. This is true even though preferential postage rates apply to nonprofit organizations and to those large volume mailers who presort their direct mail by ZIP code or by postal carrier route. Volume mailers can benefit, too, from lower average printing and production costs. There are many different direct mail designs that can be employed. Let's briefly discuss these.

Designs

Compared with other media, direct mail provides considerably more space and opportunity to tell a complete story. It can gain attention and develop an orderly and logical flow of information leading to action by the reader. Direct mail, too, has a unique capability to involve the recipient and faces less competition for attention at the time it is received than other advertising media do. It is the most scientifically testable of all media because marketers can control experimentation with variables such as format, copy, and graphics.

With adequate marketing research, direct mail affords the opportunity for positioning products to specific market segments and can, through computer and printing technology, individualize each piece to each recipient. The following example illustrates how companies effectively use market research to create a direct marketing campaign and target different consumer groups. Family-owned Lacks Home Furnishings, headquartered in Victoria, Texas, performed a customer database analysis to determine the need for two different creative versions in a recent direct marketing campaign. Research showed that 33 percent of the new homeowner prospect

FIGURE 7-2.
Lacks Uniqu Homeowner Program direct mail pieces. Used with permission of Lacks Home Furnishing and MondZoo, LLC.
Photo by Jim Kirby.
www.jimkirbyphoto.com.

population qualified as "affluent" shoppers, and the remaining 67 percent were classified as "careful" shoppers. As Figure 7-2 shows, the company targeted each shopper category with unique direct mail pieces—each one featuring different creative images. Both direct mail pieces contain the same two coupon offers to promote multiple shopping trips; however, photographs of both the home elevation and interior design are different in an effort to target the two unique market segments.

The advantages of direct mail also give it the highest cost per reader, so that marketers must always seek the highest response rate, when compared with other lower-cost media. There are three basic formats of direct mail: the self-mailer, the classic format, and the catalog.

SELF-MAILERS. A **self-mailer** is any direct mail piece mailed without an envelope. Self-mailers can range from simple postcards to tubes to a variety of different sizes and shapes of direct mail. Self-mailers can promote a single product/service or many products/services at one time. Mailing pieces promoting a single product or a limited group of related products are often called **solo mailers.** Figure 7-3 presents some examples of ShipShapes, a company specializing in the creation of unique self-mailers. ShipShapes provides customized self-mailers that really grab attention. Nearly any shape goes—a car, frog, elephant, cartoon character, floral bouquet—if you can imagine it, ShipShapes will create it! So think out-of-the-box and out-of-the-envelope and explore the many creative, colorful, and eye-catching designs associated with self-mailers.

Insert Figure 7-3 (ShipShapes Mailers) about here.

CLASSIC FORMAT. The **classic format** normally consists of six components: an outer mailing envelope, a letter, a brochure, a return device, a reply envelope and a "chit." Let's address the purpose of each component. A **chit** is an additional enclosure card or separate slip of paper that highlights a free gift or some other information, which is often printed on a different color and size of paper to make it stand out from the rest of the mailing package. The **mailing envelope** is a vital component to the success of a direct mail package, for unless the envelope receives atten-

FIGURE 7-3. ShipShapes self-mailers, Frog and car. Used with permission of ShipShapes™. Used with permission of ShipShapes™.

tion and is opened, the contents will never be revealed. For this reason, direct response advertisers often use teaser copy on the outside of a mailing envelope in order to lead the recipient inside to entice but not reveal. Figure 7-4 shows examples of how Valpak effectively uses teaser copy on its famous blue outer envelopes. In addition to teaser copy, the size, color, shape, and paper texture of the outer envelope can provide feelings of importance, urgency, prestige, or bargain to the recipient.

The principal element of the direct mail package, the **letter**, provides the primary means for communication and personalization. Databases enable personalization of letters. Letters can be narrative and intriguing or they can be factual and staccato. The P.S. (**postscript**) at the end of a letter has high visual value. The recipient will frequently read this part of the letter first. For that reason, the copywriter often uses the P.S. to restate the offer, highlight benefits, and direct the

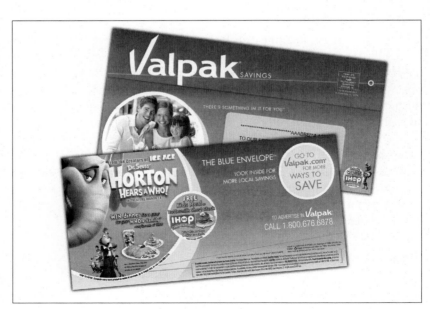

FIGURE 7-4. Valpak teaser copy. Used with the permission of Valpak.

reader to another part of the package. The **brochure** (also called a flyer, folder, or circular) is an optional piece that augments the letter (if needed) to provide product specifications, cover technical points such as pricing, provide scene-setting narrative and photographs, and dramatize and illustrate while incorporating benefits to the reader. A brochure is sometimes a physical part of the letter itself—pages two and three of a four-page letter/brochure format, for example. It can be as simple as a single sheet printed on one side only or as complicated as multi-folded brochures, giant broadsides, or multipage booklets. Headlines and illustrations are vital parts of brochures, along with adequate subheads and body copy to provide full description and entice action. Sometimes testimonials or endorsements can lend credence to product claims or report satisfied users.

Once the mailing envelope, letter, and brochure have performed their particular functions, the **response device** provides the means for action. This device can be as simple as a postage-paid return card with a mere "check off" of instructions, or it can be an order form providing for remittance or credit instructions along with specific product selections, or it can be as complex as an application for insurance, a credit card, or an investment. In any event, it should be a selling piece. It should have a name to identify it, it should be well designed, and it should contain compelling and clear-cut copy. It should be easy to complete.

The real challenge to the direct response advertiser in developing response devices is to provide, in a condensed format, all the necessary elements of the response/transaction while at the same time keeping the form logical, orderly, and simple. Involvement devices should be constructed to lure the reader into action.

Finally, unless a card is used as a response device, a separate reply envelope is usually provided as an incentive and as a convenience and to ensure privacy, especially if remittance is requested. Often, depending on the mathematics of the offer and whether curiosity seekers are to be discouraged, reply postage is prepaid. Sometimes wallet-flap envelopes incorporate an order form on the seal flap. Specialty envelopes provide an order blank combined with a reply envelope. Examples of such order forms can be found bound, as a convenience, into many mail-order catalogs. Like other elements of the classic direct mail package, the reply envelope should be designed to encourage action.

Market Segmentation

Databases are most often the distribution vehicles for direct mail. Sophisticated techniques for compiling, warehousing, and mining such databases—coupled with computer technology for most effectively using transaction, demographic, psychographic, and other data inherent to them—can pinpoint prospects and identify market segments in a highly efficient manner.[3] With such data, the direct marketer can efficiently segment house lists (active and inactive customers as well as inquirers) and compiled databases of other organizations. For example, Busch Gardens segments its database to target specific guests with customized offers and messages. Figure 7-5 shows a re-acquisition self-mailer that was sent to Busch Gardens guests who had purchased a Summer Sizzler pass the previous year, but had not renewed for the current year.

Databases are at the heart of most print media, regardless of the type used. Let's now explore some other direct response print media, including catalogs, coupons, cooperative mailings, statement/invoice stuffers, package inserts and take-one racks.

Catalogs

Certainly one of the most challenging and popular formats for direct marketers is the catalog. A **catalog** is a multipage format or booklet that displays photographs and/or descriptive details of

FIGURE 7-5. Busch Gardens Summer Sizzler self-mailer. Used with permission of Busch Gardens.

products/services along with prices and order details. A catalog can have just a few pages or hundreds of pages. Direct marketers may produce their catalogs in house or by contract with an outside agency or organization. Catalog shopping offers almost every product imaginable, from art supplies to gourmet food and drink, children's clothing, games, toys, home furnishings, perfumes, gear for camping and sporting, automotive supplies, gardening tools, jewelry, and books. You can also find the latest, greatest fashions.

Figure 7-6 presents an excellent example of creativity in catalog design. Hauser's Jewelers created its holiday catalog with a unique twist.

This 12-page booklet was designed to feature extraordinary jewelry collections as well as be a keepsake holiday recipe booklet for its customers. Each page contained a jewelry collection along with a corresponding page with a recipe and a picture of the baked good that coordinated with the colors of the jewelry. For example, the ruby collection was presented with a picture and recipe for red velvet cake and the brown Fabergé collection was shown with a picture and recipe for pecan pie. The catalog itself was a holiday greeting from Hauser's Jewelers family to each of its customers. Each recipe, shared by an associate of Hauser's Jewelers, featured a handwritten note about the recipe and how it brought back holiday memories. Let this example serve to inspire creativity in catalog design.

A notable attribute of catalog copy is succinctness, brevity, and conciseness—few words and to the point. Catalog copy goes hand in hand with design, illustration, and graphics. Pictures show it, words describe it. Descriptive words often found in catalog copy include these: *quality, genuine, fine, full, comfortable, heavy, natural,* and *best.* Like all direct marketing promotional copy, the words are arranged to spell out benefits. The words *inform* at the same time they *sell.*

Layout, including space allocation, is important. Like the store retailer who allocates shelf space and position according to the potential profitability of products displayed, a catalog retailer allocates space and position in print. Successful catalogers allocate space, including preferred positioning, such as covers, according to a product's potential profitability.

The copywriter must anticipate objections and overcome them in advance, at the same time holding the number of words used to a minimum. The catalog copy must be concise, yet it must be complete and clear. Notice the effective use of copy, design, and images in the Cheryl's catalog shown in Figure 7-7. The free shipping offer is clearly presented, as is the company's Web site and toll-free number for easy ordering. The pictures feature the products in an appetizing and appealing fashion. This catalog page inspires gift giving.

Catalogs have become a vital and productive format of direct mail. Successful catalogs rely on databases to target specialized product lines to the market segments most likely to be interested. Today's catalogs are not confined to consumer products; they also play an important role

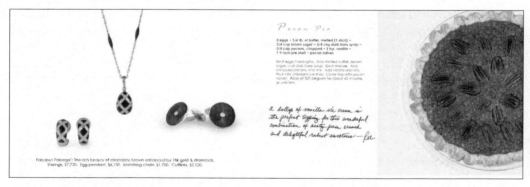

FIGURE 7-6. Hauser's Holiday catalog recipe book. Used with permission of Hauser's Jewelers.

FIGURE 7-7.
Cheryl's catalog
page. Used with
permission of
Cheryl & Co®.

in business-to-business distribution. Examples include the office product catalogs of Staples, Office Depot, Office Max and others.

Coupons

As a promotional medium—primarily for grocery, health, and beauty care products—a **coupon** is an offer by a manufacturer or retailer that includes an incentive for purchase of a product or service in the form of a specified price reduction. A major objective of coupons is to motivate buyers to try a new product or to convert occasional users into regular customers. A further objective is to increase sales so the retailer will give the product greater display space.

Coupons distributed by direct mail can be self-mailers for a single brand, enclosed in an envelope with descriptive literature, inserted in company newsletters, or combined with coupon offers—which will be discussed next. Coupon redemption rates are highest when coupons are instantly redeemable.[4]

Cooperative Mailings

Cooperative mailings provide participants, usually direct response advertisers, with opportunities to reduce mailing cost in reaching common prospects. Mass cooperative mailings frequently combine coupon offers with other direct response offers, thus sharing the total mailing cost among several advertising participants. Some cooperative mailings provide opportunities to reach market segments such as new homeowners, new families, Spanish-speaking households, or consumers in particular ZIP code clusters. As many as a dozen or more offers might be contained in a cooperative mailed to a specific market segment. Such mass cooperatives are sometimes distributed through other print media: newspapers and magazines.

Valpak, the leader in cooperative mailings nationwide, allows its clients to select from a variety of format options including coupons, flyers, and postcards to fit each client's product or service, message, and budget. Valpak is a well known and recognized cooperative direct mail program. Many consumers recognize its familiar blue Valpak envelope (shown in Figure 7-8) and look forward to sorting through the offers. Popular Valpak coupon advertisers most appealing to consumers include grocery stores, sit-down restaurants, fast food restaurants, mass retail stores, pizza, and video rentals/movie theaters.

FIGURE 7-8.
Valpak envelope.
Used with
permission of
Valpak.

Statement/Invoice Stuffers

Periodic bills and reminder statements mailed to customers of department stores, utilities, publications, and bank credit cards provide an opportunity for distributing complementary (but not competing) offers of products and services with **stuffers** inserted in the envelope with the invoice or statement. Deliverability is ensured, because most bills travel via first-class mail, and virtually everyone opens their bills in a timely fashion. The billing company implies an endorsement of the offer and, in some cases, also offers credit to make the purchase. Marketers can segment these mailings by selecting the organization sending out the bills.

Package Inserts

Package inserts are related to stuffers but offer the additional advantage of arriving when the recipient has just made a purchase. Certain direct marketers offer the opportunity for one or more direct response advertisers to include inserts with customer shipments. Gourmet meat purveyor Omaha Steaks, for example, might enclose an offer of gourmet coffee from Gevalia in its shipments. Some package shippers may even offer specific selection by product line or geographic location. Inserts might be loose or contained within a separate folder in the package.

Take-One Racks

Another method of print distribution is the use of **take-one racks** in supermarkets, restaurants, hotels, drug stores, transportation terminals, buses and trains, or other high-traffic locations. These might be placed in a cardboard display container adjacent to a cash register, or could be placed in a wire rack strategically hung on a wall in a supermarket and containing many offers. An advantage of such distribution is that those who voluntarily take a promotion piece from the rack are usually more than casually interested. Thus, the response rate from take-one rack inserts is relatively high when lower cost is considered. Even though distribution within a single rack might be quite low—say, fewer than 100 pieces per month—the number of potential outlets for racks is quite large and distribution could total into the millions.

Other print media include magazines and newspapers, with which the following sections are concerned.

Magazines

A key consideration for direct marketers, in the development of direct response advertisements for use in print media, magazines, and newspapers, is space limitation when compared to direct mail. Because print advertisements must compete with other advertisements as well as the editorial content of the print media, the headline is the most important element. Like catalog copy, the headlines of print ads must gain attention quickly and the body copy must tell the story completely yet concisely. Copy must be benefit oriented and the graphic design should lead the reader through the advertisement's elements in intended sequence. Illustrations augment copy.

Design

Direct response print advertisements must contain an attention-getting headline, compelling body copy to stimulate interest and desire, and a strong call-to-action response device that can be traced, tracked, and measured. Let's explore each of these elements in greater detail.

HEADLINES. Possibly the most important element of a direct response print advertisement is the headline.

BODY COPY. Direct response copy starts with benefits and ends with a request for action. Typical sentences are short and active, including phrases such as these:

Today more than ever . . .	Authorities have proved . . .
Fortunately for you . . .	Try it for ten days . . .
There's a new way . . .	Judge for yourself . . .

RESPONSE DEVICES. When all is said and done, the time comes to ask for the order. A good way to determine whether the advertisement can be categorized as direct response is to see whether it asks for action and how effectively it does so. Remember that a key characteristic of direct marketing is that it is measurable and accountable. Marketers measure transactions, that is, orders, inquiries, contributions, or votes. A direct response can be visiting a Web site, sending a text message, mailing a coupon or order form, phoning in an inquiry or order, traveling by going to the seller's location, or placing a request for the seller to come to the buyer's location. Many otherwise good advertisements with effective headlines and compelling body copy fall down when they do not specifically ask the reader to order the product, fill out the coupon, click on the shopping cart, or call.

An excellent example of a magazine ad with a strong call-to-action is that of Pringles "The Happy Pup." Note at the top of this magazine ad it states: "100 chips in every can. 100 ways to enjoy Pringles." This ad is "#19" and shows individuals enjoying Pringles in a fun way. Then, at the bottom of the ad it encourages the reader to "Share your way on Facebook." The magazine ad is effectively driving traffic to its Facebook Page, where it hopes people will post photographs of themselves or others enjoying Pringles in fun and innovative ways. The top 100 ways will be featured in ads for Pringles.

The terms of the offer, including price, need to be clearly stated. The response mechanism must provide a sense of *action now*. Although layout is not always easy to control, it is desirable to have right-hand coupons on advertisements that run on right-hand pages of print media (especially magazines) and vice versa for left-hand pages. The reason is obvious: it's easier to clip such a coupon if it adjoins an outside edge of the page.

INSERTS. A popular form of print advertisement in a magazine is an insert. Printing technology has made possible a great many variations for such inserts, including folding, gumming, consecutive numbering, die-cutting, and personalization on a printing press. The insert might be a multipage piece, or it can be a simple reply card bound next to a full-page advertisement and serving as the response device.

**FIGURE 7-9.
Pringles
magazine ad.**

Copy and format are important considerations for inserts in newspapers and magazines. Single-page or multipage formats are available along with special features, such as perforated coupons and gummed reply envelopes, incorporated right into the format. Inserts offer a chance for unbounded creativity for the writer and designer of direct response print.

Market Segmentation

Special-interest magazines, through their selection of content and resulting readership, serve to define market segments and even psychographic lifestyles for direct response advertisers. Categories of special-interest magazines are today virtually unlimited: class (the *New Yorker, Smithsonian,* and *Museum*), literary (*Atlantic, Harpers,* and the *New York Times Book Review*); sports (*Sports Illustrated, Ski,* and *Golf*), how-to (*Popular Mechanics, Popular Science,* and *Woodworking*), news (*Time, Newsweek,* and *U.S. News*), religious (*Christian Herald* and *Catholic Digest*), and many other diverse titles, such as *Entertainment Weekly, Self, Vanity Fair,* and *Playboy*. Figure 7-10 presents an example of a special-interest magazine, McDonald Garden Centers *Inspirations* magazine, "Four Season Solutions for Home and Garden." This publication focuses on interior and exterior lifestyle trends and designs and also contains advertisements related to home and garden improvement.

Certain national magazines—including, among many others, *New Yorker, Business Week,* and *Newsweek*—are available in demographic editions describing market segments, such as women, college students, and business executives. Some publications, including *TV Guide,* offer geographic editions that are described by ZIP code areas. Some, such as *Time,* combine both

FIGURE 7-10.
McDonald
Garden Centers
Inspirations
magazine cover.
Used with
permission of
McDonald Garden
Center.

demographic and geographic market segmentation, offering selected advertisers access to these selected groupings. Occasionally, using laser printing technology, individual ads are personalized to individual subscribers.

In terms of circulation, the top five magazines are currently AARP with 23 million (although the magazine is a benefit of membership); followed by Better Homes and Gardens with 7.9 million; Reader's Digest with 5.5 million; Game Informer at 4.7 million; and National Geographic Magazine at 4.5 million.[5]

Categories of Magazines

Magazines can be grouped by editorial content into five major categories:

1. General Mass: Characterized by high circulation and relatively low cost per thousand readers, general mass circulation magazines include *Reader's Digest, TV Guide, People,* and *National Geographic.*

2. Women's Service: Like the first category, women's service magazines are characterized by heavy circulation and reasonably low cost per thousand readers. Included are magazines such as *McCall's, Good Housekeeping, Family Circle, Seventeen,* and *Ladies Home Journal.*

3. Shelter: With selected demographics and increased cost, shelter magazines (those that focus on homes, decorating, and gardening) include *Architectural Digest, Better Homes and Gardens, House & Garden,* and *House Beautiful.*

4. Business: This category includes *Fortune, Forbes, American Banker, Business Week, Nation's Business, Fast Company,* and *Black Enterprise.*

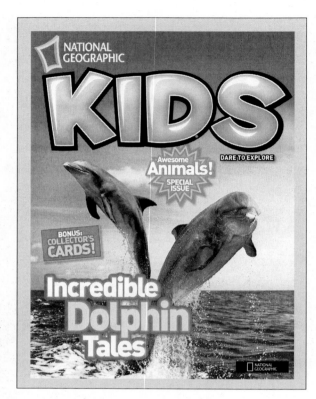

FIGURE 7-11.
National Geographic Kids Magazine. Used with permission of National Geographic Society.

5. Special Interest: With highly selected demographics and even lifestyle definition, this category would include magazines such as *Travel & Leisure, Gourmet, Ski, Golf Digest, Jogging, Modern Bride, USA Hockey, Guitar Player, Hot Rods, Car and Driver, Game Informer,* and *National Geographic Kids.* (Figure 7-11.)

Advantages and Disadvantages

Magazines can be selected to reach defined market segments: mass or class; rural, urban, or suburban; females or males; senior citizens or teenagers. Modern printing technology permits excellent reproduction at a relatively low cost per thousand circulation. Because magazines usually come out periodically—weekly, monthly, quarterly—they enjoy relatively long life and often many readers will read a single copy. Through split-run techniques in which alternative advertisements are placed in every other copy, magazines can be tested relatively inexpensively for ways to maximize direct response.

On the negative side, however, magazines offer direct marketers less space in which to tell their story than direct mail does. Additionally, **closing dates** for magazines (the date by which the magazine must receive the ad) are often considerably in advance of the issue dates and, because of staggered distribution, over a long period of time, response is usually spread out over time and thus slower.

Factors influencing the cost of magazine advertising include: the amount of space purchased; whether the ad is in color or black and white; whether the ink bleeds off the edges of the page; and the use of regional, demographic, or test market selections. Certain magazines offer discounted rates for direct response advertisers as well as special rates for categories such as publishers or schools. Sometimes, standby or "remnant" space is available at publication deadline and at substantial discounts.

Position and Timing

Although the front and back covers usually get maximum readership in a magazine, many publications do not permit direct response coupons in these preferred positions. The front portion of the magazine, assuming a full page, is preferable. A right-hand page is usually better for direct response than a left-hand page, but there are exceptions, such as the last left-hand page in the publication. Whether on a right-hand or left-hand page, the response coupon, if there is one, should always appear on the outside margin and never in the gutter (center fold) of the magazine. Inserts and bind-in response devices, reply cards or envelopes, serve to call attention to the advertisement.

Many magazines offer advertisers an opportunity, along with a special cooperative advertising rate, to have their advertisement listed and highlighted on a bingo card. A **bingo card** (also called an information card) is an insert or page of a magazine that is created by the publisher to provide a numeric listing of advertisers. Bingo cards can be bound into the magazine or loosely inserted and serve as a response mechanism for consumers to request additional information by simply circling or checking the number corresponding to each advertiser. Advertisers will often reference the bingo card in their ad with statements such as "for further information circle item 27." Consumers send completed cards directly to the publisher who, in turn, sends compiled lists of inquiries to the appropriate participating advertiser.

Aside from seasonal offers, response from magazine advertisements usually follows the normal direct marketing cycle. The strongest response occurs in January–February and September–October, with the poorest response during June–July.

Newspapers

Along with magazines, newspapers represent a major medium for distribution of printed direct response advertising. A sizable number of weekly and free newspapers are also available for use by direct marketers. Figure 7-12 presents an example of a free monthly newspaper, the *Oyster Pointer,* which provides direct marketers with excellent opportunities to promote to local consumers. The *Oyster Pointer* is a business publication that features stories about businesses and people who work within the Oyster Point Business Park. The publication is distributed throughout the local area in governmental buildings, banks, office reception areas, local restaurants, and the local airport. The *Oyster Pointer* started as an 8-page newspaper, and today it spreads news about the business park area in 32 pages. Its circulation has grown to 10,000 with a readership of more than 37,000. Direct response advertisements are highly effective in this publication.

Market Segmentation

Like magazines, newspapers help segment the market for direct response advertising although not as finely as magazines. National newspapers, such as the *Wall Street Journal, USA Today, Capper's Weekly,* and *National Enquirer,* are directed to well-defined market segments. Some national newspapers are produced via franchises in local geographic regions. For example, *Kidsville News,* a newspaper created to promote literacy among children, is published in local editions to feature stories and artwork of children in the local area. This newspaper is distributed free of charge via local schools and is an excellent medium for direct marketers to reach families with school-age children in specific geographic areas. An edition of this highly targeted newspaper appears in Figure 7-13.

Additional opportunities for market segmentation through newspapers include urban versus rural, dailies versus weeklies, commuter editions versus those home-delivered, morning versus evening editions, tabloids, comic sections, and Sunday supplements. Marketers can also

FIGURE 7-12.
Oyster Pointer
newspaper. Used
with permission
of Sylvia S.
Weinstein.

select specific types of readers by choosing the placement of direct response advertisements within the newspaper, such as in the sports, television, comic, or business sections, for example.

Categories of Newspaper Advertising

Aside from type and location of a newspaper's circulation, there are four distinct ways to reach newspaper's readers: (1) run-of-paper, (2) preprinted inserts, (3) syndicated Sunday supplements, or (4) ad notes.

RUN-OF-PAPER ADVERTISEMENTS. Although position in a newspaper can many times be specified and paid for, **run-of-paper (ROP) advertisements**—positioning the ad at the will of the newspaper—do not normally have the visual impact or dominance required for direct response advertisers. Most ROP direct response advertisements are small or appear in specific "mail-order" sections of newspapers. (Full-page direct response advertising in newspapers will, of course, increase dominance wherever placed.)

PREPRINTED INSERTS. Preprinted inserts run typically in Sunday editions or on Wednesday or Thursday mornings. The direct response advertiser usually prints them ahead of time and provides them to the newspaper according to the publication's specifications. Newspaper inserts abound and appear in a variety of formats, especially on Sundays and midweek, on Wednesdays and Thursdays, which are typically grocery shopping days for many newspaper advertisers. Coupons are a major response format used in such inserts. Direct response advertisers using

FIGURE 7-13.
Kidsville News
newspaper. Used
with permission
of Sylvia S.
Weinstein.

newspaper inserts include insurance companies, land developers, trade schools, retail stores, book clubs, magazine publishers, and film processors. A key advantage of newspaper inserts is controlled timing. In many markets, demographic selection, often by ZIP code definition, makes possible pinpointing messages to market segments.

The direct response print advertisement from Hauser's Jewelers shown in Figure 7-14 demonstrates many of the necessary elements of an effective print ad. This print ad was a newspaper insert, so it contained two sides of colorful copy. Direct response advertisements often incorporate photographs to convey visually what the words describe. The call to action "Drop everything! Head to Hauser's Jewelers" is very strong, and it is creatively pictured on a clothesline to get the prospective customer to think about Mother's Day. The Hauser's Jewelers print ad presents a compelling picture of "Splendor in the Grass" followed by the announcement of Hauser's annual pearl event. The direct response advertisement is measurable in that customers must present the ad to receive the 15 percent discount incentive on all pearl jewelry purchases. The advertised offer contains a time limit, May 7–12, which is clearly presented on both sides of the advertisement. Location and contact information is also provided on both sides.

SUNDAY SUPPLEMENTS. Mass circulation **Sunday supplements,** such as *Parade* and *Family Weekly,* are edited nationally but appear locally in the Sunday editions of many newspapers. They offer large circulation and a great deal of flexibility at a relatively low cost. One variation of

FIGURE 7-14. Hauser's direct response print advertisement. Used with permission of Hauser's Jewelers.

the Sunday supplement is the comics section, which reaches as many as 50 million households. Sunday supplements, both magazine and comic sections, have proven successful for many direct response advertisers.

AD NOTES. An **Ad Note** is a small sticker that is placed on the front page of the newspaper that can be peeled off without damaging the newspaper. These notes offer a powerful front-page top position that truly catches the reader's attention. Ad Notes are an excellent spot to place a direct response ad, such as the Hi-Ho Silver Ad Note featured in Figure 7-15. Some companies offer Ad Notes in different shapes, two-sided printing, scratch-off ink and barcoding for recording responses.[6]

FIGURE 7-15. Hi-Ho Silver ad. Used with permission of Hi Ho Silver.

Advantages and Disadvantages

Key advantages of newspapers for direct response advertisers include short closing dates and relatively fast response. A wide variety of formats is available, as well as broad coverage of geographic or demographic areas. Most newspapers now offer online editions that can be accessed from the Internet or from mobile devices via a free app, such as the Daily Press's "ON THE GO" shown in Figure 7-16. The ON THE GO application allows you to view headline articles, see photos of the articles, add your favorite article, photo or blog, view Daily Press tweets and see breaking news stories. It has Facebook, Twitter and e-mail sharing devices built-in and offers mobile text alerts to any iPhone, Android, or mobile site.

Newspapers are well known for providing strong market penetration in a local geographical area. Figure 7-17 provides an example of a direct response space ad from a local newspaper. Note the offer being presented is designed to appeal to the consumers residing in a specific geographical area (Newport News/Williamsburg, Virginia) and encourages readers to respond by visiting its Web site, or connecting on Facebook or Twitter.

Most newspapers do not have the degree of selectivity or market segmentation that direct mail offers. Therefore, most direct response ads in newspapers keep the message more generic. A disadvantage is that response from newspaper advertisements is usually short-lived because tomorrow brings another edition.

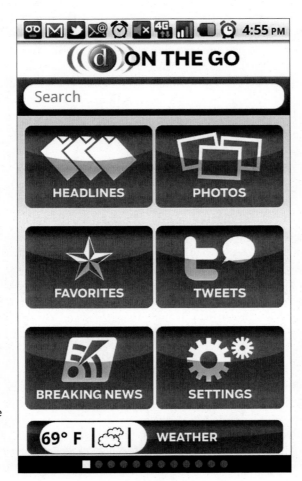

FIGURE 7-16. Daily Press iPhone screen. Used with permission of Daily Press Media Group.

FIGURE 7-17. Newport News/Williamsburg International Airport advertisement. Used with permission of Newport News/Williamsburg International Airport (PHF).

Position and Timing

There are many opportunities for **positioning** in newspapers. An obvious one is placement of a funeral service inquiry ad adjacent to the obituaries. Another is placement of automobile tire and hunting gear ads in the sports section. Most newspapers have food sections—usually on Wednesday or Thursday—and relevant ads are obvious candidates for placement there. Financial advisors and stockbrokers are appropriate advertisers in business sections.

Timing can be important, too. Seasonal interests are obvious. Sunday editions typically are read at a more leisurely pace and in a family setting. Morning editions may be more appropriate for retailers than evening editions. As already noted, Wednesday and/or Thursday may be more favorable to grocery shopping ads and weekend sport sections carry a lot of scores and other references for sports fans. Tuesdays may be relatively light days for advertising, so ads can be showcased. Friday editions may emphasize weekend activities. Of course, major news happenings (often unforeseen) can grab attention away from all the other contents.

Summary

Direct mail remains an important medium for direct marketers, relying on databases to effectively reach specific market segments. Direct mail is a selective, flexible medium, and it offers great potential for a high rate of response although it is the most expensive medium per prospect mailed. Variations of direct mail include self-mailers, classic formats, catalogs, coupons, cooperative mailings, and miscellaneous distribution, such as statement/invoice stuffers, package inserts, and take-one racks.

Printed media, other than direct mail, include magazines and newspapers. Magazines, as they have moved away from mass circulation to special-interest circulation, offer increased opportunities for market segmentation through definition of content and readership. We generally categorize magazines as general mass, women's service, shelter, business, and special interest. Thus, magazine readership can help describe markets. Although they offer high-quality printing reproduction, magazines provide direct marketers less space for their messages than does direct mail. The cost of circulation of magazines is substantially lower than that of direct mail, but response rates of individual advertisements are also much lower.

There are also a good many weekly and industry-specific newspapers (such as farm newspapers), which are also used extensively by direct marketers. Like magazines, newspapers can be segmented for direct response advertisers by geographic location, special positioning within the paper, and other factors such as morning or evening editions, and commuter or home delivery circulation. Response advertisers can use ROP (run-of-paper), preprinted inserts, or Sunday supplements.

Key Terms

direct mail

self-mailer

solo mailer

classic format

chit

letter

catalog

coupon

cooperative mailings

stuffers

package inserts

take-one racks

insert

bingo card

run-of-paper (ROP) advertisements

preprinted inserts

Sunday supplements

Ad Note

positioning

Review Questions

1. What is the major advantage of direct mail over other media for direct response?

2. Discuss the attributes of a database that could be helpful for targeting direct mail to the most likely prospects. How can these be used in developing promotion copy?

3. In what ways do contemporary mailed catalogs differ from those pioneered by Ward, Sears, and Spiegel?

4. What are two attributes of mailed catalogs that give them an advantage in direct mail?

5. Why is a coupon considered to be direct response advertising?

6. Evaluation of media for direct response advertising must relate results to costs. How might this be done?

7. Describe and show examples of these alternatives to traditional direct mail: cooperative mailings, statement/invoice stuffers, package inserts, and take-one racks.

8. Discuss the relative advantages and disadvantages of direct response advertising placed in magazines and/or newspapers.

9. Of what importance are position and timing of direct response advertising placed in magazines or newspapers?

10. How are print media being used in conjunction with high-tech digital media? Provide an example.

Exercise

Congratulations! You have just been hired as a marketing director for a specialty magazine. Your primary responsibility is to increase the number of subscribers to your magazine. Your assignment is to (1) describe the magazine and its target market; (2) create a media plan comprised of only print media; and (3) develop the rough creative materials you plan to use in the execution of the media plan. Your new boss didn't give you a budget, so be creative!

Critical Thinking Exercise

Find a print media advertisement that utilizes a multi-channel call-to-action. Follow and comply with each of the calls-to-action and describe the synergy, or lack of, between the various channels.

CASE: Busch Gardens

SeaWorld Parks and Entertainment is one of the world's top theme park companies. Its 10 parks, including the SeaWorld and Busch Gardens parks, play host to 25 million guests each year. One of the company's major bases of operation is Williamsburg, Virginia, where its Busch Gardens and Water Country USA parks are top attractions for family vacationers. Busch Gardens features some of the world's top-rated roller coasters, along with other rides, children's play areas, shows, animal encounters and seasonal events. Water Country USA is the largest water park in the mid-Atlantic region, offering rides and slides from mild to wild, plus plenty of other water-soaked fun.

As leading regional theme parks, Busch Gardens and Water Country USA appeal to both tourists, who stay overnight in the destination, and residents, who visit the parks as a day trip. The majority of these guests are families, but the parks also cater to groups and niche audiences, such as seniors and members of the military. Although visitors come from across the United States and many other countries, the largest concentration of guests come from the region stretching from New York through North Carolina, encompassing major cities including New York, Philadelphia, Baltimore, Washington D.C., Richmond, Norfolk and Raleigh-Durham.

Media Mix

To reach potential visitors, the marketing team uses a comprehensive mix of paid media, direct marketing, public relations, promotions and interactive communications. The media mix and level of activity are adjusted according to the potential of each geographic market and consumer segment. Television and radio advertising are used in most major visitor-source markets. Digital media, including online display advertising, pre-roll video, rich media and paid search, are key parts of the mix, which are targeted according to geography or behavior.

Although broadcast and digital media account for the largest portion of its marketing spending, Busch Gardens continues to use print media as a key component of its mix. Each year the park produces hundreds of unique printed pieces, including advertisements, direct mail and collateral materials. These elements provide a layer of communication that work in concert with other media by providing more information and specific purchase direction than are typically possible in a 30-second television spot or a Web banner advertisement.

Print Advertisements

Print advertisements are designed for newspapers and magazines and most have a specific call to action—a ticket offer, promotional discount or limited-time event. As shown in Figure 7-18, some advertisements are targeted to specific audiences, such as parents of young children or military families. Others are designed to drive business through ticket-sales partners, which include travel agents, credit unions and hotels.

One recent print piece ran as an insert in Thanksgiving Day editions of major regional newspapers and promoted the Christmas Town holiday event at Busch Gardens. The eight-page, four-color insert highlighted the special attractions, shows, dining and shopping available dur-

FIGURE 7-18. Busch Gardens Military Appreciation, *Parenting Magazine,* Credit Union ads. Used with permission of Busch Gardens.

ing the event in high-impact format. The timing on Thanksgiving Day coincided with the start of Christmas Town and took advantage of the high readership of advertising inserts during this edition. Attendance for Christmas Town increased more than 30 percent year-over-year, with the print insert serving as the only paid advertising in some markets.

Direct Mail

A significant part of Busch Gardens' direct-mail activity is aimed at its pass members, who purchase a pass good for unlimited admission for one or two years. To acquire new pass members, the park often uses self-mailers highlighting upcoming events and new attractions. To encourage existing members to renew their passes, the park communicates through a combination of e-mail, four-color postcards and a statement-type letter offering a discount for continued loyalty. In addition, all members receive newsletters, postcards and an annual "Fun Tracker" calendar featured in Figure 7-19, to encourage park visitation.

The Fun Tracker calendar was mailed to the "Annual Fun Card holders" segment of Busch Garden's customer database. While working on its communication plan to reacquire previous Fun Card holders, Busch Gardens chose to communicate to this group differently than in the past. Historically the theme park mailed out a small flyer to entice these guests to purchase another Fun Card. Since this group was already familiar with the park, Busch Gardens decided to illustrate the value of the Fun Card more demonstratively by showcasing by month all the events, concerts and new offerings at Busch Gardens with an annual Fun Tracker calendar. The inside cover messaging of the calendar was "we welcome you back" and stressed all the fun that could be had all spring and summer at Busch Gardens. Pass members consistently cite these printed pieces as a primary source for their knowing about events and new features at the parks.

Direct mail also is effectively used by the marketing team to reach likely tourists. These mailers are targeted both geographically and demographically and typically include a strong call to action for a vacation package or multi-day ticket for both Busch Gardens and Water Country USA. A recent direct mailing, shown in Figure 7-20, included a free, ready-to-use seven-day ticket to both parks as a powerful incentive to plan a getaway. While giving away a free ticket may seem like a money-losing proposition for the company, the mailing was successful because an average of two additional tickets were purchased for every free ticket redeemed, and each ticket resulted in almost three visits across Busch Gardens and Water Country USA.

FIGURE 7-19.
Busch Gardens
Fun Tracker
Calendar. Used
with permission
of Busch Gardens.

FIGURE 7-20. Busch Gardens and Water Country USA 7-Day Tourist Self-Mailer. Used with permission of Busch Gardens.

Conclusion

Printed collateral ranges from small information cards to large posters. Almost all pieces include a direct call-to-action and many are customized for sales outlets, geographic markets, or customer segments. The pieces provide an important layer in extending the park's messages where potential visitors work, play and seek vacation ideas. Busch Gardens' most widely distributed print piece is its annually updated park brochure, where more than 1 million copies are printed each year for use in visitor centers, hotels and sales outlets.

Even with its strong presence in broadcast and digital media, Busch Gardens and Water Country USA continue to invest heavily in print media to reach diverse consumers with customized messages, captivating images and compelling offers.

Case Discusssion Questions

1. The case indicates that Busch Gardens' visitors are from all walks of life. Explain how the company segments its markets and what communication-mix it uses to connect with potential visitors. What promotional packages does Busch Gardens offer to attract different segments of its target market?

2. Describe the television and radio advertising media that Busch Gardens uses to attract potential visitors. How are they different from digital media such as online display ads, pre-roll videos, and paid search in reaching the Busch Gardens potential target markets?

3. What is the role of print media in the company's media mix? Explain how print media compliment broadcast and digital media in Busch Gardens' communication mix.

4. Discuss the specific roles of newspaper and magazine ads in the company's overall marketing communications. What audiences do they reach?

5. Busch Gardens focuses a significant part of its media on direct-mail activities. Describe different types of direct mail such as self-mailers, newsletters, postcards, flyers, and annual "Fun Tracker" calendars that the company uses. Who are the target audiences for the company's direct mail. What are their features?

Notes

1. *Statistical Fact Book 2011* (New York: Direct Marketing Association), p. 23.

2. Ibid.

3. See Chapter 2, which deals with market segmentation strategies, and Chapter 3, which deals with database development.

4. *Statistical Fact Book 2011* (New York: Direct Marketing Association), p. 48.

5. The Association of Magazine and Media, http://www.magazine.org/consumer_marketing/circ_trends/ Retrieved May 21, 2011.

6. http://info.thewest.com.au/ratecard/index.php/adnotes, Retrieved May 20, 2011.

Utilizing Television, Radio and Digital Video

OPENING VIGNETTE: SMITHFIELD FOODS

Today's wide variety and sheer number of available cable television channels make it easy for companies to target specific types of consumers with advertisements featuring their products or services. Television advertisements have always been an effective form of "mass advertising" because they generate excellent brand awareness and enhance brand recognition. However, television advertising is also an effective form of direct and interactive marketing when the advertisement requests consumers to take some specific action or response, such as the purchase of a certain product at a store, a phone call using a specific toll-free number, or a visit to the company's Web site using the Web address presented in the ad. This is the beauty of the medium—it is most effective when used in conjunction with other media. It is also most effective when tied into the company's overall branding strategy—thus contributing to the synergy being created by

FIGURE 8-1.
Smithfield
Foods DRTV
advertisement.
Used with
permission of
Smithfield Foods.

the use of several media vehicles to drive home the message. The use of television to generate a consumer response, commonly referred to as direct response television (DRTV) advertising, is especially effective when the product or service being marketed has mass appeal and is not limited to the desires of a specific consumer group or audience. This is the case with Smithfield Foods. Let's explore how this company effectively used national cable television to market its variety of delicious meat products.

In an effort to increase brand recognition and encourage brand loyalty, Smithfield Foods established a partnership with the "queen of Southern cuisine," Paula Deen. Paula Deen, a world famous cooking guru, has endorsed the Smithfield brand. With its new celebrity spokesperson on board, Smithfield created a series of 30-second TV spots promoting a wide range of its products. As Figure 8-1 presents, each advertisement begins with the opener of "Smithfield Cooks with Paula Deen" and then proceeds into the kitchen showing Paula cooking with a Smithfield brand product. Some of the television spots take Paula out of the kitchen and put her on the road promoting Smithfield.

The objective of these DRTV spots is to entice and interest the consumer to purchase and use Smithfield products when making the excellent recipes being shared by Paula Deen. Of course, each advertisement directs the consumer to its Web site to learn more about Smithfield products. Have these direct response advertisements been effective for Smithfield? You bet! Unique visitors at its Web site increased 252 percent! In fact, because this DRTV campaign was such a success, Smithfield Foods plans to continue and expand the use of national cable television in its upcoming marketing campaign. Tune in to a cable network such as Fine Living, the Food Network, the Learning Channel, Great American Country, TBS, USA Network, and Lifetime, and you might be able to snag a few great recipes courtesy of Paula Deen and Smithfield Foods. Smithfield has successfully woven DRTV into its media mix. The company uses electronic media to create a synergistic effect in its overall marketing campaign.

Electronic media are the topic of this chapter. We explore how direct marketers use the media of television, radio, and digital video to generate a response from customers and prospective customers. We also discuss the various formats available for each medium and the advantages and disadvantages associated with using each medium for direct and interactive marketing.

Television and radio are commonly referred to as broadcast media. **Broadcast** is the most universal of communications media. Unlike telephone and print media, broadcasts reach virtually everyone and every location. Many people in the United States listen to the radio during some part of each day. Nielsen estimates the total number of households with TVs in the U.S. will climb to 115.9 million during the 2010-2011 broadcast season. [1] The average television set is used as much as 6 hours per day, and television long ago replaced the newspaper as the primary source of news.

With its universality, broadcast reaches the full range of geographic, demographic, and psychographic market segments, which are not always easily separated. Relatively high costs associated with relatively low response rates result from reaching (and paying for) nonqualified prospects. Measurability and accountability, hallmarks of direct marketing, are difficult, if not impossible, with broadcast media. Still, the potential reach is there, if it can be harnessed.

In spite of their universality, however, broadcast media—television and radio—account for only a small percentage of total expenditures for direct response advertising. Most TV advertising creatively emphasizes product brand and image rather than asking for an immediate response, the preferred advertising mode of direct marketers. However, this is changing as direct marketers experiment with and learn about the possible uses of television and radio.

In this chapter, we look at the ramifications of television, such as network, cable, and satellite transmission; then we discuss radio; and, finally, we look at digital video as a direct response and interactive medium.

Television

Television when it began, transmitted via established networks or local channels, was not an important medium for direct response advertising. But its value has increased as direct marketers have learned how to use it. Cable and satellite transmissions now provide an almost endless variety of programming and special-interest channels, defining the potential for market segmentation. Interactive modes of television provide the immediate response—along with measurability and accountability—on which direct marketers thrive.

Direct response advertisers use television in the following three ways, as we detail in this chapter:

1. To sell products or services, or promote a political candidate.

2. To get inquiries: expressions of interest or sales leads for personal follow-up.

3. To support other media: newspaper inserts or heavy penetration direct mail.

To accomplish these alternatives, direct response advertisers need to be mindful that television viewers have one of two objectives: *entertainment* or *information*. It also is important that advertisers know how to direct their messages to defined market segments so as to minimize the high cost of reaching television audiences.

Market Segmentation

When a farmer "broadcasts" seed, much of that seed lodges in moist, fertile ground and, under ideal growing conditions, it is nurtured into a living plant. Another portion of the seed is borne away by the wind or fails to achieve the proper conditions for germination for other reasons. Direct marketers using television are like the farmer sowing seed. Although television has the potential for reaching virtually everyone, it can achieve the objectives of the direct response advertiser only if it is seen in the right place at the right time under the right conditions. Market segmentation, in television as in other media, is one way to maximize direct response.

FIGURE 8-2. Professional lumberjack athletes Mark Jones and Jason Lentz compete in the stock saw discipline in the STIHL® TIMBERSPORTS® Series Midwest Professional Qualifier. Published with the consent of STIHL TIMBERSPORTS.US/ Adam Harbottle— All Right Reserved.

Television programming plays an important role in defining specific audience segments. Sports, news, comedies, westerns, mysteries, variety, documentaries, wrestling, and opera or drama can categorize and appeal to market segments of viewers and thus provide a showcase for a particular direct response offer. Other factors that can help segment markets include time of day or day of the week. Viewers of one of television's most-watched audience events each year, the Super Bowl, are large in number and broad in characteristics. On the other hand, viewers of a Clint Eastwood movie are a more narrowly defined group, and whether they watch late at night or mid-afternoon also can make a difference in the demographic and psychographic characteristics of the audience. The "reach" of a local TV station can itself describe geographic markets differentiated by ZIP code characteristics.

Offering direct response advertisers even greater opportunities for market segmentation is cable television, with hundreds of specialized channels. Highly specialized programming, "live" news, sporting events, and a variety of movie fare can help define desirable segments of cable TV audiences, as can special-interest channels, such as CNN, ESPN, the History Channel, the Country Music Channel, or even the Golf Channel.

Let's check out a great example of how a company has innovatively used cable channels and social media to target a very specific market segment, build brand awareness and drive product sales. STIHL, Inc., the best-selling brand of handheld outdoor power equipment in America, wanted to boost its brand awareness and promote both its products and its network of more than 8,000 servicing power equipment retailers to outdoor power equipment users. In 1985 STIHL established the STIHL® TIMBERSPORTS® Series which brings together the world's top lumberjacks to compete in the Original Extreme Sports competition to determine the best all-around lumberjack. The STIHL® TIMBERSPORTS® Series is seen by more than 20 million viewers annually in more than 62 countries on targeted networks such as EUROSPORT and ESPN2.

In an effort to connect with college-age consumers STIHL created the STIHL® TIMBER-SPORTS® Collegiate Series which airs on ESPNU. Winners of the Collegiate Series events earn an opportunity to compete in the Professional Series. Consumers can learn more about the different competition disciplines and competitors, view pictures, video, live events and check out ESPN airdates on its Web site, www.stihltimbersports.us. In addition, STIHL connects with followers and engages fans of both the professional and the collegiate series via social media sites,

FIGURE 8-3. Jason Lentz finishes the underhand chop discipline in 25.89 seconds at the STIHL® TIMBERSPORTS® Series Midwest Professional Qualifier hosted by Purdue University in West Lafayette, Ind. April 9, 2011. Published with the consent of STIHL TIMBERSPORTS.US/ Adam Harbottle— All Right Reserved.

including Facebook, Twitter and YouTube. Social media platforms are used to provide fans with event and athlete updates and promotional opportunities that feature local STIHL® TIMBER-SPORTS® Series events. Social media is also used to coordinate with STIHL® TIMBERSPORTS®'s partners and sponsors to promote and highlight the series.

The STIHL® TIMBERSPORTS® Series is one of the longest-running programs on ESPN garnering more than 45 million media impressions, with an advertising value topping $1.77 million. Nationally, the STIHL® TIMBERSPORTS® Series has been featured in the Boston Globe and on The 700 Club, ESPN.com, National Public Radio (NPR) and The Colbert Report. So, if you want to become a fan and follow the action, check out the STIHL® TIMBERSPORTS® on Facebook, Twitter or YouTube. It promises you a thrilling, action-packed extreme sporting event.

Characteristics of Television Time

Like empty seats on a departing airplane, television time is perishable. Furthermore, once 24 hours per day have been used within a market, coverage cannot be extended, nor can more time be manufactured or imported. Only actual viewing can be increased. This penetration of the potential market, the number of viewers, is what determines the price of commercial television time.

This price usually peaks during prime time, the early evening hours, and drops to a minimum during the wee hours of the morning. The cost of TV time is highest when the viewing audience is the largest, although the cost is often set without regard to audience composition. Prime time may not be the best time for direct response advertising unless an offer appeals to a large and diversified audience. Furthermore, large audiences attracted to a suspense-filled event like the Super Bowl are not inclined to break off watching to "call this toll-free number *now!*"

The cost of a 120-second selling commercial, as typically used for direct response advertising on television, is not an adequate indication of success unless it is related to anticipated (actual) response to the advertising. The key to maximizing such response lies in market segmentation: just who are the viewers at a particular time and how receptive are they to a direct offer?

Because television costs as well as audience segments vary, the most valid measurement for the direct marketer is **cost per response (CPR)**, not **cost per viewer (CPV)**. Nielsen audience ratings, **gross rating points (GRPs)**, and areas of dominant influence (ADI)—the glossary of TV time buying for the general advertiser—have little or no relevance for the direct marketer who wants somewhat more from direct response advertising than simply "recall." For example, GRPs are a combination of **reach** and **frequency** measures. GRPs are determined by multiplying *reach* (the number of people exposed to vehicles carrying the ad) by *frequency* (the number of insertions purchased in a specific communication vehicle within a specified time period). GRPs may be able to measure the number of people exposed to an ad; however, they cannot determine whether that ad stimulated any subsequent action (response or order). As an example, the CPV of reaching one of television's largest audiences, those watching the Super Bowl, might be quite low, but because of the diversity of this audience, the CPR could be prohibitively high.

The acronym that counts is CPR, the total cost of a direct marketing campaign divided by the number of responses that campaign generated:

$$CPR = \frac{\text{Total Promotion Budget}}{\text{Total Number of Orders/Inquires Received}}$$

Direct marketers must always relate advertising results to its costs.

Direct Marketing Uses of Television

We've said that there are three basic ways in which direct marketers use television. Let's now look at each in turn.

The first of these ways is to *sell something:* a recording, a subscription, a kitchen utensil. Consumers are ordering a broad assortment of products/services via DRTV. Direct marketers usually require a 2-minute (120-second) commercial to achieve a direct sale. Customers respond by mail or, more likely, by phone or through a Web site.

The second purpose of television for direct marketers is to *generate leads*. Leads can be generated for nearly any entity, such as companies wanting to sell products or services, non-profit organizations looking for donations, or political candidates seeking votes. These responses require a two-step process in which the commercial stimulates the original inquiry and the customer then follows up in some manner. This follow-up might be by e-mail, postal mail, telephone, SMS text, Web site visit, or personal visit. Recall the Nevada Tourism case back in Chapter 2 explored the highly effective use of e-leads. If television is used, sixty-second television commercials are normally adequate to generate such leads, although in some cases, the ad time may be shorter.

The third direct marketing use of television is as *support* of direct response advertising in another medium. This includes online advertisements or offline in newspapers or magazines such as *Cosmopolitan* and *People*. Usually 10- or 30-second commercials are adequate as reminders, with extensive repetition over a period of several days being the key to success. Support television, often purchased locally, creates interest in the offer and directs the viewer to the printed medium, which in turn provides detailed explanations as well as means for response.

Television Home Shopping

(HSN (formerly known as the Home Shopping Network) and QVC (Quality/Value/Convenience) are notable examples of TV channels devoted to the continuous sale of merchandise. Though such programming does not yet provide random access for product selection—as would a printed catalog or a Web site—technology for such interactivity is emerging. For now, these networks primarily offer products such as jewelry, cosmetics, and electronics, which are frequently purchased on impulse. These products are extensively demonstrated, priced for quick sale, and

Top 20 Infomercials of 2010		
Rank	*Product Name*	*Marketing Company*
1	P90x	Product Partners/Beachbody
2	Body Makeover	Provida Life Sciences
3	Total Gym	Total Gym Fitness LLC
4	Advertising Profits	Visionary Strategies LLC
5	Insanity	Product Partners/Beachbody
6	Nu-Wave	Heartware Home Products
7	Your Baby Can Read	Your Baby Can LLC
8	Ab Circle	Direct Entertainment Media Group
9	MaxClarity	Stiefel Laboratories Inc.
10	Shark Portable Steam Pocket	Euro-Pro
11	Shark Navigator	Euro-Pro
12	Shark Steam Pocket	Euro-Pro
13	New Body Shaper	Kymaro
14	Cash Flow Business	Dalbey Education
15	Trudeau's Free Money	Free Money
16	Lifestyle Lift	Lifestyle Lift
17	Living Well Health Master	TriStar Products
18	bareMinerals	Bare Escentuals Beauty
19	Extenze	Biotab Nutraceuticals Inc.
20	Nopalea	TriVita

FIGURE 8-4. Top 20 Infomercials of 2010.

sometimes rely on well-known personalities for credibility. Television home shoppers claim that product demonstrations were the prime motivating factor for their purchasing from television.[2]

Infomercials

Infomercials have become an important means of demonstrating and selling certain categories of products through television. These ads appear primarily on cable channels and often during early morning and late-night time slots. They usually last for 30 minutes. Featured products include exercise machines, cookware, weight-loss programs, and sundry cleaning products. Figure 8-4 provides a list of the top infomercials on national cable in 2010.

The lifespan of infomercials is somewhere between 9 and 18 months.[3] Infomercials allow customers to respond to marketers within moments of being exposed to the product and advertising. They are used by brands that are trying to sell high amounts of goods and increasing brand awareness at the same time. Marketers should focus on the benefits of products and not the features when creating an infomercial. Individuals watching the infomercial can connect more easily with benefits and in turn be more likely to purchase, rather than just hearing a list of different features. A benefit of DRTV infomercials is the fact that campaign results will be known in a quick and efficient manner. This makes tracking the ROI, cost per order, and other calculations easy to determine.

Average infomercial costs are often between $150,000 and $200,000.[4] Infomercial media tests cost about $10,000 to $15,000. If the test is successful, media expenditures will increase, which can translate into a larger ROI. For example, let's say you spend $10,000 per week on your infomercial campaign and it generates $20,000 in revenue. If you can maintain that same 2:1 **media efficiency ratio** (**MER**) and you spend $100,000 per week, then your informercial campaign will generate $200,000 in revenue per week.[5] It is also important to remember that there are additional costs associated with an infomercial campaign, such as card processing, tele-marketing, fulfillment, and other miscellaneous ones.

Advantages and Disadvantages

Television, when used for direct response advertising, can provide a wide choice of cost alterna-tives and achieve quick (but short-lived) responses. It reaches an extremely large audience and uses the combination of video and audio, simultaneously providing a sales message along with a product demonstration to deliver a lot of impact in a short time. Figure 8-4 provides a list of the Top 20 Infomercials of 2010. Note the wide range of products and services.

Television's major disadvantage is the high cost to prepare and place the ads. For example, to place a 30-second advertisement during prime time on *American Idol* will cost roughly $467,617.[6] Limited time is also one of the medium's disadvantages when product descriptions are complex or not subject to simple demonstration. Another major drawback is lack of a response device that the viewer can reference at a later time.

Radio

When radio broadcasting was still in its infancy in the 1920s, it became a major medium for direct response advertising. It was productive for books and records, as it is today, and also, in that early period, for proprietary medicines and health cures. A powerful radio station in Del Rio, Texas, with the call letters XERA, built its transmitter across the border in Mexico to cir-cumvent curtailment of its power by the U.S. government as well as regulation of its direct response advertisements. These advertisements were often "exaggerations of the truth" at best. XERA (and other stations) solicited orders for "genuine synthetic diamonds" as well as inquiries for Dr. Brinkley's "goat gland transplants" for those seeking perpetual youth. Mail-order nurs-eries, pioneers in direct marketing, offered their plants and trees, and religious groups raised funds for their evangelists through the medium of radio. Radio is still probably as effective a direct response medium as it was then, although it is minimally used today.

Market Segmentation

Even more than TV channels, individual radio stations tend to develop strong images of pro-gramming, attracting particular types of listeners. Such program formats can segment markets into an array of specific subgroups that is virtually unlimited: all music, all news, and all talk. Program format doesn't stop with just "music," however. Music can be rock, classical, easy listen-ing, country/western, show tunes, or nostalgic music-of-your-life programming. There are numerous different types of radio stations in United States, each offering a different format or program available to satisfy the listening desires of all consumers.

Listeners are loyal to certain stations, so direct response advertising, presented within an established program format by a well-known personality, derives an air of credibility or even an implied endorsement from the station announcer. (For many years, syndicated radio news com-mentator Paul Harvey provided a notable example, with his personally presented commercials for insurance and health products.) Unlike the case in television, in which viewers are constantly surfing among as many as a dozen or more favorite channels, according to the Radio Advertising Bureau, the average radio listener "tunes in regularly to less than three stations—no matter how many he can receive." Several thousand radio stations (AM as well as FM stations) provide a lot of choices, and there appears to be relatively little switching!

In addition to program format and station loyalty, another means of market segmentation through radio is by its use during particular times of the day or even days of the week. Unlike most TV viewers, radio listeners can be involved in another activity while listening to the radio, so direct marketers can reach them in an automobile, on arising, or in front of a mirror while shaving. Of course, the listener's attention is not always undivided at these times, and the real challenge to the direct marketer is to deliver a direct response instruction that the listener will recall later.

Rate Structure

A major boost for radio in direct response advertising is its relatively low cost. Whereas the economics of television dictate a maximum commercial length of 2 minutes, commercial messages on the radio can be melded with DJ chatter. Entire 15-minute information radio programs have been built around the content of a magazine, such as *National Geographic,* for which subscriptions are being simultaneously solicited. The same format has also been applied to advice for household repairs at the same time as orders are solicited for a *Home Handyman's Guide.*

Some radio stations accept per inquiry (PI) arrangements under which the station runs commercial messages, at its own discretion, in return for remuneration from a direct response advertiser for each sale or inquiry produced in this manner.

Advantages and Disadvantages

Radio is the most flexible of all response media in that it requires relatively little in the way of preparation, and it can be scheduled or the copy can be changed right up to the time the message is aired. In contrast with the cost of direct mail or other print media and the high preparatory cost of television video, radio has minimal production costs. In fact, the direct response advertiser accrues virtually no production cost if the message can be typed for reading by a local station announcer. Because the various program formats of radio are conducive to testing, the direct response advertiser can readily test alternative copy and formats at relatively low cost.

A major disadvantage of radio, like that of television, is the absence of a response device that can be referenced at some later time. Radio also lacks the visual impact afforded by direct mail and the other print media as well as by television. Also, the transmission of radio programming via satellite is significantly decreasing commercial air time and thus the opportunity to place ads. Customers pay a monthly subscription fee to receive satellite services. In the US, Sirius Satellite Radio is the dominant provider. It offers commercial-free channels and channels with limited advertising per hour compared with the minutes heard on "free" channels.[7]

Digital Video

There are a number of different factors to consider with digital video marketing. The first factor is that to be successful in digital video marketing, the video content must fit with the culture of the brand. Without this necessary component there will be no tie to the product or brand that is being marketed. This will help consumers understand where the brand is coming from and what it stands for. For example, Virginia Beach established its "Livethelife" YouTube video channel to reinforce its Live the Life brand as shown in Figure 8-5. Its YouTube site provides rich video content and entices viewers to want to learn more about Virginia Beach as a vacation destination. Its YouTube videos are an excellent way to communicate the many exciting features of Virginia Beach to prospective visitors.

Marketers must also have their target market in mind when creating digital videos, and video content should stem from consumer research. Sound consumer research will reveal the

FIGURE 8-5.
Virginia Beach
YouTube screen
shot. Used with
permission by the
City of Virginia
Beach Convention
& Visitors Bureau.

types of videos or products in which customers are most interested. Armed with that consumer information, marketers can identify other brands that already have a strong base of the customers that you wish to reach. If you have a YouTube channel, you can link to these other brands to quickly spread your message to your prospective customers.

Ideas for video content may come from many different places. Regardless of the content, the video must have both a dialogue and conversation to be effective. One of the most appealing features of digital video marketing is that it enables the company to connect its different marketing media. Driving customer traffic from videos to Web sites, social networks, and other marketing platforms is easily accomplished with video marketing.

The final factor to mention is the importance of video metrics. There are many different ways to measure the outcome of a video. Typical metrics include the following:

- Views: The number of people who click on the video to watch it.

- Uploads. The number of times the video content is posted to a server to be shared with others.

- Ratings: YouTube videos can be rated by users clicking red stars. The more and higher the ratings, the more people are viewing the video and like it.

FIGURE 8-6.
YouTube icon.

- Comments. These are text responses to a video (on a watch page) or a user (on a channel page.)
- Favorites. When people add the video to their own list of preferred videos on a YouTube watch page.
- Subscribers. Those people who pledge to support the video channel by viewing video content on a regular basis.
- Links. On the watch page, displays the five Web sites within which your video has been embedded and is receiving the highest number of clicks or views.
- Active sharing. A YouTube feature that allows you to see who else is watching a video at the same time.

Let's now explore the marketing opportunities associated with the leading video marketing channel, YouTube.

YouTube

YouTube was founded by three former PayPal employees: Chad Hurley, Steve Chen, and Jawed Karim. The idea of YouTube was proposed by Karim at a dinner party in San Francisco, and they all began working on the creation within a couple of days. The first video on YouTube, "Me at the Zoo," was shot by Yakov Lapitsky at the San Diego Zoo. It was uploaded on April 23, 2005, and within a month it had more than 684,000 views, received more than 4,400 ratings, been "favorited" more than 3,100 times and generated nearly 5,200 text comments.[8] In May 2005, a public beta test version of YouTube went live.[9] YouTube has grown rapidly since its inception in 2005 when only 8 million videos were watched each day. Today, more than two billion videos are viewed every single day. In addition, YouTube is now localized in 22 countries across 24 different languages.[10]

When YouTube was first created, the available features included the following:[11]

- Searching by username
- Linking videos from other Web pages
- Showing related videos within comments
- Introducing channels, categorizing and grouping similar content
- Embedding the YouTube video player into other Web pages
- Rating videos between one and five stars

As YouTube has grown, so have the number of features available to users. The following features have been added to the original list over the years and are very useful to marketers in this digital age of marketing:

- Insight. An analytical tool that tells you where users are coming from; their age and gender; how many times viewers rate your videos; how people discovered your video (what terms they searched on YouTube or Google); and where are the hot and cold parts of your video are through the "Hot Spot" feature.[12]

- Annotations. This features allows you to insert text notes and bubbles; links to other YouTube videos or channels; and highlighted areas, creating another way to drive traffic from YouTube to other marketing mediums such as Web sites. **Video annotations** is a way to add interactive commentary to videos by adding background information about the video and linking to related YouTube videos, channels, or search results from within a video.[13]

- Call to Action: A call to action or requests can be created as overlays for all video plays across YouTube (whether the video play is triggered by a promotion or not). The overlay will appear as soon as the video begins to play and can be closed by the user. You can use the overlay to share more information about the content of your video or to raise interest in your channel, other videos, or additional Web sites. How it works is that when users click on the overlay, they are directed to a company's Web site as specified in the overlay's destination URL.[14] In addition, nonprofit organizations in the YouTube Nonprofit Program have the opportunity to insert ads within their own videos, which could be a link to their Web site, latest campaign, or a donation page.

- Autoshare: This feature enables marketers to automatically share their company's YouTube Activity Feed to Facebook, Twitter and Google Reader. Marketers must opt-in to Autoshare to be able to perform certain actions to be shared on YouTube. AutoShare will send an update to your friends on Facebook, a tweet on Twitter, and notification in Google Reader about those actions.[15]

You are encouraged to monitor YouTube to learn about the additional features it has to offer for video marketing along with the tips available for setting up a video channel.

Setting up a Video Channel

Marketers can set up and utilize the YouTube channel to maximize their marketing efforts. A YouTube channel permits YouTube users to view your public videos, your favorite videos, and your bulletins. Your channel page also displays several links that let other people connect with you (or your brand) by sending you a message, sharing your channel with friends, or adding comments to your channel.[16] It allows all of their videos to be centralized in one location to create maximum exposure from both subscribers and channel visitors. A YouTube channel page serves as a profile page for a veteran marketer or new YouTubers.

There is a very simple process that must be followed in order to set up a YouTube channel. First, individuals or companies must visit the YouTube Web site and create an account. Registering for YouTube is free. Then they are able to upload videos that will go directly to the users of the YouTube channel. New videos can be added at any time, which enables marketers to provide video content to reflect updated information, events, or interests. For example, the Virginia Beach video shown in Figure 8-7 might have been produced and posted in response to tourist feedback indicting that they wanted to learn more about how to pick crabs. Digital videos present an ideal format to serve both customers and prospects by providing timely information.

The YouTube channel allows individuals to have a unique URL code that they can share with others. Marketers can use this URL in all of their marketing activities, including printing it on promotional materials in order to drive traffic to their YouTube Channel. The YouTube channel is where potential customers will be able to learn more about the company and the products or services that are provided. The YouTube channel also enables consumers to subscribe to a

FIGURE 8-7. Virginia Beach YouTube crab picking video screen shot. Used with permission by the City of Virginia Beach Convention & Visitors Bureau.

company's specific channel. Marketers can customize their YouTube channel so that it is more appealing to their audience.

The following are some of the different options YouTube offers for such customization:

- Posting a bulletin to be sent to subscribers that will alert them to any of your updates.

- Creating a unique title for your YouTube channel and tagging your channel with unique keywords. Individuals can type these keywords into the YouTube search and find your videos.

- Themes can be customized by selecting preset designs or by uploading unique images that will appear as the channel's background.

- Modules can be added and removed from the YouTube Channel at anytime. The available modules include: comments, moderator, subscribers, event dates, other channels, subscriptions, friends, and recent activity.

- Uploaded videos, favorites, and playlists can all be chosen to be shown or to be hidden from subscribers. In addition, you can choose your featured video and how you wish your videos to be displayed on the YouTube Channel.

In summary, customization is the key to success in digital video marketing. YouTube channels can keep subscribers coming back for more and spreading the word. Individuals coming to the channel may have only come there to watch one video, but in turn may end up watching three or four. More importantly, videos are often viral or highly shared, which is very desirable for marketers today.

Going Viral

Going viral is something that is difficult to define. Typically, **viral** means creating an infectious video that individuals will want to share with their friends, thus further promoting the video and its featured product(s). Viral videos usually generate viewers on their own when individuals who have watched the video decide to pass along the link to others. This helps garner more awareness for marketers who are looking to expose their brands with viral videos.

Videos that go viral are most often those that contain an emotional appeal or a cute factor such as animals or babies. Viral videos often have sex appeal or appeal to either the serious side of the consumer or to the humorous side.[17] Humor has been effectively used in many videos that have gone viral. One of the most outstanding humorous videos shot was for Old Spice. The "Return of The Man Your Man Could Smell Like" campaign generated the following results through the use of YouTube:[18]

- Day1: The campaign received more than 6 million views.
- Day 3: The campaign received more than 20 million views.
- Old Spice released 8 of its 11 most popular videos online.
- Day 7: The campaign received more than 40 million views.
- Twitter follower base increased by 2700 percent, while Facebook fan interaction increased by 800 percent.
- YouTube channel of Old Spice was framed as the most-viewed channel.
- The official Web site of Old Spice incurred more site traffic (300 percent.)
- The campaign drove 27 percent more sales within 6 months of launching.
- Sales were increased by 107 percent by social campaigns.

These impressive results demonstrate the power of viral videos. They also show the importance of creating viral videos for marketing activities. Viral videos provide the opportunity to create tremendous results on a cost effective basis.

Individuals view videos for different reasons. In the end, the propensity of a video going viral is based on consumer preferences. However, there is one item that can help to determine the viral nature of videos and that is social media. Think about it—videos go viral because people share them with their friends, family, and acquaintances. Social media sites are normally the battlefield where viral video fame is won. E-mail is another ingredient that should be factored into the equation of enabling a video to go viral. The following facts and statistics reveal the viral nature of videos and some considerations to help marketers create videos that will go viral.[19]

- Social video ads of 15 seconds or less are shared nearly 37 percent more than those between 30 seconds and one minute, and 18 percent more than videos over a minute.
- With more than 500 million people on the social network, Facebook dominates the share of social video. People share videos on Facebook 218 percent more than through Twitter and e-mail combined.
- People on the East Coast share more videos by e-mail than any other part of the country by 15 percent.

In conclusion, video marketing, especially via the YouTube Nation, should be an important component in a direct marketer's media mix. Video watching and sharing is a rapidly growing habit among consumers and marketers have the opportunity to tap into that force. In the words of Suzie Reider, YouTube Head of Advertising, "The Internet gave marketers the opportunity to innovate. YouTube has given marketers a platform for celebrating and amplifying nearly every marketing activation."[20]

Summary

In summary, electronic media encompasses television, radio, and digital video. Television and radio are commonly referred to as broadcast media. Broadcast media are the most universal of communications media because broadcast reaches virtually everyone and every location. There are a number of different advantages and disadvantages associated with both television and radio, as well as a number of different formats from which direct response advertisers may choose. Both media can be segmented according to different viewers and listeners. Direct response advertising on television and radio can be highly productive for direct marketers. Digital video, exemplified by video marketing on YouTube, presents a new opportunity for the direct marketer. Digital videos can and should be designed to meet the interests and tastes of specific audience segments. Digital videos offer a number of response mechanisms, enabling marketers to judge their effectiveness. Creating a video that goes "viral" can dramatically affect customer product awareness and lead to eventual purchase.

Key Terms

broadcast
cost per response (CPR)
cost per viewer (CPV)
gross rating points (GRPs)
reach

frequency
infomercials
media efficiency ratio (MER)
viral videos

Review Questions

1. Broadcast media (television and radio) are the most universal of all media, but what limits their effectiveness for direct response advertising?

2. Suggest ways to segment markets through broadcast media.

3. In what ways do direct marketers use television as a medium?

4. What is an *infomercial* on television? Describe some of the advantages and disadvantages in using infomercials for direct response advertising.

5. What are some of the most common products or services featured in infomercials?

6. In what ways is radio more efficient than TV as a direct response medium?

7. How has satellite radio changed the opportunities for direct response advertising?

8. What are the advantages of direct marketers of digital videos?

9. Where are most digital videos seen today by prospective customers?

10. What characteristics are likely to help make a video "go viral?"

Exercise

Have you ever wanted to be a "couch potato"—even for a little while? Go ahead. Sit down this evening or weekend and watch television for a couple of hours. While you're watching, write down all of the TV commercials you view. How many of them are direct response ads? What makes each advertisement a direct response ad? For those ads that are not, identify how you could convert three into direct response ads that are measurable and accountable.

Critical Thinking Exercise

Go to www.youtube.com and locate a viral video of a specific company or organization. Identify the video's source. Evaluation whether the video created positive or negative brand image for that company or organization. Provide justification to support your position.

CASE: GEICO

This case explores the benefits associated with innovative media buys for DRTV campaigns and how television can work with other media—especially telephone and online media. This case enables the student to appreciate the risk and value associated with the unique positioning strategies implemented by a direct and interactive marketer.

What you are about to read is a success story about a company that effectively uses DRTV campaigns with humorous ad appeals and innovative media buys to sell a commodity—automobile insurance. The DRTV campaigns are the products of the creative minds at The Martin Agency, located in Richmond, Virginia. These campaigns and case study are a testament to the great things that can occur when a client and an agency have a collaborative relationship. It also affirms the fact that being different and trying new things with an established medium can really pay off. Are you ready to read, learn, and think out of the box? If so, we'd like to introduce you to the client, GEICO.

GEICO (which stands for Government Employees Insurance Company) was founded in 1936. Today the GEICO companies insure more than 16 million vehicles and have assets of more than $30 billion. GEICO is ranked the third largest in the auto insurance market behind State Farm and Allstate. It is the fastest-growing auto insurers and has more than 10 million policyholders.

GEICO's success has been largely attributed to its widespread television and radio direct-response advertising campaigns. GEICO and its series of innovative and award-winning direct-response advertising campaigns use humorous ads appeals to entertain, inform and connect with customers. Let's take a closer look at a few GEICO DRTV campaigns.

Campaign: "15 minutes could save you 15 percent or more on car insurance"

The initial GEICO "15 minutes could save you 15 percent" campaign took the idea of buying automobile insurance (which doesn't seem very exciting, and the insurance product itself is probably considered an unsought good by most consumers) and turned it into a personalized, quick process with a worry-free consequence. The Martin Agency's work with this campaign was among the more innovative campaigns of the 1990s. At the time, 60- and 120-second spots were the standard TV media buys in direct marketing. Instead, GEICO ran back-to-back 15-second spots in a 30-second media buy. This media strategy of pairing two 15-second DRTV spots did a number of smart things for GEICO, including the following.

- First, it allowed smaller, customized messages to be tailored to individual market needs, creating a cafeteria menu of creative options. For example, a new market might get a spot with a message about how many new drivers sign up with GEICO every day paired with a spot focusing on price. In Washington, DC, GEICO's hometown, a different pair of service and savings messages was teamed to address specific needs in that market. Thus, segmented messages were relatively easy to execute with this new media format.

- Second, it provided two opportunities for the toll-free phone number and Web site to appear in the 30-second media buy. This longer exposure allowed the number to make a better impression, while still leaving room for the creative work to stress the brand. Most important, it contributed to the ability of each DRTV spot to generate a consumer response—the ultimate goal of a DRTV campaign.

- Third, it enabled the message to break through. Different was good, especially when battling against giants who had worked for years to build their brands. Most insurance companies' ads were similar, many incorporating "scare tactics" in their messages. However, there was no confusing a GEICO ad with another insurance company's. GEICO's unique positioning strategy effectively generated consumer awareness and placed GEICO in the minds of millions of consumers as an exciting and easy-to-deal-with insurance company. The catchy tagline "15 minutes could save you 15 percent or more" became extremely well known by consumers and it branded GEICO as the most affordable choice for consumers making auto insurance purchase decisions.

Campaign: "Gecko"

GEICO's Gecko trademark character—that cute little green lizard with a British accent—emerged to help people properly pronounce and remember the company's name, GEICO. Many people weren't sure how to pronounce it—was it pronounced "geeko" or "gecko" or what? So the

company created the Gecko to teach the world that you pronounce the company's name as "GUY-co" and history began for GEICO's Gecko. The continued use of the Gecko in GEICO advertisements was also due in part to an actors' strike at the time, which made it difficult to find humans to star in advertisements. So the little Gecko was fate for GEICO (Figure 8-8).

The Gecko was used to deliver GEICO's message with humor. It uniquely positioned GEICO as an inexpensive and fun insurance company. This was opposite of the perceptions of GEICO's competitors, which were thought of as more expensive and serious. This unique positioning strategy, combined with the cuteness and liveliness of the Gecko's personality, worked. In each ad the Gecko makes a claim in a sassy manner. For example: "I am a gecko, not to be confused with GEICO, which could save you hundreds on car insurance. So stop calling me!" Each commercial attracts the attention of the audience and generates a smile or laugh. More important, consumers remember the little Gecko, his messages, and along with it, GEICO.

FIGURE 8-8. GEICO's Gecko. Used with permission of Geico.

The animated lizard quickly became both effective and popular for GEICO. In fact, the Gecko has been named one of America's top two favorite icons. The Gecko's charismatic personality and popularity made it a natural choice to become a symbol to promote wildlife conservation for the Association of Zoos and Aquariums (AZA). As a form of cause-related marketing, GEICO's Gecko has joined the AZA with a traveling live gecko exhibit and is featured in a series of TV commercials on behalf of the AZA.

Campaign: "Caveman"

To continue the humorous appeal and drive home the fact that not only would GEICO save consumers money on car insurance, but consumers would find it easy to work with the company, GEICO introduced its Caveman campaign. The campaign objective was to convince tech-savvy 25- to 49-year-olds that shopping for car insurance was easy with the company's Web site. The Martin Agency created a series of TV commercials, each playing on the theme of a fictitious slogan: "GEICO.com. So easy, a caveman can do it" to drive the message home. Each advertisement shows modern-day cavemen in various scenarios complaining about how offensive the slogan is. The cavemen are hairy, hostile, and dressed in designer clothes. They play tennis, they visit therapists, and order fancy meals like roast duck with mango salsa. They are much more sophisticated than one would have thought—and thus the simple message The Martin Agency was trying to get across (GEICO's Web site is really easy) was wildly effective in a humorous and fun-loving way (Figure 8-9).

FIGURE 8-9.
GEICO's caveman.
Used with permission
of Geico.

GEICO's cavemen have quickly become a pop-culture phenomenon. Their popularity in TV commercials is now being extended to the Web. Launched in January 2007, the Flash site www.cavemanscrib.com allows visitors to get to know these cavemen—their personalities, preferences, and possessions. The primary purpose of the Web site is to entertain visitors. Selling auto insurance is considered secondary. GEICO receives fan mail for the cavemen, and kids dress up like them for Halloween. The cavemen ads have been so effective that the cavemen have had to fend off groupies!

Campaign: "Testimonials"

Another mini-DRTV campaign created for GEICO by The Martin Agency was the Testimonials campaign, a series of TV ads featured real customers providing testimonials to correct a misperception that lower price meant lower-quality service. To continue with GEICO's humorous appeals, each consumer was paired with a celebrity, such as Little Richard or Burt Bacharach, who helped "interpret" the testimonials.

Each advertisement contained the tag line: "Real Service. Real Savings." Also, each advertisement ended with the GEICO Web site clearly displayed—causing people to process what they had just heard from a fellow consumer and encouraging them to visit the Web site to learn more about how their needs might be better served. Because these ads used real consumers, the messages were highly believable, yet fun. They were also quite effective.

Campaign: "Sexy Grandpa"

Go to YouTube, type "Geico commercial" into the search box, and see what you find. Millions upon millions of views for car insurance commercials? What's going on here?

What's going on is that the GEICO brand has become just as engaging in the online and social landscape as it is in traditional media by introducing GEICO's "Sexy Grandpa": http://www.youtube.com/watch?v=nlVo7O2qm-4. (Figure 8-10).

FIGURE 8-10.
GEICO's sexy
grandpa. Used
with permission
of Geico.

There are three keys to GEICO's success in the digital space. One reason is brand consistency. GEICO has the same fun, slightly irreverent personality on Facebook as it does on prime time TV. Be entertaining, be engaging, and reinforce GEICO's core competency—saving people money on car insurance.

The second reason for GEICO's success is the element of surprise that has always been part of GEICO's multiple storyline approach to campaigns. This means that there is always a lot of fresh digital content for people to discover, share, and even parody. There's no better recipe for helping a brand go viral.

Finally, like other smart brands, as a marketer GEICO doesn't try to elbow its way into social conversations and digital interactions. GEICO believes that creating content that people seek out and that rewards them is a much better way to win friends and influence people.

Xtranormal is a favorite site where anyone with a computer and a keyboard can make their own movies. GEICO partnered with Xtranormal to make a series of inexpensive, lo-fi commercials made in 15 minutes or less (the time it takes to save hundreds with GEICO.)

By using a digital tool with which a younger, desirable demographic segment was already having fun, GEICO built an instant bridge between the brand and fans of the brand. Even with a limited media buy, Sexy Grandpa quickly became a top-rated video on YouTube with more than one million views. Also, a full 90-second downloadable version of the Sexy Grandpa song was made available on geico.com so people could make their own music videos, further seeding GEICO as a likeable, relevant brand in pop culture.

Conclusion

Because most of GEICO's customers work with the company through direct channels, the DRTV spots themselves needed to have personality. They were in fact the human voice for the company until the call was made and a real voice could answer. The fact that the GEICO marketing group understood this and was brave enough to be different from their competitors and embrace a humorous tone in each of its DRTV campaigns are additional reasons this brand has made its mark so effectively. Consumers were pleasantly surprised that an insurance company could make them smile. Humor can be a fine line to walk, and consumers' perceptions of humor can vary. The humor in GEICO ads pokes fun or makes light of the human condition but does not belittle the serious nature of the product. The campaigns include everything from snappy one-liners to buttons at the end and over-the-top visual exaggeration.

These GEICO campaigns have proven you should never underestimate the value of a strong call to action and never change it if it's working. The modular media and messaging needed glue to hold it all together and keep the phones ringing and the Web visits coming. The glue for most of these campaigns was a strong call to action that remained constant in every spot—"15 minutes could save you 15 percent or more on car insurance."

Have these innovative and humorous DRTV campaigns been effective in selling car insurance? You bet! While GEICO may be the number 3 company in the insurance business based on market share, it ranks number 1 in new customer acquisition and in recent polls, 91 percent of shoppers say they have seen or heard at least one GEICO message in the past 12 months. Finally, in 2010, GEICO achieved an 5.9 percent increase over the previous year in voluntary auto insurance business.

In conclusion, GEICO now owns its look, tone, and feel. No other name in the business can be substituted for GEICO. That has been the goal for the GEICO marketing group from the very first spot produced with The Martin Agency to the present. Indeed, the GEICO story is an impressive one—and one that most direct response advertisers would like to emulate. So, the next time you are faced with the task of creating a DRTV campaign—think about doing something different. Think about GEICO.

Source: This case is based on information provided by The Martin Agency, Richmond, Virginia and GEICO, Washington, D.C.

Case Discussion Questions

1. GEICO's marketing team took a great risk in agreeing to a new approach to direct response advertising. How did their approach set them apart from other insurance companies?

2. With its heavy emphasis on humor, GEICO has managed to gain the attention of many prospective customers. Was this risky? Why or why not? Could GEICO have achieved the same success without the use of humor?

3. How did GEICO differ from the norm of TV advertising and was it effective?

4. What do the GEICO's Gecko, Cavemen and Sexy Grandpa campaigns have in common? Is the target market customer the same for all three of these GEICO DRTV campaigns? Why or why not?

5. In your opinion, what could GEICO do to maintain such a spectacular marketing performance in the future?

Notes

1. "Number of U.S. TV Households Climbs by One Million for 2010-11 TV Season | Nielsen Wire."*NielsonWire.* 27 Aug. 2010. Web. 29 May 2011. <http://blog.nielsen.com/nielsenwire/media_entertainment/number-of-u-s-tv-households-climbs-by-one-million-for-2010-11-tv-season/>.

2. *Statistical Fact Book 2002* (New York: Direct Marketing Association), p. 116.

3. http://www.hawthorneinfomercialmarketing.com/FAQs.htm, retrieved, May 23, 2011.

4. Koeppel, Peter. "What You Should Know About Infomercial Production." *Infomercial DRTV Infomercial*

Media Buying TV Infomercials Infomercial ROI. Web. 29 May 2011. <http://www.infomercialdrtv.com/infomercial-production-09_07.htm>.

5. *Infomercial DRTV,* retrieved from http://www.infomercialdrtv.com/infomercial-faq.htm.

6. "2000-2011 Prime Time Ad Costs." *Media Literacy Clearinghouse: Resources for K-12 Educators.* Web. 29 May 2011. <http://www.frankwbaker.com/prime_time_programs_30_sec_ad_costs.htm>.

7. Adapted from Cara Beardi, Advertising Age, *Radio's Big Bounce* (August 27, 2001), 52; and from Roger Kerin, Steven Hartley, and William Rudelius (2009), *Marketing,* 9th ed. (New York: McGraw-Hill/Irwin), p. 526.

8. YouTube and Video Marketing: An Hour A Day, Greg Jarboe, 2009 Indianapolis, Indiana: Wiley Publishing, Inc., p. xxi.

9. Ibid., p. 7.

10. http://www.Web site-monitoring.com/blog/2010/05/17/youtube-facts-and-figures-history-statistics/, retrieved May 23, 2011.

11. YouTube and Video Marketing: An Hour A Day, Greg Jarboe, 2009 Indianapolis, Indiana: Wiley Publishing, Inc., p. 7

12. http://www.youtube.com/t/advertising_insight., Retrieved May 23, 2011.

13. http://www.youtube.com/t/annotations_about. Retrieve May 23, 2011.

14. http://www.google.com/support/youtube/bin/answer.py?answer=150471. Retrieved May 23, 2011.

15. http://www.google.com/support/youtube/bin/answer.py?answer=157215, Retrieved May , 23, 2011.

16. YouTube and Video Marketing: An Hour A Day, Greg Jarboe, 2009 Indianapolis, Indiana: Wiley Publishing, Inc., p.170.

17. http://www.marketingvox.com/humor-the-main-theme-in-julys-top-viral-videos-047508/, retrieved May 23, 2011.

18. http://www.socialf5.com/blog/2011/05/old-spice-the-most-spiced-up-social-media-campaign/, retrieved May 23, 2011.

19. http://www.movieviral.com/2011/01/27/infographics-how-videos-go-viral-and-how-social-media-users-watch-video/, retrieved May 23, 2011.

20. YouTube and Video Marketing: An Hour A Day, Greg Jarboe, 2009 Indianapolis, Indiana: Wiley Publishing, Inc., p. 7

Using Mobile, Text and Telephone for Marketing

OPENING VIGNETTE: LET'S TALK, LET'S CONNECT: OBAMA PRESIDENTIAL CAMPAIGN 2008

Barack Hussein Obama could have won a Direct Marketing Association Gold ECHO award or just about any other top award offered by the various marketing and advertising organizations for his effective political marketing campaign in 2008, but he didn't. What he did win was the most powerful position in the world: President of the United States of America. His direct and interactive marketing campaign was so incredible, in fact, many people have begun to refer to Obama as "Campaigner in Chief" instead of Commander in Chief, as he successfully secured 69 million votes and raised an unprecedented $747 million for the 2008 primary and general election campaigns.[1] Indeed, he certainly has earned both titles. (See Figure 9-1.)

What was it about his 2008 presidential campaign that earned him the highest seat in the land? The answer: An effective direct and interactive marketing campaign that simply connected with people. His campaign team unleashed a digital media assault on the American people unlike any that has been seen before. A large part of Obama's campaign strategy involved mobile, text and telephone. Let's take a peek at how the Obama campaign leveraged these media formats.

Mobile. Barack Obama was the first political candidate to create an iPhone application that made it simple for his volunteers to engage in his campaign activities anywhere they went. The free application was easily downloaded and turned the iPhone into a potent and portable field office for the Obama campaign. The application had a variety of features including the following:

- Call Friends
- Receive Updates
- Local Event (using GPS)
- Get Involved
- News
- Media
- Issues
- Countdown
- Donate Now

FIGURE 9-1. Obama Official Presidential photo.

The "Call Friends" feature was brilliant as it relied on each caller's own personal network or address book so that the person being called would be more receptive to receive a call from a friend than from a stranger—even though the call had an expressed political purpose. The application accessed a caller's address book and organized contacts by key battle ground states. The application even kept track of who had been called to prevent callers from contacting the same person twice. How handy and clever.

Text. The Obama campaign used text messaging as a platform to grow its supporter database. The key feature of the Obama texting strategy was the emphasis the campaign placed on having users "opt-in" to the SMS text list. Users were required to sign-up for the program and specify that they were willing to receive updates from the Obama campaign. Supporters could also disclose additional personal information such as their ZIP code area, which would enable the Obama campaign team to send them geographically-specific updates of events and activities happening in their local area.

Obama used text messages to share campaign news with his supporters and this helped them feel like "insiders." One example is that 2.9 million people received the campaign's text message announcing Joe Biden as Obama's running mate.[2] Supporters commonly received text messages from the Obama campaign requesting volunteers to help with a rally or event.

Phone. Even though many mistakely believe the power of the phone is behind us, personal, one-on-one phone calling was one of the most valuable ways of connecting with potential voters and volunteers for the Obama campaign. Obama's campaign team energized his many supporters and encouraged them to make phone calls on behalf of his campaign to engage people in conversations about campaign issues. Volunteers gathered in field offices to make phone calls to lists of voters provided by the campaign staff.

In addition, Obama's "Neighbor-to-Neighbor" (N2N) program was an online phonebanking tool that allowed campaign volunteers to makes phone calls on behalf of the campaign from the comfort of their own home. Obama's staff sent these volunteers manuals containing interactive scripts designed to guide the volunteer's phone conversation and enabled the user to record the caller's answers in real time. Once a call was completed, the volunteer entered the results into the N2N online system updating information to Obama's database and to the campaign's field organizers for appropriate follow up communication as necessary. The N2N program was very technical, yet easy to use, highly efficient and extremely personal.

The above is just a brief glance at some of the ways that mobile, text and phone formats can be effectively used in a political marketing campaign. In this chapter we will present many more concepts, strategies and applications associated with marketing via mobile, text and phone.

Mobile Marketing

Never leave home without your keys, wallet, and now . . . your mobile device. In the future, you may not need your keys or wallet. Many consumers never leave home or go anywhere without their mobile devices. Direct marketers must recognize this and respond accordingly. The mobile industry is undergoing significant growth and change and, consequentially, so is mobile marketing.

In recent years, the number of people who own mobile phones, and SmartPhones specifically, has grown significantly. A Warc article states that Google and Ipsos OTX surveyed 5,013 SmartPhone owners, and reported that 81 percent regularly surf the Net via this route, while 77 percent access search engines, 68 percent leverage apps, and 48 percent stream video.[3] An increasing number of individuals have the Internet at their fingertips—constantly. The way that consumers access information is beginning to switch. Savvy marketers recognize the change and are responding in many cutting-edge ways.

Location-Based Search: Google, Yahoo, & Bing Places

Recently, Google, Yahoo, and Bing introduced a new feature that is primarily for people searching on their mobile devices such as cell phones. The three search engines started aggregating data from various directories such as InfoUSA to create their own search directories. What is the difference in these search directories versus traditional directories such as the Yellow Pages? There are several:

1. These directories are already mobile ready, so when people search on their cell phone for a specific business, product or services, these pages will show up on the mobile search.

2. It is free for business owners to claim their listing and add contact information, information about the business, photos, a link to their Web site, and embed videos from YouTube.

3. Google, Yahoo, and Bing aggregate other data about the business from across the Web, such as reviews from customers, and the number of times the business is listed in other directories.

4. Business owners can make offers in the form of coupons, directly on the sites.

5. The search is location specific and geographically relevant to the place where the customer is searching.

6. There is a local map, included on the page, to show where the business is.

7. A person searching can get directions to the business based on his or her location via the GPS in the phone.

8. The person searching can push one button and call the business directly after searching.

9. All of these features give businesses a presence on the Web for FREE, whether they have a Web page or not, that shows up in mobile search.

10. As the person searches, Google remembers the searches and the businesses they interact with, so in the future, Google will show search results that are relevant to the person's likes and interest.

11. Plus, statistics are aggregated, such as the number of impressions, number of clicks, number of calls, and the business owner has access to the data.

12. Mobile search engine optimization can be used to get the business ranked higher in the mobile searches.

13. Mobile ads can be used to drive people to specific local searches.

On average, people search Google on a local level 3,387 times for every single time they open the Yellow Pages. One third of these searches are conducted on a mobile device. And 85 percent of all searches on a local level result in either the person visiting the store or purchasing a product or services. This creates a huge opportunity for marketers to engage hot prospects, while the prospect is searching for the product or service.

Google has invested heavily in the open source SmartPhone technology called the Android. Right now, the Google Android phones are the number two selling phones in the United States. Google has also developed a Google Places app that is specifically for searching Google Places. This app can be downloaded and is now pre-installed on all of their Android phones. There are also Android apps for various devices, including iPhone, iPad, Blackberry, Windows.

Mobile Web Sites

Many SmartPhone users are now accessing the Web on a regular basis through their mobile devices. This trend will likely continue in the future. Companies and organizations now have the technology to create a mobile version of their Web site. This enables consumers to easily connect with a given company at the convenience of their hand-held devices. As Figure 9-2 presents, Virginia Beach has created a mobile version of its VisitVirginiaBeach.com Website for consumers to use prior to and during their visit as a mobile research or planning tool.

Mobile Coupons

Mobile coupons are becoming mainstream. They are also an effective way to track consumers and to microtarget. Many mobile coupon redemption rates are as high as 20 percent or more, and "some claim their redemption rates from mobile coupons are eight times greater than their e-mailed coupons." [4] Mobile coupons are only likely to become popular in the future.

According to David Wachs, President of Cellit, there are five steps to a strong mobile coupon

FIGURE 9-2.
Virginia Beach
Mobile Web site
on a SmartPhone.
Used with
permission of the
City of Virginia
Beach Convention
& Visitors Bureau.

program: Offer creation, unique code generation, distribution, validation, and redemption. **Offer creation** for a mobile coupon campaign is the same as a traditional coupon campaign. The coupon must not only be convenient, the offer has to be of worth to the consumer. If it is not a unique offer (i.e., a consumer can find it elsewhere), it will not be an effective mobile campaign. Secondly, Wachs stresses the creation of completely **unique coupon codes** for each coupon. If it is a standard barcode or the same coupon code for every consumer, tracking consumer redemption can only go so far as counting the number of people who use it. Step three, **distribution**, is also critical. The coupon must be delivered to the right consumers at the right time. This means understanding customers: when and where they make their purchase decisions. The fourth step, **validation**, refers to the way that the program minimizes fraud. This may include point of purchase technology. Finally, **redemption**, may not mean only the scanning of a bar code. There are many ways to have consumers redeem mobile coupons while still maintaining the coupon's uniqueness and creating an ease of use.

Click-to-Call

Mobile campaigns have the ability to combine the search and information functions of the Internet, with the communication aspect of a mobile phone. Now, as consumers search for companies or services, they can also connect instantly through **Click-to-call.** Many companies are using Click-to-call in conjunction with sites such as Google Places, etc. Click-to-call programs work as a liaison between the consumer and a business. A consumer can search for a specific type of business, in a specific area, and can take action by making a reservation, booking, etc. right from his or her mobile device. They can click an icon, and the third party (such as Google) will connect them to the business.

Furthermore, companies can use **call metrics** in order to track phone calls and collect data. They have information on the number of "clicks" on almost every aspect of their business listing through programs such as the Google Call Metrics feature. This is a shift towards advertisements with more immediate and convenient responses. Instead of going to a Web site, consumers can connect directly to a business that meets their needs through an extremely refined search at any time and any place. Companies are using click-to-call ad campaigns in order to break through the clutter and be one of the first to gain contact with their potential customer.

Prerecorded Messages

Prerecorded messages are another way to distribute information to consumers. This usually refers to a stored voice message that one may access through various triggers. There are many ways by which prerecorded messages can be used and delivered to individuals, including text messages with links to an audio piece or through the use of a QR code which can take the recipient to the message. "QR" stands for "quick response" as these codes enable consumers to quickly connect with a company's Web site. QR codes will be covered in more depth in the following section. Prerecorded messages, if utilized carefully and sparingly, can prove to be a catchy medium to grab consumers' attention and prequalify the customer, prior to making contact with the business owner or sales team.

QR Code Campaigns

QR Codes (Quick Response Codes) are two-dimensional barcodes that can be read by barcode scanners on smart phones. These unique codes offer marketers a wide range of opportunities to increase interaction and response to traditional direct response ad campaigns and they can be created quite easily, while marketing to people instantly on their SmartPhones. There has been a tremendous surge in the use of QR codes in the past year and this growth will continue. QR code use has exploded by 1200 percent in 2010 alone.[5]

For instance, QR codes can be used on traditional print media to drive response to a specific landing page on a Web site that makes a specific offer or asks for the individual to opt in to an e-mail list in exchange for something of value, such as a coupon, a report, a discount, an online presentation, etc.

The possibilities for marketers to use QR codes are endless. For instance, retail stores can use them at the point of purchase display to drive traffic to a specific Web page to offer more information, product demonstrations, and customer reviews about a product. Businesses can use them to increase interaction on direct mail and postcards campaigns, by making specific, targeted offers on the landing page, once the QR code has been scanned with the smart phone. QR codes are spreading beyond most print advertisements, direct mail, and magazines, to billboards, magnetic car signs, table top displays and on the products themselves. These codes will be placed nearly everywhere.

An example of QR codes appearing on product labels is that of The Williamsburg Winery presented in Figure 9-3. The Williamsburg Winery recently created new labels for its line of *Winemaker's Blends.* These labels are complete with gold foil, an embossed logo, and a QR code. By scanning the QR code with a SmartPhone, the consumer will automatically be linked to a Web site featuring a 20-second video of winemaker, Matthew Meyer, describing the wine. It will be extremely beneficial for consumers to be able to know with what each blend of wine might be best served or paired when planning to serve wine with a meal.

The direct marketer can measure the success of the QR Code campaign with several metrics. Many QR Code creators can measure the number of times the QR code was scanned by a Smart-Phone or use Web tracking software, such as Google Analytics, to determine how many people

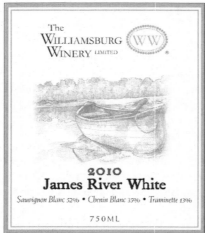

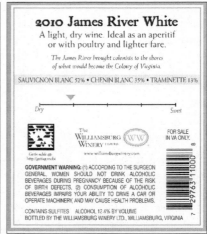

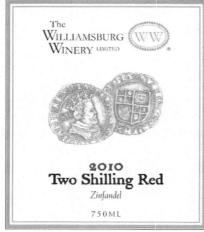

FIGURE 9-3.
Williamsburg
Winery Labels
Containing QR
Codes. Used with
permission of
The Williamsburg
Winery.

landed on a specific landing page. They can also compare how many people performed the requested action, such as opt-in to an e-mail list or purchase a product.

An example of this would be if the direct marketer mails 5,000 postcards, the postcards may have several ways for the prospect or customer to respond, such as calling a unique phone number, sending an e-mail, visiting a specific page on a Web site, or by scanning the QR code. The marketer can look at the number of responses from each of these response methods to determine the overall response rate, cost per response, and profitability of the campaign. Plus, the marketer can look at the response rate of each method to determine what the most popular way people are responding. In the future, you may see more campaigns that are just QR Code driven and will not have a multi-channel response approach to the campaign. QR codes are used to drive response and increase interaction of direct marketing campaigns in a variety ways.

QR codes may affect how consumers shop, check out and pay for products in supermarkets and other retail stores. A device that looks like a SmartPhone is being used in supermarkets and stores across the country. Perched on the handle of the shopping cart, the device scans grocery items as customers add them to their cart. Shoppers like it because it helps avoid an interminable wait in the checkout line. Retailers like it because the device encourages shoppers to buy more. The way to use QR Codes in marketing is limitless, because they are so easy to create and print, and because consumers like to use them.

Location-Based Mobile

Current mobile devices and software have allowed for the creation of location-based social networking Web sites, such as Yelp, FourSquare and WeReward. These can be referred to as **Location-based Mobile (LBM).** Many of these programs enable SmartPhone users to "check in" to a location, such as a business, and to see other friends' locations. For instance, one can use their SmartPhone to "check in" to a restaurant on Facebook Places, Yelp, FourSquare, and many others to share their location with friends. Some, such as Foursquare, employ a point system, awarding points and statuses to those who check into a location multiple times. There are also review and communication aspects to programs such as these. For instance, Yelp allows users to review businesses and share their experiences with others through rating the company and posting informative reviews.

Business owners can utilize this technology to their advantage and to drive traffic to their retail location. There are several benefits of doing this, including the following:

1. It will increase the exposure of the business via social media and within the application. Many of the apps have their own social networking aspect within them also, where people can friend each other and also see where their friends are geographically on their SmartPhones.

2. Loyalty/Frequency Programs—many of the apps allow the marketer to offer coupons. These coupons can be for first time visitors, repeat visitors, etc. This helps the business offer coupons to new customers or to repeat customers similar to loyalty cards or the physical punch cards, but they are digital and available through a SmartPhone.

3. Gather customer data such as demographic and behavioral. Many of these apps help the business profile their customers by offering data in reports such as the times when people check in, ZIP codes with direction requests to the business, how many coupons each customer has claimed, average age of each customer, male versus female, etc.

FourSquare is a leading geo-location network within the U.S. This app allows people to check in to the business, search for businesses within their geographic location, search for other friends within FourSquare who are close to them, redeem coupons, write reviews and most importantly, the app makes a game out of it for the users. This engages people's attention within Foursquare and makes it more interactive. One of the most compelling features is what is known as the "mayor" of the businesses. The person who checks in to a business the most times each quarter is given the title "Mayor." The mayor can receive special discounts, coupons, etc., that the business owner can offer the person for being the mayor.

WeReward is a newer app that is starting to become more popular. It is integrated with the customer's Facebook and Twitter accounts, so each check in goes viral on their wall. Plus, it integrates with m-commerce (mobile commerce shopping cart for cell phones) so people can make purchases directly on their SmartPhone. The unique aspect about WeReward is that it actually pays users to visit locations. The benefit to advertisers is that they only pay for actual clients.

Here is how it works. The advertiser requests that each user perform a particular task upon checking in to the business. If it were a restaurant it could be take a picture of you and your meal and submit it. The advertisers pay each person who takes the requested action. Moreover, the advertiser gets to approve each action taken on a customer-by-customer basis. So, the advertiser has complete control over which customers they want to pay. For example, the advertiser could choose to pay only the people who took quality photos. This is all based on a point system where 1 point = 1 penny. So the advertiser might pay a customer 200 points, or $2 to take a picture and upload it. The customer would get the $2 upon the business approving the photo and the customer's submission. The business would actually pay WeReward $4 for the successful action. Two dollars would go to the customer and two dollars would go to WeReward.

What does the business get in return for its investments?

1. All of the photos of all of the customers are put on the businesses page wall for others to see. The business actually owns the photos and can use them for other promotional materials.

2. Plus, once the customer has been paid, the business can e-mail him or do what is called a push notification. A push notification is a pop up message that comes over a person's SmartPhone that pops to the front any window.

3. Customer information: demographics, top customers, on what social media site the customer is sharing the photos, reviews and check-ins. Also performance metrics, such as rewards claimed, cost per reward, total reward cost, estimated average purchase, estimated total purchases, ROI, percent ROI.

Facebook Places is similar to Google Places except it has a social aspect to it. Facebook gives the advertisers many tools and will be introducing many new tools for local businesses to target customers and drive people to their businesses and Facebook local pages. Facebook gives the business owner an advertising platform, (see the digital media chapter) that is extremely targeted, enabling the business to grow a fan page or a Facebook Place page. Plus, soon Facebook will have a coupon style platform such as Groupon where people can purchase a coupon and then share it with a friend.

Companies can use these applications and Web sites as another way to track customers, gain feedback, and provide product offerings. The networking aspects of programs such as these include instant word of mouth regarding businesses. Many companies are taking advantage of these programs and providing special offers to customers who use them. These can be tailored to different customers, repeat customers, or first timers. This provides marketers with another form of segmentation. While location-based mobile continues to grow, direct marketers should adapt and increase their attention to this innovative segment of the mobile industry.

Mobile Application Development

An important topic with regard to mobile devices and the growth of SmartPhones is mobile applications. **Mobile Applications,** or mobile apps, are Internet software programs to run on handheld devices such as SmartPhones. Applications can serve a number of purposes, such as connecting a consumer to a Web site, or providing the software that enables people to perform an action on their device that they otherwise may not have been able to do. "Apps" can come in many different forms, with various programming and functions. Consumers can install apps onto their device in order to tailor it to their preferences.

Many businesses are creating applications. As the mobile industry booms, applications will continue to become an important aspect in any business's marketing plan. Applications provide a consumer with better accessibility to the business and ultimately, the product. As Oren Michels of Forbes.com states: "Apps allow businesses to leverage nearly infinite resources of information and services by satisfying one highly targeted need at a time. This avoids brand confusion and builds brand strength."[6]

Mobile Applications are very empowering to consumers. For example, Red Laser, a mobile application designed by Occipital, allows consumers with an iPhone or an Android to scan a barcode and instantly receive information about the product. This application allows a consumer, with a click of a button, to learn the price of an item, where it can be found and purchased, or even what ingredients are in a specific food. [7] This allows consumers to have access to even more information regarding specific products.

New mobile apps are being developed daily to fit consumers' desires for a carefree on-the-go lifestyle. For example, SWAGG™ is a free app that will manage offers and retail stores plastic gift cards and reward cards digitally. It lets consumers shop, send gifts, or check gift card balances simply and easily. Check out SWAGG.com and see for yourself what it can do to make your shopping easier. At the time of this writing legislation has been introduced to regulate tracking (Do Not Track) of mobile devices and major browser companies are implementing options for consumers to opt out of being tracked. Time will tell if it is passed and implemented and if it has the same impact as Do Not Call legislation has had on outbound calling.

Some mobile apps can help consumers live a healthier lifestyle. One such app is a food calorie counting app that minutes give you a caloric readout almost instantly after taking a picture of the meal with an iPhone. The app, called MealSnap, was developed by DailyBurn, a fitness social network that has created other fitness and diet-related apps for consumers. The way this app works is that it matches the pictured food items to a database of about 500,000 food items, and send the users an alert with a range of calories for the photographed meal.

In summary, there are many different types of mobile applications, and they are a growing part of the mobile industry. Direct marketers should understand the significance of the applications' ability to provide consumers with greater accessibility to information and should learn to utilize and leverage those in existence, or consider creating one.

Text Messaging

SMS Text Messaging

One of the newer forms of direct marketing is **SMS text messaging services**. SMS services allow the marketer to track open rates, manage lists, allow customers to opt in and opt out and do many of the same functions as e-mail companies. There are some differences in e-mail and SMS text messaging services, but keep in mind, whether it is Twitter, SMS texting, or other forms of instant messaging services they are all based on an e-mail type platform/system.

One of the biggest differences between e-mail marketing and text messaging is that with e-mail marketing, the average "open" rates for a house list are about 20 percent with a click-through rate of almost 7 percent, according to a survey conducted by the Direct Marketing Association.[8] Text message open rates vary depending on the source, but range anywhere from 90 percent to 98 percent.[9] Most people automatically check their mobile device when it chirps or beeps.

So how does a marketer use SMS texting to drive sales? There are several ways including the following:

1. Promote Special Events and Remind Customers about upcoming Events: A winery hosting a monthly wine tasting event can send a text message about the wine tasting to its clients an hour before the event. This can be a reminder that can get clients to visit the wine tasting. Another example is Barack Obama's 2008 presidential campaign sending text messages to promote campaign events to its supporters. Text messages such as the following were commonly used:

   > *Less than a week until Election Day on Nov. 4th! Barack needs your help.*
   > *REPLY to this msg with your 5 digit ZIP CODE for local Obama news and*
   > *voting information.*
   > —*Text message from Barack Obama, Oct. 30, 2008, 2:53 EST*[x]

2. Recoup Lost Sales. If a hairdresser has a client cancel an appointment, and the client was to get a perm in her hair, normally this dead time would now represent lost sales to the hairdresser. But with SMS texting, the hairdresser could send out a coupon to her clients letting them know she has a spot available. The coupon could be something to the effect of "*25% discount on a perm to the first 5 people who show up at the salon and show this text message.*" Depending on the size of her client list, this could actually get more people in store than just one person, which would result in additional revenue for the hairdresser, instead of having down time from a canceled appointment.

3. Coupons, Coupons, Coupons. This technique has to be used sparingly. SMS texting is still viewed by consumers as a means of personal communication, not a sales medium. So, the marketer has to be very careful, not to burn out the list and have clients unsubscribe. Any communication with clients has to be content driven and have value to the recipient or the marketer risks upsetting the clients and having them opt out of receiving the text messages from the marketer. If SMS texting is abused the marketer could lose the client totally.

4. Send People to a Specific Web page on a Web site. Most SmartPhones have Internet capabilities, so it is easy to send a text message to a customer with a link within the text message. This could be an opt in to a squeeze page that requests a name and an e-mail address that would then give the customer access to a coupon, Webinar, video, or some of form of content. It could requests customers to comment on a specific page of a Web site, etc. There are an infinite number of ways that marketers can use SMS text messages to engage customers and drive them to specific Web pages and content. As shown in Figure 9-4, the VIPER SmartStart phone app provides various messages that encourage prospective customers to visit its Web site to sign-up for the SmartStart services.

FIGURE 9-4. (left) VIPER SmartStart "go to" Webscreen message. Used with permission of DEI Holdings, Inc.

FIGURE 9-5. (right) VIPER SmartStart "tip" Webscreen message. Used with permission of DEI Holdings, Inc.

There are many other ways that SMS can be used, such as polling and voting through text messages, using giveaways to entice consumers, sharing a little humor, or providing tidbits of advice, such as the VIPER SmartStart tip provided in Figure 9-5. The methods of utilizing SMS have grown significantly, and may continue to change.

Finally, the other features that makes SMS texting direct response driven is most SMS texting services offer metrics to the marketers such as open rate, who opened, click through rate if there is a link in the message, opt out rate, who opted out, etc. Normally, the more expensive premium text messaging services offer these features to the marketer, which makes SMS texting a truly dynamic marketing platform.

In conclusion, SMS texting creates another way for marketers to interact with their clients and get them involved. It allows the business owner to drive sales, request e-mail addresses and remind clients of events. As SMS texting evolves, business owners and marketers will find more and more ways to engage and retain customers, initiate sales, and increase response at a very low price.

MMS

Multimedia Message Services (MMS) is very similar to SMS, but usually includes much more detail and elements. It may combine components such as text, images, audio, and even video to send to consumers. While SMS can be utilized by anyone who has a mobile phone capable of texting, MMS is used mainly with SmartPhones, or phones with cameras and colored screens. MMS can be used in similar ways to SMS. Coupons and promotions can be sent through MMS, as well as special event reminders. Also, MMS provides the capability to market directly to the segmented consumer with more flashy effects. Though MMS is fairly new compared to SMS, it is expected to grow as SmartPhones continue to become more popular.

How can businesses use MMS services to their advantage? With the ability to send multimedia driven messages, the possibilities far surpass regular SMS texting services and are limitless.

Imagine you are an artist and you are having a showing of your latest art at a local gallery. At the height of the show, you take a quick picture with your SmartPhone and MMS your list, with a quick audio that you record on your SmartPhone. The audio could sound something like this "I sure wish you could be here to join us. If you order from my Web site within the next hour, while the show is still going on, you will receive *Free Framing* as if you were here at my show." Then you would include a link to a landing page for the client to receive the *Free Framing* offer. This example would drive sales both online and at the gallery and it combines several different technologies, like MMS technology with online digital marketing technology. Moreover, it would not only give the artist's current clients a onetime offer, it would offer value to the client and provide social proof of the success of the show to clients, who are not at the show.

Another example would be a travel agent visiting different locations around the globe. He could use his SmartPhone to record a personal video message, while on location. He could talk about what he has done, places he has visited and then give a quick review about the destination. He could end the video with a link to his Web site, a call to action and a link to the offer page with something to the effect of: "If you book your travel package to Bermuda, by August 12th while I'm still visiting, I'll give you and your family an additional adventure of *Free Parasailing*." This allows the agent's clients to obtain a real-time review of the destination, follow him across the globe, and shows that the only reason the agent is offering this package is because the clients are virtually visiting the destination through the agent right now. Plus, the offer is automatically time sensitive, has a concrete deadline, and is only available while the agent is in Bermuda.

Response rates for both of these campaigns can be analyzed in several ways, such as:

1. The open rate of the MMS message.
2. The number of clicks on the link.
3. The number of people who purchased the offer.

These are just a examples of how a business can incorporate MMS texting into its marketing mix. The marketer can also provide incentives to clients or customers to share or forward the text message to friends and invite them to join. The marketer can then unleash the viral/word-of-mouth potential of the message. The opportunities to do so are endless and only limited by the imagination. The number of ways MMS can be used will only continue to grow as Smart-Phones become more of a commodity and the norm of the cell phone industry.

Telephone

The telephone occupies a dual position in direct marketing. Like print or broadcast media, it is a conduit for direct response marketing, and like mail or the Internet, it can carry the response itself. Thus, telephone marketing is both a marketing medium *and* a response mechanism. Telephone marketing is also referred to as teleservices or telemarketing. The objective of telephone marketing is to reach customers in a personalized interaction that meets customer needs and improves cost-effectiveness for the organization. Its scope is limited only by the imagination of the direct marketer, who can use it both for profit and nonprofit organizations as well as for individuals (such as political candidates), alone or with other marketing media, and targeted to both businesses (B2B) and final consumers (B2C). Compared to SMS and MMS, telephone communication is treated differently from regulatory points of view in terms of opt-in / opt-out, and the Do Not Call registry.

The telephone is an interactive medium, providing the flexibility and immediate response of a personal conversation. It can be especially effective when used in concert with other direct response media, such as direct mail or a Web site. Experienced direct marketers report that the phone can generate many times the response achieved by mail alone if it is used correctly and in tandem with other media. Because of the live person-to-person power of a phone call, its cost is high. When calculating telephone marketing costs, the direct marketer needs to consider not only the line (minimal these days) and hardware, but also the program design, creative development, and labor costs. The latter should include supervisory as well as clerical support costs. If the telephone is used as an alternative to a personal visit by a salesperson, as is often the case, it can be tremendously efficient.

Telephone marketing has been woven into the planning of most direct marketers. To those who know how to use them, the interactive features of the telephone are, in many cases, replacing the face-to-face contact of a salesperson's visit to a prospect or a buyer's visit to a retail location. The phone obviates the need for travel and makes it possible to talk *with* and not just *to* customers and prospects. Now, click-to-chat is replacing some of the person-to-person contact of the phone. The application of the telephone to direct marketing efforts is a powerful combination. Telephone selling is a form of personal selling, because it occurs on a person-to-person basis but without the face-to-face aspect. Businesses use telephone marketing with the sole purpose of receiving results. [10] Let's take a closer look at the two basic ways direct marketers use the telephone.

Inbound versus Outbound Calls

Telephone marketing applications may be categorized as **inbound calls,** when customers are calling to place an order, to request more information, or for customer service. Customer calls responding to DRTV or radio, service center calls, advertising responses, calls to catalog centers, after-hours sales calls, and dealer locator services requests are examples of typical inbound calls. The second category encompasses **outbound calls.** Here, organizations place calls to customers to make a sale or to offer information hoping for a later sale. These calls often deal with lead generation, appointment setting, market research fund raising, political calling, database verification, database appending, and of course sales. Outbound calls have become extremely regulated due to the national Do Not Call Registry and regulations. More will be discussed about this topic in Chapter 12. Let's discuss each application in greater detail.

INBOUND CALLS. Inbound calls are also referred to as **reactive telephone marketing** in that the initiator of the marketing communications is the customer. The customer places that call at his or her convenience to obtain information or to place an order, often using a toll-free number provided by the organization. The Federal Communications Commission has designated not only 800 numbers as *toll-free* but also the area codes 888, 877, 866 and 855.

The recent surge of the Web and Internet marketing strategies has also increased the number of inbound calls to marketers. Consumers have used the Internet to search for product or service information, and then have turned to the telephone to place orders for products and services that were presented in a company's Web site.

Toll-free telephone service has itself been a tremendous incentive to the use of inbound phone calls to respond to offers or transact an order. The marketer's direct response advertising in other media must provide incentives to encourage consumers to place inbound calls. Many of these ads point out the convenience of having a telephone order taker on hand 24 hours a day to answer questions and ensure faster deliveries or services.

The applications of inbound telephone marketing generally include: ordering or inquiring; clarifying or requesting assistance; responding immediately to an advertisement; expediting processing; locating a dealer or a product servicing location; making reservations for travel accommodations, hotel rooms, or conferences; obtaining financial data, stock prices, yields, making pledges or contributions; and obtaining warranty information.

OUTBOUND CALLS. Outbound calls are also referred to as **proactive telephone marketing** because the company is the initiator of the marketing communications. Outbound calls are generally longer in duration and require more experienced and higher-paid personnel.

The large outbound telemarketers are using T1 service. **T1** designates bandwidth and denotes a giant pipeline or conduit through which a user may send multiple voice, data, and even video signals. It supports simultaneous voice/Internet connectivity, enabling telephone sales reps (or telereps) to speak to customers while also participating in their Internet session. Instead of simply carrying one voice conversation at a time, a T1 can carry almost 100 conversations or data connections simultaneously.

Although well-prepared scripts and well-structured offers can make telephone promotion highly effective, the medium is usually most efficient if calls are directed to persons who have been prequalified in some way. These are sometimes called handraisers or leads. The reason is that the cost of an individual phone call is expensive. Therefore, when telephone marketers properly segment the market (according to a wide variety of segmentation variables) and prequalify prospects, the length of the call may be reduced and the number of positive consumer responses may be increased.

Prequalified outbound calls might include response to an inquiry, a new product offer to an existing customer, or generation of responses/transactions from a carefully selected list. **Cold**

calls (which are calls made when there is no existing relationship with, or recognition of, the direct marketer) must be carefully structured in content because, by their very nature, they usually interrupt some other activity of the person being called and can create a negative response.

Direct marketers use the telephone for a great variety of outbound call applications, including the following: generating new sales, including reorders and new product introductions; generating leads and qualifying inquiries for personal sales follow-up; serving present accounts; reactivating old customers; validating the legitimacy of orders before shipping; responding to customer service needs, including responding to complaints; surveying customers, members, donors, voters, etc.; substituting for a personal sales call. In summary, outbound calls have the ability to generate great profit when executed properly. Let's explore the advantages and disadvantages associated with telephone marketing.

Advantages and Disadvantages of Telephone

Some of the specific advantages of using the telephone as a marketing medium include the following.

- It provides *two-way communication* and *immediate feedback*. This quick feedback, often in response to a test campaign, can be of great assistance to the direct marketer in making any needed changes before the entire marketing campaign is executed.

- It is a *very flexible medium*. Although a telerep may use a prepared script, this doesn't limit the number of changes you can make to that script as needed. You may also change the message for each caller.

- It is a *productive medium*. The telephone is actually more productive than traditional personal selling when you consider the sheer number of sales calls that a rep can make by phone on a daily or weekly basis.

- Telephone marketing is a *cost-effective medium*. Although the exact costs vary depending on the type of call being placed, the average cost per call is far lower for telephone selling than for traditional personal selling.

Some of the distinct disadvantages of telephone marketing include the following.

- It is by far the most *intrusive marketing medium* used by direct marketers. Telephone marketing has a poor image among people who dislike the intrusion of marketers' outbound calling.

- Telephone marketing *lacks visual enhancement*. It is not a visual medium, and thus its power is often related to being integrated with other media.

- Telephone marketing *does not provide a permanent tangible response device*. Once again, it must be coupled with other media to provide a physical form for the customer to sign or a brochure to keep on hand to be reviewed at a later time.

Most direct marketers have concluded that although telephone marketing has its share of disadvantages, it can be a highly effective medium when properly planned and executed.

Planning a Telephone Marketing Program

To be successful in telephone marketing, telephone operators must convey a trustworthy, reliable image to the customer. Companies must train their operators to develop these skills and provide them with well-conceived scripts.

PREPARING THE TELEPHONE SCRIPTS. A **telephone script** is a call guide to assist the operator in communicating effectively with the prospect or customer. Most do not have to be read word for word; in fact, the most effective scripts are more like a detailed outline that provides structure to the conversation. Each outbound telephone call aims to deliver a sales presentation to the potential customer or client. The purpose of each inbound call is to deliver information to the customer or receive the customer's order information. Thus, different types of scripts are needed for different types of telemarketing calls. In either case, developing scripts offers the dual challenge of determining the right words to gain a favorable customer response or impression and, at the same time, minimizing the length and the cost of a call. Writing a telephone script is both an art and a science. One valuable asset of a script is the flexibility it provides, allowing the telereps to change or experiment. While most marketing media call for copy to be finalized by a certain date, scripts can be revised after a few or a few dozen calls.

TRAINING TELEPHONE OPERATORS. Many people might think that the best way to develop an effective telephone operator is to take someone with field sales experience and transfer that sales knowledge to the phone. However, in reality, this rarely works. One of the reasons field salespeople often do not make good operators is that they are accustomed to face-to-face inter-action with their customers and dislike working behind a desk. These work qualities are the exact opposite of the requirements of a telephone marketing representative.

When hiring a telephone operator, companies normally look for the following six character-istics: (1) call center experience, (2) good interpersonal skills, (3) computer literacy, (4) reliabil-ity, (5) problem-solving skills, and (6) good organizational skills:[11] Finding and retaining good telephone operators is a constant challenge for telephone marketers. In addition to high turnover rates, there has been a shrinking employment pool for this industry. Compensation for operators varies depending on such variables as industry sector, product prices, and the com-plexity of the sale.

Summary

In this chapter we examined many concepts, strategies and applications associated with market-ing via mobile, text and telephone. The mobile industry is undergoing significant growth and evolution and, so is mobile marketing. Direct marketers must recognize and respond to this mobile movement if they are to take advantage of the new opportunities presented by the mobile, text and telephone formats. These new media formats must be integrated into each mar-keter's marketing mix.

Text messaging is also used for a variety of marketing purposes and its use is rapidly grow-ing. The chapter provided an overview of both MMS and SMS text messaging as well as an overview of their similarities and differences. Telephone rounds out the chapter as it remains an important medium to be used, especially for business-to-business. The uses of both inbound and outbound call for telephone marketing are examined. As explained in the chapter, telephone marketing programs require planning and training to be executed in both a timely and cost effective manner.

Key Terms

call metrics
prerecorded messages
quick response codes
location-based mobile (LBM)
mobile applications (apps)
SMS text messaging

inbound calls
outbound calls
T1
cold calls
telephone script

Review Questions

1. Compare and contrast mobile search directories with traditional directories such as the Yellow Pages?

2. What are the five steps to creating a strong mobile coupon program?

3. Define Click-to-call and explain how consumers may use it in the marketplace.

4. Name and explain the many opportunities QR codes offer marketers. Explain what opportunities QR codes offer consumers.

5. How can business owners utilize Location Based Mobile (LBM) to drive traffic to their retail locations? What are the key benefits of doing this?

6. Identify and explain some of the ways a marketer uses SMS texting to drive sales?

7. Compare and contrast SMS and MMS texting from a marketers perspective. Why would a company use both types of text messaging?

8. How are response rates for SMS and MMS campaigns analyzed?

9. Explain the role of telephone marketing in today's highly digital and social world.

10. What are some of the most common products or services featured in infomercials. Do you think infomercials are effective? Why or why not?

Exercise

Visit a mobile phone store and investigate all of the new features of the various brands of mobile devices, including the SmartPhone and Blackberry. Compare and contrast the various brands and each of their capabilities.

Critical Thinking Exercise

QR Codes affect how consumers shop and pay for items in retail stores today. What will tomorrow bring in terms of new digital techniques? Will QR codes be replaced one day with some newer codes and even better technology? What more will the QR code or some code similar to it be able to do to assist consumers in their daily lives five years from now?

CASE: VIPER: SmartStart

Let's talk about how a mobile SmartPhone app boosted sales big-time and revitalized a long-standing brand.

VIPER® has been the undisputed heavyweight world champion of car alarms for more than 20 years. Its nearest competitor, Clifford, went bankrupt and out of business more than ten years ago and its assets were acquired by VIPER. As VIPER's tagline accurately states: NO ONE DARES COME CLOSE.®

But the car-alarm business has plateaued for many years. While still highly profitable for retailers and perceived as necessary by millions of consumers, auto theft has been trending down for some time and the category deteriorated from a "must have" to a commodity that lacks sex appeal.

In the past, VIPER car alarms and remote starters appealed to a very broad cross-section of the population. This was one of the key success drivers for the brand. Young people were over-

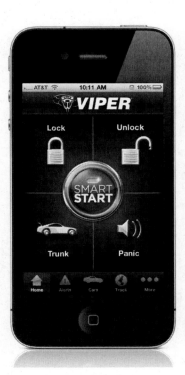

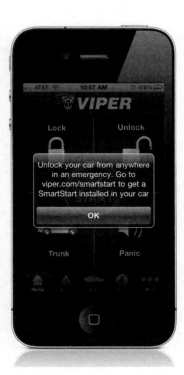

FIGURE 9-6. (left) VIPER SmartStart on a SmartPhone. Used with permission of DEI Holdings, Inc.

FIGURE 9-7. (right) VIPER SmartStart unlock screen. Used with permission of DEI Holdings, Inc.

represented only because they were more aware of the threat of car theft and content theft and more vulnerable. But young and old bought car alarms—and of course anyone in the cold weather regions is a viable target for a remote start purchase in the winter.

However, just as cellular phones were energized by the explosive functionality of the iPhone and other SmartPhones, VIPER has been re-energized by a very compelling SmartPhone app—along with integrated hardware for the car—called VIPER SmartStart.

Spearheaded by Directed Electronics Executive VP Mike Simmons, VIPER SmartStart debuted on October 12, 2009 with an article in USA TODAY, followed by more than 100 broadcast news stories. VIPER SmartStart instantly captured the imagination of the public, because it was the first app that let users start their car from virtually anywhere with their SmartPhone. (Figure 9-6.)

Within hours, Conan O'Brien and Jimmy Fallon mentioned the product in their late-night monologues. It wasn't long before Apple showcased it in their iPhone advertising, including a full page ad in *Time* and *The Wall Street Journal*, followed by a 30-second TV commercial—free advertising for VIPER that reached nearly half a billion viewers!

The product won the coveted "Best of Innovations" Award at the Consumer Electronics Show in 2010 and has continued to evolve since then, adding features as it expanded platforms, first to BlackBerry and then to the popular Android SmartPhones. The free VIPER SmartStart app is now on close to one million SmartPhones, and it's not slowing down.

However, for VIPER and parent company Directed Electronics, the good news is that VIPER SmartStart is not "just" a free app. The full-featured system, made available to paying customers, includes hardware for the car that enables drivers to lock/unlock, arm/disarm, and start their car remotely. (See Figure 9-7.) This hardware (and installation) is sold at thousands of VIPER retailers across the country, from local aftermarket shops to national retailer Best Buy, and integrates with existing VIPER car alarm and remote start systems.

FIGURE 9-8.
VIPER SmartStart
ads. Used with
permission of DEI
Holdings, Inc.

VIPER Advertising Then and Now

VIPER has a history rooted in memorable advertising. From the company's perspective, the number one driver of growth was an award winning TV commercial that ran for more than a decade. In "The Lady, the Thief and the Snake," a classy lady parks her Lexus and arms her car alarm—and we hear the voice of Directed Electronics founder (now Congressman) Darrell Issa say "VIPER Armed." A would-be thief sneaks up on the car, but is frightened away by a VIPER snake inside the vehicle. As the terrified thief scurries away, the woman returns to disarm her alarm. Many people still remember this commercial though it hasn't aired in years.

Today VIPER SmartStart advertises in the app itself. (See Figure 9-8 for some typical VIPER advertisements.) The company also buys mobile SmartPhone advertising from Google's AdMob, and on The Weather Channel (in select cold-weather markets, using "weather triggered" ads that only launch below a threshold temperature). Not to mention a growing presence on Facebook, Twitter, and YouTube. The company is leveraging new social media opportunities to reach its target demographic and spending less money on traditional advertising.

In other words, the "old media" VIPER systems (formerly advertised in the Yellow Pages, and in car audio magazines that have since gone out of business) have gotten a huge infusion of energy and excitement from "new media" VIPER SmartStart, including social networking integration—because your car needs friends too!

Results have been impressive. VIPER SmartStart also launched a GPS product allowing users to know exactly where their car is at all times on their SmartPhone—along with home control features that allow users to arm and disarm their home alarm from the VIPER app. As shown in Figure 9-9, other VIPER app innovations include shared location and roadside assistance features.

Even though VIPER SmartStart is a new product on a new platform (a SmartPhone app),

FIGURE 9-9.
VIPER SmartStart
shared location
& roadside
assistance screens.
Used with
permission of DEI
Holdings, Inc.

the company is still seeing a wide range of customers for the product, because of the broad appeal of SmartPhones, which again bodes well for the future. The core price point for a VIPER SmartStart remote start-only system begins at just $299, which is not perceived as a significant barrier to entry.

VIPER Line Extensions

For most marketers, line extensions that complement and support sales of the original product are the holy grail. VIPER has also benefited in this way, from VIPER SmartStart, then from the new VIPER SmartStart GPS, new "home control" features in the VIPER app—and now VIPER Window Film, another related product that offers synergies of:

- seasonality (summer for window tint vs. winter for remote start)
- customer acceptance (60 percent of VIPER dealers are already in the tint business)
- product category (VIPER offers a Security Film that strengthens the glass)
- technology (VIPER Window Film is non-metallic, so it doesn't interfere with radio frequency (RF) signals including the cellular signals used by VIPER SmartStart).

Even Directed's car audio brand, Orion, is part of the line extension roadmap—because when consumers enhance their ride with expensive aftermarket gear, they'd better invest in a VIPER alarm to protect it!

How did VIPER SmartStart become such an overnight success? What were the stages it undertook to move consumer from awareness to interest to desire to action? Moreover, how did the SmartStart mobile app leap so quickly from arousing consumer curiosity to achieving millions of dollars in sales revenue?

From Curiosity to Conversion: How VIPER SmartStart Leverages Mobile Technology to Generate New Customers

Let's detail the step-by-step process that enabled VIPER SmartStart to become a success.

Step 1: A free app with attractive features like SmartPark (pinpoints where your car is parked) generates awareness, intrigue and trial. VIPER continues to take advantage of all the publicity surrounding the free app, as well as consumer interest in SmartPhone apps in general to manage day-to-day activities. The synergies of the Apple TV commercial, targeted marketing efforts and a boatload of free publicity put the free app in front of millions of prospects

Step 2: Communicating in-app with the one-million plus users who have so far downloaded the free app identifies sales prospects. The company continually enhances the free features of the app, such as SmartPark.

Step 3: Offering information and incentives aids sales conversion, by inviting prospects to join the satisfied users who have the product on their cars and are enjoying the VIPER SmartStart connected lifestyle. By carefully engineering cost out of the product (both hardware and data)—and shifting some up-front costs to service plan revenue, the company reduces sticker shock and entices more users down the purchase funnel.

The long-term strategy for VIPER SmartStart is to continuously improve the value proposition both for free app users and active users—to keep generating interest from new prospects and increasing purchase conversion.

Conclusion . . . The Future

The long-term vision? Key replacement. People want their multi-functional SmartPhone with them at all times—but they don't want to carry that heavy bundle of keys. (See Figure 9-10.)

Phase one of the key replacement strategy is already in place: using the SmartPhone to unlock and start the car—and using the SmartPhone to arm and disarm the home alarm. Is it

FIGURE 9-10.
VIPER SmartStart
Future: Key
Replacement Used
with permission of
DEI Holdings, Inc.

too much to expect additional hardware to soon be created and made available to enable the SmartPhone to take the place of your bundle of keys? Stay tuned for the future.

Case Discussion Questions

1. Evaluate the car-alarm business in the United Sates. What are the characteristics of the market for car alarms, including the market size and growth? Do you think the car-alarm business has plateaued in recent years? Why? Justify your answer.

2. Conduct a SWOT analysis for VIPER®. What are the company's strengths and weaknesses? Who are the major competitors? What are their strengths and weaknesses? What are VIPER®'s competitive advantage(s) vis-à-vis other competitors?

3. Given your SWOT analysis in the above, identify key growth strategies that VIPER® may pursue in the foreseeable future. Hint: you can look into "security" as a growth theme. Likewise, you may examine "vehicle"—including automobiles—as a direction for growth.

4. VIPER® is leveraging social media to reach its target audience and to connect with the online community of visitors and fans. As such, it has a growing presence on Facebook, Twitter, and YouTube. What other social networking sites do you recommend?

Notes

1. Michael E. Toner, "The Impact of Federal Election Laws on the 2008 Presidential Campaign," in *The Year of Obama: How Barack Obama Won the White House,* ed. Larry J. Sabato (New York: Pearson Education, 2010), 149-152.

2. Rahaf Harfoush, *Yes We Did: An Inside Look at How Social Media Built the Obama Brand,* Berkley, CA: New Riders, 119.

3. "Mobile Shaping Purchases: News from Warc.com." *Warc—Ideas and Evidence for Marketing People | Warc.com.* 28 Apr. 2011. Web. 22 May 2011. <http://www.warc.com/LatestNews/News/E-mailNews.news?ID=28212>.

4. Wachs, David. "Five Steps to a Strong Mobile Coupon Program—Mobile Marketer—Columns."*Mobile Marketer—The News Leader in Mobile Marketing, Media and Commerce.* 4 Mar. 2011. Web. 23 May 2011. <http://www.mobilemarketer.com/cms/opinion/columns/9265.html>.

5. Breta, Brodie. "Mobio Reports QR Code Use Has Exploded by 1200 Percent—TNW Industry."*The Next Web—International Source for Internet News, Business and Culture.* 2 Sept. 2010. Web. 23 May 2011. <http://thenextWeb.com/industry/2011/02/09/mobio-reports-qr-code-use-has-exploded-by-1200-percent/>.

6. Michels, Oren. "Why Businesses Need Mobile Apps—Forbes.com." *Information for the World's Business Leaders—Forbes.com.* 8 Sept. 2010. Web. 23 May 2011. <http://www.forbes.com/2010/09/08/mobile-apps-Internet-technology-mashery.html>.

7. *RedLaser—Impossibly Accurate Barcode Scanning.* 2011. Web. 23 May 2011. <http://redlaser.com/>.

8. http://www.dmnews.com/marketing-e-mails-see-open-rate-of-nearly-20-says-dma-survey/article/172573/, retrieved May 20, 2011.

9. Opt It Founders on RSS Ray—Mobile Marketing Extravaganza, May 2, 2011 by Jessica Zorawski, https://www.optit.com/blog/page/2/, retrieved May 20, 2011.

10. Rahaf Harfoush, *Yes We Did: An Inside Look at How Social Media Built the Obama Brand,* Berkley, CA: New Riders, 119.

11. Telemarketing Consultant.com, *TCs' Telemarketing Outsourcing Tips,* retrieved on May 8, 2008, from http://www.telemarketingconsultant.com/Telemarketing%20Tips.html.

12. Adapted from Steve Jarvis, "Call Centers Raise Bar on Hiring Criteria," *Marketing News* 34, no. 19 (September 11, 2000); adapted from Stone, *Successful Direct Marketing Methods,* p. 147.

Utilizing Current Digital and Social Media

OPENING VIGNETTE: THE NATIONAL GEOGRAPHIC SOCIETY: *RESTREPO* MOVIE

In 2010, The National Geographic Society (NGS) launched a series of e-mail marketing campaigns to support its feature documentary *Restrepo*. *Restrepo* is a film that chronicles the deployment of a platoon of U.S. soldiers in Afghanistan's Korengal Valley. The Restrepo *documentary* was directed by American journalist Sebastian Junger and the late British/American photojournalist Tim Hetherington. (See Figure 10-1.)

Since the NGS didn't have a large budget to promote the documentary, it relied on "grassroots appeals" to generate awareness and boost in-theater attendance. First, The NGS implemented an e-mail campaign to current NGS members. The e-mails incorporated the comments of Facebook users who saw the film and posted messages on its fan page shown in Figure 10-2.

In its second e-mail campaign, The NGS brilliantly incorporated a Facebook "like" button in its e-mail campaign to encourage consumers to discuss the film on the social networks. The Facebook "like" button allowed consumers to virtually support the film directly from the e-mail, as opposed to driving recipients to the fan page. The NGS microsite for *Restrepo* encouraged consumers to sign-up for newsletters from the company, contact their local theaters to book the film, or buy tickets to see the film. The page also urged consumers to follow the film on Twitter or become a friend of the film on Facebook. The campaign strived to draw attention to the Facebook page of the movie, which now had attained a very engaged fan base.

The NGS strategically employed geographic targeting in a third e-mail campaign. As the

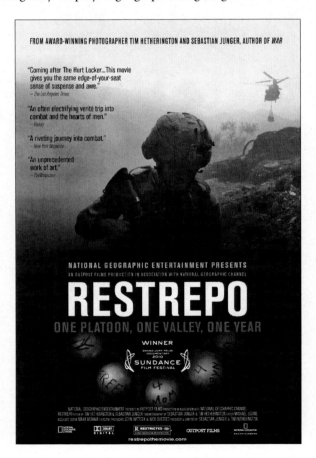

FIGURE 10-1. *Restrepo* movie poster. Used with permission of National Geographic Society.

FIGURE 10-2.
Restrepo
Facebook page.
Used with
permission of
National
Geographic
Society.

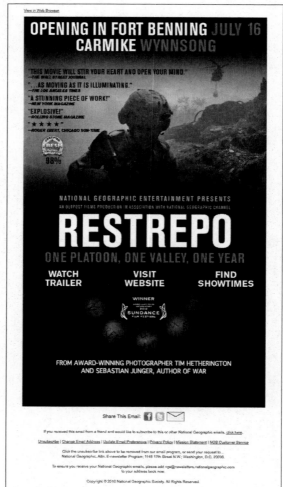

FIGURE 10-3.
Restrepo geo-
targeted e-mail.
Used with
permission of
National
Geographic
Society.

Restrepo movie opened up in different theaters around the nation, NGS sent e-mails to its members who had opted in to receive notice about its entertainment offerings. Using data from its marketing database, NGS was able to match e-mail addresses to member ZIP code areas. With this information, NGS segmented its entertainment list to create geo-based clusters around theaters where *Restrepo* was going to show. When the members received the e-mail, an example of which is shown in Figure 10-3, it told them where and when they could see *Restrepo*. The e-mail also had links to encourage people to watch the trailer, visit the *Restrepo* Web site and find show times. The very bottom of the e-mail featured the share options for Facebook, Twitter and forward to a friend. NGS implemented many of these customized geo-targeted e-mail campaigns. Using dynamic content techniques, NGS was able to basically design one e-mail, but code the e-mail to accept custom headlines naming the respective theater locations and dates, along with custom links. The main benefits of using dynamic content is that it allowed NGS to reduce the work involved in executing the e-mail campaign, and more importantly, it allowed the recipient to receive a customized, relevant message.

To measure the e-mail campaigns, The NGS analyzed click-through rates and monitored the number of consumers who became a fan on Facebook. The series of e-mail campaigns were a smashing success! The grass-roots participation of the *Restrepo* Facebook community was credited for successful ticket sales ($1.3 million to-date) and even for having theaters agree to show the film. The Facebook e-mail campaign resulted in a 40 percent open rate that translated to a lift in the "Daily New Fans" of 11 percent. The campaign also garnered an increase of 33 percent in 'Total Interactions' on a week-to-week basis. Also, the campaigns generated a ton of buzz for the film, which honors a true American hero, Juan "Doc" Restrepo, a medic who was killed in action during his deployment to Afghanistan. The buzz continued when the *Restrepo* Director, Tim Hetherington, was killed in the besieged city of Misurata, Libya on April 20, 2011.

Introduction

The digital and social media industry is evolving and growing at a rapid pace. Marketers must embrace this digital and social media revolution or they will forgo the most powerful, dynamic, personal, and cost-effective marketing force ever to emerge. This chapter will examine the concepts, strategies, tactics, platforms and capabilities associated with marketing via digital and social media. However, a word of caution is in order. Digital and social media techniques and capabilities are dynamic and continuously evolving at warp speed. You must keep abreast of the changes if you are to truly harness the power of digital and social marketing. Beware...the speed of change can be mind-boggling!

Growth and Transition

Direct marketers must not only keep up with the changes, but also be able to utilize digital and social media, as they become vital in marketing plans. More than three-fourths of individuals residing in the United States have access to the Internet[1], and the Internet is a key way to reach consumers. Approximately 85 percent of adults age 33 or younger currently use social network sites and use among older generations is on the rise.[2] Currently, 78 percent of adult Internet users visit a social media site for at least one hour per week; of those aged 18-34, 88 percent spend more than one hour, while 34 percent spent at least six hours per week.[3] These numbers are expected to continue to grow in the next few years.

The Internet also has enjoyed the fastest growth and acceptance rates of all other media. Consider the time it has taken these technologies to reach 50 million users: telephone—40 years; radio—38 years; cable television—10 years; the Internet—5 years.[4] However, Facebook's growth has been phenomenal as it added 100 million users in less than 9 months.[5]

The Internet is an interactive marketing medium for direct marketers offering information access and two-way communication with customers in real time via the computer. Interactivity is what makes marketing on the Internet different from other forms of direct marketing media. According to the Direct Marketing Association (DMA), to be considered "interactive," a new medium must meet the following three criteria:[6]

1. Consumers must be able to control when they view the products and which types of products they are viewing.

2. Consumers must be able to control the pace at which they review products. They must be able to review the product content at their leisure, reading the product literature at a pace that is convenient to them, rather than being forced to progress to the next product.

3. Consumers must be able to place an order or request additional information directly via the medium rather than having to order through another method.

The Internet began as a high-tech tool for facilitating communication between scientists and was developed under the sponsorship of the U.S. Defense Department's Advanced Research Projects Agency (DARPA). In 1969, the network, then called DARPAnet, became a reality when two nodes were linked together. By 1989, the National Science Foundation had replaced the Defense Department as the chief source of support for the network of networks, renamed NSFnet. Originally intended to facilitate research and communication within the scientific community, today the Internet has grown to include social networks and users across a wide variety of backgrounds and interests. The first widespread interest in the Internet as a vehicle for commerce occurred in 1993 when the first Web browser, Mosaic, was released and became freely accessible to the public.

Companies use the Internet to provide customer service, share information, sell goods and services, and build and strengthen customer relationships. However, most companies have established a Web site with the primary purpose of disseminating product/service information. Visit the Web site of the City of Virginia Beach Convention & Visitors Bureau featured in Figure 10-4 to experience a well-organized and easy-to-navigate Web site.

In terms of functionality, Web sites are classified as informational and transactional. Providing customer support and service straddles the two, depending on the situation. Three primary marketing activities are well suited to the Web. They include:[7]

• making information available to prospective customers,

• providing customer support and service, and

• enabling transactions to occur.

Direct marketers have been performing these activities for decades without the Internet, but now due to technological advances, they are able to transfer their knowledge and experience to this powerful interactive marketing medium. It is also very clear to many companies that merely having a Web presence is not enough. What it takes to succeed in this electronic marketplace is a clear plan for the organization to follow and execute, along with a strong commitment of both human resources and capital for the technological infrastructure to support the various online applications and digital marketing activities. Let's examine the various applications to be utilized in digital and social media marketing.

FIGURE 10-4.
Virginia Beach
Web site home
page. Used with
permission of the
City of Virginia
Beach Convention
& Visitors Bureau.

Applications

E-mail Marketing

E-mail is a part of the Internet that is separate from the Web. It is electronic communication that travels all over the world via the Internet. E-mail is an extremely successful and effective means of retaining current customers. According to the DMA 's 2010 Response Rate Trend Report, e-mail to a house list averaged a 19.47 percent open rate; a 6.64 percent click-through rate; a 1.73 percent conversion rate; with a bounce-back rate of 3.72 percent and an unsubscribe rate of 0.77 percent.[8]

Now let's analyze these numbers. With a 19.47 percent open rate to a house list this is almost one out of every five people opening the e-mail. A 6.64 percent click-through rate is the equivalent of someone actually reading an entire direct mail letter and then either calling a toll free number, visiting a Web site or sending in a response form for requesting more information.

Finally, a conversion rate of 1.73, when compared to a direct mail letter, is equivalent to a customer calling a number and ordering the product or service, placing an order on online, or mailing in an order form with a check or credit card number. In conclusion, all of these numbers are very good response rates and are comparable to some of the highest numbers in direct response. Now these statistics are averages across many industries, so it is important for direct marketers to test and measure the response rates for their own industry and for their own house list.

Some of the methods marketers can use e-mail to grow their business, generate sales and retain customers include:

1. Staying in touch with current customers.
2. Sending an e-mail newsletter.
3. Announcing a new product or service.
4. Sending an affiliate promotion.
5. Promoting a sale or event.
6. Targeting specific promotions for loyalty programs.
7. Announcing new content, such as a blog post, mp3 audio, or video on a company Web site.

Auto responders are e-mails that are automatically sent, when triggered by some variable or some event. They enable the marketer to create and set it up and then forget about it. These can be triggered by all kinds of events, such as the purchase of a new product, opt-ing in to a new list, registering for a Webinar, or pretty much any other thing the marketer wants to use them.

Here is typical scenario of how a marketer can use auto responders:

1. Consumers opt-in to a new list.
2. They are immediately sent an auto responder welcoming them and offering them the promised item.
3. Two days later, each person receives a second e-mail with additional content linked to a teaser video.
4. The third day these consumers receive a third e-mail with a link to a third video. This video may be a sales presentation asking for the sale.

Marketers can use auto responders to increase sales, build rapport for a product and provide information the person perceives as valuable. Most e-mail providers offer auto responders as part of their packages and services. As far as measuring response rates, most e-mail providers can do this. Typical metrics that can be measured include deliverability rate, open rate, click-through rate, bounce rate, and the unsubscribe rate.

There are three basic types of e-mail of interest to marketers:

1. E-mail from companies targeting promotions to specific customers. This method is most effective when it is database-driven and customized to match the needs of specific market segments of customers. This includes both B2B and B2C e-mail.
2. E-mail from the consumer to the company. This is often used for placing an inquiry or a request for additional information.
3. E-mail from the consumer to another consumer. This is the electronic version of word of mouth. This form of e-mail has also been referred to as **viral marketing** where e-mail messages are forwarded to other consumers by a consumer. In fact, the term **viralocity**

FIGURE 10-5.
Peninsula SPCA
e-newsletter.
Used with
permission of
Peninsula
Society for the
Prevention of
Cruelty to
Animals.

has been coined to measure both the number of messages and the rate of speed by which e-mail messages are forwarded by a consumer to other consumers. Research reports that about 89 percent of adult Internet users in the U.S. send content to others, with 63 percent doing so at least once a week and 25 percent share content nearly daily.[9]

E-mail is similar to traditional direct mail in that it is conducted on a one-to-one, personal basis. However, e-mail costs a lot less than traditional mail and therefore enables companies to communicate on a more frequent basis and creates a tendency to spam. In addition, consumers respond more quickly to e-mail than to direct mail, with replies normally coming from consumers within hours from the time they received the message. Likewise, this sets consumer expectations to receive responses from companies, when consumers send e-mail requests or inquiries. Consumer response for an average direct mail campaign may take weeks.

E-mail direct marketing is most productive when companies use their own customer lists instead of lists generated by third parties. Many companies have developed an e-mail list of their customers and send e-newsletters and other communication on a regular basis. For example, Figure 10-5 shows an e-newsletter that was used by the Peninsula SPCA to communicate with its "friends" and update them about recent SPCA accomplishments and request continued support. E-mail allows companies to send tailored and personalized messages to specific customers based on needs. This is both highly effective and efficient for direct and interactive marketers.

Because sending e-mail messages is easy, cheap, and fast, some companies have misused this medium. **Spam** is the term for unsolicited e-mail messages. Spam is considered the junk mail of the Internet. Direct marketers can avoid sending spam by handling customer information carefully and adhering to ethical e-mail marketing practices. Providing a way for consumers to opt in to a mailing list is a starting point for practicing ethical e-mail marketing. Direct marketers must follow the established laws and should follow DMA guidelines for using e-mail. There are many rules that marketers should follow when creating and conducting e-mail marketing. However,

FIGURE 10-6. U.S. Navy Web page.

when done right, an e-mail campaign can build profitable customer relationships at a fraction of the cost of other direct marketing methods. Creating customized e-mail marketing programs are most effective when combined with other digital media.

Let's take a look at an excellent direct and interactive marketing campaign that combined e-mail with banner ads and a customized Web site to produce impressive results. The U.S. Department of the Navy recently used a 100 percent digital direct marketing campaign to change perceptions of the role of women in the U.S. Navy. An outbound e-mail campaign targeting women aged 18 to 24 who were not attending a four-year college explained the benefits of joining the Navy, including training and money for college. Banner ads showed women in this age group in common jobs, and then showed them in a navy uniform doing exciting and important jobs like diving or fixing planes. As shown in Figure 10-6, on its Web site, Navy.com, a customized "just for women" community showcased opportunities for women in the Navy. The combined digital campaign was extremely successful with leads exceeding goals by 400 percent in 90 days, and the digital campaign increasing overall recruitment leads by 15.25 percent.

In conclusion, e-mail offers the direct marketer an inexpensive way to grow a business, generate sales and retain customers. It can be even more effective if the marketing company has a thorough understanding of its customers, based on market research. Let's discuss how this works.

Online Market Research

Primary data collection has also been enhanced by technological progress. Consumers seem to be more receptive to participating in surveys conducted via the Internet as opposed to mail and phone surveys. Thus, the Internet offers an alternative medium for executing marketing research studies on a one-to-one basis with customers. Some of the more common primary data collection techniques being implemented online include online surveys and online panels.

ONLINE SURVEYS. Online survey research is carried out by either sending electronic questionnaires to customers via individual e-mails or by posting a survey on a company's Web site. Sending questions via e-mail allows for personalization and control over the timing and distribution of the survey. E-mail surveys are also the preferred method of data collection in countries where users must pay by the hour for Internet connection because e-mail may be answered offline, whereas a respondent must be online to complete a survey on the Web.

However, Web surveys can be written in a more user-friendly fashion than e-mail, with reply buttons, drop-down menus, and blank spaces for each customer to record responses. Although Web surveys are not as easy to create as most other types of Web pages, Web surveys are converted to hypertext markup language (HTML) files and do not need lengthy printing, collating, and mailing time. **HTML** is a simple coding system used to format documents for viewing by Web clients. Web pages are usually written in this standard specification. Among its other advantages, online survey research is still relatively fast and inexpensive and can be conducted nearly instantaneously on a worldwide basis.

ONLINE PANELS. Online panels overcome the sampling and response problems associated with online surveys. **Online panels**, which are similar to focus group interviews, are discussions marketers conduct with people who have agreed to talk about a selected topic over a period of time. For example, a fitness magazine might conduct an online panel to discuss the latest available fitness equipment and obtain feedback as to the ease and effectiveness of the equipment. Normally, panelists receive a fee or gifts for their participation. Each person must complete a comprehensive survey after being accepted to participate as a panelist so that researchers have data about their characteristics and behavior. Online panels provide marketers with a supply of willing respondents about whom they already have extensive data. Thus, there is no need to ask demographic questions each time. Marketers contact panelists on a regular basis with high expectations for a positive response to their request for information. Many publishers have online panels to assist in the development of magazine content. For example, *Working Mother* magazine has an online reader advisory panel. Digital Marketing Services (DMS) has exclusive rights to millions of America Online (Aol) members for marketing research purposes. DMS provides survey opportunities to Aol members and gives respondents credits on their monthly Aol bill for participating in market research activities.

Conducting online research is important to better understand consumer behavior and to more effectively be able to connect with consumers to satisfy their needs and wants. This research is used to determine how companies can serve consumers via e-commerce.

E-commerce

The buying and selling of products online is known as **Electronic Commerce**, or **e-commerce.** However, e-commerce encompasses much more than the transactional portion of business. It can include every step of the supply chain, from advertising to order fulfillment over the Internet. Many successful companies have been built through e-commerce.

Companies such as Amazon.com, Overstock.com, and Zappos are based entirely on the Internet. Amazon was started in 1995 as an online bookstore[10], and has evolved into the top Internet retailer in the country.[11] According to its Web site, Amazon prides itself on being centered on the customer, by offering an extremely wide variety of products and increasing convenience. [12] E-commerce is becoming a huge industry, creating a new type of convenience for consumers around the world. As we'll examine in the next section, the Internet offers consumers a way to unite with others—regardless of whether or not they are there to shop, make new friends, obtain information or just to connect.

Connecting Sites

Along with e-commerce, connecting sites are becoming increasingly popular. **Connecting sites**, which are similar to e-commerce sites, can be referred to Web sites that serve as media to connect people for various reasons. They create market fronts to bring consumers to other consumers in order to trade products, information, or even to find relationships. Connecting sites serve two purposes: connecting people to products, and connecting people to people.

PRODUCT CONNECTING SITES. Auction sites and the like connect people to products. Major product connecting sites include eBay and Craigslist. eBay is an online auction Web site that serves as a liaison from consumer to consumer in order to trade products. Users can upload items to auction, view items to buy, or both. Similarly, Craigslist is a forum that allows users to post items for sale, view items, or both. Here's an example of how it works: A low-budget college student is in the market for a surfboard. Instead of driving to the nearest surf shop to pay full price for a new long-board, he simply logs onto Craigslist to look for surfboards for sale in his area. He finds a listing for a used board that he likes, and contacts the owner. They meet in the area and he pays the "lister" and straps the board to the roof of his car. He was able to find the product he wanted at an extremely low price, and the lister was able to sell an item that he no longer wanted. Consumers have access to a variety of product connecting sites. Various social networking Web sites also have the ability to connect people with products, such as Facebook Marketplace.

PEOPLE CONNECTING SITES. There are also connecting sites that connect people to people, such as dating sites, or job search sites. For instance, Match.com is an online dating company where one can create an account and profile, and view others' profiles in search of a relationship. Job sites allow consumers to create accounts and upload a resume and relevant information. They may search job listings and apply, or a company may search profiles and resumes and contact the user. Connecting sites are a growing segment of the online industry and are designed to be easy, convenient and need-satisfying for consumers.

Driving Site Traffic

Gaining Web site traffic is key for online marketing. There are many ways a direct marketer can drive site traffic, including search engine optimization, banner ads, affiliate marketing, Webinars, new video sales letters, direct response online sales letters, viral and electronic word of mouth, and various offline tactics. Utilizing social networking, which will be covered later in this chapter, is also an important way to drive traffic.

Search Engine Optimization

In the past, people used to look for products and services they needed in local phone books or directories such as the Yellow Pages. Today the Internet has changed the way people search for just about any type of information. Google's mission statement states: "Google's mission is to organize the world's information and make it universally accessible and useful."[13] With Google's technology, it is now easier and more convenient to search for these products and services via a search engine versus looking things up in a local directory. **Optimization** is the *process* of improving Web site traffic by using search engines. In general, when the link to a Web site is listed in a higher position on the search engine results page, the user is more likely to view it. Thus, search engine optimization aims at moving the link to one of the top links on the results page.

Search Engine Marketing (SEM) is the entire set of techniques and strategies used to direct more visitors from search engines to marketing Web sites. The four most common purposes for SEM use include increasing or enhancing brand awareness of products or services; selling products, services, or content directly online; generating leads; and driving traffic to a Web site.[14] Research shows more than 85 percent of companies are listed on at least one search engine.[15]

Let's explore the three different types of SEM that could be used by companies wanting to improve their Web site traffic:

1. Paid placement: Sometimes referred to as "pay-per-click" (PPC) or "cost-per-click" (CPC), paid placement advertising uses text ads targeted to keyword search results on search engines through programs such as Google AdWords and Yahoo!

2. Paid inclusion: Paid inclusion entails the practice of paying a fee to search engines and similar types of sites such as directories or shopping comparison sites, so that a given Web site or Web pages may be included in the service's directory, although not necessarily in exchange for a particular position in search engine listings. The fee structures will vary.

3. Organic search engine optimization: This form of optimization includes the use of a variety of techniques to improve how well a site or page gets listed in search engines for particular search topics.

Today, most consumers take the approach of typing in what they are searching for using key word search engines such as Safari, Bing, Yahoo! or Google. Before that, consumers often browsed through catalogs prior to visiting Internet retailers. Some consumers still do; however, that is certainly not the trend. Today, technological advances such as Like.com makes it even easier to search for items online. Like.com uses visual search engine technology that allows a consumer to search for a product with only a photo. For example, when consumers see a photograph of a sweater they really like that is worn by a celebrity online, they can search for that same sweater online by using Like.com.[16] Just imagine what other technologies lie ahead to help consumers save time and shop online.

Because of this shift in people's behaviors, it has become very important and valuable for a business to have its products and services or a company Web site show up on the *first page* of the search engines for a particular keyword that will benefit their business. How important is it to be on the first page of Google? Or what is the number one position in Google worth to a company? The number one position on Google search achieves an average of a 46.3 percent click-through rate. The number two position on a Google organic search garners 29.43 percent, while the listing in the third position gets about 19.81 percent of the clicks.[17] Thus, the closer the company is to the top—the more traffic they will receive from the organic search listing. Holding one of the top three positions on Goggle, a premium position to obtain, and maintaining this position has created a whole new opportunity for marketers known as search engine optimization (SEO).

There are three components to getting a site ranked in most search engines, and specifically in Google. They are: content, links, and activity:

Content consists of how relevant the content on the site is to the actual domain name and how relevant it is to the keyword search. For instance a site with the domain www.dogtraining.com if it has current, relevant information about dog training would be very hard to beat for the keyword search "dog training". This Web site would be very hard to knock out of the number one spot on Google by another site competing on the same dog training keyword. **Key word density** is the number of times that the key word in the search appears on that Web site. The keyword must be intertwined throughout the article or site naturally but not too often as it can be viewed as spamming the searching engines. The more times the word appears, the higher the site will rank. Site structure primarily includes the content of the Web site.

Links can be thought of as a popularity contest. This is based on the premise that the more valuable a site is, the more people will link to it. The other aspect of a link campaign is that not every link is the same. Each site has a PR value. A **PR Value** is simply how often Google or other search engines indexes a site or how often they send their spiders to index a site. **Back links** involve the quality of links, number of broken links, the anchor text, and the positioning of the link.

How do you start establishing back links to a Web site? There are many ways of doing this and each can be used as an overall traffic building and linking strategy. And each medium can help the author establish himself as an expert in his field, drive traffic from each piece of content, with the overall objective of ranking on Google's first page. Links can be established from many sources including:

- Videos: Uploading videos to various video sites with links back to the either a specific article or to the home page.
- MP3's: Uploading MP3's to the various mp3 directories with back links on the download page and within the audio content to the site.
- Article Directories: This is also known as article marketing. Writing articles with good relevant content that is keyword driven will establish you as an expert within a field after you have uploaded several articles. Each article, of course, has a link back to your site at the bottom of the page or in the resource box. You can then take the same article and upload it to multiple article directories, leveraging your time and content, while establishing you as the expert in multiple article directories.
- PDF directories: These work very similarly to article directories except they are saved as a pdf and then uploaded to a pdf directory. Keep in mind one article can be sent to multiple directories, establishing multiple links and traffic sources and people interact with each directory and download the pdf. The advantage of saving in the pdf format is that people perceive pdfs to have higher value than articles. And often people will store pdfs that they find of valuable on their hard drives. This adds to the shelf life of the pdf, often allowing the person who downloaded the pdf to go back later and reread the content, causing them to revisit the Web site.
- Press Releases: Reformatting the article and pdf into a press release can establish two things: (1) the content can be syndicated across various media, such as newspapers, radio

stations and television stations, which will allow multiple back links to the domain of the Web site; and (2) the owner of the site can receive free publicity about the company via content syndication, or radio and TV interviews.

- Commenting on other niche-related blogs and Web sites: Adding value to other blogs by commenting and then posting a link in the Web site is a very good strategy for establishing back links to a Web site and encourages people within the niche to visit your site and interact with you.

The end result of all of the linking is twofold. First, if the content is good it will establish the author as an expert across multiple directories in various media. Second, it will create traffic from each of these directories back to the Web site. And this leads us to the third part of Google's triad for getting a site ranked, which is activity.

ACTIVITY. Activity includes the length of time people stay on a Web site and how they are interacting with the Web site. Activity also addresses how often a site is updated—every day, once a week, or once a month—the more often the better. **Aging** refers to the recency of the site and is based on the date by which it was established on the Web. The newer the site, the less weight it will be given compared to already established Web sites.

There are several ways of encouraging activity on a Web site including:

- Featuring video and mp3 content on a site that allows people to consume the content, while they are on the site. This will increase the average time that people spend on the site.

- Allowing people to comment on a Web site by using a blogging platform as the Web site. Having comments on a Web site from people visiting a site communicates social proof to other visitors. We will discuss blogging in greater detail later in the chapter.

In conclusion, whether you decide to partake in search engine optimization for your own site or another company's site, keep in mind the importance of being listed on the first page of Google because not only does it help a business on a local level, but it can quickly give a business a national presence as well. Other ways to achieve awareness is by purchasing Adwords, which is the topic of the next section.

Adwords

Most of the ad platforms online that allow you to bid on keywords have one commonality: You bid on how much you will pay-per-click or per impression. So for this section we will focus on the most advanced and dynamic advertising platform and that is of Google. For Google there are two platforms that you can bid on: the Search Platform and the Content Network.

SEARCH PLATFORM. The search platform is the part of Google Adwords with which most people are familiar. Traditionally it is more expensive than the content network, but normally businesses that use the search platform are bidding on terms that people are searching. This means they are placing ads based on keywords. The people that are searching using these keywords are looking for a solution to a need or want. This makes them red hot prospects, and if the ad can grab attention, generate interest and get the person to click, then the marketer has a good chance of either getting an opt-in lead and/or converting a sale.

When the person clicks on the ad, to incorporate a direct response component the visitor can either be taken to a landing page or a sales page. The ad can send the visitor to a standard Web page, but there needs to be some sort of funnel in place or call to action that will get the person to take the desired action of the marketer.

There are three metrics that Google considers when showing the ad and when establishing the cost of the ad. They are the cost per click, quality score, and click-through rate.

Cost per click is simply how much the person is willing to bid to show the ad. This can make a difference of whether the ad will be placed on page one of Google or some other page.

Quality Score looks at a variety of factors to measure how relevant your keyword is to your ad text and to a user's search query. A keyword's Quality Score updates frequently and is closely related to its performance. In general, a high Quality Score means that your keyword will trigger ads in a higher position and at a lower cost-per-click (CPC). **Click-through rate** addresses the number of people that click on your ad. The higher your click-through rate, the more it improves your quality score. The higher the click-through rate the more often your ad will show.

There are many strategies to maximize click-through rates; these include the following.

- Ask for the click-through action. The easiest way to increase click-through is to simply ask for it.

- Animate a banner advertisement. Animation increases the likelihood that the ad will draw the user's attention and also generates more clicks than static banners, all else being equal.

- Involve the audience. The third generation of banner ads is interactive. Engage the viewers to allow them to personalize ads to their needs. Involving the viewer allows the advertiser to get to know them better, one of the primary goals of direct marketing!

- Change creative messages frequently. The nature of the Internet means that responses occur quickly, on the first few impressions. Therefore, creative wears out more quickly than with traditional media.

AD STRUCTURE. Many businesses when utilizing Google Adwords mistakenly try to sell the product or do a branding ad to push the business. To make the ad more effective remember to sell the click, not the product. There is not nearly enough space in a Google adword to do a sufficient job of selling a product or service. An effective ad structure follows the AIDA format (Attention, Interest, Desire, Action.)

In conclusion, when using Google Adwords, search network can help businesses find prospects that are searching for their product and service, while growing their lists and driving sales. Another service offered by Google related to adwords is that of the content network. In the content network, either Google will place your ads on Web sites that it believes are a match for your ad or banner ad or you can actually select the Web sites on which you want your advertisement to be shown. The content network is based more on interruption marketing similar to Facebook ads or ads in magazines. The content network allows marketers to be more creative with their ads and also allows direct marketers to place ads in various positions that target their customers. An example of this is placing a banner ad for rap music on golf sites. Most people would not understand why a company would want to place a banner ad on a site that seems to not be targeted. Once people understand that grandparents buy a lot of music for their grandchildren then this ad makes much more sense. The content network allows the marketer to do just this type of advertisement. People are not necessarily looking for the ad, but notice it as they are perusing content of interest.

Using Google suggestions of Web sites to place ads on in the content network can actually open up entire new markets for products and it will allow the marketer to test to see if the ad and product will actually pull. Once a converting offer is established, the marketer can actually start looking for other similar sites to advertise on in the same market either through the Google content network or by contacting the Web site owner directly.

Many people ignore and do not understand the content network and focus much of their campaign budget on the search network when using Google Adwords. By doing this they are missing out on a lot of traffic at a lower cost than the search network. The content network

FIGURE 10-7. Busch Gardens banner ads. Used with permission of Busch Gardens.

allows the direct marketer to place their ad on far more sites than the search network that is extremely targeted, direct and not nearly as creative as the content network.

Banner Ads

Banners and buttons basically occupy designated space that is available for rent on Web pages. **Banner advertising** is the digital analog to print ads, targeting a broad audience with the goal of creating awareness about the product or service being promoted. Banner ads are similar to space ads used in print media; however, they have video and audio capabilities because they are designed for interactive media. There are a variety of sizes that have been standardized per the Interactive Advertising Bureau. Those primary sizes include rectangles, pop-ups, banners, buttons, and skyscrapers. Banner ads must have a strong call-to-action as can be seen in the creative banner ads shown in Figure 10-7.

The goal of banner ads is twofold: first, to increase brand awareness by exposing consumers to the banner ad, and second, to maximize the "click-through" rates or "ad clicks."

Embedded ads are gaining attention, too. Embedded ads allow the viewer to receive more information without having to link to other Web sites. These ads are designed to overcome the space limitations of banners.

Affiliate Marketing

Affiliate Marketing is akin to taking word-of-mouth marketing and putting it on steroids. Today there is software that will manage relationships and actually reward people for referring people to a product or service. This reward is normally a percentage of the sale of the product or service. This percentage can range from 5 percent up to 75 percent of the sale. The more aggressive companies even pay 100 percent or even 200 percent commission on the sale price to grow their lists. Affiliate marketing is one of the fastest ways to build a list in the Internet marketing channel. The advantages of using affiliate marketing are twofold: (1) the number of opt-ins is much higher because it is endorsed traffic; and (2) it allows the company to build a list with no initial cash outlay.

Here is how it works: The company sets up what is known as a squeeze page or landing page, where there is an opt-in form and the only thing the person can do is enter their name and e-mail address or leave the page. The opt-in form traditionally offers something of value, such as a Webinar (which will be discussed in the next section.) The affiliate promotes the free content to his list and sends them to the squeeze page, where they have to opt-in. The company then has the ability to market to whoever opts in for the free content. The affiliate only makes money if the person purchases what is being offered in the Webinar. There are other strategies for using affiliate marketing, like direct sales, but this strategy is one of the smartest ways companies can leverage other companies' lists to grow their own lists with little initial investment.

Webinars

Traditionally, face-to-face sales have the highest close rate, but are also the most expensive strategy for a direct marketer to implement. Moreover, they consume the greatest amount of time. The time involved limits the number of people that can be shown the sales presentation and ultimately can be very limiting on sales, even if there is a very high close rate. However, what if you could leverage the same one-to-one relationship when selling, but multiply it times 1,000? Webinars essentially allow you to do this.

Imagine offering an hour long presentation with up to 1,000 people watching, while you are delivering good content, controlling the entire sales process, then asking for the sale, and finally answering any questions at the end to overcome any objections? Now imagine giving this same presentation up to 1,000 people at the same in the same hour all over the world, who are targeted and already prequalified to purchase. This is the power of Webinars. Webinars are essentially Web conferencing software used for sales presentations.

Here is how they work:

1. The presenting company establishes an account with a host company, such as www.gotomeeting.com.

2. Next the presenting company establishes a time that the Webinar is going to be delivered.

3. An opt-in landing page is created where people have to enter their information, in return they will get the details of how to log in to the Webinar.

4. After a person opts in to the landing page to view the Webinar an e-mail is sent from an auto responder giving the person the actual link and time and any other information needed to access the Webinar.

5. At the start time of the Webinar the prospect logs into to watch the Webinar.

6. The Web conferencing software connects all of the computers of all of the people logging in to watch the Webinar to the presenter's computer. This way each person can watch the Webinar at home, in the office or where ever they are as long as they have an Internet connection.

7. The presenter normally uses a PowerPoint presentation to go through the sales process, while talking into a USB connected microphone, plugged into their computer.

8. The presentation shows up on all of the people's computer screens that are logged into watch the presentation as it is being delivered.

9. As the Webinar is being delivered, the people watching can type in any questions, which are then sent to the presenter's computer. The presenter can answer the questions, either during the Webinar or at the end of the Webinar.

10. At the end of the Webinar there is a specific Web page that is shown where people can go and purchase the product or service being offered.

Webinars can be effectively used to build a prospect list. Let's examine a four-step process for doing so. The steps include:

1. The presenting company, A, sets up an affiliate link for the promoting company, B.

2. Company B sends an e-mail to their list with the affiliate link, asking their customers to join them on the Webinar to learn about some topic of interest to the list.

3. The link in the e-mail that Company B sent to its list is a link to the opt-in page for the Webinar.

4. When people opt-in to the Webinar, those names and e-mail address become an asset of Company A, because they can be downloaded from the Webinar software and inserted into an e-mail program such as Icontact. This allows Company A to market to them, whenever they desire in the future.

Traditionally, marketers will use a separate opt-in e-mail form, for people to actually log in to the Webinar, when it is being delivered. This serves two purposes. First, it allows Company A to measure who registered for the Webinar and how many people actually showed up. The company can then look at this number to determine its close rate and how many people actually purchased. Second, the company can segment the people who did not show up or purchase into a separate list and e-mail them details of the Webinar, when it is replayed.

Incorporating Webinars into the digital media mix is wise and can be a productive method for building a prospect list, especially when combined with affiliate marketing and e-mail marketing.

Online Direct Response Conversion Pages

The Web allows the direct marketer to target specific traffic to a specific Web page. Many online direct marketers will either send traffic to a squeeze page, long form sales letter or video sales letter. Let's look at each of these three different types of pages that are known for converting traffic into either a prospect or customer.

SQUEEZE PAGES /LANDING PAGES. Squeeze pages or landing pages are pages on a Web site that only allow the visitor to do one of two things: (1) opt-in to obtain the lead magnet being offered, or (2) leave the page all together. Squeeze pages can be presented in various formats, but the common elements of a squeeze page are:

• Headline

• Sub-headline

• Bullet points about the features and benefits of the lead magnet.

• And Opt-in Form

• Photo of the lead magnet. This can be optional, but people buy pictures and photos, so photos can boost conversion.

Keep in mind squeeze pages can come in various formats, including video squeeze pages, where instead of having the bullet points in print format, they are delivered in the video, either in presentation format or by a video of person speaking and delivering the bullet points while they are speaking.

The goal of the squeeze page or landing page has one objective and that is to get the person on the page to opt-in. This is the only objective of the squeeze page. In conclusion, using squeeze pages to require people to opt-in is a sure fire way to grow your list, while keeping the lead magnet exclusive to only those who opt-in.

LONG-FORM SALES LETTERS. One of the five components of a direct mail package is the sales letters. This is the part of the direct mail package that if done correctly builds intense demand for the product and has people yearning to grab their wallet and either visit a Web site, call a phone number, or mail in an order form to purchase whatever is being offered. However, since we are talking about digital marketing in this chapter, how can direct marketers take the same principles of the direct mail sales letter and apply them to the Web? Very easily actually, because long-form direct sale letters convert on the Web very well. Long-form direct sale letters are similar to squeeze pages, where there is just one page and the visitor to the page can only do one of two things, either purchase or leave.

The primary goal of the sales letter is to make a sale. But there are some differences to online sales letters, when compared to squeeze pages. The first is length as these letters are much longer than squeeze pages and include more components, including:

- Headline
- Sub-headline
- Testimonials
- Guarantees
- Johnson Boxes
- Call-toAction
- Offer Box: This is where is the offer is stated and a buy button appears
- Buy Button
- Videos
- MP3 Files
- Bullet Points
- Sales Graphics
- 100% Satisfaction Guarantee
- Check mark bullet points
- Stop signs

There are many other elements of an online long-form sales letter, but the most important thing to remember is they traditionally follow the same format as a normal long form direct mail letter. The main difference is the ability to incorporate a multimedia approach with graphical headlines, videos, mp3's or any other digital aspect that will help increase the conversion rate.

In conclusion, long-form sales letters are alive and well online as well in direct mail, but the main difference is online you can give them a truly multimedia component that is much harder to do offline.

VIDEO SALES LETTERS. Video sales letters are very similar to long form direct mail letters, except the sales letter is in the form of a video presentation. It is perceived as content and is more interactive than just reading a long-form sales letter. They are very similar to Webinars, but not as long. Video sales letters can be created with PowerPoint slides that are turned into a video with screen capture software. Or they can include actual video of the person doing the selling. Nearly any kind of presentation can be turned into a video sales letter. Furthermore with a simple java script, the buy button of the video sale letter can be hidden, until the appropriate time for the person to purchase. Other advantages of the video sales letters include being:

1. Much faster to create than long-form sales letters.
2. Less expensive—do not necessarily have to hire a copywriter.
3. Higher perceived value than a long-form sales letter.

FIGURE 10-8. Airport Van and Virginia Beach ad on a bus. Used with permission of Adam Baker.

FIGURE 10-9. Bananas with message sticker. Used with permission of Adam Baker.

4. Can control the sale process by eliminating video controls.

5. Can present the price correctly, because people cannot just scroll to the bottom of the presentation and see the price, like they can on a long-form sales letter.

6. Conversion rates are normally higher than long-form sales letters.

In conclusion, video sales letters are the newest form of conversion page online today, but they are quickly becoming more popular as conversion rates out-perform traditional online long-form sales letters.

Offline Tactics

A company's Web site is designed to be a powerful destination for consumers to interact with the organization and its offerings. Great effort should be placed into Web site design to make the site easy to navigate so visitors can easily and quickly locate desired information, products, services or connections. However, even the most robust and well-organized Web site cannot be successful without visitors. All marketers must realize that designing and launching a Web site is only one-half of the equation—driving appropriate traffic is the other half. Think about it this way: Would you throw a party and not send out invitations? Let's hope not.

Offline tactics are essential to drive Web site traffic. The words to remember are: *consistency* and *omniscience*. Marketers must be consistent in using their URL with unshakable consistency and place it anywhere and everywhere. Consumers should bump up against a company's brand and its URL at every turn. "Outside-the-box" thinking should be used to be creative as to where to place your URL. To assist with your idea generation, glance over the creatively placed URLs presented in Figure 10-8.

Placing an ad containing a "call to visit a Web site" might be expected on transportation vehicles, such as vans and buses, but who would have thought it would be featured on a banana? (See Figure 10-9.)

As Figure 10-10 proves, when it comes to innovatively promoting Web site traffic, the sky's the limit! So, think outside the box and determine where your company's URL should be placed in order to effectively draw Web site traffic.

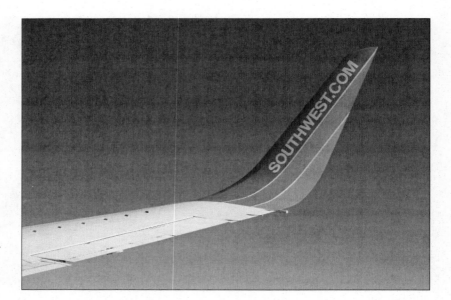

FIGURE 10-10. Southwest Airlines airplane. Used with permission of Adam Baker.

Digital Formats and Tools

Digital formats and tools are the context for information that is this generated, disseminated, and shared. A major movement behind these formats and tools is "User Generated Content" that catapulted Web applications to Web 2.0. In a report, eMarketer chronicled:

> The days of giant media conglomerates controlling the creation, distribution and monetization of content are fading. An explosion of user-generated content is reshaping the media landscape, shattering the status quo and creating new opportunities for marketers.

There are several digital and online formats and tools that every direct marketer should be familiar with as the digital industry continues to mature. These include blogs, social networks, personalized URLs (PURLS), and click-to-chat capabilities.

Blogs

A **Blog** is a Weblog, or a Web site that contains informal information and journal-like entries. There are many types of blogs, varying from those chronicling personal experiences to informational article like pieces from experts. Their scope also varies. Some blogs are about a very specific topic such as baking cakes, while others can touch on a much wider subject such as sports, or have no subject at all. In most cases, one can follow a blog and post comments to various entries. Important to marketing are product and company-based blogs, creating a type of discussion board. Direct marketers must be able to understand consumers' use of blogs, and how to utilize blogs.

Companies can utilize blogs as a means of providing information to customers and prospects. This is a form of online public relations.   **Online PR** or **E-PR** refers to any type of public relations conducted digitally. Companies may also use social networking Web sites as tool for E-PR. This will be discussed in detail in the next section. Companies use blogs in order to let their customers "know what's going on." They can use the informal nature to their advantage,

FIGURE 10-11.
Virginia Beach
Shorelines Blog
site Web page.
Used with
permission of the
City of Virginia
Beach Convention
& Visitors Bureau.

making the customer feel like they can get to know the company a bit better. Blogs can be used to discuss new products, corporate level decisions, product support, and much more.

As Figure 10-11 illustrates, the City of Virginia Beach's *ShoreLines Blog* offers visitors an opportunity to share information with its guests about upcoming events and activities.

Companies can also use blogs as a way of obtaining feedback from consumers. Many consumers discuss products in blogs, and firms should constantly monitor this form of digital word of mouth. Some companies have even begun reacting to blogs online. This also demonstrates E-PR.

Social Networks

Another digital format that each and every direct marketer should be extremely familiar with is social networks. Social networking sites are another way to connect with consumers, gain

FIGURE 10-12. Facebook icon.

insights and feedback, conduct online PR, advertise, and drive site traffic. Three important social networking sites include Facebook, Twitter, and Linkedin.

Facebook

Facebook is a social networking Web site created in 2004. Facebook now has more than 600 million users worldwide. Users create a profile and share personal information, which can be anything from interests and demographics, to pictures. Facebook users also share information on preferred products through use of the "**like**" button. Consumers can, with one click, show their preference for an advertisement, business, group, or topic.

An excellent example of how Facebook can be used to serve customers is that of Busch Gardens shown in Figure 10-13. In 2009, Busch Gardens opened its gates during the holiday season for the first time ever in its 30-year history. *Christmas Town: A Busch Gardens Celebration* was promoted as "a winter wonderland filled with holiday traditions, new surprises and park favorites that make everyone say, 'Now this is Christmas.'" When Christmas Town debuted, Busch Gardens had an active Facebook page with about 50,000 fans. The park had always supplied the fan page with exclusive content, conversed with fans constantly, and used the page for everything from providing customer service to executing giveaways. However, after the first few days of Christmas Town the fan page had turned into a priceless focus group.

The few operational kinks and shortcomings of the new event were quickly pointed out by fans on Facebook. Queue lines at some attractions were longer than what some fans deemed worthwhile. The culinary shops were often out of the most popular drinks. And even though there was plenty of praise for the overall event experience from Facebook fans, Busch Gardens did not want the few shortcomings to spoil the overall success.

Largely based on Facebook fans' feedback, a variety of major and minor changes were made to the event. Attractions were redesigned, and hot cocoa orders were doubled. Then the fans noticed. They noticed partly because Busch Gardens made the marketing decision to tell them. On Facebook, the social media team posted updates about the changes, and thanked the fans for trying to improve the event. Very quickly the fans started to appreciate the changes. Fans credited the park for a great event, and, ultimately, for listening to their guests.

Marketers can use the Facebook "like" information to microtarget consumers on Facebook. Facebook's ad platform allows you to segment your data by layering information. Let's look at a few ways that you can layer and segment data within Facebook to give you laser-like focus on targeting best customers. You may recall from Chapter 3 that marketers normally use the following five bases to segment markets:

GEOGRAPHIC. You can target by geographic region, such as country, specific states within the United States, or if you are a local business and/or if you only want your ads to run in specific cities.

DEMOGRAPHIC. You can also target by gender, age, married, unmarried, education level, occupation, new moms, widows or widowers, etc.

SOCIAL. Social segmentation is normally based on peer groups of influence. Facebook allows you to target ads to specific groups within Facebook. If you were selling flowers, you could target ads specifically to the people who have joined a horticultural group within Facebook. Ads can also be targeted towards companies. For instance if you wanted to offer jobs to employees of Microsoft or Google, you can do this by running ads targeted to these individuals or any other company that has a presence within Facebook.

FIGURE 10-13.
Busch Gardens
Facebook page.
Used with
permission of
Busch Gardens.

BEHAVIORAL. In direct marketing, behavior is often identified in list rentals by what products were purchased, average transaction size, when it was purchased, etc. This is the one area where Facebook is currently lagging behind other direct response media. But with the recent introduction of the Facebook Marketplace that allows users to bid on items, similar to eBay, it is likely to be just a matter of time before Facebook incorporates this data into the advertising platform.

PSYCHOGRAPHIC. This normally includes likes, interests and behaviors. Psychographic segmentation is another area where Facebook excels because of the *Like* button. Within Facebook you can bid on keywords such as book titles, band names, political affiliation, movie titles, religious orientation, the possibilities are almost endless. These can be very advantageous by targeting ads of your product or service toward your competitors. This can be done several ways, but say your competitor wrote a book, you could target your keywords to be the title of the book. Thus the ad would only show up to people who have listed the book on their profile or Liked the book title. This is very powerful advertising.

Facebook also introduced **Facebook Fan Pages** that allow businesses to set up a Web site within Facebook about their company, products or services. Each Facebook user can set up as many of these fan pages as he or she desires. This gives marketers a fantastic advantage, because not only could they establish a Fan Page for their companies, but could create one for each product and service they offer in addition. The ads can be targeted to individuals for each of these products and services.

Plus, Fan Pages can be customized using FHTML, which is Facebook's own HTML language. You can also customize your Fan Page using apps. Apps make the page far more dynamic, by being able to import blog posts from a Web site, import YouTube videos, Tweets from Twitter, stream live video, and offer exclusive content for fans only. Fan Pages can be used as another form of E-PR, providing information to, and staying in contact with customers.

Let's examine an example of an organization that has used Facebook Fan Pages to its advantage—the Ultimate Fighting Championship (UFC). Traditionally it offers its customers matches between its best fighters only on premium pay- per-view channels such Direct TV, live online, and via other cable providers. In addition, it offers two preliminary matches on Spike TV an hour prior to the pay-per-view. This left four or five preliminary bouts unaired on any television channel. The only people who could view these fights were people in attendance at the actual live event. In January 2011, UFC streamed two preliminary matches on its Facebook Fan Page—http://www.facebook.com/UFC. To view the matches, you were required to "Like" the UFC Fan Page.[18] This strategy enabled the UFC Fan Page to go viral on Facebook—right before the pay-per-view fights and in time for people to still order the pay-per-view. Moreover, UFC has now added previous matches and continues to add value for fans to Like its Fan Page on Facebook. Another social media aspect about this UFC example is that in February 2011 via Twitter, UFC fans expressed demand for a particular preliminary fight to be shown and as a response to this fan outpour on Twitter, the President of UFC, Dana White announced that the fight the fans were requesting would be shown on UFC's Facebook Fan Page.[19] This is just another way of using social media to reach out to your customer base and then deliver what your customers are requesting.

Finally, Facebook now has a shopping cart within Facebook where customers may purchase items and buy upgrades for games within Facebook. Surely many more options will soon come. This is just one more aspect that separates Facebook from the other social media sites and makes it more dynamic and user friendly for both the marketer and the consumer.

Twitter.

FIGURE 10-14. Twitter icon.

Twitter is a microblogging social networking Web site on which users can receive real time information through microblogs known as "**tweets.**" Users can create a Twitter account and follow various accounts that interest them, as well as posting their own information. A "tweet" is a 140 character statement which users share to stream publicly. A tweet can include a photo, video, or link.

An example of a unique social media campaign that really connects with consumers is that of PING MAN. PING MAN is a real golf-testing robot created in the 1970s by PING Golf founder Karsten Solheim. Today, PING MAN has become social and he's the talk of Twitter! To take advantage of his newfound popularity, The Martin Agency in Richmond, Virginia has created a Web series for PING MAN where he answers fan mail with the help of golf experts at PING. Text "follow PING_MAN" to 40404 and you can become a PING MAN fan yourself. You might learn a bit more about the sport of golf and even sneak a peek into the testing robot's personal life.

Businesses can create Twitter accounts as a form of E-PR in order to provide information to their customers, and to gain feedback and insight through consumers' tweets. Many businesses are using this E-PR tool in order to create a connection with customers, and positive word of mouth. For example, a consumer may tweet something either positive or negative about a product. The business may search for tweets that include its product, thank or reward those who have given positive feedback (with a coupon, shout out, etc.) or reconcile with those consumers who had something negative to say. For instance, if a consumer had an issue with a technical device, a company could tweet them a link with directions, or a number to call. As can be seen in Figure 10-16, Busch Gardens uses Twitter to connect with its customers and offer special promotions.

Here's a great example that demonstrates both the power and the speed of Twitter. In anticipation of the second year of *Christmas Town: A Busch Gardens Celebration,* the theme park's marketing team leaned on its Twitter account to generate some buzz. At the time of the promotion, Busch Gardens had been positioning its Twitter account (@BuschGardensVA) as the best place online for park guests to find exclusive offers, last-minute deals, giveaways and promo-

FIGURE 10-15. PING MAN photo and PING logo. Used with permission of PING.

FIGURE 10-16. Busch Gardens Twitter Web page.

tional information. So in October, 2010 the marketing department decided to sell Christmas Town tickets through Twitter for $5—only a fraction of the normal $21.99 price of admission. With one tweet, the offer was live:

> Hurry! Limited Time Offer. Buy a Christmas Town ticket for $5. Normally $21.99 Promo Code: BGVACT http:// ow.ly/2Ws90

There was not any public relations or other promotional support behind the offer. Still, news of the deal spread quickly from the 4,400 followers and was accelerated by a posting on a local newspaper's blog dedicated to savvy shopping. Soon after, other news organizations picked up on the promotion, including another local newspaper and television station. In six hours, more than 18,000 tickets were sold! Additionally, the theme park had proof there was strong demand for the event, the promotion generated significant publicity, and the Twitter account's profile had been boosted. That's the power of Twitter. Companies shouldn't neglect to incorporate Twitter in their social media arsenal, as it's a growing force of social networking and word of mouth.

LinkedIn

FIGURE 10-17. LinkedIn icon.

LinkedIn is the world's largest professional network with more than 100 million members worldwide and growing rapidly. A demographic profile of LinkedIn members reveals that they tend to be older (68 percent are age 35 or older), more educated (74 percent have a college or post-graduate degree), and wealthier (39 percent earn more than $100,000 annually) than average consumers.[20] In 2008, LinkedIn launched its advertising platform featuring enhanced targeting capabilities that include targeting users by geographic location, age, gender, industry and other general information.

LinkedIn allows its registered users to maintain a detailed contact list of people with whom they have some level of relationship, called *Connections*. Users can invite anyone to become a connection. This list of connections can be used in a number of ways:

- A contact network is built up consisting of their direct connections, the connections of each of their connections (termed *second-degree connections*) and also the connections of second-degree connections (termed *third-degree connections*). This can be used to gain an introduction to someone a person wishes to know through a mutual contact.

- Connections can be used to find jobs, people, and business opportunities recommended by someone in one's contact network.

- Employers can join the network to list jobs and search for potential candidates.

- Job seekers can review the profile of hiring managers and search to find out which of their existing contacts can introduce them.

- Users can post their own photos and view photos of others to aid in identification and become acquainted.

- Users can also follow different companies and can get notification about the new joining offers available. They can bookmark jobs for which they would like to apply.

PURLs

Personalized URLs, commonly referred to as PURLs, can really boost response rates when employed in direct and interactive marketing campaigns. A **PURL** is a personalized Web page or microsite that incorporates the prospect's name and is tailored to his interests based on information known about him. Personalized URL Marketing is the practice of engaging valuable prospects with their own VIP landing page. It begins with a specific Web address as one of the response channels in a mailer or direct response ad and follows it up with a series of extremely customized landing pages. When the individual visits the personalized landing page, he will find precisely the information he is looking for, which means he stays engaged at the site longer and is more likely to respond to the targeted offers presented to him. PURLs permit marketers to:

- Engage prospects and customers with personalized dialogue.
- Collect and update customer data.
- Track customer activities and preference.
- Enhance marketing campaign effectiveness.
- Analyze and measure campaign success.

In addition, PURLs enable the unique creative messages of marketers to be linked with the interactive capabilities of the Internet. Let's examine the step-by-step process of PURLs:

Step 1: Attract—Targeted prospects receive direct response communication containing a call-to-action encouraging them to visit a customized Web site or microsite.

Step 2: Connect—When prospects respond they are taken to a VIP landing page established for them containing relevant content based on their preferences.

Step 3: Engage—Prospects provide additional information that guides them through customized landing pages based on their needs and wants. This enables more meaningful dialogue with the prospect.

Step 4: Retain—The personalized nature of the interactive communication enables the marketer to create a more direct relationship with each prospect and act according to each prospect's interests.

Let's explore an example of a PURL marketing campaign that was developed by BlueSky Creative, Inc. in Cincinnati, Ohio for one of its clients. BlueSky created a PURL marketing program, called Level 10™, for a university that was seeking to connect more effectively with prospective students, as well as its alumni. Here's how it worked:

Level 10™ started with a database and printed postcards. (The university could have provided the database, or a prospect list might have been rented and used for the targeted mailing.) A customized postcard personalized to each recipient was designed for each target segment— admission candidates and alumni. The postcards encouraged each recipient to "visit his or her personalized Web site today." All of the copy and images on the postcards pertained to the university. (See Figure 10-18.)

Upon visiting their personalized URLs, individuals receive personalized thank you messages and a customized landing page designed just for them as presented in Figure 10-19. It is important to note that the degree of personalization that can be offered on the initial customized landing page is determined by the amount of information the organization knows about its target audience. Thus, in this case, the university would likely know more about its alumni than it would prospective freshmen students.

Visitors are asked to answer a few questions or provide information when they first visit their PURL Web page. The answers provided are used to determine the secondary pages to which each visitor is directed and the specific information that will be featured on these subsequent Web pages. Refer back to the interest questions to which Ryan and Beth responded and you will notice that Ryan selected "campus activities" and Beth selected "donor relations" as their respective areas of interest on their PURLs. As shown in Figure 10-20, those responses determined the following personalized Web pages for both Ryan and Beth. Now they will obtain the information in which they are most interested from the university (campus activities and donor

FIGURE 10-18. BlueSky Creative Level 10™ PURL—Admissions and Alumni postcards.

FIGURE 10-19. BlueSky Creative Level 10™ PURL—Admissions and Alumni customized landing pages.

relations, respectively) and the university can proactively communicate in order to build or strengthen its relationship with both of them.

BlueSky's Level 10™ program doesn't end there; in fact it's just the beginning. Through the information provided on the personalized Web sites, the university can more effectively respond to prospective students and alumni and engage in more meaningful dialogue with each on a personalized basis. The data reporting and analysis capabilities associated with BlueSky's Level 10™ program includes dashboard reports captured in real time 24/7; individualized analysis by unique PURL visitor detailing the pages viewed and the number of visits; customized campaign reports based on the needs of the university; hourly reports that can be used to determine future communications. In summary, one of the best ways to connect meaningfully with customers and prospects is via personalized communications. Beyond connecting with the customer or prospect, PURLs enable marketers to interact individually with prospects and respond to their expressed desires.

FIGURE 10-20. BlueSky Creative Level 10™ PURL—Admissions and Alumni personalized Web pages.

Deal-of-the-Day Online Offers/Coupons

Deal-of-the-Day Online Offers/Coupons such as Groupon, Living Social and many more are Web-based offers where typically one product is offered at a highly discounted price (50 percent or more discount) for a period of typically 24-hours or less. A customer may buy a $50 restaurant certificate for $25. The restaurant and the deal provider split the $25 with each typically taking 50 percent or in this example, $12.50.

Click-to-Chat

A relatively new customer contact channel has emerged as an important method for engaging with visitors on a company's Web site. Click-to-Chat is gaining momentum among businesses that strive to top off customer attentiveness and real time service. **Click-to-Chat,** nicknamed "**Chat**" for short, is a form of Web-based communication in which a person clicks an object (e.g., button, image or text) to request an immediate connection with another person in real-time. (See Figure 10-21.) You may have experienced it while shopping online, or conducting business with a bank. Click-to-Chat has revolutionized the Contact Center, its agents' productivity, and the interactive marketing manager's options for meaningful dialog between the corporate Web site (or mobile sites, or SMS, Twitter, Facebook, etc.) and its visitors. It enables the kind of synchronous, multitasking that customers want (personal enough to be helpful, but not as personal as a phone call). It has the added benefit of leaving behind a transcript for further review by either party, and it increases the productivity of the chat agents as they are able to handle multiple chats concurrently. Experienced agents should be able to conduct 2.5 chats, on average, concurrently with seamless consistency. Chat was first seen in 1996 and over the years Click-to-Chat has become a common feature on B2B and B2C sites. Its uses a range from cultivating leads in a pre-sales environment, to reducing abandonment within conversion, to technical support.

How does Click-to-Chat work? The two main types of chat are Button Chat and Proactive Chat. As shown in Figure 10-22, **Button Chat** is where the call-to-action is resident on the page and the visitor initiates the chat. **Proactive Chat** is where the visitor has triggered a business rule and the chat invitation 'pops in' to the page with a relevant call-to-action. Business rules can vary and include the time spent on a page or site, aggregate pages viewed, the sequence in which the pages are viewed (known as **pathing**), or even specific page combinations such as "pogo-stick-

FIGURE 10-21.
Cisco chat
messages. Used
with permission
of Paul Martson,
Cisco Systems.

FIGURE 10-22.
Cisco's Web page
with Chat button.
Used with
permission of
Paul Martson,
Cisco Systems.

ing" between product oriented pages. One interesting business rule that many financial sites employ is the **abandonment rule**. This rule is when visitors start to complete a form and then stall or close the form—at which point a proactive Chat invitation can be issued to help complete the task.

There are a number of Chat providers. Current providers include Moxie Software, Right-Now, and Oracle. One of the category leaders is LivePerson. Most implementations involve software as a service (SaaS) which is contracted for with the chat provider. The Chat provider is responsible for the hosting of certain assets such as the *routing logic*, which entails sending this chat to contact center X and that chat to contact center Y. In addition, the provider is responsible for technology to determine agent availability for the chat experience as well as the infrastructure, such as the data centers to conduct and archive the many conversations. As an example, LivePerson currently monitors 45 million sessions (visits to Web sites) per month, and transacts 14 million chats per month. There is a lot of customer interaction happening here!

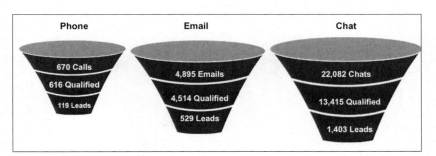

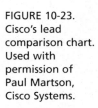

FIGURE 10-23. Cisco's lead comparison chart. Used with permission of Paul Martson, Cisco Systems.

Case in Point: Cisco

Let's explore a company that is expert at using Click-to-Chat—Cisco. Web Marketing and Strategy is a discipline within Corporate Marketing at Cisco. Its charter is to run the product/solution/services sections of *cisco.com* as well as the homepage. It is also accountable for Search (on site and organic), Video, and Chat. Cisco began a pilot chat program in 2006. It started with just a handful of pages in a specific section of the site focused on pre-sales product information for the Small and Medium Business (SMB) market. Almost immediately the executives at Cisco were surprised by the performance of Chat. Initial findings associated with Chat included:

- More people wanted to chat than Cisco expected.
- More leads were generated than forecasted, with a higher conversion rate than other tactics including telephone or e-mail communication. (See Figure 10-23.)
- Cisco agents were more productive because they were able to handle concurrent Chats. Agents on the phone can only service one customer at a time, but agents are able to "multi-chat."

Over the course of the next few quarters the number of chat placements expanded rapidly. At every checkpoint along the way the ROI was extremely healthy. Customer satisfaction was in the 90th percentile as measured in the post-chat surveys, where Cisco routinely asks for level of satisfaction with the agents and the chat experience overall.

At this time Cisco's focus turned to chatting in other countries. Scaling the program to include 43 countries and 14 languages was surprisingly not that difficult. It took about one year of effort among a few Web marketing staff and the Cisco professional services team at LivePerson. There were some tricky points with the technology, like right to left languages such as Hebrew and Arabic. And of course, the 'management' of internal stakeholders is always a challenge at a company of this size.

With the expansion phase behind Cisco, it was time to work on optimization and innovation. Optimization included changes to business rules for better outcomes, including the number of visitors who move from chat candidates to chat leads as shown in the Chat funnel in Figure 10-24.

At the Cisco contact centers—approximately eight globally—optimization included frequent reviews of transcripts to share best practices for agents. Innovation efforts came often as there was a whole universe of opportunity: What if Cisco could transfer chats to its partners to close the deal in real time? What if Cisco proactively invited visitors from other countries on its U.S. site in their local language? What if Cisco Chat could be placed on other Web sites that its customers frequent (referred to as 'watering holes')?

Today, the next big thing with Chat is establishing a handshake between Cisco's engagement scoring system and the Chat rules engine. The idea behind this is that Cisco can better target high prospect chatters if it peeks into their structured data, such as purchase history, partner sta-

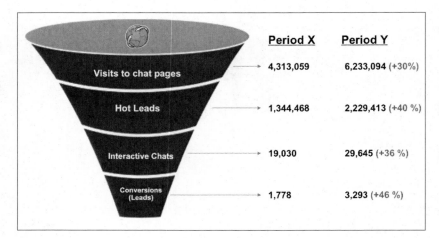

	Period X	Period Y
Visits to chat pages	4,313,059	6,233,094 (+30%)
Hot Leads	1,344,468	2,229,413 (+40 %)
Interactive Chats	19,030	29,645 (+36 %)
Conversions (Leads)	1,778	3,293 (+46 %)

FIGURE 10-24. Cisco chat funnel. Used with permission of Paul Martson, Cisco Systems.

tus, etc., combined with their on-the-site behavior such as including search terms or recency and frequency of visits.

Cisco has identified three emerging trends with Chat, including *third-party apps* that harmonize with your chat deployment to enhance functionality; *unstructured data* to better manage the content of chat transcripts; and *skill matching* to provide more intelligent routing and matching of Chat users and subject matter experts. Let's briefly discuss each of these:

THIRD PARTY APPS. Much like how a phone-based contact center might take advantage of new call features like recording, or forwarding, Chat is experiencing a period of rapid innovation around capabilities for providing a richer and more relevant experiences. Targeting by company domain is one example. If you were Cisco, wouldn't you want to know that the person chatting with you happens to work for Xerox? Add to this CRM data and it gets really exciting. If you knew what equipment your customers have bought from you in the past, you are better positioned to make the best recommendations.

UNSTRUCTURED DATA. Chat leaves behind a vast amount of text. Mining the chat transcripts for business intelligence can be very rewarding from a sentiment monitoring perspective or a training perspective or even a product development perspective. Cisco has begun to aggregate actionable data around opportunities to improve its Web content offerings.

SKILL MATCHING. Chat should be moving from a many-to-many, homogeneous experience to one of great differentiation. We've already talked about knowing more about the visitors, and therefore better targeting. As shown in Figure 10-25, the opportunity becomes matching that high-value target with an equally capable agent who may not be located in a contact center. Think of it as connecting niche questions with niche expertise or working the supply side of Chat along with the demand. Cisco's customers consistently ask for more access to its subject matter experts, whose time is extremely valuable.

Through these Chat trends Cisco is attempting to create productive and frictionless conversations that yield good business results and support its brand promise.

Measuring Site Traffic and Analytics

There are now other tools available online that will allow you to estimate how much traffic a keyword may generate for your site, Web site visitor search trends, and data about the types of people that are visiting your competitor's sites. These tools enable marketers to know who their target customers are and where to acquire new customers.

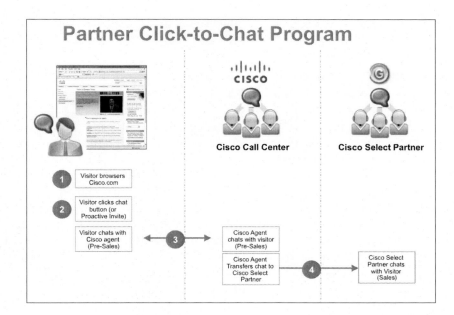

FIGURE 10-25.
Cisco flowchart.
Used with
permission of
Paul Martson,
Cisco Systems.

Google Analytics

Google provides many tools for their Adwords program that marketers can use to their advantage, and help target their customers. A few of these tools include:

GOOGLE KEYWORD TOOL. The Google keyword estimator allows people to search for keywords terms and it also offers additional keywords that are similar to the keyword. The tool also shows the level of competition for the keyword, the number of monthly global searches and the number of searches within the USA (local search). This can give the marketer a good estimate of how many searches are being performed for a keyword and if the market is large enough to even launch a product or business. Keep in mind this tool was developed to help Google Adwords users target new keywords that they may have not thought about. But a marketer can use these same tools not only for this, but also to gauge organic traffic for SEO and the overall demand for a product or service. For instance, the frequency of the term "growing tomatoes" shows over 60,500 monthly searches and 33,100 for the local or USA. The competition for this is not very strong. So a business could put together a report or pdf on growing tomatoes and offer it for either a lead magnet or an e-book to purchase, based off of just looking at the Google Keyword Tool.

GOOGLE TRENDS. Google Trends allows the marketer to type in keywords and see search results for that term based on the search volume, most popular countries and the cities where the term is being searched for, and finally the months with the most searches. This allows the advertiser to target digital individual ads in those particular cities. This saves on advertising expenses by knowing where the people are that are searching for this key term. It is also helpful by knowing which months to spend on advertising or when to increase the amount spent on advertising during months of high searches.

QUANTCAST.COM. This is an invaluable tool for targeting people and advertising. Quantcast will allow you to analyze specific Web sites and then reveal demographic and search data about the Web site. For instance after conducting a quick search for "growing tomatoes" on Google, the Web site http://www.tomatogardeningguru.com was in the third position. Upon entering the URL into Quantcast it revealed that more than 100,000 people visited the site in April 2011. It also revealed the demographics of the visiting traffic such as gender, age, race, marital status, family status, income level and education. The site also provides information on traffic frequency and business type.

WWW.SPYFU.COM. Reveals information about a site such as how much the company is spending on Adwords., the clicks per day and the cost per day. This is important because it is a gauge on the dollar amount that your competitors are spending and making each day with Google Adwords. This site also reveals other keywords that your competitors are bidding on and the other competitors bidding on the same keyword. If we continue our example and put "growing tomatoes" into SpyFu it reveals that the cost per click is 36-44 cents per click, average clicks per day 30.1-41.9, the cost per day $9.72-$20.38. It reveals that the number one advertiser is www.growingtomatosecrets.com. It also gives you search data and organic search results.

Combining these tools will give marketers an ideal picture of who their customers are. This allows the marketer to target them more effectively, save on wasted marketing to people who are likely not going to respond, and increase response rates. In the past, it would have taken companies a great deal of time, money and testing to narrow down who their customers are and learn this much about them. Today, the data is at a marketer's fingertips, and a customer profile can be generated for free in less than an afternoon for just about any product.

Clicktale

Clicktale.com is a Web site that provides marketers with a tremendous amount of information about their Web site and how their visitors are using the Web site. These analytics allow marketers to fine tune their Web site to increase conversions and improve overall performance.

Clicktale will allow marketers to do four things.

1. Watch visitors. Clicktale will record visitors as they interact on the Web site. Clicktale will actually record a video screenshot of the visitor for the entire time he or she is on the site. This allows the marketer to know exactly how people are interacting with their site by being able to watch the mouse move throughout the site.

2. View heatmaps. Heatmaps allow marketers to see the areas of the site that are most popular and where the mouse is the most.

3. Conversion Analytics. This analyzes several aspects of a Web site. It looks at sales funnels, forms, and where people are leaving the sales funnel. This allows marketers to improve the site and test different pages.

4. Demographics. This feature provides a demographic analysis of the Web site.

In conclusion, Clicktale will allow direct marketers to fine tune their Web site, increase conversions and improve the overall Web site usability.

Summary

This chapter examined the concepts, strategies, tactics, platforms and capabilities associated with marketing via digital and social media. As detailed in the chapter, digital and social media techniques and capabilities are dynamic and continuously evolving. These formats are both popular and powerful for direct marketers and must be utilized effectively to connect with customers. Marketers are challenged to keep abreast of the constant change associated with these digital formats.

The chapter proveded an overview of the marketing opportunities available with the digital media applications of e-mail, online market research, e-commerce and connecting sites. The chapter also presents the importance of driving Web site traffic and details the various methods used by marketers to generate site visitors. These methods included search engine optimization, adwords, banner ads, affiliate marketing, webinars, online direct response conversion pages and offline tactics. The chapter also examined the various digital formats available for marketers, such as blogs, social networks, PURLs, online offers and coupons, and click-to-chat. Finally, the chapter concluded with an important discussion of measuring site traffic and analytics.

Key Terms

auto responders
viral marketing
viralocity
spam
hypertext markup language (HTML)
online panels
e-commerce
connecting sites
search engine optimization
search engine marketing
key word density
PR value
backlinks
aging
adwords

cost per click
quality score
click-through rates
banner advertising
affiliate marketing
webinars
blogs
online PR
social networks
personalized URL (PURL)
click-to-chat
button chat
proactive chat
pathing
abandonment rule

Review Questions

1. What is one of the first key things that a marketer must understand when utilizing digital and social media?

2. What are the different types of online market research? How are they alike? How are they different?

3. What are the two focuses of e-commerce connecting sites? Describe some of these sites.

4. Discuss the various digital and social ways that a direct marketer can drive site traffic.

5. Compare and contrast the three types of search engine marketing?

6. What are blogs? How are they different from other online formats?

7. How can online social networks be used by a direct marketer to segment consumers? Provide an example.

8. Compare and contrast Facebook, Twitter, and LinkedIn with regard to how they may be used by direct marketers.

9. What are PURLs and how are they used by direct marketers?

10. Discuss the significance of programs such as the *Google Keyword tool, Google Trends, Quantcast.com, SpyFu.com,* and *Clicktale.com.*

Exercise

Select two different products, such as cameras, camping gear, running shoes or skateboards, and visit the Web sites of at least three different companies who sell these products. Compare and contrast the Web sites. How easily can you locate the style or model of the product for which you are interested? What types of offers or incentives are provided to encourage you to purchase? Does the site offer a blog? Can you connect to Facebook or Twitter directly from the site?

Critical Thinking Exercise

Are you on Facebook? Twitter? LinkedIn? Have you posted a blog anywhere in the past week or month or year? Why do you connect? What primary needs or wants are you satisfying by doing so? How much time are you spending on such digital and social media? Now, compare your digital and social media usage profile with that of your parents. How should marketers use both profiles to determine how digital and social media should be used as a component of its media mix?

CASE: Freecreditscore.com™ Band Search

How does a company successfully build brand awareness, create buzz, and generate new business in today's modern marketing world? It's simple. It gets social. That is precisely what Experian Consumer Direct did for its credit-monitoring business with the help of the creative minds at The Martin Agency in Richmond, Virginia.

Experian Consumer Direct was launching a new Web site and brand, freecreditscore.com™. The company had previously found great success with its freecreditreport.com® site, which had become a household name, thanks to its widely popular "spokesband" campaign. This case explores the innovative concept and Experian's digital and social media campaign.

What's a "Spokesband"?

Similar to a spokesperson, a spokesband is a band that represents a company. The spokesband is an original concept of Experian Consumer Direct and The Martin Agency. Experian's first freecreditreport.com® spokesband was a group of misfits that appeared in a series of humorous television ads crooning amusing lyrics about the woes of bad credit. The members of this spokesband were dressed in pirate costumes and shown musically greeting customers at a seafood restaurant. In other television spots the band members were featured riding bicycles and driving around town in cars and buses while singing comical tunes about the misery associated with bad credit.

These advertisements were extremely entertaining and very effective. Not only was this band wildly popular, it quickly became very successful in generating new business for Experian. Given such success, Experian wanted to continue the spokesband concept for its new brand. Therefore, it needed to find a new band to represent its new brand. This meant that Experian needed to conduct a band search. That idea served as the foundation upon which its new digital media campaign was created.

Band Search Campaign

The basic marketing idea behind Experian's Band Search campaign involved turning the search for a new spokesband into a marketing engine by using the lyrics of the songs to build awareness for the brand. The campaign sought to involve consumers in the search for a new band, while educating them about bad credit and how freecreditscore.com™ could help them. The entire Band Search campaign was used to fuel consumer interest and drive both inquiries and sales for freecreditscore.com™.

Target Market and Campaign Objectives

The freecreditscore.com™ Band Search campaign targeted approximately 40 million "down-to-earth-dreamers" who often use credit to bridge the gap between their aspirations and their financial reality. In other words, these customers are those who are in need of real financial guidance.

The three campaign objectives included:

1. To create buzz and garner enthusiasm for the band search by having 100 bands participate in the search.

2. To build awareness for the new Experian Consumer Direct brand through the band search and unique visits.

3. To convert awareness and enthusiasm for the brand into business on the freecreditscore.com™ site.

The campaign goal was to have site traffic and new orders each increase by 15 percent as a result of this campaign.

Campaign Strategy and Tactics

The creative strategy behind the Band Search campaign was simple: to attract bands to play Experian's freecreditscore.com™ songs and then encourage the bands to spread the credit-monitoring business message to their fans. The campaign encompassed a detailed step-by-step process to attract the bands and then involve consumers in the process of selecting the new spokesband. Here's how the campaign was executed:

First: The Martin Agency created five original 30-second songs, each of which seeded the new brand name and told a story about the product benefits.

Second: The freecreditscore.com™ Band Search was launched. Direct-response television and print ads, along with music industry word-of-mouth, were used to invite bands to perform songs at live auditions in major cities and online. Strategic partnerships with Gibson Guitars and Live Nation were established to add to the music legitimacy of the contest and to turn the auditions into a free opportunity for bands to perform with professional instruments in legendary venues such as The Palladium in Los Angeles. (See Figure 10-26).

Third: Four finalist bands were flown to Los Angeles to shoot music videos that served as direct-response television commercials that premiered during the 2010 Major League Baseball All Star Game. Humor was used in both the lyrics and the set designs in order to help the campaign appeal to the larger target audience. For example, online campaign promotions featured a "spokesgoat" that wore a pirate hat and gnawed on guitar cables. (See Figure 10-27.)

Fourth: The commercials drove traffic to a Web site (see Figure 10-28) where consumers could vote for their favorite band. The ads also drove sales to freecreditscore.com™ via an offer for a free credit score.

Fifth: Fans could access freecreditscore.com™ -branded social media toolkits to help them spread the word about the band contest to their friends. As shown in Figure 10-29, the toolkit included: tip sheet on how bands could promote themselves, widget on microsite, audio file of song that was professionally recorded, band search logo and professional pictures of band. All

FIGURE 10-26.
Freecreditscore.com™
Band Search casting
flyer. Used with
permission of
FreeCreditScore.com

items were sent to each band so they could self promote socially and on their Web sites. This resulted in free impressions for the company and its new brand.

Sixth: The Martin Agency produced three new direct-response commercials with the winning band in time for their nationwide red-carpet premiere at the 2010 MTV Video Music Awards celebration.

Campaign Results

Engaging consumers in the search for a new spokesband for freecreditscore.com™ proved to be incredibly successful. The Band Search campaign exceeded all of its established goals. More than 150 bands competed to be the new spokesband for freecreditscore.com™. The voting site registered more than 900,000 visits, 500,000 of which were unique visits during the campaign. Traffic to freecreditscore.com™ increased 25 percent versus pre-campaign levels and new orders were up 35 percent compared with pre-campaign levels.

Moreover, the campaign garnered more than 161,400,000 unpaid or earned media impressions with coverage from MTV, NPR, and countless local radio and television stations—many of which aired the campaign songs in conjunction with profiles of local bands. Social media impressions (from YouTube, blogs, Facebook, etc.) contributed to create tremendous "noise" for freecreditscore.com, which helped solidify the new brand name and connect with new customers.

FIGURE 10-27.
Freecreditscore.com™
Homepage goat
screen page. Used
with permission of
FreeCreditScore.com

FIGURE 10-28.
Freecreditscore.com™
Band Search Monsters
site screen page. Used
with permission of
FreeCreditScore.com

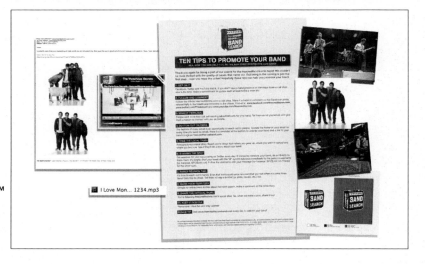

FIGURE 10-29.
Freecreditscore.com™
Band Search toolkit.
Used with
permission of
FreeCreditScore.com

Conclusion

The Band Search campaign illustrates that in today's social media world dominated by user-generated-content schemes that puts the image of a brand in the hands of consumers, successful brand-building direct-response campaigns are still possible. Not only did the Band Search campaign innovatively combine online and offline media to cement the new brand in the marketplace, it effectively drove site traffic and generated a ton of new business for freecreditscore.com™. Now that's something to croon about!

Case Discussion Questions

1. Explain the reasons behind the success of Experian's digital and social media campaign. Can you name other promotion occasions where the Experian's Spokesband and Search Band themes can be used successfully? Justify your examples.

2. Elaborate the role of Spokesband search in the Experian's campaign. Can the success of the campaign be attributed to the use of Band Search? Why or why not?

3. Discuss the elements of consumer involvement and their measures in the Experian campaigns. How consumer involvement are related to sales at freecreditscore.com

4. Compare the campaign's step-by-step execution with its three objectives: (1) creating buzz and garnering enthusiasm, (2) building awareness, and (3) converting awareness and enthusiasm to sales. Discuss the metrics that show the Experian's campaign obj

Notes

1. White, D. Steven. "Social Media Growth from 2006 to 2010." *Social Media Growth from 2006 to 2010.* 8 Aug. 2010. Web. 23 May 2011. <http://dstevenwhite.com/2010/08/08/social-media-growth-from-2006-to-2010/>.

2. DMA Statistical Fact Book 2011 (New York: Direct Marketing Association) p.109.

3. Ibid.

4. Coupey, *Marketing and the Internet*, p. 5.

5. http://www.socialnomics.net/2009/08/11/statistics-show-social-media-is-bigger-than-you-think/, Retrieved May 23, 2011.

6. *Interactive Direct Marketing: A DMA Guide to New Media Opportunities*, Introduction Section (New York: Direct Marketing Association, 2000), p. 5.

7. Mary Lou Roberts and Paul D. Berger (1999), *Direct Marketing Management*, 2nd ed. (Upper Saddle River, NJ: Prentice Hall), p. 414.

8. http://www.the-dma.org/cgi/dispannouncements?article=1451

9. Strauss and Frost, *E-Marketing*, p. 21.

10. http://www.brandinteractivism.com/2006/01/some_statistics.html, retrieved May 23, 2011.

11. Maryann Jones Thompson, "When Market Research Turns into Marketing," *Industry Standard* (August 30, 1999), 68–76.

12. "Media Kit: Overview." *Amazon.* Feb. 2011. Web. 23 May 2011. <http://phx.corporate-ir.net/phoenix.zhtml?c=176060&p=irol-mediaKit>.

13. "The Top 500 List—Internet Retailer." *Industry Strategies for Online Merchants—Internet Retailer.* Web. 23 May 2011. <http://www.Internetretailer.com/top500/list/>.

14. "Media Kit: Overview." *Amazon.* Feb. 2011. Web. 23 May 2011. <http://phx.corporate-ir.net/phoenix.zhtml?c=176060&p=irol-mediaKit>.

15. http://www.google.com/corporate/, retrieved May 18, 2011.

16. *Statistical Fact Book 2006*, p. 118.

17. Ibid., p. 113.

18. Lamb, Hair, and McDaniel, *Marketing*, p. 204.

19. http://www.seomad.com/SEOBlog/google-organic-click-through-rate-ctr.html

20. Kyte, E. Spencer. "UFC Fight for the Troops Prelims to Stream on Facebook." *The Province.* 19 Jan. 2011. Web. 24 May 2011.http://communities.canada.com/theprovince/blogs/keyboard-kimura/archive/2011/01/19/ufc-fight-for-the-troops-prelims-to-stream-on-facebook.aspx

21. Non, Sergio. "UFC to Stream Yamamoto-Johnson on Facebook—MMA Fighting Stances: Mixed Martial Arts Intelligence from the Cage and Ring—USATODAY.com." *News, Travel, Weather, Entertainment, Sports, Technology, U.S. & World—USATODAY.com.* 2 Feb. 2011. Web. 24 May 2011. <http://content.usatoday.com/communities/mma/post/2011/02/ufc-to-stream-yamamoto-johnson-on-facebook/1>.

22. http://mashable.com/2011/03/24/linkedin-overview-infographic/

## PART 3

Serve and Adapt to Customers and Markets

Fulfilling the Offer and Serving the Customer

OPENING VIGNETTE: ZAPPOS.COM

When it comes to serving customers, Zappos.com is in a class all by itself. There may not be another company on our planet that is more consumer *and* employee oriented than Zappos. Given the opportunity, Zappos won't just meet your expectations, it will far exceed them. Zappos will delight you!

FIGURE 11-1. Zappos logo. Used with permission of Zappos.

It's hard to imagine that when Zappos first began in 1999, it was a struggling online retailer that sold shoes. In fact, the name "Zappos" comes from the Spanish word for shoes, "zapatos." Today it is a subsidiary of Amazon and employs more than 2,050 people between its corporate offices located in Las Vegas, Nevada, and its fulfillment operations in Shepherdsville, Kentucky. Its gross sales are more than $1 billion and it offers a wide assortment of men's, women's, and children's clothing, handbags, house wares, and beauty supplies. Between its one million square feet of storage space spread between its two warehouses in Kentucky, Zappos's offers 1,317 brands, 143,612 styles, and 4,815,767 total products available for immediate shipment. Moreover, it physically warehouses every product item that it offers to its customers. That's quite a statement.

Zappos moved its state-of-the-art warehouse operations from California to the central location of Kentucky in order to provide more timely shipping of orders to its customers across the United States. For example, the shipping time required to send products from California to the East Coast was reduced from a week to only two days.

To really appreciate this company and its success, you must go beyond its highly efficient fulfillment operations and understand its culture. The Zappos company culture is the result of a number of wild, crazy, fun, brainy and absolutely brilliant strategic decisions made by Zappos's CEO, Tony Hsieh. He implemented a number of core values for the company that all employees embrace and live by on a daily basis. The first, and perhaps most important, is to "Deliver WOW through service." Hsieh contends "At Zappos, anything worth doing is worth doing with WOW." "WOW is such a short, simple word, but it really encompasses a lot of things. To WOW, you must differentiate yourself, which means doing something a little unconventional and innovative. You must do something that's above and beyond what's expected. And whatever you do must have an emotional impact on the receiver. We are not an average company, our service is not average, and we don't want our people to be average. We expect every employee to deliver

FIGURE 11-2. Zappos Fulfillment Center building. Used with permission of Zappos.

WOW." That should give you an idea of the vision and passion of Tony Hsieh. His "WOW" philosophy of serving Zappos's customers includes free shipping, 365-day return policy, speedy fulfillment and extremely friendly customer service that is available 24/7 and 365 days a year.

Zappos's associates are available and compassionate. They strive to make magic happen for their customers and want their customers to know that Zappos is "only a wave of a wand away and are very willing to assist in every possible way." To live up to that goal, Zappos regularly connects with its customers via numerous social media formats, such as Facebook, Twitter, blogs, and its own YouTube channel. Customer testimonials linked to the Zappos's homepage prove that its associates have gone the extra mile to serve its customers. For example, one Zappos's customer service representative helped a caller locate a nearby pizza place that would deliver after midnight, while another rep helped a customer locate a pair of boots seen in a movie. That's "WOW" customer service!

Zappos has a "people-centered" culture bursting with employees who are motivated to serve each customer with complete attention to detail. New employees are given a Zappos culture book that describes the ethos of the company with short essays written by current employees. The company employs a life coach, maintains an on-site library to encourage employees to read books, and regularly offers its employees $2,000 to quit, just to make sure that Zappos employees are working for more than just a paycheck. Indeed, Zappos employees are striving to WOW their customers and will go the extra mile to contribute to the successful customer experience.

That extra service includes helping Zappos revolutionize the online shopping experience by using amusing and useful videos to showcase its products. Zappos's employees participate in these videos by showing and talking about shoes, sandals, handbags and clothing. Zappos's employees produced about 58,000 short videos in 2010 because they determined that when a product includes a video explanation, especially one coming from a "regular" person as opposed to a supermodel, it is highly effective in helping with the online buying process. Zappos's research has found that when a product includes an employee video explanation, sales increase and product returns decrease. Today, Zappos has a sizable crew of people creating hundreds of videos each week to present to its customers.

Serving customers and prospective customers is what separates Zappos from the rest of the online retailers. As we discuss fulfillment and customer service throughout this chapter, keep Zappos in mind as the champion of companies that cares for its customers in a remarkable way. Better yet, visit its Web site and online store at Zappos.com and experience its extraordinary customer care for yourself. Brace yourself . . . you will be amazed at the "WOW" it delivers!

Fulfillment

What Is Fulfillment?

Fulfillment is the act of carrying out a customer's expectations. Strictly defined, fulfillment means sending the product to the customer or delivering the service agreed on. Loosely defined, it includes the entire dialogue (all interactions with the customer) and delivery functions. Marketers also see fulfillment as a part of the "extended product," or the intangible part of the product. For example, think in terms of the dialogue that a customer has with an organization. A customer or potential customer may communicate with the direct marketer by making an inquiry or placing an order and then expects to receive a response in a timely fashion. Likewise, customers expect their orders to be filled and delivered in a timely fashion. These dialogue and delivery activities are fulfillment.

Fulfillment is often referred to as the "back end" of the direct marketing process—the fulfillment, call center, and customer service operations. Fulfillment entails anything and everything that happens *after* the customer or prospective customer responds to some form of direct response communication from a company or organization. If a customer places an order, he or she expects delivery of the ordered item. If a prospective customer places an inquiry, he or she expects to receive the requested information. In some cases, consumers need additional information to make appropriate product or service selections. In those cases, the task of fulfillment is to provide information and assistance to empower consumers to make informed decisions. Of course, fulfillment of these requests should be handled in a timely manner. Direct marketers strive to fulfill customer and prospect desires and ensure customer satisfaction.

Many experts contend that back-end functions alone cannot make a sale but certainly can break one. More important, the lack of efficient fulfillment operations and good customer service can injure the relationship the direct marketer has with the customer and ultimately lead to the loss of that customer. Customer relationships begin when the firm receives an order. We also discuss the components of fulfillment, call centers, and customer service along with strategies to help direct marketers maximize their customer satisfaction level.

Adequate fulfillment, by minimizing the time between ordering and receiving, can alleviate two distinct handicaps inherent in direct marketing: (1) a time lag between placing an order and receiving it, and (2) a lack of familiarity with the actual product, which has been purchased remotely by mail, telephone, or online. Ultimate success in direct marketing depends on adequate fulfillment. It has been said, "The best copy, the best graphics, and the wisest choice of lists are all a sheer waste of money, time, and talent if they are not followed through with really outstanding fulfillment."[1] Let's investigate the standards direct marketers must meet to provide really outstanding fulfillment.

Traditional Fulfillment Standards

Fulfillment standards have changed over the past couple of decades. The consumer is increasingly desiring, demanding, and expecting faster turnaround times on orders and all forms of communication with companies. This is especially true of those orders and inquiries that come to the organization via the high-tech media. Consumers are busier today, they are more astute, and they procrastinate. With overnight delivery, toll-free numbers, fax machines, and the Internet, direct marketers have inadvertently encouraged customers to wait longer before placing an order because the consumer expects an immediate delivery service from the direct marketer.[2] Though not every direct marketer can provide immediate delivery services, all direct marketers must uphold certain delivery standards. The following are some typical fulfillment benchmarks that direct marketers strive to attain to ensure excellent customer service.[3]

- **Cost per Order (fully loaded):** The range is between $8 and $13 which includes both call center and warehouse costs such as direct labor, indirect labor, benefits, occupancy, packing supplies, telecom and credit card processing. This does not include shipping and handling revenue or shipping costs.

- **Order Processing Turnaround Time:** For in-stock products, 100 percent in 24 hours. Zappos.com has this down to a science and allows customers to book within a two-hour window of goods having to be passed off to UPS from its Kentucky distribution center.

- **Initial Customer Order Fill Rate:** This pertains to the percentage of customer orders shipped complete in 24 hours (or whatever its shipping standard is). Typically good performance is based on product lines, such as advanced fashion: 70–80 percent; re-orderable apparel: 80–90 percent; gifts/home: 85–95 percent; business supplies: 98–100 percent.

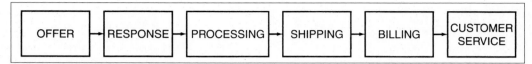

FIGURE 11-3. Fulfillment process.

- **Order Accuracy:** These targets are 99.5 percent without bar code and 99.9 percent with full inventory process bar code.

- **Inbound Receipts, Dock to Stock:** Products moving through all fulfillment processes should have 8–24 hour turnaround time.

- **Per-Hour Benchmarks:** These vary, but as noted by an industry expert, most systems should handle at least 3,100 units per hour.

- **Inventory Accuracy:** The target is 99.8–99.9 percent for bar-coded products.

The Fulfillment Process

The fulfillment process consists of the following six basic elements: offer, response, processing, shipping, billing, and customer service. Figure 11-3 shows a model of the elements involved in the fulfillment process. Let us now take a closer look at each element.

The Offer

We saw in Chapter 5 that the **offer** encompasses the terms under which a direct marketer promotes a specific product or service to the customer. To create an offer, the direct marketer first undertakes a number of activities, such as a close examination of the target customer, market segmentation, product or service research, database analysis, price determination, packaging requirements, and others. Direct marketers should properly address and direct the product/service offer and ensure that it is relevant to the needs of the addressee. This description should be adequate and fair and communicate the offer's relevance to the prospect's needs. Direct marketers should clearly state all disclosures and all options, such as sizes and colors. Direct marketers must specify credit terms. They should leave nothing to the imagination of the consumer during this initial stage.

A relevant product offering is timely and clear. Because an order form is an essential contractual document, it should be legally correct as well as distinct, simply stated, and easy to follow. When creating the order form, the direct marketer may use check-off boxes, or something equally easy to identify, for allowing customers to select size, color, or style variations and any other specialized information, such as personalization.

The Response

Direct marketers generally receive consumer responses (inquiries) or transactions (orders) via mail, phone, fax, or the Internet. If an order or inquiry is placed through the mail, fax, or Internet, it is critical that the consumer completes the order form in a full and accurate manner. The consumer must provide all information necessary for the direct marketer to fill the order. If the order or inquiry is placed via telephone, then operators need to be especially diligent in collecting order information. The way an organization handles the receipt of an order or inquiry is critical in the fulfillment process.

Processing

After receiving an order, the marketer undertakes editing and coding as well as credit checking and capturing of vital data for updating the database. The seller also prepares a series of documents such as shipping labels, billing notifications, and inventory instructions. At this stage, if there might be a delay in shipping an order, the marketer lets the customer know and anticipates any possible complaints.

Inventory control is another critical part of fulfillment operations. Direct marketers must examine inventory for quality checks prior to packaging and, if possible, after packaging as well. Computer technology can be of great assistance in processing orders. For example, at Lillian Vernon, computers are programmed to catch errors such as an invalid address or an invalid credit card. Furthermore, if an item can be personalized and the order information provided by the customer does not include personalization information, the computer flags the order and alerts the employee of the situation.[4]

Shipping

A computerized inventory control system is often the key to proper and timely shipment. Out-of-stock and back orders, requiring separate shipments later, are costly to the direct marketer and frustrating to the customer.

Back orders may even result in corrective action by governmental agencies. The Federal Trade Commission (FTC) trade regulations require all direct marketers to comply with its strict "30-day rule" guidelines regarding out-of-stock situations by notifying the customer if an item cannot be shipped within 30 days of the time it was placed. In addition, the customer must have the opportunity to cancel the order because of the out-of-stock condition. Direct marketers should not substitute a similar item to try to fulfill the sale, nor send a different color or size, without explicit authorization from the customer. If these FTC guidelines are not followed, the FTC may take punitive actions, including fining the company.

Billing

Once an order is on its way, the organization should receive payment as expeditiously as possible. If the customer did not use a credit or debit card and payment did not accompany the order, then clear billing instructions, with appropriate follow-up, are vital to ensure not only payment but also customer goodwill.

This need for clarity and accuracy also extends to proper receipt and posting of the payment, especially with extended-pay options. We often hear of computer errors, such as incorrect billings and incorrect postings, but more than likely these are human instruction errors.

Customer Service

The customer service function of the fulfillment process specifically refers to the handling of complaints, inquiries, replacements, and special problems. The high costs associated with this kind of customer service should be one of the incentives to getting it right the first time. Another more important incentive is, of course, that only a satisfied customer comes back. Therefore, because direct marketers place great importance on repeat business, they should pay great attention to detail in all aspects of the fulfillment process so as to eliminate the need to handle complaints and special problems. This care will also eliminate the risk of losing a valued customer.

However, because 100 percent quality control is often unattainable, shipping and billing errors inevitably occur, and only prompt handling and adjustment can overcome these. A customer might receive an incorrect shipment, be erroneously double-billed for a product, or be billed incessantly for a product that was returned. Though such occurrences can become extremely complicated, all should be meticulously adjusted as soon as possible.

Not all communications from customers relevant to fulfillment are complaints—many are inquiries. Many seek further information and some request additional orders. These, too, are a proper concern of the fulfillment operation and fall under the heading of customer service. Good customer service is simply good business. Some tips for providing excellent customer service are presented in Figure 11-4.

TIPS FOR PROVIDING EXCELLENT CUSTOMER SERVICE

1. *Conduct Customer Satisfaction Research.* A simple survey asking customers to indicate how well the company and its competitors are performing should be conducted on a regular basis.

2. *Simplify Your Guarantee.* Omit the confusing legal jargon and explain the refund and replacement policy in simple everyday language.

3. *Acknowledge Orders.* If merchandise cannot be shipped immediately, send a postcard acknowledgment. Many customers probably won't mind waiting a short time period for their order if they know that their order has been received and is getting careful attention by the direct marketer.

4. *Ship Merchandise More Promptly.* Most professionals believe that order turnaround time should be one week. Thus, the product should be in the customer's hands the week following the one in which the order was placed.

5. *Don't Bill Before You Ship.* Customers should be told that payment is not necessary until after the order has been received—just in case they receive an invoice prior to the merchandise they order.

6. *Acknowledge Returns and Cancellations.* When customers return merchandise, they want to be assured that the direct marketer has received it. Send a simple acknowledgment card telling the customer you received the returned goods or cancellation request, explain that it may take a couple of weeks to process it, and to disregard any invoice for the product(s) that they may receive in the interim.

7. *Answer Correspondence Promptly.* Nothing is more bothersome to the customer than having to write multiple letters or make multiple calls to get a problem straightened out with the direct marketer. Direct marketers can use a form with check-off boxes, if necessary, to make it easier for the customer to reply. Most importantly, follow through to get the problem straightened out to minimize the inconvenience of the customer.

8. *Make Complaint Resolution a Priority.* Recent research points to the fact that customers who have a complaint or problem satisfactorily resolved become *better* long-term customers than those who never had a problem. In addition, it is well documented that an unhappy customer tells many more people about their dissatisfaction than does a happy customer.

9. *Appoint Your Own Consumer Affairs Manager.* This person might be called the "customer service manager." Their job is to keep customers happy, seeing that orders go out promptly and that complaints are handled properly. This person should be empowered by the organization to make changes in policy and procedures.

10. *Make Customers Your Top Priority.* Everyone within an organization should understand the value of keeping customers satisfied and happy. Train and reward employees for good customer service.

FIGURE 11-4. Tips for providing excellent customer service.

Fulfillment Options

Options for fulfilling a customer's order include handling all of the processing within the company (in-house), outsourcing the fulfillment activities to an outside fulfillment service, and handling the fulfillment activities online, either in-house or with an outside agency. Let's see what each of these entails and how marketers choose among them.

In-House Fulfillment

Many traditional direct marketing organizations (L. L. Bean, Lands' End, Lillian Vernon, Speigel, Williams-Sonoma, Orvis, Avon, etc.) operate their own fulfillment centers. Most of these direct marketers have invested heavily in automation and bar code systems to make their fulfillment centers more efficient and improve customer service. However, as many professionals agree, automation in a fulfillment operation warehouse must benefit the customer as well as the company. Some direct marketers believe that the ability of an organization to deliver good customer service is *not* dependent on automation alone. They believe that new technology, coupled with a well-trained staff, can create good customer service.

THE IN-HOUSE WAREHOUSE PROCESS. Although some in-house fulfillment centers may differ, most traditional fulfillment warehouses operate in a similar manner. The fulfillment warehouse process normally follows the steps presented in Figure 11-5. Let's walk through the process step by step:

1. The direct marketer receives the customer's order via mail, phone, fax, or the Internet.

2. The marketer processes the order and checks inventory levels (if they have not already been checked while receiving the order).

3. The direct marketer sends several documents per order to the warehouse, including the packing slip and the picking list. The **packing slip** identifies the products to be included with the order, and the **picking list** normally provides routing information regarding the most efficient way to physically move through the warehouse and assemble the items ordered by the customer.

4. Fulfillment center personnel, often called *pickers,* physically move through the warehouse and as items are picked, the items are merged with the packing slip. The pickers check the items against the packing slip and indicate a correct match with his or her initials. The picker is responsible for order accuracy. Many fulfillment centers now use robots to pick the merchandise instead of having pickers physically walk up and down the aisles of the warehouse. For example, Swisslog, a leading warehouse operations systems provider, offers a robotics system to retrieve cartons and distribute them to appropriate picking stations featured in Figure 11-6. This system uses a 3D matrix of bins to store the goods which are then retrieved by a series of robots. The bin is brought directly to the perspn

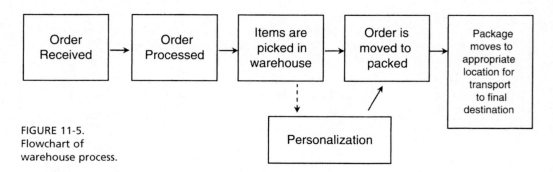

FIGURE 11-5.
Flowchart of
warehouse process.

FIGURE 11-6.
Swisslog robotic
retrieval to
picking stations.
Used with
permission of
Swisslog, Newport
News, Virginia.

doing the item picking, no walking around searching for an items location—hence the term a goods-to-person system.

5. The order then moves to a packing area, where the *packer* rechecks the products picked against the order and initials the packing slip before boxing the order. This is a second quality control checkpoint.

6. The packer packs the items into an appropriately sized carton enclosing a variety of materials, including a catalog, gift boxes, dunnage material (like foam or bubble wrap to protect products during shipment), and promotional inserts. These materials are within an arm's reach of the packer to ensure high productivity levels. As shown in Figure 11-6, warehouse employees must inspect, weigh, and scan each package before it is shipped to the customer.

7. Finally, the package moves via conveyor belt to the appropriate truck for transportation to its destination. Often, prior to the package leaving the warehouse, a warehouse supervisor randomly opens packages to check for order accuracy. This is the third quality control checkpoint.

Other warehouse activities occur simultaneously. For example, the direct marketer is collecting customer database information and updating customer records. Additionally, the warehouse is receiving shipments of products and warehouse employees are responsible for restocking the inventory as well as replenishing the packaging stations with packing materials, such as tissue paper, inserts, and bulk packing material called peanuts. Sometimes a portion of a customer's order is sent to a specific location in the warehouse to be personalized. This may involve a wide array of sophisticated machinery and trained operators to fulfill the customer's request for personalization. Let's briefly explore what is involved in personalization processes.

PERSONALIZATION. Free personalization is popular with many customers. Personalization operators must carefully read the packing slip to ensure accuracy in the personalization process.

FIGURE 11-7.
Swisslog High
Bay automated
storage. Used
with permission
of Swisslog,
Newport News,
Virginia.

Personalization processes include engraving, stamping, sandblasting, heat press transferring, embroidery, and more. Though computers run many of the personalization machines, operators are responsible for ensuring accuracy and preventing malfunction. Once the operators personalize the product, the fulfillment process continues to order processors in the picking department, where the personalized product is placed with the rest of the customer's order.

Inventory availability drives the efficiency and success of the entire fulfillment process. Occasionally a customer will not be shipped their complete order due to the inventory not being in stock. In this situation, the customer is informed that the product is on back order and will be shipped by a specified date. Most in-house warehouses store huge quantities of inventory, often stocked so high that special equipment is needed to obtain the merchandise cartons as needed. Figure 11-7 reveals the large quantity of inventory typically stored at a distribution center and the Swisslog high bay automated storage vehicle used to retrieve merchandise from the warehouse shelves.

The warehouse processes of most in-house fulfillment operations are highly sophisticated and computerized. The Zone Pick-to-light System from Swisslog shown in Figure 11-8 is a good example of the automation involved in the warehouse process. This system reduces employee picking time dramatically by having a flashing light identify the bins from which the picker must

FIGURE 11-8.
Swisslog Zone
Pick-to-light
System. Used with
permission of
Swisslog, Newport
News, Virginia.

secure an item for the order currently being packed. As goods are exhausted in the picking area, a system of storage and retrieval cranes behind each picking location automatically replenish inventory to allow non-stop order fulfillment.

Most distribution center operations use computer-originated bar codes to enable orders to be tracked and packages to be physically moved throughout the center and routed to appropriate distribution areas for timely delivery. Conveyor belts are used to swiftly transport the shipping cartons through the warehouse.

An excellent example of an in-house fulfillment center is that of Zappos.com. Its warehouse is highly automated, featuring robots that pick up and carry 1,000 to 3,000 pounds of product, depending on the robot model. These robots are in constant motion carrying one of Zappos's 3,000 storage pods to or from packing stations enabling a Zappos employee to take an item from a pod and put it a shipping box at a packing rate of 600 items per hour. That translates to one item being packed every six seconds! This is impressive fulfillment productivity with the goal of serving customers efficiently and effectively. Among the great features of robots is that, unlike humans, they don't need to take a rest break, nor do they care about air conditioning or lighting. As can be seen in Figure 11-9, telescoping conveyers are used to insert the shipping carton directly onto the delivery truck at the Zappos fulfillment center. This highly automated process aids in reducing fulfillment center operating costs while maximizing speed with which the orders get delivered to customers. This is how Zappos is able to provide superior shipping to its customers.

However, some direct marketers do not believe in this traditional in-house fulfillment process. They do not support the storage of products and having inventories sitting in a warehouse waiting for an order to be placed by the customer. They support the concept referred to as "integrated order fulfillment."

INTEGRATED ORDER FULFILLMENT. Integrated order fulfillment is an emerging business concept based on the idea that the process of building and delivering products should not begin until after the firm receives an order for them. This is in sharp contrast to the traditional fulfillment model, in which assorted products are collected and stored in the distribution center warehouse until an order arrives.

FIGURE 11-9.
Zappos cartons
loading on
delivery truck.
Used with
permission of
Zappos.

The following eight steps describe the process of integrated order fulfillment:[5]

Step 1: The direct marketer receives a customer's order via mail, phone, fax, or the Internet.

Step 2: The direct marketer processes the order. This includes logging the order into the computer system and determining whether any special promotions or discounts should be noted on the customer's invoice.

Step 3: Next, sourcing occurs. This is where the direct marketer determines where the individual products or components needed to fill the order will come from. The primary choices are the company's own production lines or an outside contract manufacturer.

Step 4: Now it is time for the direct marketer to store the product. This is the brief holding of products or components in a warehouse until their scheduled delivery or manufacture times.

Step 5: The direct marketer assembles the product. Product assembly includes the gathering of parts in a central place where they are put together to form the finished product.

Step 6: Next, the direct marketer ships the product to the customer.

Step 7: The direct marketer tracks the distribution of the product and fulfills any after-sale service needs.

Step 8: Finally, the customer grades the company on how well it performs the entire process on each individual order.

Integrated order fulfillment will not work for every organization. It is primarily designed for those direct marketers who manufacture custom-made products on a customer-by-customer basis. According to Stig Durlow, chairman and CEO of the Swedish software company Industrial Matematik International, which manufactures a popular fulfillment software system called System ESS, "Integrated order fulfillment helps companies make the jump from the industrial age to the information age by forcing everyone within the enterprise—including outside contractors—to think first about exactly what the customer has asked for before taking any action toward fulfilling a particular order."[6]

Integrated order fulfillment is carried out at the fulfillment center of well-known direct marketer and personal computer manufacturer, Dell. When a consumer places an order, Dell builds the computer precisely to the customer's specification. Dell's customers are able to select different performance options and add-ons. When a customer visits Dell's Web site or calls the company, he or she custom-designs his or her computer online or over the phone with a representative. The computer is built and shipped to the customer. Probably the most valuable thing Dell offers its customers is a customer-oriented approach to product customization that carries over to a comprehensive approach to customer service. Dell believes that each customer is unique and integrated order fulfillment is one way to serve these distinct needs.

Outside Fulfillment Centers

Once upon a time, most traditional direct marketers had their own fulfillment or distribution centers to warehouse products until picked and packed for shipment to customers. However, this traditional fulfillment model is changing. Today, many direct marketers are extending their businesses to the Web and are realizing their need to quickly convert their operating models from shipping in bulk to processing thousands of daily online orders consisting of just a few items.[7] So they are outsourcing their fulfillment operations to third-party fulfillment centers or online fulfillment providers to obtain the customer service expertise they need. Many direct marketers are moving toward the business model that management experts have dubbed the **virtual enterprise.** According to this model, the company whose name appears on any given product is primarily a marketing and customer service entity, with actual product development and distribution being handled by a broad—and sometimes far flung—network of subcontractors.[8]

ADVANTAGES OF AN OUTSIDE FULFILLMENT SERVICE. There are certain distinct advantages of hiring an outside contractor to provide back-end support versus handling fulfillment in-house. Some of those advantages include the ability of the company to focus more specifically on marketing and sales activities as opposed to warehousing and distributing tasks. Another advantage is that outside fulfillment companies are likely to have state-of-the-art fulfillment software that most direct marketers would otherwise find too expensive to acquire. A third advantage concerns financial risk. By contracting outside fulfillment services, direct marketers can treat fulfillment costs as variable costs. Thus, there will be less financial risk because fulfillment costs will be more predictable. A final advantage is that the direct marketer may receive equivalent fulfillment services at a lower cost per order than would have been the case with in-house fulfillment.

Some traditional retailers just getting started in direct marketing activities, especially those planning to use electronic media, have also decided to outsource their fulfillment operations to a third party. They quickly realize that fulfillment capabilities are outside their general core competencies. Many other direct marketers are outsourcing fulfillment operations so that they may concentrate on multichannel marketing activities, especially those tasks associated with the Web.

An Example of an Outside Fulfillment Company

Dick's Sporting Goods has looked to outside fulfillment for its e-commerce division, announcing a fifteen-year extension of its partnership with GSI Commerce in 2008. GSI Commerce provides Dick's Sporting Goods with a full range of services associated with Dick's e-commerce, customer service, fulfillment, shipping, and marketing processes. Dick's Sporting Goods began its relationship with GSI in 2001, and sales through its Web site, dickssportinggoods.com, grew significantly—more than tenfold—by 2008. Dick's Sporting Goods envisions growth of its multichannel business approach by another tenfold over the coming decade. GSI is also directing Dick's Sporting Goods toward greater innovation, such as in-store pickup and in-store ordering, to provide even more customer convenience and satisfaction.[9]

Online Fulfillment

Of all the changes that computers and information technology have brought to our modern society, few are more visible than the change in the way products and services are bought and sold. Digital media raise new managerial and customer service challenges for direct marketing organizations. Many organizations have learned the hard way that there is more to e-commerce than just opening a Web site and inviting consumers to come and shop. It is well established that the primary problem with e-commerce customer satisfaction is *fulfillment.*

Fulfillment guru Bill Kuipers sees little change in fulfillment as a result of electronic media. "You still have to warehouse, pack, and ship."[10] Kuipers believes that companies need to plan for the fulfillment process when they use the Internet. Customers shopping online have higher expectations and service standards than do their offline counterparts. Customers are looking for a quicker response to their order or inquiry. They often expect to receive a response to their online communication the same day—and no later than the next day, and they like to be able to investigate the shipping status of their orders online. These high consumer expectations can be a real fulfillment nightmare for the online direct marketer who isn't able to meet them.

Many of the benefits of the automated warehouse are provided by radio frequency identification (RFID). RFID is a technology that enables the wireless identification and subsequent tracking of products. RFID technology has been used by thousands of companies for more than a decade to support a variety of manufacturing, retailing, and warehousing processes along the supply chain. Through the transmission of radio frequencies between an RFID tag with a programmed microchip and a specialized receiving device, companies such as Target and Walmart can immediately locate items and determine inventory levels. This enables them to improve supply chain efficiency and ensure that a given product is in stock when customers want to buy it.[11] RFID can essentially provide a 70 percent improvement in counting efficiency over bar codes, and in the warehouse, that means reduced labor and human error.[12]

E-FULFILLMENT. E-fulfillment refers to the integration of people, processes, and technology to ensure customer satisfaction before, during, and after the online buying experience.[13] Online retailers have what may be the unique ability to extend the interaction with their customers by creating a memorable and distinct fulfillment experience. Unlike passive traditional media, interactive media put the consumer in control, with both positive and negative consequences. The positive include the great opportunity for building brand awareness and enhancing the relationship between customer and company. An example of e-fulfillment is Amazon.com with its entrance into the e-fulfillment market in 2008. Through its Fulfillment Web Service merchants can store their own products with Amazon's fulfillment centers and then, using a simple Web service interface, fulfill orders for the products when needed.[14] This process frees merchants from the fulfillment process, but provides them with control over inventory of their products creating practically a virtual business.[15]

The major problem with many e-commerce organizations is that they lack the needed focus and emphasis on e-fulfillment. According to Kuipers, e-commerce organizations treat fulfillment and customer service as incidental rather than fundamental. They're interested in technical capabilities—instant messages, e-mail, click-to-talk, and so on—and they don't realize that what they need most to satisfy the customer and keep the customer coming back is a polished customer fulfillment infrastructure.[16] However, that may be in part due to the fact that most organizations wanting to attract and obtain customer orders electronically don't have the fulfillment systems or infrastructures and don't want to be in the warehousing business. Therefore, these organizations normally outsource or hire third-party service bureaus to sort, pick, pack, and ship the product.

Delivery Options

Because the delivery of products is such a vital part of the fulfillment operations of direct marketers, we should look at the alternative delivery options that are available, especially those that provide individual delivery to households and businesses rather than those that handle bulk shipments. Direct marketers are concerned with product delivery, but also with the delivery of advertising and other promotion materials.

U.S. Postal Service

The volume and scope of operations of the U.S. Postal Service (USPS) is mind-boggling.[17] The USPS handles more than 169.15 billion pieces of mail annually.[18] The total number of pieces of mail attributable to direct mail in 2010 was slightly more than 90 billion, representing 53.3 percent of total mail volume.[19]

FIRST-CLASS MAIL. This category includes business reply envelopes and cards. The postage rate is higher than for the other classes but so is the cost of priority handling and individual sorting. This category of mail is the largest source of mail revenue for the USPS, although that percentage has been steadily shrinking over the past few decades. It generated 70 percent of USPS revenue in 1977, 64.6 percent in 1987, 54.1 percent in 2005, and 50.7 percent in 2010.[20]

PERIODICALS. The periodicals category consists of publications. It includes magazines, newspapers, and miscellaneous periodicals, such as classroom publications. It accounted for 4.3 percent of total mail volume in 2005. This category of mail generated 3.6 percent of USPS revenue in 1977, 4.4 percent in 1987, 3.2 percent in 2005, and 3.0 percent in 2.8 percent in 2010.[21]

STANDARD MAIL. Standard mail is the category mainly used for the distribution of direct response advertising. Although postage rates are lower per piece, mailers of this class must ZIP code their mail, sort and bundle, tie, bag, and personally deliver the sacks of mail to the post office. Thus, the direct mailer performs up to half the basic tasks normally performed by the postal service for first-class mail. Delivery is also deferred. This class accounted for 25.8 percent of total mail revenue in 2010 compared with 28.4 percent 2005. This class represents the second largest source of revenue for the USPS. Standard mail accounted for slightly more than 31.6 percent of mail volume in 2010, compared with 47.8 percent 2005.[22]

SPECIAL MAIL SERVICES. There are certain alternatives for expedited mail service of special interest to direct marketers. These include services such as Express Mail, which is guaranteed overnight service to designated destinations for items mailed prior to 5 P.M. In addition, the USPS continues to offer more online services (att www.usps.com) such as Mailing Online, Card Store, Certified Mail, and Postecs. Using NetPost, for instance, you can send professionally printed letters, postcards, and booklets that have been created on a personal computer. NetPost also offers CardStore, an ideal way to customize your business or personal message.

Alternative Delivery Systems

Although the Private Express Statutes grant the USPS a form of monopoly over first-class mail delivery, they have been in transition and now make private delivery services possible under certain conditions. Alternatives to first-class mail, permitted under the Private Express Statutes provided they meet certain criteria, include FedEx® and major airlines. FedEx® provides 8.5 million worldwide shipments daily using a fleet of 697 aircrafts and more than 80,000 motorized vehicles across some 220 countries and territories.[23]

Other alternatives for the delivery of information include telephone and the Internet, as well as additional emerging forms of electronic message transmission. Certain publications, including *Better Homes and Gardens* and the *Wall Street Journal,* among others, have been experimenting with delivery alternatives to the periodicals category of mail. These alternatives have been increasing as have the number of private firms distributing direct mail advertising, including samples, in selected markets.

Fulfillment Problems

Everybody makes mistakes—and fulfillment centers are no exception. The crucial point for the direct marketer is becoming aware of the mistake and fixing it promptly—making it right for the customer so that the final impression is a positive one. Keep in mind that the fulfillment experience often determines whether the customer will respond to the next sales offer.

What are some common sources of fulfillment problems and how can direct marketers attempt to avoid these mistakes? Let's examine these two important issues.

Sources of Fulfillment Problems

Many of the most common fulfillment problems originate in the warehouse. These problems can occur in many ways. Let's look at some of the potential sources of fulfillment problems:

- Accuracy of the order: Delivering the wrong product to the customer is a costly mistake. It may result in losing the customer's future business as the customer has lost a certain degree of confidence in the direct marketer.

- Package presentation: Packaging is an extension of the company's image, and sloppy packaging communicates a poor image. Small details like the correct position of the label on the mailing carton and the neatness of the outer carton seal are important. Even more important is the product placement within the package—making sure that the product is upright or positioned the best way to ensure it reaches the customer in good condition.

- Speed of delivery: In today's electronic age, customers demand faster delivery than ever before. However, accuracy cannot be sacrificed for speed. Therefore, the fulfillment challenge is to process and fill orders as efficiently as possible.

- Stock availability:Delivering what you offer is the ultimate role of fulfillment. Maintaining an accurate inventory system and an adequate amount of inventory is crucial to fulfillment success. Back orders commonly result not only in the loss of a sale but also loss of a customer.

- Return processing:It would be wonderful if every product a customer ordered was received and kept. The fact is that many products get returned for many different reasons and direct marketers must process these returns in a timely and professional manner.

Other common fulfillment problems come from areas outside the warehouse and are commonly related to customer database files. Included in this category of fulfillment mistakes are not thanking the customer for the order, sending the customer an invoice *after* payment has already been sent, misspelling the customer's name, and using the incorrect prefix (for example, using Mr. or Ms. instead of Dr.). Mistakes like these can make the customer skeptical and could result in the loss of future business.

Ways to Avoid Fulfillment Problems

Fortunately, direct marketers can take simple steps to avoid fulfillment problems and actually assist the organization in exceeding consumer expectations. Although many of these may seem like common sense marketing, not all direct marketers exercise these steps. The ways to avoid fulfillment problems include the following:

- Pay careful attention to the packing slips and picking lists to ensure that orders get filled accurately and expediently.

- Include a toll-free number for customer service in a prominent place on the catalog, direct-mail piece, Internet site, or packing slip with the order. If your toll-free phone line is too expensive because too many calls are coming in, then maybe you've got too many service problems. So fix them.[24] However, you should encourage your customers to call you even if the problem is small.

- Hire a professional, well-trained customer service staff. If your customers are important to you, make sure their interaction with your organization is a positive experience. Nothing is more frustrating for a consumer than dealing with an inept customer service representative. The more positive you can make the customer experience the greater the probability the customer will return and purchase from your organization again. Smart direct marketers ensure repeat business by establishing customer service standards and monitoring customer service representatives (often via tape-recorded phone calls) to measure and control the service level.

- Establish quality control measures for each phase of the fulfillment process. From order receiving to warehousing, from order processing to shipping and delivery, from picking and packing to handling customer complaints, each part of the fulfillment process is important and you should establish and monitor quality control standards that focus on the customer. Service levels are shaped by the needs of the target audience, the desired image of the company, and management's ability to define and implement the necessary programs and systems in the operation.[25] Setting up these quality control standards, communicating them to all employees, and monitoring their performance and ultimate effect on customer satisfaction is a proactive approach to delivering quality service and to avoiding fulfillment problems before they begin.

Call Centers

A **call center** is a dedicated team supported by various telephone technological resources to provide responses to customer inquiries.[26] Some marketers think of call centers as the "telephonic front door" to the company or the main access point for obtaining information or placing an order. In essence, the call center is the formal entity of an organization, or representing an organization, that handles communication with any type of stakeholder. Regardless of whether a customer is placing an order, calling to check on the status of an order, inquiring about new products or services, seeking technical support, or placing a complaint, the call center should provide a seamless communication process and quality service.

In addition to receiving phone orders, the call center provides answers for customers who call with questions or problems they may have concerning a product or an order. For example, Pittsburgh-based PNC Bank has devised a customer rating program that automatically activates when customers contact its National Financial Services Center. It uses software that requires customers to enter their PIN or Social Security number. The bank determines the customer's identity and analyzes that person's past transactions with the bank and places the customer into one of several preset based segments. Callers with basic transactions are transferred to an entry-level representative. Callers with complex financial histories are given to handlers with a specific expertise. A "most valuable customer" is routed to a relationship consultant—one of 30 or 40 service representatives deemed the bank's very best.[27]

Call centers can operate (1) within the company or in-house; (2) outside the company, when calls are made or taken by a teleservice outsourcing firm; or (3) a combination of both. Each type of call center organization has similar functions, yet all have unique features and challenges. The decision about how to carry out telemarketing activities ultimately is a function of the company's financial situation and the nature of its telemarketing program. A major factor in determining whether to establish the call center in-house or outsource it is the expected pattern of calls. When customer orders are expected to come into the company all at once (or within a relatively short time interval), it becomes difficult to staff the call center to receive and process each order on a timely basis. This is when outsourcing begins to look attractive because nothing is worse than putting your customers "on hold." Only outsourcers with thousands of positions can handle such call volume effectively. According to Peppers and Rogers, "Customers today are accustomed to having their needs met immediately, completely, conveniently, and inexpensively."[28]

Organizations measure the level of customer dissatisfaction by calculating the rate of **call abandonment,** the number of callers who hang up before being served by a sales representative. Companies strive to keep this rate as low as possible. However, during peak calling times, consumers may abandon a higher percent of the calls. To reduce customer frustration, many companies route incoming calls through interactive voice response equipment to capture preliminary information and balance the workload among teleservice agents. Nonetheless, even one missed call can lead to the loss of a sale and, more important, the loss of a customer. At these times outside service centers should handle customer orders. Let's examine both in-house and outsourced call centers.

In-House Call Center

In-house call centers require substantial investment in facilities and equipment. Direct marketers can place outbound calls or receive inbound calls from the same call center due to advances in telephone and computer technology. The process of setting up an in-house call center and managing an ongoing program entails many activities. These include (but are not limited to) obtaining support from top management, setting goals and objectives, developing scripts and guides, recruiting and training personnel, designing a productive work environment, developing measurement systems, testing systems and procedures, and reporting and controlling the operation. Personnel issues comprise a sizable portion of this process—from obtaining support of top management to reporting and controlling the operation.

The biggest advantage of establishing an in-house call center is the degree of control the company has over the telemarketing operations. The biggest disadvantages of an in-house call center are the time it takes to properly train representatives and the large financial burden. Many in-house call centers, especially those B2C organizations that offer seasonal products, rely on a large number of seasonal, part-time, or flex-time employees.

Outside (Oursourced/Outsourcing) Call Centers

Outsourcing formally refers to the process of having all call center activities handled by an outside organization or a teleservice outsourcer. The primary advantage of outsourcing for the marketer is a reduction in expenses and capital outlays. Most call center outsourcers are larger than in-house call centers and can more easily accommodate a large volume of seasonal orders. Additionally, because of their size, they offer lower costs and provide better formal training for telephone operators than in-house call centers. In addition, most call center outsourcers tend to use the most advanced technology available to stay efficient.

There are five main advantages to using an outside service bureau to conduct a company's telemarketing program:

1. Low initial investment: marketers pay for the telemarketing program on a short-term basis only.
2. Elimination of hiring needs: marketers eliminate the day-to-day managerial tasks associated with hiring employees.
3. Fixed operating costs: with a defined rate schedule provided by the call center outsourcer.
4. Quick start-up: shorter lead times for implementing the telemarketing program.
5. Time flexibility: 24-hour, 7-day-a-week service for inbound calling and, as required by the FTC, restricted hours for outbound calling.

There are also disadvantages associated with call center outsourcers:[29]

1. Lack of direct control: the company does not have the same degree of control over an external organization.
2. Lack of direct security: because of the remote location of the call center outsourcer, the company cannot keep its customer information in its exclusive possession. However, most call center outsourcers take great security measures.
3. Lack of employee loyalty. employees possess greater loyalty to the call center outsourcer than to the company that they are representing on the telephone.
4. Mass-market approach. service bureaus are high-volume businesses, thus the quality of the sales pitch for any single company could suffer.
5. Caliber of personnel. often call center outsourcers pay less than in-house call centers, thus the quality of personnel is affected.

Regardless of the aforementioned disadvantages, many telemarketing companies successfully outsource their call center activities to service bureaus. In fact many outsource their call center operations to call centers in international locations as the geographic location has an impact on its operating costs.

The Importance of Customer Service

Each customer wants to be satisfied. **Customer satisfaction** has been defined as the extent to which a firm fulfills a consumer's needs, desires, and expectations.[30] Contrary to what many believe, the customer doesn't care about what has to happen behind the scenes to get the product or service delivered on time. The customer is primarily interested in what the marketer can do to satisfy his or her needs.

Direct marketers know that simply providing a quality product or service is not enough. So they have begun to create strategies designed to move goods from factories and warehouses directly to the customer in the shortest possible time and at the lowest possible cost, using the level of service to differentiate their organization from others. Customer service also enables the organization to exceed rather than simply meet the customer's expectations. Delivering high-quality customer service can enable the direct marketer to develop a long-term relationship with each customer, which is, after all, the ultimate goal of direct marketing. In essence, the task of **customer relationship management (CRM)** as discussed earlier in Chapter 2, is a big-picture approach that integrates sales, order fulfillment, call center operations, and customer service and coordinates and unifies all points of interaction with the customer, throughout the customer life cycle and across multiple channels.

Business doesn't end when an order is received. In fact, most direct marketers believe that is when it begins. Let's take a look at the customer service strategies direct marketers implement before and after a customer places an order. What does a customer experience when shopping online?

Imagine you are sitting at your computer in the comforts of your home. You have just connected to Zappos online (www.zappos.com). Stop there for a moment. How did you get to this point? This is also a part of customer service—because serving the customer begins with researching and analyzing the customer's needs and wants. A great deal of business planning, consumer research, and historical sales analysis has gone into determining which products are offered to customers and how the items are displayed on the Web pages. In addition, great care has been put forth to organize and design the Web site so you, the customer, can easily navigate and shop from it. Zappos strives to make the site easier for you to use by not having to enter information more than once. Zappos uses the customer information that you enter to help the company help you quickly find information, products and services, create content that is most relevant to you, and alert you to new information, products and services that might be of interest to you. The company also offers a "How Do You Like Our Website" feedback link to gather information that can be used to better serve you in the future.

Once you make a product selection the Web site may offer additional related products or services. This is an example of up-selling, cross-selling, and suggestive selling. Any of these suggested items may be added to your shopping cart with a simple click. Then the Web site visually displays your updated shopping cart. This point provides another cross-selling opportunity with an offer to purchase some inexpensive unrelated items. Think of this as offering impulse items—similar to those that are located near the checkout counters in traditional retail stores.

Once you make your final selections, you proceed to a checkout stage where the Web site totals the order, adds shipping and handling fees, and verifies personalization (if applicable). The shipping and billing addresses are determined, as is the method of payment. Most direct marketers offer several payment methods to enable each customer to select the preferred method. Next, Zappos sends you an order confirmation. This is an opportunity for the company to thank the customer and to provide the order number in case the customer has an inquiry about that particular order. It also enables Zappos's customers an option to sign up for its weekly newsletter.

What happens next? Within a day or two, Zappos may send you an e-mail providing details about the status of your online order. This is an additional opportunity for the direct marketer to thank you for your order and to provide an update. In addition, it allows the company to remind you about its customer service priority and how its products carry a 100 percent money-back guarantee. In sum, it enables the direct marketer to strengthen the relationship it has with the customer.

Zappos enters the information collected about you and your transaction data into its customer database. The company will use this information to target future direct response communications to you and better serve you in the future. From this point on, the direct marketer will communicate with you on a regular basis. Each time Zappos contacts you via some direct response media (e.g., an outbound e-mail, phone call, or catalog), the contact and response (if applicable) will help further the customer relationship. Although we've used an online example here, all customer service activities are similar whether online, through a catalog, or via a telephone contact. The main purpose of all back-end functions is to serve the customer more effectively. When carried out well, such back-end functions can strengthen customer relationships and encourage customers to continue to purchase from the organization.

Beyond waiting for the customer to repeat purchase, how do direct marketers determine the

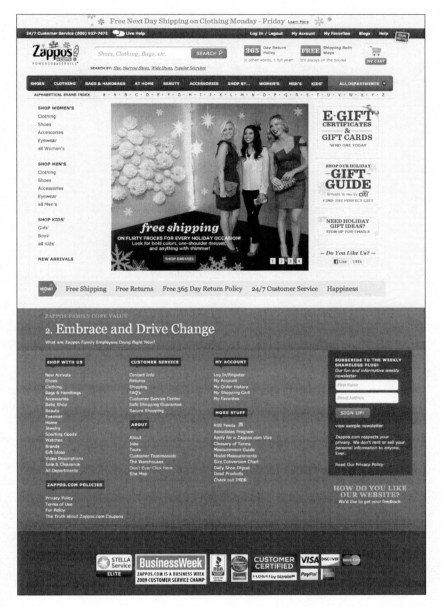

FIGURE 11-10. Zappos.com home page. Used with permission of Zappos.

strength of their relationship with the customer? How does a direct marketer assess the level of service the customer is receiving from their organization? How will direct marketers determine whether their relationship with each customer can be improved? How can they know what is best for the customer? The next section details how direct marketers can evaluate customer satisfaction levels.

Evaluating Customer Satisfaction Level

Direct marketers can evaluate the level of customer satisfaction in a number of ways. First, they might begin by pretending they are the customer. Every organization likes to think they are doing a good job of serving their customers. But savvy direct marketers investigate this from both sides of the relationship. Are inquiries processed in a timely manner? Are customer com-

Please tell us how we rated:	Excellent	Good	Fair	Poor
Knowledgeable Phone Operators	❑	❑	❑	❑
Promptness of Delivery	❑	❑	❑	❑
Overall Impression of Service	❑	❑	❑	❑
Other Comments:				

FIGURE 11-11. Sample customer survey.

plaints addressed as quickly and as professionally as they should be? Is delivery time as expedient as you promised the customer it would be? Direct marketers determine the answers to these questions in two ways:

1. Place an inquiry, order, or a complaint with the organization under a fictitious name and experience firsthand the level of customer service your organization really delivers.

2. Send periodic follow-up surveys consisting of only a few questions designed to address a customer's fulfillment experience. Questions might address the speed, accuracy, and degree of staff friendliness the customer experienced when interacting with the organization. An example of a brief customer survey designed for assessing the fulfillment experience is shown in Figure 11-11.

Regardless of how you obtain this information, it is critical to perceive the fulfillment experience from the customer's point of view. This experience and any subsequent action you take should lead to an improved relationship with the customer.

A strong focus on CRM is crucial to the success and profitability of every direct marketing organization. Many professionals believe that it may be necessary to make CRM part of the broader concept of customer management because the whole organization must support and participate in customer relationship maintenance. These words from Robert McKim, CEO of MS Database Marketing, sum up the value of customer relationship marketing:

> Gone are the days of empty 'customer is king' lip service. The key to the new rules of success is the ability to address each customer's idiosyncrasies and needs, balanced with their current and future value to the company. Firms that do this can differentiate themselves from the competition, forge long-term customer relationships, engender customer loyalty, stop attrition and enjoy success in the 21st century.[31]

The next section provides suggestions and examples of how to keep customers happy.

Keeping Customers Happy

At the foundation of customer service is the simple notion of *keeping the customer happy*. Only a satisfied customer is a happy customer. Only a satisfied customer will come back and purchase from your organization again and again. However, keeping customers happy does not happen by accident. Direct marketers need to constantly keep abreast of the customer's changing needs and wants and must always strive to satisfy these. Some classic suggestions for keeping customers happy are shown here.

• Remember that the customer is always right.

• Don't promise something you cannot deliver.

• Inform your customers about how to return products.

- Inform your customers about how to complain.
- Test your own service.
- Date and record all customer correspondence.
- Investigate your competitor's offerings on a regular basis.
- Exercise care in billing and collection.[32]

Many companies go out of their way to exceed customer expectations and delight the customer. Let's look at an example of great customer service. One holiday season a customer ordered two Towers of Treats from the Harry and David Specialty Foods and Gifts catalog to have delivered to two neighbors. The customer had placed the order in time to have the packages arrive the day or two prior to seeing the neighbors at a dinner party. The packages didn't arrive before the date of the dinner, nor did they arrive before the holiday. When the customer found this out, she phoned the company. The customer service department was very professional and apologetic and offered to resend the ordered items that had not arrived. Within a week, the packages were received by each of the neighbors and the customer received a note of thanks for both her order and her patience, another apology for the inconvenience, *and* a free gift. Mistakes happen, but how they are handled can either contribute to a positive customer experience or reinforce a negative one.

Good customer service is an important part of fulfilling the customer's expectations.

Summary

Fulfillment encompasses all the activities a company has with a customer after the initial order has been placed. It can also be defined as the final impression left with the customer. In the fulfillment process, there is a chance for additional communication with a customer, including making available promotional materials and/or new catalogs included in the shipment of an order. Being attentive to detail in the fulfillment process should generate satisfied customers and future business for the organization. Customer service and fulfillment activities are vital to the success of any direct marketing organization. They may not be glamorous, but they are the guts of direct marketing. There are six steps in the fulfillment process—offer, response, processing, shipping, billing, and customer service. Direct marketers may select from various fulfillment options, including in-house fulfillment, outside fulfillment centers, and online fulfillment, to serve its customers. In addition, direct marketers must select from the various delivery options, available for shipping products to consumers. These delivery options include multichannel distribution, USPS, and alternative delivery systems.

Direct marketers should recognize the most common fulfillment problems along with ways to avoid these problems.

Another key aspect of fulfillment involves call center operations. Call centers can operate within the company, outside the company, or a combination of both. Regardless of where the call center is located, qualified personnel are the key to effectively serving the customer.

The importance of customer service begins with an understanding of customer satisfaction and CRM. Direct marketers follow a step-by-step process to ensure customer relationships are managed properly. Direct marketers use personal experience and surveys to determine whether the organization is providing good customer service and keeping customers happy. Good customer service, correct order entry, and prompt order delivery generates satisfied customers and repeat buyers.

Key Terms

fulfillment	e-fulfillment
offer	call center
packing slip	call abandonment
picking list	outsourcing
integrated order fulfillment	customer satisfaction
virtual enterprise	customer relationship management (CRM)

Review Questions

1. List and describe the six steps of the fulfillment process.
2. Discuss some common fulfillment problems along with actions direct marketers may take to avoid future fulfillment problems. Why don't all direct marketers exercise these preventive measures?
3. What are some of the ways a firm can keep their customers happy? Describe from your own personal experience the actions direct marketers have taken to keep you happy.
4. Describe the relationship between fulfillment and customer service.
5. Describe how the traditional fulfillment model is changing.
6. Compare the advantages and disadvantages between in-house fulfillment and outside fulfillment services. Name some companies that are using the different types of fulfillment services.
7. List and explain the eight steps of the integrated order fulfillment concept.
8. What is the function of a call center? How does it fit within the fulfillment process?
9. Explain some of the primary challenges associated with operating a call center?
10. Describe the ways a company can interact with its customers to strengthen those relationships and maximize customer satisfaction.

Exercise

You are an employee of a small clothing boutique that also distributes a catalog. You work in the fulfillment department. Currently the company uses in-house fulfillment, but you learn that your boss is considering using an outside fulfillment service to meet demand, in part because it may be less expensive. Business has grown rapidly since the company has gone online and is now receiving online orders. Voice your opinion on the matter of outside fulfillment. Should the company keep fulfilling orders in-house or should they use an outside fulfillment source? What about the call center functions—should those also be outsourced? What variables would impact your decision? Be sure to give specific reasons to support your position on the matter.

Critical Thinking Exercise

Visit www.zappos.com and any other online retailer and examine how each company addresses customer issues and concerns. Compare and contrast. What strategies and tactics are being effectively employed? Explain. What might each company do to enhance its customer service?

CASE: 1-800-FLOWERS.COM

This case provides real stories of how 1-800-FLOWERS.COM has made its customers the top priority and how it has been able to motivate its employees to embrace this customer orientation. The roles of changing technology and changing consumer needs have led the company to become a successful multichannel direct marketer. This case illustrates the important role that high-quality customer service and employee motivation play in building a successful enterprise. Jim McCann, CEO of 1-800-FLOWERS.COM, demonstrates how his company combines recognition of people with technology to build a highly profitable direct marketing business.

The original 1-800-FLOWERS was started by a group of successful businessmen from Dallas, Texas. The founders spent $30 million during their first year of business and built the world's largest telemarketing center. This call center consisted of million-dollar telephone switches, state-of-the-art computer systems, 700 workstations, and a detailed bridge command center to oversee the entire operation. The operation was housed in 55,000 square feet of office space. A network of 6,800 "fulfilling florists" were paid on a commission basis to create, package, and deliver the orders received by the 1-800-FLOWERS telecommunications call center.

Sounds great? You bet! Was it profitable? No way! With that kind of killer overhead and nobody with a burning desire to manage the business on a daily basis, the company lost money right from the start. What was missing in the business start-up was a focus on the customer. The original owners failed to establish relationships with their customers.

One day, in walks Jim McCann, then owner of Flora Plenty, a successful 14-store retail chain of florists in New York. Flora Plenty was doing extensive telemarketing for its retail chain, plus it was one of the fulfilling florists for 1-800-FLOWERS. McCann had a passion for serving the customer, and he sincerely believed in the 1-800-FLOWERS concept. He thought the company could be highly successful if managed properly. Thus, on November 6, 1984, after a few years of negotiation, McCann bought 1-800-FLOWERS for $7 million, and managed it first as a partnership, then later as sole proprietorship. The acquisition gave McCann the right to use the 1-800-FLOWERS phone number but left him buried in debt and scrambling to create a makeshift operation for the new company with very little overhead. In the beginning McCann himself went back to answering the phone: "Thank you for calling 1-800-FLOWERS, how can we help you today?"

McCann knew the three big challenges that were ahead for this troubled business:

1. At that time, toll-free numbers were still new to most consumers, and it was going to take time to build consumer confidence in purchasing via toll-free technology.

2. Most consumers were not aware of 1-800-FLOWERS yet often had a need to purchase flowers. Thus, brand awareness would need to be developed such that consumers thought about 1-800-FLOWERS whenever they had the urge to buy flowers.

3. Most important, there was the challenge of building relationships with customers—one at a time—to gain their loyalty for a lifetime. McCann realized that if he were going to make a business out of something impersonal like buying flowers over the telephone, he would have to create a personal relationship with *every* caller. The sale would be almost secondary.

When McCann first bought the business, it was a lousy deal: several million dollars of debt and a telephone number with a not very good track record. One of the keys in turning 1-800-FLOWERS into a success story in the world of telemarketing has been getting people to want to buy flowers over the phone for someone they really care about. In 1992, as 1-800-FLOWERS entered online commerce (www.1800flowers.com), the company had to give people a reason to want to be in its virtual store. See Figure 11-12 for the company's Web site.

FIGURE 11-12. 1-800-FLOWERS.COM Web site.

The company added personal contact and entertainment to the value equation to make people want to visit its site. McCann credits the fact that 1-800-FLOWERS was named the single most successful business operation on the Web in 1996 to the lessons he learned ten years earlier in telemarketing. He believes the Internet fulfills the same functions as any other retail system, so the jump from telemarketing to modem marketing was a natural one for 1-800-FLOWERS. On the Internet, as with telemarketing, a company must have strong infrastructure to keep track of inventory, process orders, secure billing, and deliver the product. Above all, the business must focus on people.

Today, the company is called 1-800-FLOWERS.COM and people are still its top priority. Training and motivating customer service representatives to provide top-notch customer service are critical to ensure long-term customer relationships. How does 1-800-FLOWERS.COM motivate its customer service representatives? Here are a few examples:

- It is not uncommon for managers to place smiley face stickers on a customer service representative's computer whenever the customer service representative has been seen smiling while on the phone with a customer. Customers can tell a smiling, happy person over the phone, and it makes the customer experience more enjoyable. Thus, the customer service representative is rewarded simply for smiling.

- Like many companies, 1-800-FLOWERS.COM monitors customer service representative phone calls. However, the primary reason for the monitoring is to reveal strengths to be shared with others. This ensures the quality control of customer service representatives and provides clues on how to sharpen the script and improve customer service.

- Public praise of the customer service representative is also common at 1-800-FLOW-ERS.COM. In fact, the company purchased a refrigerator door and mounted it on the wall at the entrance to the customer service area. Whenever a customer service representative was found doing something noteworthy, the manager wrote it up and stuck it to the door with a magnet.

- There is a legends book at 1-800-FLOWERS.COM. This book is filled with stories of associates going the extra mile to please a customer. This book is given to new customer service representatives as a part of their training—it provides the rules for working in customer service. The new employees are told that if what they are doing to serve a customer is not worthy of being included in the Legends book, then they are probably not doing enough.

In summary, old-fashioned rules have been the guiding light to McCann in building 1-800-FLOWERS.COM into a successful business. McCann believes in putting a premium on people and making an emotional contact—by planting emotional seeds that will yield sales and build customer relationships far in excess of a simple sale. The company tries to please each and every customer. If a customer isn't happy, company policy is to "find out what it will take to make the unsatisfied customer happy, then do it." The 1-800-FLOWERS.COM "100% SMILE Guarantee™" policy is unique to the floral industry: "If at any time, you are not satisfied with the product you ordered, we will replace it. Or refund your money. Or do whatever it takes to ensure that you, the customer, are happy and will continue to be a customer of ours in the future, as we are here to help you deliver a smile."

Technology also plays a key role in the success of 1-800-FLOWERS.COM. The company uses technology to:

1. process orders more quickly,

2. confirm product delivery more accurately,

3. remind customers of birthdays and anniversaries more faithfully, and

4. free employees to devote themselves to creating customer relationships.

Figure 11-13 shows an example of how 1-800-FLOWERS.COM electronically communicates with its customers. Once a customer places an order, she instantly receives an order confirmation and thank-you e-mail. Follow-up e-mails are sent to update that customer on the status of her order and ultimately confirm delivery.

In addition, 1-800-FLOWERS.COM sends out regular e-mail offers to its customers featuring weekly specials or holiday reminders. Figure 11-14 presents examples of these special offers. Notice how the company effectively promotes its free reminder service.

As McCann puts it, "Computers aren't friendly, people are." Technology is very effective at improving a business, but too much technology can depersonalize a business—which is a bad thing. Over the years, 1-800-FLOWERS.COM has investigated new telephone technology and has experienced both positive and negative outcomes. Technology allowed the company to adjust the length of the phone ring. During the busiest times (Mother's Day, Valentine's Day, and Christmas), customer service representatives had the alternatives of putting people on hold with canned music or letting the phone ring. Since it was already established that people like to have their telephone call answered by the third ring, 1-800-FLOWERS.COM simply extended each ring from 6 seconds to 9 seconds. The company found that there was no perception of a longer

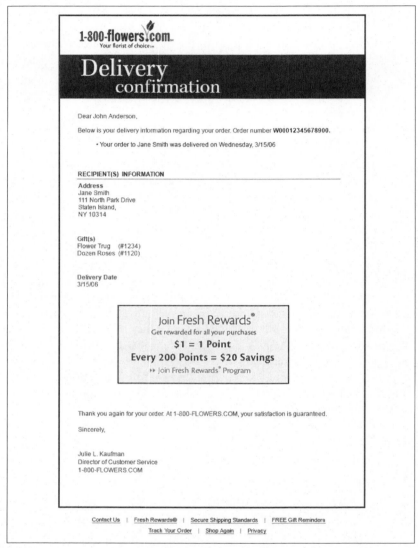

FIGURE 11-13. 1-800-FLOWERS.COM delivery confirmation example.

wait, so with the same number of rings, it was able to serve customers during peak seasons without turning them off with too many rings or too much "elevator music." This same technology enabled the company to pick up the phone before the caller even heard a ring—but callers thought it was downright creepy, as if the company knew what the customer was doing before they did it. Therefore, although technology would allow the company to eliminate phone rings, 1-800-FLOWERS.COM chose to stay with the old-fashioned ring cycle because people felt comfortable with it.

What began as a simple, toll-free number is now a well-established brand. 1-800-FLOWERS.COM has blossomed into a successful direct marketer with a database of loyal customers and a nationwide network of BloomNet florists who have been handpicked to fulfill. The company has become a multichannel direct marketer. It now sells its products via phone, Internet, on-site retail stores, and even catalogs. Figure 11-15 shows a couple of 1-800-FLOWERS.COM catalogs.

FIGURE 11-14.
1-800-FLOWERS.COM Outbound E-mail offers.

The 1-800-FLOWERS.COM call center, once a bunch of crates and boards and telephones down in the basement of a Queens, New York, floral shop, now has the capability to handle millions of calls and Internet orders per week. With unparalleled attention to customers, motivated employees, and modern technology, 1-800-FLOWERS.COM, the world's largest florist, is poised to continue its direct marketing success story well into the future.

In conclusion, according to McCann, "Today 740,000 people are celebrating their birthdays, tomorrow another 740,000 will be celebrating theirs. If you'd like to make one or two of them feel terrific on their special day . . . I know a 1-800 number you can call!" Of course, if you prefer, you may place your order by visiting its Web site instead at 1-800-FLOWERS.COM.[33]

FIGURE 11-15. 1-800-FLOWERS.COM catalog covers.

Case Discussion Questions

1. Discuss how 1-800-FLOWERS.COM became a direct marketing success story. What were the main ingredients in its success?

2. Why did 1-800-FLOWERS.COM become a multichannel direct marketer, instead of specializing solely in telemarketing? How should the company use these channels to support one another?

3. What role did technology play in assisting the company in achieving its goals? Has improved technology always lead to success for 1-800-FLOWERS.com? Support your answer with specific details and examples.

Notes

1. Robert D. Downey, "Proper Fulfillment—Image with the Proper Stuff," *Direct Marketing* (July 1985), 28.

2. Jack Schmid, "How the Back End Drives the Bottom Line," *Target Marketing* 13, no. 5 (May 1990).

3. F. Curtis Barry & Company, Benchmarking Fulfillment ShareGroups, 2007. http://www.fcbco.com/articles-whitepapers/trends-in-fulfillment.asp, retrieved May 5, 2011.

4. Lillian Vernon (1996). *An Eye for Winners* (New York: HarperCollins).

5. Sidney Hill, "Integrated Order Fulfillment for the Virtual Enterprise," dmnews.com, February 1998, retrieved on May 10, 2000, http://www. manufacturingsystems.com.

6. Ibid., p. 3A.

7. Susan Reda, "Customer Service, Brand Management Seen as Key Aspects of On-Line Fulfillment," *Stores* (October 2000), 44.

8. Hill, "Integrated Order Fulfillment for the Virtual Enterprise."

9. http://www.gsicommerce.com/news_events/news_releases/gsi_commerce_and_dicks_sporting_goods _extend_e_commerce_agreement_with_new_/

10. Jonathan Boorstein, "Customer Service: Fulfillment 101," *Direct,* May 2, 2000, retrieved May 2000, http://www.directmag.com/Content/monthly/200/2000050119.htm.

11. http://www.aimglobal.org/technologies/RFID/what_is_rfid.asp, retrieved May 12, 2011.

12. http://ezine.motorola.com/ezine/enterprise?title=Indiana+Jones+and+the+Automated+%0AWare-house&a=554, retrieved May 12, 2011.

13. Reda, "Customer Service, Brand Management," pp. 40–44.

14. http://www.informationweek.com/news/206905010, retrieved May 12, 2011.

15. http://aws.amazon.com/fws/, retrieved May 12, 2011.

16. Boorstein, "Customer Service: Fulfillment 101."

17. All statistics are based on *The Statistical Fact Book 2006,* 28th ed. (New York: Direct Marketing Association), pp. 200–215.

18. http://www.usps.com/financials/anrpt10/ar2010_finance_5.htm., retrieved May 12, 2011.

19. DMA Statistical Fact Book 2011, New York: Direct Marketing Association, p. 23.

20. http://www.usps.com/financials/anrpt10/ar2010_finance_5.htm., retrieved May 12, 2011.

21. http://www.usps.com/financials/anrpt10/ar2010_finance_5.htm., retrieved May 12, 2011.

22. http://www.usps.com/financials/anrpt10/ar2010_finance_5.htm., retrieved May 12, 2011.

23. http://about.fedex.designcdt.com/our_company/company_information/fedex_corporation, p. 8. Retrieved May 12, 2011.

24. John M. Chilson, "The Top 10 Fulfillment Mistakes," *Folio: Magazine for Magazine Management* 27, no. 7 (May 1998), 61–62.

25. Jeffrey A. Coopersmith, "Customer Service: The Final Link," *Catalog Age* 5, no. 7 (July 1988), 76.

26. Bobette M. Gustafson, "A Well-Staffed PFS Call Center Can Improve Patient Satisfaction," *Healthcare Financial Management* 53, no. 7 (July 1999), 64.

27. *Sales & Marketing Management* 151, no. 9 (September 1999), 26.

28. Ibid.

29. Ibid., pp. 39–40.

30. William D. Perreault Jr. and E. Jerome McCarthy (2009), *Basic Marketing: A Global Managerial Approach,* 17th ed. (New York: Irwin McGraw-Hill), p. 5.

31. Robert McKim, "Is CRM Part of Customer Management?" dmnews.com, March 13, 2000, retrieved on May 10, 2000, http://www.dmnews.com/archive/2000-03/7058.html.

32. Adapted from Stanley J. Fenvessy (1979), "Introduction to Fulfillment," in *Direct Marketing Manual* (New York: Direct Marketing Association), p. 500:1.

33. Case adapted from Jim McCann and Peter Kaminsky (1998), *Stop and Sell the Roses: Lessons from Business & Life* (New York: Ballantine Books). Updated based on information provided by 1-800-FLOWERS.COM, 2008.

## CHAPTER 12

Understanding the Industry's Environmental, Ethical, and Legal Issues

OPENING VIGNETTE: GREEN IS ALWAYS IN FASHION AT MACY'S

In 2010 Macy's Inc., was ranked #5 in *Newsweek* magazine's "Top 100 Greenest Companies in America." The company continues to commit resources and initiatives that will contribute to a more sustainable environment for future generations. This long-standing and highly reputable department store has become a Recyclebank® Rewards Program Partner.

In an effort to become more environmentally friendly, Macy's has taken a number of important "green" steps thus far. These steps include:

• Powering up a 3.5 megawatt, high-efficiency solar power system on the roof of its Goodyear, Arizona, fulfillment center which will be one of the largest of its kind in the U.S.

• Leading the industry in rolling out LED lighting in its stores to conserve energy.

• Increasing the use of sustainable building materials in construction projects by 20 percent.

These activities are excellent, and they are only the beginning as Macy's partnership with Recyclebank has only just begun.

FIGURE 12-1. Macy's logo. Used with permission of Macy»s

What's even more exciting about Macy's new green initiatives is that the company is encouraging its customers to join the mission to go green. In partnership with Recyclebank, Macy's is offering its customers an opportunity to earn big rewards for going green. Macy's customers are encouraged to go to Recyclebank.com to learn how they can earn points for Macy's rewards by living an environmentally-friendly lifestyle.

Macy's is a leader in helping to raise public awareness about environmental protection. Macy's was recognized by ForestEthics for reducing its mailing and overall paper consumption, as well as for the increased use of recycled and certified paper. In fact, the Environmental Protection Agency (EPA) has rated Macy's as one of its top 20 partners for generating the most green electricity on site. Finally, Macy's is to be commended for creating a customer rewards program that encourages and motivates its customers to exercise more environmentally-friendly behavior.

In this chapter we will discuss the environmental, ethical, and legal issues and regulations that affect the business practices of marketers. Raising environmental consciousness and exercising environmentally-friendly behavior are two of the more recent focuses of most marketers today. We will also explore "The Green 15" which are a set of business practices that the DMA has established to assist its members in becoming more environmentally friendly.

The regulatory environment of direct marketing includes the two very important areas of ethical and legal issues. **Ethics** are the moral principles of conduct governing the behavior of an individual or a group. **Morals** are often described in terms of good or bad. To be *ethical* in marketing means to conform to the accepted professional standards of conduct. However, you might ask, what exactly are the "accepted professional standards of conduct"?

This chapter discusses ethics and the ethical behavior expected of direct marketers as set forth by the Direct Marketing Association (DMA) along with the law as it pertains to direct marketing activities. The legal regulations affecting direct marketing activities on the federal, state, and local levels primarily deal with three broad legal issues: intellectual property, security, and privacy. We detail the legal issues in each of these three areas in this chapter, after an overview of the ethical aspects of direct marketing.

Environmental Issues

Protecting the environment is an important issue for direct marketers. The DMAs around the world are taking a lead role in shaping the industry by partnering with other organizations to create environmental standards. The UK DMA, for instance, has developed an alliance of like-minded member companies to partner with BSI British Standards to create the first standard for environmental performance in the field of direct marketing.[1] The U.S. DMA has taken a lead on this issue, starting in 2005 with the formation of a Committee on Environment & Social Responsibility (CESR) comprised of DMA member organizations. In January 2007, the DMA launched an Environmental Planning Tool & Policy Generator (www.the-dma.org/envgen). In May 2007, the DMA board of directors passed an Environmental Resolution. That same month, the DMA also announced a nationwide "Recycle Please" campaign. For more information on these major milestones, please visit the DMA's Environmental Resource Center at: www.the-dam.org/environment. The following section provides an overview of the key environmental issues.

The DMA's Environmental Resolution and "Green 15" Program

The U.S. DMA has taken a stance on protecting the environment by promulgating greener marketing practices with its Environmental Resolution and new green goal to reduce waste and carbon. The main objectives of this initiative include the following:

1. Offering notice and choice to mail recipients, and implementing effective list hygiene and targeting strategies into marketing practices.

2. Questioning paper suppliers where the paper comes from, to protect forests and to ensure the wood was harvested legally.

3. Reviewing direct mail and direct marketing pieces, testing and downsizing where appropriate.

4. Encouraging packaging suppliers to submit alternate solutions for environmentally preferable packaging.

5. Purchasing office papers, packaging, and packaging materials made from recycled materials with postconsumer content.

The DMA's newest Green Goal states that "the percentage of paper recovery for standard mail and magazines be 70 percent by 2020 as measured by the Environmental Protection Agency Municipal Solid Waste Report." [2]

The DMA has also created a nationwide public education campaign called "Recycle Please" that asks all DMA members to display prominently the "Recycle Please" logo, shown in Figure 12-2, in their catalogs and direct mail pieces to encourage consumers to recycle them after reading. The DMA coordinated with the Envelope Manufacturers Association and the Magazine Publishers of America and launched this campaign in 2007.[3] The DMA hopes this campaign will overcome the lack of public awareness that catalogs and mixed paper can be recycled.

The other objective of this campaign is to improve the overall recycling/recovery rate of used catalogs and direct mail in the United States. Increasing recycling and recover activity benefits our environment by:

- making efficient use of raw material.
- reducing the amount of new fiber that must be obtained from wood to make new paper products.
- conserving valuable global resources.
- decreasing landfill waste.
- reducing greenhouse gas emissions from incinerators and landfills.[4]

RECYCLE PLEASE ▷

recycleplease.org

FIGURE 12-2. DMA "Recycle Please" logo. Used with permission of The Direct Marketing Association.

The DMA enacted a resolution calling on members to implement and benchmark a set of 15 business practices called "The Green 15."[5] These practices address the areas of paper procurement and use; list hygiene and data management; mail design and production; packaging; and recycling and pollution reduction. Figure 12-3 provides an overview of the Green 15. The program has met with success. According to the DMA's office of Consumer Relations, "The U.S. Postal Service has recorded a 14.1 percent drop in Undeliverable-as-Addressed mail in standard mail (as a percentage of total volume). As a result, the Earth has benefited from associated carbon and greenhouse gas savings that now exceed 201,979 metric tons, or nearly 20.2 percent of the total goal which the DMA set for itself by 2013."[6] In summary, the DMA is making a concerted effort to move its members along the continuum of ongoing environmental improvement. These standards are a part of its commitment to corporate responsibility and its efforts to promote sustainable and ethical business practices, which is the topic of the next section.

Ethics of Direct Marketing

A different kind of e-business is receiving an increasing amount of attention from the direct marketing community. In this case, the "e" doesn't stand for *electronic,* it stands for *ethics,* and direct marketers are paying close attention. Ethics are concerned with morality: the rightness and wrongness of individual actions or deeds. As former Supreme Court Justice Potter Stewart once said, "Ethics is knowing the difference between what you have a right to do and what is the right thing to do." A **code of ethics** is a set of guidelines for making ethical decisions.

The DMA's Guidelines for Ethical Business Practice

The DMA has established a detailed code of ethics for direct marketers. These guidelines are intended to provide individuals and organizations in direct marketing in all media with generally accepted principles of conduct. These are self-regulatory measures as opposed to governmental mandates. Visit www.dmaresponsibility.org/Guidelines to obtain updated versions of these guidelines. Figure 12-4 provides an overview of DMA's guidelines for ethical business practice.

The DMA Corporate Responsibility Department

In addition to providing guidelines for ethical business practices, the DMA sponsors several activities in its Corporate Responsibility Department. The Mail Preference Service (MPS) offers

Paper Procurement & Use

1. Encourage your paper suppliers to increase wood purchases from recognized forest certification programs.
2. Require your paper suppliers to commit to implementing sustainable forestry practices that protect forest ecosystems and biodiversity as well as provide the wood and paper products that meet industry needs.
3. Ask your paper suppliers where your paper comes from before buying it with the intent of not sourcing paper from unsustainable or illegally managed forests.
4. Require your paper suppliers to document that they do not produce or sell paper from illegally harvested or stolen wood.
5. Evaluate the paper you use for marketing pieces, product packaging and internal consumption to identify opportunities for increased environmental attributes.

List Hygiene & Data Management

6. Comply with DMA Guidelines for list management, including: Maintaining in-house do-not-market lists for prospects and customers who do not wish to receive future solicitations from you. Using the Mail Preference Service (MPS) monthly for consumer prospect mail. Providing existing and prospective customers with notice of an opportunity to modify or eliminate direct mail solicitations from your organization in every commercial solicitation.
7. Maintain "clean" mailing lists by using USPS or commercial equivalent files where applicable for: ZIP Code correction; address standardization; change of address, address element correction, delivery sequence file and/or address correction requested.
8. Apply predictive models and/or Recency-Frequency-Monetary (RFM) segmentation where appropriate.

Mail Design & Production

9. Review your direct mail and printed marketing pieces, and test downsized pieces when and where appropriate.
10. Test and use production methods that reduce print order overruns, waste allowances and in-process waste.

Packaging

11. Encourage packaging suppliers to submit alternate solutions for environmentally preferable packaging, in addition to quoting prices on approved or existing specifications.

Recycling & Pollution Reduction

12. Purchase office papers, packing and packaging materials made from recycled materials with post-consumer content where appropriate.
13. Integrate use of electronic communications (email, Web and intranets) for external and internal communications.
14. Ensure that all environmental labeling is clear, honest and complete, so that consumers and business customers may know the exact nature of what your organization is doing.
15. Participate in DMA's "Recycle Please" campaign and/or in another recycling campaign and/or demonstrate that your company or organization has in place a program to encourage recycling in your workplace and/or your community.

FIGURE 12-3. DMA Green 15. Used with permission of The Direct Marketing Association.

consumers assistance in decreasing the volume of national advertising mail they receive at home. The Telephone Preference Service (TPS) offers consumers assistance in decreasing the number of national phone calls received at home. The E-Mail Preference Service (EMPS) is designed to assist consumers in decreasing the number of unsolicited e-mail offers received. In essence, the DMA supports a consumer's right to choose the channel by which he or she would prefer to shop. The DMA's consumer page for registering with the Preference Services is www.DMA-Choice.org. The DMA also publishes a variety of publications designed to assist direct marketers in complying with federal and state regulations. Visit the DMA Web site at www.the-dma.org to obtain a list of such publications and information sources. The DMA has established both the Guidelines for Ethical Business Practice and an office of corporate responsibility to assist direct marketers in developing and maintaining consumer relationships that are based on fair and eth-

The Terms of the Offer
Honesty and Clarity of Offer - Article #1
Accuracy and Consistency - Article #2
Clarity of Representations - Article #3
Actual Conditions - Article #4
Disparagement - Article #5
Decency - Article #6
Photographs and Artwork - Article #7
Disclosure of Sponsor and Intent - Article #8
Accessibility - Article #9
Solicitation in the Guise of an Invoice or Governmental Notification - Article #10
Postage, Shipping, or Handling - Article #11

Advance Consent Marketing
Article #12

Marketing to Children
Marketing to Children - Article #13
Parental Responsibility and Choice - Article #14
Information from or about Children - Article #15
Marketing Online to Children Under 13 Years of Age - Article #16

Special Offers and Claims
Use of the Word "Free" and Other Similar Representations - Article #17
Price Comparisons - Article #18
Guarantees - Article #19
Use of Test or Survey Data - Article #20
Testimonials and Endorsements - Article #21

Sweepstakes
Use of the Term "Sweepstakes" - Article #22
No Purchase Option - Article #23
Chances of Winning - Article #24
Prizes - Article #25
Premiums - Article #26
Disclosure of Rules - Article #27

Fulfillment
Unordered Merchandise or Service - Article #28
Product Availability and Shipment - Article #29
Dry Testing - Article #30

Collection, Use, and Maintenance of Marketing Data
Collection, Use, and Transfer of Personally Identifiable Data - Article #31
Personal Data - Article #32
Collection, Use, and Transfer of Health Related Data - Article #33
Promotion of Marketing Lists - Article #34
Marketing List Usage - Article #35
Responsibilities of Database Compilers – Article #36
Information Security - Article #37

Online Marketing
Online Information - Article #38
Commercial Solicitations Online - Article #39
E-Mail Authentication – Article #40
Use of Software or Other Similar Technology Installed on a Computer or Similar Device – Article #41
Online Referral Marketing - Article #42
E-Mail Appending to Consumer Records - Article #43

FIGURE 12-4. DMA ethical guidelines. Used with permission of The Direct Marketing Association.

Telephone Marketing
Reasonable Hours - Article #44
Taping of Conversations - Article #45
Restricted Contacts - Article #46
Caller-ID/Automatic Number Identification Requirements – Article #47
Use of Automated Dialing Equipment - Article #48
Use of Prerecorded Voice Messaging - Article #49
Use of Telephone Facsimile Machines - Article #50
Promotions for Response by Toll-Free and
Pay-Per-Call Numbers - Article #51
Disclosure and Tactics - Article #52

Fundraising
Article #53

Laws, Codes, and Regulations
Article #54

FIGURE 12-4. continued.

ical principles. With these ethical guidelines, the DMA is encouraging all direct marketers to act in a morally correct business manner and to safeguard basic consumer rights.

Basic Consumer Rights

Consumers possess the following basic human rights: (1) the right to safety, (2) the right to be informed, (3) the right to selection, (4) the right to confidentiality, and (5) the right to privacy.[7] Direct marketers should respect and safeguard these rights. Let's look at each.

The Right to Safety

The **right to safety** entitles consumers to be safe from both physical and psychological harm. They cannot be harassed or made to feel bad if, for example, they declined a phone request to purchase a product or service. These circumstances may cause the consumer to experience undue stress.

The Right to Information

The **right to information** includes the consumer's right to receive any and all pertinent or requested information. This includes the right to be informed about all stages of the direct marketing process. It is an obligation of direct marketers to fully disclose what they intend to do with the consumer's name and address once it is put onto a mailing list. In addition, direct marketers should provide the consumer with an explanation of why they collect information about consumers and their lifestyles.

The Right to Selection

The **right to selection** includes a consumer's right to choose or make decisions about his or her buying behavior. In other words, the consumer can accept or reject any offer from a direct marketer or a telemarketer, be it a request to purchase a product or service, subscribe to a magazine, attend a meeting, donate to a charitable organization, or vote for a political candidate. Consumers cannot be made to feel forced into taking an action against their wishes.

The Right to Confidentiality

The **right to confidentiality** is a consumer's right to specify to a given company that information they freely provide should not be shared. Like information disclosed in a physician–patient or attorney–client relationship, information a consumer provides to a direct marketing organization with expressed confidentiality must not be shared. Savvy direct marketers know that to be successful they must build long-term relationships with their customers based on trust. This trust must not be betrayed. Direct marketers can uphold the consumer's right to confidentiality by developing proper security measures (electronic watermarks, firewalls, digital signatures, authentication, data integrity, encryption, etc.) to protect the security of the proprietary data the direct marketer has promised to safeguard.

Suppose a nonprofit organization specifically stated in its printed materials that it will not share the names of donors with other charitable organizations, and then it turns around and rents its donor lists! This is unethical and constitutes a breach of confidentiality.

The Right to Privacy

The final basic consumer right, the right to privacy, is probably the most noteworthy consumer right affecting direct marketers. The **right to privacy** has been defined as the ability of an individual to control the access others have to personal information. Because of the heightened awareness and controversy over the matter, along with the legal ramifications of the consumer's right to privacy, we discuss privacy issues later in the chapter in more detail than the other four basic consumer rights.

Legislative Issues

The three primary areas where legislation has been designed to safeguard consumer rights are intellectual property, security, and privacy.

Intellectual Property

Intellectual property is defined as products of the mind or ideas.[8] Some examples include books, music, computer software, designs, and technological know-how. The protection of intellectual property afforded by copyrights, patents, trademarks, and databases is the province of several governmental agencies. Under copyright laws, a copyright owner has the exclusive right to distribute copies of the protected work. Thus, third parties are not permitted to sell, rent, transfer, or otherwise distribute copies of the work without the express permission of the copyright owner. Several channels currently exist for businesses to prevent unauthorized usage of protected material. The American Intellectual Property Law Association (AIPLA) is a national bar association constituted primarily of intellectual property lawyers in private and corporate practice, government service, and the academic community.[9] The AIPLA is one of the organizations available to assist direct marketers in protecting intellectual property.

Given the freedom of the Internet, protection of trademarks has recently become even more difficult. The Internet's focus on visual advertisements will increase the likelihood of a conflict over trademark rights as more company logos, slogans, brand names, and trademarks are appearing in Web sites. Therefore, this area of intellectual property protection must also be one of the top concerns for direct marketers.

With the introduction of faster computer applications and hard drives with larger capacity for data storage, a new kind of intellectual property has emerged—a database. Data collection, both online and offline, has soared in the past decade. However, intellectual property protection of an organization's database is a volatile area. Businesses are being caught between the threats of unauthorized access by hackers (which we discuss with regard to security in the next section), requirements to disclose certain data collected to law enforcement agencies, and consumer privacy concerns about data collection (which we discuss later in the privacy section).

Security

In addition to creating and storing databases, companies must also secure their databases from unauthorized access and outside damage. Failure to do so may cause the direct marketer much embarrassment, pain, and potential liability for breaches in security. Although technology exists to provide security via password controls and firewalls, these are not completely dependable, and security breaches may still occur.

For example, Carmichael Lynch, a public relations and advertising firm, accidentally published its administration password on its Web site. The slip-up went undetected for six months. During that time, unauthorized visitors could have accessed e-mail addresses and passwords for almost 12,000 people who had just registered on the American Standard Web site, or the names, addresses, and vehicle information of 75,000 luxury car and SUV owners.[10]

In another mishap, publishing giant Ziff-Davis Media suffered a security lapse that exposed the personal data of thousands of magazine subscribers. In restitution, the company agreed to pay $100,000 to the New York State Department of Law and $500 each to the 50 customers whose credit card information had been disclosed.[11]

In response to these types of incidents, a California law known as SB 1386 became the first state law to address security breaches. This law requires government agencies, businesses, and anyone else who stores personal information to notify the California resident when the data have been accessed. The purpose of SB 1386 is to give California residents adequate time to check their credit ratings and protect themselves against identity theft.[12]

Privacy

Consumers are more concerned about privacy today than ever before. There are two terms that should be distinguished concerning privacy today. Privacy and data/security breach are both discussed in this section, however they are two separate and distinct issues that may require separate legislation. **Privacy** refers to a level of control consumers have over information provided. **Data/Security Breach** pertains to the safeguarding and securing of data from unauthorized access or damage, as mentioned in the security section above. Privacy legislation has existed for a long time. Let's review the history of this important legislation.

Privacy Legislation

Privacy protection actually began being discussed over a century ago, in 1890, when Samuel Warren and Justice Brandeis wrote a law review article advocating that a person should be protected from having personal matters reported by the press for commercial reasons. That marked the beginning of what many know today as a consumer's right to privacy. In the 1950, laws protected citizens from allowing public organizations to intrude on their private matters. However, these laws did not protect consumers against a private organization's use of personal information. Still, it wasn't until recent years that privacy issues became increasingly visible.

From the explosion of credit cards and personal computers to the advent of SmartPhones to the new marketing realities in social media today, the process of direct marketing has attained new heights of marketing success. With this phenomenal success, businesses have also faced scrutiny on numerous aspects of the privacy issue. Whatever the root, the concern over information privacy has been going on for decades. Back in the late 1970s, prior to most technological advances, the following appeared in a newspaper:[13]

> They know about you. They know how old you are.
>
> They know if you have children. They know about your job.
>
> They know how much money you make, what kind of car you drive,
>
> what sort of house you live in and whether you are likely to prefer paté
>
> de foie gras and champagne or hot dogs and a cold beer.
>
> They know all this and much, much more.
>
> And you know how?
>
> They know your name.
>
> What they have done with it is very simple:
>
> they have added it to a mailing list.

Though it was an exaggeration (at the time), this excerpt is evidence of a widely held concern that a list is a conduit through which personal information is transferred from one direct marketer to another. Although this may be true, as you should realize from the material contained in Chapters 2 and 3, to a direct marketer a list is an instrument for describing a market segment. Market segments enable direct marketers to target appropriate promotional offers to consumers, thus reducing the amount of irrelevant marketing communication each consumer receives. This is good for both direct marketers and consumers. Information technology has made it possible for marketers to design promotional campaigns directed at different segments of prospective and current customers. From a marketing and customer service perspective, the purpose of gathering consumer information is to achieve greater selectivity and to make direct response advertising more relevant to the recipient. The use of personal information enables marketers to develop closer relationships with customers that foster brand loyalty and better customer service. However, regardless of the noble purpose information serves for direct marketers, privacy issues have now become legal matters.

Marketers have always had an interest in knowing consumer information, dating back to the days of corner "mom and pop" stores when everyone knew everyone else and their families and their business. Today is no different. Marketers still want to know about their customers to serve them better. Technology makes it easier to do that. With the swipe of a customer loyalty card, consumers receive discounts on purchases or earn bonus points toward free gifts while retailers download information about customer purchasing preferences and habits. From there, with a few clicks of the mouse or strokes on the keyboard, the purchase information can be shared with any number of interested parties—for a fee. Technology has made direct marketing database activities easier and more efficient. However, before direct marketers start thinking beyond this, they have to realize that along with advances in technology come additional legislative regulations. Perhaps the best-known legislation regarding privacy has come from the Privacy Protection Study Commission.

Privacy Protection Study Commission

The concern of the U.S. consumer and Congress over the broad issue of privacy, including the subject of mailing lists and databases, culminated in the **Privacy Act of 1974.** This act established the Privacy Protection Study Commission to determine whether the various restrictions on what the federal government could do with personal information, as provided in the Privacy Act, should also be applied to the private sector. Significantly for direct marketers, Section V (c), B (i) of the act directed the commission to report to the president and Congress on whether an organization engaged in interstate commerce should be required to remove from its mailing list the name of an individual who does not want to be on it.

In July 1977, after months of hearing testimony and studying the issues, the commission issued its 618-page *Report from the Privacy Protection Study Commission*. Chapter 4 of this report was devoted entirely to the subject of mailing lists. The commission basically concluded that the appearance of an individual's name on a mailing list, so long as that individual has the prerogative to remove it from that list, was not in and of itself an invasion of privacy. In reaching this conclusion, the commission observed "that the balance that must be struck between the interests of individuals and the interests of direct marketers is an especially delicate one." The commission also noted the economic importance of direct mail "to nonprofit organizations, to the champions of unpopular causes, and to many of the organizations that create diversity in American society."

Agreeing that the *receipt* of direct mail is not really the issue but how the mailing list record of an individual is used, the commission further recommended that a private sector organization that rents, sells, exchanges, or otherwise makes the addresses or names and addresses of its customers, members, or donors available to any other person for use in direct mail marketing or solicitation should adopt a procedure whereby each customer, member, or donor is informed of the organization's list practice. In addition, each consumer should be given an opportunity to indicate to the organization that he or she does not wish to have his or her address or name and address made available for such purposes.[14]

These were the privacy issues of the past. Now direct marketers must prepare for handling the privacy issues of the future. Let's take a look at privacy today.

Privacy Today: Antispam Laws

Spam is defined as unwanted, unsolicited bulk commercial e-mail messages. It has also been referred to as junk e-mail. Most people today complain about spam. Recipients find it annoying; Internet service providers say it clogs up and slows down the online systems; and many direct marketers claim it is ruining e-mail as a legitimate media channel. The minutes e-mail recipients spend clicking through unwanted e-mail messages add up quickly in a nation with millions of Internet users. However, spam is a worldwide issue. It accounts for 14.5 billion messages globally per day, which translates into about 45 percent of all e-mails.[15] This worldwide phenomenon of spam had to start somewhere. There is some speculation about who actually sent out the first spam e-mail and when it happened. The first "tasteless" spam e-mail was most likely sent out in 1996 by Dave Rhodes. Rhodes was a college student who advertised a pyramid scheme in his e-mail messages. The message was relayed to all newsgroups on Usenet. Thousands of users were hit with a message that read, "MAKE MONEY FAST!" It's said that Rhodes made a substantial amount of money from several people chasing an elusive dream. The most interesting twist of the story is the great possibility that Rhodes never existed. The university that he supposedly attended had no records of him. Because chain letters began as early as the 1970s, it's very probable that someone else copied the format onto a computer and distributed it via Usenet under an alias.[16]

Internet providers have tools for blocking spam; however, these filtering programs are often time-consuming and ineffective. Senders of spam are finding ways to defeat the filtering software simply by misspelling key words that trigger the filters. To get consumers to open these e-mail messages, the senders of spam also use a variety of attention-getting subject lines and sender names in the "from" field of the e-mail message. Some examples include: "Claim Your Prize" or "Payment Past Due" or "You Have Won." This is where the law comes into play. When the subject line of an e-mail message misrepresents its point of origin or the nature of the message itself, it is considered deceptive.

The CAN-SPAM Act of 2003 sets requirements for everyone involved in sending commercial e-mails. This act also states various penalties for spammers and companies whose products are advertised as spam. The CAN-SPAM Act gives the power to the consumer to ask the e-mail sender to stop sending e-mails to the consumer's address. The U.S. Federal Trade Commission (FTC) has the power to enforce the act, which came into effect on January 1, 2004. CAN-SPAM gave the Department of Justice (DOJ) the power to enforce criminal sanction for noncompliance. The main provisions of The CAN-SPAM Act are that it:

- bans false or misleading header information.
- prohibits deceptive subject lines.
- requires that the advertising e-mail give recipients an opt-out method.
- requires that commercial e-mail be identified as an advertisement and include the sender's valid physical postal address.[17]

Additionally, in October of 2010, the DMA and other leading advertising trade associations created the "Advertising Option Icon" and the Digital Advertising Alliance, in order to give the consumer more options and control over advertisements that they receive. The icon is placed on billions of ads online that are behaviorally targeted. Consumers may click on the icon to discover why they received an ad, and continue to opt out of a majority of behavioral advertising. According to the DMA, the goal of this program is to enable consumers who desire to "opt out" of receiving online ads, the opportunity to do so. This program includes 100 percent of the behavioral online advertising.[18] Visit www.aboutads.info to view the program.

Federal and state legislation covering the broad range of privacy issues today is rapidly changing. The legal environment concerning spam is also constantly changing. For updated legislative information contact the Internet Alliance at www.internetalliance.org or visit the spam laws Web site at www.spamlaws.com. Direct marketers must constantly monitor key information sources.

Annoyance and Violation

To get at the heart of privacy concerns, you have to understand two basic consumer perceptions: **annoyance** and **violation**.[19] People feel annoyed because they receive too many unsolicited marketing communications, and they feel violated because they believe too much information about their personal lives is being exchanged between marketers without their knowledge and/or consent. Many consumers want to place restrictions on the amount of information that may be collected, warehoused, and shared about them. However, not all consumers feel the same way. Some are willing to disclose personal information to marketers, providing they receive something in return. This may include a targeted offer that meets the consumer's needs and desires, or informative updates on a certain topic of interest to them. In fact, it has been determined that a consumer's willingness to disclose personal data may actually depend on the type of information being disclosed.

Type of Information

The degree of control or the amount of restriction an individual wants to have over his or her personal information may depend on the *type* of information requested. We can divide personal information into four different categories: general descriptive information, ownership information, product purchase information, and sensitive/confidential information.[20] Let's discuss each of these types of information and look at some examples of each category.

GENERAL DESCRIPTIVE INFORMATION. General descriptive information is the easiest to obtain. Often considered demographic or classification information, it includes race, height, age, gender, level of education, and occupation. Consumers are the least restrictive with this category of information and usually provide marketers easy access to this data.

OWNERSHIP INFORMATION. Ownership information contains data about the various products the consumer owns. Consumers consider some belongings to be status symbols, like a home, an expensive automobile, or an American Express Platinum travel and entertainment credit card. Consumers generally place moderate restrictions on the release of these data, and it is believed that some may want to share this data to achieve greater self-esteem or status.

PRODUCT PURCHASE INFORMATION. The information contained in the product purchase information category includes a variety of purchase activity data, including magazine subscription information, credit record information, and lifestyle information obtained from such purchases as vitamins, cat food, hunting and fishing equipment, or certain medications. This category is similar to the ownership information category; however, these purchases are not necessarily considered to be status symbols. Consumers generally place moderate restrictions on this information category.

SENSITIVE/CONFIDENTIAL INFORMATION. The final category of information contains facts about an individual that are considered to be most private: sensitive/confidential information such as annual income, medical history, Social Security number, driving records (including any motor violations), and home value. Consumers are most restrictive with this category of information and usually exercise the strongest control over the release of these facts.

Consumer Privacy Segments

Not *all* consumers possess the same feelings and opinions about privacy issues, regardless of the type of information. Just as information can be grouped into categories, consumer opinions and behaviors toward information privacy can be categorized as well. In fact, research conducted by Alan Westin of Columbia University and Lou Harris Organization/Equifax has concluded that consumers may be grouped into three possible segments (the privacy unconcerned, privacy fundamentalists, and privacy pragmatists) when it comes to their feelings about privacy.[21] Let's take a closer look at these segments.

PRIVACY UNCONCERNED. The privacy unconcerned group represents about 20 percent of the population and consists of those who literally do not care about the issue of privacy at all. They are aware of the benefits of giving information for marketing purposes and enjoy the information and opportunities they receive in exchange for it. These consumers say their lives are an open book. They feel they have nothing to hide. They welcome most contacts by businesses, nonprofits, and others and have little concern about information about them being transferred from one organization to another. This group is most likely to be receptive to the activities of direct marketers.

PRIVACY FUNDAMENTALISTS. The privacy fundamentalists also make up approximately 20 percent of the population. These individuals are likely to take the point of view that they own their name, as well as all the information about themselves, and that no one else may use it without their permission. This group includes activists who will write letters to their congressional representatives or the editor of a local newspaper about privacy. They may call companies and file complaints on this issue. Direct marketers should be certain to purge these consumers from their lists because they are the least receptive to direct marketing activities.

PRIVACY PRAGMATISTS. The **privacy pragmatists** represent approximately 60 percent of U.S. consumers. They look at the contact, the offer, and the methods of data collection and mentally apply a cost/benefit analysis to make a determination about a marketer's use of information.

They ask themselves:

- What benefits can I get from this?
- Are there choices that I would not otherwise have?
- Is there an opportunity for me?
- Can I get a product or an offer that is valuable to me?
- What harm can come from this? For example:
  —Will I be inconvenienced in some way?
  —Will I be embarrassed or feel discomfort?
  —Will I be disadvantaged in some way?

Pragmatists will allow their buying patterns to be tracked by supermarkets, if they get valuable coupons or other deals in return. They have no problem with a catalog company providing its list to another organization or company so long as they appreciate the subsequent offers they receive. They will receive telemarketing calls from an organization they patronize and respond to an offer they consider valuable. The privacy pragmatists represent the majority of consumers in the United States. Developing relationships with these customers is an important strategy for the direct marketer to take. So what have companies done to respond to consumer's privacy concerns?

Corporate Response to Privacy

The **chief privacy officer (CPO)** is the newest arrival in corporate hierarchies, the new white knight of the twenty-first century. Like the CEO and the CIO, the CPO is overseeing something very important in the corporation: *privacy!* The CPO is responsible for protecting the sensitive information the corporation collects, from credit card accounts to health records.

Privacy executives have an open-ended job. They must guard against hackers and articulate uses for sensitive personal, financial, or medical information. They must not only set guidelines, they must figure out how to communicate those guidelines to customers and employees. Figure 12-5 shows the privacy policy booklet the J.C. Penney Company distributes to its customers. Hiring CPOs to oversee privacy matters may be the price of doing business in today's corporate world as consumers and government officials more aggressively sue companies over breach of privacy cases.

Many companies already have information privacy policies and actively communicate these to their customers. Take, for example, the following privacy notice provided to customers at Universal Bank:[22]

> Keeping customer information secure is a top priority for all of us at Universal Bank. We are sending you this privacy notice to help you understand how we handle the personal information about you that we collect and may disclose. This notice tells you how you can limit our disclosing personal information about you. The provisions of this notice will apply to former customers as well as current customers unless we state otherwise.

Universal Bank goes on to provide their customers with a "Privacy Choices Form," which allows them to select one of the following four choices and return the form to the bank:[23]

1. Limit the personal information about me that you disclose to nonaffiliated third parties.
2. Limit the personal information about me that you share with Citigroup affiliates.
3. Remove my name from your mailing lists used for promotional offers.
4. Remove my name from your telemarketing lists used for promotional offers.

FIGURE 12-5. JCP privacy policy. Used with permission of J.C. Penney Company, Inc.

Like Universal Bank, many direct marketers have become proactive in handling information privacy issues. Perhaps no organization is more proactive than the DMA. The DMA initiated a Privacy Promise in 1999 that provided public assurance that all members of the DMA follow certain specific practices to protect consumer privacy. The practices were designed to have a major impact on those consumers who wish to receive fewer advertising solicitations. DMA updated and expanded its Privacy Promise and now requires its members to adhere to the Commitment to Consumer Choice (see www.DMACCC.org).

FIGURE 12-6.
Examples of
notice language.
Used with
permission of The
Direct Marketing
Association.

> A. "We make our customer information available to other companies so they may contact you about products and services that may interest you. If you do not want your name passed on to other companies for the purpose of receiving marketing offers, just tell us by contacting us at _____, and we will be pleased to respect your wishes."
>
> B. "We make portions of our customer list available to carefully screened companies that offer products and services we believe you may enjoy. If you do not want to receive those offers and/or information, please let us know by contacting us at _____."

FIGURE 12-7.
Examples of
In-House suppress
language. Used
with permission
of The Direct
Marketing
Association.

> A. "If you decide you no longer wish to receive our catalog, send your mailing label with your request to _____."
>
> B. "We would like to continue sending you information only on those subjects of interest to you. If you don't wish to continue to receive information on any of the following product lines, just let us know by _____."
>
> C. "If you would like to receive our catalog less frequently, let us know by _____."

The DMA Commitment to Consumer Choice

In 2008, the DMA initiated its redefined preference Web site, DMAchoice. This site addresses consumers' need for choice across a multitude of channels, not just mail. The primary mission of DMAchoice is to give consumers the opportunity to make what they receive more relevant to their needs and interests. This Web site's purpose is to educate consumers and enable them to make more informed decisions about their preference choices. The Commitment to Consumer Choice includes the following four components:[24]

1. Provide customers, donors, and prospects with notice that they may eliminate or modify their future receipt of direct mail solicitations "in every marketing offer" (see Figure 12-6 for examples of notice language).

2. Honor consumers' opt-out requests within 30 days, and for a period of at least three years, not to receive further mailings or have their contact information transferred to others for marketing purposes.

3. Disclose, on the consumer's request, the source from which the marketer obtained personally identifiable data about that consumer (see Figure 12-7 for examples of in-house suppress language).

4. Update mailing lists using DMA's MPS suppression file each month.

In addition, the DMA has developed privacy principles and guidelines for those direct marketers operating online sites. The next section explores these principles.

The DMA Online Privacy Principles

While millions of consumers have been quick to embrace technology, consumers have called for regulation. Some consumers view online data collection as an invasion of privacy that, at best, inundates them with spam and, at worst, risks putting their financial or personal information in the hands of potential employers, lenders, or insurance companies. Most consumers freely provide their e-mail address or shopping preferences in exchange for better customer service. However, they don't expect marketers to share the information without their consent and use it to target them for other offers (especially from other companies).

DMA Online Privacy Principles state that all marketers operating online sites should:

UNSUBSCRIBE: Please use this link to unsubscribe—Or please write UNSUBSCRIBE in the e-mail subject heading and reply to this e-mail.

FIGURE 12-8. Example of opt-out notice.

1. make available their information practices to consumers in a *prominent place* on their Web site; and

2. furnish consumers with the opportunity to opt out of the disclosure of such information. An example of an opt-out notice is shown in Figure 12-8. In addition, the online notice should be easy to find, easy to read, and easy to understand.

The DMA privacy policy specifically expects the online notice to perform the following seven tasks:[25]

1. Identify the marketer.

2. Disclose the marketer's e-mail and postal addresses.

3. State whether the marketer collects personal information online from individuals.

4. Contain a disclosure statement regarding the *information collected*.

5. Contain a disclosure statement regarding the *uses of such information*.

6. State the nature and purpose of disclosures of such information and the types of persons to which disclosures may be made.

7. Explain the mechanism by which the individual may limit the disclosure of such information.

With these privacy principles for online marketing activities in place, it is up to direct marketers to ensure that their programs include responsive personal information protection practices.

Third-Party Privacy Intervention: Infomediaries

Infomediaries are companies that act as intermediaries or third parties by gathering personal information from a user and providing it to other sites with the user's approval. These companies vary in their methods; each attempts to provide consumers with a type of privacy assistance by enabling consumers to control and limit access to their personal information when shopping online.

Critics of infomediaries claim that these companies fail to provide enough protection and that they have the potential to exploit what they claim to protect. The World Wide Web Consortium, the Washington-based organization that sets standards for the Internet, has developed a "Platform for Privacy Preferences Project," also known as P3P. This program enables web browsers and consumers to easily read a company's privacy practices and even to "automate decision making based off of these when appropriate,"[26]

Now that we have reviewed the main privacy issues affecting direct marketers and the various DMA and corporate responses to these issues, we explore the regulatory authorities that are charged with enforcing these rules.

Regulatory Authorities of Direct Marketing

By their very nature, direct marketing promotional activities, as they inform and persuade, often in very large numbers, are highly visible. The volume of direct mail grew rapidly over the past few decades. As it grew, some of it was branded as junk mail by those people who received it and did not find it relevant, by those individuals who resented its intrusion, and even by those businesses that represented competing advertising media. This, coupled with the development and advances in telephone equipment, fiber optic cables, satellite transmissions, and the Internet, enabled direct marketers to transfer consumer data from internal or external databases to user databases quickly and easily and at low costs. During this period of proliferation of direct marketing, abuses by individual organizations ultimately resulted in intervention by regulatory authorities.

The Federal Communications Commission (FCC) and the Federal Trade Commission (FTC) have issued several very important trade regulation rules and guides that affect direct marketing as well as advisory opinions about unfair competition in the form of misleading or deceptive acts or advertising. State and local governments also intervene in advertising and selling practices as do the U.S. Postal Service, Better Business Bureaus, trade associations, the advertising media, and ultimately consumers themselves. Let's look more closely at each.

Federal Communications Commission

The FCC is an independent U.S. government agency directly responsible to Congress. It was established by the Communications Act of 1934 and is charged with regulating interstate and international communications by radio, television, wire, satellite, and cable.[27] The FCC enforces the Telephone Consumer Protection Act (TCPA), originally passed in 1992, and its rules governing telephone marketing.[28] From a telephone marketer's point of view, the most significant part of the TCPA regulations concern commercial solicitation calls made to residences. Direct marketers making those calls are required to do the following:

- Limit the calls to the period between 8 A.M. and 9 P.M.
- Maintain a do-not-call list and honor any consumer request to not be called again. The FCC permits one error in a 12-month period. The FCC worked closely with the FTC in enforcing the National Do Not Call Registry, which we discuss a little later in this section.
- Have a clearly written policy, available to anyone on request.
- If you are a service bureau, forward all requests to be removed from a list to the company on whose behalf you are calling.

A call is exempt from the TCPA if the call

- is made on behalf of a tax-exempt nonprofit organization.
- is not made for a commercial purpose.
- does not include an unsolicited advertisement, even if it is made for a commercial purpose.
- is made to a consumer with whom the calling company has an "established business relationship."

The TCPA prohibits both for-profit and nonprofit marketers from using an automatic phone dialing system (including predictive dialers) to call any device when the called party is charged unless that called party has given prior express consent. Therefore, marketers using automatic dialing systems should not call consumers' or businesses' cellular phones, pagers, or toll-free numbers unless they have been given permission to do so. The FCC also has created strict rules concerning the use of fax machines for marketing purposes. We discuss the TCPA in greater detail later in the case at the end of this chapter.

In addition, the FCC, in concert with the FTC, enforces the National Do-Not-Call (DNC) Registry. This registry permits consumers to sign up via the telephone by calling (888) 382-1222 or online at www.donotcall.gov to declare that they do not wish to receive telephone marketing calls. Section 310.2 of this new federal DNC legislation provides for an established business relationship exemption. Thus, direct marketers may still call customers who appear on the registry providing they are calling on them

- within 18 months of their last purchase, transaction, shipment, end of subscription/membership, or
- within three months of their last inquiry or application.

Exemptions to the DNC legislation have also been made for most business-to-business calls, including nonprofit organizations, airlines, some financial institutions, and insurance companies (to the extent regulated under state law), and third-party marketers calling on their behalf are required to honor in-house suppress requests.[29] Visit the FCC Web site at www.fcc.gov/cgb/donotcall to obtain updates on the National DNC Registry.

Federal Trade Commission

The major federal legislation regulating the promotional activities of direct marketing is the FTC Act, together with its Wheeler-Lea Amendment. The FTC is charged with regulating content of promotional messages used in interstate commerce. In Section 5(A), intended to prevent unfair competition, the Wheeler-Lea Amendment to the FTC Act strengthened this provision by making it a violation of the law whenever such competition injured the public, regardless of its effect on a competitor. The amendment also prohibited false, misleading, or deceptive advertising by enumerating four types of products in which advertising abuses existed and in which the public health could be directly affected: foods, drugs, cosmetics, and therapeutic devices.[30]

In October 1995, the FTC and the DMA produced a checklist for direct marketers. It was written for mail, telephone, fax, and computer order merchandisers to give them an overview of rules or statutes that the FTC enforces. Visit the FTC Web site to obtain complete details and updates of FTC rules and regulations at www.ftc.gov. Figure 12-9 provides a brief overview of these rules.

Those direct marketers using online media must be aware of and comply with the FTC regulations. The four elements in the FTC's privacy policy for online direct marketing are:[31]

1. **Notice:** Web sites should provide consumers clear and conspicuous notice of their information practices, including what information they collect, how they collect it, how they use it, whether they disclose the information to other entities, and whether other entities are collecting information through the site.

2. **Choice:** Consumers should be offered choices as to how their personal information will be used beyond completing a transaction.

3. **Access:** Consumers should be offered reasonable access to the information that a Web site gathers about them, including the opportunity to review such data and correct or delete data.

4. **Security:** Organizations that have Web sites should take reasonable steps to protect the security of information they gather from their consumers.

Online marketing activities are not alone in receiving FTC attention. As the case at the end of this chapter explains, direct marketing activities using fax machines are being regulated as the FTC enforces the TCPA. Although in some cases their actions have been controversial, the FTC has become much more aggressive in its enforcement, especially when false or deceptive advertising is sent. All direct marketers should take note of the FTC rules and regulations prior to carrying out their marketing activities and utilizing various media.

Advertisements: Product Offers and Claims All products and/or services advertised must be advertised truthfully. The FTC Act prohibits unfair or deceptive advertising.

Mail and Telephone Orders In order to comply with the Mail or Telephone Order Merchandise Rule ("MTOR"), you must have a reasonable basis for stating or implying that you can ship within a certain time when you advertise mail or telephone order merchandise.

Telemarketing If your business uses either inbound or outbound interstate telephone calls to sell goods or services, you must comply with the new Telemarketing Sales Rule (TSR) and Do-Not-Call laws.

900 Numbers All providers of 900 numbers must comply with the FTC 900-Number Rule requiring that they disclose the cost of the call.

Delayed Delivery Rule This rule provides that, if the marketer believes that goods will not be shipped within 30 days of receiving a properly completed order, an advertisement must include a clear and conspicuous notice of the time in which delivery is expected to be made.

Negative Option Rule This trade regulation rule, effective June 7, 1974, governs pre-notification negative option sales plans. Under negative option plans, sellers notify buyers of the periodic selection of merchandise to be shipped.

Guides Against Deceptive Guarantees The FTC promulgated seven guides on April 26, 1960, for the purpose of self-regulatory adoption by marketers in their advertising of guarantees. These guides are intended to ensure that the buyer is fully apprised of the conditions governing any guarantee.

Guides to Use of Endorsements and Testimonials These FTC guides, which became effective May 21, 1975, relate to the use of expert and organizational endorsements and testimonials in advertising.

Advisory Opinion on Dry Testing An advisory opinion issued by the FTC on March 27, 1975, allows such dry testing under very strict guidelines to ensure that the potential customer is in no way misled about the terms of the offer.

Mailing of Unordered Merchandise Coming under a category of fraud and deception is the mailing of unordered merchandise, sent without the prior expressed request or consent of the recipient, an unfair method of competition, and an unfair trade practice in violation of the FTC Act.

Guides Against Deceptive Pricing Made effective January 8, 1964, these guides cover offers stating reductions from a "former," "regular," "comparable," "list price," or "manufacturer's suggested retail price."

Guides Against Bait and Switch Advertising The four guides against bait and switch advertising that were issued by the FTC on December 4, 1959, define this type of advertising as that which is "alluring but insincere in offering to sell a product or service which the advertiser in truth does not intend or want to sell."

Guide Concerning Use of the Word "Free" This guide issued by the FTC on December 16, 1971, is intended to prevent deceptive or misleading offers of "free" merchandise or services if, in fact, such is available only with the purchase of some other merchandise or service.

Advisory Opinion on the Use of the Word "New" This advisory opinion, issued on January 4, 1969, is concerned with merchandise that has been used by purchasers on a trial basis, returned to the seller, refurbished, and resold as new.

Advisory Opinion on Disclosure of Foreign Origin Merchandise Direct marketers, when advertising or promoting goods of foreign origin, must clearly inform prospective purchasers that such goods are not made in the United States if, in fact, the goods originate elsewhere.

Warranties The FTC is empowered by the Magnuson-Moss Warranty Act, effective July 4, 1975, with enforcement. Although no organization is required to give a written warranty and state a minimum duration for a warranty, the National Retail Merchants Association, in summarizing the act and the FTC rules relative to it, describes the following responsibility of direct marketers under the act: Catalog or mail order solicitations must disclose for each warranty product either the full text of the warranty or notice that it may be obtained free upon written request.

Online Direct Marketing Due to the information explosion, online direct marketing activities have become one of the focal points of the FTC. In fact, the FTC has produced a four element "Privacy Policy" in an effort to assist companies in telling their customers what information they are collecting, how they will use it, what security is in place, and how consumers can opt out of providing information.

FIGURE 12-9. An Overview of the FTC rules and regulations for direct marketers.

U.S. Postal Service

Through its Inspection Service and in compliance with the Private Express Statutes, the U.S. Postal Service has established rules and regulations that impact the promotional activities of direct marketers. The Inspection Service is constantly on the lookout for fraud and deception through the mail; the Private Express Statutes, by granting the U.S. Postal Service a form of delivery monopoly, determine classification and cost of promotional matter that can be circulated outside the postal monopoly.

State and Local Regulation

Certain organizations using direct marketing strategies, including insurance companies, small lending associations, banks, and pharmaceutical companies, are closely regulated by state legislation, especially relative to promotion and pricing tactics. State legislators have become increasingly active in consumer issues and in privacy matters such as those that affect mailing lists and promotional use of the telephone. The matters of state sales and use taxes, as they relate to taxation of advertising and promotional services, are also of vital concern to direct marketers.

An example of state and local regulations that affect direct marketing activities is the Truth in Advertising legislation. Truth in Advertising was fashioned after a model statute first proposed in 1911. Most states have so-called truth in advertising legislation that governs the conduct of promotional activities in intrastate commerce.

Private Organizations

Better Business Bureaus, the history and influence of which go back more than half a century, are located in most major cities and are sponsored by private businesses and organizations to prevent promotional abuses though commonsense regulation. Likewise, trade groups, along with the DMA, have promulgated ethical guidelines for use by their members and others desiring to adhere to them.

The Future: Self-Regulation or Legislation

Many believe that these issues are merely generational, and, as technology continues to advance, the concerns will fade away. Many privacy debates may seem irrelevant down the road. However, while these issues remain hot topics today, there are two methods for dealing with them—self regulation or legislation.

Self-Regulation

The preferred method to deal with the issues of the regulatory environment is through self-regulation by direct marketers. The DMA has attempted to assist member companies in complying with federal and state regulations, as well as industry self-regulatory responsibilities, attempting to lead the way for its members to meet their customer privacy expectations.

Years ago, Donn Rappaport, chairman of the American List Counsel, presented an eight-step self-regulation plan for direct marketers to follow. The basic guidelines of that plan are still relevant today. Figure 12-10 provides an overview of Rappaport's plan.[32] For newer guidelines, please see DMA's Strategic Plan provided on its Corporate Responsibility Department's Web site.

Legislation and Permission Marketing

Permission marketing obtains the consent of a customer before a company sends out a marketing communication to that customer via the Internet. In other words, permission marketing

1. ***Allow the consumer some measure of control over what lists or types of lists his or her name is on.*** Include a notice in every marketing communication stating your list rental practices and offering to remove the name of anyone who prefers that his or her name not be released to other mailers.
2. ***Ensure that we know who's renting our lists and what they are planning to do with them.*** Direct marketers must pay close attention to list renters that plan to combine your file with other files, abstracts, or overlays.
3. ***Review all third-party cooperative arrangements with regard to list rights.*** From time to time, a credit card processor will lay claim to the names of people who charge mail-order purchases to their credit cards. Remember, they are your customers regardless of how they paid. Be wary of any arrangement that dilutes your rights of ownership.
4. ***Make sure that information is used for the purpose for which it was gathered.*** In other words, if you sell women's clothes and happen to sell a significant volume in large sizes, use that information to develop more large-size business. Don't rent your large-size customer names to a weight-loss program.
5. ***Stop scaring consumers unnecessarily over how much personal data on them is actually available.*** For example, Pacific Bell Telephone Company once began promoting its customer file with the announcement: "Now a business list from the company that has everyone's number." Is this kind of claim really worth the scare it may instill in the consumer?
6. ***Eliminate deceptive or misleading direct mail.*** Does direct mail that looks like an official document from the IRS really work in the long run? Even if it did, it's deceptive and it raises suspicion about the direct marketing industry.
7. ***Use personalization wisely.*** There is a fine line between familiarity with the consumer and an invasion of their personal privacy. Keep in mind that certain types of personal data should not be included in personalization.
8. ***Make sure that the consumer is not ripped off or compromised by the dissemination of personal data.*** Since consumers are serious about the issue of personal privacy, direct marketers must safeguard against privacy abuses.

FIGURE 12-10. Donn Rappaport's Eight-Step Plan for direct marketers. Used with permission of Donn Rappaport.

gives the consumers control over what online communications come to them. It is a parallel to opt-out procedures, whereby the consumer must opt in to receive marketing messages from select organizations seeking to communicate with the consumer. Permission marketing must start with consumers' explicit and active consent to receive online commercial messages and always give consumers the option to stop receiving messages at any time.

Summary

Upholding ethical guidelines in carrying out direct marketing activities is crucial to the present and future success of the direct marketing industry. The three primary areas of legislative oversight include intellectual property rights, security, and privacy. Privacy is the area of greatest concern for direct marketers. Privacy issues encompass personal privacy, information privacy, and offline and online privacy—including spam. The opt-in and opt-out mechanisms along with permission-based marketing are some of the ways consumer privacy issues are being addressed. In addition, security concerns have arisen greatly over the past several years because of security breaches—companies are addressing these concerns as well. Direct marketers must be mindful of the consumer's right to safety, information, selection, confidentiality, and privacy.

The regulatory environment is both dynamic and uncontrollable. Direct marketing regulatory authorities include the FCC, FTC, U.S. Postal Service, state and local entities, and private organizations. The FCC oversees the Telephone Consumer Protection Act. The FTC rules govern advertisements, mail and telephone orders, telemarketing, delivery, negative option rule, guarantees, endorsements and testimonials, testing, merchandise mailing, pricing, bait and switch advertising, use of the words *free* and *new,* disclosures of foreign origin merchandise, warranties, and online direct marketing. Direct marketers must maintain compliance with the many laws affecting direct marketing activities while not losing sight of the bottom-line objective: maximizing customer relationships and customer satisfaction while sustaining a profitable business. The preferred method to deal with issues in the regulatory environment is through self-regulation by direct marketers.

Key Terms

ethics
morals
code of ethics
right to safety
right to information
right to selection
right to confidentiality
right to privacy
intellectual property
privacy
data/security breach

Privacy Act of 1974
spam
annoyance
violation
privacy unconcerned
privacy fundamentalists
privacy pragmatists
chief privacy officer (CPO)
infomediaries
permission marketing

Review Questions

1. What is the purpose of the DMA's guidelines for ethical business practice?
2. List and briefly explain the five consumer rights.
3. What is a chief privacy officer (CPO)? What is her or his primary role in an organization?
4. What are the four components of the DMA's Commitment to Consumer Choice?
5. Explain the role of infomediaries and why some consumers might object to them.
6. What are the names and recommendations of some of the private organizations that provide ethical guidelines for direct marketing?
7. Explain the Privacy Act of 1974 and its impact on direct marketers.
8. What is spam? Why are there so many negative feelings toward spam? What is currently being done to eliminate spam?
9. What is the current status of the FCC/FTC Do Not Call Registry?
10. Using the online legal sources provided in the chapter, provide a legal update on permission marketing and spam as they affect direct marketing activities.

Exercise

Imagine you are the first CPO for a major credit card company. Your organization, like all credit card companies, unfortunately has the typical reputation of selling your customers' information to various firms. You want to change the reputation your company has regarding this matter so that you may gain a competitive edge over your competition. What do you think are some of the regulations and ethical codes you are subject to follow set forth by legislation, private organizations, and organizations such as the FTC? Also explain steps that your company can take to regulate itself that aren't currently being taken by other companies.

Critical Thinking Exercise

How might the continuing technological developments in marketing affect the ethical or legal issues pertaining to consumer privacy? What can direct marketers do to alleviate these concerns? Identify a company or organization that is responding to consumer privacy concerns today. Overview what that company or organization is doing and predict what it might do in the future to continue to address consumer privacy concerns.

CASE: Snow Companies

Very few marketers have more ethical and legal regulations imposed on their marketing activities than those who operate in the pharmaceutical and biotech industry. As Figure 12-11 details, this industry is highly regulated, both externally and internally. Compliance is the name of the game.

Just think of the sophisticated web of key players in this industry and how each player affects the actions of one another. Those key players include patients, doctors, pharmaceutical companies, medical trade associations, insurance companies, and the government.

The need for ethical use of patients' medical information is quite obvious in this industry as each patient's medical records are private. These are highly sensitive documents that must be kept strictly confidential. However, the mirage of legal restrictions imposed on the marketing of branded pharmaceutical drugs is simply mind-boggling. This case will present the challenges and marketing strategies associated with pharmaceutical marketing.

Federal Regulations

The ethical and legal regulations associated with pharmaceutical marketing make "business as usual" vastly different from that of nearly any other industry. The pharmaceutical industry is one of the most highly regulated industries. The Food and Drug Administration (FDA) Center for Drug Evaluation and Research has a division dedicated to establishing and policing guidelines for all pharmaceutical marketing communications. The mission of the Division of Drug Marketing, Advertising, and Communications (DDMAC) is to protect the public health by assuring prescription drug information is truthful, balanced, and accurately communicated. DDMAC has a team of reviewers who are responsible for reviewing prescription drug advertising and promotional drug labeling to ensure that the information contained in those promotional materials is not false or misleading. DDMAC goes beyond the monitoring of pharmaceutical print and broadcast advertisements; they also travel to major medical meetings and pharmaceutical conventions to monitor promotional exhibits and activities.

These legal restrictions include the following:

- Substantiation of Claims—Claims stated in the approved Product Information (PI) have been proven in several phases of clinical trials prior to approval. The FDA reviews the data and convenes panels of experts to review the findings prior to approving the drug to be manufactured and marketed.

FIGURE 12-11. External and internal regulator flowchart. Used with permission of the Snow Companies.

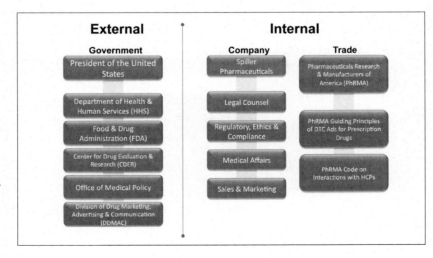

- Fair Balance—When benefits of a product are stated, the risks must also be stated with equal time or space for identical emphasis. The fair balance requirement for DTC ads prohibits ads that convey a deceptive impression of the risk and benefits from the overall presentation of information.

- Overstatement of Efficacy—No statements beyond those in the PI are allowed, nor superlative interpretations of those claims. The FDA regularly sends warning letters or issues fines for promotional materials that exaggerate the efficacy of a product or make an unsubstantiated claim of superiority over another product.

Not so long ago (1990s) pharmaceutical sales representatives of various pharmaceutical companies would call on physicians with an arsenal of free gifts and offer plush benefits, such as free lunches, dinners, weekend trips, tickets to theater productions, and even circus tickets or amusement park passes for the physician and his or her entire family. In 2002, the Pharmaceutical Research & Manufacturers of America (PhRMA) established specific guidelines that affect the direct marketing practices of pharmaceutical companies to physicians.

The Code on Interactions with Health Care Professionals are PhRMA guidelines specific to live interactions between pharmaceutical companies and medical providers. These guidelines have imposed spending limits on meals, speaker training and speaker program guidelines, and the distribution of promotional merchandise. To comply with PhRMA guidelines, pharmaceutical sales representatives cannot leave a single pen, notepad, or mug bearing the name or logo of a pharmaceutical brand behind after they make an office sales call or they will be in violation with PhRMA regulations. Items given to healthcare professionals must not be of substantial value ($100 or less) and they must be educational in nature (such as medical reference books) and benefit patients in the long term.

With a decrease in the variety of marketing activities legally and ethically permitted by pharmaceutical sales reps, many pharmaceutical marketers are now placing more emphasis on direct-to-consumer (DTC) marketing. As Figure 12-12 presents, investments in direct marketing activities in this industry have been rising for decades and are expected to continue to grow in the future.

Direct-To-Consumer (DTC) Marketing

Have you ever wondered about the drug your doctor prescribed to you or a loved one? Do you ever wish you could talk to someone who has a similar condition? Have you ever researched a condition you or a loved one has in advance of a doctor's visit to be better prepared to ask the right questions? If you've answered "yes" to any of these questions, you are among the hundreds of millions of people across the nation who have helped to make DTC or direct-to-patient

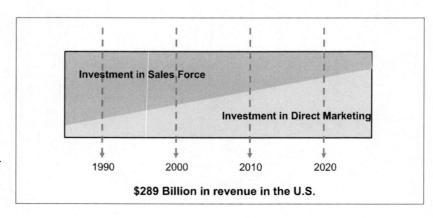

FIGURE 12-12. Investment graph. Used with permission of The Snow Companies.

(DTP) pharmaceutical and biotechnology marketing a burgeoning endeavor. DTC/DTP pharmaceutical advertising is considered to be any marketing communication for prescription drugs that directly targets the final consumer or individual patient, as opposed to promotions that target the physicians who write prescriptions. DTC/DTP marketing is currently allowed only in the United States and New Zealand. Other countries allow a variety of unbranded educational programs, such as grants for support groups or disease awareness events.

While most consumers desire more information on the products they take or have been prescribed, the U.S. Food and Drug Administration (FDA) closely regulates this type of communication. In addition, PhRMA has created specific guidelines to which pharmaceutical companies must follow. PhRMA's *Direct-to-Consumer Advertising about Prescription Medicines* are guidelines specific to direct promotion to consumers of prescription medications. These guidelines address the use of actors in television and print advertisements, the content of advertisements, and lead time before DTC advertising for a new product may begin.

Products in other industries that pose significant health and occupational risks to individuals do not have the same level of scrutiny as do pharmaceuticals. Before a promotional piece can be created for a pharmaceutical product, it needs to undergo an internal review by the pharmaceutical company. Typically, there is a review team for each brand or therapeutic area within the company. These review committees may be called different things:

- Joint Review Committee (JRC)—typically used when co-promoting multiple products
- Promotional Review committee (PRC)
- Review Committee (RC)
- Communication Committee Review (CCR)

As shown in Figure 12-13, most review committees are made up of the same key players—legal, medical, regulatory—each tasked with different prime directives and each viewing the promotional material through the lens of their personal experience.

Each and every pharmaceutical advertisement or item that will be seen by either a physician or a consumer must go through an extensive and rigorous review process. An example of this detailed process is revealed in Figure 12-14. This process may take months and require several revisions before the ad or item obtains the necessary approval to be used in marketing.

Given the stringent federal regulations and scrutiny imposed on the direct marketing of pharmaceutical products, innovation is a prerequisite for success in this space. One company

Players	Prime Directive
General Counsel (Legal)	Are we breaking the law?
Compliance & Ethics (Regulatory)	Does this stay within the boundaries of our label and of agreed upon oversight (DDMAC, PhRMA)?
Medical Affairs	Is the information medically sound? Do we have data to support the claim?
Marketing & Sales	Is this strategic?

FIGURE 12-13. Players/Prime Directive flowchart. Used with permission of The Snow Companies.

FIGURE 12-14.
Review process
flowchart. Used
with permission of
The Snow
Companies.

that has found a way to innovate and create value for clients is Snow Companies, a DTC/DTP
and word-of-mouth health care marketing agency.

Snow Companies Patient Ambassador Program

Brenda Snow, pictured in Figure 12-15, founded the Snow Companies (formerly named Snow
and Associates) in 2001 and developed its proprietary Patient Ambassador™ program. After
Snow was diagnosed with multiple sclerosis, she became frustrated at how little was being done
to help educate, empower, and engage people like herself.

The company identifies, develops, trains, and manages Patient Ambassadors, who are people
with a medical condition who have undergone legal, regulatory, and storytelling training. They
help provide a human face to the disease conditions and brands they represent. Patient Ambassadors help raise awareness of treatment options and educate others about therapy choices by
sharing their personal stories. In this role, they become a resource for other patients with the
same condition under the guidelines established by the FDA. This powerful and persuasive personal communication has proven to be a success and has helped Snow Companies become a successful marketing force in the pharmaceutical and biotech industry.

FIGURE 12-15.
Brenda Snow, The Snow
Companies Founder. Used
with permission of The
Snow Companies.

The Snow Companies employ a variety of direct marketing
strategies in the execution of tactics to support clients including
direct mail, outbound and inbound telephone marketing, e-mail
marketing, Internet marketing, and social networking to reach target audiences. Patient Ambassadors are used in a mixture of online
features, including webisodes, YouTube videos, and features on
sponsored Web sites. Web initiatives, as a percent of a brand's tacti-
cal mix, continue to rise due to decreasing brand budgets. This
means that there is increasing scrutiny for effectively measuring
marketing spending and the desire to target specific patient segments. Further, although face-to-face interactions have the greatest
impact on behavior, patients are increasingly leveraging the Internet, and specifically social media, for health topics such as a specific
disease or treatment.

Despite successfully using Patient Ambassadors in content
online, such as posting approved material on a program Facebook

site, or listing Local Patient Outreach Programs (LPOPs) for their social network to attend, there are still restrictions. Although DTC marketing has moved online and will remain there for the foreseeable future, there is one area where communications are limited or tentative: social media. Pharmaceutical companies producing online video content have disabled YouTube commenting, for example, due to HIPAA concerns over the "friends" and "subscribers" functions which might reveal the identity (and diagnosis) of those parties. Depending on the content of a channel's posted videos, i.e. branded vs. unbranded information, additional restrictions may be made related to disclaimers, share functions, and friends/subscribers options

Besides patient privacy issues, another major concern for the pharma and biotech industry is reporting of adverse events, or side effects, via the Internet. Members of the industry are required to report AEs within 24 hours of receiving information that fits four criteria: an identifiable reporter, patient, drug name, and adverse event. These requirements increase the burden on any marketing initiatives from a financial and resource perspective, as constant surveillance would be mandatory. The subsequent surveillance and anticipated results must be weighed to determine if this is an avenue which is positive for the brand. Additionally, Facebook, the unquestioned leader in social media, has made screening responses more challenging by lifting the ability to prescreen comments in 2011. This decision makes it even more challenging for pharma companies to engage with their consumers directly, due to the increased risks related to the other regulatory guidelines.

The FDA has been studying social media for several years but has not issued any substantive social media guidelines, which would help provide a framework for marketing decisions. Due to that, pharmaceutical and biotech marketers have been wary about pursuing any large-scale social networking projects until they have a more concrete idea of what the FDA will permit. In most instances, social media endeavors have been leveraged as one-off extensions to supplement existing marketing tactics versus a stand-alone business driver.

In any case, whether a brand chooses to engage in these mediums or not, in order to remain authentic, real patients should be a major part of the brand's tactics. The more involved these brand Ambassadors are, the stronger the messages, brand resonance, and subsequent marketing results. Snow continues to look for new, yet safe, approaches to social media and pharma marketing and will continue to propose and develop new ways to leverage the conversations patients are having online, with Patient Ambassadors at the center of those efforts.

Because of the highly regulated nature of the industry, all of the company's activities come under tough scrutiny from regulatory, legal, and medical reviewers who closely monitor all of these activities to ensure compliance. One of the most effective methods used by Snow Companies is live events, which are high-touch and very resonant with the people who attend. LPOPs are targeted educational symposia for patients, caregivers, family members, and friends to learn about a specific condition and possible treatments for that condition. Snow uses direct marketing tactics to promote LPOPs and find people who are interested in learning more about their condition and interacting with others living with it.

At these events, a Patient Ambassador shares his or her personal story of their trials and tribulations of living with a chronic medical condition with the event attendees. They also share their philosophy of taking charge of their health to inspire others, as well as share tips and advice for their specific condition. Disease and treatment information is presented by a health care professional as well. The program attendees can also meet others living with the same condition or opt-in for relationship marketing programs for more information. Through these programs, Snow is able to amplify brand messages, such as treatment compliance, not settling, and being proactive with health care providers, while still remaining compliant to the industry guidelines.

Snow Companies is an excellent example of an organization that has found a way to be highly successful by effectively employing myriad direct and interactive marketing strategies and tactics within the constraints of a strict regulatory environment.

Case Discussion Questions

1. Discuss the factors contributing to the popularity of direct-to-customer (DTC) marketing in the pharmaceutical industry. Explain the advantages and disadvantages of direct-to-customer marketing of prescription drugs to patients, physicians, and pharmaceutical companies.

2. Describe the number of reviews a pharmaceutical product has to go through before it is marketed to the public. Explain how each review committee is made up and the rationale behind it.

3. Discuss the Snow Companies and the Patient Ambassador™ program developed by Brenda Snow. Who are the Patient Ambassadors and what role(s) do they play in the marketing of pharmaceutical and biotech products? Explain the communication techniques that they use.

4. Discuss why the role of social media is limited in the DTC marketing communications of pharmaceutical products. What are the concerns with HIPAA (the Health Insurance Portability and Accountability Act) compliance?

5. Why are pharmaceutical and biotech marketers wary about using large-scale social networking to promote their products? Explain the advantages and disadvantages of social networking in marketing pharmaceutical and biotech products.

Notes

1. *New Environmental Standard on Direct Marketing,* September 21, 2007, http://www.bsi-global. com/en/About-BSI/News-Room/BSI-News-Content/Disciplines/Environmental-Management/DMA-PAS/ (May 7, 2008).

2. Direct Marketing Association, Washington D.C. Office, personal communication, May 5, 2011

3. Melissa Campanelli, *EMA Unveils 'Please Recycle' Campaign,* July 2007, http://www.dmnews.com/ EMA-unveils-Please-Recycle-campaign/article/html(April 16, 2008).

4. Direct Marketing Association, *Recycle Please,* http://www.the-dma.org/recycle (April 16, 2008).

5. Direct Marketing Association, *The Green 15: Benchmarking Environmental Progress,* http://www.the-dma.org/green15/overviewDMAgreen15.pdf (April 16, 2008).

6. Direct Marketing Association. Washington D.C. Office, personal communication, May 5, 2011

7. Adapted from Carl McDaniel, Jr., and Roger Gates Contemporary Marketing Research, 2nd ed. (New York: West Publishing Co., 1993).

8. Charles W. L. Hill, Global Business Today (New York: McGraw-Hill/Inrwin, 2002), p. 50.

9. American Intellectual Property Law Association, www.aipla.org>.

10. Ibid.

11. "Help Wanted: Steal This Database," Wired News, January 6, 2003; Elaine M. LaFlamme, "Know the liabilities of Data Collection," New Jersey Law Journal (March 14, 2003), www.law.com>.

12. ZDNet.Co.Uk, California's S.B. 1386 Requires Notification of Customers When Unencrypted Data Are Stolen: Law Exempts Encrypted Data, November, 2005. http://whitepapers.zdnet.co.uk (April 11, 2008).

13. James Kindall, "Lists Help Build Dosier on You," Kansas City Star, September 5, 1978, p. 1.

14. Adapted from The Privacy Protection Study Commission, Report from the Privacy Protection Study Commission (Washington, DC: GPO, July 1977), p. 147.

15. Spam Statistics and Facts, 2009. http://www.spamlaws.com/spam-stats.html, Retrieved May 19, 2011.

16. Spam Laws, *Spam Origin* http://www.spamlaws.com/spam-origin.html (April 16, 2008).

17. Federal Trade Commission, *The CAN-SPAM Act: Requirements for Commercial Emailers,* Washington, DC. http://www.ftc.gov/bcp/conline/pubs/buspus/canspam.shtm (April 16, 2008).

18. vDirect Marketing Association. Washington D.C. Office, Personal communication. May 5, 2011

19. Saul Hansell, "Virginia Law Makes Spam, With Fraud, A Felony," New York Times, April 30, 2003, sec. C, p. 1, col. 5.

20. Karl Dentino, "Taking Privacy into Our Own Hands," Direct Marketing (September 1994).

21. Richard A. Hamilton and Lisa D. Spiller, "Opinions about Privacy: Does the Type of Informatin Used for Marketing Purposes Make a Difference?" International Journal of Voluntary Sector Marketing 4, no. 3 (September 1999): 251–264.

22. Page Boinest Melton, "Business Trends to Watch", Virginia Business (February 2001), 78–81.

23. Universal Bank, Important Information Regarding Your Privacy (2001), 1.

24. Ibid., 5.

25. The Direct Marketing Association, Inc., "Online Marketing Privacy Principles and Guidelines," July Direct Marketing Associations, New York, NY, July 1997, pp. 3–9.

26. W3C Platform for Privacy Preferences Initiative. Technology and Society Domain. "Enabling Smarter Privacy Tools for the Web" 21 May 2011. http://www.w3.org/P3P/

27. http://www.fcc.gov/

28. Adapted from the Direct Marketing Association, *Telephone Consumer Protection Act (TCPA),* http://www.the-dma.org/guidelines/tcpa.shtml (September 17, 2003).

29. Direct Marketing Association, *10 Steps to Making a Sale Under the FTC's New Telemarketing Sales Rule,* DMA Telemarketing Resource Center, http://www.the-dma.org/government/teleresource center.shtml (September 12, 2003).

30. The Federal Trade Commission, Privacy Online: Fair Information in The Electronic Marketplace (Washington, DC: GPO, May 2000).

31. Direct Marketing Association, "The FTC's New Telemarketing Sales Rule: Q & A's," http://www.the-dma.org (September 12, 2003).

32. Kristen Bremner, "CA Assembly Passes Amended Privacy Bill," Direct Marketing News, September 17, 2003.

## CHAPTER 13

Exploring and Adapting Direct and Interactive Marketing Strategies around the World

OPENING VIGNETTE: BODY PARTS DIRECT

If you are like most college students, you are often strapped for cash. What that small detail translated into was an opportunity for the Bank of New Zealand to target college students with a wildly creative direct marketing campaign called "Body Parts." The name of the campaign alone arouses curiosity, right? Well, allow us to satisfy your curiosity and reveal the details about this brilliant direct marketing campaign.

Most banks believe that the student market is a highly important one to target. Are you wondering why? It seems odd since most students do not have much money to be saved or invested. However, it is as a student that most customers begin a relationship with the bank that they are likely to stay with for many years. Therefore, establishing relationships with students is seen as investing in future profitability for banks. It makes good sense. Therefore, most banks offer lucrative incentives, such as MP3 players or cash sign-on bonuses, to get students to open an account. In New Zealand, many students are a bit cynical toward overt marketing, therefore banks have to be extra creative and strategic when developing and executing their marketing campaigns.

Bank of New Zealand sought out AIM Proximity to help it meet the challenges associated with marketing to students. The campaign objective was to open 6,500 new accounts, with a stretch target of 10,000 accounts—which was the same campaign objective as the previous year, but with the added challenge of a 10 percent reduction in the promotional budget over last year. With the student consumer culture in mind, AIM Proximity and Bank of New Zealand constructed a campaign to appeal to students' desire to *get something*. They wanted something different and unique—something that would really appeal to students. The answer was to develop a program where students could obtain discounts and get free stuff all year (as opposed to just once) to make their frugal life more enjoyable.

The offer featured Bank of New Zealand's Campus Pack, which is a student bank account with a free student discount card. The bank offered additional incentives to students to encourage them to open a Campus Pack account. The campaign was executed through a variety of traditional direct response media, such as print and direct mail, as well as some nontraditional media, such as mobile bank stands on campus, street posters plastered around campus, banner ads on student Web sites, inserts in new student orientation bags, and street theater–style stunts on campus. The campaign was creative, bold, and fun. As Figure 13-1 presents, all of the creative

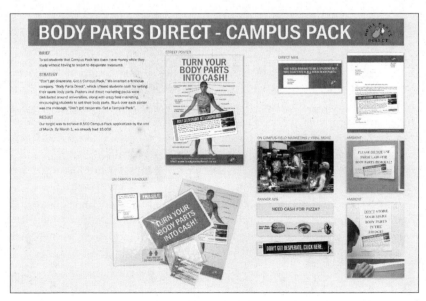

FIGURE 13-1.
Body Parts Direct
Campus Pack.
Used with
permission of
Bank of New
Zealand.

materials used in the campaign featured the same basic message—"You don't have to sell your body parts for cash—don't get desperate, get a Campus Pack instead."

The agency invented a fictitious company, Body Parts Direct, which offered students cash for selling their spare body parts. This was crazy marketing—but fun! Need extra cash for pizza? Consider selling an eyebrow! The call to action was to visit Bank of New Zealand's Web site, visit a branch office, or text message the company. The campaign was so effective that Bank of New Zealand opened 18,138 new accounts, far surpassing the stretch target of 10,000.[1]

This campaign is proof that highly creative and effective direct and interactive marketing campaigns are being used all over the world. That is the topic of this chapter. We explore international versus domestic direct marketing strategies, factors entering into the decision to market internationally, modes of market entry, and international direct marketing infrastructure needed to be successful in international direct and interactive marketing. In addition, this chapter enables you to explore how direct and interactive marketing strategies are being employed in geographical regions around the world. We hope you enjoy the international voyage!

Direct and Interactive Marketing around the World

The world is getting smaller. Facing saturated U.S. markets, many companies are looking overseas to achieve increased sales volume and greater profits. Over the past two decades, global trade has climbed from $200 billion a year to more than $7 trillion.[2] Although those are the two reasons frequently named by organizations seeking international business, other reasons include the hope of expanding into new markets, diversification, achieving economies of scale, and business survival. World exports of merchandise products increased 22% (from $12.5 trillion to $15.2 trillion in a single year); world exports of commercial services increased 8% (from $3.4 trillion to $3.7 trillion).[3] The United States' trade with the world was $3.2 trillion in 2010.[4] The top trade partners for the United States in 2010 were Canada at $525.3 billion, China at $456.82 billion, Mexico at $392.98 billion, Japan at $180.89 billion, and Germany at $130.88 billion.[5] Today, nearly half of the global brands are headquartered outside of U.S. borders. According to a study by Goldman Sachs, it is estimated that by 2050 the "BRIC" economies of Brazil, Russia, India, and China will in all likelihood surpass that of today's six largest economies, thus creating a new world order.[6] Revenue generated by international direct marketing activities has continued to increase over the years.

The Internet is one of the reasons many companies have entered international markets via direct exporting. Marketing on the Internet through a Web site is the same thing today as opening a global business with a worldwide audience. Unlike traditional exporting, which began with brokers and other intermediaries who assisted companies in generating international sales from preselected foreign countries, a Web site is immediate and inexpensive. However it does not permit much selectivity in choosing markets. Research has shown that 77.4 percent of the population in North America has Internet access, and that 86.5 percent of Internet users are located outside of North America.[7] This may often lead to fulfillment problems for direct marketers, who don't have the distribution network or capability of fulfilling international orders in some countries.

There are four compelling reasons for direct marketers to decide to go international in their marketing efforts. These are: limited growth opportunities in the domestic market, shared global values, the high cost of new product development, and competitive forces.[8] The potential of many international markets is extremely attractive for direct marketers and has been for a number of years. International direct marketing is not new. Let's take a short look at the use of direct marketing around the world.

According to the Direct Marketing Association (DMA) *Fact Book,* the oldest known catalog was produced by Aldus Manutius of Venice in 1498 and listed the titles of 15 texts Manutius had published.[9] Next came seed and nursery catalogs, the earliest known mercantile gardening catalog being a printed price list issued by William Lucas, an English gardener. But it was in Germany that direct marketing truly has its roots. Germany had a parcel post system by 1874, and a collect on delivery (COD) system by 1878. The first known European consumer catalog was distributed in 1883, about the same time that Richard Sears was creating his first catalog in the United States.[10]

By 1912, a German businessman, August Stuchenbrok, produced a 238-page catalog—which was five years before Leon Bean (of L. L. Bean) sold his first pair of boots.[11] One of the largest catalog houses in the world is also owned by a German company, Otto Versand, who owns Spiegel, Eddie Bauer, and Newport News, among others.

Differences between Domestic and International Direct Marketing

What makes international direct marketing different from domestic direct marketing? Market uncertainty is one of the biggest differences. The uncertainty of different foreign business environments is due to differences in infrastructure, technology, competitive dynamics, legal and governmental restrictions, customer preferences, culture, accepted payment methods (such as the use of credit cards), and many additional uncontrollable variables. These factors make many direct marketers hesitate to leap into international markets, regardless of their potential.

To ensure success in foreign markets, direct marketers must first research the cultural differences of the prospective market. Primarily, the culture being examined needs to be recognized as being either a collectivist or individualistic society. In a **collectivist culture** emphasis is placed on the group as a whole. History, family ties, loyalty, and tradition are revered above individual accomplishments. Societies sharing strong attributes of collectivism include cultures like those of Latin America, Asia, and the Middle East. In **individualistic cultures,** the value lies on the achievements and successes of the individual person. Independence and a strong sense of self take priority over any group focus. Cultures such as the United States, Europe, Canada, and Australia display this individualistic quality. For example, Tang, the orange-flavored powdered drink, was marketed successfully in the United States as an orange juice substitute. However, in France, Tang had to be marketed as a refreshment beverage because the French do not normally drink orange juice at breakfast. Thus, customer preferences driven by cultural differences dictated the marketing strategy.[12]

Different country laws can also dictate marketing strategies. For example, in Europe there are many restrictions on advertisements for cigarette and tobacco products, alcoholic beverages, and pharmaceutical products. Ads for other products may also be regulated. Advertisements in the United Kingdom cannot show a person applying an underarm deodorant. Therefore, ads are modified to show an animated person applying the product.[13] In addition, many Western European countries allow partial nudity in late-night television advertisements. There may be tremendous opportunities in foreign markets, but direct marketers must conduct careful, calculated research before they venture abroad.

Making the Decision to Go International

Various researchers have offered tips or processes to follow when deciding to begin international direct marketing activities. Today, it has become increasingly important to pursue **global market segmentation (GMS)** as a starting point for going global. GMS can be defined as the process of identifying specific segments, country groups, or individual consumer groups across countries of potential customers who exhibit similar buying behaviors.[14] The following five-step approach is a synthesis of the many processes suggested for screening, selecting, and marketing to an international country:[15]

Step 1: Assess Your International Potential

Direct marketers must analyze their domestic position in their industry to provide an indication of the strength of their foundation and resource base from which they can expand. A part of this assessment is determining whether there are adequate external resources to assist them in penetrating international markets. Some of these external resources may include *expert advice and counseling*. Many organizations exist in the private and public sector to assist firms in beginning an international marketing program. Some of these resources include the following:

- Bureau of the Census (www.census.gov)
- CIA—Country Fact Sheets (www.cia.gov)
- DMA Global Knowledge Network Services (www.the-dma.org)
- Forefront Corporation (www.forefrontinternational.com)
- GroupM (www.groupm.com)
- Market Development Cooperator Program—MDCP (www.ita.doc.gov/td/mdcp)
- Partners International (www.partnersinternational.com)
- U.S. Chambers of Commerce—AMCHAMS (www.uschamber.org/intl/amcham.la.htm)
- U.S. Department of Commerce—Foreign Trade Highlights (www.doc.gov)
- U.S. Department of State (www.state.gov)
- U.S. Market Development Group (www.usmarketgroup.com)
- U.S. Small Business Administration (www.sba.gov)
- U.S. Trade Information Center (1-800-USA TRADE)

In addition, many industry trade associations and graduate business programs at universities provide assistance to companies beginning international marketing activities.

Step 2: Conduct Market Research

Conducting market research is critical to understanding the cultural differences and market nuances that may exist between and among countries. Identifying potential overseas markets involves a great deal of time, effort, and research. However, given the vast amount of data available about each foreign market, researching a single market is likely to provide information overload. Savvy direct marketers sort through all the data and determine the pertinent information they need to analyze the potential of a foreign market.

Direct marketers must determine whether consumers have a basic need for their products/services and whether the resources necessary for them to carry out local business activities are available. International direct marketers must understand the local color of the destination country, including such information as what consumers buy, why they buy, how they pay for it, and what motivates them to make a purchase. At a minimum, direct marketers must understand local buying behavior, typical payment methods, advertising practices, and privacy laws. The customers in other countries are not Americans who simply live abroad. They have different cultures, different tastes, and different needs and wants and must be segmented accordingly. For example, Europe is highly diverse in terms of geography, language, economic development, spending habits, disposable income, and so on. Therefore, direct marketers structuring their approach as if there were one unified European Union will likely fail.

Direct marketers must also research the national business environment of the target country including its cultural, political, legal, and economic situation. Determine whether the language, attitudes, religious beliefs, traditions, work ethic, government regulation, government bureaucracy, political stability, fiscal and monetary policies, currency issues, cost of transporting goods, and the country image are understandable and conducive to doing business there.

The state of a country's infrastructure must be factored into the potential for success in that country's market. Infrastructure is normally a leading indicator of economic development and must be in place to support the direct marketer. A country's **infrastructure** represents those capital goods and services that serve the activities of many industries. At a minimum, the infrastructure analysis should include the following essential services: transportation, communications, utilities, and banking. There are really three infrastructure pillars that support the international direct marketing industry—the publishing industry, the transportation industry, and advances in high technology.[16] Because of its importance, we discuss infrastructure in greater detail later in this chapter. Market research should also investigate the potential market or site to determine the suitability of the market for the particular product or service. Would the product succeed in this market? Certain locations may not be acceptable due to the lack of resources available for marketing a specific product or service. Therefore, direct marketers must conduct a detailed country-by-country analysis to properly select which markets to penetrate. Market research for each country under consideration can be boiled down to the following primary international market indicators: population, political stability, GDP/inflation, distribution of wealth, age distribution, currency, tariffs and taxes, and computer ownership. Let's look briefly at each.

POPULATION. Direct marketers should consider the size of the population segments that fit their targeted prospect profile. Direct marketers should take into consideration a country's population along with its overall wealth. For example, direct marketers should be cautious in entering a country with a large population but little monetary wealth. Direct marketers may prefer entering a market with a small population that has a high per capita gross domestic product (GDP), such as Singapore.

POLITICAL STABILITY. The political stability of a country becomes extremely important for those direct marketers planning to establish a physical presence there. In addition, political shifts in power and leadership may affect foreign exchange rates and tariffs.

GDP/INFLATION. The rate of inflation of a country affects the purchasing power of consumers within a country and is closely related to the country's GDP. GDP stands for **gross domestic product,** which is the total market value of all final goods and services produced within a nation's borders in a given year. When assessing a country's GDP and inflation rates, most direct marketers look for annual trends going back as far as five years.

DISTRIBUTION OF WEALTH. Direct marketers must assess the distribution of wealth in a country to determine whether there are a substantial number of consumers who are able to afford the product or service. As in the United States, some international countries, such as Mexico, have the situation where the top 10 percent of the population possesses more than 50 percent of the wealth. Thus, the size and viability of a market in any country depends on the target market customer's disposable income.

AGE DISTRIBUTION. An analysis of age distribution assesses both the average longevity of the citizens as well as the age breakdown of the population. The age structure of a population affects the nation's key socioeconomic issues. Countries with young populations (high percentage under age 15) need to invest more in schools, whereas countries with older populations (high percentage aged 65 and over) need to invest more in the health sector.[17] For example, a population comprised primarily of young adults is great if you are marketing soft drinks; however, if you are marketing automobiles, the likelihood of these young people having the income to purchase the product is considerably lessened.

CURRENCY. An assessment of the currency of a foreign country includes an evaluation of the convertibility and ease of exchange of currency, inflation rates, and credit card penetration. While currency and payment method may be separate issues, they may be related in some countries. For example, in 2005, 86 percent of Mexican consumer purchases were still made in cash. This lack of credit card usage was attributed to Mexican citizens' inability to afford the high interest rates accompanying credit cards, which at times exceeded annual interest rates of 39 percent![18]

TARIFFS AND TAXES. How difficult and expensive is it to bring goods across a country's international border? Do local regulations such as tariffs and taxes favor locally produced goods and services over imported ones? These are the types of questions with which direct marketers must be concerned when deciding to go international.

COMPUTER OWNERSHIP. How widely are computers used, and how many computer users have Internet access? In many countries, the majority of consumers do not have easy Internet access. This poses a problem for direct markers who seek to create a virtual business.

POSTAL/DELIVERY SERVICES. This category includes the postal system as well as private delivery alternatives. Some areas to address include the following:

1. Adequacy of the change-of-address system available;

2. The existence of parcel COD system;

3. The existence of a track-and-trace system for parcels; and

4. The level of sophistication and format of the postcode system.

If any of these researched items do not satisfy a business's requirements or justify the modifications necessary to carry out necessary marketing activities in that country, then perhaps that country should be eliminated from further business consideration.

Step 3: Select Your Trading Partners

Based on the research collected and analyzed in step two, careful analysis should provide an indication as to which markets would be receptive to the particular product and/or service. Direct marketers should select the market or site that holds the greatest potential for successful international marketing. Although many companies are anxious to get an international direct marketing campaign started, it can be extremely taxing on a company. Most experts suggest targeting only one country at a time. Multicountry rollouts are very difficult to execute successfully.

This is the step of the process that may require traveling to those countries or markets that have been selected. During these field trips, direct marketers should investigate the nuances of the market and perform a competitor analysis. Many countries select neighboring countries for trading partners or they select those countries that share a common language and culture.

Step 4: Develop an International Direct Marketing Plan

Direct marketers should create a detailed marketing plan itemizing their long-term goals along with the competitive niche the firm is attempting to fill. They should structure the marketing plan

FIGURE 13-2. Peruvian Connection home page. Used with permission of The Peruvian Connection.

to cover a two- to five-year period, along with a competitor analysis. This plan should detail communication and distribution strategies. For example, direct marketers must determine the media mix for communicating the promotional message. Keep in mind that internationally, postal reliability and postal rates may limit mail-order offerings, including the use of many catalogs.

Regarding distribution strategies, direct marketers must determine whether they will have a physical presence in the country. Although many international consumers look for U.S. products on the basis of reputation and prestige, they also want the feel of a local presence. This translates into the need to have a local in-country return address along with customer addresses without country codes, response call centers handled in the native language, country- and language-specific Web sites, prices quoted in local currencies, and so on. However, given today's technological advances, it is possible for U.S. direct marketers to create a "virtual" local presence if the firm cannot attain a physical presence. (This is attained by making the intangible tangible.)

The Peruvian Connection is another example of the many direct marketers using multi-channel fulfillment. It obtains inquiries for its catalog from its Web site, direct mail, and magazine ads. It has retail stores in selected locations, where it sells surplus stock. A good many new sales now originate at its Web site, the home page of which appears in Figure 13-2.

Step 5: Begin International Direct Marketing Activities

Implementing a direct marketing plan is expensive and time-consuming. However, for many direct marketers, it is very well worth it. As direct marketers begin to implement their strategies, revisions may be necessary. The international business environment is extremely unpredictable. It is a dynamic environment that must be constantly monitored. Therefore, as direct marketers begin international direct marketing activities, they will need to continue researching and analyzing the changing business environment.

With all the necessary research and preparation, of course, direct marketers entering foreign markets still do so with greater risk than they face when entering the domestic marketplace. Thus they should slowly, not hastily, penetrate one country's market at a time. International direct marketing is all about differences. It should be no surprise then that different foreign market entry strategies exist. We now turn to market entry modes.

Modes of Market Entry

There are six basic modes of market entry for penetrating an international market: exporting, licensing, joint venture, contract manufacturing, direct investment, and management contracting.

Exporting

An **exporting** company sells its products from its home base without maintaining any of its own personnel overseas. IBM used direct exporting to expand its global distribution of products like the OS/2 Warp operating system to businesses and consumers in Japan.[19] Many successful, well-known direct marketers, such as L. L. Bean, conduct their international marketing via direct exporting from their respective home bases. L. L. Bean is located in Freeport, Maine, yet fulfills orders from customers all over the world. However, sometimes the company must have a local mailing address because some customers are reluctant to place orders and send money overseas. For example, in Japan, L. L. Bean works with McCann Direct, the specialized direct marketing division of McCann-Erickson Hakuhodo, Japan's largest foreign advertising agency. When L. L. Bean places ads for its catalogs in Japanese media, those catalog orders are sent locally to McCann Direct. McCann Direct then forwards the orders to L. L. Bean's headquarters in Maine, where all the orders for catalogs or products are fulfilled.[20] L. L. Bean also has a distribution arrangement with UPS for parcel fulfillment. [21]

Licensing

Licensing occurs when a **licensor,** a company located in the host country, allows a foreign firm to manufacture or service a product or service for sale in the **licensee's** country. Licensing is similar to franchising in that a local business in an international country becomes authorized to manufacture or sell specific brand products for another company. Franchising is a form of licensing that has grown rapidly in recent years. The right to use a patent or trademark must be granted to a foreign company under the license agreement contract. The most common licensing agreements occur when a direct marketer allows a firm in a local country market to reproduce a direct marketing catalog in the local language. An example of a direct marketer using licensing agreements to market internationally is that of Orvis. It markets its outdoor clothing, accessories, and fishing equipment by mailing 50 million catalogs a year through four different titles, and operates about 50 retail stores in the United States. [22] In addition, they have more than 20 stores in the United Kingdom.[23] Orvis sells through catalogs, a network of 500 independent dealers worldwide, and its Web site. It also partners with select licensees.[24] In fact, if you go to its Web site, www.orvis.com, you can obtain a listing of its worldwide dealer network along with a listing of international market opportunities Orvis wants to pursue in the future.

Joint Venture

A **joint venture** is created when two or more investors join forces to conduct a business by sharing ownership and control. It is similar to a partnership. Companies understand that marketing alliances with a foreign company can provide a number of benefits. These benefits include easy access to a foreign market, elimination of tariffs and quotas, faster growth and market coverage, and ability to penetrate markets that normally would have been closed to wholly owned enterprises. Joint ventures are normally a win-win situation for each of the partners. For example, Recreational Equipment Inc. (REI) and Austad's, a golf supply cataloger, worked out a cooperative venture with one another and mailed their catalogs together to names on both of their Japanese lists.[25] Another example of a joint venture is that of E*TRADE. E*TRADE, a U.S. Internet-based stockbroker, entered into a joint venture with Softbank Corporation of Japan to offer online investing services in Asia. E*TRADE also entered into a second joint venture with Electronic Share Information in Great Britain.[26]

Contract Manufacturing

Many times, a company will outsource or contract with a local manufacturer to produce goods for the company. This strategy, known as **contract manufacturing,** enables companies to take advantage of lower labor costs and faster market entry, while avoiding local ownership problems, and satisfying legal requirements that the product must be manufactured locally for it to be sold in that country. For example, visit the Web site of Texas Instruments at www.ti.com and click on TI Worldwide and you will learn that TI has manufacturing sites and sales and support offices located in Europe, Asia, Japan, and the Americas.[27] While you're there, take note of the selection of TI Web sites featuring different languages designed to serve its international customers.

Direct Investment

Direct investment occurs when a company acquires an existing foreign company or forms a completely new company in the foreign country. For example, Walmart currently has more than 9,000 retail stores, with 60 banner names in 15 countries. Sales in 2010 were $405 billion and the company employed 2.1 million associates worldwide.[28] For the Fiscal year that ended in January 2011,Walmart International drove $109 billion in sales, which is 26 percent of the Company's three business units (Walmart U.S., Walmart International, and Sam's Club). This same year, 458 new stores were added and there was an international net sales increase of 12 percent. [29]The German company Otto Versand, for example, became the largest mail-order company in the world by buying existing companies or building new ones. Otto Versand owns mail-order companies or is part owner of direct marketing firms in Belgium, France, Italy, Japan, Spain, and the United States.

Management Contracting

In **management contracting** local business people or their government sign a contract to manage the foreign business in their country's market. An example of management contracting is Day-Timers, a U.S. firm located in East Texas, Pennsylvania. Day-Timers uses direct mail to market to millions of businesspeople in the United States. However, it opened offices in Australia, Canada, and the United Kingdom and hired local employees to manage its foreign business locations because it needed to have people who were familiar with the culture and could handle incoming phone calls.[30]

Direct marketers must carefully weigh the advantages and disadvantages of each method and determine which is best for their company. The choice of mode of market entry depends in the end on many factors, one of which we address next.

International Direct Marketing Infrastructure

Direct marketers must assess the degree of sophistication of each country's direct marketing infrastructure with the goal of determining how well they can use it to implement direct marketing activities. Some questions and issues direct marketers might investigate include:

- Does the country have an active DMA?
- What is the degree to which the support services (printing and publishing services, transportation or package delivery services, postal services, and technological services) are present?

List Availability
Quality of Postal Service
Average Postage Costs
Percentage of Mail Friendly Households
Internal or External Database
Average Direct Mail Cost per Piece
Availability of In-Line Personalization
Standardized Addresses
Postal Codes
Inbound Telemarketing Availability
Outbound Telemarketing Availability
Availability of Credit Cards
Response Channel Opportunities

FIGURE 13-3.
Direct marketing
infrastructure.

- How sophisticated is the credit card and banking system in the country?
- Is there an established pattern of purchasing via familiar direct channels?
- What legislative issues will affect direct marketing activities?

Figure 13-3 provides an itemized list of the direct marketing infrastructure needed to support international direct marketing activities. Let's briefly look at some of the infrastructure supporting international direct marketing activities.

Lists and Databases

Lists of both consumer and business customers are normally available for most countries, although different kinds of lists are available in different countries. Direct mail and e-mail lists are important tools for a global direct marketer. However, the list industry (with the exception of Australia, the United Kingdom, Canada, and New Zealand) remains far less developed than that offered within the United States and list sharing among mail-order companies is nearly unheard of.[31] For example, in Europe, there are multinational lists and local lists. In China, lists of factories, ministries, professional societies, research institutes, and universities are available, though quite expensive.[32] A number of vendors in the United States offer international lists, but the quality will vary. It is good practice to test a small representative sample of any list before renting it. Because mailing lists in Russia are so unreliable, Hearst Corporation bypassed direct mail and opted for newsstand sales to distribute the first issues of *Cosmopolitan* to the consumer market.[33] However, Magnavox CATV, which markets cable television equipment, has increased its international mailings to support its many trade shows in developing regions.[34]

Also be aware that a number of laws pertain to information privacy—which normally affects direct marketing list and database activities. Canada's Personal Information Privacy and Electronic Documents Act has had significant impact on direct marketers on both sides of the border.[35] Lists and databases are clearly key areas of importance to international direct marketers.

Fulfillment

Distributing products to the customer is one of the prime difficulties associated with international direct marketing. Direct marketers have two main distribution options available to them—ship products from the home location, or establish a bulk distribution operation overseas. Those direct marketers using their home location have three basic options for distributing products: (1) the U.S. Postal Service (USPS) international mail; (2) non-USPS postal delivery via a foreign postal administration, such as the Royal Mail; or (3) consolidators within the United States (such as Worldpak, Global Mail, and FedEx) that act as service agents for the international direct mailer.

Besides distribution issues, fulfillment concerns also include the determination of payment options. In the United States, most direct marketers offer consumers the option to pay by credit card, check, or money order. These are not necessarily the standards in foreign markets. Credit card penetration is considerably lower in other countries than it is throughout the United States. In addition and unlike the United States, many consumers in foreign countries primarily use their credit cards for vacation purposes only. Checks, direct debit, bank transfers (wire services), and invoicing are other payment options to be considered.

Another growing option for transferring money between buyers and sellers is through online transactions facilitated by companies such as PayPal—a company of the online auction Web site eBay. The company, through online processes, enables its members to "send money without sharing financial information, with the flexibility to pay using their account balances, bank accounts, credit cards or promotional financing." Nearly 98 million active user accounts are maintained in some 190 worldwide markets. The company customizes its Web site for 21 individual markets and handles 25 different international currencies.[36]

An additionally important fulfillment issue is customer service. Direct marketers must make their return policies simple and easy to understand, as well as have toll-free numbers available for consumers to place inquiries or complaints. Local fulfillment centers should be established to handle orders for foreign countries with language barriers. For example, U.S. inventory for Lands' End's U.K., German, and Japanese catalogs is shipped in bulk to local operations in the United Kingdom and Japan. The U.K. fulfillment center handles orders originating from its U.K. catalog and German-language catalog, and the Japanese fulfillment center handles orders for its Japanese-language catalog.[37]

Determining the locations for fulfillment centers and deciding whether to centralize fulfillment operations are among the other decisions international direct marketers must make. Garnet Hill and Paper Direct have centralized fulfillment. Garnet Hill is a consumer apparel cataloger that fulfills orders to customers in about 20 different countries from its centralized facility in Franconia, New Hampshire. Paper Direct is a leading direct marketer of preprinted papers and supplies for the laser and desktop publishing industry and offers more than 3,000 items through four separate catalogs to customers in 35 countries, fulfilling all orders from three distribution centers located in Lyndhurst, New Jersey; Hinckley, England; and Northmead, Australia.[38] Visit the Web site of Paper Direct (www.paperdirect.com) and you will learn that Vista Papers, based in Leicestershire in the United Kingdom, is the exclusive European supplier of Paper Direct products (www.paperdirect.com.uk).[39]

Media

Direct marketers must determine the most effective media mix based on consumer preferences in each foreign market. Media decisions are based on a number of market specific factors, such as media availability, legal restrictions, literacy rates, and cultural factors. A country's level of economic development may also enter into the media mix decision. For example, literacy rates, TV and computer ownership, and sophisticated technology usage tend to be lower in less developed countries. Mature countries with high broadband usage appear to be converging on a

FIGURE 13-4.
Virginia Beach
French site. Used
with permission
by the City of
Virginia Beach
Convention &
Visitors Bureau.

norm. However, Internet advertising revenue does not include all investments, like advertiser investment in building Web sites.[40]

Canadian tourists represent a sizeable portion of summer travelers to Virginia Beach. Thus, a media plan specifically to attract Canadians from Ontario and Quebec is executed via radio, print, television, and targeted online formats such as e-mail. As presented Figure 13-4, Virginia Beach offers its Canadian tourists a dedicated microsite in French language.

Shipping products overnight and using telephone marketing may also be difficult in less developed countries. In these countries, the establishment and maintenance of databases may prove difficult. In some countries the price of postage is very low; in others, it is quite expensive. In many developing countries the mail system is slow and not secure. For example, in Mexico, there is a dearth of mailboxes and the system is very slow, although improving. In Argentina, mailboxes are considered a luxury and most residents do not have them. Therefore, mail is often delivered directly underneath the door. In an effort to increase delivery to residents, the Argentinean postal service charges lower rates for items that would fit underneath residents' doors. Telecom Argentina saved on postage and chose to capitalize on this cost-saving opportunity by creating innovative mail pieces targeting different market segments. A variety of designs were created, including flat items such as pencil cases which were mailed to students, along with innovative flat sea waves which washed under doors promoting "a flood" of Internet savings through the company's Web site. This campaign won a Silver ECHO award for its creativity and achieved a response of 3.2 percent, which was more than double the goal set by Telecom Argentina.[41]

E-mail marketing can offer direct marketers lower development costs and excellent targeting. E-mail is an efficient and cost-effective alternative to direct mail. E-mail is growing significantly. The European e-mail market is expected to grow by 12 percent annually and hit 2.3 billion   in 2012.[42] Because of the international growth of e-mail usage, companies such as Silverpop, a major e-mail marketing provider, have begun preparations to extend their services outside North America.[43]

In addition, e-mail marketing can provide a faster response—just compare a direct mail campaign that typically takes months to roll out to an e-mail campaign that may take only weeks to execute. E-mail newsletters are a recommended first step into international e-mail marketing, because their circulation tends to be greater than that for solo campaigns. However, to successfully implement e-mail marketing, direct marketers must be aware of each country's local privacy laws.

International acceptance for direct response television (DRTV) has grown. Latin America has become one of the first regions outside the United States to be explored. To successfully use DRTV, direct marketers must be keenly aware of the media landscape, including the key TV stations, cable, and satellite opportunities; the role of third-party negotiators (representatives); federal regulations concerning advertising and infomercials; audience trends; media penetration; and viewing share.[44] Direct marketers normally have two options when launching a DRTV campaign—(1) set up local operations on their own, or (2) use an established DRTV international company.

General Motors used a DRTV campaign in Argentina supported with a series of follow-ups via direct mail, phone, and fax. The campaign, designed to increase test drives and sales of the Astra, offered consumers a free video by calling a toll-free number. The results were phenomenal. Astra's market share in Argentina increased from 5 to 11 percent.[45]

Telemarketing is another medium for direct marketing overseas; however, it is more limited than in the United States and varies greatly from country to country. In many countries, such as Japan, telemarketing is perceived to be too aggressive. As is the case with other types of media, the successful use of telemarketing depends on the level of sophistication of the telecommunications infrastructure.

SMS text messaging is being met with great success in some international markets. In the Chinese capital of Beijing, Coca-Cola executed a summertime campaign where participants could text their predictions of the following day's high temperature. The participant who had the most accurate predictions won the first prize of a year's supply of Coke. The 34-day campaign generated 4 million SMS messages and 50,000 mobile downloads of a new Coke ringtones.[46] Another effective SMS campaign was that of Smirnoff's mobile sweepstakes in the United Kingdom where Smirnoff offered a free dance CD in every six-pack of Smirnoff ICE. Inside the CD was also a unique code and instructions to SMS the code to a special number to learn if they might have won a vacation package. This successful campaign generated more than 200,000 responses.[47]

Creative

In the process of developing the creative materials for any international direct marketing campaign, the four words of wisdom seem to be *research, test, translate,* and *adapt.* Visit the Web site of Nestlé in Peru (www.nestle.com.pe) and you will see how the company effectively translated its Web site for Peruvians. It is critical to present your promotional message in words and images to which your audience can relate. That is why direct marketers must properly research their audience, testing the offer and the copy, carefully translating the message into the proper language, and adapting to the local nuances of different cultures. Words that are entirely appropriate in one country's language are inappropriate and insulting in another. Certain colors, symbols, and designs may also be inappropriate to use in a marketing campaign.

One well-known example of a company adapting to local cultural differences is that of the Coca-Cola Company. In Japan, the word *diet* has a negative impression, because Japanese women do not like to admit they are drinking a product for weight loss. Therefore, the Coca-Cola Company revised the brand name of Diet Coke to "Coca-Cola Light" and successfully introduced and positioned the product in Japan as a soft drink for figure maintenance as opposed to weight loss.[48] Another example of the need to adapt to different cultures and consumer lifestyles is that of N.W. Ayer's Bahamas tourism campaigns designed for the European market. While the overall campaign focused on clean water, beaches, and air, it incorporated different appeals for select European markets. It emphasized sports activities to the German market, and it used humorous ads in the United Kingdom.[49]

To get maximum results, direct marketing campaigns must use promotional appeals that motivate prospects. However, consumer motives vary country by country, and what works in one market may not work in another. Direct marketers using the Web as a marketing medium must also be aware of the legal regulations that vary by country. For example, Germany sued Benetton for "exploiting feelings of pity" with one of its online campaigns.[50] Again, careful market research and cultural adaptation is the key to developing successful creative materials. For example, U.S. consumers are more receptive to advertisements that affect the emotional or even sensual aspects of their decision-making process, whereas the Japanese are more comfortable with logical and rational appeals. Then again, U.S. consumers are said to be far more conservative than are Canadians and Europeans. Regardless of whether the message appeal is emotional, rational, conservative, or liberal, it must be produced to maximize the response from the targeted customer. Cultural adaptation is crucial to the success of the direct marketing campaign when developing the creative appeal.

An excellent example of creativity that was effective was a direct mail campaign executed in India. Seagrams wanted to reinvigorate the image of its Chivas Scotch whisky brand in India. Therefore the company invited the country's most famous figures to an elite art show and sale in which Chivas would be promoted. To convince famous guests to attend, a lavish invitation was created. The invitation was designed to look like an artist's portfolio and contained high-quality miniature prints as a preview of the works on sale at the show. The campaign was a great success. The invitation itself became a collectible item, and 90 percent of those invited attended the event. Furthermore, 60 percent of the art displayed was sold.[51]

One of the first measures a direct marketer can take to ensure cultural adaptation is to determine the country's receptiveness to direct marketing activities. Let's look briefly at the indicators used in this assessment.

FIGURE 13-5.
Two Virginia
Beach banner ads.
Used with
permission by the
City of Virginia
Beach Convention
& Visitors Bureau.

Geographical Area Analysis

Canada

Most Canadians are very familiar with products and services from the United States because the majority of Canadians reside within 100 miles of the U.S. border. In fact, Canada and the United States have many things in common—they even share a professional ice hockey league. However, there are some distinct differences that direct marketers should bear in mind when marketing to Canadians. For example, Canada is officially bilingual in English and French. However, in Quebec, local language laws require all advertising materials to be printed in French. As Figure 13-5 shows, Virginia Beach banner ads were translated into French to be used to promote its vacation destination to prospective tourists in Quebec, Canada. Both ads creatively encourage Canadians to take a vacation to Virginia Beach and leave the cooler Canadian climate behind.

Taxes and duties assessed in Canada are another area of difference. Three taxes may come into effect when a U.S. company ships products to Canada. These are as follows:[52]

1. The Goods and Services Tax (GST): A 5 percent tax on the total value of the parcel. This tax is applied to all goods imported into Canada with the exception of prescribed property such as magazines, books, or similar printed publications.

2. The Harmonized Sales Tax (HST): Dependent on the province and includes a single tax which combines both GST and PST.

3. The Provincial Sales Tax (PST): A province dependent tax (around 8 percent) on the parcel's total value. The provincial retail sales tax rates vary from province to province, as do the goods and services to which the tax is applied and the way the tax is applied.[53]

Duties, or charges imposed on shipments based on a country of origin and commodity, are also imposed by Canada. Under the North American Free Trade Agreement, products manufactured outside the United States or Mexico are subject to duty charges when shipped to Canada. Shipments of noncommercial goods at Can$20 or less are exempt from duties because they fall into an international category of low value shipment.

Canadians are experiencing the same societal pressures as their neighbors in the United States (single-parent families, two parents working outside the home, constant time pressures) that make the ability to shop from home appealing. Privacy issues are also on the rise. However, unlike the U.S. DMA, which has been a proponent of industry self-regulation with regard to pri-

FIGURE 13-6.
Busch Gardens
Canadian ads in
English and
French languages.
Used with
permission of
Busch Gardens.

vacy, the Canadian Marketing Association has been active in calling for federal privacy legislation. Other differences between the United States and Canada include cultural ones. For example, Canadian direct marketing appeals don't normally include appeals to patriotism and vanity as U.S. appeals often do.

When marketing to Canadian consumers, often companies may use two versions of the same advertisement with one translated into French for those Canadians who speak French. An example of two ads promoting Busch Gardens as a family vacation destination for Canadian residents appear in Figure 13-6. Note the ads are identical with the exception of language.

Europe

The European Union currently represents 495 million consumers.[54] According to European Union External Action, bilateral trade between the European Union and U.S. amounts to more than $1 billion a day. Each partner creates jobs for about 6 million workers on each side of the Atlantic, and EU-US trade accounts for almost 40 percent of world trade.[55] The European Union

FIGURE 13-7. Guinness "A Passion Shared" direct marketing campaign. Used with permission of Guinness

is made up of 27 different countries with 23 official languages, cultures, and legal systems.[56] Direct marketers are advised to conduct an in-depth study of each country prior to conducting business in that country.

Differences between U.S. and European markets also exist. For example, European stores are not open seven days a week, as many are in the United States. In fact, many European stores maintain hours and service levels that most U.S. consumers would find unacceptable. For example when actual vacation time is calculated, workers average 7.9 weeks in Italy, 7.8 in Germany, and 7 weeks in France, whereas in the United States, the average is 3.9 weeks.[57] Is Europe still an attractive avenue for direct marketing? The answer is, you bet! There are many successful U.S. direct marketers in Europe including Lands' End, Viking, and Allstate Insurance, as well as successful European direct marketers.

An example of a successful direct mail and print campaign in Europe is that of Diageo Ireland's Guinness Relationship Marketing program. Diageo Ireland needed to regain lost market share from competing lagers and ciders that were strongly associated with sporting and music events through sponsorships. To accomplish this task, the company created its own event, "poker night," and chose to communicate with customers on a personal level by sharing stories about the history and heritage of the Guinness product and its bond with consumers. As shown in Figure 13-7, this campaign, "A Passion Shared," helped convert in-pub drinkers of Guinness to also become at-home Guinness drinkers, a vital change in the market, and generated an increase of 17 percent of Guinness consumption.[58]

French direct marketing for consumer products and services is one of the world's largest, growing at a rate of 20 percent annually to reach $30 billion in 2007. The total number of Internet users in France and the total number of commercial Web sites has increased drastically. Currently, there are approximately 45 million Internet users in France, 21 million of whom made an average purchase of $124 in 2007.[59] Among total direct marketing sales, France has the highest rate of Internet sales in Europe. France experienced an increase in online sales of products and services of 37 percent between 2005 and 2006. This attests to the significant role that the Internet will play in future direct marketing sales.[60] Despite the high level of spending on mail-order products, most Europeans are not bombarded with direct mail as are U.S. consumers. The United Kingdom's national postal service, Royal Mail, has made an effort to counter this trend of using fewer direct mailings, however. Through use of "DM Sales," Royal Mail has launched dis-

FIGURE 13-8. Euro intermail direct mail. Used with permission of Euro Intermail.

counts of twenty percent for direct mail items in an effort to encourage marketers to utilize new, expanded campaign tactics, such as the distribution of samples.[61]

Some factors affecting direct marketing activities in Europe include:

- **Postal requirements**— formats, location of the window, teaser copy on the outer envelope— must comply with local postal authorities, which differ by European country. Euro Intermail, the leading full-service direct mail company in Italy, is finding great success by designing innovative direct mail pieces for its clients while still complying with the local postal regulations. Many of the direct mail packages it has created have used clear see-through outer envelopes, personalized messages, compelling copy, and small premiums, such as a free pencil or coin. Figure 13-8 provides an example of one of Euro Intermail's creative direct mail pieces.

- **Data protection** is far more stringent in Europe than it is in the United States. Throughout Europe, an opt-out provision is mandatory at the point where you collect data. Until recently, individual countries had their own privacy legislation—which varied from country to country. However, now a Europe-wide privacy directive is in place and must be adopted by every European Union country.[62]

- **Mailing restrictions and policies** may differ by European country. For example, in the United Kingdom, each direct mail package must be approved by the Advertising Standards Authority.

- **The list industry** is strong in Europe. Multinational lists include names and data about individuals who are usually responsive to direct mail offers, speak English, and are internationally minded. The list selections available, output formats, and guarantees equal U.S. standards. Multinational lists allow the direct marketer to test many countries at the same time without incurring additional fees. Local lists tend to be more numerous and offer greater selections.

- **The Benelux,** which includes the countries of Belgium, Netherlands, and Luxembourg, is ideal for direct marketing because of its well-developed direct marketing infrastructure. Lists, payment options, and call centers are all quite advanced in this region of Europe.[63]

Latin America

The population of Latin America is 580 million across 33 countries, and total trade with the U.S. approaches $500 billion—twice that of the European Union. Different dialects of Spanish are spoken across Latin America, and Portuguese is spoken in Brazil.[64] Overall, the direct marketing industry—commercial and business-to-business—is growing at a rate of about 40 to 50 percent per year in most of Latin America.[65] Latin America is a continent of countries made up of very different direct marketing infrastructures. It cannot be treated as a single market except on paper.

For direct marketers, Brazil is the most sophisticated market in Latin America. Brazil accounts for nearly 60 percent of the total South American GDP, and has grown continuously— 7.5 percent in 2010 and a predicted four to five percent in 2011. With growing per-capita income and 193 million consumers, Brazil offers great opportunity for direct marketers.[66] The lists and databases available there are of fairly high quality. However, fewer public sources of data are available in Latin America than in the United States. With the exception of Brazil, direct marketing is largely underdeveloped in terms of the number of agencies and telemarketing companies in Latin America. However, Latin America is not expected to follow the path the United States did in *slowly* developing sophisticated direct marketing machinery. The Internet will likely enable Latin America to make revolutionary strides quickly in direct marketing development.

An example of a successful online direct marketing campaign in Spain is that of the 2007 Gold ECHO award–winning campaign "The Factory of Dreams" created by the ad agency Uncommon (Havas Group). This multimedia campaign conducted for ESIC, one of Spain's leading business schools, targeted teens contemplating business school. The campaign entailed the distribution of flyers for career events and invited students to play an online interactive game called the Dream Factory. The game led prospects through a series of various challenges faced by professionals in the world of public relations, marketing, and business. Daily text messages prompted players to return to the site to learn more about a prospective career with another game. The campaign was a huge success and generated nearly double the expected online visits, and 65 percent of those who registered for ESIC online played the game.[68]

Although the direct marketing industry in Latin America trails that of the U.S., the outlook is promising. One reason for this is that the amount of communication one Latin American consumer receives is much less than what is received by a typical U.S. or European consumer. For example, the average household in Mexico receives only six or seven pieces of mail per month.[69] Therefore, the amount of communication clutter is significantly reduced. It is also true, however, that mail services in Mexico are considerably slower than in the United States.

Latin American consumers are very receptive to products made in the United States and have recently shown acceptance of DRTV media as well. Some successful DRTV marketing campaigns in Latin America include the following:[70]

- AB Flex, one of the fitness industry's top-performing products, generated more than $10 million of sales in a nine-month period.

- Murad International Skin Care generated more than $7 million in sales in Mexico alone. The brand awareness generated created an extremely successful continuity program and catalog.

A large part of Mexico's population of 114 million subsists below the poverty line. It's the top 10 percent that commands 36.3 percent of the nation's wealth. This may be of concern to direct marketers. Though the percentage of the population under 15 has fallen in recent years to 30 percent, this relatively high figure still provides strong opportunity for direct markers to make inroads with younger consumers and build lasting relationships. [71]

Building relationships is important in direct marketing, and this is especially so in Latin America, where consumers crave personal contact and *confianza* (trust). Many Americans find the Latin American perspective on human-space and physical interaction somewhat alarming. They are not nearly as conscious of body-space as Americans are; thus, physical contact is quite common. For example in most Latin American countries, it is expected for men conducting business from the second meeting onward to greet one other with an *abrazo* or hug or sometimes even with a kiss on the cheek. Most business deals will not develop until a friendship has been established. Unlike in the United States, time is not money in Latin America.

Asia

Asia has a population of more than 4 billion consumers and millions of businesses.[72] Companies such as consumer products leader Procter & Gamble Co. have capitalized on growing product demand in this massive market, accelerating growth and extending its customer base. The Asian market generated 15 percent of P&G's $79 million revenue in 2010, but the company hopes to rely even more extensively on the region in the coming years to help more than double total global revenues to $175 million by 2015. Considering Asia's diverse population and unique culture, P&G intends on offering products for all levels of buying behavior—from billionaires to those living on less than one dollar per day. P&G's Asia Group president, Deb Henretta, states that "I don't believe you can win in Asia by simply taking Western mindset and Western business models and plopping them into Asia. We've taken on a bit of a rallying cry—being as common as possible, but as different as needed" to satisfy varying cultures and customer demands. By offering both "pennies-priced" shaving tools and advanced, high-end cosmetics and shampoos, P&G is accomplishing this balance necessitated by the Asian market.[73]

Catalog marketers have struggled with the Asian market for more than a decade. The major challenges include the lack of reliable mailing lists, a scarcity of local talent, inadequate phone systems, and the inability to fulfill orders through traditional retailers. Among the lessons many direct marketers have learned in Asia is that you must treat each country separately and understand the local laws and policies. All Asian markets are not equally attractive. Recent research shows that the more accessible Asian countries for direct marketers include South Korea, Taiwan, Hong Kong (China), and Japan.[74]

However, one of the major challenges faced by Americans and other Western international companies is a propensity to lump together these markets and assume that all Asian consumers have similar tastes and preferences. This is not true and is an unwise assumption made by companies seeking to enter these markets. Each market demonstrates different preferences toward marketing and often differs in its consumer buying behavior. Let's take a closer look at each of these markets.

SOUTH KOREA. Direct buying in South Korea is growing considerably, with South Koreans importing almost $30 billion in U.S. goods annually, and importing over $400 billion total annually.[75] Sales from direct selling have grown by 2 to 3 percent annually in recent years, leading some companies to adopt more appropriate marketing strategies.[76] For instance, Hong Joon-Kee, Chairman of the Korea Direct Selling Association and CEO of Woongjin Coway Co. Ltd, a global leader in health and environmental-related lifestyle products such as water purifiers, notes strong increases in both door-to-door sales and multi-level marketing strategies. "The Korean direct selling market is one of the largest markets around the world," he says. Indeed, the country generated an additional $840 million in sales in 2009, and Woongjin Coway attributes a significant portion of that growth to "doorway traffic."[77]

Furthermore, U.S. products are desirable to South Koreans because most of the population is concentrated in cities, especially near Seoul, which accounts for about 20 percent of the entire population.[78] These urban consumers tend to possess a stronger desire to keep up with the latest innovations in technology and trends in fashion. For example, Life's Good (LG), the world's top producer of air conditioners and one of the top three players in washing machines, refrigerators, and microwaves, introduced the Kimchi refrigerator in this market. Kimchi, a spicy cabbage concoction, is very popular in Southern Korea. However, the problem was the dish's odor is so strong that it penetrates all surrounding food items when it is stored in the refrigerator. Therefore, LG used in-depth localization to target the southern Korean community. This approach emphasizes understanding the idiosyncrasies of key local markets by opening in-country research, manufacturing, and marketing facilities. Their efforts paid off when the new Kimchi refrigerator became all the rage in South Korea.[79]

TAIWAN. The direct marketing infrastructure in Taiwan is not fully developed. List availability is very poor and telemarketing is available, but not yet popular. Although the postal service is of very good quality, there is no bulk discount rate for mailings. Direct marketing in Taiwan should expand as its infrastructure improves.

CHINA. Direct marketing in China is relatively new, but growing. With 1.3 billion people, China has great potential for direct marketers with heavy concentrations of wealth in mostly coastal cities.[80] However, like Taiwan, its direct marketing infrastructure is lacking. Although the middle class is growing, the vast majority of the Chinese population has little money, no credit cards, no telephones, and no direct way to receive merchandise. Surprisingly, information privacy is very strict in China, and there are privacy code laws in place. Anyone caught breaking the privacy code laws may be subject to a prison term.

JAPAN. Japan is one of the most advanced countries in the Pacific Rim. Its direct marketing infrastructure is superior to that of its Asian counterparts. Direct mail, telemarketing, home-shopping programs, and even infomercials continue to grow in popularity. The Internet was the most used ad medium by 86.5 percent in Japan in 2004.[81] Japanese consumers used the telephone (59.4 percent), mail (13.9 percent), and Internet (8.8 percent) when ordering products in 2004.[82] Online retail in Japan is expected to grow to $50 billion by 2015, but the country's consumers have lagged behind other developed markets in their willingness to embrace the electronic method of shopping. Instead, consumers in Japan enjoy more of a physical shopping experience. That said, the online market for physical goods in Japan has expanded to an estimated $30 billion—a sharp increase from the $1.3 billion in online sales in 1999. When Domino's Pizza, for instance, launched an online ordering system for home delivery in 2004, the company set a target usage rate of 5 percent. Instead, more than 35 percent of sales for Domino's in Japan are now received through the Internet.[83]

Regarding direct marketing, an example of a highly successful marketing campaign in Japan is that of DHL Japan. Faced with customers who increasingly regarded air express services as commodities, DHL Japan wanted to build loyalty among its customers via a campaign with an emotional appeal. The campaign included year-round greeting cards mailed to customers depicting a seasonal scene with a DHL vehicle or airplane in one of the major International cities of the world, such as Melbourne in the summer or New York at Christmas. Customers were captured by the beautifully illustrated cards and the campaign exceeded all targeted projections, garnering an ROI of 700 percent.[84]

Egypt

Direct marketing in Egypt is in the early stages of development. Lists of business organizations are available in a directory referred to as KOMPASS. This list contains information such as the nature of business, address, phone number, and key personnel. Also some key highlights about each company are offered, such as number of employees, annual revenues, date of establishment, and legal form of operations. Most direct marketing activities are based on out-bound telemarketing calls to customers. These databases are based on purchases of databases. There are no strict laws and regulations for information privacy in Egypt. Many companies share information with other companies maybe for a fee. Consumers in Egypt are not very concerned about sharing their private information for marketing purposes.

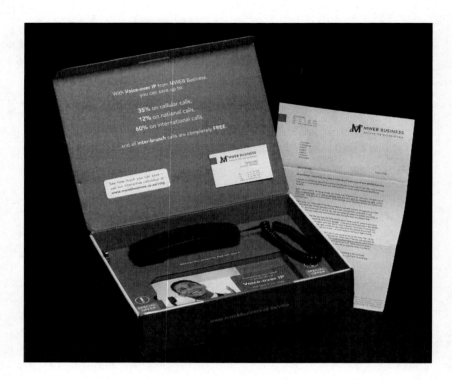

FIGURE 13-9.
MWEB's Voice
Box direct mail
package. Used
with permission
of Primaplus.+

Africa

The African continent is home to around 1 billion people.[85] The largest country in terms of population is Nigeria, with a population of more than 155 million.[86] More than 47 percent of Africa's population is between the ages of 5 and 24. With a large percentage of the population uneducated, the literacy rate varies from one country to another.[87] There is very limited computer access and also low Internet penetration. That said, the middle class in Africa has increased notably. Today's middle class includes 34.3 percent of the population—about 313 million people—compared to 27.2 percent of the population—about 196 million people—in 2000. The emergence of a stronger middle class has increased consumption expenditures in Africa to a third of those in developing European countries.[88] In fact, Africa's middle class has grown larger than that of India, and the "invasion" of stores such as Walmart and KFC has begun. An estimated 220 million new consumers will be present in Africa by 2015, and international corporations are preparing to capture this demand.[89] High commodity prices have helped drive Africa's economy, while "better infrastructure, improved governance and the creation of jobs through private investment have helped drive the growth of the middle class."[90]

The North African countries are considered to be the most developed in Africa. Yet there are some countries that exhibit different characteristics. Africa has the fastest growing mobile market in the world. Seven out of ten telephones in Africa are mobile. Direct marketing is considered to be a new phenomenon for many African countries and does not exist in most African markets.

South Africa is considered to be one of the most developed nations in the African continent. There is a direct marketing association in South Africa. This association regulates direct marketing practices and ensures that the rights of consumers and the organizations are protected.

Direct marketing activities in South Africa are growing rapidly. Examples of effective campaigns are those of MWEB. Recently MWEB executed the following two unique direct marketing campaigns with totally different objectives and target markets. "The Voice Box" campaign, created by the Primaplus Agency, targeted a business community in South Africa that was paying extremely high telephone rates but was shy about adopting new technologies. MWEB introduced its ADSL VOIP product to select CFOs and medical doctors, sending them a substantial 3D pack that gave them a unique way to try the new phone service. As shown in Figure 13-9, the pack came with a telephone, which rang as soon as the box was opened and directed them to a designated account manager. The campaign was highly effective with this hard-to-convert audience and achieved an outstanding 60 percent response rate.[91]

The other successful direct mail campaign, called "Babushkalopes," was created for MWEB by Ogilvy One Cape Town. In the South African market, where broadband services are new, the objective of this campaign was to ensure that MWEB's dial-up customers converted to its new broadband service before the competition reached them. To achieve this, a direct mail campaign was built around the theme of the bigger world available through broadband. The mailing conveyed that message with a series of envelopes within envelopes, each of which unfolded to reveal a larger envelope, which resulted in a large poster promoting the product. The campaign was a success, with 9 percent of all consumers receiving the mailing opting to upgrade their service to broadband.[92]

Summary

International direct marketing is on the rise. Many U.S. businesses are seeking to expand by penetrating international markets. In doing so, direct marketers must keep in mind the many unique differences between domestic and foreign markets. Many researchers offer suggestions for how to enter a foreign market. These steps include assessing your international potential, conducting market research, selecting your country markets, developing an international marketing plan, and implementing your international marketing strategies. Careful market research, including an assessment of consumer needs, direct marketing infrastructure, and political, economic, and business environments, is necessary prior to commencing international direct marketing activities.

Direct marketers must make decisions involving the mode of market entry—direct exporting, licensing, joint venture, contract manufacturing, direct investment, or management contracting—that they will employ. Direct marketers must make a careful examination of the unique infrastructure needed to support direct marketing operations, including an analysis of lists and databases, fulfillment operations, media, and creative. The direct marketing infrastructure varies by country market and each market must be thoroughly researched and analyzed.

Key Terms

collectivist culture	licensor
individualistic cultures	licensee
global market segmentation (GMS)	joint venture
infrastructure	contract manufacturing
gross domestic product (GDP)	direct investment
exporting	management contracting
licensing	duties

Review Questions

1. What makes international direct marketing different from domestic direct marketing?

2. Why are companies looking outside the United States to do business?

3. Describe the different modes of market entry that can be used to enter a foreign market.

4. Discuss the primary infrastructure necessary for international direct marketing activities to be carried out with success.

5. Name some of the ways direct marketers have adapted to cultural differences when marketing internationally.

6. Identify and explain the five-step approach direct marketers should follow when marketing to an international country.

7. How do the media preferences vary by country markets? Which country is attractive for DRTV?

8. Compare and contrast direct mail and e-mail as international direct marketing mediums. Which one would be most appropriate to use when marketing in Canada? Europe? Latin America? Asia?

9. Discuss fulfillment operations. What advantages do both centralized and decentralized fulfillment operations offer international direct marketers?

10. Overview the history of direct marketing around the world. Be sure to explain when and where it began and how it grew.

Exercise

The U.S.-based motorcycle company that you are now employed with wants to expand its business overseas. Using the market research issues described in this chapter, describe how the company should go about doing this. Based on your analysis, which countries might be considered likely candidates for international expansion? Provide an explanation to support your selections.

Critical Thinking Exercise

Many marketing campaigns translate effectively across international markets, while some do not. Select two different direct marketing campaigns that were successful in the United States and apply them to three different country markets. Discuss whether or not each would be effective in the respective country and how might each one be modified to be successful in each market.

CASE: Chevrolet EUROPE'S Dream Garage

This case demonstrates how a number of considerations must be made in conducting a direct marketing campaign in multiple country markets. It illustrates the techniques of an online campaign implemented simultaneously in five countries. Finally, it showcases the creativity and successful execution of a campaign designed to connect and engage consumers with a well-known American brand—Chevrolet.

Overview

Chevrolet relaunched in Europe in 2004 with a new range of cars. (See Figure 13-10). In 2010 the brand was still not very well known by the European consumer, with about a 3 percent mar-

FIGURE 13-10. Chevrolet Europe 2011 Model Range included on the Dream Garage site. Used with permission of Cheverlot Europe.

FIGURE 13-11. Chevrolet Dream Garage instructions and unveiled cars Web page. Used with permission of Cheverlot Europe.

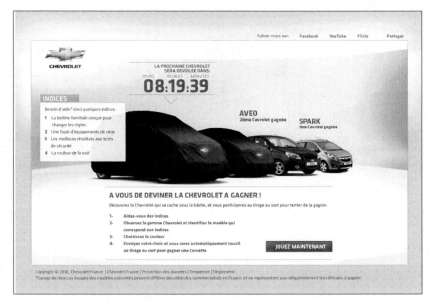

ket share and buyer consideration was relatively low. Thus, there was a need to improve brand awareness and educate the car buying public about the new range of models offered by Chevrolet and the character or personality of the brand.

The "Chevrolet Dream Garage" project was conceived as an online-only campaign designed to tackle these challenges in five major European markets. The budget to achieve the campaign objectives was small—(two million Euros)—and had to cover everything including media, Web sites, legal, prizes, etc.

The "Dream Garage" was a competition to win a Chevrolet car. A dedicated microsite was created for this. A total of five cars could be won, split over five competition rounds (each one lasting two weeks). Four of the five cars were displayed with covers on them on the site and a competition entrant would have to "*Guess the Car to Win the Car*" (model name and color). The fifth car was the legendary Corvette. (See Figure 13-11.) At the end of each round, the car was unveiled and a draw (or lottery) took place to pick a winner among all those entrants who guessed correctly.

Bonus Round

Round five was setup as a bonus round that was a straight lottery, where previous activity in the competition affected the number of chances the user had to win the Corvette. For Rounds 1-4, the user would guess all the elements, including the model and color of the cars, but the Bonus round required no such thing. If a person competed in any of the previous four rounds, they

FIGURE 13-12. Dream Garage Refer-a-Friend Facebook Web page. Used with permission of Cheverlot Europe.

would receive a "ticket" to the bonus round, effectively one extra ticket for each competition entry in the previous rounds.

FaceBook and E-Mail

To make the campaign more viral, Chevrolet chose to offer an extra entry ticket to each participant who referred five friends by e-mail or Facebook after completing a round (rounds 1-4). (See Figure 13-12.) Therefore a person could earn a maximum of eight "tickets" (or entries) into the Corvette Bonus Round. Note: A person could only enter each round (1-4) once. No multiple entries were allowed.

A Facebook tab was also created for Facebook pages in each market so those people who "liked" Chevrolet via this channel could also enter the competition without needing to leave the Facebook platform. The App was all but identical to the microsite. An automated e-mail would also be sent to each entrant at the end of the round informing them the next round had begun.

Markets and Local/Central Implementation

A total of five country markets were chosen: France, Germany, Italy, Poland and Spain. They were all chosen on the basis of local legislation (for an online competition and lottery), media costs per market, market size, and past performance in other brand campaigns.

Centrally, Chevrolet Europe oversaw the project conception and implementation. All elements such as competition mechanics, concept and design were handled centrally. Locally, the markets were responsible for translating all copy (microsite, T&Cs, and banners) as well as proofing all imagery to ensure the model trim levels were displayed correctly as well as any other local product differences.

The country markets that managed their own Facebook pages communicated news on the Dream Garage competition to their followers in a manner they felt most appropriate. Some markets, for example, would post updates on how long a particular round had left before it closed, others' responded to fans' questions without providing any additional hints on what the color and model were.

FIGURE 13-13. Chevrolet Dream Garage competition end Web page. Used with permission of Cheverlot Europe.

Why Online Only?

It was decided that the campaign would be online only due to the following reasons:

- Measurability—can measure all interactions and performance
- Scalability—in case they were to operate this again in additional markets
- Viral Quality—to encourage entrants to share the Dream Garage with as many friends as possible
- Costs

Campaign Results

The campaign generated more than 195,000 competition entries over an eight-week period in five country markets, of which 40 percent were re-entries. This shows an excellent degree of engagement between the user and Chevrolet as part of this competition. The campaign also performed far better than Chevrolet had expected, outperforming previous Dream Garage campaigns (conducted in 2007 and 2008) which were run both online and offline. (See Figure 13-13.)

As a direct result of the banner campaigns, Chevrolet achieved more than 50,000 conversions, which translated into more than 25 percent conversion rate (including test drives, dealer searches, brochure requests, etc.) on the main brand sites (e.g., www.chevrolet.fr).

Case Discussion Questions

1. For years Chevrolet was primarily a great American Brand and in recent years it invested in building its global presence. Chevrolet Europe has used the "Dream Garage Campaign" to increase the brand's awareness, knowledge and move prospects along the purchase funnel. If you were Chevrolet Europe Marketing, what enhancements would you suggest in the Dream Garage Campaign to increase awareness, consideration and ultimately purchase in the diverse countries in the European Community and why?

2. In moving the Dream Garage Campaign, across countries in Europe, what must Chevrolet consider besides language and why? What are examples of problems that have occurred with other countries?

3. Can you think of other measures to evaluate the campaign effectiveness based on the objectives stated in the case, i.e., to improve brand awareness and educate the car buying public about the new range of models offered by Chevrolet? Discuss your proposed measures.

4. Can you help the campaign manager with metrics to evaluate the viral element of the campaign? Broadly explain measures for traffic building goals, conversion / engagement goals, 3rd-party site reach goals, and multi-channel marketing goals for the direct marketing campaign discussed in the case.

Notes

1. Adapted from the *Direct Marketing Association International ECHO Awards 2006.*

2. Charles W. Lamb, Joseph F. Hair Jr., and Carl McDaniel (2008), *Marketing,* 9th ed. (Mason, Ohio: Southwestern), p. 106.

3. "WTO | 2011 Press Releases—Trade Growth to Ease in 2011 but despite 2010 Record Surge, Crisis Hangover Persists—Press/628." *World Trade Organization—Home Page.* Web. 23 May 2011. <http://www.wto.org/english/news_e/pres11_e/pr628_e.htm>.

4. "U.S. Trade Tops $3 Trillion in 2010, Nearing 2008 Record." *WorldCity: Connecting Greater Miami's Multinational Business Community.* 11 Feb. 2011. Web. 23 May 2011. <http://www.worldcityweb.com/trade-connections-listing/766-us-trade-tops-3-trillion-in-2010-nearing-2008-record>.

5. "FTD—Top Trading Partners." *Census Bureau Home Page.* 11 Feb. 2011. Web. 23 May 2011. <http://www.census.gov/foreign-trade/statistics/highlights/top/top1012yr.html>.

6. Bob Stone and Ron Jacobs (2008), *Successful Direct Marketing Methods,* 8th ed. (New York: McGraw-Hill), p. 148.

7. "North America Internet Usage Statistics, Population and Telecommunications Reports." *Internet World Stats—Usage and Population Statistics.* 27 Mar. 2011. Web. 23 May 2011. <http://www.internetworldstats.com/stats14.htm>.

8. Richard N. Miller (1995), *Multinational Direct Marketing: The Methods and the Markets* (New York: McGraw-Hill), pp. 7–8.

9. Ibid., p. 2.

10. Ibid.

11. Ibid.

12. Michael R. Czinkota and Ilkka A. Ronkainen (2004), *International Marketing,* 7th ed. (Mason, Ohio: Southwestern), p. 539.

13. Ibid., p. 545.

14. V. Kumar and Anish Nagpal (2007), *Marketing,* 29th ed. (New York: Irwin/McGraw-Hill), p. 174.

15. Adapted from John J. Wild, Kenneth L. Wild, and Jerry C. Y. Han (2003), *International Business,* 2nd ed. (Upper Saddle River, NJ: Prentice Hall); adapted from William J. MacDonald, "Five Steps to International Success," *Direct Marketing* 61, no. 7 (November 1998), 32–35; Rainer Hengst, "*Plotting Your Global Strategy,*" *Direct Marketing* 63, no. 4 (August 2000), 52–54; and Richard N. Miller, "Where in the World... How to Determine the Best Market for Your Product or Service," *Target Marketing* 24, no. 3 (March 2001), 57.

16. Miller, *Multinational Direct Marketing,* pp. 6–7.

17. Central Intelligence Agency (2007), *2008 World Factbook* (New York: Skyhorse Publishing), p. 346.

18. Stone and Jacobs, *Successful Direct Marketing Methods*, p. 58.

19. Lawrence J. Gitman and Carl McDaniel (2002), *The Future of Business* (Mason, Ohio: Southwestern),p. 81.

20. Czinkota and Ronkainen, *International Marketing*, p. 318.

21. Reed, Ted. "UPS: We Took L.L. Bean Account From FedEx—TheStreet." *Stock Market Today—Financial News, Quotes and Analysis—TheStreet.* 09 Feb. 2009. Web. 23 May 2011. <http://www.thestreet.com/story/10462893/1/ups-we-took-ll-bean-account-from-fedex.html?puc=_tscrss>.

22. Hoovers Web site, retrieved in February 2008, http://www.hoovers.com/orvis-company/—ID__89473—/free-co-profile.xhtml.

23. "Orvis Stores: Retail Locations in the UK." *Orvis UK Official Store: Quality Men's Clothing, Women's Clothing, Fly Fishing Gear, Dog Beds, Luggage, Travel, Shooting, and Gifts; Since 1856.* Web. 23 May 2011. <http://www.orvis.co.uk/intro.aspx?subject=328>.

24. "The Orvis Company, Inc. | Company Profile from Hoover's." *Hoovers | Business Solutions from Hoovers.* Web. 23 May 2011. <http://www.hoovers.com/company/The_Orvis_Company_Inc/xsckyi-1.html>.

25. H. Katzenstein and W. S. Sachs (1986), *Direct Marketing*, 2nd ed. (New York: Macmillan), p. 417.

26. Gitman and McDaniel, *The Future of Business*, p. 83.

27. Texas Instruments Web site, retrieved in September 2003, http://www.ti.com.

28. "Walmartstores.com: About Us." *Walmartstores.com.* Web. 23 May 2011. <http://walmartstores.com/aboutus/>.

29. "Walmart 2011 Annual Report." Web. 22 May 2011. <http://walmartstores.com/sites/annualreport/2011/financials/Walmart_2011_Annual_Report.pdf>.

30. Terry Brennan, "Day-Timers Makes Foray into U.D. with First 100,000-Piece Mail Test," *DM News*, November 15, 1989, p. 14.

31. Stone and Jacobs, *Successful Direct Marketing Methods*, p. 164.

32. Czinkota and Ronkainen, *International Marketing*, p. 318.

33. MacDonald, "Five Steps to International Success," p. 35.

34. Czinkota and Ronkainen, *International Marketing*, p. 318.

35. Beth Negus Viveiros, "As the World Turns," *Inside the DMA* (2002), D19.

36. "About PayPal—PayPal." *PayPal Press Center—PayPal.* Web. 23 May 2011. <https://www.paypal-media.com/about>.

37. Lawrence Chaido and Lisa A. Yorgey, "The Back-End of Global Delivery: How to Transport Your Products around the World," *Target Marketing* 21, no. 9 (September 1998), 64–66.

38. Paper Direct Web sites, retrieved in February 2008, http://www.paperdirect.com.

39. Ibid. and http://www.paperdirect.com.uk.

40. "All Change: Marketing in Addressable Media," *Interaction* (April 2007), 24.

41. *The DMA ECHO Winners Program 2007* (New York: Direct Marketing Association), p. 39.

42. Jennings, Rebecca. *European E-mail Marketing Spend Hits ?2.3 Billion In 2012.* 28 Aug. 2007. Web. 23 May 2011. <http://www.forrester.com/rb/Research/european_e-mail_marketing_spend_hits_%26%23x20ac%3B23_billion/q/id/43165/t/2>.

43. "Secrets and Lies about International E-mail Marketing :: BtoB Magazine." *BtoB Magazine: Marketing News and Strategies for BtoB, Direct & Internet Marketing.* 8 May 2008. Web. 23 May 2011. <http://www.btobonline.com/apps/pbcs.dll/article?AID=/20080508/FREE/922962543/1116/FREE>.

44. Priya Ghai, "Southward Bound," *Target Marketing* 24, no. 5 (May 2001), 64.

45. Stan Rapp, "Something New Under the Advertising Sun," *DMA Insider* (Fall 2002), 10–14.

46. NewPhase Mobile Marketing, 2008. http://newphasemobile.com/campaign_examples.php

47. Ibid.

48. Czinkota and Ronkainen, *International Marketing*, p. 257.

49. Ibid., p. 552.

50. Rose Lewis, "Before You Advertise on the Net—Check the International Marketing Laws," *Bank Marketing* (May 1996), 40–42.

51. *DMA ECHO Winners Program 2007*, p. 87.

52. Lisa A. Yorgey, "Navigating Taxes and Duties," *Target Marketing* 22, no. 10 (October 1999), 76.

53. Susan Munroe, About.com: Canada Online, *Provincial sales tax-PST*, retrieved in February 2008, http://canadaonline.about.com/od/personalfinance/g/pst.htm.

54. "EUROPA—Living in the EU." *EUROPA—The Official Web site of the European Union*. Web. 23 May 2011. <http://europa.eu/about-eu/facts-figures/living/index_en.htm>.

55. "EU-US Relations." *European Union External Action*. Web. 23 May 2011. <http://www.eurunion.org/eu/Table/EU-US-Relations/>.

56. EUROPA Web site, "Education and Training," retrieved in March 2008, http://ec.europa.eu/education/policies/lang/languages/index_en.html.

57. Lamb, Hair, and McDaniel, *Marketing*, p. 112.

58. *DMA ECHO Winners Program 2007*, p. 81.

59. "Selling U.S. Products and Services." *U.S. Commercial Service—United States of America Department of Commerce*. Web. Retrieved 23 May 2011. <http://www.buyusa.gov/france/en/115.html>.

60. U.S. Commercial Service, "Direct Marketing and E-Commerce Business to Consumer—Best Prospect 2008," retrieved in February 2008, http://www.buyusa.gov/france/en/207.html.

61. "Keeping you up to date." *Royal Mail—Personal* Customers. Web. Retrieved 23 May 2011. <http://www2.royalmail.com/customer-service/customer-news#Royal%20Mail%20announces%20DM%20sale%20to%20help%20advertisers>.

62. Erika Rasmusson, "The Perils of International Direct Mail," *Sales & Marketing Management* 152, no. 4 (April 2000), 107.

63. Lisa A. Yorgey, "Direct Marketing in the Benelux," *Target Marketing* 22, no. 7 (July 1999), 40.

64. Jason Bremner, Carl Haub, Marlene Lee, Mark Mather, and Eric Zuehke. "World Population Highlights: Key Findings from PRB's 2009 World Population Data Sheet." *Population Reference Bureau—Population Bulletin* 64, no. 3 (September 2009).

65. *World Almanac and Book of Facts*, p. 67.

66. Laura Loro, "Zeroing in on Latin America: Infrastructure Varies by Nation, But Marketers Say Opportunity Huge," *Business Marketing* 83, no. 1 (January 1998) 19.

67. "Fact Sheet on U.S. Relationship with Central and South America." (15 March 2011). *United States of America Embassy—IIP Digital*. Web. Retrieved May 23, 2011. <http://iipdigital.usembassy.gov/st/english/article/2011/03/20110315105216su0.2035443.html#axzz1MiWvpPKT>.

68. *The DMA ECHO Winners Program 2007*, p. 23.

69. Traverso, "A Global Perspective," p. 8.

70. North American Publishing Company, "Southward Bound," *Target Marketing*, 24, no. 5 (May 2001), 64.

71. CIA Web site, "The World Fact Book," retrieved in May 2011, <https://www.cia.gov/library/publications/the-world-factbook/geos/mx.html>.

72. Ibid., p. 845.

73. Dan Sewell. (8 April 2011). "P&G's Asian Chief: Growth is Speeding Up." *ABC News/Money*. Web. Retrieved May 23, 2011. <http://abcnews.go.com/Business/wireStory?id=13328714>.

74. Rainer Hengst, "Plotting Your Global Strategy," *Direct Marketing* 63, no. 4 (August 2000), 52–57.

75. CIA Web site, "The World Fact Book," retrieved in May 2011, https://www.cia.gov/library/publications/the-world-factbook/geos/ks.html.

76. "Direct Selling—South Korea—Market Report—new market research report." (30 March 2011). *Wooeb News*. Web. Retrieved May 23, 2011. <http://news.wooeb.com/NewsStory.aspx?id=713452>.

77. Katherine B. Ponder. (March 2011). "Direct Selling's Billion-Dollar Markets." *DirectSellingNews.com*. Web. Retrieved May 23, 2011. <http://www.directsellingnews.com/index.php/entries_archive_display/direct_sellings_billion_dollar_markets1>.

78. Hengst, "Plotting Your Global Strategy," p. 55.

79. Elizabeth Esfahani (2006), "Thinking Locally Succeeding Globally," *Annual Editions International Business,*14th ed. (New York: McGraw-Hill), p. 86.

80. *World Almanac and Book of Facts*, p. 760.

81. *DMA Statistical Fact Book 2006*, p. 190.

82. Ibid.

83. Brian Salsberg. (2010). "The New Japanese Consumer. *McKinsey Quarterly*. Web publication. Retrieved May 23, 2011. <http://www.marketingpower.com/ResourceLibrary/Documents/Content%20Partner%20Documents/McKinsey%20and%20Company/2010/japanese_consumer.pdf>.

84. *The DMA ECHO Winners Program 2007*, p. 27.

85. "2009 World Population Data sheet." *Population Reference Bureau*. Web. Retrieved May 23, 2011. <http://www.prb.org/Publications/Datasheets/2009/2009wpds.aspx>.

86. CIA Web site, "The World Fact Book," retrieved in May 2011, https://www.cia.gov/library/publications/the-world-factbook/geos/ni.html.

87. Ibid.

88. Mthuli Ncube, Charles Leyeka Lufumpa, and Désiré Vencatachellum. 20 April 2011. "The Middle of the Pyramid: Dynamics of the Middle Class in Africa." *AfDB Chief Economist Complex*. Web Publication. Retrieved May 23, 2011. <http://www.afdb.org/fileadmin/uploads/afdb/Documents/Publications/The%20Middle%20of%20the%20Pyramid_The%20Middle%20of%20the%20Pyramid.pdf>.

89. Holly Richmond. (19 January 2011). "Walmart, KFC, and others fight over Africa's new middle class." *Grist—A Beacon in the Smog*. Web. Retrieved May 23, 2011. <http://www.grist.org/article/2011-01-18-walmart-kfc-and-others-fight-over-africas-new-middle-class>.

90. Peter Wonacott. (May 2011). "Continental Shift—Global Businesses Battle to Tap Africa's New Middle Class Wealth." *The Wall Street Journal—Classroom Edition*. Web. Retrieved May 23, 2011. <http://www.wsjclassroom.com/cre/articles/11may_intl_africa.htm>.

PART 4

Applications, Examples and Careers in Direct and Interactive Marketing

Domino's Pizza:
Growing Sales with Technology

Since 2007, Domino's customers have been able to visit its Web site and browse the menu to build their own pizza and add sides such as Buffalo Chicken Wings or Chocolate Lava Crunch Cakes. Customers can watch the simulated image of the pizza they are ordering. The image changes as they select a different pie size, choose a sauce and add pepperoni, black olives and other toppings. They can also watch the price when the order changes and ingredients get added or removed and when they apply a coupon.

Domino's Web site also allows customers to track orders with updates. Once the order is placed, a "pizza tracker" communicates with customers in real time and through a bar graph when their order is being processed, baked, checked and sent out for delivery. Over twenty-five percent of all Domino's orders are placed online through the company Web site, which is great for impulse purchases according to Dennis Maloney, Domino's VP of Multi-Media Marketing. The CEO, Patrick Doyle, explains that when customers order pizza online " . . . it enhances the ticket, as we can remind them [via pop-up windows] that we sell drinks, chicken wings and chocolate cake, too" (Change at Domino's, 2010; Domino's Pizza Investor Presentation, 2010).

OH YES WE DID.

FIGURE 1. Domino's Pizza logo with tagline.

Domino's online presence extends well beyond its own Web site. The company understands the critical importance of reaching out to its target market using social media. To stay in touch with its customers, Domino's uses major social media such as Facebook, MySpace, Twitter, and YouTube. Through its corporate account, for example, Domino's monitors Twitter feeds around the clock to hear from followers about its brand, products, and services. The company methodically uses social media to review, respond, and react to what fans and followers post. A company representative, for example, responds with instructions on how to ask for a refund if a customer is dissatisfied with the product. Domino's also uses Facebook to make special offers, news, and reminders to place an order. "Digital media affords you the opportunity to go much more in-depth and be much more transparent with your message," says Russell Weiner, Chief Marketing Officer. "We want people to know that we have nothing to hide and that we have a better pizza." (Change at Domino's, 2010).

This case has been coauthored by Matthew H. Sauber, David W. Marold and Alicia N. Anderson. Used with permission of the coauthors.

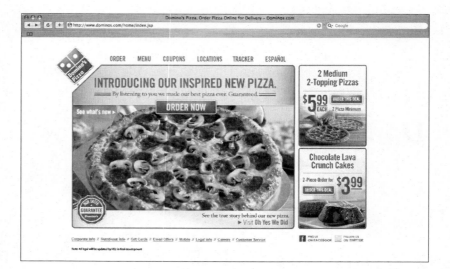

FIGURE 2.
Domino's Home page.

Company Background

In 2010 Domino's Pizza celebrated its golden anniversary by opening its 9000th store globally. The company has come a long way since its humble beginning. In 1960, brothers Tom and Jim Monaghan borrowed $500 to purchase DomiNicks, a local pizzeria in Ypsilanti, Michigan (Boyer (2007). Eight months later, Jim Monaghan traded his share of the restaurant for a Volkswagen Beetle. In 1965, Tom renamed the business "Domino's Pizza, Inc." (Our Heritage, 2008).

The restaurant had minimum seating, making delivery essential for success. Initially, Tom Monaghan hired laid off factory workers as drivers, compensating them based on commission. With an efficiency focus, the menu was reduced from subs and small pizzas to only offering "regular pizza." The business concept took off, leading to expansion through franchising and the first franchise store opened in 1967 (Domino's Pizza, Inc., 2008).

Expansion

The company continued with its expansion, overcoming challenges including a fire destroying company headquarters in 1968 and a legal battle headed by Domino's Sugar over trademark infringement (Amstar Corporation, 1980). Originally, Monaghan added dots to the logo for each new franchise opened. With the aggressive expansion rate the idea became impractical. There were 200 franchises in operation by 1978. Domino's opened its 1000 stores five years later. In 1983, Domino's opened its first international store in Winnipeg, Canada (Figure 3). This paved the way for a global expansion of 1,000 pizzerias overseas—in Europe, Australia, South America, Africa, and Asia—by 1995. In 1997, Domino's opened its 1,500th overseas location (Domino's Pizza Investor Presentation, 2010).

After 38 years of ownership, Tom Monaghan announced his retirement and sold Domino's Pizza to Bain Capital, Inc. in 1998 (Domino's Founder to Retire . . . , 1998). A year later, the company named David A. Brandon Chairman and Chief Executive Officer (Domino's Pizza, Inc., 2008). The company went public in 2004.

Domino's marked the opening of its 8000 and 9000 franchise stores in 2006 and 2010 respectively (Domino's Open 9000th Store, 2010). The company has franchised stores in all 50 U.S. states and 62 foreign countries (Domino's Pizza Investor Presentation, 2010).

As of January 3, 2010, the company reported 8,999 stores in operation worldwide, of which

1960	Tom Monaghan and his brother, James, purchased "DomiNick's," a pizza store in Ypsilanti, Mich. Monaghan borrowed $500 to buy the store.
1965	Tom Monaghan, renamed the business "Domino's Pizza, Inc."
1967	The first Domino's Pizza franchise store opened in Ypsilanti, Michigan
1968	First Domino's store outside of Michigan opened in Burlington, Vermont
1978	The 200th Domino's store opened.
1983	Domino's first international store opened in Winnipeg, Canada. The 1,000th Domino's store opened. The first Domino's store opened on the Australian continent, in Queensland, Australia.
1985	The first Domino's store opened in the United Kingdom, in Luten, England. The first Domino's store opened on the continent of Asia, in Minato, Japan.
1988	The first Domino's store opened on the South American continent, in Bogota, Columbia.
1989	Domino's opened its 5,000th store.
1990	Domino's Pizza signed its 1,000th franchise agreement.
1995	Domino's Pizza International opened its 1,000th store. First store opens on African continent, in Cairo, Egypt.
1996	Domino's launched its first Web site (www.dominos.com).
1997	Domino's Pizza opened its 1,500th store outside the United States
1998	Domino's launched HeatWave®, a hot bag using patented technology that keeps pizza oven-hot to the customer's door. Domino's Pizza opened its 6,000th store in San Francisco, California. Tom Monaghan announced retirement and sold 93% of the company to Bain Capital, Inc.
1999	David A. Brandon was named Chairman and Chief Executive Officer of Domino's Pizza.
2000	Domino's Pizza International opened its 2,000th store outside the United States.
2003	Domino's became the "Official Pizza of NASCAR." Domino's was named Chain of the Year by *Pizza Today*. Domino's introduced it Pulse Point of Sale, a touch screen ordering, system.
2005	Domino's Pizza Australia opened its 400th store in Aspley, Brisbane. Domino's Pizza United Kingdom opened its 400th store in Wadsley Bridge, Sheffield.
2006	Domino's opened its 8,000th store by simultaneous opening the 5,000th U.S. store in Huntley, Illinois and the 3,000th international store in Panama City, Panama.
2007	Domino's rolled out online and mobile ordering in the United States.
2009	Domino's ranked No. 1 in customer satisfaction per the annual American Customer Satisfaction Index (ACSI). Domino's introduced Pizza Tracker.
2010	Domino's changed its pizza recipe "from the crust up". J. Patrick Doyle became Domino's Chief Executive Officer Domino's opened its 9000th in New Dehli India Domino's ranked No. 1 in Keys Brand taste test

FIGURE 3. Domino's milestones.

	Domestic Company-Owned Stores	Domestic Franchise Stores	Total Domestic Stores	International Stores	Total
Store counts:					
Store count at					
September 6, 2009	481	4,456	4,937	3,949	8,886
Openings	—	49	49	140	189
Closings	(14)	(45)	(59)	(17	(76)
Transfers	(1)	1	—	—	—
Store count at					
January 3, 2010	466	4,461	4,927	4,072	8,999
Fourth quarter 2009					
net growth	(15)	5	(10)	123	113
Fiscal 2009 net growth	(23)	(97)	(120)	346	226

Source: Domino's Pizza, Inc., www.dominos.com

FIGURE 4. Domino's Pizza Stores Wordwide as of January 3, 2010.

4,072 were international and 4,927 were domestic stores. Of the domestics stores 466 were company owned and 4,461 were franchise stores (Figure 4).

Domino's same store sales grew 1.4% domestically and 3.9% internationally in the 2009 4th quarter. The growth rate was smaller (.5%) for domestic stores and more robust (4.3%) for international stores for 2009 as a whole (Figure 5). Although Domino's does not provide quarter or annual sales forecast, the management believes that the following year-over-year growth rates are achievable over the long term:

Domestic same-store sales:	1%–3%
International same-store sales:	3%–5%
Net units store growth	200–300
Global retail sales growth	4%–6%

International Growth

Domino's received 40 percent of sales from the company's international division in 2009. The proportion was expected to grow and surpass the domestic sales in the next three to five years according to the company (Domino's Pizza Investor Presentation, 2010). The company reports many years of same-store sales growth in its international operations. The key growth areas are the top ten markets (Exhibit 4) where Domino's has used master franchises—well-financed local businesses with the rights to own, operate many stores and franchise branches as chains. Domino's Pizza Enterprises, for example, owns and operates stores in Australia, New Zealand, France, Belgium, and the Netherlands. The master franchises for the UK and Ireland are publicly traded as Domino's Pizza UK & IRL (Litterick , 2010).

Industry Overview

Categorically, Domino's Pizza belongs to the Quick-Service-Restaurant (QSR) industry. The QSR industry consists of restaurants with fast food service and limited menus of moderately priced and cooked to order items. The U.S. QSR pizza category is highly competitive, large, and

Fiscal	Fourth Quarter of 2009	Fiscal Year 2009
Same store sales growth: (versus prior year period)		
Domestic Company-owned stores	+0.9%	(0.9)%
Domestic franchise stores	+1.5%	+0.6%
Domestic stores	+1.4%	+0.5%
International stores	+3.9%	+4.3%
Global retail sales growth: (versus prior year period)		
Domestic stores	+7.4%	+1.3%
International stores	+28.1%	+3.3%
Total	+16.4%	+2.2%
Total (on a 52-week basis)	+7.8%	(0.3)%
Global retail sales growth: (versus prior year period, excluding foreigncurrency impact)		
Domestic stores	+7.4%	+1.3%
International stores	+21.6%	+14.4%
Total	+13.5%	+7.1%
Total (on a 52-week basis)	+4.9%	+4.6%

Source: Domino's Pizza, Inc., www.dominos.com

Figure 5. Domino's domestic and global sales (Fiscal year 2009)

FIGURE 6. Domino's Top 10 international markets.

Domino's Top 10 International Markets

- Mexico*
- United Kingdom*
- Australia*
- South Korea
- Canada
- India*
- Japan
- France
- Taiwan
- Turkey

*These indicate publicly traded companies in their home countries

Source: 2010 Chain of the Year, *Pizza Today*, June 2010, www.pizzatoday.com

FIGURE 7.
Honolulu
Hawaiian Pizza.

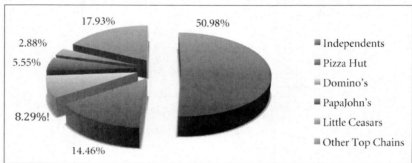

FIGURE 8.
U.S. Market
Share.

Source: Pizza Power: Report 2009, *PMQ Pizza Magazine,* September 2009.

fragmented. With sales of $33.5 billion in the twelve months ended November 2009, the U.S. QSR pizza category is the second largest category within the $230.1 billion U.S. QSR sector. The pizza category is primarily comprised of delivery, dine-in, and carryout (Domino's Annual Report, 2010). Approximately *three billion* pizzas are sold in the U.S. each year (Bloomenfield and Associates, 2010). On average, each man, woman, and child in America eats 46 slices, (23 pounds), of pizza per year (Package Fact, 2010).

About 59 percent of pizza outlets in the United States are independently owned. They control 51 percent of the industry sales (Exhibit 5). A recent survey reports that 54% of consumers prefer independent stores to chains (2010 Chain of the Year, 2010). The Big Four—Pizza Hut (14.46%), Domino's (8.29%), Papa John's (5.55%), and Little Caesars (2.88%)—as a collective unit, have kept steady sales and market share during the recession.

Pizza Hut

Pizza Hut is a division of Yum! Brands, Inc., the world's largest restaurant company in terms of system restaurants with more than 37,000 restaurants in over 110 countries and territories and more than 1 million associates. Yum! is ranked No. 239 on the Fortune 500 List, with nearly $11 billion in revenue in 2009 (Yum! Brand Annual Report, 2009).

Pizza Hut, based in Dallas, Texas, is America's first national pizza chain, established in 1958.

It is the world's largest pizza chain with more than 7,500 restaurants in the United States and over 5,600 restaurants in 97 countries and territories around the world. Pizza Hut became the first national chain to offer pizza delivery on the Internet in 1994. It offered online ordering in all its U.S. locations in 2007 and mobile ordering, through text messaging and web-enabled cell phones, in 2008. Specializing in Pan Pizza, Thin 'N Crispy® Pizza, Hand-Tossed Style Pizza and Stuffed Crust Pizza, Pizza Hut was celebrated as America's Favorite Pizza in 2007.

Faced with 9% decline in same-store sales in 2009, Pizza Hut responded by cutting its pizza prices and rolling out a "$10 any way you want it" promotion that resulted in a dramatic improvement in sales. The company's long term strategy is to transform the brand from "pizza' to "pizza, pasta and wings." They are focusing on improving the speed of their service and have added a new mobile application ahead of their major competitors (2009 Yum! . . . , 2009).

Papa John's

Since opening its first pizzerias in 1985, Papa John's has grown to be the third largest U.S. pizza chain. Headquartered in Louisville, Kentucky, the company had 3,469 restaurants in operations, as of December 2009, of which 614 were corporate owned and 2,167 were franchised restaurants operating in all 50 states and 688 restaurants in 29 countries (Papa John's Annual Report, 2009). Papa John's international development pipeline projects the opening of 1200 new restaurants in the next eight years. Their sales were down 2.3% in the 12 months ended March 31, 2010 (Standard & Poor's Stock Report, 2010).

Papa John's long-term business goal is to build the strongest brand loyalty of all pizza restaurants. The company's key strategies are based on a menu of high-quality pizza along with side items, efficient operating and distribution systems, team member training and development, national and local marketing, developing and maintaining a strong franchise system, and international operations (Domino's Annual Report, 2010).

Papa John's "traditional" domestic restaurants are delivery and carryout operation that serves defined trade areas. As such, Papa John's is the closest competitor to Domino's.

Papa John's advertising slogan and brand promise is, "Better Ingredients. Better Pizza." Domestic Papa John's restaurants offer a menu of high-quality pizza along with side items, including breadsticks, cheese sticks, chicken strips and wings, dessert items and canned or bottled beverages. Papa John's traditional crust pizza is prepared using fresh dough (never frozen). Papa John's pizzas are made from a proprietary blend of wheat flour, cheese made from 100% real mozzarella, fresh-packed pizza sauce made from vine-ripened tomatoes (not from concentrate) and a proprietary mix of savory spices, and a choice of high-quality meat (100% beef, pork, and chicken with no fillers) and vegetable toppings.

In 2001, Papa John's became the first national pizza company to offer online ordering and was the first pizza company to surpass $1 billion in online sales and now has recently surpassed $2 billion in sales (Domino's Annual Report, 2010). In addition to placing orders online at papajohns.com, customers can place order via text messaging and mobile web capabilities of cell phones.

Domino's

Based in Ann Arbor, Michigan, Domino's Pizza is the number one pizza delivery chain in the United States. The company pioneered the pizza delivery business and has built the brand into one of the most widely recognized consumer brands in the world. The Domino's Pizza® brand was named a Megabrand by *Advertising Age* magazine in 2009. Domino's was also ranked number one in customer satisfaction in a survey of consumers of the U.S. largest limited service restaurants, according to the annual American Customer Satisfaction Index (ACSI).

Domino's operated a network of over 9000 franchised and company-owned stores in all 50 states and 62 international markets. The company had global retail sales of over $5.6 billion in 2009, comprised of $3.1 billion domestic sales and over $2.5 billion international sales (Horovitz, 2010).

Domino's business model emphasizes on-time delivery of quality pizza. The model entails: (1) delivery-oriented store design with low capital requirements, (2) a concentrated menu of pizza and complimentary side items, (3) a network of committed owner-operator franchisees and (4) a vertically integrated supply-chain system. Revenues are largely driven form sales through company-owned stores and at franchise levels, comprised of royalty payments and supply-chain revenues.

Domino's operates primarily within the U.S. pizza delivery market. Its $10.3 billion of sales accounted for approximately 31% of total U.S. QSR pizza delivery sales in the twelve months ended November 2009. Domino's and its top two competitors account for approximately 45% of the U.S. pizza delivery market—based on reported consumer spending—with the remaining 55% market share attributable to regional chains and individual establishments (Horovitz, 2010).

Domino's also competes in the carryout market, which together with pizza delivery comprise the largest components of the U.S. QSR pizza industry. The U.S. carryout pizza had $13.8 billion of sales in the twelve months ended November 2009. Although Domino's primary focus is on pizza delivery, it is also favorably positioned to compete in the carryout segment given its strong brand identity, convenient store locations, and affordable menu offerings (Domino's Annual Report, 2010).

Domestically, Domino's competes against regional and local pizzerias as well as the national chains of Pizza Hut® and Papa John's. These companies generally compete on the basis of product quality, location, image, service and price. They also compete on a broader scale with quick service and other international, national, regional and local restaurants. In addition, the overall food service industry and the QSR sector in particular are intensely competitive with respect to product quality, price, service, convenience and concept. The industry is often affected by changes in consumer tastes, economic conditions, demographic trends and consumer disposable income (Horovitz, 2010).

According to Dennis Maloney, Domino's Vice President of Multi-Media Marketing, "the recessionary economic climate has contributed to less delivery and more carryout and home cooked and frozen food, substituting for some QSR purchases." (Phone Interview with Dennis Maloney, 2011).

Competitive Analysis Summary

Pizza Hut is the number one pizza chain in the world. It competes in delivery, carryout and sit-down segments of QSR. The recession of 2009 took its toll on Pizza Hut as its sit-down restaurants were hit harder than other segments. Pizza Hut responded by cutting its pizza prices and rolling out a "$10 any way you want it" promotion. It is transitioning itself to be known for pizza, pasta and wings. It also sees itself as a leader in technology and was the first to introduce an application for iPhone.

Papa John's has grown to be the third largest U.S. pizza chain in the 25 years since it was established. It competes in the delivery and carryout segments and as such it is the closest competitor to Domino's. Papa John's advertising slogan and brand promise is: "Better Ingredients. Better Pizza." It is generally agreed that it lives up to its quality promise. In 2001, Papa John's also focused on technology and it became the first national pizza chain to offer online ordering and was the first pizza company to surpass $1 billion in online sales and recently surpassed $2 billion

FIGURE 9. Pacific veggie pizza.

in sales. In addition to placing orders online at papajohns.com, customers can place their order via text messaging and mobile web devices.

Domino's is No. 1 in delivery and No. 2 in the overall pizza chain sales after Pizza Hut. Domino's is striving to be No.1 in technology and to improve the perception of the taste of its pizza and the value it provides to consumers. Domino's Pulse system is arguably the best system in the industry and a demonstration of its leadership in Point of Purchase Database Marketing. The launch of the new pizza recipe and a new menu with 80% changed items between 2008 and 2010 have contributed to sales increases and changing perceptions. Evidence of the industry recognition of the change at Domino's is that in June, 2010, Domino's was named "2010 Chain of the Year" by *Pizza Today*.

Customer Profile

Although pizza is a favorite meal for all Americans, young and old, and more than 95% of population eats pizza, there are variations in consumption based on age, household size, and income. Mintel surveys reports that 21% of people in the 18-24 age category purchase pizza more than three times a month, compared to only 7% of those aged over 65 (Pizza Power Report, 2009).

Among households with children, 20% purchase pizza more than 3 times a month, compared to 12% of those households with no children. Research also indicates that households with annual income of $100,000 and beyond are more likely to prefer pizza from independent, local pizzerias, while households with children are more likely to visit a pizza chain (Corporate Porfile, 2010).

Buying Behavior

U.S. consumer pizza-buying behavior was negatively impacted in 2009 because of the difficult economic environment. As such, consumers reduced their discretionary spending during 2009 in response to increased unemployment and adverse economic conditions. As a result, the QSR Pizza industry sales were approximately 1.0% lower in 2009 compared to 2008. Cost-conscious consumers are opting for less-expensive pizza choices at QSRs and the low-end of the market appears to be saturated. Thus, pizza chains aiming higher growth are targeting consumers from high-income households (Corporate Profile, 2010)

Other buying trends indicate that consumers are shifting dining-out occasions toward break-fast and lunch and away from dinner in recent years. Consumers are also being attracted to alter-native dinner meals from non-pizza QSR chains, including the ones focusing on fresh sandwiches. Many casual diners began using other restaurants that emphasize carryout and curbside meals.

Value consciousness is perhaps the biggest trend among QSR customers. Consumers look for value meals at nearly every QSR outlets, big chains, and small independents. A recent survey by the National Restaurant Association (NRA) reported that 75% of consumers would patronize full-service restaurants more often if they offered discounts for frequent dining or for dining on slow days of the week.   The NRA survey also reported that 44% of consumers are more likely to make a restaurant choice based on the restaurant's energy and water conservation practices. Some QSR chains are showing leadership in green initiatives by conserving energy and reducing water use (Corporate Profile, 2010).

Focus on healthy food, for adults and children, is a trend that will stay here. Seventy-six percent of those who were surveyed by the NRA reported that they are trying to eat healthier meals in restaurants compared to two years ago.   Forty-five percent said they would frequent quick-serve restaurants more often if the restaurant offered expanded menu of healthy items for children.   Large chains have answered the call by adding salads, flatbreads, whole-wheat crusts, salad-topped pizza, locally grown produce, and organic items to their menu in order to appeal to health conscious consumers (Corporate Profile, 2010).

In its report, "A look into the Future of Eating," the NPD group has forecasted that healthy foods, especially the ones labeled "organic," will be among the fastest growing consumption trends in the next decade.   On the other hand, Mintel's research reports that 84% of surveyed consumers consider pizza as indulgence and they do not care if it is healthy or not (Corporate Profile, 2010).

Domino's SWOT Analysis

Strengths

- *Cost-efficient store model* is characterized by a delivery and carry-out oriented store design, low capital requirements, and a focused menu of quality, affordable pizza, and other com-plementary items. At the store level, the simplicity and efficiency of operations provide advantages over competitors who, in many cases, also focus on dine-in.

- *Strong brand awareness.* The Domino's Pizza® brand is one of the most widely recognized consumer brands in the world. Consumers associate the brand with the timely delivery of affordable pizza and other complementary items.

- *Domino's PULSE™ point-of-sale system.* Domino's PULSE™, the proprietary point-of-sale system, is installed in every company-owned store in the United States and substantially in all of the domestic franchise stores. Features of Domino's PULSE™ point-of-sale system include:

   —Ability to implement centralized promotional activities throughout the marketing mix, including couponing and flyers as well as communicating back to the consumers in the manner they communicated;

—Touch screen ordering, which improves accuracy and facilitates more efficient order taking;

—A delivery driver routing system, which improves delivery efficiency;

—Improved administrative and reporting capabilities, which enable store managers to better focus on store operations and customer satisfaction;

—Enhanced online ordering capability, including Pizza Tracker, which was introduced in 2007 and Pizza Builder, which was introduced in 2008;

• *Successful new pizza recipe* with subsequent successful taste tasting and higher sales results

Weaknesses

• Perception by many that Domino's pizza ranks near the bottom on taste;

• Because Domino's business model is heavily dependent upon deliveries, there are areas of the country that it is difficult for the company to expand to and serve;

• Extended menu that may reduce effectiveness of delivery and great service that Domino's is renowned for.

Opportunities

• Great prospects for international expansion in densely populated parts of the world;

• Opportunity to differentiate the brand in terms of health, nutrition, and environmental sustainability;

• Opportunity for growth domestically upon economic recovery in the United State;

• Opportunity for expansion by acquiring local and independent pizza stores

Threats

• Lingering economic doldrums hamper profitability and growth;

• Stronger competition from pizza chains, independents, and take-and-bake options as well as OSR categories other than pizza;

• Healthy eating trend and organic food consumption

Domino's Growth Strategy

Growth is Domino's top business mandate domestically and internationally. The company uses two primary strategies, menu and technology, to grow domestically.

Menu-based Growth Strategy

Domino's has expanded its menu significantly since 2008. To attract the launch crowd, it added the Oven-Baked Sandwiches line in 2008 in direct competition with Subway. The company also rolled out several BreadBowl Pasta varieties in response to the pasta line from Pizza Hut.

Domino's also expanded its pizza line by launching the American Legends—a line of six specialty pizza varieties featuring 40 percent more cheese than its regular pizza, cheesy crust, and premium toppings–in 2009. The addition of the American Legends was to strike a balance in Domino's pizza offerings to premium oriented customers according to the CEO, Patrick Doyle.

In January 2010, Domino's launched a new pizza recipe to change its reputation from what was one of the bottom of the barrel. It even ran a "self-flogging" advertising campaign that showed that customers commented on Domino's Pizza crust tasting like cardboard and its sauce like ketchup. The new recipe has been credited for Domino's sales rebound in 2010 (Horovitz, 2010).

Starting from scratch, Domino's changed "part of core," beginning with crust up. In the new crust it added butter, garlic, and parsley. The new cheese was shredded instead of diced mozzarella, with a hint of provolone. And the new sauce was made sweeter, with a red pepper kick.

Domino's communicated the arrival of the new pizza to its customers on every box it delivered:

"DOMINIO'S NEW PIZZA. 50 YEARS IN THE MAKING

> Our hand-tossed pizza is new. It's not a slightly-altered version of the old pizza. It's not the same old product in a fancy wrapper. It's completely new pizza from the crust up. And we're pretty doggone proud of it. Because while it doesn't take long for you to get one, it's taken us 50 years to create a pizza of this perfectitude. Fifty years worth of listening to feedback, tasting cheeses, crafting sauces and trying every possible combination of combinations we could think of. So what's new about it? For starters, everything: our cheese made with 100% real mozzarella and flavored with just a hint of provolone. Our sauce with a dose of spicy red pepper to put a spring in your step. And our garlic-seasoned crust with a rich, buttery taste. Now you may be wondering, is it really different? Will it be as good as they say? Is 'perfectitude' actually a word? Well, there's only one way to find out. Take a bite. Then if someone asks if we actually abandoned our old recipe and completely revamped our pizza, you can tell'em . . . Oh yes we did."

In a national taste test, sponsored by Domino's and which appeared on their Web site, three out of five people preferred the taste of Domino's pepperoni pizza, sausage pizza, and extra cheese pizza over Papa John's and Pizza Hut's. Domino's used social media to announce the new arrival by it "Pizza Turnaround" documentary on YouTube, showing how they listened to customers who complained about the "old" recipe and how they developed the "new" recipe.

The company's 2010 first–quarter financial results indicate that the new recipe is a hit with the customer. Domino's domestic same-store sales grew a staggering 14.3 percent in the first quarter, while international same-store comparables were up 4.2 percent (2010 Chain of the Year, 2010).

Technology-Based Growth Strategy

Domino's has developed a reputation for innovation in business processes. It pioneered the corrugated cardboard boxes and 3-D car-top signs that are synonymous with the pizza industry. The company strengthened their efficiency with the time saving invention of the Spoodle, a combination of a spoon and ladle. To ensure that customers received the best pizza, the Domino's HeatWave Hot Bag was introduced. This technology utilizes electro-magnetic energy and 3M Thinsulate Insulation to deliver pizza hot and without excess moisture (Corporate Profile, 2010). To improve their daily operations, the Domino's Pulse Point of Sale system was introduced in 2003 (Domino's Pizza . . . , 2003). The touch-screen ordering system significantly improved the accuracy and efficiency of order taking.

1996	Launched its first Web site, www.dominos.com
1998	First ordering through interactive television
1999	Direct ordering through Quickorder.com
2004	Launched its dedicated Web site for digital marketing
2006	Received Revolution Award as the Best Online Retailer
2007	Launched mobile commerce by introducing SMS pizza ordering service

FIGURE 10.
Domino's digital
pioneering.

Early Adoption of Online Technology

Dominos Pizza has led the restaurant industry as an early adapter of online technology to reach customers. It utilized Internet marketing as early as 1996 by launching its Web site www.dominos.com (Making Pizza since 1960 . . . , 2010). The first ordering method deviating from the standard call-and-place norm began two years later through a television set (Exhibit 6). In 1998, Domino's launched this new ordering method with Open, the "world's first interactive TV platform" in the United Kingdom (Strategic Play . . . , 2005). In the following year, Domino's began a partnership with Quickorder.com, allowing customers to place a delivery or pick-up order directly through the Internet. The user's order was automatically routed to the closest store's point-of-sale system, with a confirmation e-mail sent to the customer (Connor, 2000).

Domino's hired AKQA, an innovative agency with a focus on digital marketing, to create a functional Web site to stimulate online ordering in 2004 (Agency of the Year . . . , 2004). The agency's successful feat won Domino's Pizza recognition in the digital marketing world by 2006, with a nomination for a Revolution Award as the Best Online Retailer (Revolution Award . . . , 2006). In July 2007, Domino's began their exploration of mobile commerce by introducing a SMS pizza ordering service (Domino's Pizza . . . , 2007). To place an order, the customer was required to set up an account online with a keyword attached to their favorite orders and the delivery address. An option for credit card or cash upon delivery allowed the consumer payment flexibility. To place the order for delivery through their mobile phone, the customers sent their chosen word in a text message to 61212 (Domino's Pizza UK, 2007).

Improvements followed the establishment of e-commerce and m-commerce sales channels. Mobile ordering advanced to an application accessible with web-enabled phones at the end of 2007. The expanded sales channel allowed customers more spontaneity in ordering, choosing their desired pizza and side items from the mobile screen. The option of entering an online ordering ID and Password was available to accelerate repeat ordering transactions (Ross, 2007).

In 2007, Domino's reconfigured its online ordering application to include the Pizza Tracker. This monitoring system allowed the customer to view the progressive action of the pizza creation process in real time, from order placement to leaving the store for delivery. Traditional ordering advanced as well with the Pizza Tracker technology. This system was made available to customers who used smart phones to order. Once the order was placed, the customer could monitor it through the Pizza Tracker icon on the Domino's Web site (Domino's Launches . . . , 2008).

The "Build Your Own Pizza" feature began to enhance the Internet user's experience in 2008, allowing the customer to create a progressive photo of their pizza with chosen toppings. The ordering system enhancement was combined with other features to assist the store operations. The improved point of sale system provided the restaurant with delivery route maps and optimal scheduling assistance (Jargon, 2009).

FIGURE 11.
Online order
pizza builder.

In 2008, Domino's entered another television-based sales outlet, TiVo. After viewing a Domino's Pizza commercial, TiVo users can click on the "I want it" icon to place an order for pick-up or delivery. They can use the Pizza Tracker to watch the progress of their pizza on their TV screen (Liddle, 2008).

Domino's aggressive mobile commerce expansion occurred in 2009. The company entered into a partnership with Air2Web to provide an opt-in mobile coupon service, tailored to the customer's ordering history (Butcher, 2009). In August 2009, a new version of the mobile Web site was released, specially designed for iPhone, Android, and Palm Pre users. This mobile site mirrored the web platform by providing the Pizza Tracker with menu visualization, order graphics, and ability to browse and apply available coupons that the customer used (Domino's Pizza Launches . . . , 2009).

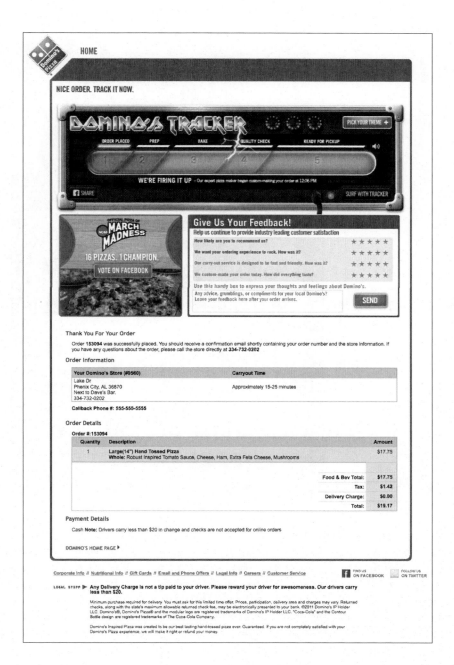

FIGURE 12.
Domino's pizza
tracker.

New Media Strategy

Although television accounts for more than 90% of Domino's media spending, the company is increasingly utilizing new media, such as online advertising, e-mail, mobile, search, and social networking, to connect with its younger customers. Domino's recently tripled its online advertising spending to promote its new menu and delivery service across a broad range of sites such as Amazon, Ask, Facebook, MySpance, Yahoo, college Humor, Yellow Pages as well as sites from local newspapers.

E-mail marketing at Domino's ranges from a variety of special deals, promotional offers, and coupons to new menu item introduction and menu suggestion for special occasions (e.g.,

FIGURE 13.
Domino's mobile
site.

lunch, family gathering, gift) to just a simple reminder to order from Domino's. Established customers typically receive weekly e-mail with promotional deals and suggestions.

Domino's search marketing was catching up with its archrival, Pizza Hut. It demonstrated a strong showing in organic search—a testimony to the company's effective advertising and strong Web site experience—as opposed to paid search where Pizza Hut made a bigger commitment.

Mobile is one of the fastest growing elements of new media that all the three pizza chains are paying attention to. Although, mobile marketing at Domino's is a small proportion compared to online marketing via the Internet, the company reports that it is growing at an average rate of 20% per month. The growth rate dovetails mobile commerce, the fast growing area of retail purchases in the United States. Shoppers were expected to order $2.2 billion worth of merchandise using cell phones in 2010, $1 billion more than 2009 and five times more than 2008, according to ABI Research Inc., a New York technology research firm. To respond to the rapid growth in mobile shopping, 30% of retailers have installed mobile-commerce Web site (Mattioli, 2010).

Domino's has taken a different approach toward its mobile media. Instead of developing smart phone application to provide access to mobile ordering, Domino's has decided to streamline its Web site for mobile access. The advantage of the site is that it requires few clicks for mobile ordering and no downloading or registration for access. By visiting http://www.

FIGURE 14.
Domino's
Facebook page.

dominos.com, customers can create order by tapping "Express Ordering" or "Create Your Own Pizza," examining the menu, special offers and coupons, and using the Pizza Tracker upon placing order.

Domino's social media strategy is a broad ranging program that encompasses Facebook, Twitter, and YouTube. Domino's engagement in social media was hastened in April 2009 when a prank video, posted on YouTube, showed two employees were abusing and mishandling the food they were preparing in a franchise kitchen. The video quickly spread all over the Internet and received more than a million views in less than 24 hours on YouTube. Domino's President properly responded and discredited the prank in another video posted on YouTube. The company also set up a twitter account, shortly after the incident, and started answering the questions addressed to Domino's.

Domino's continued using social media to announce the arrival of its new-recipe pizza by its "Pizza Turnaround" documentary on YouTube. They also showed the success of their taste test by beating Papa John's and Pizza Hut on a "Celebrate" page. And they had a "Stop Puffery" campaign, also on Twitter, which made fun of Papa John's (Domino's Pizza Rewards . . . , 2010).

Domino's integrated its social media campaign on Facebook by encouraging consumers to try its new-recipe pizza. An interactive contest, "Taste Bud Bounty Hunters," rewarded Facebook users with free food for getting their friends to try the new pizza recipe. On the Web site, pizzaholdouts.com, photos were displayed of the top bounty hunter contestants and those pizza holdouts with "wanted taste buds".

Challenges Ahead

As a $5.6 billion company with 170,000 employees and more than 9,000 stores in 62 countries, Domino's Pizza Inc. is readying to celebrate its 50th anniversary. Basking in the company's

FIGURE 15. Domino's Logo without tagline.

success, the management is realistically thoughtful about the list of challenges ahead. On the top of that list are the state of the economy and the maturity of the U.S. pizza market. The question before the management is whether the same-store growth performance is domestically sustainable and achievable in the near future. Per company reports, the U.S. sales rose slightly, from $3 billion to $3.1 billion in 2009. It is expected that quick-service restaurants fare slightly better than full-service restaurants in the coming year, according to the National Restaurant Association. Because of the lingering slowdown in the economy, however, the average amount spent per order won't increase appreciably as consumers continue to hold tight to their wallets.

The international growth is one area that management is hopeful about. Currently over 40% of the company revenues are from the international operation. The proportion is expected to pass 50% in the next three to five years.

The success of Domino's new recipe has created momentum for the brand whose maintaining is subject to proper marketing strategy and execution. Since 2008, Domino's significantly expanded its menu to include multivariety Oven-Baked Sandwiches, BreadBowl Pasta, and the American Legends line of specialty pizza. While the additions contribute to higher sales and growth at store level, they may complicate order processing, preparation, and delivery as well. Whether the expanded menu would slow down Domino's fast delivery and great service when the economic recovery begins and business picks up remains to be seen.

Case Discussion Questions

1. Discuss Domino's point-of-sale (POS) ordering system. What are the advantages of the new system, for Domino's, its franchisees, and its customers?

2. Analyze the pizza home delivery market. What are the market size and growth? Who are the major competitors? What are Domino's competitive advantages and disadvantages? Evaluate Domino's growth potential in the pizza home delivery market.

3. With the advent of online and mobile ordering, the rivalry among Domino's, Pizza Hut, and Papa John's has been heightened in the past three years. Each company claims that its online/mobile ordering system is as easy to use as blinking. You can engage in online shopping and purchasing by browsing the menu, ordering a pizza, and tracking your pizza in real time from order to delivery on their Web site. You can also search for deals, valuable information on nutrition, health, and environment. So, what else can you do on these Web sites? Check it for yourself by visiting Domino's, www.dominos.com; Pizza Hut, www.pizzahut.com; and Papa John's, www.papajohns.com. Browse the menu, go over menu items, and decide on a meal from different types of pizzas, side items, and drinks. Check out the listing of various toppings that are offered. Examine the nutritional value of the menu items. After choosing your meal, try to place an order by clicking on the order tab. How many steps do you have to go through before completing your order? What information do you have to decide on, such as delivery versus carryout? After you place your order, can you track it online from submission to delivery? What other communication / information do you receive after the completion of the delivery? Evaluate your experience with each Web site you visited. Which site is easier to use? Which site is user-friendlier? Is ordering pizza online better or worse than ordering pizza over the phone? Why?

4. Domino's recently announced the launch of a new version of its mobile ordering Web site, http://mobile.dominos.com. The enhanced version is optimized to access Google's Android operating system, used by iPhone, Palm Pre and others. Discuss the enhancements of the new ordering site and its marketing implications.

5. What types of data does Domino's collect when it transacts with customers online? Identify at least *five* different ways that Domino's can use customer data to increase sales and market share.

6. Discuss Domino's recent marketing activities using social media. Compare Domino's social-media strategies vis-à-vis those of Pizza Hut and Papa John's. Address Domino's advantages and shortcomings in using social media. How do you think Domino's can leverage social media to better connect with its customers and advance its brand?

References

2009 Yum! Brands Annual Customer Mania Report, 2009.

2010 Chain of the Year, *Pizza Today*, June 2010, www.pizzatoday.com.

"Agency of the Year: Digital Agency of the Year—Best of the Rest". *Dow Jones*. 15, December 2004.

"AMSTAR CORPORATION, Plaintiff-Appellee, v. DOMINO'S PIZZA, INC. and Atlanta Pizza, Inc., Pizza Enterprises, Inc. and Pizza Services, Inc., Hanna Creative Enterprises, Inc., Defendants-Appellants.". United States Court of Appeals for the Fifth Circuit. 2 May 1980. http://altlaw.org/v1/cases/525090.

Blumenfeld and Associates, 2010.

Boyer, Peter J. (19 February 2007). "The Deliverer". *The New Yorker*. http://www.newyorker.com/reporting/2007/02/19/070219fa_fact_boyer.

Butcher, Dan. "Domino's Pizza Exec: Mobile Commerce Growing at Astounding Rate". *The Mobile Marketer*. 4, September 2009. http://www.mobilemarketer.com/cms/news/commerce/4102.print.

"Change at Domino's." nyse magaine.com, 2010. http://www.nysemagazine.com/dominos.

Connor, Deni. "QuickOrder Brings Domino's Pizza to You in 30 minutes or Less". *Network World*. 6, March 2000.

"Corporate Profile". Domino's Investor Relations, 2010. http://phx.corporate-ir.net/phoenix.zhtml?c=135383&p=irol-homeprofile.

Domino's 2010 Annual Report, 2010.

"Domino's Founder to Retire, Sell Stake". *Los Angeles Time*. 26 September 1998. http://articles.latimes.com/1998/sep/26/business/fi-26500.

"Domino's Launches Revolutionary Customer Tool: Pizza Tracker ™; Industry-Leading Technology Allows Customers to Follow Progress of their Order Online—Even if they Order by Phone". *PR Newswire (U.S.)* 30, January 2008.

"Domino's opens 9000th store". *Nation's Restaurant News*. 11, March 2010. http://www.nrn.com/breakingNews.aspx?id=380448&menu_id=1368

"Domino's Pizza & Breakaway Roll Out of New Pulse POS System". *Pizza Marketplace*. 5, February 2003. http://www.pizzamarketplace.com/article.php?id=2277.

"Domino's Pizza Enables Ordering by SMS". *New Media Age*. 26, July 2007.

"Domino's Pizza, Inc." *Datamonitor Company Profiles*. Datamonitor. 12 November 2008. http://www.datamonitor.com/store/Product/dominos_pizza_inc?productid=1744376E-79E5-49F9-9298-F128768A73E5.

Domino's Pizza, Inc. (2008). "David A. Brandon Biography". Press release. http://phx.corporate-ir.net/phoenix.zhtml?c=135383&p=irol-govBio&ID=115901.

Domino's Pizza Invester Presentation, January 2010. http://phx.corporate-ir.net/External.File?item=
    UGFyZW50SUQ9MjY5Mjh8Q2hpbGRJRD0tMXxUeXBlPTM=&t=1

"Domino's Launches Revolutionary Customer Tool: Pizza Tracker ™; Industry-Leading Technology Allows
    Customers to Follow Progress of their Order Online—Even if they Order by Phone". *PR Newswire
    (U.S.)* 30, January 2008.

Domino's Pizza Rewards the 'Taste Bud Bounty Hunters'. *Restaurant News.Com.* 11, May 2010.
    http://www.restaurantnews.com/dominos-pizza-rewards-the-taste-bud-bounty-hunters/

Domino's Pizza UK (2007). "Domino's Pizza Launches UK's First Ever Text Message Pizza Order Service".
    Press Release. http://www.dominos.uk.com/media_centre/pdf/Text%20Ordering.pdf.

Horovitz, Bruce (May 5, 2010) "New pizza recipe did wonders for Domino's sales". USA Today.
    http://www.usatoday.com/money/industries/food/2010-05-05-dominos05_ST_N.htm Retrived 2010-
    06-18

Jargon, Julie. " Business Technology: Domino's IT Staff Delivers Slick Site, Ordering System—-Pizza Chain
    Rolls Out Point-of-Sale System in U.S. Stores to Woo Customers, Streamline Online Orders". *Wall
    Street Journal.* 24, November 2009.

Liddle, A. "Domino's Pioneers 'Couch Commerce,' Expands its Ordering Options with New TiVo Partner-
    ship." *Nation's Restaurant News.* 1, December 2008.

Litterick, David (February 23, 2008). "Colin Halpern sells £4 m slice of Domino's Pizza". *The Daily Tele-
    graph.* http://www.telegraph.co.uk/money/main.jhtml?xml=/money/2008/02/23/cndomino123.xml.

"Making Pizza Since 1960 . . .". Domino's Pizza Inc.. http://www.dominosbiz.com/Biz-Public-EN/Site+Con-
    tent/Secondary/About+Dominos/History/.

Mattioli, Dana (June 11, 2010). "Retailers Answer Call of Smartphones". *The Wall Street Journal.*
    http://online.wsj.com/article/SB10001424052748704749904575292

"Our Heritage". Domino's Pizza, Inc.. 2008. http://www.dominos.com/Public-EN/Site%2BContent/Sec-
    ondary/Inside%2BDominos/Our%2BHeritage/.

Packaged Facts, New York, 2010.

Papa John's 2009 Annual Report, 2009.

Phone interview with Dennis Maloney, Domino's Multi-Media Marketing Vice President, 2011.

"Pizza Power Report, 2009". PMQ Pizza Magazine, September 2009, www.pmq.com

"Revolution Awards 2006: Is Your Work in the Running?". *Revolution.* 28, February 2006.

Ross, J. "Domino's, Papa John's Look to Build Clientele Via Text Message Ordering". *Nation's Restaurant
    News.* 10, December 2007.

Standard & Poor's May 15, 2010 stock report, 2010.

"Strategic Play—Domino's Pizza: Speedy Delivery". *New Media Age.* 14, April 2005.

Yum! Brands 2009 Annual Report, 2009.

Peninsula Society for the Prevention of Cruelty to Animals (PSPCA)

In 1824, New York resident Henry Bergh decided he could no longer sit idly by and watch a street merchant beat his defenseless horse. On that day, the first SPCA was born. Named the ASPCA, or the American Society for the Prevention of Cruelty to Animals, this organization became the first of its kind to exist for the sole purpose of helping make the world a better, safer place for tens of millions of companion pets.

Since that time, hundreds of SPCAs and Humane Societies have been formed across the United States to serve their communities' needy and homeless animals. While the primary goal of these

FIGURE 1. PSPCA logo.

organizations is to find new homes for homeless pets, they also provide humane animal care education to pet owners, make available low-cost medical services to indigent families, and care for sick and injured stray animals.

SPCAs generally have small staffs and largely rely on volunteers and private donations to operate. Given that these organizations must raise their own money, they often lack the funds necessary to employ skilled employees or to even engage in the most basic business practices. Modern-day tactics such as direct and interactive marketing are often overlooked or are simply not considered due to a lack of time or money. This was the case for the Peninsula SPCA located in Newport News, Virginia.

Peninsula SPCA

Founded in 1962, the Peninsula SPCA (PSPCA) became the only facility in a four-city region to provide sheltering and adoption services. By 2004, The Peninsula SPCA needed some help in the area of marketing. Meet Vicki Rowland, who at the time was a 24 year-old college graduate with a love of animals and a keen understanding of direct and interactive marketing. Vicki, pictured in Figure 2, joined the PSPCA as the new Marketing Director in 2006. The Peninsula SPCA did not have a complete direct and interactive marketing strategy in place. Vicki was there to solve this problem. With research on "best practices" of national and regional SPCAs and humane societies as well as the knowledge of the PSPCA's need to increase fundraising and adoptions,

The initial version of this case was coauthored by Lisa Spiller and Carol Scovotti. This revised version has been coauthored by Lisa Spiller, Vicki Rowland, and Kaitlin Rogers. Used with permission of the coauthors.

Vicki prepared the marketing strategy and overall plan for the Peninsula SPCA. The marketing plan had two goals: to increase animal adoptions and to increase funds raised. The "increase funds raised" goal was largely driven by direct marketing principles. This overall goal was segmented into multiple objectives and numerous supporting strategies which included creating both a direct mail program and special fundraising events. As Vicki began to get organized, she knew that since the heart of direct and interactive marketing is a customer or client database, her initial efforts should be focused on creating the PSPCA's first real customer database.

The Database

Vicki investigated several database software solutions and evaluated each on several criteria: ability to synchronize with the PSPCA's sheltering software, importing/exporting functionality, reporting tools, and price. Ultimately, WiseGuys™, by Database Marketing Solutions, Inc., was selected as it was "user-friendly" and able to be customized to meet PSPCA's needs.

The next task was to import existing donor names and addresses from Excel into the new database. Vicki

FIGURE 2. Vicki Rowland.

established source codes and match codes for each unique customer record, enabling the PSPCA team to analyze which sources provide the most responsive and profitable donors. The next step was to determine appropriate customer segmentation criteria, which would enable messages to be tailored and targeted to each unique segment. Vicki realized she needed additional information in order to create a sound segmentation strategy. A team of volunteer market researchers from the marketing department of her alma mater, Christopher Newport University, began surveying more than 15 of the top SPCAs across the country to learn how they segmented their databases. The results showed that most SPCAs were not segmenting their databases—a result of a lack of time and inability to integrate current marketing practices. Of the few SPCAs that did, the following segments were identified: Donors and Prospect Donors. For the PSPCA, these segments are primarily sub-segmented by gift history, which as shown in Figure 3, is based on monetary donations.

The final step in the database development process was to establish ways to generate leads and train volunteers to enter new data. Data entry took much longer than Vicki envisioned, but it was well worth the effort. Vicki created processes to capture new names of people adopting, visiting the PSPCA, and/or participating in a fundraising event. As the database and special events developed, so did the usefulness of the database. Vicki was able to see all recent donors, and she was able to send direct mail pieces to these donors asking for the exact amount they donated in the past. The direct mail pieces also provided an opportunity for what is called database lift. These donors had three options: donate the same amount, donate $10 more, or donate $20 more than their usual. This provided donors the opportunity to increase donations, which helps the PSPCA segment donors while receiving larger donations.

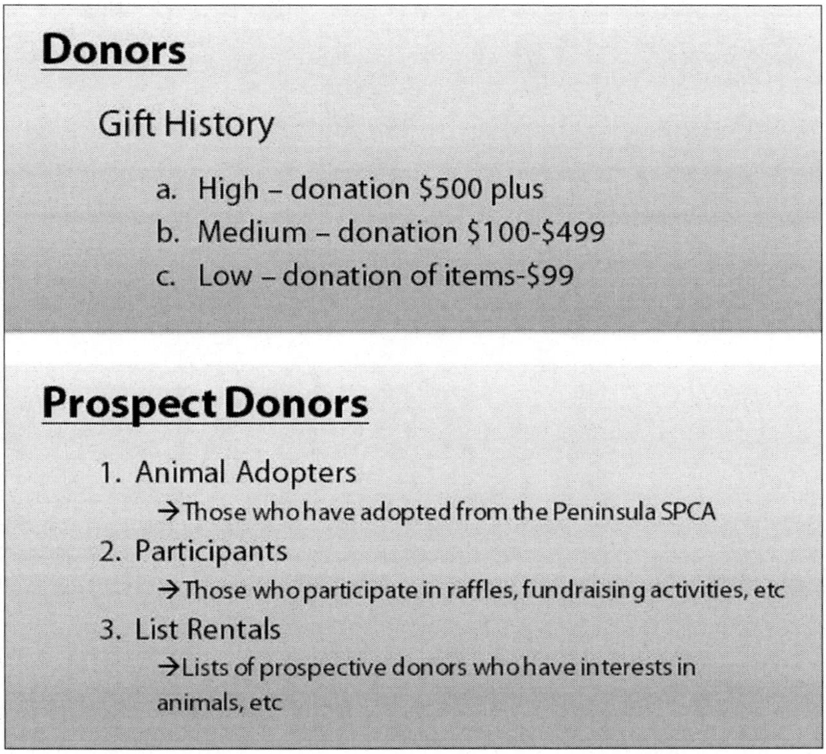

Donors

Gift History

a. High – donation $500 plus
b. Medium – donation $100-$499
c. Low – donation of items-$99

Prospect Donors

1. Animal Adopters
   → Those who have adopted from the Peninsula SPCA
2. Participants
   → Those who participate in raffles, fundraising activities, etc
3. List Rentals
   → Lists of prospective donors who have interests in animals, etc

FIGURE 3.
Donor gift history.

The Marketing Plan

Direct Mail Program

Research revealed that the optimal frequency of direct mail solicitations was four to six times per year. Therefore, the direct mail plan was built around executing four direct mail solicitations per year. However, as the database grew, the PSPCA expanded direct mail solicitations to six per year. One of the six solicitations includes an annual report, which provides information about the PSPCA to interested donors.

The most successful direct mail piece each year is the Holiday Fund Drive. It appears that donors are willing to give a little bit extra around the holiday season, so the Peninsula SPCA benefits from this increase in donations. The Holiday Fund Drive direct mail piece, as pictured in Figure 4, features an emotionally appealing letter from the director as well as "gift certificates," which show the donor's name and how much was donated. These certificates were displayed in the PSPCA's front office to show the giving nature of its donors.

As Figure 5 illustrates, direct mail solicitations are not created equal and there are many factors that contribute to their success. As shown, the Holiday Fund Drive mailings seem to have the most success. The timing of direct mail pieces is especially sensitive, and the holiday season is one of the best times to appeal to donors.

Some solicitations mailings are important to donors, but do not receive as many donations in response. For example, the Annual Report/Newsletter mailed in January 2011 was not wildly successful, but it was vital to maintain donor relationships. This direct mail piece showcased success stories, included a letter from the Peninsula SPCA Board of Directors addressing the new direction of the organization, and featured important and positive adoption numbers for the organization. This piece gave donors an inside look into the Peninsula SPCA, and it gave them

Dear Liz & Susan,

Do you remember the holiday gifts you gave last year? For many, it can be difficult to remember all the gifts we give and receive over the course of a year. Chances are, many of the neckties and sweaters we gave last year have also been forgotten by the recipients.

Here at the Peninsula SPCA we remember the gifts we receive from caring friends like you because your gifts to the animals for whom we care SAVE LIVES. Your support enables us to provide much needed food, medical care and shelter to animals who would be lost without us.

Together, this is what we have accomplished since 2004.

- Found homes for more than 21,516 animals
- Reunited over 9,719 lost pets with their families
- Total Lives we have saved on the Peninsula is 31,225

As you work on your gift list this year, may I suggest another gift of $10 or more to help the Peninsula SPCA. It's a terrific way to honor friends and family and I am certain it's a gift you will remember and be very proud of for the entire year. Share with your loved ones the difference your support makes every day in the lives of homeless animals.

So, please think the hundreds of other animals in our care and send your Holiday Fund Drive gift today. Returning one, two or all three of the enclosed Gift Certificates will make an immeasurable difference in the lives of so many deserving animals.

(over, please)

FIGURE 4.
Holiday fund
drive mailer.

FIGURE 5.
Response rate
analysis table.

Date	Mailing	Number Mailed	Response Rate	Funds Raised	Cost	Net Income
April 2006	Helping Discarded Pets is What We Do	7,389	7.10%	$19,415	$2,500	$16,915
Sept. 2006	Operation: On the Run & Having Fun!	7,390	7.24%	$21,089	$2,500	$18,589
Jan. 2007	Together, We Changed Lives	8,794	4.97%	$14,759	$3,300	$1,459
June 2007	PVA/SPCA Clinic Fund	46,00	.80%	$22,885	$24.00	($1,115)
	(SPCA Donors)	8,806	2.7%	$13,860	$4,594	$9,266
	(Pet Owner Prospects)	37,194	.34%	$9,025	$19,406	($10,381)
Sept. 2007	Never Again (Disaster Planning)	9,548	4.16%	$16,985	$3,000	$13,985
Dec. 2007	Holiday Appeal	9,548	6.00%	$27,500	$3,000	$24,500
Oct. 2008	October Mailing	1,719	16%	$9,453	$1,031	$8,422
Nov. 2008	Holiday Fund Drive	16,792	21%	$38,371	$8,266	$30,105
Mar. 2009	Spring Fund Drive	2,044	22%	$14,968	$1,212	$13,756
June 2009	Summer Fund Drive	1,879	12%	$9,333	$1,160	$8,173
Aug. 2009	Fall Fund Drive	2,708	14%	$7,412	$1,531	$5,881
Nov. 2009	Holiday Fund Drive	2,273	25%	$22,214	$1,341	$20,873
Mar. 2010	Spring Fund Drive	2,268	17%	$12,496	$1,338	$11,158
July 2010	Summer Mailing	2,268	19%	$16,033	$1,338	$14,695
Aug. 2010	August Mailing	2,268	13%	$10,055	$1,338	$8,717
Sept. 2010	Falling in Love	2,210	17%	$14,110	$1,303	$12,807
Nov. 2010	Holiday Fund Drive	18,035	4%	$34,801	$8,300	$25,781
Jan. 2011	Annual Report/Newsletter	3,035	5%	$7,165	$1,850	$5,315
Feb. 2011	Winter Fund Drive	3,035	11%	$10,111	$1,362	$8,749
Mar. 2011	Spring Fund Drive	18,035	3%	$16,191	$8,300	$7,891

insight into how their generous donations would be spent. Figure 6 shows a portion of the PSPCA's Annual Report/Newsletter for 2011.

Tracking and analyzing response rates is important. The dip in response rates in June, 2007 is likely to be attributable to an attempt to cultivate new donors. In an effort to expand its donor base, Vicki reached out to the veterinary community to solicit its clients. Since clients of vet clinics own pets, Vicki and her PSPCA team speculated that they would be sympathetic towards the PSPCA's mission and willing to support it financially. Several veterinarians in the area provided Vicki with their customer lists, which the PSPCA used to roll out a direct mail piece requesting a donation. She knew that prospective solicitations often lose money in the short run; however, the lifetime value of each donor far exceeds the initial gift, so effective prospecting can be a lucrative long-term investment. In this instance, a 0.34 percent response rate was achieved, which translated to 112 new donors. Vicki and the team saw this tactic more as a means of generating awareness and "planting seeds for the future" rather than an unsuccessful direct mail effort.

Overall, the PSPCA direct mail campaigns were highly effective in both strengthening relationships with its donor base and generating funds for the shelter. However, Vicki and her team were not solely focusing on direct mail campaigns to generate both awareness and funds for the PSPCA; they were also busy planning special events.

Special Fundraising Events

Part of the new marketing plan was to create and implement profitable fundraising events. The question Vicki faced was: what kind of event to conduct? To determine the most successful fundraising events, Vicki again surveyed top SPCAs across the country. Results indicated that the flagship fundraiser of most SPCAs was a pledge walk and a formal gala including pets, with top SPCAs earning between $75,000 and $100,000 for each event.

The premise of the pledge walk is to get individuals to register, become excited about the cause, and raise money from their friends and family. Participants have many ways to raise money. They may ask in person, mail requests, hold their own mini-fundraisers at work, school, church, etc. Participants can also easily create an interactive, personal fundraising webpage that allows participants to e-mail their requests, complete with a picture of their pets. Team formation is encouraged and prizes are awarded for top individual and team fundraisers.

So, how could this simple idea yield hundreds of thousands of dollars in donations for the PSCPA? The answer is simple: it's a direct marketing extravaganza! Rather than using a mass request to ask thousands of people for money, a pledge walk provides a fun way for individuals to make personal requests on behalf of the PSPCA. The beauty of this approach is that each

FIGURE 6. Annual report/newsletter.

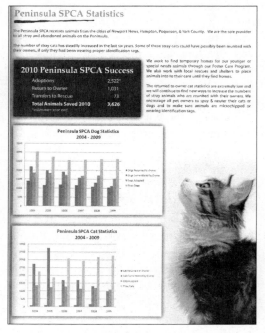

request is a highly targeted, one-on-one plea to the hottest leads of all—friends and family. In addition to requesting donations, registered individuals also ask for their friends and family to register themselves, thus exponentially expanding the PSPCA team's reach.

PSCPA PAWS FOR A CAUSE DOG WALK & FESTIVAL.—The PSPCA launched its first dog walk, "Paws for a Cause Dog Walk & Festival," with great anticipation in 2007. Following the advice of the Tampa Bay SPCA, the PSPCA's focus was on recruiting walkers to fundraise on its behalf. Additionally, Vicki approached many local businesses to sponsor the event and donate via in-kind contributions so that 100 percent of funds raised from the walkers would benefit the animals. With the help of everyone at the PSPCA and many volunteers, a massive festival was put together to draw non-participants to witness the walk, which also featured local rescue groups, pet-related vendors, canine games and contests, and canine demonstrations. Figure 7 presents the flyer used to promote this special event.

The event was a resounding success and has raised more than $235,000 collectively over its four years! The Paws for a Cause Dog Walk & Festival has grown in the number of animal lovers and PSPCA supporters, which has made it a very successful event. Since its success, Vicki has added the 5K Fun Run and other dog-related attractions to the overall event.

FIGURE 7.
Paws for a Cause
dog walk &
festival flyer.

PSCPA FUR BALL. Each December, Vicki begins to prepare and send out Fur Ball invitations. These invitations, featured in Figure 8, go to recent donors as well as past Fur Ball attendees. The Peninsula SPCA Fur Ball is a black tie, red carpet fundraiser for animal lovers and their pets. This event attracts people from the entire community, and some out of state guests. These guests enjoy a night filled with dinner, dancing, a live band, both a silent and live auction, and an exciting pet parade down the red carpet. The human guests are not the only ones dressed up; many of the dogs sport black ties and dresses to make the evening even more of a spectacle.

The Peninsula SPCA Fur Ball has gained success since its beginning in 2008. The event had a net profit of nearly $94,000 in its fourth annual event in 2011. The Peninsula SPCA relies on its donors to help run the organization. Funds raised makes up a large amount of the operating budget. Reaching these donors through special events, direct mail, and digital and social media are ways the Peninsula SPCA remains a part of the community.

Outreach Programs & Strategies

The PSPCA has embraced the wonders of technology to reach donors, customers, and volunteers. Vicki had a great idea to utilize online live-streaming Webcams to showcase the PSPCA animals available for adoption. Vicki secured sponsorship for the webcams from its local newspaper, The Daily Press. The program began with a Live Kitty Webcam, and after its immediate success of more than 30,000 views per month, the Daily Press sponsored a Live Dog Webcam. These webcams have allowed the public to view certain adoptable cats and dogs any time of the day or night—if you have that kind of time! This has been a great solution to finding loving homes for adoptable animals.

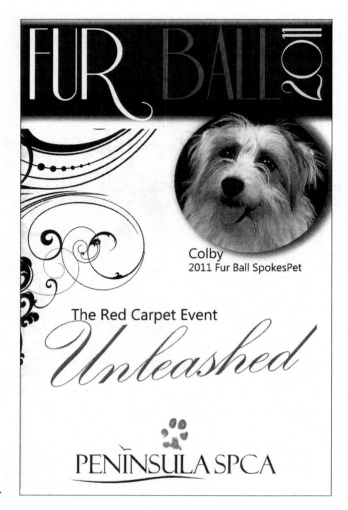

FIGURE 8.
Fur Ball program.

The PSPCA finds many ways to showcase adoptable animals. Adoptable pets are featured on the PSPCA Web site and updated daily by the adoption team. The animal management software, PetPoint, allows PSPCA staff to incorporate photos, videos, and descriptions for each pet through a pet search tool called Petango. Recently, Vicki had the idea to post foster animals in addition to the adoptable animals. This is a great solution to showcase animals that will become adoptable in the near future.

The Foster Care Program is vital to the mission of the PSPCA. Animals that would otherwise be humanely euthanized are able to have a second chance in a loving environment. Some animals, specifically kittens and puppies, are too small or too young to be adopted when they first arrive at the PSCPA shelter. These animals are placed in foster care along with other animals that are not quite ready for adoption. There are many factors that make specific animals candidates for foster care, such as age, weight, temperament, and health issues. Some animals just need some tender loving care instead of being stuck in the shelter. The PetPoint software makes it possible to make these animals "viewable" on the PSPCA website so potential adopters can see animals that will become available in the near future.

Animals in foster care are not limited to the PSPCA's website, but they are also showcased

FIGURE 9.
Peninsula SPCA
Facebook page.

on Facebook. In 2009, the PSPCA created its first Facebook page, and it has been instrumental in spreading the mission of the PSPCA. As Figure 9 shows, the PSPCA Facebook page makes it easier for the PSPCA to communicate with its supporters, allows the PSPCA to showcase adoptable animals, and keeps fans updated on day-to-day events. Today, the PSPCA has more than 2,300 fans on Facebook. The PSCPA has expanded its Facebook pages to target specific interests including its Foster Care Program, Paws for a Cause fundraising event, and the PSPCA Petting Zoo. Each one of these pages is different, but they all work together to keep the community informed on what's happening at the PSPCA. The main PSPCA Facebook page is linked to its Twitter account, so each update automatically goes to Twitter simultaneously. The overall goal for the Peninsula SPCA's social media utilization is to interact with its donors, customers, and volunteers in as many ways possible.

The Outcome—Year One

As the successes and continued challenges of the PSPCA's marketing efforts illustrate, direct marketing is not a success-only journey. The PSPCA team has learned several important lessons along the way. Since it is often a marketer's goal to maximize profit on every marketing activity, it is important to recognize the role that measuring and analyzing results play in ensuring that those tactics that are effective are repeated, while those tactics that are not effective are eliminated. It is also vital to recognize the importance of performing solid research to avoid investing in activities that are likely to fail.

At the end of its first year, Vicki and the PSPCA team raised more than $165,000 from its marketing activities and projected raising more than $250,000 in its second year. Just as importantly, however, the team's marketing efforts began the critical strategy of forming thousands of relationships with community members—people who may well become future donors, future volunteers, and hopefully, future families for the homeless animals of the Virginia Peninsula.

The Case Challenge: Adoption Guarantee Vision

When Henry Bergh established the first Society for the Prevention of Cruelty to Animals (ASPCA) in 1824, primarily to prevent carriage horse abuse in the days before automobiles, he feared what would come of the ASPCA when he was gone. Following his death, the ASPCA signed contracts with New York City to run the dog pound. By 1910, the ASPCA was doing little more than impounding dogs and cats on behalf of the city, with all but a small percentage put to death. The guaranteed source of income provided by contracts enabled SPCAs and humane societies to abandon their advocacy to prevent cruelty in order to administer dog control for cities and counties. Sadly, many humane societies and SPCAs did little more than euthanize dogs and cats within the past decade or so.

The revolutionary break from municipal contracts began with San Francisco SPCA Director, Richard Avanzino. In 1988, Avanzino signed the society's final animal control contract with the city and gave notice it would not be renewed. Until then, every city had an SPCA or humane society that signed an agreement to conduct services on behalf of city animal control. In addition, these shelters became financially dependent and in most cases the level of funding was inadequate to perform the services required. The private fundraising efforts of these transforming shelters increased substantially since the funds were being used for lifesaving methods instead of animal control services.

The Peninsula SPCA has been the *sole* provider for homeless animals on the Virginia Peninsula, which includes Newport News, Hampton, York, and Poquoson municipalities. The contracts between the PSPCA and the local municipalities have created two dynamic business models. The Virginia State Law identifies a pound for the purpose of impounding or harboring seized, stray, homeless, abandoned, or unwanted animals. In addition, according to Virginia State Law, an animal shelter including a humane society, animal welfare organization, or a society for the prevention of cruelty to animals operates for the purpose of finding permanent adoptive homes for animals (Virginia Comprehensive Animal Law Handbook, 2009). Dr. Richard Chance, Executive Director Peninsula SPCA states, "There was conflict, ethical conflict—the tasks required from contracts were taking them outside of our mission."

One of the many challenges for the Peninsula SPCA was getting the Board of Directors committed to the new vision and mission. According to Dr. Chance, the Peninsula SPCA's Board of Directors organized a strategic planning meeting about three years ago. The board was trying to accomplish change without ending the municipal contracts and continue working with two different business models. "Why attempt a strategic plan that you cannot possibly accomplish?" challenged Dr. Chance. "If we remain true to our mission, people will get behind it because they know we are really advocating for the animals."

An Adoption Guarantee organization commits to save all the healthy and treatable animals under its care, with euthanasia reserved only for the unhealthy & untreatable animals. There are four different types of animal categories: healthy, treatable—rehabitable, treatable—manageable, and unhealthy & untreatable (Maddie's Fund, 1999). The problem across the nation is that healthy and treatable animals are being euthanized daily. According to the Humane Society of the United States' Web site, six to eight million cats and dogs enter U.S. shelters every year and four million cats and dogs (about one every eight seconds) are put down in U.S. shelters every year. It's difficult to put a number on a cat or dog's life. This is the hard truth.

Ultimately, the PSPCA Board of Directors made the decision to become an Adoption Guarantee organization and end contractual obligations with the municipalities by year 2013. There were four significant problems that accelerated the need for change:

1. The municipalities trapping and euthanizing feral cats.

2. Crowded conditions and inability to house all animals brought into the shelter by animal control.

3. The imbalance between funding provided and the number of animals the Peninsula SPCA was required to handle.

4. The resources required to fulfill the requirements of the animal control contracts detracted from the PSPCA performing its own mission.

The PSPCA has been operating as an adoption and animal control business for years. By year 2013, this new direction will bring the PSPCA to a new level of branding and expectations from the Peninsula community. The PSPCA will no longer provide animal control services and will not be known as the place where animals are being euthanized. The PSCPA will be branded as the Adoption Center on the Peninsula. Thus, this new brand or identity of the PSPCA will generate higher expectations from both the greater community and within the internal organization. Becoming an Adoption Guarantee facility gives the PSPCA unlimited potential when it comes to gaining new donors.

Case Decision Problems

Case Decision #1—Creating a New Brand Identity

The new vision of the Peninsula SPCA to become an Adoption Guarantee facility will create major changes within the internal organization and external environment. The Peninsula SPCA's mission states: "The mission of the Peninsula SPCA is to advocate and provide for the humane care and welfare of animals. We are committed to finding a loving home for every orphaned pet in our community." This mission still applies, but the Peninsula SPCA as a whole needs a *new* brand identity.

It is important to understand how execution of the new vision will affect the relationship between the Peninsula SPCA's organizational design and its external environment. Just as important is how the external environment will directly affect the organization's performance and culture. The new vision and strategies implemented to support that vision will ideally set the standards for the Peninsula SPCA. When the implementation of the new vision takes place, the other relationship elements, e.g., staff standards, organizational culture, customer service, fundraising and development, etc., will indirectly be enhanced. The objective is to align the organizational design with its new direction as an adoption guarantee organization. How might the Peninsula SPCA get everyone within the organization involved in an Adoption Guarantee culture?

The Peninsula SPCA does not currently have a specific tagline. This could be helpful when creating the new brand identity for the organization. Vicki knows the tagline needs to be short and sweet, but what would appeal to the organization, the donors, and to the community?

Decision #2—Cultivating New Donors and Prospects

Another major issue that had to be addressed was cultivating new donors and prospecting new donors. The Peninsula SPCA has a wide range of donors, but there are many more to be acquired and engaged in the new mission. Acquiring new donors who have not previously supported the Peninsula SPCA, who have an interest in animal welfare, and individuals who are especially engaged in the new vision are great ways to begin cultivating new relationships. Increasing the number of donors will be vital to the Peninsula SPCA's new vision. Because the

Peninsula SPCA will no longer provide animal control services as of July 2013, the organization's funding will be cut by 50 percent, and new fundraising efforts will need to be implemented.

Decision #3—Developing and Expanding Life Saving Programs

The Peninsula SPCA has many programs to provide not only for the humane care and welfare of animals, but also to promote awareness. These programs, however, need to grow as the organization grows to become an Adoption Guarantee facility. The foster care program provides care for animals that are not yet adoptable, such as young kittens and puppies as well as sick animals.

The volunteer program is another vital component of the Peninsula SPCA. Volunteers help the Peninsula SPCA with its day-to-day activities, assist at fundraising events, and participate in off-site adoption events. However, the Peninsula SPCA will have to rely much more on volunteers when it becomes an Adoption Guarantee facility in 2013. This means the number of active volunteers needs to increase. Active volunteers are those who are reliable, who are able to dedicate hours to the Peninsula SPCA, and who make the Peninsula SPCA part of their normal work routine.

Creating a new brand identity reflecting the new vision, cultivating new donors, and developing and expanding life saving programs are important to the PSPCA. However, all of these initiatives must work together as a whole. There are many things to do before July 2013, and the PSPCA needs to be ready. As you can see, Vicki had many questions for which she desired answers.

Case Discussion Questions

1. How should the Peninsula SPCA showcase its new vision? How should it be branded? How can the Peninsula SPCA educate the community? How can donors best be reached about the new vision? Should the communications plan be altered to fit this new mission?

2. What might be a great new tagline for the organization? How could Vicki go about testing taglines for the Peninsula SPCA? How can the PSCPA use the new tag line to increase animal adoptions?

3. How could new donors be reached? What sort of offers should be sent to these donors? How might Vicki prioritize donor contacts with both current and prospective donors?

4. How could the PSPCA expand its foster care program? How could this program be further promoted? Who should be the target market for the foster care program? What type of offer(s) should be used in an attempt to attract new foster care program participants?

5. How can the PSPCA increase its number of active volunteers? How can these volunteers be reached? How should the PSPCA appeal to these volunteers?

Developing a Direct and Interactive Marketing Campaign Featuring The Martin Agency

If you think it takes a Madison Avenue address to become a national success in advertising, think again . . . and meet The Martin Agency! The Martin Agency is an award-winning full-service advertising agency that is becoming well known for creating pop culture icons such as the GEICO gecko and GEICO's cavemen. The Martin Agency was named *Adweek*'s Agency of the Year in 2009. How did this successful company begin, and how does it create award-winning direct and interactive marketing campaigns? That's the topic of this appendix. We take a behind-the-scenes look at how The Martin Agency puts together award-winning campaigns for its clients. First, let's meet this famous advertising agency.

The Martin Agency

The agency began in 1968 as a small shop doing mostly print work in a Southern city far removed from the sophisticated East and West Coast cosmopolitan centers of New York and Los Angeles. It is located in the heart of Richmond, Virginia's Shockoe Slip, a historic area of restored warehouses. The red-brick headquarters is set on a quaint cobblestone square, with a circular drive surrounding the water fountain that once was used by dray horses. Historic on the outside? You bet! But once you step inside the building it is bursting with energetic, creative minds, high tech, contemporary furnishings, and fine art. This proves that in a wired world, geography doesn't really matter. The external setting of The Martin Agency may be a bit subdued, but its staff of over 600 associates is certainly not.

The Martin Agency was founded by a couple of local ad executives, David Martin and George Woltz. They quickly snagged the bright talent of Harry Jacobs, who, in turn, recruited a young writer, Mike Hughes, to the company. Under this dynamic creative duo, the agency quickly became noticed. Its first national high-visibility campaign was the popular "Virginia Is for Lovers" in 1972. By 1981, the agency was ranked as one of *Advertising Age*'s top ten creative shops. In the 1990s, The Martin Agency moved beyond regional advertising, landing national accounts, such as Mercedes-Benz, Wrangler jeans, and Saab. Today, Hughes heads the company as president. He is a creative giant in the industry. *Adweek* has named him one of the "nine best creative directors in America" and *The Wall Street Journal* named him one of the country's "creative leaders." Hughes is joined at the helm by John B. Adams Jr., who is the agency's chairman and CEO, and John Norman, Chief Creative Officer. This dynamic trio may lead the agency, but it takes a brilliant, visionary, and hard-working staff to serve its clients in such fine, creative, and successful fashion. Today the agency's client list includes GEICO, Walmart, Discover Card, Pizza Hut, B.F. Goodrich, American Cancer Society, Hanes, Comcast, and many others.

FIGURE A-1.
The Martin
Agency.

Now let's pretend that we are a new client of The Martin Agency and we have engaged them to plan and develop an award-winning direct and interactive marketing campaign for us. What will happen first? Whom will we meet? What's next? What series of stages will the campaign development take? How will we know whether it is a successful campaign? Let's explore the steps involved in planning and developing a direct and interactive marketing campaign via The Martin Agency.

Campaign Development Process

Initial Consultation

Welcome to The Martin Agency! Your initial meeting is about laying the foundation for a relationship that will produce great work that generates great results. Award-winning direct and interactive campaigns aren't stumbled on—it takes insightful and productive client and agency teams working together to hatch big ideas that motivate actions and elevate brands to a higher status. Like any personal relationship, the best relationships foster a high level of openness, trust, and respect.

Your initial meeting is with your agency ownership team, which is a seasoned group of agency leaders assigned specifically to your account. Ownership team members are from the areas of account management, strategic planning, media, and creative and provide the vision and direction for the account. A partner in the agency oversees the ownership team, looking over the account and providing you with senior-level accountability and the ability to marshal agency resources on your behalf.

What is covered in the first meeting? The opportunity for the brand. Every brand has an opportunity to extend itself from its current equity and grow, and the first meeting is focused on uncovering that opportunity. A large amount of data and knowledge are presented and discussed to come to a shared understanding of your company's business/category dynamics, current equity, core competencies, and any consumer insights you have. With a solid handle on the business and opportunities for your brand, the next step of campaign planning begins.

FIGURE A-2.
Ownership team
meeting at the
whiteboard.

Campaign Planning Meeting

Campaign development begins with establishing the best agency and client team for the task. The agency ownership team assigns an account director who is the main contact with your company and oversees the process of campaign development from beginning to end. In a full service agency, the account director manages all aspects of the relationship from making sure objectives are established to ensuring the execution will achieve the best results.

At the campaign planning meeting, campaign goals are established, metrics for success are determined, potential target audiences are discussed, budget and timing are outlined, and the protocols for working together are defined. The discussion produces the necessary ingredients for a campaign strategy to be formed. It is exciting, with both agency and client teams embarking on a creative process that can have a monumental impact on your business.

Strategic Development

A direct and interactive marketing campaign needs to rise out of solid strategy. At this stage, you'll meet a strategic planner who, alongside key creative, media, account management and analytics staff, establishes the approach to reaching the campaign objective. Elements of a direct and interactive strategy include targeting, offer, and creative methods that are derived from insights about consumers and the category of your company. A test-then-rollout approach may also be considered.

Strategy development is often a collaborative process, so you are encouraged to share past strategies and their effectiveness, competitive strategies and positioning, data from an in-house database (if you have it) to lend support or challenge the strategic approach, and an understanding of operationally how a campaign might be deployed and who it might impact, for example, a sales force.

Market research is often conducted at this stage. Research helps inform the best strategic approach with the audience you're targeting. Research will reveal the strength of your brand, attitudes and perceptions, key drivers of use for your product, how the audience consumes media, and whether your strategy will likely produce the results you're looking for. Budgets and timing of research vary, so you can expect to talk through options that best fit the campaign strategy.

Also at this stage, since it is likely that there will be digital aspects to the project, 'discovery' related to needs analysis, requirements definition, technical specifications, suitable vendors, site

FIGURE A-3.
Strategic
development.

FIGURE A-4.
The creative
development
process.

map/flow, and information architecture are explored. Budgets for all aspects of the campaign are submitted and the expected return on that investment is projected.

Creative Development

Now the fun really begins. Direct and interactive creative development is as much of a science as it is an art form. The creative director will work with copywriters and art directors to bring out the strategy in a creative expression that prompts actions from the target audience. The creative director maintains a balance between using proven techniques and challenging old conventions.

The strategic planner and creative director will produce a document called a creative brief. This succinct document sets up the creative opportunity within the strategic direction and is what the copywriters and art directors use as a touchstone when coming up with great ideas. Brainstormed, then filtered ideas are refined for a creative presentation to your team.

Creative concepts are presented, complete with the rationale for why they will succeed.

FIGURE A-5.
The creative
development
process.

Creative directions are discussed and are often put into quantitative or qualitative testing to verify that the work will resonate with the target audience. In many instances, the creative is put
into a live-market situation to determine its effectiveness with the offer and specific audiences
the work is intended to reach and create an action from. A creative idea is selected by both the
agency and client team and the process shifts from idea generation to execution.

Campaign Execution

Creative ideas need to be delivered in targeted ways. This is where it all comes together. At this
point, the media strategy turns into ideas for media execution that serve as the basis for a completed media plan. A media buyer will join the team along with a production manager to set the
wheels in motion for the campaign to be executed.

This stage is all about the details. Schedules, checklists, specifications, and production all
come together to produce a finished campaign. An account manager referees this process
between your team and the agency team, making sure everything is taken care of. Multimedia
producers, particularly ones that know how to bring digital work to life, are key to the process.
This is when digital concepts move into the coding phase, the motion designers are called in, it is
determined how and which elements should be tracked, engineering is done on sites, beta testing
and quality assurance is run, bugs are fixed, and all legal reviews are finalized before creative is
deployed to live servers. Any pretesting before roll-out will occur, with results poured back into
the communications to refine it for optimization.

Meetings happen all along the way, typically with daily or weekly status get-togethers.
Finally everything has been reviewed, approved, and can be sent to media for distribution. A
communications lawyer makes sure there is no trademark or messaging issues, and the public

FIGURE A-6.
Polishing the
idea.

relations department is put into action to generate buzz and excitement about the new work if it is an open-to-the-public campaign.

Tracking and Learning

Campaigns have the benefit of generating tangible results—which are fed back into future strategies, testing, and execution, but are also used to optimize the campaign as it runs. Leading this area will be The Martin Agency's director of analytics, who will not only report on the results of the campaign but also analyze it for optimization. The maintenance, monitoring, measuring and reporting that happen once a campaign launches are as important as the planning and strategic development that happen in the beginning. It allows The Martin Agency to adjust the creative, the media, and the offer "on the fly" to get the best possible results for your marketing expenditure.

Throughout the campaign and at its conclusion, you'll see a results "dashboard" with response rates, conversions, and a return on the investment calculation. Results will be analyzed by segment, demographics, and past behavior. When the results are very strong, it may be eligible to win an industry award, such as a Direct Marketing Association ECHO (the Oscars of the direct marketing industry).

Conclusion

The process of planning and developing a direct and interactive marketing campaign can take as little as four weeks or last as long as eight months, depending on client objectives and creative challenge. The key to developing a truly successful campaign is that it must meet your company's stated objectives. Is there fun in this process? Sure! But developing creative campaigns also takes a great deal of vision, research, and hard work. As you've seen from the process, it takes many talented people to create a successful direct and interactive marketing campaign. If you are thinking of a career with an advertising agency, such as The Martin Agency, please review Appendix B:

FIGURE A-7.
A patio meeting
at The Martin
Agency.

Careers in Direct and Interactive Marketing. There we provide descriptions of the many different career positions available in direct and interactive marketing.

Note: The information contained in this appendix has been generously provided by The Martin Agency, Richmond, Virginia. The authors are grateful for the valuable ongoing contributions of the Martin Agency to higher education. We especially recognize Barbara Joynes, Partner, Integrated Services and J. P. LaFors, former Vice-President/Account Director, for their work on this Appendix.

Careers in Direct and Interactive Marketing

Select Direct and Interactive Marketing Career Positions and Descriptions
Careers in Direct and Interactive Marketing in Agencies
Direct and Interactive Marketing Career Resources

Select Direct and Interactive Marketing Career Positions and Descriptions

Account Executive, Advertising Agency
Group Account Director, Advertising Agency
Account Supervisor, Advertising Agency
Account Executive, Advertising Agency
Group Account Director, Advertising Agency
Market Research Director
Marketing Manager Business Products/Services
Media Planner/Analyst
Marketing Manager Consumer Products/Services
Art Director, Catalog
Copywriter, Catalog
Catalog Marketing Manager, Consumer
Catalog Marketing Manager, Business-to-Business
Creative Director, Catalog
Catalog Circulation Manager
Catalog Marketing Director, Business-to-Business
Catalog Marketing Director, Consumer
Telesales Director, Outbound (B2B)
Telesales Director, Outbound (Consumer)
Telesales Director, Inbound
Telesales Manager, Inbound
Telesales Manager, Outbound (B2B)
Telesales Manager, Outbound (Consumer)
Circulation Director, Consumer Magazine
Creative Manager, Consumer Promotion
Circulation Manager, Trade Magazine
Circulation Manager, Newsletter
Marketing Manager, Internet
Search Engine Optimization Manager

Web Marketing Manager
Web Site Manager
Director of Ecommerce
Database Analyst
Database Director
List Manager, Corporate
Database Manager

Account Executive, Advertising Agency

The ambassador of an advertising agency in its relationship with clients, the Account Executive serves a triple role as the liaison officer, consummate marketing advisor, and eyes and ears of the agency's management team.

DUTIES. Assigned to specific clients, the Account Executive is responsible for advising the client, and the development and execution of programs designed by the agency, including direct mail, space ads, television, e-marketing, and in some agencies, catalogs. Works with creative directors, art directors and copywriters, media experts, market researchers, and production and traffic professionals to ensure maintenance of media schedule within budgetary guidelines. Responsible for reflecting client thoughts and the final acceptance of agency's program.

Group Account Director, Advertising Agency

The last word on the client accounts under his or her direction, this person has the final approval of all agency client projects. This person is the primary contact to senior-level marketing professionals on the client side, and must meet with expectations while ensuring the integrity of the agency's beliefs.

DUTIES. Oversee the development of the internal and client business strategy, build external relationships while maintaining internal ones, develop expertise in a client's product/service and industry, oversee account reviews and analysis, participate in new business development and pitches, provide input for annual and quarterly revenue forecasts, negotiate contractual agreements between client and agency.

Account Supervisor, Advertising Agency

Account Supervisors rely on long days and their depth of knowledge for solving marketing problems for the agency's clients, maintaining a friendly and profitable relationship, and the supervision of Account Executives.

DUTIES. Responsible for development of the staff, day-to-day supervision and monitoring of agency account executives, and the strategic development and implementation of client programs within budgetary guidelines. Guides marketing, creative, media and production activities and participates in securing client approval of cost estimates. As a senior manager, participates in the acquisition of new clients as a member of the new business team. With a keen understanding of the realities of agency competition, insures maximum cost-effectiveness for clients and relentlessly pursues the achievement of client goals.

Market Research Director

Always in demand, even in the ancient epoch of the slide rule, the market research professional has risen in eminence with the development of the computer and analytical tools and now plays a leading role in all phases of direct marketing.

DUTIES. Responsible for evaluation, analysis, and implementation of research and statistical techniques to develop marketing insights and improve marketing plans, increase response rates, minimize credit risks, and decrease buyer attrition. Develops and initiates market segmentation programs using demographic, psychographic, and usage data. Conducts front- and back-end analysis and product performance measures. Tracks competitor mailing and product programs. Prepares reports for departmental needs. Presents forecasts to management. May supervise staff of manager(s) and analyst(s).

Marketing Manager Business Products/Services

All businesses are consumers, but the reverse is not always true. Because there are fewer businesses, business marketers face great challenges in the marketplace, including, for one, continually finding new buyers for their products.

DUTIES. Responsible for the maximum penetration of a universe limited by the scope of the product, develops promotional direct marketing materials for the generation of profits. Supervises all testing and the creation of creative output ranging from, but not exclusive to, direct mail, card decks, bouncebacks, statement stuffers, billing inserts, as well as any e-marketing and response space advertising, generally in trade and business publications. Analyzes promotions and digests reports from research staff. Supervises assistants, decides on internal lists and external list recommendations. Maintains mailing schedules.

Media Planner/Analyst

Long after the lights have dimmed in other offices, this professional evaluates the past and ponders the future to ensure that the next direct marketing or telesales program achieves its goals, within an established budget.

DUTIES. For the needs of the client, recommends the size and scope of myriad media options, including but not restricted to direct mail, space, TV, broadcast, co-op vehicles, package inserts, and, more recently, cable and Internet promotions. Maintains current status reports of promotion budget, plans media schedules, and proposes new test vehicles and formats. Meets with list brokers, space salespeople, and other media vendors. Analyzes front- and back-end results on a timely basis, determines seasonal trends, and maintains an alertness for statistical inferences and variances in response rates.

Marketing Manager Consumer Products/Services

Hitting a target that's always shifting, demographically and geographically, is the specialty and challenge of the consumer direct marketer. Lifestyle changes, aging populations, and dual-income families impact all promotions.

DUTIES. Responsible for the development of the budget. Determines the marketing position and pricing, directs creative department in production of a myriad of direct marketing promotional vehicles, including but not limited to direct mail, space advertisements, e-marketing efforts, freestanding inserts, bouncebacks, billing, and package inserts and even matchbook covers. Participates in the selection of product or services sold, credit and collection policies, list approval. Reviews results of front- and back-end analysis, sometimes presented by research department and uses information to improve profit picture.

Art Director, Catalog

Generally under intense time pressure, the Art Director gives the catalog its direction and aura. Also acts as the conciliator between the merchandising and marketing experts, a function that's never written on job specs.

DUTIES. Responsible, under the leadership of the Creative Director, for the look and feel of a catalog, the Art Director constantly struggles with "square inch" formulas for space allocation made by marketing and merchandising executives. Designs with copy and, in the great majority of catalogs, photographic and/or graphic images, to make presentation of a three-dimensional product within the limited confines of a printed page. Also responsible for revisions and additions to an existing format or other promotional offering and in some cases the company Web site. Experienced with paper, type, photography, illustrations, and printing.

Copywriter, Catalog

When consumers read what the catalog copywriter wrote, they feel you have found a solution, or captured a dream, as well as touched a product or smelled a fragrance. Copywriters know the power of words to create sales.

DUTIES. Working within the most stringent confines of inches, brings to life a valve, or a suit, or a book, without deviation from the specifications, the quality, essence, or contents of the product, often enhancing it with the benefits. Frequently working from a specifications sheet, writes for a printed page, often but not always accompanied by a photograph or illustration. Creates on paper (or in cyberspace) an image for the consumer at home or a buyer in the office. Details particulars of the product or the service offered in the catalog or Web site, and answers questions before they are asked, and with skill, reduces returns.

Catalog Marketing Manager, Consumer

Working in a universe shifting in taste and lifestyle, the Consumer Catalog Manager is challenged daily to explore new marketing techniques and products. It's a fortuitous day when challenges don't come hourly.

DUTIES. With profit and loss responsibilities, develops short- and long-range marketing plans and goals, projecting sales, growth, and profit objectives. Determines pricing, directs creative output, supervises media including Web site and e-marketing efforts, list decisions, oversees telesales department, determines market research requirements, and maintains mailing schedules with production department. Vigilant for new products at trade shows and maintains contact with customer service for ideas in improving or adding to product line. Monitors market share and competitive and noncompetitive "books."

Catalog Marketing Manager, Business-to-Business

Equivalent to a product manager in a consumer package goods environment, the Business-to-Business Marketing Manager for a catalog is responsible for day-to-day marketing, creative, and operations of one catalog. Or often, two, or three.

DUTIES. Carries profit and loss responsibilities for a high-volume catalog or a number of smaller ones, generally under the guidance of the catalog marketing director. Develops and executes budget. Decides the positioning, theme, pricing, marketing approach, creative thrust, and media selection. Supervises production by internal or external facilities to ensure mailing schedules. Reviews fulfillment procedures to maintain expeditious delivery of customer orders. Confers with research department and is conversant and knowledgeable in recency/frequency/monetary analysis and its descendants.

Creative Director, Catalog

When dozens of products, in many instances hundreds, must be presented appealingly on a printed page to entice orders, you have an insight into the Herculean task facing the Creative Director of a catalog.

DUTIES. Within the limits of a page and budgetary considerations, directs copywriters, art directors, traffic department, and often production in the theme, design, and execution of layouts for catalogs. Uses photography and/or illustrations to reflect and achieve marketing objectives. Frequently acts in the same function for multiple catalogs targeted at diverse market segments. Responsible for order forms, direct mail packages, space advertisements, television, Web sites, cable, packaging, corporate house organs, and ancillary creative materials, particularly if retail operations are involved.

Catalog Circulation Manager

No business has a better understanding of the importance of acquiring new subscribers, and retaining the old, and their lifetime value, than does direct marketing. In this universe, the Circulation Manager rules.

DUTIES. With creative insight, develops and tests many media, including direct mail packages, e-marketing efforts, list rentals and exchanges, space ads, statement stuffers, bouncebacks, package and freestanding inserts, and alternative media programs to acquire new customers. Responsibility for cost and profitability of acquisition efforts. Develops greater analysis and utilization of internal database. Establishes inquiry programs to develop circulation. Maintains contact and negotiates with list brokerage firms and list managers. Knowledgeable in merge-purge, enhancement techniques, and segmentation.

Catalog Marketing Director, Business-to-Business

Profit and loss responsibility for catalog sales to businesses, governments, and institutions, generally in a market niche or segment, with a range of propriety and distributory items. Continually seeks new markets.

DUTIES. Formulates budget and develops long- and short-term strategic marketing plans and policy. Supervises marketing managers and manages teams of creative, merchandising, list, production, research, customer service, and telesales professionals. Evaluates market share and monitors competition. Continually explores customer database to develop new products. Examines development of new markets by entry into markets defined by Standard Industrial Codes. Explores alternative media for customer acquisition. Monitors sales of ancillary products to broaden catalog or launch new ones.

Catalog Marketing Director, Consumer

This is the direct marketing executive charged with the profit and loss responsibilities for the company's sale of products and/or services by catalog to consumers at home. Enjoys dividing existing catalogs and conquering a new audience.

DUTIES. Prepares and executes corporate marketing plans, budgets, and short- and long-term strategies and pricing policy. Evaluates, tests, and retests new and old media. Assesses, develops, and tests new products to expand market share or introduce new catalogs or programs. Supervises department heads responsible for creative, merchandising, marketing, market research, lists and telesales, and reviews operations and fulfillment activities. Represents the corporation at industry functions. Keeps abreast of legislative and postal regulations as they affect catalogs or telesales and e-marketing efforts.

Telesales Director, Outbound (B2B)

From an ugly duckling into a beautiful swan, telesales has taken added importance and status as a marketing tool that profitably sells products and services to other businesses. A growing discipline with new players.

DUTIES. Complete marketing, strategic, and operational responsibility, including profit and loss, for integration of telesales into corporate marketing mix. Coordinates telesales with other method of sales and distribution. Monitors effectiveness of programs. Establishes personnel policies, training methodology, and motivation techniques. Directs sales activities toward meeting set goals. Supervises script and call guide strategies and performance ratios. Evaluates and recommends installation of new equipment. Responsible for facility planning, systems design, and cost control.

Telesales Director, Outbound (Consumer)

Calling consumers at home, at what may be an inconvenient time, is always delicate, but having them enjoy buying your product or service is the unique talent of the Telesales Director whose programs combine poise with sales.

DUTIES. Profit and loss responsibility for an outbound call center. Facility planning, equipment selecting, systems design, and cost control. Integrates telesales into total marketing mix and coordinates function with other avenues of sales and distribution. Establishes personnel policies, incentive or motivational plans, directs training activities, and establishes and maintains performance standards and records. Awareness of stress factors and methods to alleviate them. Manages the overall effectiveness of the department and produces progress and productivity reports for upper level management.

Telesales Director, Inbound

The Inbound Department is often the only personal contact a company has with its customer. Everyone relies on this leader to keep customers loyal and happy to buy again, while monitoring productivity and morale.

DUTIES. Complete strategic and operations responsibility for the inbound division including the integration of the inbound function with order processing and fulfillment. Development of up-selling and cross-selling techniques and programs. Establishes acceptable levels of call handling, including rates for abandonment, busy signals, and time in queue. Responsible for scheduling, setting staff levels, and putting systems into place to measure and control allowable cost per order. Selection of telephone equipment, switches, line configurations, facility planning, and cost control.

Telesales Manager, Inbound

In the trenches with the troops, always alert to potential problems, acts as the eyes and ears of the order department to ensure proper staffing, without overstaffing, and maintains a professional atmosphere in a stressful environment.

DUTIES. Supervisory responsibility for a staff of Telesales Representatives (TSRs), often headed by supervisor(s), responsible for orders and inquiries. Implements and monitors the telesales order entry system and develops policies pertaining to fulfillment of orders. Oversees clerical and administrative support staffs. Responsible for the instruction of TSRs on product features and pricing. Schedules staff for optimum handling of incoming calls. Conducts performance reviews. Presents daily, weekly, and monthly reports on activity to management.

Telesales Manager, Outbound (B2B)

A three-star general in the sales department, the Telesales Manager works with the troops, ensuring their health, wealth, happiness, and contribution to the profits of the company. No day passes without a new challenge.

DUTIES. Responsible for planning, implementing, and managing the Telesales department and its programs. Duties include recruitment, training, and motivating staff in sales, sales techniques, and product awareness. Structures incentive and motivation programs to reduce turnover. Develops operational procedures. Monitors productivity standards and individual quotas. Directs list selection and analysis activities. Develops direct mail campaigns to support the Telesales effort and ensures cooperation and synergy between the department and the field sales force.

Telesales Manager, Outbound (Consumer)

Under the watchful eye of the Telesales Director, upper management, and the rest of the world, Telesales Managers who sell to the consumer at home watch their team with vigilance while reducing turnover and improving the bottom line.

DUTIES. Frequently conducted during the afternoon and evening hours, responsibilities focus on staffing, training, and monitoring the production of a sales force, comprised frequently of part-timers. Develops recruitment programs beyond "help-wanted" ads and adds to staff with candidates at shopping malls, college campuses, "open houses" and other nontraditional sources. Directs training and motivational sessions to improve productivity. Supervises scripts, develops and monitors budget, and recommends lists and direct marketing programs. Monitors calls to ensure quality standards.

Circulation Director, Consumer Magazine

The marketing function in any organization represents one of life's supreme challenges, but when a company's every move is highlighted in the trade, and sometimes in the public press, the job takes on new dimensions. Enter the Circulation Director.

DUTIES. Part of a three-legged executive stool with the editor and advertising manager, the Circulation Director builds the base on which the publication thrives or flounders. A marketing professional with profit and loss responsibilities, determines circulation budget and long- and short-term strategy, and usually serves as an advisor and consultant to the editor and publisher. Responsible for the identification of the target audience, circulation acquisition, marketing policy and pricing adjustments, creative strategy and implementation, renewals, newsstand sales, fulfillment, and audits.

Creative Manager, Consumer Promotion

The amazing fecundity of the human mind is evident in the activities of the Circulation Manager, diligently seeking to make substantive inroads to build circulation through the use of every promotional vehicle.

DUTIES. Involved in acquisition and retention programs, and works with the circulation director and/or manager, plans and executes promotions, using all media, including direct mail, insert cards, gift subscriptions, take-ones, blow-in and bind-in cards, newsstand, television and space advertising, as well as e-marketing efforts. Tests and analyzes promotions. Deals with vendors to develop premiums. Frequently involved in list promotions to develop additional rental activity, including e-mail lists. Works with creative department and list specialists, computer service bureau, lettershops, and production departments to ensure scheduled mailings.

Circulation Manager, Trade Magazine

Squeezing blood from a stone is an easy task compared to the challenges handed to the Circulation Manager of trade magazines, competing for the advertising dollar. Of course, they are confined by audit regulations to a limited audience.

DUTIES. Yearly budget preparation and planning and execution of circulation acquisition programs, including creative, list selection, print orders and production and lettershop activities to ensure scheduled mailings. Front- and back-end analysis of promotions. Knowledge of audit regulations, generally BPA. Qualification and reverification of paid and/or nonpaid subscribers, preparation of audit materials for publisher's statement, and monitoring of telesales. Supervision of customer service and development of research information for editorial and advertising departments.

Circulation Manager, Newsletter

Each day the newsletter Circulation Manager goes home saying, "Well, at least we don't have to worry about advertisers." But that's small solace when you worry about renewals and new subscribers.

DUTIES. Full profit and loss responsibilities for single or multiple newsletters, generally highly specialized. Directs artists and copy writers, staff, and/or freelancers in the development of new packages for reader acquisition and renewal and billing series. Supervises production and in some cases Web site and Internet marketing efforts as well as lettershop activities to ensure mailing schedules and fulfillment procedures. Heavily involved in the search for affinity lists, compiled or response, for expansion of markets. Proficient in the analysis of promotion results, pricing of publication(s), and postal regulations. Supervises the telesales activities.

Marketing Manager, Internet

The Internet channel is drawing many new recruits to the field of direct marketing. The traditional direct marketing manager's sibling, the Internet Marketing Manager, has emerged as a very desirable position managing a source that is growing by leaps and bounds. The opportunities afforded by the Internet channel in terms of cost efficiency, flexibility, and reactivity are just beginning to be fully recognized.

DUTIES. Access and use all relevant research and sales support tools to stay current in the online marketplace. Drive sales and customer retention through the Web site experience. Recommend product, content, and marketing programs to support company marketing plans. Monitor and report on the online sales and traffic results for the Web site. Build infrastructures and processes for enabling and executing Web contacts. Work closely with the marketing and IT teams to drive and execute various projects.

Search Engine Optimization Manager

Top ten positioning in search engines is the most effective form of online marketing. Mystery shrouds how to accomplish this. Enter the Search Engine Manager.

DUTIES. With the vast majority of all new visitors to a Web site originating from major search engines, it is essential that every business implement a search engine optimization marketing campaign that allows customers to find them ahead of the competition. The Search Engine Optimization Manager develops and maintains keyword phrases that have a high amount of search traffic, conducts site analysis to ensure the site is user-friendly and optimized, reviews text writing to maximize search engine ranking, and creates a program in which links are utilized. It takes skill and time to ensure that the Web site is ranked above competitors, while still achieving maximum return on investment.

Web Site Manager

The Web site is the storefront, or at least the corporate brochure, for the organization, and it takes a savvy professional to present it well. An effective Web Site Manager keeps them coming back again and again.

DUTIES. Responsible for developing and executing marketing communications focusing on building the company's Web site customer base. Responsible for growth of page impressions, unique users, Web subscribers, and registered users against target. Studies the analysis of site traffic and user surveys to gain understanding of customer purchase patterns. Responsible for the overall "look and feel" of the site and ensuring consistency with the company's brand image. Works closely with advertising technology vendors and partners to ensure advertising is delivered effectively and efficiently. Keeps abreast of Web-related developments and evaluates new revenue opportunities.

Database Analyst

At the right hand of the database manager, the Database Analyst knows the inner workings of the database like no other. The ability to manipulate raw data so that diverse audiences can use it is a special skill.

DUTIES. Responsible for interpreting information and reporting results. Compiling and analyzing metrics on customer file; responsible for queries to the operational system, data cleansing/hygiene, integration and data quality assurance. Recommends lists for internal decisions, pricing, positioning, and marketing. Evaluates and reports on data source, analysis of data, requests sample data, executes list hygiene plan, merge-purge literacy. Reports and recommends test strategies. Knowledge of SAS or related programs. Responsible for database integrity issues, including NCOA, LACS, Telematch updates.

Database Director

Without the talents of this person, the database would be just a mountain of unrelated facts. It takes a professional with a special talent to make the information tell its story.

DUTIES. Oversees the development and implementation of database marketing operation solutions that support marketing and customer relationship management campaigns. Establishes corporate data strategy and strategic focus including written policies and procedures for database marketing. Oversees segmentation and targeting, including list strategy and media plan recommendations, matrix design and cell population, list purchases and merge-purge management, and developing technical specifications. Evaluates data vendors or internal staff capability for database enhancement, modeling, profiling, integrated database creation/management, and data warehousing.

List Manager, Corporate

Most professionals state that a direct mail promotion is composed of three elements: creative, product, and list. For the list professional, the list comes first, second, and third, and then come creative and product, or product then creative.

DUTIES. Recommends lists for internal marketing decisions. Responsible for pricing, positioning, and marketing the rental of the house file to other firms. Liaison with clients and brokerage community to increase rentals of house lists. Direct execution of list promotions by direct mail, space, and personal visitations. Schedules, selects, and staffs trade shows. In some companies, also responsible for the list acquisition function, both response and compiled. Analyzes list performance, establishes merge-purge standards. Works with computer department, service bureau, and lettershops.

Database Manager

With few ancestors, but beginning a dynasty, the professional Database Manager has become the toast of all marketers and is wooed for the profits they bring.

DUTIES. Designs and enhances databases, in alliance with the marketing department and research professional, incorporating significant information including but not limited to customer psychographic and demographic attributes, purchasing patterns and preferences. Develops models, including response, predictive, conversion, and zip, providing insight for marketing decisions to increase sales, market share, and profitability. Expert at segmentation and list enhancement techniques. Ability to use information to gain meaningful insight into customer purchase motivation.

Salary Information

Crandall Associates, an executive recruiting firm, provided all of the career position descriptions included in the first section of this appendix. In addition, they can provide salary information for each of the above career positions.

Copies of the full salary guide with 60 functions and regional salary variations are available for $75 from Crandall Associates, 44 South Bayles Avenue, Suite 316, Port Washington, NY 11050, (516) 767-6800. The guide can be ordered online at www.crandallassociates.com.

Note: The information contained in this section of the Appendix has been generously provided by Crandall Associates, Washington, New York. The authors are grateful to Wendy Weber, President, Crandall Associates, for her contributions to this Appendix section.

Careers in Direct and Interactive Marketing in Agencies

Whether you are interested in marketing, management, or finance, there is something for you in the direct and interactive agency industry. Agencies are businesses, just like any other. Although there are a lot of specialized functions unique to helping agencies create the work that they do, there are also many of the same career opportunities that you might find in any other industry:

- Human Resources: staffing, payroll, and benefits
- Accounting: billing, receivables, financial administration
- Facilities Management: everything from running the mail room to planning office parties
- Information Services: technology infrastructure

But what makes these jobs a little different in an agency environment is that they require an extra degree of *creativity*. When you are dealing with a very creative staff, the environment needs to be that much more creative (Facilities Management). Hiring and benefits needs to have that extra special touch (Human Resources). Connectivity to each other, clients, and what's going on in the world is key (Information Services). Sometimes you even need to figure out how to creatively finance the running of the business (Accounting).

Of course, there are many jobs that are unique to the way agencies work. Each agency may have different titles, but essentially the jobs fall into the following categories.

Account Management

Account Managers are the liaison between the client and the agency and are responsible for the agency's relationship with the client. Account Managers are expected to know their client's business inside-out.

Entry-level positions, such as Account Coordinators or Assistant Account Executives, are responsible for preparing competitive analyses, monitoring budgets, analyzing data, and developing monthly billing reports. Successful Account Managers will be strong in three areas as they grow through their careers: organizational skills, strategic thinking, and relationship skills, both with clients and within the agency.

Account Managers rely heavily on another function that helps move work through the agency. Project management, or traffic, it is a great place to start in an agency if you're not sure what you want to do, but you want to (1) learn how an agency works and (2) become familiar with all of the different departments. You will surely accomplish both of those as an Assistant Project Manager, because this job is responsible for scheduling the jobs an agency has to do, moving the work around the agency, and making sure everything stays on time. This role is vital to every agency, and the people who do it are super-organized and great motivators and negotiators.

Strategic Planning

Strategic Planners ensure that all strategic and creative initiatives undertaken by the agency on behalf of a client are strategically sound by incorporating a variety of tools, some qualitative and some quantitative. Planners review secondary research, design and implement primary research, and synthesize their findings. This helps them write sound creative "briefs," which guide the creative department in its idea generation.

Assistant Account Planners or Junior Planners are responsible for reviewing and synthesizing secondary research sources, drafting research proposals, learning to analyze quantitative data, and writing and editing reports. Planners must have excellent analytical, writing, and verbal skills, as well as the ability to present in a manner that influences and leads others around a great idea.

Increasingly, User Experience Planners, who use primary research to determine how consumers engage with online media to create the optimal consumer experience, are part of the planning department, as opposed to a separate interactive department. This makes a campaign much more holistic when planners are working together to think about all aspects of the work and what a consumer's experience will truly feel like.

Creative

Copywriter and Art Director are the two creative positions most people are familiar with. To get these positions in an agency, most entry-level hires probably went to a graduate or portfolio school to develop their "book" (a portfolio of work to demonstrate their creative capability). The Copywriter and the Art Director are the ones who work on the agency's campaigns, the work that requires "concepts."

But there are other opportunities within a creative department where people with excellent technical skills can find entry-level opportunities (especially given the boom in the digital space):

Studio Artist: This position works with all graphics needs of the agency, especially those in 2D; requires proficiency in Quark, PhotoShop, and Illustrator and/or Freehand.

Digital Designer: Understands how a Web site comes together; is responsible for art concepts in the production of Web sites; has a basic understanding of HTML programming as it relates to design.

Flash Developer: Responsible for HTML and graphic production as it relates to programming e-mails, landing pages, and microsites. Should be conversant in action scripting, the latest version of Flash, click tagging for online banner ads, and file optimization.

HTML Programmer/Developer: Converts project specifications and statements to detailed logical charts for coding into computer language.

Interaction Designer: Helps ensure that the ideas of the art director are translated into workable ideas online; requires sound fundamentals in information architecture, but must also have a fresh enough design sense to keep all user interfaces and user experiences innovative while maximizing usability.

Media

As you've learned, the single most important thing in direct marketing is targeting, so the media department is a very important department. Very keen, strategic minds reside here. If you are interested in solving puzzles (where to find the prospect?), like to play with numbers (how much can I get for the fewest dollars?), and love to analyze and optimize (did it work? what worked best? how could it work better?), then media might be the right part of the agency for you.

Assistant Media Planners spend much of their day meeting with representatives of various media and list companies, doing research about those companies' offerings—learning about the demographics of the readers/watchers/listeners/mailing lists of those reps. These assistants are often given the responsibility to pull together the initial recommendation for how a client's budget should be allocated.

Assistant Media Buyers do the opposite of planning the purchases—they actually do the negotiating and buying! Assistants will be given smaller projects or markets, but they will place the buy, monitor its progress, track spending and results, optimize the buy, prepare reports, and resolve billing issues. (Note: In smaller agencies, the roles of planner and buyer are often combined.)

Analytics

The data analytics group is often closely tied to the media group in a direct and interactive agency, because so much of what is done is tied to results. While the senior management in an analytics group often consists of people with doctorate degrees, there are opportunities for entry-level candidates.

An entry-level analyst will compile and analyze data from secondary sources, as well help design and execute primary research. Enhanced computer skills will include knowledge of database software and statistical software.

Production

Last but not least are the terrific people who produce all of the work that has been created. Some of the work can be created digitally by the folks in the creative department. Other assets must be created either with in-house production resources or through outside resources.

The production department maintains a file of directors, photographers, film companies, printers, lettershops, premium companies, box makers—anything and anybody that can help them produce whatever the creative department can dream up.

Assistant producers for video, art, events, branded content, and online create job dockets, prepare bid sheets, manage estimates as they come in, monitor status of jobs daily, create weekly status reports, coordinate with the talent department on talent releases, and manage billing (to cite a few responsibilities).

Talent payment coordinators maintain all broadcast agreements, prepare talent payment vouchers/authorizations, estimate reuse fees, and prepare talent contracts.

Note: The information contained in this section of the appendix has been generously provided by The Martin Agency, Richmond, Virginia. The authors are grateful to Barbara Joynes, Partner, Integrated Services at The Martin Agency, for her work on this Appendix section.

Direct and Interactive Marketing Career Resources

Investigate the following resources to obtain additional information about direct and interactive marketing careers:

- **DMA Job Bank, http://www.the-dma.org/jobbank.** This online resource offers job seekers and DMA member companies looking to fill positions a state-of-the-art online job bank. It matches direct marketing employers and qualified candidates. It allows you to post a résumé and search for career positions. The job bank also contains articles with valuable links to job and career articles.

- **Marketing Jobs For Students—www.MarketingJobsForStudents.com.** This online interactive resource offers students career assistance and helps them to gain a competitive advantage. A range of topics are offered such as:

  —How to distinguish yourself from other marketing students and marketing professionals;

  —How to position yourself in your ideal field;

  —How to get an interview, instead of just waiting for a call;

  —How to negotiate your salary;

  — Much more to help you when searching for a marketing job.

- **Other online resources include:**
  —CareerBuilder.com
  —nytimes.com
  —hotjobs.com

Note: The information contained in this final section of the appendix has been generously provided by the Direct Marketing Association (DMA) and the Direct Marketing Educational Foundation (DMEF). The authors are grateful to Jeff Nesler of the DMEF for his assistance with the Appendix, and to the DMA and DMEF for their constant support of and commitment to direct marketing education and career placement.

Glossary

abandonment rule when visitors start to complete a form and then stall or close the form—at which point a proactive Chat invitation can be issued to help complete the task.

ad note a small sticker that is placed on the front page of the newspaper that can be pealed off without damaging the newspaper.

adwords keywords used to describe or promote something.

affiliate marketing a type of marketing that will manage relationships and actually reward people for referring people to a product or service.

aging the recency of the site.

allowable margin (also known as advertising allowable) the amount of money that can be spent to get an order while still permitting some left over for media costs and the designated profit to be made.

alternative hypothesis the hypothesis that is determined when a null hypothesis is proven wrong.

annoyance in marketing terms, it is the way people feel when they receive too much unsolicited marketing communications.

auto responders e-mails that are automatically sent, when triggered by some variable or some event.

backlinks the quality of links, number of broken links, the anchor text, and the positioning of the link

banner advertising the digital analog to print ads, targeting a broad audience with the goal of creating awareness about the product or service being promoted.

big idea the idea that becomes the company's logo, slogan, or tagline. It is the highlighted unique selling point or creative expression that is the focal point of a whole promotional campaign.

bingo card an insert or page of a magazine that is created by the publishers to provide a numeric listing of advertisers (also called an "information card").

blog Web sites that contain up-to-date, continuous information, which is posted for all viewers to read.

brand marketing marketing that boosts knowledge of a company or product's name, logo, or slogan.

break even the point at which the gross profit on a unit sale equates to the cost of making that unit sale.

broadcast media television and radio that can be used as methods for direct response advertising.

business-to-business (B2B) direct marketing the process of providing goods and services to industrial market intermediaries, as opposed to ultimate consumers.

button chat the call-to-action is resident on the page and the visitor initiates the chat.

call abandonment the number of callers in telemarketing that hang up before being serviced by a sales representative.

call center a dedicated team supported by various telephone technological resources to provide responses to customer inquiries.

call metrics used to track phone calls and collect data.

catalog a multipage direct mail booklet that displays photographs and/or descriptive details of products/services along with prices and order details.

cause-related marketing a commercial activity by which businesses and charities or causes form a partnership with each other to market an image, product, or service for mutual benefit.

chi-square (c^2) test a statistical technique for determining whether an observed difference between the test and the control in an experiment is significant.

chief privacy officer (CPO) a corporate officer whose responsibility it is to protect the sensitive information the corporation collects, from credit card accounts to health records.

chit an additional enclosure card or separate slip of paper that highlights a free gift or some other information.

classic format a direct mail package consisting of an outer envelope, letter, circular, order form, and a reply envelope.

click-through rates the number of times a user clicks on an online ad, often measured as a function of time.

click-to-chat a form of Web-based communication in which a person clicks an object to request an immediate connection with another person in real-time.

code of ethics a code that generally serves as a guideline for making ethical decisions.

cold calls a telemarketing term that indicates there is no existing relationship with or recognition of the direct marketer by the customer or potential customer.

collectivist culture a culture in which emphasis is placed on the group as a whole.

compiled lists prospect lists that have been generated by a third party or market research firm via directories, newspapers, public records, and so on. These individuals do not have a purchase response history.

connecting sites serve as media to connect people for various reasons.

continuity selling offers that are continued on a regular (weekly, monthly, quarterly, annually) basis (also called "club offers").

contract manufacturing the process by which a company contracts a local manufacturer to produce goods for the company.

control group a group of subjects on which the experiment is not conducted.

conversion the movement of a prospective customer to a definite buying customer.

conversion rate the rate at which leads are converted into sales.

cookie an electronic tag on the consumer's computer that enables the Web site to follow consumers as they shop and recognize them on return visits.

cooperative mailings provide participants, usually noncompeting direct response advertisers, with opportunities to reduce mailing cost in reaching common prospects.

copy appeal the essential theme, which generally stems from fundamental human needs, of the whole promotion or campaign.

cost of goods sold all costs related to manufacturing or producing a good or service.

cost per click how much the person is willing to bid to show the ad.

cost per inquiry (CPI) (also known as cost per lead, or CPL) promotion costs divided by the number of inquiries (people who responded but did not yet order).

cost per response (CPR) the total promotion budget divided by the total number of orders and/or inquiries received.

cost per viewer (CPV) the total promotion budget divided by the total number of people in the viewing audience.

coupon an offer by a manufacturer or retailer that includes an incentive for purchase of a product or service in the form of a specified price reduction.

cross-selling an important characteristic of direct marketing where new and related products (or even unrelated products) are offered to existing customers.

customer database a list of customer names to which additional information has been added in a systematic fashion.

customer lifetime value (CLTV) the discounted stream of revenue a customer will generate over the lifetime of his or her relationship or patronage with a company.

customer loyalty programs programs that encourage customer repeat purchases through program enrollment processes and the allocation of awards and/or benefits, sponsored by the organization or firm.

customer relationship management (CRM) a business strategy to select and manage customers to optimize value.

customer satisfaction the extent to which a firm fulfills a consumer's needs, desires, and expectations.

data/security breach the safeguarding and securing of data from unauthorized access or damage.

data mining the process of using statistical and mathematical techniques to extract customer information from the customer database to draw inferences about an individual customer's needs and predict future behavior.

database analytics the direct marketer analyzes customer information housed within the customer database to draw inferences about an individual customer's needs.

database enhancement adding and overlaying information to records to better describe and understand the customer.

degrees of freedom the number of observations that are allowed to vary.

demographics identifiable and measurable statistics that describe the consumer population.

dependent variable a variable on whose outcome or effect the research is interested.

direct investment the process whereby a company entering a foreign market acquires an existing company or forms a completely new company.

direct mail the leading printed medium that direct marketers use for direct response advertising.

direct marketing a database-driven interactive process of directly communicating with targeted customers or prospects using any medium to obtain a measurable response or transaction via one or multiple channels.

duties a tax charged by a government, especially on imports.

e-fulfillment the integration of people, processes, and technology to ensure customer satisfaction before, during, and after the online buying experience.

electronic commerce (e-commerce) the completion of buying and selling transactions online.

ethics a branch of philosophy, a system of human behavior concerned with morality: the rightness and wrongness of individual actions or deeds.

experiment a procedure designed to measure the effect of change (often called a "test" by direct marketers).

exporting when a company sells its products from its home base without any personnel physically located overseas.

fixed costs costs associated with a business that do not vary with production or number of units sold.

frequency the number of ad insertions purchased in a specific communication vehicle within a specified time period.

fulfillment the act of carrying out a customer's expectations by sending the ordered product to the customer or delivering the service agreed upon.

Geographic Information System (GIS) a computer system capable of obtaining, storing, analyzing, and displaying geographically referenced information known according to position.

global market segmentation the practice of identifying particular segments, country groups, or individual consumer groups across countries of potential customers who display similar behaviors in buying.

Global Positioning System (GPS) a segmentation tool that associates latitude and longitude coordinates with street addresses.

gross domestic product (GDP) total market value of all final goods and services produced in a certain year within a nation's borders.

gross rating points a mathematical value computed by multiplying reach by frequency that measures the number of people exposed to an ad.

gross sales total sales made.

hotline names the most recent names acquired by specific list owners, but there is no uniformity as to what chronological period "recent" describes.

house lists lists of an organization's own customers (active as well as inactive) and responders.

hypertext markup language (HTML) a simple coding system used to format documents for viewing by Web clients.

hypothesis testing an assertion about the value of the parameter of a variable (the researcher decides) on the basis of observed facts such as the relative response to a test of variation in advertising.

inbound calls a category of telemarketing where customers are placing calls to the organization to place an order, request more information or to obtain customer service.

independent variable a controllable factor in an experiment.

individualist culture a culture in which emphasis and value is in the individual.

industrial goods products that are generally used as raw materials or in the fabrication of other goods.

infomediaries companies that act as third parties by gathering personal information from a user and providing it to other sites with the user's approval.

infomercial a relatively long commercial in the format of a television program, to inform view-ers of a featured product.

infrastructure is normally a leading indicator of economic development of a country and includes the essential services that support business activities.

insert a popular form of print advertisement commonly used in a magazine or newspaper.

integrated order fulfillment a term based on the idea that the process of building and delivering products should not begin until after an order has been taken.

intellectual property products of the mind or ideas.

involvement devices devices used in direct response advertising to spur action by involving the reader; examples would be tokens, stamps, punch-outs, puzzles, and so on.

joint venture two or more investors join forces to conduct a business by sharing ownership and control.

key code a unique identifier placed on the response device or order form prior to mailing a promotional piece to track and measure results.

key word density the number of times that the key word in the search appears on that Web site.

layout the positioning of copy and illustrations in print media to gain attention and direct the reader through the message in an intended sequence.

letter the principal element of the direct mail package that provides the primary means for communication and personalization.

licensee the foreign business that enters into an agreement and becomes authorized to manufacture or sell specific brand products in its country on behalf of a licensor.

licensing similar to franchising, local businesses become authorized to manufacture or sell specific brand products for another company.

licensor a company located in the home or domestic country that permits overseas manufacturing to occur.

lifetime value of a customer (LTV) the discounted stream of revenue a customer will generate over the lifetime of his or her relationship or patronage with a company (also called "customer lifetime value").

list brokers those who serve as intermediaries who bring list users and list owners together.

list compilers organizations that develop lists and data about them, often serving as their own list managers and brokers.

list managers managers who represent the interest of list owners and have authority and responsibility to be in contact with list brokers and list users on behalf of list owners.

list owners those who describe and acquire prospects (as market segments) who show potential of becoming customers.

location based mobile (LBM) program that enables SmartPhone users to "check in" to a location, such as a business, and to see other friends' locations.

mail order a transaction within a channel, characterized by the absence of a retail store or a salesperson; direct channel from producer to user.

management contracting the process whereby a contract is signed with local foreign people or the foreign government to manage the business in the country market.

market penetration the proportion of customers to some benchmark.

market segmentation a marketing strategy devised to attract and meet the needs of a specific submarket where the submarkets are homogeneous.

market segments placing people (customers or potential customers) into homogeneous groups based on certain attributes such as age, income, stage in the family life cycle, and so on.

match code abbreviated information about a customer record that is constructed so that each individual record can be matched, pairwise, with each other record.

matchback the procedure by which an order response is tracked back to the starting place (catalog or offer) from which it was generated.

media efficiency ratio (MER) a ratio that is calculated by dividing infomercial sales by the media cost.

merge-purge a computerized process used to identify and delete duplicate names/addresses within various lists.

micro-targeting the creation and direct delivery to customers of customized winning messages, proof points, and offers, and accurately predicting their impact.

mobile applications Internet software programs to run on hand held devices such as SmartPhones.

morals the judgment of the goodness or badness of human action and character.

motivations needs that compel a person to take action or behave in a certain way.

multibuyer an individual whose name/address appears on two or more response lists simultaneously.

multichannel distribution refers to a marketer using several competing channels of distribution to reach the same target customers.

negative option the shipment of a product is sent automatically unless the customer specifically requests that it not be.

net profit (also known as net profit margin) the amount of money the company retains after the fixed costs are subtracted from the gross revenues and before taxes.

nixie mail that has been returned by the U.S. Postal Service because it is undeliverable as addressed.

North American Industry Classification System (NAICS) an industrial classification system using a six-digit code that focuses on production activities.

null hypothesis the statistical hypothesis that there is no difference between the means of the groups being compared.

offer the terms under which a specific product or service is promoted to the customer.

online panels online discussions marketers conduct with people who have agreed to talk about a selected topic over a period of time.

online PR any type of public relations conducted digitally.

optimization the process of improving Web site traffic through the use of search engines.

outbound calls a category of telemarketing where firms place calls to prospects or customers.

outsourcing a telemarketing term referring to the process of having all call center activities handled by an outside organization or a service bureau.

package inserts printed offers of products and services that arrive when the recipient receives an order that he or she had purchased.

packing slip a form or document that identifies the products to be included with the order.

partner relationship management (PRM) the generation of greater value to customers through companies' cooperation and close work with partners in other companies or departments.

pathing the sequence in which the pages are viewed.

permission marketing the process of obtaining the consent of a customer before a company sends out online marketing communication to that customer via the Internet.

personalized URL (PURL) a personalized Web page or microsite that incorporates the prospect's name and is tailored to his interests based on information known about him.

picking list a list identifying each item on an order list and serves as a routing guide to move the picker efficiently through a warehouse.

political micro-targeting combining groups of voters based on information about them accessible through databases and the Internet to target them with specific messages.

positioning a marketing strategy that enables marketers to understand how each consumer perceives a company's product or service based on important attributes (also known as "product positioning").

positive option the process whereby the customer must specifically request shipment of a product for each offer in a series.

PR value how often Google or other search engines indexes a site or how often they send their spiders to index a site

pre-recorded messages a stored voice message that one may access through various triggers.

preprinted inserts newspaper advertisements that are usually printed ahead of the newspaper production and are distributed with the newspaper.

price elasticity the relative change in demand for a product given the change in the price of the product.

price penetration a strategy used if the direct marketer wants to maximize sales volume.

price skimming a strategy used when the objective of the price is to generate the largest possible return on investment (ROI) where the price must be set at the highest possible level to "skim the cream" off the top of the market and only target a select number of consumers who can afford to buy the product/service.

privacy refers to a level of control consumers have over information provided.

Privacy Act of 1974 an act that determined whether limits on what the federal government could do with personal information should be applied to the private sector as well.

privacy fundamentalists people who believe that they own their name, as well as all the information about themselves, and that no one else may use it without their permission.

privacy pragmatists people who look at the contact, offer, and the methods of data collection and apply a cost/benefit analysis to make a determination about a marketer's use of information.

privacy unconcerned those who literally do not care about the issue of privacy at all.

proactive chat the visitor has triggered a business rule and the chat invitation 'pops in' to the page with a relevant call-to-action.

product differentiation a strategy that uses innovative design, packaging, and positioning to make a clear distinction between products and services serving a market segment.

product positioning a marketing strategy that enables marketers to understand how each consumer perceives a company's product or service based on important attributes (also called "positioning").

psychographics the study of lifestyles, habits, attitudes, beliefs, and value systems of individuals.

quality score measures how relevant your keyword is to your ad text and to a user's search query.

quick response codes two-dimensional barcodes that can be read by barcode scanners on smart phones.

random assignment a component of a valid experiment that refers to the fact that both control and experiment group subjects must be assigned completely randomly so that differences between groups occur by chance alone.

reach the number of people exposed to a particular media vehicle carrying the ad.

recency/frequency/monetary (R/F/M) a mathematical formula used to evaluate the value or sales potential of customers or prospects.

reference groups the people a consumer turns to for reinforcement.

reference individuals the people a consumer turns to for advice.

response lists lists of those who have responded to another direct marketer's offer.

return on investment (ROI) a popular tool of measurement in business, this is the net profit divided by the average amount invested in the company in one year.

right to confidentiality a consumer's right to specify to a given company that information that they freely provide should not be shared.

right to information includes the consumer's right to receive any and all pertinent or requested information.

right to privacy the ability of an individual to control the access others have to his or her personal information.

right to safety a right by the consumer to be protected from physical or psychological harm.

right to selection a consumer's right to choose or make decisions about his or her buying behavior.

run-of-paper advertisements (ROP) small advertisements that appear in the regular section of the newspaper where positioning of the ad is at the will of the newspaper.

salting the process whereby a direct marketer places decoys, which are either incorrect spellings or fictitious names, on a customer list to track and identify any misuse (also called "seeding").

search engine an index of key words that enables Web browsers to find what they are looking for.

search engine marketing the whole set of techniques and strategies used to direct more visitors to marketing Web sites from search engines.

seeding the process whereby a direct marketer places decoys, which are either incorrect spellings or fictitious names, on a customer list to track and identify any misuse (also called "salting").

self-mailer any direct mail piece mailed without an envelope.

service bureaus groups that provide data processing, data mining, outsourcing, online analytical processing, and so on to support the interchange of lists and database information.

SMS text messaging allow the marketer to track open rates, manage lists, allow customers to opt in and opt out and do many of the same functions as e-mail companies.

social networks Web sites used to connect with consumers, gain insights and feedback, conduct online PR, advertise, and drive site traffic.

solo mailer direct mail pieces that promote a single product or limited group of related products.

source code the media, media vehicle, or means by which the person has responded to become a customer.

source data the information contained in a customer database.

spam unsolicited e-mail messages.

split test a test where at least two samples are taken from the same list, each considered to be representative of the entire list, and used for package tests or to test the homogeneity of the list.

stealth marketing communications secrecy in that direct marketers can communicate with small market segments or individual customers without competitors or other customers having knowledge of it.

storyboard a series of illustrations that show the visual portion of a TV commercial.

stuffers printed offers of products and services that are inserted in the envelope with invoice or statement.

Sunday supplements mass circulation sections that are edited nationally but appear locally in the Sunday editions of many newspapers.

T1 a giant pipeline or conduit through which a user may send multiple voice, data, or video signals.

take-one racks an alternative method of print distribution where the printed material is placed on a display rack.

telephone script a call guide used by telemarketers to assist a telephone operator in communicating effectively with the prospect or customer.

test a term that direct marketers may use for experiment.

till-forbid (TF) an offer that prearranges continuous shipments on a specified basis and are renewed automatically until the customer instructs otherwise.

transactional data the information contained in a customer database.

Type I error results when the decision maker rejects the null hypothesis (even though it is true).

Type II error occurs when the decision maker accepts the null hypothesis (when it is not true).

unit margin (also known as unit contribution, unit profit, or trade margin) the amount of money each sale provides to cover fixed costs.

up-selling the promotion of more expensive products or services over the product or service originally discussed or purchased.

variable costs costs that vary with production and number of units sold.

violation in marketing terms, is the way people feel when they believe too much information about their personal lives is being exchanged between marketers without their knowledge and/or consent.

viral marketing a form of electronic word of mouth where e-mail messages are forwarded from one consumer to other consumers.

viralocity measures both the number of messages and the rate of speed by which e-mail messages are forwarded by a consumer to other consumers.

virtual enterprise a company that is primarily a marketing and customer service entity, with actual product development and distribution handled by a broad network of subcontractors.

webinar Web conferencing used for sales presentations.

Index

Racom Communications Order Form

QUANTITY	TITLE	PRICE	AMOUNT
_____	Contemporary Direct and Interactive Marketing, 3rd Ed., **Spiller/Baier**	$69.95	_____
_____	The *IMC Handbook*, **J. Stephen Kelly/Susan K. Jones**	$49.95	_____
_____	*Creative Strategy in Direct & Interactive Marketing, 4th Ed.*, **Susan K. Jones**	$49.95	_____
_____	*Innovating . . . Chcago Style*, **Thomas Kuczmarski, Luke Tanen, Dan Miller**	$27.95	_____
_____	*The New Media Driver's License*, **Richard Cole/Derek Mehraban**	$24.95	_____
_____	*Aligned*, **Maurice Parisien**	$24.95	_____
_____	*How to Jump-Start Your Career*, **Robert L. Hemmings**	$19.95	_____
_____	*This Year a Pogo Stick . . . Next Year a Unicycle!*, **Jim Kobs**	$19.95	_____
_____	*Follow That Customer*, **Egbert Jan van Bel/Ed Sander/Alan Weber**	$39.95	_____
_____	*Internet Marketing*, **Herschell Gordon Lewis**	$19.95	_____
_____	*Reliability Rules*, **Don Schultz/Reg Price**	$34.95	_____
_____	*The Marketing Performance Measurement Toolkit*, **David M. Raab**	$39.95	_____
_____	*Successful E-Mail Marketing Strategies*, **Arthur M. Hughes/Arthur Sweetser**	$49.95	_____
_____	*Managing Your Business Data*, **Theresa Kushner/Maria Villar**	$32.95	_____
_____	*Media Strategy and Planning Workbook*, **DL Dickinson**	$24.95	_____
_____	*Marketing Metrics in Action*, **Laura Patterson**	$24.95	_____
_____	*Print Matters*, **Randall Hines/Robert Lauterborn**	$27.95	_____
_____	*The Business of Database Marketing*, **Richard N. Tooker**	$49.95	_____
_____	*Customer Churn, Retention, and Profitability*, **Arthur Middleton Hughes**	$44.95	_____
_____	*Data-Driven Business Models*, **Alan Weber**	$49.95	_____
_____	*Branding Iron*, **Charlie Hughes and William Jeanes**	$27.95	_____
_____	*Managing Sales Leads* and *Sales & Marketing 365*, **James Obermayer**	$56.95	_____
_____	*Creating the Marketing Experience*, **Joe Marconi**	$49.95	_____
_____	*Coming to Concurrence*, **J. Walker Smith/Ann Clurman/Craig Wood**	$34.95	_____
_____	*Brand Babble*, **Don E. Schultz/Heidi F. Schultz**	$24.95	_____
_____	*The New Marketing Conversation*, **Donna Baier Stein/Alexandra MacAaron**	$34.95	_____
_____	*Trade Show and Event Marketing*, **Ruth Stevens**	$59.95	_____
_____	*Accountable Marketing*, **Peter J. Rosenwald**	$59.95	_____
_____	*Contemporary Database Marketing*, **Martin Baier/Kurtis Ruf/G. Chakraborty**	$89.95	_____
_____	*Catalog Strategist's Toolkit*, **Katie Muldoon**	$59.95	_____
_____	*Marketing Convergence*, **Susan K. Jones/Ted Spiegel**	$34.95	_____
_____	*High-Performance Interactive Marketing*, **Christopher Ryan**	$39.95	_____
_____	*Public Relations: The Complete Guide*, **Joe Marconi**	$49.95	_____
_____	*The Marketer's Guide to Public Relations*, **Thomas L. Harris/Patricia T. Whalen**	$39.95	_____
_____	*The White Paper Marketing Handbook*, **Robert W. Bly**	$39.95	_____
_____	*Business-to-Business Marketing Research*, **Martin Block/Tamara Block**	$69.95	_____
_____	*Hot Appeals or Burnt Offerings*, **Herschell Gordon Lewis**	$24.95	_____
_____	*On the Art of Writing Copy*, **Herschell Gordon Lewis**	$39.95	_____
_____	*Open Me Now*, **Herschell Gordon Lewis**	$21.95	_____
_____	*Marketing Mayhem*, **Herschell Gordon Lewis**	$39.95	_____
_____	*Asinine Advertising*, **Herschell Gordon Lewis**	$22.95	_____
_____	*The Ultimate Guide To Purchasing Website, Video, Print & Other Creative Services*, **Bobbi Balderman**	$18.95	_____

Name/Title_____

Company _____

Street Address _____

City/State/Zip _____

Email _____ Phone _____

Credit Card: ☐ VISA ☐ MasterCard
 ☐ American Express ☐ Discover

☐ Check or money order enclosed (payable to Racom
 Communications in US dollars drawn on a US bank)

Subtotal	_____
Subtotal from other side	_____
8.65% Tax	_____
Shipping & Handling	_____

$7.00 for first book; $1.00 for each additional book.

TOTAL _____

Number _____ Exp. Date _____

Signature _____

Racom Communications, 150 N. Michigan Ave, Suite 2800, Chicago, IL 60601
312-494-0100, 800-247-6553, www. Racombooks.com

Racom Communications Order Form

QUANTITY	TITLE	PRICE	AMOUNT
_____	Contemporary Direct and Interactive Marketing, 3rd Ed., **Spiller/Baier**	$69.95	_____
_____	The *IMC Handbook*, **J. Stephen Kelly/Susan K. Jones**	$49.95	_____
_____	*Creative Strategy in Direct & Interactive Marketing, 4th Ed.*, **Susan K. Jones**	$49.95	_____
_____	*Innovating . . . Chcago Style*, **Thomas Kuczmarski, Luke Tanen, Dan Miller**	$27.95	_____
_____	*The New Media Driver's License*, **Richard Cole/Derek Mehraban**	$24.95	_____
_____	*Aligned*, **Maurice Parisien**	$24.95	_____
_____	*How to Jump-Start Your Career*, **Robert L. Hemmings**	$19.95	_____
_____	*This Year a Pogo Stick . . . Next Year a Unicycle!*, **Jim Kobs**	$19.95	_____
_____	*Follow That Customer*, **Egbert Jan van Bel/Ed Sander/Alan Weber**	$39.95	_____
_____	*Internet Marketing*, **Herschell Gordon Lewis**	$19.95	_____
_____	*Reliability Rules*, **Don Schultz/Reg Price**	$34.95	_____
_____	*The Marketing Performance Measurement Toolkit*, **David M. Raab**	$39.95	_____
_____	*Successful E-Mail Marketing Strategies*, **Arthur M. Hughes/Arthur Sweetser**	$49.95	_____
_____	*Managing Your Business Data*, **Theresa Kushner/Maria Villar**	$32.95	_____
_____	*Media Strategy and Planning Workbook*, **DL Dickinson**	$24.95	_____
_____	*Marketing Metrics in Action*, **Laura Patterson**	$24.95	_____
_____	*Print Matters*, **Randall Hines/Robert Lauterborn**	$27.95	_____
_____	*The Business of Database Marketing*, **Richard N. Tooker**	$49.95	_____
_____	*Customer Churn, Retention, and Profitability*, **Arthur Middleton Hughes**	$44.95	_____
_____	*Data-Driven Business Models*, **Alan Weber**	$49.95	_____
_____	*Branding Iron*, **Charlie Hughes and William Jeanes**	$27.95	_____
_____	*Managing Sales Leads* and *Sales & Marketing 365*, **James Obermayer**	$56.95	_____
_____	*Creating the Marketing Experience*, **Joe Marconi**	$49.95	_____
_____	*Coming to Concurrence*, **J. Walker Smith/Ann Clurman/Craig Wood**	$34.95	_____
_____	*Brand Babble*, **Don E. Schultz/Heidi F. Schultz**	$24.95	_____
_____	*The New Marketing Conversation*, **Donna Baier Stein/Alexandra MacAaron**	$34.95	_____
_____	*Trade Show and Event Marketing*, **Ruth Stevens**	$59.95	_____
_____	*Accountable Marketing*, **Peter J. Rosenwald**	$59.95	_____
_____	*Contemporary Database Marketing*, **Martin Baier/Kurtis Ruf/G. Chakraborty**	$89.95	_____
_____	*Catalog Strategist's Toolkit*, **Katie Muldoon**	$59.95	_____
_____	*Marketing Convergence*, **Susan K. Jones/Ted Spiegel**	$34.95	_____
_____	*High-Performance Interactive Marketing*, **Christopher Ryan**	$39.95	_____
_____	*Public Relations: The Complete Guide*, **Joe Marconi**	$49.95	_____
_____	*The Marketer's Guide to Public Relations*, **Thomas L. Harris/Patricia T. Whalen**	$39.95	_____
_____	*The White Paper Marketing Handbook*, **Robert W. Bly**	$39.95	_____
_____	*Business-to-Business Marketing Research*, **Martin Block/Tamara Block**	$69.95	_____
_____	*Hot Appeals or Burnt Offerings*, **Herschell Gordon Lewis**	$24.95	_____
_____	*On the Art of Writing Copy*, **Herschell Gordon Lewis**	$39.95	_____
_____	*Open Me Now*, **Herschell Gordon Lewis**	$21.95	_____
_____	*Marketing Mayhem*, **Herschell Gordon Lewis**	$39.95	_____
_____	*Asinine Advertising*, **Herschell Gordon Lewis**	$22.95	_____
_____	*The Ultimate Guide To Purchasing Website, Video, Print & Other Creative Services*, **Bobbi Balderman**	$18.95	_____

Name/Title_____

Company _____

Street Address _____

City/State/Zip _____

Email _____ Phone _____

Credit Card: ☐ VISA ☐ MasterCard
              ☐ American Express ☐ Discover

☐ Check or money order enclosed (payable to Racom
  Communications in US dollars drawn on a US bank)

Subtotal	_____
Subtotal from other side	_____
8.65% Tax	_____
Shipping & Handling	_____
$7.00 for first book; $1.00 for each additional book.	
TOTAL	_____

Number _____ Exp. Date _____

Signature _____

Racom Communications, 150 N. Michigan Ave, Suite 2800, Chicago, IL 60601
312-494-0100, 800-247-6553, www. Racombooks.com